RETHINKING, REPACKAGING, AND RESCUING WORLD TRADE LAW IN THE POST-PANDEMIC ERA

This book explores the ways to 'rethink', 'repackage' and 'rescue' world trade law in the post-COVID-19 era. Using the COVID-19 pandemic as an important context, the book makes original and critical contributions to the growing debate over a range of emerging challenges and systemic issues that might change the landscape of world trade law in the years to come. The book asks: do these unprecedented times and challenges call for reengineering the world trading system and a further retreat from trade liberalisation?

The authors offer a rigorous and insightful analysis of whether and how the existing trade institutions and/or rules, including their latest developments, may provide room to deal with pandemic-induced trade-related issues, sustainable development goals, future crises and other existential threats to the multilateral trading system.

The book reinforces the importance of international cooperation and the pressing need to reinvigorate the world trading system. The pandemic has provided a unique opportunity for governments to rebuild the political will needed for such cooperation. One should never let a serious crisis go to waste.

Studies in International Trade and Investment Law: Volume 25

Studies in International Trade and Investment Law

Series Editors

This series offers a forum for publication of original and scholarly analyses of emerging and significant issues in international trade and investment law – broadly understood to include the whole of the law of the WTO, the public international law of foreign investment, the law of the EU common commercial policy and other regional trade regimes, and any legal or regulatory topic that interacts with global trade and foreign investment. The aim of the series is to produce works which will be readily accessible to trade and investment law scholars and practitioners alike.

Recent titles in this series:

Free Trade and Cultural Diversity in International Law
Jingxia Shi

Tied Aid and Development Aid Policies in the Framework of EU and WTO Law: The Imperative for Change
Annamaria La Chimia

Balancing Human Rights, Environmental Protection and International Trade: Lessons from the EU Experience
Emily Reid

Public Procurement and Labour Rights: Towards Coherence in International Instruments of Procurement Regulation
Maria Anna Corvaglia

The China-Australia Free Trade Agreement: A 21st-Century Model
Edited by Colin Picker, Heng Wang and Weihuan Zhou

Regional Economic Integration and Dispute Settlement in East Asia: The Evolving Legal Framework
Anna G Tevini

The EU, World Trade Law and the Right to Food: Rethinking Free Trade Agreements with Developing Countries
Giovanni Gruni

Patent Games in the Global South: Pharmaceutical Patent Law Making in Brazil, India and Nigeria
Amaka Vanni

The Nationality of Corporate Investors under International Investment Law
Anil Yilmaz Vastardis

The Regulation of Product Standards in World Trade Law
Ming Du

Investors' International Law
Edited by Jean Ho and Mavluda Sattorova

Rethinking, Repackaging, and Rescuing World Trade Law in the Post-Pandemic Era

Edited by
Amrita Bahri
Weihuan Zhou
and
Daria Boklan

•HART•
OXFORD • LONDON • NEW YORK • NEW DELHI • SYDNEY

HART PUBLISHING

Bloomsbury Publishing Plc

Kemp House, Chawley Park, Cumnor Hill, Oxford, OX2 9PH, UK

1385 Broadway, New York, NY 10018, USA

29 Earlsfort Terrace, Dublin 2, Ireland

First published in Great Britain 2021

A catalogue record for this book is available from the British Library.

A catalogue record for this book is available from the Library of Congress.

Library of Congress Control Number: 2021940351

ISBN: HB: 978-1-50995-169-7
ePDF: 978-1-50995-171-0
ePub: 978-1-50995-170-3

Typeset by Compuscript Ltd, Shannon

FOREWORD

Following the wise advice of Winston Churchill never to waste a good crisis, the contributors to *Rethinking, Repackaging and Rescuing World Trade Law in the Post-Pandemic Era* look at the multiple crises currently confronting the world trading system and enquire what lessons can be learned from these crises for the future. Each of the contributors to this book as well as its editors should be congratulated for doing so. Looking ahead and 'dreaming' of better days is often the best, if not the only, antidote against despair and depression in distressed times. As the title already reveals, this book is divided into three parts. The first part, entitled 'Rethinking World Trade Law and the Pandemic' deals with the trade-related measures taken by WTO Members in response to the COVID-19 pandemic and what these responses (be it in the form of export restrictions, subsidies or otherwise) tell us about the adequacy of the current WTO rulebook and the WTO's ability to resolve related disputes. It should not come as a surprise that an unprecedented crisis such as the COVID-19 pandemic reveals new weaknesses and puts the spotlight on well-known deficiencies. The contributions in the second part of this book, which is entitled 'Repackaging World Trade Law and Sustainable Development', discuss the future of world trade law in light of the need to ensure that economic development is both environmentally and socially sustainable. To make development sustainable is a daunting challenge but one that we must embrace. The four contributions in this part of the book each show, from a different perspective, how trade and trade rules can play a role in achieving the sustainability of economic development. The third and final part of this book, entitled 'Rescuing World Trade Law and Other Fundamental Challenges' focuses on some aspects of other challenges currently facing the global trading system, such as the WTO dispute settlement crisis and the geopolitical superpower confrontation over economic hegemony between the United States and China. While it should be possible to overcome – in one way or another – the WTO dispute settlement crisis in the next few years, the geopolitical confrontation between the United States and China is likely to be with us for decades to come. Trade and trade rules can and should contribute to the common effort to 'manage' this confrontation and prevent it from getting out of hand. As the editors recognise in chapter one, it is 'unrealistic for this book to address all the challenges' facing the world trading system. However, this book does an excellent job in addressing a number of aspects of some of these challenges. When reading this book, it is unlikely that you will agree with all of the analysis of the current crises and challenges or with the 'solutions' suggested. This book will, however, give you much food for thought and further discussion on how to rethink, repackage and rescue world trade law.

Peter Van den Bossche
Bern, 13 March 2021

ACKNOWLEDGEMENTS

We would like to thank the authors of this volume for their valuable contributions. We would also like to thank Elena Murashko (Legal Expert, Ministry of Economic Development of the Russian Federation) for her excellent assistance with editing and formatting. This project would not have been possible without the platform we have received from Law Schools Global League (LSGL) to collaborate on research assignments with experts from LSGL member schools. Under the LSGL Presidency of Professor Amnon Lehavi and Professor Gonçalo Matias, and on the encouragement of Professor Laura Carlson, we were invited to launch the International Trade & Investment Law Working Group at Stockholm University in February 2019. Since then, the group members have worked together to foster capacity-building and awareness in the field of international trade and investment law through joint teaching projects, exchange of faculties, joint publications and the organisation of seminars and conferences. Details on our current members and ongoing activities can be found at the LSGL webpage.

Most contributions in this book were presented at the LSGL Summer Academic Conference titled 'The 3R Initiative: Re-thinking, Re-packaging and Rescuing World Trade Law'. The conference was jointly organised by the LSGL's International Trade & Investment Law Working Group and the National Research University Higher School of Economics (Moscow) in July 2020. We thank Professor Peter Van den Bossche for giving the keynote speech and HE Ambassador Chad Blackman, Professor L Alan Winters and Professor Joost Pauwelyn for chairing the panels and their useful comments at this conference. Finally, we are thankful to Professor Gregory C Shaffer for his guidance on packaging this project in its current form.

CONTENTS

PART II
REPACKAGING WORLD TRADE LAW AND SUSTAINABLE DEVELOPMENT

PART III
RESCUING WORLD TRADE LAW AND OTHER FUNDAMENTAL CHALLENGES

ABOUT THE CONTRIBUTORS

Editors

Amrita Bahri is Assistant Professor at the Instituto Tecnológico Autónomo de México (ITAM) and Co-Chair Professor for the WTO Chair Programme (Mexico). She is the Founding Chair of the International Trade & Investment Law Research Group (Law Schools Global League, LSGL) and Founding Member of the South Asian International Economic Law Network (SAIELN). She has authored the monograph *Public Private Partnership for WTO Dispute Settlement: Enabling Developing Countries* (Edward Elgar Publishing, 2018). Her academic articles are published in prestigious journals including the *Journal of International Economic Law*; *World Trade Review*; *Journal of World Trade*; *Trade, Law & Development*; *Global Trade & Customs Journal*; and the *Journal of International Trade Law & Policy*. Working with the International Trade Centre's (ITC) team, Amrita designed the very first framework to measure gender-responsiveness of free trade agreements. She explains this framework in ITC's policy paper titled 'Mainstreaming Gender in Free Trade Agreements'.

Daria Boklan is Professor of National Research University Higher School of Economics, Moscow. She is the Chair of the International Trade & Investment Law Research Group of Law Schools Global League and Convener of the Interest Group on International Environmental Law of the European Society of International Law. Dr Boklan has been a member of the expert group, drafting the Treaty on Eurasian Economic Union. She has more than 50 academic articles including those published in prestigious journals such as the *World Trade Review*; *Journal of World Energy Law & Business*; *Environmental Earth Science*; and the *Russian Law Journal*.

Weihuan Zhou is Associate Professor, Director of Research and an inaugural member of the Herbert Smith Freehills China International Business and Economic Law (CIBEL) Centre, Faculty of Law and Justice, UNSW Sydney. He is the author of *China's Implementation of the Rulings of the World Trade Organization* (Hart Publishing, 2019) and a co-editor of *Non-market Economies in the Global Trading System: The Special Case of China* (Springer, 2018) and the *China–Australia Free Trade Agreement: A 21st Century Model* (Hart Publishing, 2017). His work has appeared in all the top journals in the field of international economic law and in some of the best journals in the broader field of international law (such as the *American Journal of International Law* and the *International & Comparative Law Quarterly*). His work has been cited widely, including in European Parliament briefings and reports of the Parliament of Australia and Australia's Productivity Commission, and by leading scholars in his field. He is currently Co-Secretary of the Society of International Economic Law (SIEL).

Contributors

Luana Almeida is a Brazilian lawyer and holds a Master's degree in Globalisation and Law – specialisation International Trade and Investment Law – from Maastricht University. Luana has been a trade and sustainability consultant and a corporate social responsibility specialist. She has also worked at the Directorate-General for International Partnerships at the European Commission. Luana has published articles on topics such as international investment law and WTO law.

Mariana Clara de Andrade holds a PhD in Public International Law (University of Milano–Bicocca). Mariana has been a research intern at the PhD Support Programme in the WTO, a guest researcher at the Max Planck Institute Luxembourg for International, European and Regulatory Procedural Law, and at the University of Geneva. She holds an LLB and LLM in Law and International Relations from the Federal University of Santa Catarina (Brazil).

Michelle R Sanchez-Badin is Assistant Professor at FGV São Paulo School of Law (Brazil), and its Law and Development postgraduate programme. Coordinator of FGV/SP Center of Global Law and Development, and of the WTO Chair in Brazil. Current director of the *Red Latinoamericana de Derecho Económico Internacional* and of the Brazilian chapter of the International Law Association, and founding member of the Society of International Economic Law (SIEL). Ongoing awarded research scholarships: FAPESP 2018/00498-2; FAPESP 2019/08878-2; IPEA 0078/2020.

Jan Bohanes is Senior Counsel at the Geneva-based Advisory Centre on WTO Law (ACWL), where he advises developing country and LDC governments on all matters relating to WTO law, including WTO litigation before WTO dispute settlement bodies. Previously, he worked at the WTO Appellate Body Secretariat and in the Geneva office of Sidley Austin LLP. He also teaches trade law at the Graduate Institute of International and Development Studies and other academic institutions.

Luyao Che is Assistant Professor and a supervisor for Master's students at the School of International Law, China University of Political Science and Law (CUPL). She holds a Master in Laws (LLM) degree from Renmin University of China, and PhD from the University of Nottingham. Her current research focus is on the legal implications of contemporary state-directed economic institutions and their impacts on the development of the international economic order.

Ru Ding is Associate Professor at the School of International Law of China University of Political Science and Law. Dr Ding holds a Doctor of Juridical Science (SJD) from Georgetown University Law Center, an LLM from Duke University

School of Law and a BA in Law from Tsinghua University School of Law. She has interned at the Appellate Body Secretariat and the Economic Research and Statistics Division of the World Trade Organization (WTO). She was a visiting scholar at Harvard University Law School. Her research interest covers WTO law, trade remedy rules and rules on state-owned enterprises.

Ilaria Espa is Assistant Professor of International Economic Law at USI, Senior Research Fellow at the World Trade Institute (WTI) in Bern and Adjunct Professor at the Catholic University of the Sacred Heart in Milan. Former Marie Curie fellow and member of the WTI-based NCCR Trade Regulation Programme (2013–17) and Adjunct Professor at the Department of Environmental Science and Policy of the University of Milan (2015–20), Ilaria holds a PhD in International Law and Economics from Bocconi University (2013).

Magali Favaretto Prieto Fernandes is a PhD student in Law and Development – FGV Direito SP. She holds a Master's degree in International Economic Law – Washington College of Law – American University (2001). Her experience in the area of law has an emphasis on public international law and international trade law.

Alexandra R Harrington is the Executive Director of the Center for Global Governance and Emerging Law and a Visiting Assistant Professor of Law at Albany Law School, New York, where her teaching focuses on international law issues. She is also Research Director of the Centre for International Sustainable Development Law and the Director of Studies for ILA Colombia. She has held two Fulbright terms in Canada at the Balsillie School of International Affairs, focusing on global governance issues.

Meredith Kolsky Lewis is Professor of Law and Vice Dean for International and Graduate Programs at the University at Buffalo School of Law, State University of New York, where she directs the Cross-Border Legal Studies Center. She is also an Associate Professor of Law at the Victoria University of Wellington Law School.

Lorenza Mola is Associate Professor of International Law at the University of Turin, Department of Law. She holds a PhD in International Economic Law from 'Bocconi' University (Milan, Italy). She is currently the scientific director of the Master of Laws in International Trade (University of Turin and ITC–ILO, in partnership with IUSE, UNCITRAL and UNIDROIT). Her most recurrent teaching and research fields are in international investment law, international human rights law, and the law of EU external relations.

María Manuela Moccero is a lawyer and academic with experience in international trade law and commercial negotiations. She is Legal Consultant at the Market Access Division of the Ministry of Foreign Affairs, International Trade and Worship of Argentina and former Legal Consultant at the International Economic Dispute Settlement Division of the same ministry. Between 2008 and 2010 she was Coordinator of the MERCOSUR Secretariat. She is also a graduate and postgraduate teacher and regularly speaks on topics relating to international trade law, regional integration processes and WTO Agreements.

Cristina Poncibò is Professor of Comparative Private Law at the Law Department of the University of Turin, Italy. She is currently coordinator (Contracts) of the Master of Laws in International Trade, jointly organised by Turin University and the ITC–ILO, in partnership with IUSE, UNCITRAL and UNIDROIT.

Jan Yves Remy currently serves as Deputy Director of the Shridath Ramphal Centre for International Trade Law, Policy and Services (SRC) of the University of the West Indies Cave Hill Campus. She lectures in the SRC's Masters in International Trade Policy (MITP) programme, in the areas of international trade law, regional integration law and e-commerce; and conducts outreach and research on behalf of the Centre. She previously worked as Senior Associate at Sidley Austin LLP (Geneva and Washington DC) and Legal Officer at the Appellate Body of the WTO.

LIST OF ABBREVIATIONS

ADR	Alternative dispute resolution
ANVISA	Brazilian Health Regulatory Agency
AoA	Agreement on Agriculture
APEC	Asia Pacific Economic Cooperation
CISG	United Nations Convention on Contracts for the International Sale of Goods
CPTPP	Comprehensive and Progressive Agreement for Trans-Pacific Partnership
CTEO	Chief Trade Enforcement Officer
DSB	Dispute Settlement Body
DSM	dispute settlement mechanism
DSU	Dispute Settlement Understanding or Understanding on Rules and Procedures Governing the Settlement of Disputes
EIDL	Economic Injury Disaster Loan
EUA	Emergency Use Authorisation
FAO	Food and Agriculture Organization
FTA	free trade agreement
FTAAP	Free Trade Agreement of the Asia-Pacific
GATS	General Agreement on Trade in Services
GATT	General Agreement on Tariffs and Trade
GHG	greenhouse gases
GVCs	global value chains
ICT	information and communication technology
IFAM	International Freight Assistance Mechanism
ILO	International Labour Organization

IMDRF	International Medical Devices Regulators Forum
IMF	International Monetary Fund
INMETRO	National Institute of Metrology, Quality and Technology
IP	intellectual property
LIFIDC	food-import-dependent countries
MDSAP	Medical Device Single Audit Program
MES	market economy status
MFN	most-favoured nation
MNES	multinational enterprises
MOCs	market-oriented conditions
MPIA	Multiparty Interim Appeal Arbitration Arrangement
NAFTA	North American Free Trade Agreement
NMEs	non-market economies
npr-PPM	non-product related PPM
OECD	Organisation for Economic Co-operation and Development
OMA	orderly marketing arrangements
PECL	Principles of European Contract Law
PPE	personal protective equipment
PPMs	process and production methods
RCEP	Regional Comprehensive Economic Partnership
RTA	regional trade agreement
SCCs	sustainability contractual clauses
SCM Agreement	Agreement on Subsidies and Countervailing Duties
SDG	sustainable development goal
SG Agreement	Agreement on Safeguards
SMEs	small and medium-sized enterprises
SOEs	state-owned enterprises
SPS Agreement	Agreement on the Application of Sanitary and Phytosanitary Measures

STEM	science, technology, engineering and mathematics
TBT Agreement	Agreement on Technical Barriers to Trade
TCAs	transnational company agreements
TPP	Trans-Pacific Partnership
TPRM	Trade Policy Review Mechanism
TRIPS	Agreement on Trade-Related Aspects of Intellectual Property Rights
UN	United Nations
UNFCCC	United Nations Framework Convention on Climate Change
USTR	United States Trade Representative
VCLT	Vienna Convention on the Law of Treaties
VER	voluntary export restraints
WFP	World Food Programme
WHO	World Health Organization
WTO	World Trade Organization

LIST OF WTO PANEL AND APPELLATE BODY REPORTS

Short title	Full case title and citation	Page No.
Argentina–Financial Services	*Argentina–Measures Relating to Trade in Goods and Services*, Report of the Panel (9 May 2016) WT/DS453/R	224
Australia–Tobacco Plain Packaging	*Australia–Certain Measures Concerning Trademarks, Geographical Indication and other Plain Packaging Requirements Applicable to Tobacco Products and Pack*, Report of the Panel (28 June 2018) WT/DS435/R, WT/DS441/R, WT/DS458/R, WT/DS467/R28	145–46
	Australia–Certain Measures Concerning Trademarks, Geographical Indications and Other Plain Packaging Requirements Applicable to Tobacco Products and Packaging, Report of the Appellate Body (29 June 2020) WT/DS435/AB/R, WT/DS441/AB/R	187, 192
Brazil–Tyres	*Brazil–Measures Affecting Imports of Retreaded Tyres*, Report of the Panel (17 December 2007) WT/DS332/R	138–39, 141, 146, 156–57
	Brazil–Measures Affecting Imports of Retreaded Tyres, Report of the Appellate Body (17 December 2007) WT/DS/AB/332	50
Canada–Aircraft	*Canada–Measures Affecting the Export of Civilian Aircraft*, Report of the Panel (14 April 1999) WT/DS70/R	60
Canada–Autos	*Canada–Certain Measures Affecting the Automotive Industry, Report of the Panel (19 June 2000) WT/DS139/R, WT/DS142/R*	229
	Canada–Certain Measures Affecting the Automotive Industry, Report of the Appellate Body (19 June 2000) WT/DS139/AB/R, WT/DS142/AB/R	224

EC–Bananas III	*European Communities–Regime for the Importation, Sale and Distribution of Bananas*, Report of the Panel (25 September 1997) WT/DS27/R/ECU	223–24
	European Communities–Regime for the Importation, Sale and Distribution of Bananas, Report of the Appellate Body (25 September 1997) WT/DS27/AB/R	230
EC–Chicken Cuts	*European Communities–Customs Classification of Frozen Boneless Chicken Cuts*, Report of the Appellate Body (27 September 2005) WTO/DS269/AB/R	137
EC–Seal Products	*European Communities–Measures Prohibiting the Importation and Marketing of Seal Products*, Report of the Panel (16 June 2014) WT/DS400/AD/R	23, 82
	European Communities–Measures Prohibiting the Importation and Marketing of Seal Products, Report of the Appellate Body (16 June 2014), WT/DS400/AB/R, WT/DS401/AB/R	141–42, 223, 225
EU–Energy Package	*European Union and its Member States–Certain Measures Relating to the Energy Sector*, Report of the Panel (circulated 10 August 2018) WT/DS476/R	85–86, 224, 229
India–Solar Cells	*India–Certain Measures Related to Solar Cells and Solar Modules*, Report of the Appellate Body (14 October 2016) WT/DS/AB/456	50
Japan–Alcoholic Beverages II	*Japan–Taxes on Alcoholic Beverages*, Report of the Panel (1 November 1996) WT/DS8/R, WT/DS10/R, WT/DS11/R	215
	Japan–Taxes on Alcoholic Beverages, Report of the Appellate Body (1 November 1996) WT/DS8/AB/R, WT/DS10/AB/R, WT/DS11/AB/R	134–35, 214–15
Japan–Trade in Semi-Conductors	*Japan–Trade in Semi-Conductors*, GATT Panel (4 May 1988) 24L/6309 – 35S/116	225
Korea–Various Measures on Beef	*Korea–Measures Affecting Imports of Fresh, Chilled and Frozen Beef*, Report of the Appellate Body (10 January 2001) WT/DS/AB/161	50

US–Tuna II	*United States–Measures Concerning the Importation, Marketing and Sale of Tuna and Tuna Products*, Report of the Panel (13 June 2012) WT/DS381/R	158
	United States–Measures Concerning the Importation, Marketing and Sale of Tuna and Tuna Products, Report of the Appellate Body (13 June 2012) WT/DS381/AB/R	158
	Unites States–Measures Concerning the Importation, Marketing and Sale of Tuna and Tuna Products (Recourse to Article 21.5 of the DSU), Report of the Appellate Body (11 January 2019) WT/DS381/AB/RW/USA, WT/DS381/AB/RW2	50

1

Rethinking, Repackaging and Rescuing World Trade Law in the Post-Pandemic Era

WEIHUAN ZHOU, AMRITA BAHRI AND DARIA BOKLAN

I. Introduction

The world trading system, established under the auspices of the World Trade Organization (WTO), is facing an unprecedented crisis. The COVID-19 pandemic is not the only cause, nor the most fundamental one, although it has significantly intensified this crisis. Anti-globalism and protectionism had been on the rise before the outbreak of the pandemic, leading to an expansion of trade barriers and on many occasions beggar-thy-neighbour policies adversely affecting global trade and international relations.[1] The most telling example has been the dramatic change in trade policies of the United States (US) under the Trump administration. This change has led to not only escalating trade tensions between the US and China[2] and rising tariffs in the guise of national security against other countries including US allies triggering retaliatory actions,[3] but also a shift away from multilateral cooperation more generally. As far as trade data is concerned, trade restrictive measures in G20 economies had doubled between mid-October 2017 and mid-January 2020 (compared with the previous review period).[4] In 2019, world merchandise trade went through a slight decline of 0.1 per cent in volume terms (3 per cent in value) after rising by 2.9 per cent in 2018. In the same year, the

[1] A González, 'Role of trade ministers at the WTO during crises: Activating global cooperation to overcome COVID-19' in S Evenett and R Baldwin, *Revitalising Multilateralism Pragmatic Ideas for the New WTO Director-General* (London, CEPR Press, 2020) 80; M Solís, 'The post COVID-19 world: Economic nationalism triumphant?' (*Brookings*, 10 July 2020), www.brookings.edu/blog/order-from-chaos/2020/07/10/the-post-covid-19-world-economic-nationalism-triumphant/.

[2] W Zhou and H Gao, 'US–China Trade War: A Way Out?' (2020) 19 *World Trade Review* 605.

[3] D Boklan and A Bahri, 'The First WTO's Ruling on National Security Exception: Balancing Interests or Opening Pandora's Box?' (2020) 19 *World Trade Review* 135.

[4] WTO, 'Report on G20 trade measures' (29 June 2020), www.wto.org/english/news_e/news20_e/report_trdev_jun20_e.pdf.

pace of the increase in world commercial services trade also slowed down significantly from 9 per cent in 2018 to 2 per cent.[5]

The impact of the pandemic on the world economy has evidently been catastrophic with 220 countries or territories affected, over 62 million confirmed cases and 1.4 million confirmed deaths as of 1 December 2020.[6] The highly restrictive containment measures that countries have unilaterally adopted to combat the spread of the disease, and the wide array of fiscal, monetary and trade policies adopted to maintain domestic economic resilience and stimulate recovery,[7] have caused sudden, extensive and enduring disruptions to international trade. The WTO estimates that the volume of world merchandise trade will shrink by 9.2 per cent in 2020,[8] leading to a collapse of global trade even worse than the 2008–09 global financial crisis.[9] The World Bank forecasts a 5.2 per cent contraction in global GDP this year, which, if materialised, would be the deepest recession since the Second World War.[10] Considerable uncertainties remain around the prospects of world trade and the global economy in the years ahead.

The history of world trade has amply demonstrated that unilateralism and protectionism are mutually destructive, and instead that international cooperation is the way to resolve disagreements on trade-related issues and eventually to build long-term peace and prosperity.[11] To deal with the pandemic-induced unilateral (and at times protectionist) measures, many have rightly called upon governments to take collective action.[12] However, as the only global institution that promotes international cooperation on trade liberalisation and regulation, the WTO is now fighting for its relevance.

At this critical juncture, trade negotiators, policymakers, scholars and other stakeholders are intensively debating the role of the WTO in international cooperation on trade policymaking and dispute resolution as well as alternative options. This book contributes to this debate by offering one of the first collections of articles that explore and develop the discussion over a range of fundamental and systemic

[5] 'Trade set to plunge as COVID-19 pandemic upends global economy' (WTO, 8 April 2020), www.wto.org/english/news_e/pres20_e/pr855_e.htm.

[6] 'Coronavirus disease (COVID-19) pandemic' (World Health Organization), www.who.int/emergencies/diseases/novel-coronavirus-2019.

[7] 'COVID-19: Measures affecting trade in goods' (WTO), www.wto.org/english/tratop_e/covid19_e/trade_related_goods_measure_e.htm; 'Policy Responses to COVID-19' (International Monetary Fund), www.imf.org/en/Topics/imf-and-covid19/Policy-Responses-to-COVID-19.

[8] 'Trade shows signs of rebound from COVID-19, recovery still uncertain' (WTO, 6 October 2020), www.wto.org/english/news_e/pres20_e/pr862_e.htm.

[9] 'Trade set to plunge as COVID-19 pandemic upends global economy' (WTO, 8 April 2020), www.wto.org/english/news_e/pres20_e/pr855_e.htm.

[10] World Bank, 'Pandemic, Recession: The Global Economy in Crisis' (June 2020), www.worldbank.org/en/publication/global-economic-prospects.

[11] See generally, DA Irwin, *Against the Tide: An Intellectual History of Free Trade* (New Jersey, Princeton University Press, 1996); DA Irwin, *Clashing over Commerce: A History of US Trade Policy* (Chicago, University of Chicago Press, 2017).

[12] See, eg, R Baldwin and SJ Evenett (eds), *COVID-19 and Trade Policy: Why Turning Inward Won't Work* (London, CEPR Press, 2020).

challenges faced by international trade and the multilateral trading system using the COVID-19 pandemic as an important context.

II. The WTO and the Pandemic: Fundamental Challenges for International Trade Regulation

Many of the fundamental challenges that the WTO currently faces have been long-standing or emerging issues since before the pandemic. These include, for example, the tensions between trade and non-trade interests, non-market economies (NMEs) and state-led market distortions, the widespread use of industrial policies and subsidies, the abuse of security exceptions, the ineffectiveness of the WTO's transparency and notification mechanisms, the need for inclusive and sustainable growth, and the proliferation of free trade agreements (FTAs). These issues have called into question the efficacy and adequacy of the current WTO rules in addressing existing and emerging issues, the reforms that might be needed, the appropriateness of the institutional framework and decision-making process of the WTO (such as the rule of consensus) in supporting such multilateral negotiations of reforms, and how regional trade negotiations and agreements may serve as a stepping stone rather than a stumbling block to more inclusive negotiations at the multilateral level.

At the same time, the WTO's dispute settlement mechanism (DSM), which has long served to protect the enforceability, certainty and predictability of world trade rules and a rules-based approach to dispute resolution, is gradually losing its legitimacy and effectiveness due to the loss of a functional Appellate Body caused by the US continuous blockage of the appointment of new Appellate Body members.[13] Despite the agreement to a 'multi-party interim appeal arbitration arrangement' (MPIA) among some WTO Members as a temporary replacement for the Appellate Body, the absence of the Appellate Body has created an irreplaceable loophole in the DSM and has already led to the abuse of the right of appeal as some major Members (particularly the US and the European Union (EU)) increasingly resort to the practice of 'appealing into the void' to avoid binding decisions and implementation of unfavourable rulings.[14]

All the aforesaid challenges predate the pandemic and will persist after it. A solution to the pandemic-induced measures or issues would not provide an

[13] A Bahri, 'Appellate Body Held Hostage: Is Judicial Activism at Fair Trial?' (2019) 53 *Journal of World Trade* 293; W Zhou and H Gao, '"Overreaching" or "Overreacting"? Reflections on the Judicial Function and Approaches of WTO Appellate Body' (2019) 53 *Journal of World Trade* 951.

[14] See, eg, *United States–Countervailing Measures on Softwood Lumber from Canada*, Notification of an appeal by the United States under Article 16 of the DSU (29 September 2020) WT/DS533/5; *European Union–Cost Adjustment Methodologies and Certain Anti-Dumping Measures on Imports from Russia*, Notification of an appeal by the European Union under Articles 16.4 and 17.1 of the DSU and under rule 20(1) of the Working Procedures for Appellate Review (1 September 2020) WT/DS494/7.

adequate response to these challenges. Nevertheless, the pandemic has amplified the impact of some of these issues, bringing them to the fore in the current policy and academic debate. Set out below are some of the most prominent:

- The wide-ranging trade restrictions, especially on the export of personal protective equipment, medicines and other essential supplies, have led to massive disruptions in global supply chains and a shortage of essential goods. These measures range from outright export bans, other forms of quantitative restrictions, additional inspections and quality checks, to new procedures on licensing or registration, to discourage exports. These trade-restrictive and distortive practices have led to a growing debate about how the WTO rules may be applied to facilitate trade while leaving the flexibility for governments to fulfil domestic economic and regulatory needs especially in times of crisis.
- The widespread use of industrial policies and subsidies for economic recovery has generated increasing concerns about their impact on trade and their compatibility with existing trade norms. These subsidies have taken a variety of forms including a direct transfer of funds (for example, wage support and other recovery funds), tax exemptions and deductions, preferential loans or loan waivers, etc. While these subsidies are applied to address the economic consequences of the pandemic, they may well have a longer-term effect on trade. Therefore, there is a pressing need for governments to discuss how to address them in a collaborative manner and in ways that strike a balance between disciplining trade-distortive subsidies and preserving policy space for their legitimate use.[15]
- More broadly, the pandemic has intensified the ever mounting concerns about the sustainability of economic growth and international trade. More so than ever before, governments are reiterating the fundamental importance of ensuring that trade rules and multilateral cooperation leave the regulatory space needed by governments in the pursuit of economic growth and sustainable development. The discriminatory and trade-restrictive measures adopted during the pandemic, affecting both imports and exports, have intensified the long-standing and fundamental challenge as to how WTO rules and exceptions may be interpreted and applied in a way that balances trade and non-trade interests. Despite this challenge, the current crisis presents a golden opportunity to rethink the nexus between trade and sustainable development

[15] See, eg, P Draper et al, 'Industrial Subsidies As A Major Policy Response Since The Global Financial Crises: Consequences And Remedies' (21 November 2020) Policy Brief, T20 Saudi Arabia, t20saudiarabia.org.sa/en/briefs/Documents/T20_TF1_PB3.pdf; B Hoekman and D Nelson, 'Rethinking international subsidy rules' (2020) *World Economy*, onlinelibrary.wiley.com/doi/full/10.1111/twec.13022. For a detailed analysis of the applicability of current WTO rules on Chinese subsidies in the high-tech sector and proposals for future negotiations of industrial subsidies, see W Zhou and MM Fang, 'Subsidizing Technology Competition: China's Evolving Practices and International Trade Regulation in the Post- Pandemic Era' (2020) University of New South Wales Law Research Series No 20-66, papers.ssrn.com/sol3/papers.cfm?abstract_id=3737272.

and to explore how trade policies may contribute to 'building back better' in the post-COVID-19 world.

Many other issues are less related to the pandemic but no less significant. Below are some major examples:

- Issues relating to NMEs, the role of governments in the market including the use of state-owned enterprises as a policy instrument, and related protective, distortive and anti-competitive behaviour, practices and implications, will continue to impose immense pressure on the WTO to provide a multilateral solution. While some WTO rules have provided tools to address these issues, there is a shared belief among major Western economies that these rules need to be updated and further developed. In contrast, countries with a different economic and growth model, particularly China, have consistently opposed the concept of NMEs and any country-specific discriminatory rules and practices. This divide remains a fundamental challenge for the multilateral trading system.
- The US–China trade tensions are likely to continue under the Biden administration precisely around the NME issues mentioned above and other related issues such as industrial policies and subsidies. These issues are not addressed in the US–China Phase One Trade Deal[16] (Phase One Deal) reached in January 2020 to ease the two-year-long bilateral trade war[17] and will remain at the centre of the escalating US–China competition and future trade policymaking.
- At the same time, the Phase One Deal has created many issues of WTO inconsistency and a dispute resolution framework that favours a confrontational approach to the settlement of disputes.[18] These issues have the potential to significantly undermine the central role of the WTO in international trade regulation and dispute resolution.
- While the MPIA is intended to provide a temporary solution to the Appellate Body impasse, it remains to be seen whether it may actually fill the gap and maintain the effectiveness and legitimacy of the DSM. As an arrangement among only a small portion of WTO Members, it not only leaves considerable uncertainties as to what the other Members may do in disputes, but also provides no guarantee that a MPIA party Member would not abuse the right of appeal (as the EU, a founding member of the MPIA, has just done).[19]

[16] Economic and Trade Agreement Between the Government of the United States and the Government of the People's Republic of China (Washington DC, 15 January 2020) (Phase One Deal).

[17] For a brief discussion of this deal, see W Zhou and H Gao, 'US–China Phase One Deal: A Brief Account' (*Kluwer Regulating for Globalization Blog*, 22 January 2020), regulatingforglobalization.com/2020/01/22/us-china-phase-one-deal-a-brief-account.

[18] See W Zhou, 'WTO Dispute Settlement Mechanism Without the Appellate Body: Some Observations on the US–China Trade Deal' (2020) 9 *Journal of International Trade and Arbitration Law* 443.

[19] See above (n 14).

Moreover, the growing use of the MPIA would trigger questions about precedent (ie, whether the existing case laws should be applied in a consistent manner), the value of decisions of MPIA arbitrators in WTO jurisprudence, etc. Therefore, the MPIA appears to have created more problems than it has solved.

- Deficiencies in the WTO's institutional framework and decision-making process have long been criticised. For instance, the 'consensus' rule, whereby decision-making under the WTO requires an agreement by all Members, has weakened the capacity of the organisation to further trade liberalisation and update its rulebook in response to cutting-edge issues. Lately, the Appellate Body paralysis and the stalemate in the appointment of a new Director-General of the WTO have further exemplified the ineffectiveness of this rule.[20] Another example relates to weaknesses in the WTO's transparency mechanism, particularly whether the mechanism may induce proper notifications and provide a desirable level of transparency, awareness and predictability of trade policy developments.
- The difficulties and failures associated with WTO negotiations have incentivised like-minded countries to resort to negotiations at sub-multilateral levels leading to the rapid expansion of bilateral, plurilateral and mega-regional trade agreements such as the Comprehensive and Progressive Agreement for Trans-Pacific Partnership (CPTPP) concluded in 2018 and the Regional Comprehensive Economic Partnership (RCEP) concluded in 2020. As these FTAs continue to deepen and broaden the level and scope of trade liberalisation and develop new rules to tackle existing and emerging issues, they increasingly challenge the relevance of the WTO rules and multilateral trade negotiations. At the same time, however, FTA negotiations cast light on how WTO Members may create workarounds to seemingly existential obstacles to multilateralism by looking beyond consensus and reinvigorating their will to find common solutions. These efforts and achievements may contribute to building the political will needed for international cooperation at the multilateral level.

III. The Aim and Structure of this Book

It is unrealistic for this book to address all the challenges outlined above. By focusing on some selected major issues, this book explores ways to 'rethink', 'repackage' and 'rescue' world trade law in the post-COVID-19 era. The underlying objective is to revive the governance of international trade and make it relevant and resilient to the existing and emerging challenges and developments. To ensure that the multilateral trading system remains relevant, it is important to rethink the existing

[20] 'Members indicate strong preference for Ngozi Okonjo-Iweala as DG but US objects' (WTO, 8 October 2020), www.wto.org/english/news_e/news20_e/dgsel_28oct20_e.htm.

rules and exceptions in a way that provides sufficient flexibility for WTO Members to respond to the pandemic, to future crises and to legitimate policy needs more generally. To maintain the resilience of the system amidst growing concerns about its lack of sustainability and inclusiveness, it has become increasingly important to repackage (ie, further develop) the trade rulebook in ways that accommodate the sustainable development goals (SDGs). In addition, efforts must also be made to address the other important (but less pandemic-related) issues faced by the system if it is to be rescued. Taken together, these efforts will play a significant role in regaining shared faith in multilateral cooperation for trade rule-making and dispute resolution.

Accordingly, this book is divided into three parts with each addressing one area of the challenges identified above.

A. Rethinking World Trade Law and the Pandemic

The pandemic is driving many countries – some of which were once the architects and designers of the current world trading system – to further retreat from global economic integration.[21] It has proliferated discontent about globalisation, free trade and the need to regulate it in a multilateral manner. It has demonstrated that long-lasting trade relations can fracture overnight in exceptional times, and that globalisation comes with a risk of being overly reliant on partners that may refuse to trade in certain situations.

In an environment with uncertain alliances and lack of international cooperation, countries are increasingly contemplating ways to reduce economic interdependence. National security, public health, food security and other concerns have become grounds for unilateralism and protectionism. In response to the current crisis, countries seem poised to reinforce the movement towards de-globalisation. Given the coverage of this crisis, a multilateral solution is needed. Although the WTO does not seem prepared to manage this crisis, it provides a forum for governments to do so via cooperation.

In an effort to rethink the role of the WTO and the current trade rules, part I of this book explores some of the most prominent trade-related issues arising from the pandemic and offers detailed analysis of the relevant rules and exceptions. It includes chapters that provide an overview of trade-related measures adopted by countries during the pandemic, and more focused discussions of export restrictions on food commodities and implications for food security, the scope of the existing WTO rules for pandemic-induced subsidies, the WTO's jurisdiction over certain health and environmental issues generated by the pandemic, and the prospects of addressing pandemic-triggered trade measures through international cooperation under the WTO.

[21] Baldwin and Evenett (n 12).

Jan Bohanes (chapter two, 'An Overview of Trade-Related Measures Taken by WTO Members During the COVID-19 Pandemic and a Few Reflections Thereon') opens the discussion by reviewing the range of measures adopted by governments around the world in response to the pandemic. This is followed by a discussion of the impact of these measures on international trade and their potential compatibility with WTO rules. This chapter shows how the existing rules may provide the flexibility for the use of trade and domestic measures in times of crisis.

Ilaria Espa (chapter three, 'Export Restrictions on Food Commodities During the COVID-19 Crisis: Implications for Food Security and the Role of the WTO') tackles a more specific issue that has attracted growing attention during the pandemic, that is, export restrictions and food security. After a review of the various types of pandemic-induced export restrictions and their impact on food security, this chapter offers a critical analysis of the flexibilities in the existing WTO rules for the adoption of these restrictions. It argues that many of these measures lack a rational nexus to the current health emergencies. It then puts forward some suggestions for improving the transparency and notifications of export restrictions more generally as one of the most crucial aspects of rethinking the world trading system.

Ru Ding (chapter four, 'Time to Reform the Non-Actionable Subsidy Rules in the WTO: The COVID-19 Subsidies and Beyond') focuses on discussing selected 'COVID-19 subsidies' in three major jurisdictions, the US, the EU and China, and their consistency with the WTO subsidy rules. Based on this discussion, this chapter calls for the reintroduction of the so-called 'non-actionable subsidies' which expired in 1999 and in particular the creation of a category of such subsidies for 'disaster relief' to provide the flexibility needed by governments to use subsidies to deal with natural disasters.

Alexandra R Harrington (chapter five, 'Rethinking WTO DSB Jurisdiction in Light of Pandemic, Climate Change and Other Evolving Threats') shifts the focus from WTO rules to the DSM. This chapter offers an insightful analysis of the WTO's adjudication of environment and health-related issues, the development of the relevant jurisprudence, and the criticisms that the WTO has attracted over the years. It then reflects on the potential deficiencies of the DSM in response to the pandemic and similar issues/situations (such as climate change) and proposes to make a structural change to the DSM through the creation of specialised panels to adjudicate matters falling within the environment and health-related exceptions under the WTO.

The final chapter in part I, by Michelle R Sanchez-Badin and Magali Favaretto Prieto Fernandes (chapter six, 'The WTO and Brazil's Trade Responses Amid the Pandemic: Can Transparency Overcome Populism?'), is dedicated to the issue of transparency including a review of transparency mechanisms under various WTO Agreements and a detailed case study of Brazil's fulfilment of these transparency requirements during the pandemic. It highlights the importance of coordination between different WTO committees to maintain and improve the effectiveness of the WTO's transparency mechanisms.

B. Repackaging World Trade Law and Sustainable Development

Trade liberalisation is not the ultimate goal of the WTO but merely an instrument to achieve the goals embedded in the Marrakesh Agreement Establishing the WTO concluded in 1994.[22] Sustainable development is one such goal. Over time, the term 'sustainable development' has become far better understood and accepted as a concept that relates to trading interests. There is a growing realisation that trade needs to be sustainable to ensure that countries can reconcile trade liberalisation with their important national interests. It needs to be inclusive so as to better include and benefit marginalised players. The Addis Ababa Agenda of Action,[23] the UN's 2030 Agenda for Sustainable Development[24] and the WTO's Joint Declaration on Trade and Women's Economic Empowerment[25] have all recognised international trade as an important instrument to achieve the SDGs.

FTAs have also shown an impressive accommodation of SDGs. In 2011, the WTO estimated that 75 per cent of countries had negotiated FTAs that included provisions on human rights.[26] In 2019, more than 60 per cent of trade agreements in force had included commitments on labour rights protection.[27] Currently, over 70 FTAs (out of 306 in force) have an explicit commitment on gender equality.[28] In addition, governments have increasingly resorted to trade agreements to cooperate on environmental matters by including environmental protection and climate change-related provisions in various trade agreements and economic partnerships.[29]

The pandemic has intensified discussions on the nexus between trade and globalisation on the one hand, and non-trade values such as environment protection, food security, labour standards, inequality etc. on the other. It has shown that national and global economies function better when they are inclusive and

[22] Preamble of the Marrakesh Agreement Establishing the World Trade Organization (Marrakesh, 15 April 1994).

[23] 'Third International Conference on Financing for Development (FfD3)' (United Nations, 13–16 July 2015), www.un.org/esa/ffd/ffd3/conference.html.

[24] 'Transforming our world: the 2030 Agenda for Sustainable Development', UNGA Res 70/1 (25 September 2015).

[25] WTO Ministerial Declaration, 'Buenos Aires Joint Declaration on Trade and Women's Economic Empowerment' (12 December 2017), www.wto.org/english/thewto_e/minist_e/mc11_e/genderdeclarationmc11_e.pdf.

[26] SA Aaronson and JP Chauffour, 'The Wedding of Trade and Human Rights: Marriage of Convenience or Permanent Match?', WTO Research and Analysis, www.wto.org/english/res_e/publications_e/wtr11_forum_e/wtr11_15feb11_e.htm.

[27] International Labour Organization, 'Social dimensions of free trade' (2015), www.ilo.org/wcmsp5/groups/public/---dgreports/---inst/documents/publication/wcms_228965.pdf, 20.

[28] Author's own calculations. See A Bahri, 'Gender Mainstreaming in Free Trade Agreements: What have we Achieved, and what More is Needed for Inclusive Post-Pandemic Recovery?', ch 10 in this book.

[29] OECD, 'Assessing the Effectiveness of Environmental Provisions in Regional Trade Agreements: An Empirical Analysis' (2 September 2018), www.oecd-ilibrary.org/environment/assessing-the-effectiveness-of-environmental-provisions-in-regional-trade-agreements_5ffc615c-en.

sustainable, where inequalities are addressed and sustainability considerations properly accommodated.[30] This has led to a growing interest in further understanding the nexus between trade and sustainable development, with topics such as circular economy, gender equality, climate change and plastic pollution acquiring prominence in trade policy debates.

Against this backdrop, part II of this book broadens the discussions beyond pandemic-related measures and issues to explore the interrelation between international trade and sustainable development. It includes chapters which discuss the interaction between domestic and international law and between public and private law when it comes to achieving sustainability through international trade, the EU's Green Deal as a way to bring trade and sustainability together (SDG 7[31] and SDG 13),[32] the compatibility of the Paris Agreement with the existing WTO rules (SDG 13),[33] and the inclusion of gender equality considerations in FTAs (SDG 5).[34]

Lorenza Mola and Cristina Poncibò (chapter seven, 'Trade and UN SDGs 2030: The Interplay between Public International Law and Contract Law') open the discussion with a broad conceptual perspective by focusing on conceptualising the role of public international law and private law and their interactions and contributions to improving the delivery of SDGs in global trade. This chapter argues that innovative repackaging of public and private law offers a way to accommodate environmental and trade interests within the perspective of sustainability.

Daria Boklan (chapter eight, 'Combating Climate Change under the WTO: Exploring the Relevance of Process and Production Methods') tackles specific issues relating to process and production methods (PPMs) in the context of discussing the nexus between multilateral trade norms and climate change. This chapter evaluates the scope of WTO rules, especially the non-discrimination rules, the general exceptions and the rules on technical barriers, for its Members to fulfil their commitments under the Paris Agreement and particularly SDG 13. It argues that the Paris Agreement and the WTO Agreements serve different objectives and are complementary in terms of their distributional consequences of climate change policies.

Luana Almeida (chapter nine, 'The EU Green Deal and International Trade Law: Bringing Trade and Sustainability Together') provides a detailed case study of the European Green Deal which seeks to reinforce the EU's commitments under a number of SDGs including Goal 7 (affordable and clean energy), Goal 11 (sustainable cities and communities) and Goal 12 (responsible consumption and

[30] K Kuhlmann et al, 'Re-conceptualizing Free Trade Agreements Through a Sustainable Development Lens'; 'A Contribution to the Policy Hackathon on Model Provisions for Trade in Times of Crisis and Pandemic in Regional and other Trade Agreements' (27 July 2020), www.unescap.org/sites/default/files/145%20Final-Team%20Katrin%20Kuhlmann-USA.pdf.

[31] UN 2030 SDG 7: Affordable and Clean Energy (n 24).

[32] ibid, UN 2030 SDG 13: Climate Action.

[33] ibid.

[34] ibid, UN 2030 SDG 5: Gender Equality.

production). After a careful review of the Green Deal and its implementation, this chapter discusses whether this deal may be reconciled with WTO rules and jurisprudence and the EU's efforts to shape the rules in FTAs to provide room for the deal.

The final chapter in part II, by Amrita Bahri (chapter ten, 'Gender Mainstreaming in Free Trade Agreements: What have we Achieved, and what More is Needed for Inclusive Post-Pandemic Recovery?'), explores the interplay between FTAs and SDG 5 by focusing on analysing how FTAs can accommodate gender equality considerations and contribute to building back an inclusive economy in the post-COVID-19 world. It addresses two major questions: (1) whether gender equality considerations are a part of existing FTAs, and (2) how FTAs may be improved to encourage women empowerment. In response to the first question, this chapter discusses some best practices of mainstreaming gender considerations in the existing FTAs between countries in North America and the EU. To address the second question, the chapter puts forward recommendations for future FTAs to strengthen women empowerment and inclusive growth, also offering some guidance for multilateral negotiations.

C. Rescuing World Trade Law and Other Fundamental Challenges

As mentioned above, many of the challenges that the WTO faces are not caused by the pandemic. For example, the failure of the WTO to facilitate trade negotiations and the dysfunctional DSM are challenges that the WTO has been trying to address since before the pandemic. Despite the ongoing crisis in the WTO, it remains to be the only forum for multilateral negotiations on trade-related issues (such as digital trade, fishery subsidies) and for the resolution of trade disputes based on rules (as opposed to power). Accordingly, it has the potential to continue to play an essential role in combating protectionism and unilateralism while promoting gains from trade and cooperation.[35] Thus, instead of letting the WTO die and then trying to rebuild it again, governments should work together to rescue and further develop it.

Accordingly, part III of this book turns to some of the most current and controversial issues that are less pandemic related and hence have not been addressed in the previous sections. It contributes to the ongoing discussions about how to reinvigorate the multilateral trading system through chapters that discuss challenges and opportunities for the DSM, the US–China Phase One Deal and the issues it creates for the WTO, the MPIA and its implications for the DSM and WTO

[35] For a recent discussion of the fundamental function of the WTO and how that function has been fulfilled by WTO tribunals in adjudicating disputes and developing WTO jurisprudence, see W Zhou, 'In Defence of the WTO: Why Do We Need A Multilateral Trading System?' (2020) 47 *Legal Issues of Economic Integration* 9.

jurisprudence, issues relating to NMEs and China, and the US approaches to the Trans-Pacific Partnership (TPP, and now the CPTPP) and lessons for multilateral cooperation.

Jan Yves Remy (chapter eleven, 'The Current State of Dispute Settlement at the WTO: How Did We Get Here and What Next?') reviews the evolution of the DSM with a focus on the Appellate Body, the criticisms of it and the general features of the MPIA. While it identifies some concerns about the MPIA and potential deviations from it, it sees the opportunities for the MPIA to play a positive role in maintaining the WTO's rules-based approach to dispute resolution in the absence of a functional Appellate Body.

Mariana Clara de Andrade (chapter twelve, 'Precedent in the MPIA: What Role for Consistency and Predictability?') provides a more detailed discussion of the MPIA with a focus on the provisions and the drafting history that shed light on the issue of precedent. It explores whether MPIA arbitrators may follow and apply the existing case law and how they may play a role in further developing WTO jurisprudence. While it suggests that the DSM needs to be adapted to new realities, it believes that MPIA arbitrators should strive to ensure consistency and predictability in trade law so as to safeguard the value of, and regain the trust in, the multilateral trading system.

Maria Manuela Moccero (chapter thirteen, 'Is the Phase One Deal the Emergence of a "New Generation" of Bilateral Trade Agreements that Challenge the WTO?') offers a fresh analysis of the US–China Phase One Deal and the challenges that it may pose to the WTO including whether the deal may be captured by the WTO Agreement on Safeguards, the potential breaches of the non-discrimination principles, and the justifiability of these breaches under the FTA exceptions contemplated in Article XXIV of the General Agreement on Tariffs and Trade (GATT) and Article V of the General Agreement on Trade in Services (GATS). It calls for updates to some of these WTO rules to prevent managed trade arrangements from undermining the core principles of the multilateral trading system.

Luyao Che (chapter fourteen, 'China's Response to the "Market-Oriented Conditions" Proposal for WTO Reform and its Implications in the (Post-) COVID-19 Era') tackles the controversial and systemic issue of NMEs through a critical analysis of the 'market-oriented conditions' proposed by the US, the EU and Japan for WTO reforms and China's possible responses to this joint proposal. It establishes a conceptual framework for this discussion which categorises the relevant issues and responses into three levels: legal instruments, institution and underlying ideology. Under each level, it develops some general propositions and approaches for a multilateral response to the concerns about NMEs.

The final chapter of this book, by Meredith Kolsky Lewis (chapter fifteen, 'Winning Strategy or Own Goal? Reflections on the United States Exiting the Trans-Pacific Partnership'), goes beyond the WTO to critically review the US withdrawal from the TPP and the implications for the US and other (CP)TPP countries. This analysis from national and regional perspectives is a significant addition to the book by demonstrating how sub-multilateral cooperation, such as the CPTPP, may offer valuable guidance for WTO Members to rescue their trade liberalisation objectives, even in an era of populism, pandemic and other challenges.

IV. The Way Forward

The pandemic has created a worldwide crisis that requires a collective response by all nations involved. Multilateral cooperation on international trade regulation and dispute resolution is indispensable not only to that response but also to the long-term peace and prosperity of the world economy. This book has benefited from rigorous and insightful discussions of some of the most significant challenges faced by the multilateral trading system by a very diverse group of authors in terms of their areas of expertise, professional backgrounds and regions. It is our hope that this book will offer a valuable source and abundant food-for-thought for academics, researchers, policymakers, trade negotiators, students and other stakeholders in debating the future of the WTO and the ways to construct an architecture for regulating international trade more generally.

This is not the first time we have been in a crisis. The 1930 Smoot–Hawley Tariff and the 2008–09 global financial crisis, for example, also had destructive impacts on trade and international relations. Through collective efforts, governments succeeded in bringing the world economy back to (a new) normal. Despite the arguably larger impact of COVID-19, international cooperation is what is needed to, and what can reinvigorate, the world trading system. The pandemic has provided a unique opportunity for governments to rebuild the political will needed for such cooperation. One should never let a serious crisis go to waste.

PART I

Rethinking World Trade Law and the Pandemic

2

An Overview of Trade-Related Measures Taken by WTO Members During the COVID-19 Pandemic and a Few Reflections Thereon

JAN BOHANES

I. Introduction

Virtually all governments around the world have reacted to the COVID-19 pandemic by adopting a range of legislative and regulatory measures that either directly regulate or at least affect international trade.

Viewed through the lens of international trade law, the measures applied to goods trade can be broadly categorised into (1) trade-restrictive measures, (2) trade-enhancing or trade-facilitating measures, and (3) subsidies. This chapter provides an overview of the types of measures in each of those categories and a brief discussion of the disciplines under the law of the World Trade Organization (WTO) that apply to each type of measures.

This chapter examines only goods trade-related measures. It therefore does not discuss the many COVID-19 related measures that directly or indirectly affect trade in services. Of course, this does not mean that trade in services has escaped the consequence of the coronavirus pandemic. To the contrary, many service sectors have been affected by the crisis itself or governmental responses to the crisis. To begin with, the various forms of lockdowns and quarantines have resulted in a collapse of both supply and demand for countless service sectors, for instance tourism[1] and gastronomy services as well as the transportation and shipping industry, which has been particularly affected by governmental restrictions

[1] See, eg, R Wolfe, 'Exposing governments swimming naked in the COVID-19 crisis with trade policy transparency (and why WTO reform matters more than ever)' in R Baldwin and SJ Evenett (eds), *COVID-19 and Trade Policy: Why Turning Inward Won't Work* (London, CEPR Press, 2020); Ministry of Economy of Fiji, 'Economic and Fiscal Update Supplement to the COVID-19 Response Budget Address' (26 March 2020), macmap.org/OfflineDocument/Covid19/COVID_FJI_1.pdf.

on the movement of personnel, including restrictions on crew change, with a particularly pronounced impact on sea transport and by extension trade in goods.[2] On the other side of the ledger, governments have also reacted to the pandemic by adopting measures facilitating service transactions, for instance by relaxing prudential measures concerning minimum capital and liquidity requirements[3] or the facilitation of the international movement of health workers and the facilitation of telemedicine.[4]

Similarly, intellectual property (IP) protection as the third 'pillar' of WTO law has also been impacted by a number of COVID-19 related measures. For instance, some WTO Members have expedited or facilitated patent examination procedures (for example, concerning deadlines and fees) for applications relating to medicines or technologies relevant for treating COVID-19.[5] Other measures on the IP front include publication of patent-related information and drug approval status in order to facilitate COVID-19 research[6] or publication of lists of patents and applications relating to COVID-19 that are available for licensing.[7] Moreover, at the international level, governments have endorsed initiatives led by international organisations (for instance the World Health Organization) that, for instance, call on governments and other key stakeholders to pool data and IP rights relevant for the development of vaccines, diagnostics and other tools to combat COVID-19.[8] Discussions at the WTO have also included proposals by some Members to waive certain provisions of the Agreement on Trade-Related Aspects of Intellectual Property Rights (TRIPS Agreement) for the prevention, containment or treatment of COVID-19.[9]

This chapter is structured as follows. Section II deals with trade restrictions, which are further subdivided into export and import restrictions, respectively. Section III addresses trade facilitating measures, divided into border measures (tariffs and non-tariff measures) and internal measures (taxes and non-fiscal regulation, including technical requirements). Section IV examines subsidies. Section V examines transparency requirements under WTO law, specifically publication and notification requirements. Section VI concludes.

[2] See the discussion about the impact of COVID-19 related measures on the shipping industry in I Heiland and KH Ulltveit-Moe, 'An unintended crisis in sea transportation due to COVID-19 restrictions' in R Baldwin and SJ Evenett (eds), *COVID-19 and Trade Policy: Why Turning Inward Won't Work* (London, CEPR Press, 2020).

[3] See, eg, Canada: 'COVID-19: Measures affecting trade in services' (WTO), www.wto.org/english/tratop_e/covid19_e/trade_related_services_measure_e.htm.

[4] 'How WTO Members have used trade measures to expedite access to COVID-19 critical medical goods and services' (WTO, 18 September 2020), www.wto.org/english/tratop_e/covid19_e/services_report_16092020_e.pdf, 10.

[5] ibid 9.

[6] ibid.

[7] ibid.

[8] See the World Health Organization, 'Making the response to COVID-19 a public common good, Solidarity Call to Action', www.who.int/emergencies/diseases/novel-coronavirus-2019/global-research-on-novel-coronavirus-2019-ncov/covid-19-technology-access-pool/solidarity-call-to-action.

[9] Communication from India and South Africa: 'Waiver from Certain Provisions of the TRIPS Agreement for the prevention, containment and treatment of COVID-19' (2 October 2020) IP/C/W/669.

II. Trade Restrictions

A. Export Restrictions

i. Types of Measures Taken

The vast majority of goods trade-restrictive measures taken in response to the COVID-19 pandemic have been export restrictions. The goods covered by these measures have been, for the most part, health-related goods such as personal protective equipment (PPE) – gowns, masks, gloves, goggles and respirators – other medical consumables such as sanitisers and other chemical products, medical devices and machines, as well as pharmaceutical products. Another product category subject to extensive export restrictions has been agricultural commodities and food products.[10] The database of COVID-19 related measures on the WTO website includes also (temporary) restrictions on the export of certain other commodity products, for instance, timber[11] and toilet paper.[12] A significant share of these measures did not remain in place for a long time; according to the WTO; just over one-third of the COVID-19 trade-restrictive measures implemented by G20 countries had been repealed by mid-May 2020.[13]

The declared or implicit policy motivation behind these measures has been of course to address actual or potential shortages of these goods and to safeguard an adequate domestic supply. Complementary objectives include the prevention of hoarding and price-gouging.

The precise legal form of these export restrictions varies. Some governments have introduced outright export bans (zero export quotas). These export bans may concern all exports of a particular product, but in some instances have affected only parallel exports.[14] WTO Member governments have also imposed export quotas or export licensing/authorisation requirements.[15]

[10] Some of the products affected include cooking oil, rice, pasta, chicken eggs, sugar, iodised table salt, feed (hay, straw, mixed feed, bran and grain feed), laboratory equipment, test kits, cane or bean sugar; bakery, pastry and biscuit products, unposted bread, empty capsules from starch leaf used for medicines, waffles with lid, dried pasta from flour, from starch, starch extracted from potatoes and similar products.

[11] This restriction appears to have been introduced by Kazakhstan: 'COVID-19: Measures affecting trade in goods' (WTO), www.wto.org/english/tratop_e/covid19_e/trade_related_goods_measure_e.htm.

[12] 'Export Prohibitions and Restrictions' (WTO, 23 April 2020), www.wto.org/english/tratop_e/covid19_e/export_prohibitions_report_e.pdf; 'WTO report finds growing number of export restrictions in response to COVID-19 crisis' (WTO, 3 April 2020), www.wto.org/english/news_e/news20_e/rese_23apr20_e.htm.

[13] 'Report on G20 trade measures' (WTO, 29 June 2020), www.wto.org/english/news_e/news20_e/report_trdev_jun20_e.pdf, 2.

[14] See the example of parallel pharmaceutical exports from the UK, 'COVID-19: UK restricts parallel export of nearly 200 drugs, threatening its biopharma industry' (*Pharmaceutical Technology*, 13 May 2020), www.pharmaceutical-technology.com/comment/uk-parallel-export-covid-19/. Parallel exports occur when for instance wholesalers buy medicines already placed on the market in a particular country and export them to sell them in another country. The restriction on parallel exports prevents wholesalers

It is probably safe to assume that a number of export restrictions may have been introduced on a more informal basis and without the transparency and publicity that would accompany formal regulatory action. For instance, it would appear that at least some governments (publicly or behind closed doors) pressured domestic producers not to export their products – in particular, medical goods – and instead to reserve all these goods (or a certain percentage of them)[16] for the domestic market.[17]

Yet other measures have included outright requisitioning and takeover by the government of stockpiles of medical products.[18] In that case, legally speaking, the measure is not a trade measure (border measure), but rather a general measure that affects both domestic and foreign transactions.[19] However, in those cases, one can reasonably expect that international trade transactions would tend to experience greater disruptions than domestic transactions.

Export restrictions with the objective to ensure quality standards have been imposed by the government of China. After several Chinese shipments of medical products were rejected by European buyers as allegedly being of insufficient quality, the Chinese government, solicitous of preventing reputational damage to the relevant domestic industry, imposed regulation on a range of products, such as COVID-19 test kits, surgical masks, surgical preventive clothing, ventilators and infrared thermometers. Pursuant to these regulations, exports were authorised only if, broadly speaking, the product satisfied both Chinese standards as well as the standards of the importing country. Other products, in particular non-surgical masks, could be exported only if the importer filed a declaration that acknowledged the non-medical intended usage of the product. The purpose of this requirement was to induce importers to ensure that the buyers and end-users were aware that these masks were intended for non-medical use and thereby to avoid legal responsibility for product misuse in the importing countries.[20]

from buying the pharmaceuticals at issue cheaply in the home market and selling them abroad for a profit. Parallel exporting and hoarding of medicines can create or worsen medicine shortages.

[15] Many examples of export prohibitions, export quotas and export licensing requirements can be found on a dedicated portion of the WTO's website that tracks COVID-related measures, based both on Members' notifications and the WTO Secretariat's own research activities. 'COVID-19: Measures affecting trade in goods' (n 11). On 23 April 2020, the WTO also published a Secretariat Note that describes export prohibitions and restrictions. See WTO, 'Export Prohibitions and Restrictions' (n 12).

[16] CP Bown, 'COVID-19: Trump's curbs on exports of medical gear put Americans and others at risk' (*PIIE, Trade and Investment Policy Watch*, 9 April 2020), www.piie.com/blogs/trade-and-investment-policy-watch/covid-19-trumps-curbs-exports-medical-gear-put-americans-and.

[17] See ibid; see also R Baldwin and SJ Evenett (eds), *COVID-19 and Trade Policy: Why Turning Inward Won't Work* (London, CEPR Press, 2020).

[18] These kinds of actions have been reported from France, China and Chinese Taipei. See SJ Evenett, 'Flawed prescription: Export curbs on medical goods won't tackle shortages' in R Baldwin and SJ Evenett (eds), *COVID-19 and Trade Policy: Why Turning Inward Won't Work* (London, CEPR Press, 2020) 51.

[19] See Baldwin and Evenett (eds), *COVID-19 and Trade Policy* (n 17).

[20] ZA Zhang et al, 'COVID-19: Key Issues When Sourcing Pandemic Prevention Supplies from China' (*White & Case*, 1 May 2020), www.whitecase.com/publications/alert/covid-19-key-issues-when-sourcing-pandemic-prevention-supplies-china.

ii. Applicable WTO Rules

WTO rules on export restrictions mirror to some extent those on import restrictions. Quantitative restrictions (prohibitions and quotas) are generally prohibited but may be permissible or justified for particular policy purposes. In contrast, tariff-based restrictions are permitted. Indeed, the freedom to impose tariffs on exports is even greater than on the import side, given that no export tariff bindings exist.[21] Members can therefore impose export tariffs at any level, including at levels that will effectively prohibit imports and have the same economic effect as export prohibitions.[22]

However, the preference in WTO law for tariffs and the aversion to quantitative restrictions is not absolute. Export restrictions are permitted under WTO law during food shortages and other emergencies, to the extent they cover 'essential' products in situations of 'critical shortages' (Article XI:2(a)).[23] The term 'essential' has been interpreted as 'absolutely indispensable or necessary products'.[24] The term 'critical shortages' has in turn been interpreted as 'situations or events that may be relieved or prevented through the application of measures on a temporary, and not indefinite or permanent, basis'.[25] The right of WTO Members to take this type of measure is somewhat tempered by Article 12 of the Agreement on Agriculture, which requires that Members introducing any new export prohibitions or restrictions on foodstuffs 'give due consideration' to potential effects on importing Members.[26] Members that have explicitly or implicitly relied on this provision as a basis for their COVID-19 related export restrictions would therefore argue that the pandemic has led to critical shortages in essential products such as medical equipment and PPE.

[21] Members subject to export tariff restrictions on at least some products include Afghanistan, Bulgaria, China, Croatia, Estonia, Georgia, Kazakhstan, Latvia, Nepal, Russian Federation, the Kingdom of Saudi Arabia, Ukraine, Tonga and Viet Nam. During the ultimately doomed Doha negotiations, some Members made negotiating proposals aimed at establishing tariff bindings for export tariffs. It may also be noted that some preferential trade agreements include provisions that limit the use of tariff-based export restrictions.

[22] This differential treatment of quantitative and tariff-based export restrictions might appear as somewhat contradictory, but it bears recalling that the same phenomenon can arise on the import side where a Member has a very high import tariff binding (for instance on agricultural products). The reason for this differential treatment is a long-standing policy preference for tariffs over quantitative restrictions, given the greater distortive effects of the latter. See J Pauwelyn, 'Export restrictions in times of pandemic: Options and limits under international trade agreements' in R Baldwin and SJ Evenett (eds), *COVID-19 and Trade Policy: Why Turning Inward Won't Work* (London, CEPR Press, 2020).

[23] Art XI:2(a) of the General Agreement on Tariffs and Trade (GATT), Marrakesh Agreement Establishing the World Trade Organization, Annex 1A (Marrakesh, 15 April 1994).

[24] *China–Measures Related to the Exportation of Various Raw Materials*, Report of the Appellate Body (22 February 2012) WT/DS394/AB/R, WT/DS395/AB/R, WT/DS398/AB/R, para 326.

[25] *China–Measures Related to the Exportation of Various Raw Materials*, Report of the Panel (22 February 2012) WT/DS394/R, WT/DS395/R, WT/DS398/R, para 7.306.

[26] See Art 12 of the Agreement on Agriculture, Marrakesh Agreement Establishing the World Trade Organization, Annex 1A (Marrakesh, 15 April 1994). The Member introducing these restrictions should also provide a notification to other WTO Members about the prospective duration and nature of the measure.

Both import and export restrictions are permissible for purposes of applying 'standards or regulations for the classification, grading or marketing of commodities in international trade' (Article XI:2(b)).[27] The meaning of the term 'commodity' has not been clarified by WTO case law. It is therefore difficult to predict how a WTO panel would decide the question of whether the above-mentioned Chinese export restrictions – intended to ensure compliance with quality standards – are covered by this provision. The Panel in *China–Audiovisuals* noted the definition of commodity as being '[A] thing of use or value; spec. a thing that is an object of trade, esp. a raw material or agricultural crop'; or 'a thing one deals in or makes use of'.[28] That Panel also stated that an evolutionary understanding of that term should include not only tangible goods but also digital products. By analogy with that reasoning, one could ask whether widely produced medical goods such as surgical masks or ventilators could also be covered by the term 'commodity' under Article XI:2(b).

Quantitative export restrictions can also be justified under Article XX of the GATT. For instance, medical goods in short supply would – depending on the particular circumstances – potentially qualify as measures necessary to protect human life or health within the meaning of Article XX(b). Furthermore, Article XX(d) permits trade-restrictive measures that are necessary to enforce other WTO-consistent regulations. Put differently, Article XX(d) permits trade-restrictive measures that serve as necessary means to achieve a WTO consistent regulatory goal. Article XX(d) could therefore conceivably justify export restrictions such as the above-mentioned Chinese export restrictions, for instance where these restrictions are intended to ensure compliance with medical regulations as well as with consumer protection and information requirements. However, this argument would have to clear the hurdle of the somewhat murky jurisdictional limitations under Article XX. Recall that, under a health-driven export restriction, the regulating Member would argue that the purpose of the restriction is to protect the public health of the exporting country's population in the exporting country's territory. In contrast, under quality-control measures such as the Chinese measure, the regulating country would be acting presumably with a view to safeguard the quality of exported products and thus for the purpose of protecting the health of consumers outside its jurisdiction. WTO case law has so far been unclear on the jurisdictional limits of Article XX, and the leading case to date is still the almost 20-year-old and carefully hedged finding by the Appellate Body under Article XX(g) in *US–Shrimp Turtle*.[29]

[27] Art XI:2(b) of the GATT.

[28] *China–Measures Affecting Trading Rights and Distribution Services for Certain Publications and Audiovisual Entertainment Products*, Report of the Panel (19 January 2010) WT/DS363/R, para 1179.

[29] In that dispute, the Appellate Body did not rule that WTO Members could pursue the legitimate policy objective only with respect to their own territories. However, it did not also state affirmatively that concerns for the protected regulatory concern outside its jurisdiction could also justify a WTO Member's measures. This balancing act was achieved by emphasising that turtles – the protected species – migrated throughout international waters, passing also through the territorial waters of the

Another justification – a work-around for any potential jurisdictional limitation – could be the public moral exception Article XX(a), a provision that has been interpreted rather extensively over the recent years. For one, WTO adjudicative bodies have been fairly generous in finding that a rather large universe of measures fit conceptually under the label of protecting 'public morals'. For instance, tariff-based border measures allegedly designed to combat money laundering[30] and recently, United States (US) additional duties on China[31] have been found to qualify, in theory, as measures designed to protect public morals. Moreover, this line of case law also permits the regulating Member to address phenomena happening outside its jurisdiction, as long as these foreign phenomena affect the moral perceptions held by the regulating Member's population.[32] However, this does not mean that any and all measures will survive scrutiny under Article XX(a). Measures have been found to fail the Article XX(a) test when they restrict the importation of products that are unrelated to the proffered moral concerns.[33]

Finally, a WTO Member might also argue that COVID-19 related measures are justified on national security grounds. The precise interpretative contours of Article XXI are still subject to litigation, but the emerging case law seems to converge on a wide Member discretion embedded in a limited and objectively defined set of circumstances. According to the existing case law, these circumstances are primarily those of a military and law-and-order-based nature. However, the scope of the term 'other emergencies in international relations' in the phrase 'war and other emergencies in international relations' in Article XXI(b)(iii) awaits further fleshing out in the case law.

Any (quantitative) export restrictions justified by any of the above-mentioned provisions should in principle be non-discriminatory. Thus, Article I and, to the extent it can be meaningfully applied, Article XIII of the GATT 1994 would provide relevant guidance in this respect. Thus, for instance, to the extent that Article XIII applies, it would permit allocation of country-specific quotas, subject to the detailed parameters set out in Article XIII, such as historical trade patterns.

regulating Member. *United States–Import Prohibition of Certain Shrimp and Shrimp Products*, Report of the Appellate Body (6 November 1998) WT/DS58/AB/R, para 133.

[30] See, for instance, *Colombia–Measures Relating to the Importation of Textiles, Apparel and Footwear* (DS461).

[31] *US–Tariff Measures on Certain Goods from China*, Report of the Panel (15 September 2020) WT/DS543/R.

[32] This was the case, for instance, in *European Communities–Measures Prohibiting the Importation and Marketing of Seal Products* (DS400, DS401) or in *US–Tariff Measures on Certain Goods from China* (n 31). WTO adjudicatory bodies have emphasised that 'public morals' reflect the standards of right or wrong prevailing in a given WTO Member and that the content and scope of this concept may vary from one WTO Member to another, influenced by each Member's systems and scales of values. See *US–Tariff Measures on Certain Goods from China*, Report of the Panel (n 31) para 7.116.

[33] See, for instance, *US–Tariff Measures on Certain Goods from China* (n 31) paras 7.194, 7.201, 7.215 and 7.231.

iii. Further Reflections

Leaving aside the strictly legal arguments, it is not likely that WTO panels would take an overly strict approach to trade measures taken in response to the COVID-19 pandemic or a comparable crisis. Similarly, WTO Members would be probably hesitant liberally to file disputes against each other over their respective emergency measures during a crisis like the COVID-19 pandemic. Political or legal complaints will probably remain reserved to isolated instances of obviously abusive and disproportionate measures. Moreover, given the pace of WTO dispute settlement proceedings – or the likely similar pace of dispute settlement proceedings under bilateral or regional trade agreements – it is unlikely that any government would expect to obtain an immediate remedy that would be of practical relevance for addressing the crisis at hand. Nevertheless, should some of the export restrictions remain in effect despite clear improvements in the current situation, it cannot be excluded that some disputes on those issues may indeed be brought.

Since the outbreak of the COVID-19 crisis, commentators – especially economists – have expressed criticism of the many export restrictions.[34] Commentators have also pointed to the conspicuous fact that a number of European Union (EU) Member States imposed export restrictions on each other, which some have criticised as contrary to intra-EU solidarity.[35] The criticism – in part based on the experience with export restrictions imposed during the 2008–09 crisis – has highlighted concerns such as the alleged ineffectiveness of export restrictions in inducing greater domestic supply of the relevant products[36] (at least in the absence of complementary measures), the creation of incentives for smuggling,[37] the resulting shortages at the international level,[38] the disruptive effects on global value chains of trade flows worth almost $US 2 trillion,[39] and the destabilising effect of these measures on the international availability and international prices of the relevant products.[40] Commentators have also expressed concerns about ethical implications of impeding access of net-importing countries to medical supplies and food,[41] the fact that export restrictions may continue to

[34] See, eg, CP Bown, 'How the G20 can strengthen access to vital medical supplies in the fight against COVID-19' (*PIIE, Trade and Investment Policy Watch*, 15 April 2020), www.piie.com/blogs/trade-and-investment-policy-watch/how-g20-can-strengthen-access-vital-medical-supplies-fight; Bown, 'Trump's curbs on exports of medical gear' (n 16).

[35] Bown, 'How the G20 can strengthen access to vital medical supplies' (n 34).

[36] WJ Martin and JW Glauber, 'Trade policy and food security' in R Baldwin and SJ Evenett (eds), *COVID-19 and Trade Policy: Why Turning Inward Won't Work* (London, CEPR Press, 2020); Evenett, 'Flawed prescription' (n 18) 54.

[37] See WTO, 'Export prohibitions and restrictions' (n 12) 1–2.

[38] See ibid 1.

[39] WTO, 'Report of the TPRB from the Director-General on Trade-Related Developments' (10 July 2020) WT/TPR/OV/W/14, 2, 7.

[40] WTO, 'Export prohibitions and restrictions' (n 12) 8.

[41] See ibid 3; Bown, 'How the G20 can strengthen access to vital medical supplies' (n 34). Jamaica, for example, imports more than half of its total imports of particular medical equipment from the US.

be applied even after the crisis that triggered them abates ('stickiness');[42] as well as the political complications and potential loss of trust between trading partners.[43] Moreover, it has been argued by some that countries that previously relied on international trade will grow distrustful of their ability to rely on imports to satisfy their demand. These countries may therefore be tempted to impose not only retaliatory export restrictions,[44] but also erect import barriers in order to foster domestic industries to have their domestic needs satisfied during the next crisis.[45]

A good example of mutual interdependence – and thus of the risks as well as intended and unintended consequences of export restrictions – is the US and China. Both countries are locked into a mutual pattern of trade in medical products, as they import and export from each other several products that have been crucial to combating the fallout from the pandemic.[46] The same applies to the US relationship with certain Latin American countries.[47]

Over the longer run, the criticism goes, export restrictions – or the lack of predictability surrounding export restrictive regulations – might negatively impact on corporate investment decisions. Many if not most companies invest with a view to producing goods that will subsequently supply not only the host country, but also export markets. For those potential investors, the prospect that host governments will make liberal use of export restrictions will hardly act as an incentive to make these investments.

Many economists are similarly critical of calls to 'repatriate' global supply chains.[48] Commentators have pointed out that the cost-containment thanks to international trade – with more than a million different medical technologies used worldwide, over 8,000 generic drugs, widespread offshore outsourcing of many medical services, and extensive manufacturing taking place in a number of emerging economics around the world – 'is essential for financing large-scale health programmes'.[49]

[42] Committee on Agriculture, Communication from Japan, Israel, the Republic of Korea, Switzerland and The Separate Customs Territory of Taiwan, Penghu, Kinmen And Matsu: 'Overview of Export Restrictive Measures – Analysis of Actual Cases in Recent Years' (16 December 2019) JOB/AG/175. According to the Communication almost 90 export-restrictive measures remained in place after the 2007–12 period, after which the world food market was no longer in a critical shortage situation.

[43] A Stellinger, I Berglund and H Isakson, 'How trade can fight the pandemic and contribute to global health' in R Baldwin and SJ Evenett (eds), *COVID-19 and Trade Policy: Why Turning Inward Won't Work* (London, CEPR Press, 2020) 24.

[44] Bown, 'Trump's curbs on exports of medical gear' (n 16).

[45] WTO, 'Export Prohibitions and Restrictions' (n 12) 9; SJ Evenett and LA Winters, 'A trade bargain to secure supplies of medical goods – Preparing for a second wave of COVID-19' (*Global Trade Alert*, 27 April 2020), www.globaltradealert.org/reports/52.

[46] See, eg, Bown, 'How the G20 can strengthen access to vital medical supplies' (n 34).

[47] Bown, 'Trump's curbs on exports of medical gear' (n 16). For instance, Mexico supplies $349 million (24 per cent) worth of US imports of protective garments for American doctors and nurses.

[48] R Baldwin and SJ Evenett, 'Introduction' in R Baldwin and SJ Evenett (eds), *COVID-19 and Trade Policy: Why Turning Inward Won't Work* (London, CEPR Press, 2020); Stellinger, Berglund and Isakson (n 43).

[49] Stellinger, Berglund and Isakson (n 43).

In April 2020, the then-EU Commissioner for Trade, Phil Hogan, proposed a 'plurilateral agreement that would lead to a level playing field, including the possible permanent liberalisation of tariffs on medical equipment'.[50] Echoing that call, an interesting recent scholarly contribution proposes a grand bargain between WTO Members whereby exporting Members promise not to impose export restrictions whereas importing Members promise not to revert to pre-crisis import restricting measures.[51]

A recent plurilateral declaration of some 24 WTO Members states that these countries will not impose export restrictions in order to ensure the orderly functioning of supply chains. According to the statement, these Members collectively account for 63 per cent of global exports of agriculture and agri-food products and 55 per cent of global imports of agriculture and agri-food products.[52] The statement emphasises the need not to disrupt global supply chains and to preserve 'the ability of Members to import agriculture and agri-food products to meet their domestic needs'.[53] These Members pledge to 'exercise restraint in establishing domestic food stocks of agricultural products that are traditionally exported so as to avoid disruptions or distortions in international trade' and not to impose agriculture export restrictions and refrain from implementing unjustified trade barriers on agriculture and agri-food products and key agricultural production inputs.[54] The declaration also states that

> emergency measures related to agriculture and agri-food products designed to tackle COVID-19 must be targeted, proportionate, transparent, and temporary, and not create unnecessary barriers to trade or disruption to global supply chains for agriculture and agri-food products. Any such measures are to be consistent with WTO rules.[55]

Declarations of this kind can play an important complementary role given that the international regulatory framework is rather permissive. Given that the legal rules do not limit the ability of governments to take trade-disruptive action,

[50] 'Introductory statement by Commissioner Phil Hogan at Informal meeting of EU Trade Ministers' (*European Commission*, 16 April 2020), ec.europa.eu/commission/commissioners/2019-2024/hogan/announcements/introductory-statement-commissioner-phil-hogan-informal-meeting-eu-trade-ministers_en.

[51] Evenett and Winters (n 45).

[52] Committee on Agriculture, Statement from Australia, Brazil, Canada, Chile, Colombia, Costa Rica, European Union, Hong Kong, China, Japan, Korea, Malawi, Mexico, New Zealand, Paraguay, Peru, Qatar, Singapore, Switzerland, The Separate Customs Territory of Taiwan, Penghu, Kinmen and Matsu, Ukraine, United Kingdom, United States and Uruguay: 'Responding to the COVID-19 pandemic with open and predictable trade in agricultural and food products' (22 April 2020) WT/GC/208, G/AG/30.

[53] ibid para 1.2.

[54] ibid para 1.6 (b).

[55] ibid para 1.6(d). A similar declaration was made by seven countries – New Zealand, Singapore, Canada, Australia, Chile, Brunei and Myanmar – emphasising the 'importance of refraining from the imposition of export controls or tariffs and non-tariff barriers and of removing any existing trade restrictive measures on essential goods, especially medical supplies'. See 'Joint ministerial statement' (25 March 2020), www.trademinister.gov.au/minister/simon-birmingham/media-release/joint-ministerial-statement-australia-brunei-darussalam-canada-chile-republic-union-myanmar-new-zealand-and-singapore.

governments have to resort to this type of signalling to provide assurances to trading partners that they will refrain from taking trade-restrictive measures.

One final important aspect concerns transparency, which is discussed in section V below. All COVID-19 related trade-restrictive measures of a quantitative nature require notification to the WTO in accordance with the 2012 'Decision on Notification Procedures for Quantitative Restrictions'.[56] Measures relating to foodstuffs should also be notified to the Committee on Agriculture. However, according to the WTO itself, compliance with these requirements has been incomplete.[57]

Many commentators emphasise how existing and new monitoring and reporting mechanisms could reassure governments what supplies are available, in which countries and whether they are being distributed fairly.[58] It is also interesting to note that many governments, when regulating exports, may not be fully aware of the disruptive impact that these restrictions have on global supply chains. Despite many theories to the contrary, governments may sometimes have insufficient information and may take regulatory action without being fully aware of the downstream effects in the corporate world. This is in part because many multinational companies are not enthusiastic about sharing relevant information for reasons of business confidentiality. Where the concerns of these enterprises can be overcome and information is shared more generously between private and public sectors, greater knowledge about particular global value chains on the part of regulators might have a beneficial impact on future crisis management. Moreover, concerns by governments about reliability of available information might trigger greater demands for re-nationalisation of the supply chains. This is not an outcome preferred by economic commentators, as they fear that this would typically not enhance cost efficiency.[59]

Recommendations of commentators also include setting up a reporting system for each member's production capacity, output, domestic demand, stockpiles, exports and imports. A system along those lines already exists for agriculture, with a view to managing global food supplies and addressing famine outbreaks in the face of natural disasters.[60]

B. Import Restrictions

i. Types of Measures Taken

Import restrictions in the first stages of the COVID-19 crisis were aimed at preventing the spread of the virus. Thus, in addition to travel bans, a number of

[56] WTO Council for Trade in Goods, 'Decision on notification procedures for quantitative restrictions' (22 June 2012) G/L/59/Rev.1.
[57] WTO, 'Export Prohibitions and Restrictions' (n 12) 2.
[58] Bown, 'How the G20 can strengthen access to vital medical supplies' (n 34).
[59] ibid.
[60] ibid.

countries introduced import bans or tight import restrictions typically on live animals and animal products. These bans targeted either a broad range of products from particular affected regions or certain species considered to be risky, such as exotic and decorative animals, including insects, arthropods, amphibians, reptiles and live fish. Some Members required COVID-19 tests for these imports.[61]

Beyond these immediate crisis measures, most governments did not impose wide-ranging additional import restrictions to protect their domestic industries, at least not in the first half of 2020. There are probably two main reasons for this. First, consistent with the evolution of the crisis in its first few months, governments were more concerned with ensuring an adequate supply of essential products (medical and food-related). Thus, most measures taken on the import side – as explained – were import facilitating measures. These measures are addressed below in section III.

Second, given the severe reduction in trade, it would appear that most governments have not (yet) felt extensive pressures from import-competing industries to impose trade restrictions, at least at the time of writing.[62] However, that situation might change as trade volumes recover and if the economic crisis continues to unfold. In this respect, economic research points to the overall not excessively negative experience with the 2008–09 crisis where governments largely shied away from a public 'tit-for-tat protectionist spiral' and instead engaged in low-profile 'murky protectionism'.[63] The question is whether in the current climate, with the political and institutional challenges in current international trade governance, the same forbearance can be expected.

Nevertheless, a few (developing) governments have already taken import restrictive measures by way of a response to the COVID-19 pandemic. By and large, these measures appear to have been intended to respond to the worsening of general economic conditions and, in particular, their adverse effects on governmental finances. Many developing countries are moreover affected not only directly by worsening business conditions, but also by the drying up of remittances, on which their economies depend.[64]

Thus, for instance, Sri Lanka introduced temporary restrictions on imports of certain products, including some agricultural produce and ethanol, and prohibited commercial banks from facilitating the importation of vehicles, in order to ease pressure on the balance of payments and the exchange rate.[65] Fiji increased

[61] For examples, see Committee on Sanitary and Phytosanitary Measures, 'Notification of Emergency Measures by the Russian Federation' (3 February 2020) G/SPS/N/RUS/178, (31 March 2020) G/SPS/N/RUS/178/Corr.1; Committee on Sanitary and Phytosanitary Measures, 'Notification of Emergency Measures by Indonesia' (20 March 2020) G/SPS/N/IDN/132.

[62] SJ Evenett, 'What's next for protectionism? Watch out for state largesse, especially export incentives' in R Baldwin and SJ Evenett, *COVID-19 and Trade Policy: Why Turning Inward Won't Work* (London, CEPR Press, 2020) 184–85.

[63] Baldwin and Evenett, 'Introduction' (n 48) 3.

[64] Fiji, 'Economic and Fiscal Update Supplement to the COVID-19 Response Budget Address' (n 1) para 3.1.

[65] Central Bank of Sri Lanka, 'The Central Bank of Sri Lanka introduces Urgent Measures to Ease the Pressure on the Exchange Rate and Prevent Financial Market Panic due to the COVID-19 Pandemic' (19 March 2020), www.cbsl.gov.lk/sites/default/files/cbslweb_documents/press/pr/press_

the applicable 'fuel surcharge', in response to a shortfall in governmental revenue and the worsening trade balance.[66] A similar duty increase on fuel was imposed by the Philippines, citing the need to ensure adequate government resources.[67] Kazakhstan imposed an import ban on cement clinker, allegedly due to declining demand (and hence the need to support local industry).[68] These kinds of measures may grow in number and scope should the economic crisis extend into the future.

ii. *Applicable WTO Rules*

Health-based import restrictions designed to address the entry and spread of the COVID-19 virus would appear to fall under the SPS Agreement[69] and would normally be justified, given the obvious health motivations underpinning them. If these measures were analysed under the GATT 1994, they would most likely fall under and be inconsistent with Article XI:1, but would be justified by Article XX(b). Any differences in the precise treaty language notwithstanding, the analysis under both sets of provisions would be informed by the same facts and public health policy considerations.

Economically motivated tariff measures are of course justified to the extent that the increased tariffs are within a Member's scheduled tariff bindings. Beyond these tariff bindings, and to the extent these measures are quantitative restrictions, they would have to fall within one of the GATT exceptions. This could be, for instance, Article XII or XVIII:B which would justify balance of payments-related measures. Alternatively, these measures would have to be taken as trade remedy measures (anti-dumping or countervailing duties or safeguard measures) after the requisite investigations by domestic authorities. Indeed, economic scholars and commentators expect these types of measures to increase in scope and number should the economic crisis continue. The advantage of these kinds of measures is that, in comparison to, for instance, broad balance of payments-related restrictions, they target specific products and thus permit a more targeted response to domestic demands for protectionism. Finally, it remains to be seen to what extent governments might be tempted to invoke the national security exception under Article XXI of the GATT 1994.

20200319_the_central_bank_of_sri_lanka_introduces_urgent_measures_to_ease_the_pressure_on_the_exchange_rate_e.pdf; See also International Monetary Fund, 'Policy Responses to COVID-19' (as of 24 October 2020), Sri Lanka, www.imf.org/en/Topics/imf-and-covid19/Policy-Responses-to-COVID-19#S.

[66] Fiji, 'Economic and Fiscal Update Supplement to the COVID-19 Response Budget Address' (n 1).

[67] Executive Order of the President of the Philippines No 113 (2 May 2020), www.officialgazette.gov.ph/downloads/2020/05may/20200502-EO-113-RRD.pdf.

[68] 'Cement Exporters in Distress as Kazakhstan Bans Imports' *Financial Tribune* (6 May 2020), financialtribune.com/articles/domestic-economy/103231/cement-exporters-in-distress-as-kazakhstan-bans-imports.

[69] Agreement on the Application of Sanitary and Phytosanitary Measures, Marrakesh Agreement Establishing the World Trade Organization, Annex 1A (Marrakesh, 15 April 1994) (SPS Agreement).

III. Trade-Facilitating Measures

A number of COVID-19 related measures taken by WTO Members were or are intended to facilitate imports, primarily those of medical and food products. As of September 2020, 40 WTO Members (including 12 G-20 Members) have either temporarily removed or at least deferred payments of duties, taxes and charges on COVID-19 critical medical goods and other essential supplies.[70] A number of other trade-facilitating measures have been taken. This suggests that international trade is part of the solution of supply challenges in the context of the COVID-19 crisis, rather than part of the problem. Indeed, according to the WTO, trade in COVID-19 related products has grown by almost 40 per cent in the first half of 2020.[71]

Legally speaking, these trade-facilitating measures can be broadly categorised as action pertaining to, respectively, border measures and internal measures.

A. Border Measures

i. Reductions in Tariffs and Other Border Charges

Many governments have waived or temporarily suspended import tariffs. This includes also the prominent example of the US which, after some reported initial hesitation, temporarily suspended some of its 'trade war' tariffs applicable to products imported from China.[72] Other border charges have also been suspended, for instance, customs fees.[73] Certain governments have also waived the application of trade remedies such as anti-dumping duties.[74]

A number of governments have introduced measures that assist in the process of paying for customs debts. For instance, some WTO Members have agreed to defer the payment of import duties, for example, by extending time frames for payment of certain customs debts and related taxes,[75] by creating a temporary moratorium on default interest on late payments of customs duties,[76] or by temporarily postponing the time to deposit certain estimated duties, taxes and fees.[77]

[70] WTO, 'How WTO Members have used trade measures to expedite access to COVID-19 critical medical goods and services' (n 4) 1.
[71] ibid 2.
[72] Bown, 'Trump's curbs on exports of medical gear' (n 16).
[73] Japan and Malaysia, 'COVID-19: Measures affecting trade in services' (WTO), www.wto.org/english/tratop_e/covid19_e/trade_related_services_measure_e.htm.
[74] For instance, Argentina and Brazil, see ibid.
[75] ibid Spain.
[76] ibid Switzerland.
[77] ibid US.

ii. Non-Monetary Import Facilitating Measures

On the non-monetary side, governments have increased import quotas,[78] eliminated certain products (in particular medical equipment and PPE) from the list of products subject to non-automatic import licensing requirements,[79] or simplified and expedited the import licensing approval process.[80] Other measures have included establishing priority clearance channels,[81] temporary suspension of the requirement to file certain import-related documents,[82] simplified import and export declaration forms,[83] or a direct prioritisation of customs clearance for relief goods relating to COVID-19 countermeasures.[84] A number of measures have also been undertaken to facilitate the processing of transit transactions, benefiting landlocked countries.[85]

An important aspect of these measures has been a greater recourse to electronic documentation.[86] In an ideal world, this could potentially become one of the lasting positive legacies of the COVID-19 crisis, since more extensive use of electronic documents will provide customs authorities with an opportunity to achieve greater familiarity and comfort of customs administrations with electronic documentation.

International organisations such as the World Bank have offered their own guidance on how to simplify and streamline border formalities during the pandemic.[87] Greater reliance on electronic documents is one of the recommendations in that document.

iii. Other Measures

Beyond the immediate conditions and logistics of import transactions at the border, some governments have taken active measures to facilitate imports by assisting importers and exporters to negotiate freight matters. For instance, Australia created the so-called International Freight Assistance Mechanism (IFAM) in order to respond to the collapse of international airfreight capacity in and out

[78] ibid Switzerland.

[79] ibid Argentina, Singapore, Brazil.

[80] ibid China.

[81] 'Trade Costs in the time of global pandemic' (WTO, 12 August 2020), www.wto.org/english/tratop_e/covid19_e/trade_costs_report_e.pdf, 7.

[82] Argentina, 'COVID-19: Measures affecting trade in services' (WTO), www.wto.org/english/tratop_e/covid19_e/trade_related_services_measure_e.htm.

[83] ibid, Japan.

[84] ibid.

[85] ibid.

[86] China and Eurasian Economic Union, 'COVID-19: Measures affecting trade in services' (WTO), www.wto.org/english/tratop_e/covid19_e/trade_related_services_measure_e.htm.

[87] World Bank, 'Trade and COVID-19 Guidance Note Managing Risk and Facilitating Trade in the COVID-19 Pandemic' (30 March 2020), documents1.worldbank.org/curated/en/751981585606039541/pdf/Trade-and-COVID-19-Guidance-Note-Managing-Risk-and-Facilitating-Trade-in-the-COVID-19-Pandemic.pdf.

of Australia as a result of the COVID-19 pandemic. IFAM assisted importers by, for instance, aggregating cargo loads, negotiating with airlines and dealing with partner governments to facilitate clearances and improve transparency of freight costs during the pandemic. IFAM did or does not provide individual funding for exporters or importers, and exporters are required to make a financial contribution towards the increased cost of their freight.[88]

B. Internal Measures

i. Domestic Taxes

A number of governments have decided to eliminate certain domestic taxes on particular products, such as VAT, excise and sales taxes. At least in some instances, this elimination of domestic taxes related to both domestic and imported products without distinction[89] and on imported products only in other instances,[90] for example, when imported by or on behalf of particular institutions[91] or distributed free of charge.[92]

ii. Non-Fiscal Regulation, in Particular, Technical Regulations and Standards

An area that has seen extensive trade-facilitating action has been that of technical regulations and standards. According to the WTO, two-thirds of the measures notified by WTO Members in the early stages of the COVID-19 pandemic relate to standards and regulations (ie, technical barriers to trade and sanitary and phytosanitary measures).[93] Given the sometimes patchy compliance record of WTO Members with notifications obligations, it is not clear whether this percentage accurately reflects the share of these measures 'on the ground'. However, there can be no doubt that a relaxation of technical regulations and requirements in particular on medicinal products has been widespread.

[88] Australia, 'COVID-19: Measures affecting trade in services' (WTO), www.wto.org/english/tratop_e/covid19_e/trade_related_services_measure_e.htm.

[89] See, eg, ibid, Brazil's elimination of the IPI (Imposto sobre Produtos Industrializados).

[90] ibid, Temporary exemption of VAT on imports of ethyl alcohol, Dominican Republic.

[91] eg, Canada is waiving tariffs and sales taxes on all goods imported by or on behalf of public health agencies, hospitals and testing sites, and first response organisations (eg, police, fire and local civil defence groups, including medical response teams) (1 April 2020) G/MA/W/145; see also, Commission Decision (EU) 2020/491 on Relief from Import Duties and VAT Exemption on Importation Granted for Goods Needed to Combat the Effects of the COVID-19 Outbreak During 2020 [2020] C/2020/2146, OJ L103I.

[92] Japan, 'COVID-19: Measures affecting trade in services' (WTO), www.wto.org/english/tratop_e/covid19_e/trade_related_services_measure_e.htm.

[93] 'Standards, Regulations and COVID-19 – What Actions Taken by WTO Members?' (WTO, 20 May 2020), www.wto.org/english/tratop_e/covid19_e/standards_report_e.pdf.

These measures primarily concern trade in PPE, medical equipment and food. Examples include streamlining certification, authorisation and other procedures for medical goods, to allow a wider range of products to enter the market more quickly, while still ensuring continued health and safety protection. These measures could even go as far as exempting certain products (ie, PPE) from conformity checks and market authorisation requirements altogether.[94] These measures thus broaden market access for PPE and medical devices which otherwise would not comply with all the applicable technical regulations, but the use of which is considered necessary to protect health due to the pandemic, as long as certain core objectives are safeguarded.

For instance, the EU Commission issued a Recommendation that Member States temporarily authorise PPE products even where all the steps towards obtaining the required CE marking have not yet been completed, provided that health and safety levels were maintained.[95] The US Food and Drug Administration issued new Emergency Use Authorisation (EUA) whereby certain respirators and other products not previously approved for use in the US could be used in hospitals.[96] Ukraine established a procedure for processing applications and authorising the placing on the market of PPE and medical goods that otherwise did not fully conform to its technical regulations.[97] Similarly, Canada temporarily authorised the marketing of certain products that do not fully meet its labelling or packaging requirements.[98]

These measures demonstrate that, in times of crises, governments are ultimately willing to rely on other countries' technical standards and accept them, at least to some extent, as 'equivalent' to their own. This kind of recognition of foreign standards is explicitly envisaged both in the TBT and SPS Agreements,[99] but is not as widespread as many trading companies and nations would desire. It remains to be seen whether after a return to a more normal trading environment, the experience

[94] See, eg, Committee on Technical Barriers to Trade, 'Notification of Switzerland' (16 April 2020) G/TBT/N/CHE/245.

[95] 'Accordingly, to address the shortage of PPE necessary in the context of the COVID-19 outbreak, where non-CE marked PPE are intended to enter the EU market, the relevant market surveillance authorities should evaluate the products and, if they are found to be compliant with the essential health and safety requirements laid down by the relevant Regulation should take measures allowing the placing of such PPE on the Union market for a limited period of time or while the conformity assessment procedure with the notified body is being carried out'. See Commission Recommendation (EU) 2020/403 on Conformity Assessment and Market Surveillance Procedures within the Context of the COVID-19 Threat [2020] C/2020/1712, OJ L/79I, para 24.

[96] 'FAQs on the EUAs for Non-NIOSH Approved Respirators During the COVID-19 Pandemic' (US Food and Drug Administration, as of October 2020), www.fda.gov/medical-devices/emergency-situations-medical-devices/faqs-euas-non-niosh-approved-respirators-during-covid-19-pandemic.

[97] Committee on Technical Barriers to Trade, 'Notification by Ukraine' (1 April 2020) G/TBT/N/UKR/162.

[98] Committee on Technical Barriers to Trade, 'Notification by Canada' (14 April 2020) G/TBT/N/CAN/609.

[99] Arts 2.7 and 6.1 of the Agreement on Technical Barriers to Trade, Marrakesh Agreement Establishing the World Trade Organization, Annex 1A (Marrakesh, 15 April 1994) (TBT Agreement); Art 4 of the SPS Agreement (n 69).

with COVID-era equivalence recognition will have induced a greater willingness among governments to enter more liberally into equivalence agreements.

iii. Applicable WTO Disciplines

WTO disciplines do not constrain governmental efforts at facilitating trade, except by demanding that any such regulation be designed and applied in a non-discriminatory manner. Thus, the most-favoured nation (MFN) principle and the national treatment principle are both relevant.

MFN would therefore require that any border or internal trade-facilitating measures apply equally to all trading partners. Thus, tariff reductions on medical and food products must be applied equally to like products from all sources. Suspension or elimination of customs requirements and formalities must apply equally to all WTO Members, assuming that the products at issue and any attending circumstances are like. Similarly, any internal tax reductions and streamlining of technical certification procedures must apply equally to products of all WTO Member, assuming of course that the products at issue objectively qualify for the treatment at issue. Thus, for instance, where a Member decides to apply a simplified technical certification and authorisation procedure for foreign products as long as these products satisfy a basic minimum safety standard, all products that satisfy that basic standard must benefit from the simplified certification and authorisation procedure. In addition, the regulating Member must ensure that importers of any product have an adequate opportunity to demonstrate that their product satisfies that basic minimum safety requirement.

National treatment requires treatment no less favourable to imported products than to domestic products. Thus, internal tax reductions or temporary tax suspensions concerning sales of domestic products must also be granted on the sales of 'like' imported products. Similarly, any suspension or simplification of technical certification and authorisation procedures must benefit domestic and imported products equally, to the extent that the products are like.

As noted above, it is interesting to reflect in this context on those WTO disciplines that mandate trade-facilitating measures. The Trade Facilitation Agreement encourages or in some instances requires measures that facilitate and expedite customs clearance (for example, greater use of electronic documentation), as do the SPS and TBT Agreements when encouraging Members to enter into mutual recognition or equivalence agreements. The regulatory response to the COVID-19 pandemic shows, in a number of areas, what kind of trade-facilitating measures are possible. Of course, this does not mean that these regulatory responses have any strictly legal implication for assessing Members' compliance with WTO provisions that require trade-facilitating measures. The COVID-19 pandemic is and remains an exceptional set of circumstances in which many Members' regulatory responses reflect a trade-off between competing policy considerations, for instance, accepting potentially a lesser degree of product safety in order to ensure adequate supply of essential products in an emergency situation. That trade-off will be (legitimately) different when the pandemic is no more or is under greater control. However, as a matter of policy, one can only hope that governments around the world may take as much inspiration as possible from what the pandemic has shown to be feasible trade facilitating measures and may apply also in normal times.

IV. Subsidies

A. Measures Taken by WTO Members

As governments design stimulus measures for economies hit by the COVID-19 crisis, it remains to be seen how these measures will fit into the regulatory framework of the SCM Agreement.[100] Most G20 member countries have passed or committed to fiscal stimulus packages to respond to the coronavirus pandemic. In terms of the size of the stimulus packages, a number of WTO Members' actions dwarf previous comparable initiatives. For instance, Japan appears to have passed the largest fiscal stimulus package, of almost 120 trillion Yen, which amounts to about 21.1 per cent of its GDP.[101] The corresponding percentage amounts for the US, Brazil, Canada and Australia amount to, respectively, 11.2, 11, 9.8 and 8.5 per cent.[102]

A recent list published on the WTO website contains 575 support measures notified by 34 WTO Members (counting the EU as one Member, which accounts for 35 per cent of the notifications).[103] Not all these measures involve subsidies or subsidy-type measures, but many would appear to involve some form of financial assistance. Many of these measures appear to apply on an economy-wide or industry-neutral basis (for example, industry-neutral relief measures for small or medium-sized enterprises (SMEs) or enterprises in financial difficulties) or instead target non-producer recipients, for instance households. Nevertheless, some measures do appear to provide targeted aid for specific industries, for instance the PPE industry, the farming sector[104] (including for specific products such as rice, fruits and vegetables, or pig or bovine meat producers), the forestry and fisheries sector, food producers, airlines, tourism/hospitality, transport, finance and services.

[100] Agreement on Subsidies and Countervailing Measures, Marrakesh Agreement Establishing the World Trade Organization, Annex 1A (Marrakesh, 15 April 1994) (SCM Agreement).

[101] 'Value of COVID-19 fiscal stimulus packages in G20 countries as of October 2020, as a share of GDP' (*Statista*, October 2020), www.statista.com/statistics/1107572/covid-19-value-g20-stimulus-packages-share-gdp/.

[102] ibid.

[103] 'COVID-19: Support measures' (WTO, as of October 2020), www.wto.org/english/tratop_e/covid19_e/trade_related_support_measures_e.htm.

[104] Concerns about support measures in the agricultural sector were also expressed at the special meeting of the Committee on Agriculture on 18 June 2020, as well as about increased activities of WTO Members in the area of stockpiling. 'COVID-19 and Agriculture: A Story of Resilience' (WTO, 26 August 2020), www.wto.org/english/tratop_e/covid19_e/agric_report_e.pdf, 7.

Some assistance programmes involve the promotion of exports or financial support for exporters or export transactions, in particular, trade finance.

According to the Organisation for Economic Co-operation and Development (OECD) Employment Outlook 2020, even under an optimistic scenario for the evolution of the pandemic, the OECD-wide unemployment rate may reach 9.4 per cent in the fourth quarter of 2020. This would exceed all the highest rates of unemployment since the Great Depression. Average employment in 2020 is projected to be between 4.1 per cent and 5 per cent lower than in 2019.[105] As of early October 2020, estimates of global GDP assume a 4.8 per cent contraction,[106] which would constitute the worst drop since the Second World War.[107] The WTO's most recent prediction is that the volume of global merchandise trade will shrink by 9.2 per cent as compared with 2019.[108] Many WTO Members will likely continue to believe that these figures will require large-scale governmental intervention. Multilateral organisations have echoed these views to some extent, highlighting in particular the need to ensure sufficient trade finance.[109]

B. Applicable WTO Disciplines

WTO law contains an elaborate set of rules designed to achieve a balance between WTO Members' right to provide subsidies and the need to ensure that these subsidies do not cause inappropriate harm to another Member's economic interests. The WTO subsidies legal framework rests primarily on the Agreement on Subsidies and Countervailing Duties (SCM Agreement) and is complemented by certain special rules pertaining to agricultural products (Agreement on Agriculture) and certain provisions in the GATT 1994.

In a nutshell, the SCM Agreement defines subsidies as specific forms of governmental action (financial contributions) that provide an economic benefit to the recipient (benefit). Where these subsidies are 'specific' – which means they are granted to particular companies, industries or groups of industries and are not available 'horizontally' throughout the economy – the SCM Agreement regulates them. Subsidies contingent on export performance or on the use of domestic products over imported products are prohibited. Other subsidies are permitted, unless

[105] 'Tackling coronavirus (COVID-19): Contributing to a global effort' (OECD), www.oecd.org/coronavirus/en/.

[106] 'Trade shows signs of rebound from COVID-19, recovery still uncertain' (WTO, 6 October 2020), www.wto.org/english/news_e/pres20_e/pr862_e.htm.

[107] 'DDG Wolff: Open markets essential to global economic recovery' (WTO, 9 October 2020), www.wto.org/english/news_e/news20_e/ddgaw_09oct20_e.htm.

[108] 'Trade shows signs of rebound from COVID-19' (n 106).

[109] See, for instance, 'Heads of WTO and development banks voice support for trade finance amid COVID-19 crisis' (WTO, 1 July 2020), www.wto.org/english/news_e/news20_e/trfin_01jul20_e.pdf; 'WTO, ICC and B20 call for action to narrow the growing trade finance gap' (WTO, 7 July 2020), www.wto.org/english/news_e/news20_e/trfin_08jul20_e.pdf.

they cause economic harm to other Members, in the form of 'injury', 'nullification or impairment of benefits' and 'serious prejudice', for instance in the form of price suppression, lost sales or other forms of market displacement. WTO Members aggrieved by another Member's subsidies can initiate disputes at the WTO or they may elect to impose countervailing duties after a domestic countervailing investigation. The Agreement on Agriculture goes beyond the SCM Agreement in the sense that it provides for absolute monetary caps on the total amount of subsidies that can be granted in any given year (referred to as aggregate measurement of support).

It is not possible to provide meaningful analysis about COVID-19 related support measures without addressing the details of any given support programme. Nevertheless, in the light of the above descriptions, certain general comments can be made. First, from the perspective of avoiding WTO disputes, non-industry specific subsidies and non-export contingent (and non-local content) subsidies stand the best chance of not raising concerns under WTO law and not becoming the target of countervailing duties imposed by other WTO Members. Thus, financial support for the benefit of SMEs that is not conditional on export performance or local content requirements should as a general principle be regarded as non-specific, and therefore neither challengeable nor countervailable.

In contrast, measures intended to increase the production of certain critical goods, in particular medical equipment, necessary to address future (new) waves of the COVID-19 pandemic, would necessarily have to be industry specific. To recall, economists have emphasised that export restrictions are not suited for inducing greater levels of production and that, in particular in the short run, governments may be required to subsidise those producers.[110] Subsidies of this kind can be expected to have some trade effects, in that they could increase exports or displace imports. However, much would depend on the precise nature and circumstances of these measures.

V. Transparency Requirements

According to WTO Deputy Director-General Wolff, the pandemic has shown the importance of institutionalised transparency and cooperation.[111] In a nutshell, WTO transparency revolves around requiring Members to publish domestic measures that affect trade and requiring notification to the WTO. Both these requirements, working together, enable other WTO Members and private traders to become acquainted with the measures being adopted. They also enable an informed public debate about policies and measures, and in particular they enable those negatively affected by these measures to raise any relevant issues.

[110] Bown, 'How the G20 can strengthen access to vital medical supplies' (n 34); Baldwin and Evenett, 'Introduction' (n 48) 10.

[111] 'Open markets essential to global economic recovery' (n 107).

A. General Publication Requirement under Article X:1 of the GATT

WTO Members are under a general requirement under Article X:1 of the GATT 1994 to publish all goods trade-related[112] regulation of general application.[113] All of the above-mentioned categories of measures are therefore covered under Article X:1. In terms of timing, the publication is required to occur 'promptly'. Where a measure introduces a more onerous requirement in comparison to the previously applicable law (for example, a higher duty or a more onerous requirement), the measure shall not be enforced before it has been published. Finally, the publication should be made 'in such a manner as to enable governments and traders to become acquainted with them'.

B. Publication Requirements in Other WTO Agreements

In addition to Article X:1 of the GATT 1994, certain other goods-related WTO Agreements feature their own publication requirements. For instance, the SPS Agreement requires timely publication of all SPS measures[114] and, as a general rule, requires a 'reasonable interval between the publication of a sanitary or phytosanitary regulation and its entry into force',[115] with a view to permitting producers in exporting Members to adapt to the new requirements of the importing Member. A similar requirement applies under the TBT Agreement,[116] including the requirement under Article 2.12 to permit a 'reasonable interval' between publication and entry into force, in order to permit traders to get acquainted with and adapt to the new measures.[117] Pursuant to a 2001 Ministerial Decision, the phrase 'reasonable interval' means a period of normally not less than six months. Article 2.12 along with this Ministerial Decision was invoked in a WTO dispute as the basis of a claim that a regulating Member had acted inconsistently with its obligations by not respecting the six-month time period. The Appellate Body held that the Ministerial Decision amounted to a 'subsequent agreement' between WTO Members within the meaning of Article 31.3(a) of the Vienna Convention on the Law of Treaties.[118]

[112] More precisely, Art X:1 of the GATT refers to measures 'pertaining to the classification or the valuation of products for customs purposes, or to rates of duty, taxes or other charges, or to requirements, restrictions or prohibitions on imports or exports or on the transfer of payments therefor, or affecting their sale, distribution, transportation, insurance, warehousing inspection, exhibition, processing, mixing or other use'.

[113] More precisely, this category of measures covers '[l]aws, regulations, judicial decisions and administrative rulings of general application'.

[114] Para 1 of Annex B to the SPS Agreement (n 69).

[115] ibid para 2 of Annex B.

[116] Art 2.11 of the TBT Agreement (n 99).

[117] ibid Art 2.12.

[118] *United States–Measures Affecting the Production and Sale of Clove Cigarettes*, Report of the Appellate Body (24 April 2012) WT/DS406/AB/R, para 267; Art 31.3(a) of Vienna Convention on the Law of Treaties (Vienna, 23 May 1969).

This means that the six-month period is effectively binding and – bar urgent circumstances – must be observed when implementing trade-restrictive regulation covered by the TBT Agreement. Of course, COVID-19 related scenarios may often precisely involve 'urgent circumstances', such that Article 2.12 is of limited significance for situations of this kind.

C. WTO Notification Requirements

WTO Members fall under a range of requirements to notify their trade measures to the WTO. The main WTO notification requirement is set out in the Decision on Notification Procedures, which contains an Indicative List of categories of measures required to be notified.[119] This Decision applies jointly with notification obligations set out in the various WTO Agreements, for instance Article 2.9 of the TBT Agreement or Article III(3) of the General Agreement on Trade in Services (GATS).

Quantitative restrictions are also required to be notified pursuant to the 2012 Decision on Notification Procedures for Quantitative Restrictions.[120] This notification requirement applies both on the import and export side and specifies in great detail the notification procedure as well as the type of information that WTO Members are obliged to provide.

Yet another notification provision is Article 12 of the Agreement on Agriculture.[121] This provision requires Members to notify the Committee on Agriculture of any prohibitions or restrictions on foodstuffs introduced pursuant to the carve-out in Article XI:2(a) of the GATT 1994.

Compliance of WTO Members with these notification requirements has occasionally been criticised as insufficient, in particular with respect to subsidies.[122] Although many COVID-19 related measures have been notified to the WTO, it is of course difficult to assess to what extent WTO Members have respected all their notification requirements in the context of the COVID-19 pandemic. However, there can be no doubt that compliance with notification requirements is not only an important part of a WTO Member's adherence to WTO norms, but also of huge practical significance to other WTO Members and imports and exporters around the world. The WTO itself has emphasised these points in one of its COVID-19 related publications.[123]

[119] WTO, 'Decision on Notification Procedures, adopted by the Trade Negotiations Committee at the Uruguay Round', www.wto.org/english/docs_e/legal_e/33-dnotf_e.htm.

[120] WTO, 'Decision on notification procedures for quantitative restriction' (n 56).

[121] Art 12 of the Agreement on Agriculture (n 26).

[122] See, for instance, the US Communication to the General Council and the Council for Trade in Goods, containing a proposal for a General Council decision to strengthen compliance with WTO transparency and notification requirements. Communication from the United States: 'Procedures to Enhance Transparency and Strengthen Notification Requirements under WTO Agreements' (12 March 2018) JOB/GC/148/Rev.1.

[123] See 'Transparency – Why it Matters at Times of Crisis' (WTO, 7 April 2020), www.wto.org/english/tratop_e/covid19_e/transparency_report_e.pdf.

VI. Conclusion

The COVID-19 epidemic has motivated all WTO Members to implement a broad range of trade-related measures, both on the import and export side, pertaining primarily to medical goods and agro-food products. Given that the pandemic is far from over, it can be expected that a number of these measures will continue to apply, even if the initial category of emergency measures (such as export restrictions) have been relaxed or withdrawn, partially or in their entirety.

By and large, even at the height of the pandemic, it did not appear that governments were being much constrained by WTO law (or FTA law, for that matter) in terms of their policy choices. This may be due, first, to the fact that international trade law – and WTO law more than FTA law – provides WTO Members with a wide margin of discretion in how to react to emergency situations, in particular on the export side. Second, beyond the strictures of the law, it would be unrealistic to expect that WTO Members would initiate dispute settlement action against each other, such that even excessive use of the existing policy space is unlikely to be effectively policed, at least during the peak of the emergency situation. Indeed, the fact that a number of WTO Members considered it useful to issue political declarations in which they promised to each other (and to other Members) not to take export-related restrictive measures signals that at least some Members felt that trade-restrictive action permitted as a matter of WTO law would not lead to a collective outcome that would be optimal as a matter of policy.

Nevertheless, as the memory of the immediate emergency situation and the related product shortages fades and goods such as medical supplies (PPE, medical machinery, pharmaceuticals) are no longer in short supply, it remains to be seen whether some of the measures implemented during the pandemic – including some restrictive measures – will continue to apply and will give rise to disagreements between WTO Members.

At a broader level, as the epidemiological situation shows little sign of improving and may result in a protracted economic crisis, it remains to be seen whether WTO Members will feel compelled to resort to more widespread trade-restrictive action in response to the general economic climate. Some of the measures described above point in that direction, but it remains to be seen what the majority of Members will do as time goes on. It will also be interesting to see how the trade-related measures taken in the short, medium and long run compare with the measures taken during and after the 2008–09 crisis.

On the trade facilitating side of the ledger, it may be interesting to observe how the COVID-19 experience will influence WTO Members' willingness, for instance, to accept more generally electronic documentation (customs clearance documents, health certificates, etc). Similarly, it remains to be seen whether mutual recognition, or even equivalence, of technical and health measures will become more widespread due to the greater resort to these policies during the COVID-19 crisis.

It also remains to be seen to what extent the vast financial support measures put in place by governments around the world will translate into trade-related tensions. Many of the support measures put in place have been provided on a horizontal, cross-cutting basis, and may therefore not fall directly under WTO rules that discipline 'specific' subsidies. However, other support measures have targeted particular industries and could therefore conceivably give rise to the imposition of countervailing measures or trigger WTO disputes.

Compliance of WTO Members with transparency and notifications also remains an important element in how the multilateral trading system deals with the regulatory responses to the pandemic. WTO Members have published and notified a vast array of trade-related measures. It is not clear whether this represents full or partial compliance with the relevant WTO rules, but there can be no doubt that transparency and timely information flows are crucial to avoid unnecessary adverse impact on importers and exporters on the ground.

3

Export Restrictions on Food Commodities During the COVID-19 Crisis: Implications for Food Security and the Role of the WTO

ILARIA ESPA

I. Introduction

The COVID-19 pandemic is an unprecedented public health challenge of 'potentially biblical' economic consequences.[1] Since its outbreak, governments have faced inevitable disruptions in the supply of critical medical products due to the labour shortages caused by the lockdowns and other containment measures introduced to fight the spread of the virus.[2] Despite the fundamental need to preserve international trade and global value chains for ensuring an adequate supply of such essential products, countries have increasingly resorted to uncooperative trade policy instruments like export restrictions in the attempt to mitigate critical shortages at the domestic level.[3]

The use of such instruments has also rapidly spread to other sectors not immediately affected by COVID-19, such as the food sector, due to concerns

[1] M Draghi, 'Draghi: We Face a War Against Coronavirus and Must Mobilise Accordingly' *Financial Times* (25 March 2020), www.ft.com/content/c6d2de3a-6ec5-11ea-89df-41bea055720b.

[2] For an overview, see among others R Baldwin and SJ Evenett (eds), *COVID-19 and Trade Policy: Why Turning Inward Won't Work* (London, CEPR Press, 2020); S Evenett, 'Tackling Coronavirus: The Trade Policy Dimension' (*Global Trade Alert*, 11 March 2020), www.globaltradealert.org/reports/50.

[3] See Jan Bohanes, 'An Overview of Trade-Related Measures Taken by WTO Members During the COVID-19 Pandemic and a Few Reflections Thereon', ch 2 in this book. See also, among others, S Evenett, 'Sickening thy neighbour: Export restraints on medical supplies during a pandemic' (*VoxEU*, 19 March 2020), voxeu.org/article/export-restraints-medical-supplies-during-pandemic; SJ Evenett, 'Flawed prescription: Export curbs on medical goods won't tackle shortages' in R Baldwin and SJ Evenett, *COVID-19 and Trade Policy: Why Turning Inward Won't Work* (London, CEPR Press, 2020); 'Export Prohibitions and Restrictions' (WTO, 27 April 2020), www.wto.org/english/tratop_e/covid19_e/export_prohibitions_report_e.pdf.

over potential disruptions in global food markets.[4] However, the proliferation of export restrictions risks exacerbating the potential food security implications of the pandemic, with devastating consequences on low-income, food-import-dependent countries (LIFIDC).[5]

Against this backdrop, this chapter focuses on the nexus between COVID-19 induced export restrictions and food security. Section II sheds light on the impact of the COVID-19 crisis on food security. Section III then explains how and to what extent such an impact may be amplified by the use of export restrictions on food commodities. Section IV examines how such measures are treated under World Trade Organization (WTO) rules and highlights the main limitations of existing disciplines. Section V critically discusses the latest reform initiatives which seek to address such limits in light of food security implications and the more general crisis of the WTO.

II. COVID-19 and Food Security

Unlike previous pandemics like the 1918 Spanish Flu, the COVID-19 crisis did not have an immediately noticeable impact on the levels of food production. As Martin and Glauber have aptly noted, 'the worst mortality effects are not on people in their prime working age' and, furthermore, 'in contrast with the avian flu and swine flu pandemics, there is no direct impact on livestock'.[6] According to the most recent statistics, global food stocks and production levels for key staples (for example, rice, wheat and maize) are indeed at or near all-time highs,[7] and food prices have remained relatively low since the outbreak of the pandemic[8] due to the favourable conditions of global food markets at the beginning of 2020.[9] Prolonged containment measures and disruptions to supply chains may however reverse this

[4] See, inter alia, A Espetia, N Rocha and M Ruta, 'COVID-19 and Food Protectionism: The Impact on the Pandemic and Export Restrictions on World Food Markets' (2020) World Bank Group Policy Research Working Paper 9253, elibrary.worldbank.org/doi/pdf/10.1596/1813-9450-9253; J Hepburn et al, 'COVID-19 and Food Export Restrictions: Comparing Today's Situation to the 2007/08 Price Spikes' (2020) IISD and IFDRI Policy Brief, www.iisd.org/system/files/2020-08/covid-19-food-export-restrictions.pdf; C Kuryama, 'Export Restrictions and Food Security in the Context of the Pandemic' (2020) APEC Policy Brief No 33, www.apec.org/Publications/2020/05/Export-Restrictions-and-Food-Security-in-the-Context-of-the-COVID-19-Pandemic.

[5] Espetia, Rocha and Ruta (n 4) 5.

[6] WJ Martin and JW Glauber, 'Trade Policy and Food Security' in R Baldwin and SJ Evenett (eds), *COVID-19 and Trade Policy: Why Turning Inward Won't Work* (London, CEPR Press, 2020). It is, however, expected that there will be 'some impact on the production of nutrition-dense products such as fruits and vegetables and on production and processing of livestock products that involve teams working in close proximity' (see ibid). This is, for instance, what happened recently in Germany: United States Department of Agriculture, 'Germany: COVID-19 Will Change German Livestock Industry' (6 July 2020): www.fas.usda.gov/data/germany-covid-19-will-change-german-livestock-industry.

[7] 'World Food Situation' (FAO, 8 October 2020), www.fao.org/worldfoodsituation/csdb/en/.

[8] 'Food Price Index' (FAO, 8 October 2020), www.fao.org/worldfoodsituation/foodpricesindex/en/.

[9] Espetia, Rocha and Ruta (n 4) 2.

picture and ultimately lead to a decline in food supplies and inventories and a parallel increase in food prices.[10]

Such a scenario would have devastating consequences on food security for two main reasons. First, the pandemic occurred at a particularly delicate historical moment when it comes to food security: in the last five years, the number of chronically hungry people has been steadily increasing, reaching a high of 800 million according to the latest data published by the World Food Programme (WFP).[11] Among these, those who risk starvation are estimated to be around 135 million.[12] While this state of affairs has multiple and complex causes,[13] the Executive Director of the WFP, David Beasley, has recently reported that an additional 130 million people could be pushed to the brink of starvation by the end of 2020 due to coronavirus. According to Beasley, the pandemic also risks becoming the worst global humanitarian catastrophe since the second post-war period and, ultimately, a 'hunger pandemic'.[14]

Second, those estimates do not take into account the impact of COVID-19 on jobs and incomes, that is, the economic effects induced by the pandemic on food security. According to the WFP, the number of acutely food-insecure people could increase by more than 80 per cent by the end of 2020, with a disproportionately disruptive effect on the most vulnerable communities located in developing and least developed economies, which are already exposed to the highest risk of food insecurity (for example, countries like Ethiopia, whose wealth largely depends on the tourism sector, or South Sudan, which relies on oil for 98.8 per cent of its total exports).[15] Accordingly, Beasley called for greater international collaboration to avoid the WFP's worst scenarios: the prospects of famine in about three dozen countries; the death of about 30 million people who depend directly on international food aid for their livelihood. Significantly, he not only stressed the urgency to secure more funding to support life-saving humanitarian assistance, but also insisted upon the need to ensure that international supply chains remain operational, including by ensuring that trade flows are kept open.[16]

[10] ibid 3.

[11] United Nations World Food Programme (WFP), 'Global Report on Food Crises' (2020), www.wfp.org/publications/2020-global-report-food-crises.

[12] ibid 2. This loom picture is in sharp contrast to the goal to eliminate hunger as enshrined in the Sustainable Development Goal No 2 'Zero Hunger'. For a complete recollection on the SDG2 targets and indicators and a discussion on the progress towards them, see United Nations, 'Sustainable Development Goals Report 2019', unstats.un.org/sdgs/report/2019/The-Sustainable-Development-Goals-Report-2019.pdf, 24.

[13] Among them, the desert locust swarms in Africa, the wars in Syria and Yemen, the increasingly numerous crises in countries such as South Sudan, Burkina Faso, Lebanon, the DRC, Sudan, Ethiopia, and the effects of climate change-related extreme weather events. 'WFP Chief Warns of Hunger Pandemic as COVID-19 Spreads, Statement to UN Security Council' (WFP, 21 April 2020), www.wfp.org/news/wfp-chief-warns-hunger-pandemic-covid-19-spreads-statement-un-security-council.

[14] ibid.

[15] ibid.

[16] ibid.

Indeed, an increasing body of evidence has demonstrated the crucial role of trade in preserving the availability and affordability of food, especially for developing and least developed countries that are dependent on food imports.[17] And yet, since the outbreak of the pandemic an increasing number of governments have purported to meet immediate domestic needs by introducing export restrictions, which actually risk exacerbating the initial effects of the COVID-19 shock on global food supplies and prices.[18]

III. Rationale and Effects of Export Restrictions on Food Commodities

Despite the proliferating number of statements urging governments to refrain from imposing export restrictions amid the pandemic,[19] the food sector got exposed to a new wave of export restrictions at the most critical time of the COVID-19 crisis.[20] According to the latest data, 22 countries resorted to export restrictions in 2020, primarily in the typical forms of quantitative restrictions such as export bans and, to a lesser extent, export quotas (normally administered through non-automatic licensing systems), minimum export prices and export duties.[21] The goods affected by these restrictions are mostly key staples such as rice, wheat, maize, and less frequently other products such as cooking oils and eggs.[22]

Although the number of imposing countries remained significantly lower than the number of countries that applied export restrictions on essential medical

[17] Espetia, Rocha and Ruta (n 4) 5–9; 'COVID-19 and Agriculture: A Story of Resilience' (WTO, 26 August 2020), www.wto.org/english/tratop_e/covid19_e/agric_report_e.pdf.

[18] Espetia, Rocha and Ruta (n 4) 5.

[19] See, inter alia, 'Joint Statement by QU Dongyu, Tedros Adhanom Ghebreyesus and Roberto Azevêdo, Directors-General of FAO, WHO and WTO' (WTO, 31 March 2020), www.wto.org/english/news_e/news20_e/igo_26mar20_e.htm. A number of WTO Members have also committed to an open and predictable trade in agricultural and food products: Statement from Australia; Brazil; Canada; Chile; Colombia; Costa Rica; European Union; Hong Kong, China; Japan; Republic of Korea; Malawi; Mexico; New Zealand; Paraguay; Peru; Qatar; Singapore; Switzerland; the Separate Customs Territory of Taiwan, Penghu, Kinmen and Matsu; Ukraine; United Kingdom; United States; and Uruguay: Responding to the COVID-19 Pandemic with Open and Predictable Trade in Agricultural and Food Products (22 April 2020) WT/GC/208.

[20] The agricultural sector has regularly been subject to waves of export restrictions due to cyclical factors. For more details, see I Espa, *Export Restrictions on Critical Minerals and Metals: Testing the Adequacy of WTO Disciplines* (Cambridge, Cambridge University Press, 2015) 11–22. Importantly, however, this is seemingly the first time the wave is triggered by the use of export restrictions in sectors that are totally unrelated to agriculture, that is, the sector of medical devices. See WTO, 'Export Prohibitions and Restrictions' (n 3) 8.

[21] See the 'COVID-19 Food Trade Policy Tracker' compiled by the International Food Policy Research Institute (IFPRI), www.ifpri.org/project/covid-19-food-trade-policy-tracker. See also, inter alia, Hepburn et al (n 4) 3.

[22] ibid. Hepburn et al offer a full list of food products subject to restrictions in addition to key staples: 'lemons, eggs, turnips, beer, and spirits, … pulses, flour, other grains, onions, garlic, beans, milk powder, vegetable oil, cheese, and yogurt'.

supplies,[23] the impact was high since production of food commodities is highly concentrated geographically.[24] For example, Russia is the largest wheat exporter and imposed export quotas which were exhausted by mid-May. The same applies to Ukraine and Kazakhstan which, together with Russia, account for about a third of all wheat exports globally.[25] Similarly, in the case of rice, the top five exporters account for 75 per cent of world exports, with India being the largest exporter accounting for 25 per cent of world rice exports. Vietnam, which is responsible for approximately 16 per cent of the global rice supply, imposed an export ban in March, replaced by a quota system on 11 March 2020.[26] More generally, the top 50 countries most affected by COVID-19, on average, account for about two-thirds of global food exports; and in the case of key staples, the average is even higher when considering the exports coming from the top 10 countries most affected by COVID-19.[27]

The traditionally declared objective of these measures is to protect domestic consumers from shortages in domestic supply and from price increases in food commodities for food security purposes.[28] The recent food crises of 2007–08 and 2010–11 have shown, however, that these may well be short-term effects which may be offset by: (i) the so-called boomerang effect of export restrictions, according to which the domestic supply of the restricted product may ultimately decline due to the export restriction and the resultant price reduction; (ii) the so-called domino effect, according to which countries affected by export restrictions may retaliate by imposing similar restrictions in an attempt to keep domestic prices low, ultimately leading to higher world prices which worsen the prospects for food security.[29]

According to recent studies, the effect of the export restrictions applied during the food crises since the second half of the 2000s has caused a 40 per cent increase in the price of rice, a 20 per cent increase in the price of maize and a 10 per cent increase in the price of wheat.[30] Based on latest estimations, a similar effect could materialise should export restrictions continue escalating. A recent study by the World Bank, in particular, finds that '[r]egardless of the size of the initial impact of

[23] World Customs Organization, 'List of National Legislation of Countries that Adopted Temporary Export Restrictions on Certain Categories of Critical Medical Supplies in Response to COVID-19', www.wcoomd.org/en/topics/facilitation/activities-and-programmes/natural-disaster.

[24] Overall, the IFPRI estimated that export restrictions have been applied on $US 21 billion in food products, which represent nearly 227,000 billion Kcal: Hepburn et al (n 4) 2.

[25] See Martin and Glauber (n 6) 96.

[26] ibid 96–97.

[27] 'Database on COVID-19 Trade Flows and Policies' (World Bank, 2 April 2020): www.worldbank.org/en/data/interactive/2020/04/02/database-on-coronavirus-covid-19-trade-flows-and-policies.

[28] For a more complete recollection, see Espa, *Export Restrictions on Critical Minerals and Metals* (n 20) 14.

[29] WTO, 'Export Prohibitions and Restrictions' (n 3) 8; see also, 'Why export restrictions should not be a response to COVID-19: Learning lessons from experience with rice in Asia and the Pacific' (FAO, 1 June 2020): www.fao.org/3/ca9362en/ca9362en.pdf; Hepburn et al (n 4).

[30] K Anderson and S Nelgen, 'Trade Barrier Volatility and Agricultural Price Stabilization' (2011) 40 *World Development* 36.

COVID-19, escalating trade restrictions would multiply the initial shock on world export supplies and food prices by a factor of 3'.[31] This means that overall there could be a decline in the global export supply of food ranging between 5.2 per cent and 13.8 per cent, that is, a contraction similar to the 2008–09 crisis, which would once again affect the LIFIDC countries (for example, Tajikistan, Azerbaijan, the Arab Republic of Egypt, the Republic of Yemen and Cuba).[32]

In light of the above it is encouraging that, at the time of writing, most imposing countries have recently phased out export restrictions on food commodities.[33] At the same time, the COVID-19 crisis is far from over, with the spread of new variants forcing countries to impose new containment measures and restrictions. Given how rapidly and pervasively governments resorted to export restrictions at the outbreak of the pandemic, it is reasonable to assume that such measures will likely rise again as soon as countries feel excessively vulnerable to the effects of new disruptions. The latest escalation has indeed shown how easy it was for governments to introduce export restrictions in spite of existing WTO rules and transparency requirements.

IV. WTO Rules Governing Export Restrictions on Food Commodities

The use of export restrictions on food commodities is governed by WTO law under the General Agreement on Tariffs and Trade (GATT)[34] and the Agreement on Agriculture (AoA).[35] These agreements lay down both substantive and procedural rules. It is essential that these rules are applied to minimise the potentially disruptive effects of export restrictions on food security.

A. Substantive WTO Rules

Export restrictions are unlawful under Article XI:1 of the GATT, which requires Member States to eliminate any type of quantitative restrictions having a limiting effect on (imports and) exports, irrespective of their legal status or of whether they de jure or de facto, potentially or actually, limit exports.[36]

[31] Espetia, Rocha and Ruta (n 4) 5.

[32] ibid.

[33] See the 'COVID-19 Food Trade Policy Tracker' (n 21). See also 'Joint Statement on Agriculture Export Prohibitions or Restrictions Relating to the World Food Programme' (21 January 2021) WT/L/1109.

[34] General Agreement on Tariffs and Trade (GATT), Marrakesh Agreement Establishing the World Trade Organization, Annex 1A (Marrakesh, 15 April 1994).

[35] Agreement on Agriculture, Marrakesh Agreement Establishing the World Trade Organization, Annex 1A (Marrakesh, 15 April 1994).

[36] For a recollection of how broadly Art XI has been interpreted in WTO jurisprudence, see Espa, *Export Restrictions on Critical Minerals and Metals* (n 20) 169–75.

However, export restrictions on food commodities (or other 'essential' products) may be justified under Article XI:2(a) of the GATT if they are applied 'temporarily' to prevent or remedy situations of 'critical shortage'.[37] Governments have repeatedly resorted to this exception as a justification for the application of export restrictions on essential medical supplies, and hence have increasingly asserted that this exception can be applied similarly to the restrictions on food exports.[38] However, it is submitted that the latter would unlikely fulfil the 'critical shortage' requirement under Article XI:2(a).[39] The fundamental reason is that, at least so far, there is no concrete prospect of disruption in the availability of key staples: food levels are still adequate; the production outlook for key staples is expected to remain good[40] since production is mostly 'mechanised, requiring relatively little labour input, and tak[ing] place in areas with dispersed, already physically distanced, rural populations'.[41] The same holds true for international transport and the distribution of key staples.[42]

In other words, there may very well be the classical scenario where the imposition of export restrictions in and of itself contributes to exacerbating food security risks due to the effects of such measures on prices and quantities available in the markets as well as on supply chains.[43] For this very reason, it also seems quite unlikely that such measures would be justified under GATT general exceptions (ie, Article XX of the GATT) or the national security exceptions (ie, Article XXI of the GATT).

Under the former, the necessity test informing the most suitable exception, that is, Article XX(b),[44] would require a weighting and balancing exercise taking into

[37] ibid 180–84.

[38] WTO, 'Export Prohibitions and Restrictions' (n 3) 8–9; see also Jan Bohanes, An Overview of Trade-Related Measures Taken by WTO Members During the COVID-19 Pandemic and a Few Reflections Thereon', ch 2 in this book.

[39] Most of the measures are also likely to fall short of the 'temporarily applied' requirement. This is mainly due to the fact that even those measures that governments have indicated as temporary may last much longer than necessary. In the case of the export restrictions applied during the recent food crises, for instance, export restrictions lasted longer than expected in most cases and, in more than a third of cases, they are still in place. WTO 'Export Prohibitions and Restrictions' (n 3) 7–8.

[40] FAO, 'World Food Situation' (n 7).

[41] Martin and Glauber (n 6) 95.

[42] ibid. In the words of Martin and Glauber, 'dry bulk commodities … can be loaded, shipped, and discharged with minimum human-to-human interaction'. In the same vein, see Espetia, Rocha and Ruta (n 4) 17.

[43] Espetia, Rocha and Ruta (n 4) 17–18.

[44] Under Art XX(b) of the GATT, WTO Members can seek to justify measures that are 'necessary to protect human, animal or plant life or health'. Another potentially relevant exception is Art XX(j) of the GATT, which allows WTO Members to defend measures that are 'essential to the acquisition or distribution of products in general or local short supply; Provided that any such measures shall be consistent with the principle that all contracting parties are entitled to an equitable share of the international supply of such products, and that any such measures, which are inconsistent with the other provisions of the Agreement shall be discontinued as soon as the conditions giving rise to them have ceased to exist. The CONTRACTING PARTIES shall review the need for this sub-paragraph not later than 30 June 1960'. Although the latter justifies measures that are 'essential' rather than 'necessary', the Appellate Body clarified that the two standards imply a very similar test in that they require a strong

account three main factors: (i) the importance of the interests or values at stake; (ii) the extent of the contribution to the achievement of the measure's objective (ie, public health due to improved food security); and (iii) the trade-restrictiveness of the measure at issue as compared with other reasonably available alternatives achieving the same level of contribution.[45] The first requirement appears relatively easy to meet given the highest degree of importance attached to the goal of protecting human life or health.[46] What seems more difficult to argue successfully is that export restrictions on food commodities 'bring about' or are 'apt to make' a 'material contribution' to the achievement of food security.[47] This is because, as shown above, they do not only occur at a time when food supplies are not tight but they have also been projected to affect negatively both export supplies and prices in global markets.[48] This conclusion holds true when considering the highly trade-restrictive nature of most of the export restrictions at issue.[49] Even assuming, *arguendo*, that the export restrictions on food commodities introduced in the context of the pandemic be considered provisionally justified under Article XX(b) of the GATT, the chapeau would require that there is no 'arbitrary or unjustifiable discrimination', that is, discrimination that 'bear[s] no rational connection' with the objective of the measure and that arises 'between countries where the same conditions prevail'.[50] The requirements of the chapeau seem also quite difficult to satisfy to the extent that the measures at issue have been proven to disproportionally affect LIFIDC countries, that is, those countries that are most vulnerable to the effects on supplies and prices which are associated with the imposition of export restrictions on food commodities.[51] In this connection, it seems likely that the deterioration of food security prospects induced by the imposition of export restrictions may suffice to ascertain the existence of discrimination which not only defeats their declared/intended objective, but also occurs among countries that are especially vulnerable from a food security perspective.

nexus between the measure at issue and its policy goal: *India–Certain Measures Related to Solar Cells and Solar Modules*, Report of the Appellate Body (14 October 2016) WT/DS/AB/456, paras 5.62–5.63. In the case of Art XX(j) of the GATT, moreover, there is the additional requirement that the measure be temporary and not prevent other members' access to an 'equitable share of the international supply' of food commodities. While this requirement has not yet been interpreted by WTO dispute settlement bodies, it is likely that it will imply an assessment of various factors, including the availability of adequate food export supplies in the global market, the importance of the imposing country as an exporter in the world market and its influence on global food prices.

[45] *Korea–Measures Affecting Imports of Fresh, Chilled and Frozen Beef*, Report of the Appellate Body (10 January 2001) WT/DS/AB/161, para 164; *Brazil–Measures Affecting Imports of Retreaded Tyres*, Report of the Appellate Body (17 December 2007) WT/DS/AB/332, para 156 (*Brazil–Tyres*).

[46] See, among others, *Brazil–Tyres*, Report of the Appellate Body (n 45) para 179.

[47] ibid para 151.

[48] See Espetia, Rocha and Ruta (n 4) 5.

[49] See section III in this chapter.

[50] *Brazil–Tyres*, Report of the Appellate Body (n 45) paras 227–30. See also *United States–Measures Concerning the Importation, Marketing and Sale of Tuna and Tuna Products (Recourse to Article 21.5 of the DSU)*, Report of the Appellate Body (11 January 2019) WT/DS381/AB/RW/USA, WT/DS381/AB/RW2, para 7.136.

[51] See Espetia, Rocha and Ruta (n 4) 5.

As to the national security exceptions, Article XXI(b)(iii) of the GATT may be invoked to seek justification for export restrictions on food commodities that '[Members] consider necessary for the protection of [their] essential security interests taken in time of war or other emergency in international relations'. In this scenario, an imposing Member would need to argue that the pandemic constitutes an 'emergency in international relations' and that food security is an 'essential security interest' within the meaning of Article XXI(b)(iii) of the GATT. According to the Panel Report in *Russia–Traffic in Transit*, the 'emergency in international relations' requirement refers to 'an objective state of affairs' that is

> a situation of armed conflict, or of latent armed conflict, or of heightened tension or crisis, or of general instability engulfing or surrounding a state [giving] rise to particular types of interests for the Member in question, ie defence or military interests, or maintenance of law and public order interests.[52]

The Panel expressly clarified, however, that

> political and economic differences between Members are not sufficient, of themselves, to constitute an emergency in international relations for the purposes of subparagraph (iii) … unless they give rise to defense and military interests, or maintenance of law and public order interests.[53]

The same analytical framework was espoused in the subsequent Panel Report in *Saudi Arabia–Protection of Intellectual Property Rights*.[54] In this connection, export restrictions on food commodities may hardly be considered to meet this requirement to the extent that, as argued above, they are not only disconnected from the immediate needs of the health emergency;[55] they also have disruptive effects on global value chains and world food prices.[56] For the same reasons, it also appears unlikely that export restrictions meet the minimum requirement of plausibility woven into the 'essential security interests' clause.[57]

In conclusion, existing WTO rules do capture the landscape of export restrictions on food commodities adopted in the contest of the pandemic, while at the

[52] *Russian Federation–Measures Concerning Traffic in Transit*, Report of the Panel (26 April 2019) WT/DS/R/512, paras 7.76–7.77 (*Russia–Traffic in Transit*).

[53] ibid para 7.75.

[54] *Saudi Arabia–Measures Concerning the Protection of Intellectual Property Rights*, Report of the Panel (16 June 2020) WT/DS/R/567, paras 7.241–7.252.

[55] This is irrespective of the fact that the COVID-19 emergency may, in itself, qualify as a 'crisis' within the meaning of Art XXI(b)(iii) of the GATT. This is in fact directly relevant for the prospects of justification of export restrictions which are themselves connected to the health crisis, eg, the export bans imposed on medical supplies.

[56] V Lapa, 'GATT Article XXI as a Way to Justify Food Prohibitions Adopted as a Response to COVID-19?' (2020) 15 *Global Trade and Customs Journal* 340.

[57] According to the Panel in *Russia–Traffic in Transit*, the obligation of good faith requires that a Member invoking Art XXI(b)(iii) of the GATT 1994 articulates the essential security interests said to arise from the emergency in international relations sufficiently enough to demonstrate their veracity (see *Russia–Traffic in Transit*, Report of the Panel (n 52) paras 7.130–7.135) and, furthermore, that the measure/s at issue meet a minimum requirement of plausibility in relation to the proffered essential security interests (ibid paras 7.138–7.139).

same time providing for a set of flexibilities which are aimed at accommodating the use of such measures during times of food security crises. The present state of the world food markets, on the one hand, and the disconnect between the COVID-19 emergency and the introduction of food export restrictions to date, on the other hand, make it however implausible that such measures may be successfully justified under existing GATT exceptions. In other words, and importantly, the latest escalation in the use of export restrictions on food commodities is not the result of inexistent or insufficient WTO disciplines on the substantive side. Rather, as explained below in section IV.B, it could occur mostly because of the poor level of transparency maintained during the COVID-19 pandemic.

B. WTO Rules on Transparency

Although it seems highly implausible that, in the context of the current crisis, countries will challenge food export restrictions before the WTO dispute settlement system,[58] their potential WTO inconsistency, discussed above in section IV.A, makes the monitoring of these measures crucial as a matter of transparency. This is even more so in the case of export restrictions on food commodities which may be decisive for the food security of net-importing countries.[59]

For this reason, export restrictions on food commodities, which are allegedly applied under the purview of Article XI:2(a) of the GATT, are subject to specific notification and consultation requirements in accordance with Article 12:1 of the AoA:

> 1. Where any Member institutes any new export prohibition or restriction on foodstuffs in accordance with paragraph 2(a) of Article XI of GATT 1994, the Member shall observe the following provisions:
>
> (a) the Member instituting the export prohibition or restriction shall give due consideration to the effects of such prohibition or restriction on importing Members' food security;
>
> (b) before any Member institutes an export prohibition or restriction, it shall give notice in writing, as far in advance as practicable, to the Committee on Agriculture comprising such information as the nature and the duration of such measure, and shall consult, upon request, with any other Member having a substantial interest as an importer with respect to any matter related to the measure in question. The Member instituting such export prohibition or restriction shall provide, upon request, such a Member with necessary information.
>
> 2. The provisions of this Article shall not apply to any developing country Member, unless the measure is taken by a developing country Member which is a net-food exporter of the specific foodstuff concerned.

[58] This is even more so considering that the Appellate Body is no longer operational at the time of writing, and that its paralysis is furthermore jeopardising binding and automatic dispute settlement in the WTO. See I Espa, *The (WTO and) Appellate Body Crisis: What Ways Forward?*, Italian Ministry of Foreign Affairs (forthcoming).

[59] See WTO, 'Export Prohibitions and Restrictions' (n 3) 9; Espetia, Rocha and Ruta (n 4) 5.

3. The provisions of this Article do not apply to developing Member countries, unless the measure is introduced by a developing Member country which is a net exporter of the specific food in question.

Accordingly, the notification and consultation requirements are rather weak in that: (i) there is no strict time frame within which Members shall notify the measure, but only the obligation to proceed 'as soon as possible'; (ii) the consultation obligation remains conditional upon an explicit request by an importing Member State; and (iii) there is no obligation to review the measure if consultations fail.

In light of the weaknesses of Article 12.1 of the AoA, it is not surprising that such requirements have been very poorly complied with by WTO Members irrespective of the numerous calls for more transparency made by multiple stakeholders, and also by the Director-General of the WTO.[60] Significantly, the WTO itself has reported that only three notifications have been filed in compliance with Article XI:2(a) of the GATT, respectively from the Kyrgyz Republic, Macedonia and Thailand, in an internal document prepared by the Secretariat.[61] The WTO has also admitted to relying on external sources compiled and updated by other international organisations or entities to monitor the current situation.[62] In other words, the WTO does not appear to be capable of internally monitoring compliance with its own provisions through the mechanisms that were specifically envisaged for this very purpose under the relevant WTO rules on transparency.

As already noted by many scholars, the current notification system is problematic not only in general but also with specific reference to the issue of export restrictions.[63] As far as export restrictions on food commodities are concerned, furthermore, the system is even more problematic to the extent that: (i) such measures are not only unrelated to the immediate needs of the health emergency, but also likely to run counter to applicable WTO rules; and (ii) they are likely to contribute to deteriorating food security conditions as well as causing disruptions to supply chains in the food sector.[64]

For these reasons, the transparency of export restrictions, more generally, and the notification and consultation requirements applicable to export restrictions on food commodities, more specifically, should be prioritised in any trade reform agenda aimed at making the WTO more resilient going forward. As regards the latter, importantly, a number of reform proposals have already been tabled as from

[60] WTO, 'Export Prohibitions and Restrictions' (n 3) 9–10.

[61] ibid.

[62] Among them are international organisations such as the World Customs Organization and the OECD, inter-agency platforms such as the Agricultural Market Information System, and other initiatives led by scientific and/or academic institutions such as the COVID-19 FOOD Trade policy TRACKER developed by the IFPRI and the Global Trade Alert compiled by the University of St Gallen.

[63] See, inter alia, G Adinolfi, 'A Tale of Two Crises: Quali Risposte dell'Organizzazione mondiale del commercio alla pandemia da COVID-19?' in P Acconci and E Baroncini (eds), *Gli effetti della pandemia Covid-19 su commercio, investimenti e strumenti finanziari: Una prospettiva italiana* (ALMA-DL AMSacta, 2020), amsacta.unibo.it/6440/1/ACCONCI_BARONCINI_Gli_effetti_emergenza_Covid19_su_commercio_investimenti_occupazione.pdf.

[64] Martin and Glauber (n 6) 97.

the late 2000s by a number of international bodies and institutions, from the WTO itself to the United Nations Food and Agriculture Organization (FAO) and the G20. Such proposals have explored avenues to strengthen the procedural requirements envisaged under Article 12.1 of the AoA insofar as they provided for, inter alia: (i) a prior notification obligation with strict and binding time frames; (ii) the obligation to demonstrate that the introduction of export measures has no appreciable effect on food aid for LIFIDC countries; and (iii) the obligation to enter into consultations is, in all cases, matched with the obligation to suspend the implementation of the measure during consultations as well as the obligation to accept the binding arbitration of a 'standing committee of experts' if consultations are not concluded within a reasonable time.[65] Although such proposals have remained unattended to date, they arguably provide a starting basis to advance the issue of transparency of export restrictions (on food products) at the WTO.

V. Conclusions

This chapter has shown that the proliferation of export restrictions on food commodities resulting from the COVID-19 pandemic was not the result of a lack of substantive WTO rules but rather facilitated by the weaknesses in WTO transparency requirements – and, particularly, the current system of notifications – applicable to export restrictions on food products. Such weaknesses have contributed to delaying awareness of the scope and coverage of export restrictions applied in the sector amid the COVID-19 pandemic in spite of their food security implications.

Against this backdrop, the need to support the calls for WTO transparency reforms is arguably one of the strongest takeaways from the COVID-19 crisis, not only in general[66] but also with specific reference to the issue of export restrictions on food commodities. This is even more so in light of the lack of progress which characterises virtually any area of normative action within the WTO.[67] After all, achieving greater transparency is arguably the most concretely tangible objective that the WTO can still – and hence all the more must – fulfil in order to avoid a legitimacy crisis that seems almost unavoidable under the present circumstances.[68]

[65] For a complete recollection, see Espa, *Export Restrictions on Critical Minerals and Metals* (n 20) 17–22.

[66] See, for instance, 'WTO Members Consider Transparency Reforms at Goods Council Meeting' (WTO, 10 July 2019), www.wto.org/english/news_e/news19_e/good_10jul19_e.htm.

[67] Keynote speech by Professor P Van den Bossche, 'Will the WTO Survive COVID-19, Economic Nationalism and Superpower Confrontation?' at 'The 3R Initiative: Re-thinking, Re-packaging and Rescuing World Trade Law' (Online Academic Conference by Law Schools Global League, in association with National Research University Higher School of Economics, 17 July 2020).

[68] OE Fitzgerald (ed), *Modernizing the World Trade Organization* (Centre for International Governance Innovation, 2020) A CIGI Essay Series, www.cigionline.org/sites/default/files/documents/ModernizingWTO_EssaySeries-web.pdf.

Importantly, an improvement of the WTO's transparency and notification mechanism would contribute not only to effectively governing protectionist attempts that have an impact on the most vulnerable countries and on the food security prospects of their populations;[69] it would also enhance the efficiency and legitimacy of the system as a whole. This is therefore a critical aspect of rethinking the world trading system in the post-pandemic era.

[69] Espetia, Rocha and Ruta (n 4) 5.

4

Time to Reform the Non-Actionable Subsidy Rules in the WTO: The COVID-19 Subsidies and Beyond

RU DING*

I. Introduction

The COVID-19 pandemic is presenting the world trading system with unprecedented challenges. According to the World Trade Organization (WTO), the 2020 trade volume will fall 9.2 per cent on 2019 levels and global GDP will contract by 4.8 per cent.[1] As one of the major coordinators of global governance, the WTO was not prepared for the global health catastrophe caused by the pandemic. As the Deputy Director of the WTO Alan Wolff noted:

> [T]he WTO, created 25 years ago, and the multilateral trading system, created nearly 75 years ago, did not have a packaged, ready-made, off-the-shelf response to a pandemic. There had been nothing this lethal, this global, for one hundred years.[2]

Nevertheless, the WTO acted swiftly to facilitate information-sharing on export prohibition measures and tariffs on medical goods, and to release reports and guidance for e-commerce, trade in services, and micro, small and medium-sized enterprises.[3] Scholars in economics and law presented timely works on how the WTO and its rules may help WTO Members utilise trade to save lives and jobs.[4]

* The author would like to thank Weihuan Zhou for his valuable feedback, and Tianyi Xie, Fei Wang and Sicong Ge for their valuable helpful research assistance. This research is funded by the Institute of Governance Studies (IGS), Tsinghua University.

[1] 'Trade shows signs of rebound from COVID-19, recovery still uncertain' (WTO, 6 October 2020), www.wto.org/english/news_e/pres20_e/pr862_e.htm.

[2] 'DDG Wolff: Policy Coordination Needed to Address Pandemic Challenges' (WTO, 20 April 2020), www.wto.org/english/news_e/news20_e/ddgaw_20apr20_e.htm.

[3] See these reports or database information: 'COVID-19 and World Trade' (WTO), www.wto.org/english/tratop_e/covid19_e/covid19_e.htm.

[4] For examples, R Baldwin and BW di Mauro (eds), *Economics in the Time of COVID-19* (London, CEPR Press, 2020); J Pauwelyn, 'Export Restrictions in Times of Pandemic: Options and Limits under International Trade Agreements' (30 April 2020), ssrn.com/abstract=3579965; JA Hillman, 'Six Proactive Steps in a Smart Trade Approach to Fighting COVID-19' (*Think Global Health*, 20 March 2020), www.thinkglobalhealth.org/article/six-proactive-steps-smart-trade-approach-fighting-covid-19.

Chapter two of this book provides a comprehensive overview of measures in response to COVID-19. There is, however, inadequate study on subsidy measures in response to COVID-19. Evenett cautioned from a trade policy perspective that there was the potential for state financial support becoming too large and causing trade distortion.[5] The WTO Members' economic stimulus measures will certainly have a significant impact on trade during and after the pandemic. The WTO rules on subsidies and countervailing measures are likely to capture some of these measures as 'prohibited subsidies' or 'actionable subsidies'. The measures that potentially fall within the definition of 'subsidy' under Article 1.1 of the Agreement on Subsidies and Countervailing Measures (SCM Agreement)[6] are referred to in this chapter as 'COVID-19 subsidies'. It means that WTO Members could respond with domestic countervailing investigations of exported products that have benefited from the COVID-19 subsidies, or directly file a dispute at the WTO to challenge these subsidies.[7]

COVID-19 subsidies have become a global economic phenomenon and many of them are large in scale. Based on the International Monetary Fund (IMF)'s database of 197 economies' 'policy responses to COVID-19' (IMF Database), 196 of these economies have implemented fiscal, monetary, or exchange rate-related policies to maintain and revive their economies.[8] Taking fiscal policies as an example, the government of Japan adopted the Emergency Economic Package Against COVID-19 on 7 April 2020, which amounted to JPY¥117.1 trillion, accounting for 21.1 per cent of Japan's 2019 GDP.[9] And this was only one of the four fiscal packages implemented by Japan. The government of the United States (US) provided three stages of stimulus totalling about $US 2.9 trillion, amounting to around 14.5 per cent of US GDP in 2019.[10] Such large-scale domestic economic support will have significant impacts on international trade and global competition in the post-pandemic era.[11]

There are two tiers of legal issues on COVID-19 subsidies under the WTO rules. The first tier is a positive analysis regarding whether these measures are prohibited or actionable under the SCM Agreement. The second tier concerns a normative analysis of whether the COVID-19 subsidies, or some of them, should be justified as not actionable through reviving the currently expired rules on 'non-actionable subsidies'

[5] S Evenett, 'What's Next for Protectionism? Watch out for State Largeness, Especially Export Incentives' in R Baldwin and SJ Evenett (eds), *COVID-19 and Trade Policy: Why Turning Inward Won't Work* (London, CEPR Press 2020).

[6] Agreement on Subsidies and Countervailing Measures, Marrakesh Agreement Establishing the World Trade Organization, Annex 1A (Marrakesh, 15 April 1994) (SCM Agreement).

[7] ibid. Rules on domestic countervailing investigations are in Part V of the SCM Agreement; rules on challenging directly at the WTO are in Art 7 (remedies to actionable subsides); and Art 4 (remedies to prohibited subsidies).

[8] The economy that did not implement any economic policy responses to COVID-19 is Eritrea, based on the data updated on 2 December 2020. 'Policy Responses to COVID-19' (International Monetary Fund), www.imf.org/en/Topics/imf-and-covid19/Policy-Responses-to-COVID-19#C.

[9] ibid.

[10] ibid.

[11] Evenett (n 5) 185.

under the WTO. The first-tier question requires an analysis of WTO Members' practice based on existing WTO rules, jurisprudence and practices.[12] With respect to the latter question, the existing literature on 'non-actionable subsidies' provides a foundation for conducting preliminary normative analysis. Robert Howse, Gary Horlick, Luca Rubini and other scholars have voiced the need to reform the WTO subsidy rules, in particular, to introduce specific exceptions for legitimate subsidies.[13]

Through an analysis using information from the IMF Database and the official documents of the WTO Members, this chapter finds that many of the COVID-19 subsidies implemented by the European Union (EU), the US and China would potentially be considered as either actionable or prohibited subsidies. This chapter argues that the WTO rules on subsidies need reform to provide flexibility for governments to deal with public health crises such as COVID-19. The remainder of the chapter consists of four parts. Section II analyses whether the current COVID-19 subsidies are actionable or even prohibited under the WTO rules, using some major measures adopted by the EU, the US and China as case studies. Section III examines the rationales for justifying some of the COVID-19 subsidies from the perspectives of human rights, economic efficiency and development. Section IV proposes ideas in formulating new rules on 'non-actionable subsidy for disaster relief'. Section V concludes.

II. Are Current Covid-19 Subsidies Prohibited/Actionable?

A. The Governing Rules

Under Article 1 of the SCM Agreement,[14] a measure is a subsidy when 'the government'[15] provides a 'financial contribution'[16] to firms, and such financial

[12] 'WTO jurisprudence' means relevant WTO Appellate Body reports, Panel reports, and arbitral awards and decisions; 'WTO practice' means information relating to the background and application of provisions, including relevant decisions and other significant activities of WTO Committees, Councils and other relevant WTO bodies. 'WTO Analytical Index: Interpretation and Application of WTO Agreements', www.wto.org/english/res_e/publications_e/ai17_e/ai17_e.htm.

[13] R Howse, 'Do the World Trade Organization Disciplines on Domestic Subsidies Make Sense? The Case for Legalizing Some Subsidies' in GA Bermann et al (eds), *Law and Economics of Contingent Protection in International Trade* (Cambridge, Cambridge University Press 2009); SZ Bigdeli, 'Resurrecting the Dead – The Expired Non-Actionable Subsidies and the Lingering Question of Green Space' (2011) 8 *Manchester Journal of International Economic Law* 2; L Rubini, 'Rethinking International Subsidies Disciplines: Rationale and Possible Avenues for Reform' (*The E15 Initiative*, November 2015), e15initiative.org/publications/rethinking-international-subsidies-disciplines-rationale-and-possible-avenues-for-reform/; G Horlick and PA Clarke, 'Rethinking Subsidy Disciplines for the Future: Policy Options for Reform' (2017) 20 *Journal of International Economic Law* 673.

[14] The SCM Agreement, which is the main source of rules on subsidy-related measures and the countervailing measures under the WTO, governs only trade in goods. The General Agreement on Trade in Services (GATS) has no substantive obligations on service subsidies. The Agreement on Agriculture provides special rules for subsidies in agriculture.

contribution confers 'benefit'[17] to the recipient. The 'benefit' test asks whether the government's financial contribution provides the recipient an advantage vis-a-vis the market.[18] Moreover, for this 'subsidy' to be actionable under the rules, it must be 'specific', either de jure or de facto, ie, the subsidy is legally targeted at or is in fact provided only or disproportionately to a particular industry or enterprise or group of industries or enterprises.[19]

If all the aforementioned criteria are met, then the measure is an 'actionable subsidy', sometimes referred to as 'yellow light subsidies'. It means that if WTO Member A can show that imports from Member B have received such 'actionable subsidies' and have caused 'adverse effect' to it or other WTO Members, then Member A can request the WTO dispute settlement processes for a legal remedy to remove the subsidy or the adverse effect of the subsidy. Under certain circumstances Member A may take countervailing measures unilaterally to counteract the adverse effects of the subsidies.[20]

Another category is 'prohibited subsidies' or 'red light subsidies' which are considered by the negotiators as most distortive to international trade and thus are illegal per se. Any WTO Member can challenge such subsidies directly without proving adverse effects or specificity, which are presumed. These include subsidies that are contingent upon export performance or the use of domestic goods over imported goods.[21]

Besides actionable and prohibited subsidies, there used to be a category of 'non-actionable subsidies' contemplated in Article 8.2 of the SCM Agreement, also known as 'green light subsidies'. This category expired in 1999.[22] Non-actionable subsidies refer to certain types of subsidy that, while fulfilling the criteria of 'actionable subsidy', can be justified under the rules. WTO Members shall not seek a remedy against such subsidies through multilateral or unilateral measures. Members can still seek consultation with the subsidising Member, but the

[15] Here the term 'government' is used in a broad sense. It encompasses the concept of public body, and also a private body when the government entrusts or directs the private body. Art 1 of the SCM Agreement (n 6). There is a body of literature on the definition of 'public body', 'private body' and 'government'. See for examples, R Ding, '"Public Body" or Not: Chinese State-Owned Enterprise' (2014) 48 *Journal of World Trade* 167; G Messenger, 'The Public–Private Distinction at the World Trade Organization: Fundamental Challenges to Determining the Meaning of "Public Body"' (2017) 15 *International Journal of Constitutional Law* 60.

[16] The concept of 'financial contribution' covers a wide range of measures, from direct cash payment to tax reliefs to equity infusion or loan guarantees, or provision of goods and services etc. Art 1.1(a)(1)(i)–(iv) of the SCM Agreement (n 6).

[17] ibid Art 1.1(b).

[18] '[A] financial contribution will only confer a "benefit", ie, an advantage, if it is provided on terms that are more advantageous than those that would have been available to the recipient on the market'. *Canada–Measures Affecting the Export of Civilian Aircraft*, Report of the Panel (14 April 1999) WT/DS70/R, para 9.112.

[19] Art 2 of the SCM Agreement (n 6).

[20] Member A needs to prove 'injury' to its own domestic industry for imposing unilateral countervailing measures. ibid Art 5.

[21] ibid Arts 3 and 4.

[22] Horlick and Clarke (n 13) 686.

subsidising Member does not have an obligation to remove the subsidy and there are several procedural hurdles to use countermeasures against such non-actionable subsidies.[23] Article 8.2 sets out three types: (1) assistance for research and development activities; (2) assistance for disadvantaged regions; and (3) assistance to implement new environmental requirements.[24] This generalisation is broad, but the actual rules, as noted by some developing WTO Members like Venezuela and Cuba, are preconditioned with stringent requirements and ceilings, making this list of little practical use in carrying out effective development policies.[25]

Under the SCM Agreement, there are no general exceptions or justifications, such as Article XX of the General Agreement on Tariffs and Trade (GATT), that provide policy space for measures taken for public health or other legitimate considerations. Scholars have been debating about whether Article XX can be applied to the SCM Agreement, an issue that remains unsettled under the current WTO jurisprudence.[26]

The first legal enquiry is: which one of the above categories of subsidies – red, yellow or green – may capture the existing COVID-19 subsidies? The rules on green light subsidies have expired, so under the current rules, green subsidies would be deemed actionable. The section below discusses whether any of the COVID-19 subsidies would be non-actionable under the expired rules. If the rules were effective, there can be a prediction of how many measures may be justified if the rules on green light subsidies were revived.

The EU, the US and China, the three WTO Members with the largest trading volumes in goods and services, are selected for a case study. Table 4.1 shows the basic information of the three Members' economic conditions during the pandemic and their policy responses. The IMF provides information on three types of measures: fiscal measures, monetary measures and exchange rate policy. The analysis below focuses on fiscal measures and their legal status under the SCM Agreement.

Table 4.1 General Information on the EU, China and the US Situation of COVID-19 and Policy Response[27]

WTO Member	No of confirmed cases	No of deaths	Impact on economy in the first quarter	2020 real GDP growth annual per cent change	Fiscal measure
US	13,385,755	266,043	– 6.8%	– 4.3%	$US 2.8 trillion
EU	11,735,894	272,041	– 3.0%	– 7.2%	€4.3 trillion
China	93,668	4,750	– 6.8%	+ 1.9%	RMB 4.8 trillion

[23] Art 9 of the SCM Agreement (n 6).

[24] ibid Art 8.

[25] Howse (n 13) 101.

[26] The 2006 World Trade Report of the WTO Secretariat, in its legal analysis, suggests: '[w]hile Article XX in principle would apply to subsidies, the more specific rules of the SCM Agreement in any case are explicitly geared to remedying trade distortions from subsidization'. Also, '[t]he lack of

B. The Case of the EU

i. EU and Member States' Measures

For the EU, there are economic stimulus packages implemented at both the Union level and at Member States' level. At the Union level, the current policy responses can be discussed in three categories. The first includes the 'safety net measures' which are the EU's initial policy responses to the COVID-19. The second and third categories are recovery and development proposals of the European Commission, including the instrument of 'Next Generation EU' and the 'Multiannual Financial Framework'. Table 4.2 illustrates the amounts of the three categories of policy. The 'safety net measures' consists of three sets of measures including:

> (1) the European Stability Mechanism (ESM) provides Pandemic Crisis Support (based on existing precautionary credit lines) up to 2 percent of 2019 GDP for each euro area country (up to €240 billion in total) to finance health-related spending; (2) €25 billion in government guarantees to the European Investment Bank (EIB) up to €200 billion in finance to companies, with a focus on small and medium enterprises (SMEs); and (iii) to create a temporary loan-based instrument (SURE) of up to €100 billion to protect workers and jobs, supported by guarantees from EU Member States. The Pandemic Crisis Support from the ESM has become operational and the European Council has adopted the SURE.[28]

Table 4.2 EU's Budget Policies for Recovery from COVID-19[29]

Policy	**Amount**
Safety nets measures: SURE/ESM Pandemic Crisis Support/EIB Guarantee Fund for Workers and Businesses	€540 billion
Next Generation EU	€750 billion
Multiannual Financial Framework 2021–27	€1100 billion

textual support for such a reading, however, makes it unlikely that the Appellate Body would accept an Article XX defense to a claim under the SCM Agreement'. ibid 98.

[27] 1. WHO, WHO Coronavirus Disease (COVID-19) Dashboard, data on confirmed cases and deaths updated on 2 December 2020. WHO does not provide data of EU in general, so the information is adopted from European Centre for Disease Prevention and Control, which was updated on 2 December 2020.
2. The GDP contraction in Q1-2020 is compared to Q1-2019, IMF policy tracker of the Policy Responses to COVID-19.
3. 2020 real GDP growth annual percent change, IMF, World Economic Outlook, October 2020.
4. The column of the amount of fiscal stimulus is calculated based on the information provided by the IMF policy tracker of the Policy Responses to COVID-19. The number does not include the programs without specified amount. The amounts of different programs are cumulated in order to show the general situation. EU fiscal measures include both policies implemented by the European Commission and EU member states' state aid. The number was updated on 2 December 2020.

[28] IMF, 'Policy Responses to COVID-19' (n 8).

[29] Source: ibid.

The 'Next Generation EU' is essentially a package of economic stimulus to boost the recovery of the EU common market. The European Council reached a political agreement on the 'Next Generation EU' recovery fund on 21 July 2020.[30] This package consists of three pillars, among which the first pillar is to support recovery through grants and loans for EU Member States and grants for rural development. The second pillar is for incentivising private investment mainly through a solvency support instrument, and the third pillar is for health programmes, development projects, humanitarian aid and other projects, which are aimed at preparing for future similar health crises.[31] The 'Next Generation EU' is supported by financing, not from the Member States, but from money raised on the private financial markets through issuing state-backed bonds for 2021–24.[32]

Moreover, the European Commission proposed the multiannual financial framework for the EU budget from 2021 to 2027. This budget proposal put forward not only an emergency aid reserve fund, but also a 'European Globalisation Adjustment Fund' to support the labour market to adjust to any financial or economic crisis.[33]

At the state level, EU Member States' subsidy policies are legally restrained by the State Aid rules of the Union. On 19 March 2020, the European Commission published the 'Temporary Framework for State aid measures to support the economy in the current COVID-19 outbreak' (Temporary Framework for State-aid).[34] It is a temporary derogation from the normal time State Aid rules and allows Member States to take extraordinary measures that would not legally be allowed in usual times. The European Commission later adopted three amendments to the framework on 3 April, 8 May and 29 June respectively,[35] in order to expand the scope of coverage of the original framework. Under the amended Temporary Framework for State-aid, EU Member States may adopt the following types of COVID-19 State aid under detailed conditions:

1. Aid in the form of direct grants, repayable advances, or tax advantages (section 3.1 of the Temporary Framework; amended to be titled 'limited amounts of aid' in 2nd amendment).
2. Guarantees on loans (section 3.2 of the Temporary Framework).
3. Aid in the form of subsidised interest rates for loans (section 3.3 of the Temporary Framework).

[30] ibid.

[31] 'Recovery plan for Europe' (European Commission), ec.europa.eu/info/live-work-travel-eu/health/coronavirus-response/recovery-plan-europe/pillars-next-generation-eu_en.

[32] 'The EU Budget Powering the Recovery Plan for Europe' (European Commission, 27 May 2020), ec.europa.eu/info/sites/info/files/factsheet_1_en.pdf.

[33] ibid.

[34] 'State aid: Commission adopts Temporary Framework to enable Member States to further support the economy in the COVID-19 outbreak' (European Commission, 19 March 2020), ec.europa.eu/commission/presscorner/detail/en/ip_20_496.

[35] Amendment documents are available at 'State aid rules and coronavirus' (European Commission), ec.europa.eu/competition/state_aid/what_is_new/covid_19.html.

4. Aid in the form of guarantees and loans channelled through credit institutions or other financial institutions (section 3.4 of the Temporary Framework).
5. Short-term export credit insurance (section 3.5 of the Temporary Framework).
6. Aid for COVID-19 relevant research and development (section 3.6, 1st amendment).
7. Investment aid for testing and upscaling infrastructure (section 3.7, 1st amendment).
8. Investment aid for the production of COVID-19 relevant products (section 3.8, 1st amendment).
9. Aid in the form of deferral of tax and/or of social security contributions (section 3.9, 1st amendment).
10. Aid in the form of wage subsidies for employees to avoid lay-offs during the COVID-19 outbreak (section 3.10, 1st amendment).
11. State injection of equity to firms (78*bis* and 78*ter*, 3rd amendment).[36]

Based on the IMF Data, national level liquidity measures, including schemes approved by the European Commission under temporary flexible EU State Aid rules, has amounted to about €3 trillion.[37]

The Temporary Framework for State-aid has some distinctive characteristics. First, it imposes a time limit on State aid. Direct grants, repayable advances, or tax advantages shall be granted no later than 31 December 2020.[38] The Temporary Framework is justified by the 'current exceptional circumstances and will not be applied after 31 December 2020'.[39] Second, it sets out a specific cap of State aid in different forms. For example, direct grants cannot exceed €800,000 per undertaking. Third, it requires reporting from Member States within 12 months from the moment of granting.[40]

ii. Analysis of the EU's Measures under the SCM Agreement

The EU and its Member States' COVID-19 fiscal measures to a large extent could potentially be characterised as either 'actionable' or 'prohibited' subsidies. At the Member State level, the State-aid programmes under the Temporary Framework for State-aid are provided by the government, or through a funding mechanism that can be attributable to the government (the 'government' test), in the form of 'financial contribution' ('financial contribution' test), and can be more favourable than the market rate depending upon whether a market rate is identifiable (the 'benefit' test), and are specific to certain industries or undertakings that are adversely impacted by COVID-19 (the specificity test). Thus, they may potentially fall within the category of 'actionable subsidies' under the SCM Agreement. Other WTO Members may challenge these subsidies at the WTO or impose countervailing duties on those subsidised European exports.

[36] The list incorporated some parts of the amendments and is not exhaustive.
[37] IMF, 'Policy Responses to COVID-19' (n 8).
[38] Point 22.d of the 'Temporary Framework on State Aid' (n 35).
[39] ibid point 39.
[40] ibid point 34.

Among those measures permitted under the Temporary Framework, the export credit insurance may fall within the category of 'prohibited subsidies'. Article 3.1(a) of the SCM Agreement sets out the definition of an export subsidy as a form of prohibited subsidy, and Annex I of the SCM Agreement provides an illustrative list of export subsidies. Item (k) of Annex I states:

> The grant by governments (or special institutions controlled by and/or acting under the authority of governments) of export credits at rates below those which they actually have to pay for the funds so employed (or would have to pay if they borrowed on international capital markets in order to obtain funds of the same maturity and other credit terms and denominated in the same currency as the export credit).[41]

The above 'export credit insurance' could fall within this category if it can be proved that the rates exporters get are below those on international capital markets.

One counterargument is that all these governmental support programmes are not providing any 'benefit' since, at the global crisis, there is no 'market' in the ordinary sense to compare with either domestically or internationally. For example, the Temporary Framework for State-aid also stipulates that for 'short-term export credit insurance' the aid cannot be justified if only

> a large well-known international private export credits insurer and a national credit insurer produce evidence of the unavailability of such cover; or at least four well-established exporters in the Member State produce evidence of refusal of cover from insurers for specific operations.[42]

This legal design may provide an argument that since there is no availability of commercial alternatives, such support does not constitute a 'subsidy' since there is no benefit conferred. This can be referred as an 'absence of a market benchmark' argument. In the WTO dispute *Canada–Feed-in-Tariff Program*, the Appellate Body reasoned that the government 'created' the renewable energy generation market, and there would be no market absent the government's intervention.[43] Following this logic, one might argue that in a pandemic, there is no market if absent government support, and thus when identifying the market benchmark, the investigation authority must take into account the government's support as an internal rather than external factor of the market benchmark. However, whether all the forms of aid at the EU Member State level could apply this argument is an open question. It depends on how the aid is designed and the comparable market situations in both domestic and international markets when the aid is granted.

The aid to research and development (R&D) seems to fall within the 'non-actionable' subsidy category of the SCM Agreement. However, the rules on R&D subsidies, as one type of the expired non-actionable subsidies, require that the assistance for research activities should cover no more than 75 per cent of the costs of industrial research or 50 per cent of the costs of pre-competitive development

[41] Annex I (k) of the SCM Agreement (n 6).

[42] s 3.5 of the 'Temporary Framework on State Aid' (n 35).

[43] *Canada–Certain Measures Affecting the Renewable Energy Generation Sector*, Report of the Appellate Body (24 May 2013) WT/DS412/AB/R, WT/DS426/AB/R, para 5.185.

activities.[44] The R&D aid under the Temporary Framework can cover 100 per cent of eligible costs for fundamental research and shall not exceed 80 per cent of eligible costs for industrial research. The 80 per cent cap is higher than the maximum amount allowed under the SCM Agreement. Therefore, the R&D aid for COVID-19 research could still be actionable even if the 'non-actionable subsidy' provisions were revived.

Comparing with aid at the Member State level, the EU-level programmes are more problematic through the lens of the SCM Agreement. For example, the 'Next Generation EU' and the multiannual budget plans are long-term subsidy schemes that are clearly geared towards industrial promotion rather than simply recovery from the COVID-19 pandemic. As noted by EC President von der Leyen: 'These investments will not only preserve the outstanding achievements of the last 70 years but will also ensure that our Union is climate neutral, digital, social and a strong global player. This is Europe's moment'.[45]

Meanwhile in the introduction of the 'Next Generation EU', the goals are to 'recover' and also 'emerge stronger', and the projects should at the same time accelerate the 'twin green and digital transitions' which are industrial plans of the EU.[46] Since these are long-term programmes,[47] the above-mentioned argument of 'absent of a market benchmark' during the pandemic can hardly apply when the markets start to normalise around the globe.

In all, the EU COVID-19 subsidies at both Union and Member State level may constitute actionable or prohibited subsidies under the SCM Agreement. Even applying the expired rules on non-actionable subsidies, many of the EU Member States' State aid may still be actionable, since they would not fulfil the preconditions to qualify as non-actionable subsidies.

C. The Case of the US

i. US Fiscal Policies

The US has provided a three-package fiscal policy response, with a total of $US 2.9 trillion, to COVID-19 through three pieces of legislation. Table 4.3 illustrates the amount of each package.

[44] Art 8.2 of the SCM Agreement (n 6).

[45] 'Overview of the Commission's response, Economic measures' (European Commission), ec.europa.eu/info/live-work-travel-eu/health/coronavirus-response/overview-commissions-response_en#economic-measures.

[46] 'Making Europe's businesses future-ready: A new Industrial Strategy for a globally competitive, green and digital Europe' (European Commission, 10 March 2020), ec.europa.eu/commission/presscorner/detail/en/ip_20_416.

[47] Z Darvas, 'Three-Quarters of Next Generation EU Payments Will Have to Wait until 2023' (*Bruegel*, 10 June 2020), www.bruegel.org/2020/06/three-quarters-of-next-generation-eu-payments-will-have-to-wait-until-2023/.

Table 4.3 US Fiscal Policy in Response to COVID-19[48]

Policy	Amount
Paycheck Protection Program and Health Care Enhancement Act	$US 483 billion
Coronavirus Aid, Relief and Economy Security Act (CARES Act)	$US 2.3 trillion
Coronavirus Aid Preparedness and Response Supplemental Appropriations Act	$US 8.3 billion

The first Act – the Paycheck Protection Program and Health Care Enhancement Act (Paycheck Act) – has two main Divisions. Division A in the Act provides additional lending authority for certain Small Business Administration programmes in response to COVID-19; and Division B provides Fiscal Year 2020 supplemental appropriations for the Department of Health and Human Services and the Small Business Administration in response to COVID-19.[49] Under such authorisation by the Act, funding is provided to programmes including:

> (i) US$321 billion for additional forgivable Small Business Administration loans and guarantees to help small businesses that retain workers; (ii) US$62 billion for the Small Business Administration to provide grants and loans to assist small businesses; (iii) US$75 billion for hospitals; and (iv) US$25 billion for expanding virus testing.[50]

The second package is under the CARES Act, which amounts to $US 2.3 trillion. It intends to provide emergency assistance to individuals, families and businesses.[51] The forms of assistance include loan forgiveness, direct grants, waiver of a prepayment penalty to small and medium enterprises, delay in paying tax, loans and loan guarantees.[52] Under the CARES Act, the supporting package goes to small enterprises, as well as 'severely distressed sectors' including passenger air carriers, cargo air carriers, business critical to maintaining national security, and facilities established by the US Federal Reserve Board.[53] The CARES Act also supports research and development through waiving a reporting requirement for projects over $100 million.[54]

The Coronavirus Aid Preparedness and Response Supplemental Appropriation Act (the Supplemental Appropriation Act) targets the programmes relating to vaccine development and manufacturing, grants to health agencies, evacuation of embassies and humanitarian assistance to other countries.[55]

[48] Source: IMF, 'Policy Responses to COVID-19' (n 8) the US.

[49] 'Paycheck Protection Program and Health Care Enhancement Act', Public Law No: 116-139 (US Congress, 24 April 2020), www.congress.gov/bill/116th-congress/house-bill/266/text.

[50] IMF, 'Policy Responses to COVID-19' (n 8).

[51] 'Coronavirus Aid, Relief, and Economic Security Act or the CARES Act', Public Law No: 116-136 (US Congress, 27 March 2020), www.congress.gov/bill/116th-congress/house-bill/748.

[52] ibid.

[53] ibid Title IV Economic Stabilization and Assistance to Severely Distressed Sectors of the United States Economy, Division A.

[54] ibid Part III Innovation, Title III, Division A.

[55] 'H.R.6074 – 116th Congress (2019–2020): Coronavirus Preparedness and Response Supplemental Appropriations Act' (US Congress, 3 April 2020), www.congress.gov/bill/116th-congress/house-bill/6074.

ii. Analysis of US Fiscal Policies under the SCM Agreement

Some of the US policies would not be considered 'actionable' subsidies under the SCM Agreement. For instance, the reimbursement to healthcare and the enhancement of testing ability under the Paycheck Act, and the support for healthcare providers under the CARES Act, are not actionable since they are financial support in the service sector, while the SCM Agreement of the WTO only governs trade in goods.

Some policies may be 'actionable' or even 'prohibited' depending on the exact design of the measure. The $US 50 billion Economic Injury Disaster Loan (EIDL) and the $US 10 billion EIDL grants under the Paycheck Act, for instance, would be actionable if they are provided to specific enterprises, industries or regions.[56] The tax delays, grants, loans, or loan guarantees for businesses under the CARES Act would likely constitute 'financial contributions' in the form of 'direct transfer of funds' and 'government revenue that is otherwise due is foregone' as contemplated under Article 1.1(a)(1) of the SCM Agreement. Some of these fiscal supports may be challenged as providing 'benefit' that is 'specific' to certain industries or enterprises, for example, the funding for specified 'severely distressed sectors' mentioned above in the CARES Act. The CARES Act under section 3101 requires the National Academies of Science, Engineering, and Medicine to examine and report on the security of the US medical product supply chain, including US dependence on critical drugs and devices from other countries. The suggested strategies for consideration include 'encourage domestic manufacturing'.[57] This rule, if implemented, may lead to domestic contingent subsidisation measures, prohibited under Article 3.1(b) of the SCM Agreement.

The counterargument in the analysis of the EU policies also applies here. One can argue it is impossible to evaluate whether the financial contribution is providing a 'benefit' since there is 'absent of a market benchmark' during the pandemic. Others might challenge this counterargument by using the 'out-of-country' benchmark[58] concept and suggest that an investigating authority may choose a market with similarly situated conditions to evaluate whether such financial support is providing any advantage. This out-of-country benchmark argument should be approached with great caution since it would presumptively ignore the diversity of countries' standards in health policies and systems.

The funding for research, development and manufacturing of medicines for COVID-19 under the Paycheck Act and the Supplemental Appropriation Act

[56] Paycheck Act (n 49).

[57] s 3101 CARES Act.

[58] Out-of-country benchmark methodology means that in a countervailing measure investigation, the investigation authority calculate the 'benefit' from a financial contribution not using the price of country of origin of the imported product but using the market price of another country or region. Under the WTO jurisprudence, only under limited circumstances, can an investigation authority use out-of-country benchmark. *United States–Final Countervailing Duty Determination with respect to certain Softwood Lumber from Canada*, Report of the Appellate Body (17 February 2004) WT/DS257/AB/R, para 93.

might be 'non-actionable subsidies' presuming the rules were revived. However, as in the EU's case study, it depends on the exact design of the programmes and whether they meet the preconditions for being treated as non-actionable subsidies.

D. The Case of China

i. *China's Fiscal Policies*

The IMF Data shows China provided an estimated RMB 4.2 trillion of discretionary fiscal measures in multiple forms, including (i) increased spending on epidemic prevention and control; (ii) production of medical equipment; (iii) accelerated disbursement of unemployment insurance and extension to migrant workers; (iv) tax relief and waived social security contributions; and (v) public investment.[59] The TMF Group provided a non-exhaustive list in English of measures taken by the Chinese central-level government and provincial governments.[60]

The State Council of China publishes and updates the latest administrative orders or notifications regarding COVID-19 on its website. However, unlike the EU and the US, where the measures may be found in legislative documents, the Chinese fiscal policies are currently made and implemented at the level of each administrative agency. These measures are administrative regulations that have a lower hierarchy than legislation and do not need approval through the legislative branch. Table 4.4 sets out some examples of the central-level administrative fiscal policies.

Table 4.4 Examples of China's Fiscal Measures in Response to COVID-19[61]

Policy	Administrative agency(ies) that issued the order	Amount	Time frame
Tax Reduction and Waiver[62]	Ministry of Finance, and State Taxation Administration	For severely impacted industries, the tax carry-over term extends from 5 years to a maximum of 8 years	1 January 2020–31 December 2020[63]

(continued)

[59] IMF, 'Policy Responses to COVID-19' (n 8).

[60] 'Government Support Schemes for COVID-19' (*TMF Group*, as of July 2020), www.tmf-group.com/en/news-insights/coronavirus/government-support-schemes/#C.

[61] Source: The State Council, The People's Republic of China, www.gov.cn/zhengce/.

[62] 'Notification on Tax Measure regarding COVID-19' [关于支持新型冠状病毒感染的肺炎疫情防控有关税收政策的公告], Doc No 8 (6 February 2020), www.chinatax.gov.cn/chinatax/n810341/n810755/c5143465/content.html.

[63] 'Notification on the Implementation Time Frame of the Tax Policy in response to COVID-19' [关于支持疫情防控保供等税费政策实施期限的公告],DocNo28(5May2020),www.gov.cn/zhengce/zhengceku/2020-05/29/content_5515981.htm.

Table 4.4 ***(Continued)***

Policy	Administrative agency(ies) that issued the order	Amount	Time frame
Reduction of Electricity Cost[64]	Development and Reform Commission	State-owned electricity companies' lower prices by 5%	1 February 2020–30 June 2020
Reduction of Rent[65]	State-owned Assets Supervision and Administration Commission (SASAC)	For SMEs that rent plants from central state-owned enterprises, the renting SOE shall waive three-months' rent in the first half year	First half year of 2020
Low interest loans, reduction or waiver of fees to small and medium enterprises[66]	State Administration for Market Regulation, Development and Reform Commission, Ministry of Finance etc	RMB 300 billion low interest rate loan; reduction of taxes and fees	Tax reduction policy with regard to value-added tax is from 1 March to 31 May 2020. The others are effective until the end of the year

ii. Analysis of China's Policies under the SCM Agreement

China's policies to increase spending on epidemic prevention and control or subsidies directly to unemployed workers are less likely to be challenged as actionable subsidies since they function as social safety-nets and do not have a direct impact on production.

In contrast, the tax and rent reduction, electricity rates subsidies and low interest rates are likely actionable. The distinctive aspect of these Chinese measures is that the state agencies direct state-owned enterprises (SOEs) to provide fiscal support to other companies. A Member may approach this scenario in two

[64] 'Development and Reform Commission, Notification on Temporarily Reduce the Electricity Cost' [国家发展改革委关于阶段性降低企业用电成本支持企业复工复产的通知], Doc No 258 (22 February 2020), www.gov.cn/zhengce/zhengceku/2020-02/22/content_5482141.htm.

[65] 'State-owned Assets Supervision and Administration Commission, Notification to Facilitate Micro, Small and Medium Enterprises to Reduce Rent' [关于进一步做好服务业小微企业和个体工商户房租减免工作的通知], Doc No 158 (20 May 2020), www.gov.cn/zhengce/zhengceku/2020-06/03/content_5516981.htm.

[66] 'State Administration for Market Regulation, Development and Reform Commission, Ministry of Finance, Ministry of Human Resource and Social Security, Ministry of Commerce and People's Bank, Guiding Opinion to Support Individual Business' [加大对个体工商户扶持力度的指导意见], Doc No 38 (28 February 2020), www.gov.cn/zhengce/zhengceku/2020-02/28/content_5484720.htm.

different ways. One way is to prove that such an action may be considered as 'government ... directs or entrusts a private body to carry out' financial contributions under Article 1.1(a)(1)iv.[67]

The other way is to prove that the SOEs involved constitute a 'public body' under Article 1.1(a)(1).[68] Following the WTO jurisprudence, whether an entity is a 'public body' hinges on whether it 'possesses, exercises or is vested with governmental authority'.[69] In other words, the key criterion concerns whether the entity performs a governmental function.[70] In this scenario, one might argue that the SOEs that are vested with a function to provide aid to enterprises might be considered as 'public bodies' in performing this particular activity.[71]

Even if an investigation authority found these executive policies were financial contributions, a similar argument may apply to these Chinese measures as in the EU and US case regarding the 'benefit' analysis. One may argue that since there is no reasonable market to be the benchmark, there is no subsidy. However, an investigation authority might ignore such argument and consider the fiscal support in response to COVID-19 as actionable subsidies.

III. The Rationales to Justify Covid-19 Subsidies

A. The Right to Life Rationale

There could be multiple rationales from different perspectives to justify COVID-19 related subsidies. The first rationale is rooted in a fundamental human right – the right to life. When facing a global crisis that poses risks to the entire human society, the priority is to save life.[72] Thus, all states have a duty to protect human life through measures they can take, including subsidies in a broad sense to enhance the health facilities and to secure people's needs for food, medicine and other necessities. Howse and Nicolaidis have suggested a global subsidiarity view of

[67] The US in its request for consultation argued that the Chinese companies selling coal or electricity to the downstream producers were 'private bodies' directed or entrusted by the Chinese government. *Request for Consultation by the United States, China–Subsidies to Producers of Primary Aluminium* (17 January 2017) WTO/DS519/1.

[68] For an introduction of the 'public body' problem relating to SOEs, please see Ding, '"Public Body" or Not' (n 15).

[69] United States–Definitive Anti-Dumping and Countervailing Duties on Certain Products from China, Report of the Appellate Body (25 March 2011) WTO/DS379/R/ABR, para 317.

[70] ibid para 318.

[71] There is a debate over whether the 'public body' determination should be activity-based or entity-based, see R Ding, 'Interface 2.0 in Rules on State-Owned Enterprises: A Comparative Institutional Approach' (2020) 23 *Journal of International Economic Law* 637, 656.

[72] A Guterres, 'COVID-19 and Human Rights: We Are All in This Together' (UN, 23 April 2020), www.un.org/en/un-coronavirus-communications-team/we-are-all-together-human-rights-and-covid-19-response-and.

the WTO system.[73] Under this view, the WTO rules, besides respecting WTO Members' policy choices, would also take into account certain global community goods that are widely recognised and reflected in general public international law and some of its specialised regimes like biodiversity and human rights.[74]

The right to life rationale would allow policy space for certain types of COVID-19 subsidies. For the above-mentioned fiscal measures of the EU, US and China, the R&D support for medicines and vaccines would fall within the definition of 'subsidy' under the SCM Agreement. Even though the 'absent of market benchmark' counterargument is available, it is still within the discretion of an investigation authority and is arguably highly unpredictable.

This chapter argues that the rules should specifically require that certain types of R&D subsidy in response to pandemics shall not be countervailed by any Members, in order to prevent a scenario of 'punishing the life-saving measures'. Building upon the right-to-life rationale, the subsidies for R&D of medicines or vaccines against COVID-19 should be justified under the rules.

B. The Rationales from Economic Analysis Perspectives

The other rationale for COVID-19 subsidies can be analysed from an economic perspective. Standard economic theory, that is the neoclassical approach, offers rationales for 'good subsidies' that can improve the outcome of the market. These rationales include:

> Providing a more equitable distribution of economic well-being: resources to poor and underprivileged;
>
> Correcting for the failure of the market mechanism to create an efficient allocation of goods and services.[75]

From this perspective, some of the COVID-19 subsidies are justified for securing these benefits. State aid to R&D of COVID-19 medicines would be justified under this rationale as well. Even under normal market conditions, there is a market failure of capturing the total cost of the research and development of novel medicines, and thus governmental funds and prizes are implemented frequently. As we can see from the case studies, the EU, US and China all have programmes to support the development and production of COVID-19 medicines and vaccines. Companies like Gilead received tens of millions in governmental aid for developing Remdesivir which is a medicine believed to be effective in curing COVID-19.

[73] R Howse and K Nicolaidis, 'Enhancing WTO Legitimacy: Constitutionalization or Global Subsidiarity?' (2003) 16 *Governance* 73.

[74] ibid 98.

[75] RK Triest, 'The Economics of Subsidies for Community Development: A Primer' (1 July 2011) *Smart Subsidy for Community Development*, joint publication of the The Federal Reserve Bank of Boston and The Aspen Institute, www.bostonfed.org/publications/one-time-pubs/smart-subsidy-for-community-development.aspx 10.

As recognised by one US congressman, it would be impossible to develop the drug if there were no direct public investment and tax subsidies.[76] At a critical time like the COVID-19 pandemic, more extreme measures should be allowed, as time is of the essence. Therefore, from the perspective of the maximisation of welfare, the COVID-19 R&D subsidies should be justified. Both the human right rationale and the economic efficiency rationale call for this justification.

Due to the expiration of the non-actionable subsidy rules, the current SCM Agreement no longer provides rules for this justification. Moreover, even if the 'non-actionable' subsidy rules were revived, the EU's R&D projects, as the analysis above has shown, cannot fulfil the requirements since the projects exceed the percentage cap (75 per cent of the cost of industrial research) in the rules. This suggests that the future WTO subsidy rules need to have a more flexible arrangement of the R&D subsidies in cases of imminent health crises or other disasters.

A different strand of economic analysis, or the 'industrial policy' argument and neo-developmentalism argues for a more progressive role for subsidy programmes. For developmental purposes, the government should move beyond applying Pigovian taxes or subsidies, and apply strategic policies to enable industrial development.[77] Whether this perspective should be taken into consideration for future WTO subsidy rules is beyond the context of COVID-19 but a more general question on industrial policy.[78] This however does inspire some ideas with respect to those COVID-19 subsidies that are essentially industrial policies. For example, the 'Next Generation EU' budget proposal to promote 'green and digital Europe' have clear industrial policy intentions beyond disaster relief. There is, thus, an issue about to what extent these industrial policy subsidies in response to COVID-19 should be justified under WTO rules. Are industrial policies to reboot the economy following a pandemic different from other industrial policies? What are the boundaries between them? These are difficult questions behind the phenomena of COVID-19 subsidies.

Drawing upon a study in disaster economics, this chapter suggests that the rules may need to distinguish between precautionary, relief and recovery policies. Dari-Mattiacci and Faure in their paper argue that a distinction should be made between three classes of activity involved in disaster management: precaution, relief and recovery. Precautionary efforts are made ex ante; relief efforts are made in the immediate aftermath of a disaster; and recovery efforts are made ex post after the disaster and are intended to return conditions to those that prevailed ex ante. Dari-Mattiacci and Faure argue that the 'relief' or immediate government

[76] 'Taxpayers paid to develop remdesivir but will have no say when Gilead sets the price' *Washington Post* (26 May 2020), www.washingtonpost.com/business/2020/05/26/remdesivir-coronavirus-taxpayers/.

[77] D Rodrik, 'Industrial Policy for the Twenty-First Century' (2004), papers.ssrn.com/abstract=617544.

[78] Zhou and Fang suggest that the rules on industrial policy should shift from the 'one size-fits-all' approach to country-specific approach through a scheduling method, W Zhou and MM Fang, 'Subsidizing Technology Competition: China's Evolving Practices and International Trade Regulation in the Post-Pandemic Era' (2020) University of New South Wales Law Research Series No 20-66, papers.ssrn.com/sol3/papers.cfm?abstract_id=3737272.

interventions, compared with long-term recovery plans could be less likely to lead to over-supply by the government.[79] Recognising that this finding should be confirmed further by more empirical-based analysis, this chapter suggests that long-term recovery plans require more scrutiny than those immediate recovery plans. This requires that long-term COVID-19 subsidies nevertheless be subject to the same disciplines as applied to other subsidies. Taking into consideration the underlying theoretical and policy arguments, and also the nuances in existing practices, the following section puts forward an approach to resolve the tension between the policy space needed for disaster relief and the effectiveness of the disciplines on subsidies and countervailing measures in the WTO.

IV. A Preliminary Proposal: A New 'Non-Actionable Subsidy' Category

It is submitted that the future reforms of the WTO subsidy rules should incorporate special provisions on disaster relief and achieve a proper balance between the right to subsidise and the right to counter the trade effects of such subsidies. There are potentially two alternative approaches to help achieve such balance. One approach is to revive and revise the rules on 'non-actionable subsidy' to incorporate certain disaster relief subsidies. Another approach is to incorporate the general exception of Article XX of the GATT 1994 into the SCM Agreement to justify certain subsidies that are necessary to protect human, animal or plant life or health. The first approach is preferred. As noted above, whether Article XX applies to the SCM Agreement remains controversial. Considering the abundance of existing WTO jurisprudence on Article XX of the GATT, the latter approach would foreseeably bring too many variables into the already complicated legal analysis under the SCM Agreement framework. The Article XX approach is certainly worth further examination, but given the limited space, this chapter will focus on the first approach, leaving the discussion of the latter for another occasion.

This chapter proposes that future WTO rules on subsidies might introduce a new category of 'non-actionable subsidies on disaster relief'.[80] The concept of disaster may be defined through an exemplary list that encompasses disasters like fires and droughts, and also public health crises like the COVID-19 pandemic. At the same time, the rules shall require temporal limitations and impose transparency requirements on such subsidies. The temporal limitation is based on the analysis above regarding the difference between relief and recovery policies. The transparency requirements are crucial for identifying the specific scope and effect of a subsidy. If these two requirements are not fulfilled, then the disaster relief subsidies may still fall within actionable or prohibited categories.

[79] G Dari-Mattiacci and M Faure, 'The Economics of Disaster Relief' (2015) 37 *Law & Policy* 180.
[80] Horlick and Clarke suggested the same idea in their article in 2017. Horlick and Clarke (n 13) 681.

Substantive requirements on the quantity or effect of the non-actionable disaster relief subsidies can be difficult to craft. Horlick and Clarke suggested that the safe harbour for disaster relief subsidies 'shall allow the industry or economy to return to its pre-disaster state'.[81] However, taking the COVID-19 pandemic as an example, since the size and conditions of each economy differ to a great extent, it is almost impossible to find a proper substantive test for finding the justifiable number of COVID-19 subsidies. A substantive test will require a judgement of the appropriateness of a WTO Member's response to the COVID-19 pandemic, which could be highly debatable, uncertain and even biased. Thus, this chapter argues that a proper and pragmatic approach is to qualify the scope of justifiable disaster relief subsidies by formalistic requirements on time frame and transparency, rather than through any substantive requirements.

The case studies above have provided some examples of how these requirements may be implemented in practice. On the temporal limitation, for example, some of the Chinese policies set an explicit time frame for fiscal aid while others are more flexible at the beginning. For instance, the reduction of electricity cost policy was effective from 1 January 2020 to 30 June 2020. In contrast, the tax reduction policy in its original form would be effective for as long as necessary depending on the circumstances, but in a later notification, the expiration date was set at 31 December 2020.[82] Another example is the EU's Temporary Framework for State-aid. Under this framework, the EU Member State's aid in the form of direct grants, repayable advances, or tax advantages shall be granted no later than 31 December 2020.[83] For each type of aid under the Temporary Framework for State-aid, there is a specified time limit. It states in the text that the special framework is justified by the 'current exceptional circumstances and will not be applied after 31 December 2020'.[84] The appropriate temporal requirements can be based on analysis of previous practice by WTO Members. The time frame may not necessarily be a settled number of months or years, but rather a range of time periods. Members' practices in relation to COVID-19 subsidies could provide a valuable database for drafting such requirements.

On the substantive requirements, each WTO Member shall determine its own standard. Such substantive requirements may include the general objective, the forms and the quantitative caps of the COVID-19 subsidies. There could, however, be some basic principles. The objective for the EU's State-aid control on COVID-19 is to ensure

> that the EU Internal Market is not fragmented and that the level playing field stays intact. The integrity of the Internal Market will also lead to a faster recovery. It also avoids harmful subsidy races, where Member States with deeper pockets can outspend neighbours to the detriment of cohesion within the Union.[85]

[81] ibid.
[82] See Table 4.4 above.
[83] Point 22.d of the 'Temporary Framework on State Aid' (n 35).
[84] ibid point 39.
[85] ibid s 1.2.

Although the rules at the multilateral level do not necessarily share the same value foundation as the EU rules, the aim to 'avoid harmful subsidy races' and also to avoid harmful countervailing measure races can be basic principles for the new rules.

This approach also suggests a transparency mechanism for the 'non-actionable' disaster relief subsidy. For instance, the EU Temporary Framework for State-aid requires reporting from Member States within 12 months from the moment of granting and annual reports.[86] WTO Members providing the disaster relief subsidies shall have the obligation to keep records of them and shall make the records available for potential countervailing measure investigations or disputes at the WTO.

In a word, under this suggested approach, a WTO Member may have a safe harbour for its disaster relief subsidy by fulfilling both the temporal and transparency requirements. This means that in practice, if a WTO Member's non-actionable disaster relief subsidies are being countervailed in another WTO Member, then the former WTO Member may either challenge in the domestic system of the latter Member or bring a dispute against the latter Member at the WTO to request a removal of the countervailing measures.

V. Conclusion

When facing a global health crisis like COVID-19, states need more policy space than at usual times to take extraordinary measures. Fiscal measures, some of which can be defined as 'subsidies' under the SCM Agreement are important policy tools to counter nationwide or global social and economic crises. The existing WTO rules on subsidies and countervailing measures fail to foresee such a scenario and thus lack a ready mechanism to facilitate WTO Members' policy responses to crises like the COVID-19 pandemic. Many of the Members' fiscal and monetary policies during and post the crisis may face the risk of being targeted by each other's countervailing duties.

This chapter, through a case study-based analysis, argues that the WTO rules on subsidies need reform to adapt to a post-COVID-19 era. This chapter suggests that there should be a new category of 'non-actionable subsidy for disaster relief' in future WTO rules on subsidies. If the WTO rules incorporate provisions on disaster relief, then the rules need to balance between the right to provide assistance and the right to counter the effects of such assistance, since some of the assistance may nevertheless have distortive effects on trade. This chapter suggests that the rules should incorporate time-frame limitations and transparency requirements. Such new rules on disaster relief subsidies may be reached through either joint declaration, decisions by the WTO Ministerial Conference, or through a new round of negotiations by WTO Members. It is the hope of this chapter that COVID-19 provides the WTO and other international institutions with an opportunity to update the rules that can enable us to rise stronger as a shared community.

[86] ibid point 34.

5

Rethinking WTO DSB Jurisdiction in Light of Pandemic, Climate Change and Other Evolving Threats

ALEXANDRA R HARRINGTON

I. Introduction

Although existing as a named entity for only a year at the time of writing, and as a recognised pandemic for even less, the COVID-19 virus has already caused significant damage and change to the global economy and global community as a whole. At the societal level, millions have been infected,[1] over a million have lost their lives,[2] and countless livelihoods have been forever disrupted. At the economic level, projections estimate that the impact could surpass that of the Great Depression and the World Wars, with concerns over the 'second wave' of infections in late 2020/21 pushing out anticipated economic recovery times even further.[3] Just as the inception of the pandemic at the opening of a new decade could not be anticipated, the terminal point cannot be known, although it is clear that the impact will last far beyond the date on which the virus can be treated or prevented.

This chapter examines the impact of the pandemic from the perspective of the World Trade Organization (WTO) Dispute Settlement Body (DSB) system. Even before the pandemic, the DSB system faced critical compositional and existential threats, especially as the inability to convene appellate panels has hobbled the assigned functions of the system.[4] While this is, beyond doubt, a dangerous situation in the best of times, uncertainty in terms of dispute settlement during uncharted territory at the international trade level can be seen as potentially devasting to a global economy struggling to recover. If there is to be a source of potential

[1] See 'COVID-19 Dashboard' (Johns Hopkins University & Medicine, Coronavirus Resource Center), coronavirus.jhu.edu/map.html.

[2] ibid.

[3] See 'Tackling Coronavirus (COVID-19): Contributing to a global effect' (OECD), www.oecd.org/coronavirus/en/.

[4] See 'Azevedo seeks WTO members' views on how to meet increasing demand for dispute settlement' (WTO, 28 October 2015), www.wto.org/english/news_e/spra_e/spra94_e.htm.

utility, this chapter asserts that it comes in the form of providing a moment to reflect on ways to reform the system not only to address current threats, including the pandemic, but also future threats to destabilising global trading regimes.

After discussing the dispute settlement system used by the WTO and the evolution of complaints involving public health and environmental protection exception claims in section II, section III of this chapter discusses various impacts of the pandemic on national and international trade and trade law. Section IV then asserts that the pandemic, as well as projections for coming climate change-related disasters, highlights the need for structural and juridical reform of the WTO dispute settlement system.

II. DSB Background and Jurisprudence

A. WTO DSB Structure

In 1995, when the WTO formally came into existence as an international organisation, there had already been a well-established international trade law under the General Agreement on Trade and Tariffs 1947 (GATT).[5] This had functioned as the governing trade law system throughout the majority of the Cold War, enabling largely Western states and allies to foster a capitalism-based global trade system.[6] However, it did so in a vacuum which lacked an overarching organisational structure and a dedicated system in which to address disputes between states. In the years following the collapse of the Soviet Union and the entrance of additional state participants in the international trading sphere, the need for a more organisation-focused international trade regime came into being.[7] This culminated in the creation of the WTO and the core trade treaties that form its legal texts.[8]

A critical aspect of the WTO's function is the organisation's ability to bring states together to agree on trade law and policies. At the heart of this is not only the capacity of the WTO to create legal norms through treaties, but also to provide a neutral forum to which states can bring their trade-related grievances rather than attempting to handle them in an incongruous and disorganised system. In this vein, the WTO's structure includes a dedicated DSB for Member States to use in the event disagreements arise with other WTO Member States regarding trade and associated policies and practices.[9] In the 25 years since its inception, the DSB has received nearly 600 complaints thus far.[10]

[5] See 'The GATT years: from Havana to Marrakesh' (WTO), www.wto.org/english/thewto_e/whatis_e/tif_e/fact4_e.htm.
[6] ibid.
[7] ibid.
[8] Marrakesh Agreement Establishing the World Trade Organization (Marrakesh, 15 April 1994).
[9] See Understanding on Rules and Procedures Governing the Settlement of Disputes (DSU), Marrakesh Agreement Establishing the World Trade Organization, Annex 2 (Marrakesh, 15 April 1994).
[10] 'Dispute settlement gateway' (WTO), www.wto.org/english/tratop_e/dispu_e/dispu_e.htm.

Structurally, the DSB contains a hybrid litigation-arbitration system, beginning with the requirement that a state file a request for consultations with another Member State in the event of a trade dispute.[11] During the consultation phase, the DSB has the capability to assist the disputing Member States in settling the complaint through good offices, mediation and the ability to convene these states for general discussion purposes.[12] In many instances, the dispute at issue is resolved during this phase, in which case the complaint is deemed to be settled and there is no need for further organisational involvement.[13]

If, however, the complaint cannot be settled in the consultation phase, the process moves forward to the filing of an official complaint, which then triggers the convening of an expert panel to hear the complaint and make a determination.[14] Both sides have the ability to file responsive documents at the outset of the panel phase.[15] Additionally, other interested Member states that have similar concerns or a particular interest in the outcome of the complaint may be included as third-party participants and provide written statements at this point.[16] Should there be identical claims brought against the same Member State by several other states, there is also the option to have them consolidated at this point.[17]

Once the Panel Report is issued, the Member States involved have the ability to work together to ensure that the terms set out by the Panel's decision are complied with.[18] Alternatively, these states have the ability to appeal some or all of the Panel Report to a separately convened Appellate Body, which serves as the highest level of appeal available in the system.[19] The Appellate Body has the ability to uphold or reverse some or all of the Panel Report.[20] Should a Member State fail to comply with the terms of the accepted Panel Report or Appellate Body report, the harmed Member State has the ability to seek enforcement through negotiations and, should these remain unsuccessful, to seek authorisation from the WTO to impose retaliatory tariffs or other measures as deemed appropriate.[21]

What is evident from this procedure is that there is a formalised and highly structured system for addressing disputes between states arising in the WTO context. What is also evident, and of particular relevance to this chapter, is that the system used is not intended to function with great speed. Indeed, a review of the disputes brought through this system highlights that, where issues are not settled

[11] WTO Secretariat, *A Handbook on Dispute Settlement System*, 2nd edn (Cambridge, Cambridge University Press, 2017), www.wto.org/english/res_e/publications_e/dispuhandbook17_e.ht.
[12] ibid 50–57.
[13] ibid.
[14] ibid 57–60.
[15] ibid 78.
[16] ibid 66–70.
[17] ibid 61–63.
[18] ibid 130–31.
[19] ibid 104–10.
[20] ibid 105–08.
[21] ibid ch 5.

during the formal process, the settlement of these complaints can take years. At the same time, the increased use of the DSB suggests that the structural limitations on time efficiency and ability to respond to critical issues will only become more onerous over time, leading to additional questions as to the integrity of the process. As discussed below, should there be a number of complaints stemming from the COVID-19 pandemic or, in the future, from disasters such as those associated with climate change, the current DSB system is not well positioned from a structural perspective.

B. WTO DSB Jurisdiction and Relevant Jurisprudence

i. Jurisdiction

As a creation of the WTO, the DSB's jurisdiction is bound by the parameters of the organisation's structure. In this context, the DSB's jurisdiction is limited to the terms of the core international trade law treaties existing under the WTO's system.[22] In addition, there are limitations on the ways in which elements that might be construed as extraneous to trade and the terms of the specific agreement may enter into the DSB process, be they as grounds for commencing a complaint, defences to a complaint, or juridical rationales.[23]

As a general matter, given the narrow scope of the DSB's jurisdiction in terms of treaty law, there is little space for the inclusion of outside, non-trade related considerations in the Panel and Appellate Body proceedings and reports. However, several WTO treaties have created a space in which to validate state action to protect public health, safety and welfare in the face of a legitimate concern and it is within this space that complaints regarding state practices allegedly conducted for health and environmental protection have found an increasing shelter. The main clause from WTO Agreements which provides some latitude and has been used to admit more progressive and holistic considerations within the trade regime is GATT's Article XX.[24]

This space provides an opportunity for less traditional issues that impact on and relate to international trade to enter into the sphere and generate jurisprudence that becomes highly persuasive in future situations. It might perhaps be obvious, but must be reiterated, that the health aspects of these jurisprudential trends are critical to understand before discussing the potential impacts of the COVID-19 pandemic on trade law and the findings of the DSB. At the same time, given the scientific projections regarding and already observable changes resulting from climate change and environmental degradation, DSB jurisprudence

[22] 'Resolving trade disputes between WTO members: WTO Dispute Settlement' (WTO), www.wto.org/english/thewto_e/20y_e/dispute_brochure20y_e.pdf; Annexes 1–4 of the Marrakesh Agreement (n 8).

[23] *WTO Handbook* (n 11).

[24] Art XX of the General Agreement on Tariffs and Trade (GATT), Marrakesh Agreement Establishing the World Trade Organization, Annex 1A (Marrakesh, 15 April 1994).

regarding the ability of states to use environmental concerns and sustainable development-related laws and policies to justify challenged practices from a trade law perspective is vital. For these reasons, this section frames the chapter by providing an understanding of relevant DSB jurisprudence to date.

ii. Relevant Jurisprudence Regarding Health and Environmental Concerns

In the context of evaluating environmental laws enacted to protect marine life – sea turtles and dolphins, respectively – which allegedly placed unfair and discriminatory barriers to trade and market access on developing states, the DSB has created allowances where environmental concerns may be valid.[25] As the Panel noted while holding the contested legal measures to protect sea turtles invalid under the GATT, the intent was not to foreclose efforts at environmental protection but rather to ensure that a unilateral approach to regulation which required all states to adopt the same standard without a negotiated treaty or other system would not be upheld.[26]

This was reflective of concerns over discrimination and unfair burdens on states, especially developing states which are often unable to afford the requisite elements of a law. At the same time, the *Shrimp–Turtle II* Panel Report clarified that, regardless of the motivation behind contested measures, the Article XX provisions 'must not frustrate or defeat the purposes and objects of the General Agreement and the WTO Agreement or its legal obligations under the substantive rules of GATT by abusing the exception contained in Article XX'.[27] These views were largely endorsed by the Appellate Body Report, although the Report did include statements endorsing standards for issues such as exhaustible natural resources which were set through the decision-making processes of United Nations (UN) and other international treaty body systems.[28]

Similarly, early cases involving public health concerns and international trade have established areas of leniency in which Article XX of the GATT can allow for the implementation of protective policies. A critical example of this is the *European Communities–Asbestos* complaint, in which Canada asserted that the stringent French restrictions and bans on asbestos being placed on its markets were violative of WTO law.[29] After evaluating the well-established threat to human

[25] BS Chimni, 'WTO and Environment: Shrimp-Turtle and EC-Hormones Case' (2000) 35 *Economic and Political Weekly* 1752; S Pratt, 'Note: The WTO Sea Turtle Decision' (1999) 26 *Ecological Law Quarterly* 815.

[26] Chimni (n 25) 1754.

[27] *United States–Import Prohibition on Certain Shrimp and Shrimp Products*, Report of the Panel (6 November 1998) WT/DS58/R, para 7.40.

[28] *United States–Import Prohibition on Certain Shrimp and Shrimp Products*, Report of the Appellate Body (6 November 1998) WT/DS58/AB/R, para 132; Chimni (n 25) 1756.

[29] *European Communities–Measures Affecting Asbestos and Products Containing Asbestos*, Report of the Panel (5 April 2001) WT/DS135/R; *European Communities–Measures Affecting Asbestos and Products Containing Asbestos*, Report of the Appellate Body (5 April 2001) WT/DS135/AB/R.

health posed by the use of asbestos, the Panel and Appellate Body decided that states had discretion in how to regulate the importation and sale of them within their territories.[30]

In the *EU–Seal Products* case, the EC placed specific bans on seal-based products, hunted predominantly in Canada and Norway and sold in Europe as well as Canada, due to the alleged public morality issues associated with the practice of hunting the young seals used in these products.[31] In addition, Canada and Norway, which are not part of the European Communities (EC), alleged that the treatment of their products created technical barriers to trade and favoured seal products which originated in EC states.[32] The challenged EC regulations were claimed to have been enacted to promote the sustainable management of marine resources as well as limited protections for European Indigenous communities, explaining that:

> The EU Seal Regime prohibits the placing of seal products on the EU market unless they qualify under certain exceptions, consisting of the following: (i) seal products obtained from seals hunted by Inuit or other indigenous communities (IC exception); (ii) seal products obtained from seals hunted for purposes of marine resource management (MRM exception); and (iii) seal products brought by travellers into the European Union in limited circumstances.[33]

Ultimately, the Appellate Body found that there was no technical barrier to trade issue presented under the terms and application of the EU Seal Regime.[34] Further, the Panel Report and the Appellate Body Report concluded that the EU Seal Regime falls within the ambit of Article XX(b) of the GATT.[35] However, in terms of design, the Appellate Body found the EU Seal Regime to be legally flawed and that

> the European Union has not demonstrated that the EU Seal Regime, in particular with respect to the IC exception, is designed and applied in a manner that meets the requirements of the chapeau of Article XX of the GATT 1994.[36]

As a result, the ultimate determination of the Appellate Body was that the EU Seal Regime was not allowable under the Article XX exceptions due to construction rather than premise of the regulations.[37] While this case in particular was founded on the public morals provisions of Article XX, it nevertheless has import for cases involving health and environmental concerns given that many of the arguments regarding seal hunting parallel arguments made for conservation of other species in the environmental law context.

[30] MC Cordonier Segger and M Gehring, 'The WTO and Precaution: Sustainable Development Implications of the WTO Asbestos Dispute' (2003) 15 *Journal of Environmental Law* 289; KR Srinavas, 'WTO and Asbestos: Dispute Settlement at Work' (2001) 36 *Economic and Political Weekly* 3442, 3443.

[31] *European Communities–Measures Prohibiting the Importation and Marketing of Seal Products*, Report of the Panel (16 June 2014) WT/DS400/AD/R.

[32] ibid para 1.5.

[33] ibid para 1.4.

[34] ibid para 6.1(a).

[35] ibid para 6.1(c).

[36] ibid para 6.1(d)(i).

[37] ibid para 6.1(d)(iii).

In *China–Rare Earths*, the European Union (EU), Japan and the United States (US) challenged the severe restrictions on exporting rare earths minerals – vital for the production of key technology – from China.[38] As these minerals are only located in a handful of states, the assertion was that limitation on exportation of these products was particularly deleterious to the international economy and to the states which serve as direct manufacturers of products that form a core component of the Chinese economy.[39] The contested measures related to export duties on these minerals as well as the imposition of strict restrictions on access and imposition of quotas.[40] However, the arguments put forward by China asserted that these restrictions and duties fell under the rubric of Article XX exceptions since they were purportedly enacted for the purposes of protecting the environment and natural resources.[41] Indeed, there was also an assertion that these practices were intended to further the Chinese national sustainable development policy, although these assertions were dismissed as being too late in time to have been relevant in the creation and implementation of the restrictions.[42]

While the Panel Report stressed that environmental concerns could fall within the legitimate framework of an Article XX exception in certain circumstances, these circumstances need to be thoroughly articulated and connected to the purposes and implementation of the contested legislation.[43] Notably,

> the Panel found and acknowledged that the mining processes associated with the minerals in question could, and indeed had, caused environmental damage in China that, in turn, resulted in threats to the health of humans and other forms of life.[44]

Despite this, in *China–Rare Earths*, the Panel Report found that the measures taken were not the least restrictive measure available and thus failed an essential element of the 'necessity' test.[45] As has been explained, 'what was missing was an established, articulable nexus between the export restrictions put in place by the Chinese government and the environmental and health damage it was purportedly seeking to rectify and prevent'.[46] Further, the *China–Rare Earths* Panel established that 'exhaustible natural resources' which can merit protection on environmental conservation grounds under Article XX are not established through a bright line rule but rather through an open-ended definition that is in essence context dependent. In this context, the Panel provided that 'measures may "relate to the

[38] *China–Measures Related to the Exportation of Rare Earths, Tungsten, and Molybdenum (Complaint by the United States, the European Union, and Japan*, Report of the Panel (29 August 2014) WT/DS431/R, para 2.2 (*China–Rare Earths*).
[39] ibid.
[40] ibid.
[41] ibid paras 7.31, 7.157.
[42] ibid paras 7.167–7.168.
[43] ibid para 7.117.
[44] ibid para 7.150.
[45] ibid para 7.114.
[46] AR Harrington, 'Sustainably: the SDGs and the Dispute Settlement at the World Trade Organization' (2020) 15 *McGill Journal of Sustainable Development Law* 38.

conservation of exhaustible natural resources" even if they are not directly imposed on those resources … provided that they support or contribute to the conservation of an exhaustible natural resource'.[47]

Additionally, in *United States–Certain Measures Relating to the Renewable Energy Sector*, India challenged many sub-national decisions made by a number of US states which, it was alleged, were discriminatory against producers of renewable energy and components used in the generation of renewable energy not from the US at issue.[48] These measures included tax incentives and rebates for the use of renewable energy generated through locally sourced services and conduits.[49] There were several critical issues at stake in this complaint. First, the question of sub-national unit ability to implicate the larger state body which, although not a new issue, takes on new characteristics in the renewable energy sector.[50] Second, whether there is WTO DSB jurisdiction to hear complaints regarding legislation that has subsequently been amended after the complaint itself was initiated at the WTO level.[51] Third, whether there is concomitant WTO DSB jurisdiction over complaints regarding amendments enacted after the complaint was filed but allegedly having bearing on the issues raised.[52] And fourth, the fundamental question of the ability of the sub-national units to enact and implement the contested measures as they relate to the generation and marketability of renewable energy sources.[53]

The jurisdictional issues in the complaint were addressed by examining the nexus between the measure complained of, the amendments and the ability of these measures to resurface in the future.[54] Ultimately, the Panel found that many of the complained of sub-national measures were violative of the GATT terms and ordered the US to remedy these issues.[55] In each of the contested practices implemented at the sub-national level in this complaint, there were at the very least facial connections with environmental concerns and efforts to establish affordable, renewable energy sources that are clean and sustainable. Given the nature of federal systems and the allocation of competencies between national and sub-national entities, the issues raised here have the ability to occur in the renewable energy context throughout the world. This adds to the importance of this decision in the fields of energy generation and environmental policies that encompass renewable energy generation and use. Additionally, and as discussed below, the post-pandemic recovery plans implemented by many WTO Member States emphasise funding and support for renewables and related environmentally

[47] *China–Rare Earths*, Report of the Panel (n 38) para 7.250.

[48] *United States–Certain Measures Relating to the Renewable Energy Sector*, Report of the Panel (circulated 27 June 2019) WT/DS510/R.

[49] ibid paras 2.1–2.69.

[50] ibid s 7.3.

[51] ibid s 7.1.

[52] ibid.

[53] ibid s 7.4.

[54] ibid paras 8.1–8.2.

[55] ibid para 8.4.

supportive policies. The *United States–Certain Measures Relating to the Renewable Energy Sector* precedent thus has a potentially significant role to play in determining the validity of these measures from an environmental exception perspective in the future.

iii. Emerging Sustainability Concerns in WTO Jurisprudence

In recent years, there have been calls for structural reform of the DSB. Many of these calls have been based on issues of funding and resource consumption at the organisational level and for those states participating in the dispute settlement process. Initially, the focus of the WTO on reforming the DSB was on largely procedural methods to reduce some of the time-related issues and allow for more condensed processes of involving experts and offering other pleadings.[56] In the more recent phase, focus has shifted to the internal structure of the DSB itself, including the number of panels convened, the retention of additional legal personnel to assist in the conduct of the dispute settlement proceedings, and emphasising transparency in all levels of proceedings.[57] Additionally, the recent decision of the US to effectively block the functioning of the appellate system has emphasised many of the issues with the implementation and governance design of the DSB.[58]

As some authors have noted, issues such as the transition to renewable and sustainable energy sources represent international law constructs that touch on trade and investment as well as environmental and human rights concerns.[59] In this scenario, it is quite likely that the current international trade and investment regimes will need to be updated – either at the treaty level or through decisions of the DSB – to reflect the interlinked elements of the renewables sector.[60]

Indeed, while they have not been brought under Article XX of the GATT, there are a number of complaints currently pending before the WTO which could have the effect of accommodating environmental, health and other sustainability concerns under the realm of the WTO. For example, the *European Union and its Member States–Certain Measures Relating to the Energy Sector* complaint challenges the ways in which the 'Third Energy Package', principally involving

[56] 'DDG Jara reports on consultations to enhance efficiency of panels' (WTO, 13 March 2012), www.wto.org/english/news_e/news12_e/ddg_13mar12_e.htm.

[57] 'Azevedo seeks WTO members' views on how to meet increasing demand for dispute settlement' (n 4).

[58] See United States Trade Representative, 'Report on the Appellate Body of the World Trade Organization' (2020), ustr.gov/sites/default/files/Report_on_the_Appellate_Body_of_the_World_Trade_Organization.pdf.

[59] See C Voigt, 'WTO Law and International Emissions Trading: Is there Potential for Conflict?' (2008) 2 *Carbon & Climate Law Review* 54; T Cottier, 'Renewable Energy and WTO Law: More Policy Space or Enhanced Disciplines?' (2014) 5 *Renewable Energy Law and Policy Review* 40; ME Rancourt, 'Promoting Sustainable Biofuels Under the WTO Legal Regime' (2009) 5 *McGill Journal of International Sustainable Development Law and Policy* 73; RA Waltman, 'Amending WTO Rules to Alleviate Constraints on Renewable Energy Subsidies' (2016) 23 *Willamette Journal of International Law and Dispute Resolution* 367.

[60] Cottier (n 59).

several Eastern European states and the access restrictions it places on the market participants in the natural gas sector, can be applied in conformity with WTO law given the alleged potential for competitive bias.[61] Given the importance of natural gas access in the generation of energy and participation in current and future iterations of the energy markets, there is a significant chance that a decision in this complaint will have an impact on the way in which energy is conceptualised and regulated through the WTO system. In terms of renewable energy generation and promotion at the national and sub-national level, the pending case of *United States–Certain Measures Related to Renewable Energy* brought by China demonstrates that these forms of issues were prevalent at the time in the years following the Paris Agreement on climate change, to say nothing of the coming spate of focus on post-pandemic recovery measures which also address the promotion of renewable energies and green economies.[62] At the same time, this complaint highlights the roles which political sub-units can play in international trade law and implementation, particularly in situations relating to environment and health.

As noted above, the *China–Rare Earths* dispute established a more nuanced understanding of the ways in which environmental and natural resource conservation arguments can be appropriately framed under Article XX of the GATT. In 2016, the US and EU filed similar complaints against China regarding similar restrictions on non-rare earths minerals, namely 'antimony, chromium, cobalt, copper, graphite, indium, lead, magnesia, talc, tantalum, and tin'.[63] Although there are no responsive pleadings in this complaint to date, a conceivable line of defence would be in the invocation of Article XX(g) of the GATT, providing for an exception 'relating to the conservation of exhaustible natural resources if such measures are made effective in conjunction with restrictions on domestic production or consumption'.[64] In this situation, there would again be an opportunity for the DSB to provide additional contours to restrictions on expendable natural resources.

III. COVID-19 Pandemic and Pandemic Recovery: Impacts on Trade and Trade Law

Although the COVID-19 virus is still quite new, the impacts it has brought to the world and to state and sub-national units have been overwhelming and complex. As has been well established, the existence and gravity of a second wave of the virus

[61] See *European Union and its Member States–Certain Measures Relating to the Energy Sector*, Request for the Establishment of a Panel by the Russian Federation (28 May 2015) WT/DS476/2.

[62] *United States–Certain Measures Related to Renewable Energy*, Request for Consultations by China (16 August 2018) WT/DS563/1.

[63] See *China–Export Duties on Certain Raw Minerals*, Request for the Establishment of a Panel by the United States (14 October 2016) WT/DS508/6; *China–Duties and Other Measures Concerning the Exportation of Certain Raw Minerals*, Request for the Establishment of a Panel by the European Union (27 October 2016) WT/DS509/6.

[64] Art XX(g) of the GATT (n 24).

will determine the severity of a prolonged economic downturn but, regardless, there has been and will continue to be a massive economic impact.[65] The results of this impact will extend beyond the point where a vaccine or proven medical treatment for the virus can be introduced to the market, and indeed there are many sectors of the economy which have arguably been forever altered. This has triggered a number of responses at the governmental level, ranging from sector-specific assistance plans and packages to interventions from central banking authorities in order to provide economic stimuli and reduce potentially onerous taxes, particularly for citizens.[66]

Even from the vantage point of only months, it is possible to observe phases of action taken by states and the global community across a number of sectors, notably international trade, in direct response to the pandemic and the economic and societal fallout from it. From the outset, the WTO and Organisation for Economic Co-operation and Development (OECD) have highlighted that many states placed increased tariffs and trade restrictions on products deemed to be essential at the national level and/or products which were subject to increased regulation upon their importation.[67] However, as more information about the virus has become available, these measures have often been relaxed or removed.[68]

Of fundamental importance in global, national and sub-national efforts to stop and treat COVID-19 is the medical supply industry.[69] In the realm of international trade, the WTO's tariff schedules have been credited with providing for lower cost imported supplies in many Member States, and has allowed for, at least in theory, an increase in and timely access to these supplies.[70] However, there are other WTO Member State jurisdictions in which tariffs on medical products have been placed at a higher rate, potentially restricting market access to life-saving supplies.[71] Further, in an effort to ensure that there are sufficient medical supplies within their jurisdiction, from the outset of the pandemic Member States have implemented export bans, particularly on personal protective equipment, respirators, hand sanitiser and soap products.[72] Some of these were lifted after the initial weeks of the

[65] 'Report on G20 Trade Measures' (WTO, 29 June 2020), www.wto.org/english/news_e/news20_e/report_trdev_jun20_e.pdfwww.wto.org/english/news_e/news20_e/report_trdev_jun20_e.pdf; 'Trade falls sharply in first half of 2020' (WTO, 22 June 2020), www.wto.org/english/news_e/pres20_e/pr858_e.htm; Committee for the Coordination of Statistical Analysis (CCSA), 'How COVID-19 is changing the world: a statistical perspective' vol I (13 May 2020); CCSA, 'How COVID-19 is changing the world: a statistical perspective' vol II (1 September 2020).

[66] 'Report on G20 Trade Measures' (n 65) 73–74.

[67] WTO, OECD & UNCTAD, 'Joint Summary: Reports on G20 Trade and Investment Measures' (29 June 2029), unctad.org/system/files/official-document/unctad_oecd2020d23_summary_en.pdf, 2.

[68] ibid.

[69] CCSA, 'How COVID-19 is changing the world' vol I (n 65) 24; 'Export Prohibitions and Restrictions' (WTO, 23 April 2020), www.wto.org/english/tratop_e/covid19_e/export_prohibitions_report_e.pdf.

[70] CCSA, 'How COVID-19 is changing the world' vol I (n 65) 24.

[71] ibid; 'Export Prohibitions and Restrictions' (n 69).

[72] See Notification from Albania (27 March 2020) G/MA/QR/N/ALB/1/Add.1; Algeria, Direction Générale des Douanes – Instruction No 111/PM (22 March 2020); Notification from Thailand (30 March 2020) G/MA/QR/N/THA/2/Add.2; Notification from Bangladesh (16 April 2020) G/MA/QR/N/BGD/1; Notification from Bangladesh (29 May 2020) G/MA/W/156; Notification from Belarus,

virus' spread;[73] however their use has set a precedent which could become important in the face of a second wave and any potential for long-term virus activity. Indeed, as at the time of writing this chapter in early November 2020, COVID-19 infection numbers have begun to rise astronomically at the global level and it is foreseeable that the measures which have been rescinded could be put back in place.[74] At the same time, the prospect of an effective COVID-19 vaccine becoming available raises the prospect of future efforts to limit exports of the vaccine.[75]

As the pandemic has spread and continues to infect additional people worldwide, the travel and tourism sector has been profoundly impacted. This necessarily includes a dramatic impact in the global airline sector, resulting in unparalleled efforts by governments to provide financial support to their domestic carriers.[76] Further, the pandemic has had, and is estimated to continue having, lasting impacts on the food and agriculture sector, including food safety elements.[77] Although current analysis by the FAO and other international organisations demonstrates a dichotomy in the types of harm suffered by developed and developing states in these spheres, the overall impact is clear and likely to be lasting.[78] As the WTO has already observed, there has been an increase in the number of questions and consultations sought with the Committee on Agriculture and some states have begun to implement new measures to bolster food security and continued food access within their territories.[79] Similarly, at the beginning of the pandemic and continuing on with declining intensity, states began to implement

Permanent Delegation of Belarus (15 April 2020) and Decision of the Council of Ministers No 149 (17 March 2020); Notification from Brazil (3 June 2020) G/MA/QR/N/BRA/2/Add.1; Notification from Colombia (2 April 2020) G/MA/QR/N/COL/1; Notification from Costa Rica (17 April 2020) G/MA/QR/N/CRI/3/Add.1; Notification from Cyprus (16 June 2020) G/MA/QR/N/EU/4/Add.3; Notification from Estonia (16 June 2020) G/MA/QR/N/EU/4/Add.3; Notification from Israel (6 May 2020) G/MA/QR/N/ISR/1; Notifications from Republic of Korea (22 June 2020) G/MA/QR/N/KOR/2/Add.1/Corr.1 and (20 July 2020) G/MA/QR/N/KOR/2/Add.3; Notification from Paraguay (29 May 2020) G/MA/QR/N/PRY/1/Add.1; Notification from Peru (23 June 2020) G/MA/QR/N/PER/2; Notification from Romania (16 June 2020) G/MA/QR/N/EU/4/Add.3; Notification from Slovak Republic (16 June 2020) G/MA/QR/N/EU/4/Add.3; Notification from Thailand (2 April 2020) G/MA/QR/N/THA/2/Add.3; Notifications from Ukraine (9 June 2020) G/MA/QR/N/UKR/4/Add.5 and (10 July 2020) G/MA/QR/N/UKR/4/Add.6.

[73] Argentina, Decreto Nos 301/2020 (19 March 2020) and 625/2020 (29 July 2020); Ministerio de Desarrollo Productivo Resolución Nos 140/2020 (6 April 2020) and 367/2020 (24 July 2020); Notifications from the European Union (7 May 2020) G/MA/QR/N/EU/4/Add.2 and (16 June 2020) G/MA/QR/N/EU/4/Add.3; Notification from France (16 June 2020) G/MA/QR/N/EU/4/Add.3; Notification from Moldova (29 May 2020) G/MA/QR/N/MDA/1/Add.1; Notification from Norway (5 June 2020) G/MA/QR/N/NOR/1/Add.1.

[74] See 'Animated Maps' (*Johns Hopkins University & Medicine, Coronavirus Resource Center*), coronavirus.jhu.edu/data/animated-world-map.

[75] See J Gallagher, 'Covid vaccine: First "milestone" vaccine offers 90% protection' *BBC News* (9 November 2020), www.bbc.com/news/health-54873105.

[76] CCSA, 'How COVID-19 is changing the world' vol I (n 65) 19; CCSA, 'How COVID-19 is changing the world' vol II (n 65) 16.

[77] CCSA, 'How COVID-19 is changing the world' vol I (n 65) 34.

[78] ibid.

[79] WTO, 'Report on G20 Trade Measures' (n 65) 3; Notification from the Kyrgyz Republic (31 March 2020) G/AG/N/KGZ/8.

importation bans on live animals and some foodstuffs originating in China.[80] In some instances, these bans were expanded to include other areas which became virus hotspots, including Iran and Italy.[81]

The imposition of lockdown and mandatory quarantine measures across the world has resulted in shifts in the use of technology, particularly online access, digital services, digital trade and electronic education. There are many short and long-term impacts of this transition for trade – and are likely to be more as society moves into the latter stages of the pandemic and post-pandemic recovery period.[82] As in many situations discussed, these impacts will vary based on the context of each state and its needs. However, as measures such as reduced fees to access technology, the creation of new customers for electronic services, and the need for additional business and supply-side capacity become entrenched, this will result in additional market opportunities. In this situation, attempts to restrict access to these markets to protect consumer pricing or even consumer data could result in significant WTO implications. At the same time, as the WTO itself has noted:

> [T]he pandemic has highlighted the importance of digital technologies in general, but also several vulnerabilities across the world. The resulting experiences and lessons are relevant to various discussions in the WTO, including those on electronic commerce, which could benefit from looking at greater international cooperation to facilitate the cross-border movement of goods and services, narrow the digital divide, and level the playing field for micro, small and medium-sized enterprises (MSMEs).[83]

At the same time, digitalisation is being incorporated as a significant element of climate change laws and policies, notably in the context of the 2019 European Green Deal.[84] In conjunction with this, there is a discernible trend among WTO Member States in terms of implementing new foreign investment restrictions during the pandemic. This is of particular importance in several sectors, including technology, banking and financial services, telecommunications services, health services (including telemedicine) and transportation services.[85] In other instances, the pandemic period has seen a rise in general foreign investment restrictions across multiple sectors.[86]

Taken together, these efforts to promote and protect domestic industries and ensure access to vital products for national populations first and foremost

[80] See Notification from the Russian Federation (3 February 2020) G/SPS/N/RUS/178; Notification from Kazakhstan (28 February 2020) G/SPS/N/KAZ/59; Notification from Indonesia (20 March 2020) G/SPS/N/IDN/132.

[81] See Notification from Mauritius (23 March 2020) G/SPS/N/MUS/18.

[82] 'E-Commerce, Trade and the COVID-19 Pandemic' (WTO, 4 May 2020), www.wto.org/english/tratop_e/covid19_e/ecommerce_report_e.pdf.

[83] ibid 2; 'Trade in Services in the Context of COVID-19 Pandemic' (WTO, 28 May 2020), www.wto.org/english/tratop_e/covid19_e/services_report_e.pdf.

[84] See Commission, Communication to the European Parliament, the European Council, the Council, the European Economic and Social Committee and the Committee of the Regions 'The European Green Deal' COM (2019) 640.

[85] WTO, 'Report on G20 Trade Measures' (n 65) 91.

[86] ibid 91–92.

demonstrate the power of a threat – be it public health related or otherwise – to cause states to step back from their long-term commitments to multilateralism in the trade context. These efforts are understandable from the societal perspective and from the perspective of domestic law, in which the obligation is on the state to act as the guardian of its people. However, when implemented without due consideration and incorporation of WTO treaties or when left in place for longer than is arguably necessary to address the prescient threat, these measures give rise to the potential for numerous complaints at the DSB level.

IV. Rethinking the WTO DSB for Current and Future Threats

The confluence of the COVID-19 pandemic and impacts on international trade in the short and long-term is striking. As noted above, the shifting nature of international and national responses can be seen in the initial bans on certain goods from states heavily impacted by the virus and in the export restrictions on medical and relate hygiene equipment. Since some of the focus has moved from these concerns to ensuring the continued existence and viability of essential industries such as airlines and tourism, the measures implemented at the national level to achieve this may give rise to contests alleging WTO law violations in the future. At the same time, it must be recalled that these are measures at least arguably implemented in the face of an overwhelming and developing threat, in this instance to public health. This opens the door to the possibility of a number of complaints at the DSB level which relate to the COVID-19 pandemic and are justified in part through invocation of Article XX(b).

Similarly, national and regional – in the case of the EU – laws and policies for post-pandemic recovery are essential for the continued economic stability of nations. And those post-pandemic recovery packages which seek to ensure that 'building back better' includes incentivising green and climate-friendly technologies such as renewable energy are vital to ensure that states meet their international commitments and their national functions.[87] However, as the above discussion has illustrated, these types of measures may also give rise to DSB proceedings.

The COVID-19 pandemic represents the potential for achieving watershed structural and juridical change in the WTO DSB system at a time when it is already under scrutiny and review. In the future, the potential for complaints regarding discriminatory and other forms of WTO law violations as a result of pandemic and pandemic recovery related measures is quite high. Indeed, although the global community has attempted to work together to address the concerns raised by

[87] For updated information on the economic policies adopted in response to the pandemic, see 'Policy Responses to Covid-19: Policy Tracker' (IMF), www.imf.org/en/Topics/imf-and-covid19/Policy-Responses-to-COVID-19#B; 'Covid-19 Law Lab' (WHO), covidlawlab.org/.

the pandemic, it is clear that there is a core connection between national reaction, recovery plans and pandemic governance. This has been highlighted across the international system, with the open session of the UN General Assembly in September 2020 emphasising the need to move past purely national interests to fight the pandemic and noting that this is not the time to implement trade or other restrictive measures.[88]

In this context, the decisions taken to protect human health could be contested at the DSB level and would likely be defended through a focus on the various Article XX exceptions discussed in this chapter. To date, successive DSB Panel and Appellate Body decisions have begun to craft an understanding of how these exceptions are to be used; however, in the face of pandemic decision-making, it is likely that these contours will have to be further refined and in rather short order. This will, in turn, result in juridical change within the DSB system. The issue will be whether this change is best served by leaving these decisions to the individual panels or seeking a WTO pandemic waiver that would serve to absolve certain national actions from negative findings based on necessity. Given the difficulties in finding agreement on the pressing items discussed over successive rounds of the Doha negotiations, the latter option is likely less viable. A primary example of this can be seen in the inability of the Doha negotiation rounds within the WTO system to result in significant policy innovations or legal responses to the issues contained in the Doha Ministerial Declaration, including issues such as agricultural practices and intellectual property laws and policies.[89]

With this in mind, and mindful as well of the current and anticipated future threats to the global trading system, and indeed the global community as a whole, it is perhaps time to examine alternative methods of reforming the DSB from a structural perspective. At the moment, there are a number of panels in the system; however other than the appellate panels, there are few specialised panels. Those specialised panels in existence are generally concentrated in certain areas having little expertise in the grounds asserted for an Article XX claim.

Against this background, it is proposed that at least two separate categories of specialised panels be created to evaluate current and future Article XX claims from the outset, serving essentially as a screening phase. The first of these panels would be convened to examine claims involving measures which are alleged to have been directly related to the pandemic and immediate post-pandemic response, largely those with significant responsive claims invoking Article XX(b) as a justification. In this way, there would be the ability for the Panel to certify whether the Article XX claim is being properly invoked against a highly nuanced background rather than flooding the panels with potentially similar claims that could result in differing outcomes. As has been seen in other arbitral settings, these

[88] United Nations, 'Report of the Secretary-General on the Work of the Organization' (2020), www.un.org/annualreport/.
[89] See 'The Doha Round' (WTO), www.wto.org/english/tratop_e/dda_e/dda_e.htm.

results can be disastrous for all involved.[90] The second proposed panel, anticipating significant climate change-related national policies which preference national industries or producers or place significant restrictions on foreign industries or producers, would be convened to examine Article XX(g) claims involving environmental and climate-related justifications, including those relating to sustainable development.[91]

Again, these are nuanced areas and have the ability to become repetitive in the future, thus justifying the creation of a body having a dedicated expertise. Given the specialised knowledge needed to assess both the claimed health or environmental justification and the relationship to international trade law, it is suggested that the members of these panels be designated by the Secretariat based on their knowledge in medicine and public health or environment and sustainable development.

In terms of functioning and evaluation, it is suggested that both panels be empowered to examine the general claims regarding health or environmental need as well as claims of heightened exigency such as a pandemic or the aftermath of an environmental disaster (such as a massive hurricane or forest fire). This suggestion is made as a response to the reality that even within nuanced areas of expertise, there are gradations of necessity and immediate threat which can be seen as justifying more drastic deviations from WTO trade law. Further, the suggestion would allow the specialised panels to accommodate new threats in the health and environment realms which are perhaps speculative or even not anticipated at present, yet may pose significant challenges in the future. In this way, the suggestion incorporates an inherent sustainability which would not require additional actions by the WTO in order to be responsive. At the same time, these suggested panels would be grounded in the jurisprudence of the DSB, particularly the cases discussed above, to provide context and a reliable basis for the generation of legal arguments and future precedent.

V. Conclusion

The COVID-19 pandemic has fundamentally changed the ways in which international law, economics and society functions. It poses critical questions to future conceptions of trade law and acceptable deviations from it during emergencies. These are existential questions in themselves, yet are only the beginning in what scientists and experts expect to be an increasingly devastated system of climate

[90] For a discussion of the results of inconsistency in the application of arbitral findings arising from the same issues in Argentina, see AR Harrington and A Kent, 'The Plea of Necessity Under International Customary Law: A Critical Review in Light of the Argentinean Cases' in K Miles and C Brown (eds), *Evolution in Investment Treaty Law and Arbitration* (Cambridge, Cambridge University Press, 2011).

[91] The anticipatory element might not in fact be a long wait, given the commitment of many states to measures such as carbon neutrality – or even carbon negativity – within the context of the Paris Agreement on climate change.

change-related disasters. Some of these will be slow-onset events while others will be rapid onset. Regardless, they will have stark impacts individually and collectively, requiring an international trade law system capable of addressing national responses which could potentially breach the terms of the WTO's treaty system.

This chapter discussed the ways in which the WTO DSB system has addressed environmental and health-related issues brought under the exceptions of Article XX of the GATT, how this jurisprudence has evolved, and the capacity of these types of claim to be brought in the context of pandemic responses as well as potential future climate change-related event responses. Building from this, the chapter then suggested ways in which ongoing efforts to create structural change in the DSB system could be used to create new panel groups empowered to hear initial assertions of Article XX and related exceptions before convening a fully-fledged panel for the complaint. In this way, the chapter has sought to shift the dialogue from the need to implement structural change in the WTO DSB context per se, to an understanding of how pandemic and other predicted future disaster responses can be seen as compelling a pre-emptive structural shift. It also shows that the WTO needs to evolve and adapt to this changing environment and for new realities to remain relevant. If it does not evolve at this stage, its members may employ more retreats from and attacks against multilateralism in the years to come.

6

The WTO and Brazil's Trade Responses Amid the Pandemic: Can Transparency Overcome Populism?

MICHELLE R SANCHEZ-BADIN AND
MAGALI FAVARETTO PRIETO FERNANDES

I. Introduction: International Trade and Trade Policies Matter

The COVID-19 pandemic has challenged states in their resources and capacity to swiftly formulate effective public policies. Along with travel restrictions and lockdowns, governments have strived to conduct testing, prevent contagion, treat citizens and minimise mortality rates. They have also strived to guarantee access to medicines, personal protection equipment (PPE) and medical devices, among other actions. In the context of the current pandemic, not only are health policies of importance, but also foreign economic policies. Such policies have been used to mitigate negative spillover effects of the current pandemic. In particular, policies serving to safeguard the stable and safe flow of trade and services in a globalised economy ensure the accessibility of basic supplies required to deal with the pandemic.

This chapter addresses the international trade and trade-related policy responses to ensure access to medical supplies, by assessing the role of the World Trade Organization (WTO) in safeguarding transparency and coordinating Members' actions. The chapter analyses how the coordinated work promoted by the WTO with domestic agencies may contribute to overcoming policies of populist leaders in denial of the crisis and at odds with the values and norms of the WTO as a multilateral institution. The picture portrayed here first provides a case study of Brazil's domestic response to the pandemic and the impact of its measures on international trade. The results of the case study analysis indicate a coordination between Brazil's domestic institutions and the relevant WTO committees to respond to this crisis. The findings also highlight the utility of the WTO's current and previous efforts to enhance transparency, notifications, technical work and supervision.

In order to develop this analysis, the chapter is organised in three further sections. Section II describes and explains how international trade regulation became a central topic amid the pandemic, by contrasting examples of export bans and restrictions imposed on PPE and pharmaceutical products to trade facilitation measures adopted in support of the COVID-19 response – such as reduction of import tariffs, exemption of anti-dumping and other remedies duties. Section III discusses the role of the WTO in the pandemic, particularly its efforts to guarantee transparency through notifications of measures taken by governments, and to facilitate cooperation among countries in a critical time filled with populist temptations. Section IV examines in greater depth the trade policies and regulatory measures taken by domestic technical agencies in Brazil, as a representative case, testing the hypothesis that the WTO institutional framework and processes have been important towards overcoming the grossly inadequate policies of populist leaders in denial of the pandemic. Section V sets forth some concluding remarks.

II. National Trade Policy Responses to COVID-19

The pandemic has brought unforeseeable circumstances to states. It will take time for researchers to fully comprehend the drivers behind and depth of the variety of states' policy responses witnessed globally and their potential impacts at both national and international levels.

The pandemic has led to a widespread shortage of medical supplies. Countries are in a battle over access to PPE such as surgical masks, respirators, goggles and facial shields, as well as ventilators and a gamut of medical devices and pharmaceutical products. Goods described as critical and in severe shortage have already been highly traded before the pandemic, totalling about $US 597 billion, or 1.7 per cent of total world trade in 2019.[1] However, a few countries were leaders in the export of these products. Based on 2019 world trade data, Germany, the United States (US), and Switzerland supply 35 per cent of medical products, while China, Germany and the US export 40 per cent of PPE.[2]

Global supply chains require sourcing inputs and raw materials from one country to another, carrying out trials and inspections in different countries and ensuring they are produced in compliance with recognised laboratory practices, standards and conformity assessment procedures. This means that trade policies adopted by countries involved in the supply chain, especially the main suppliers and destination markets, have a considerable impact on the timely supply of basic

[1] 'Transparency – Why it Matters at Times of Crisis' (WTO, 7 April 2020), www.wto.org/english/tratop_e/covid19_e/transparency_report_e.pdf.

[2] 'Trade in Medical Goods in the Context of Tackling COVID-19, Information Note' (WTO, 3 April 2020), www.wto.org/english/news_e/news20_e/rese_03apr20_e.pdf.

goods, calling for collective actions by all nations involved to address disruptions in supply chains.[3]

As the pivot of multilateral trade regulation, the WTO has adapted and mobilised its transparency efforts under its Trade Policy Review Mechanism (TPRM). The TPRM mandate was extended in 2009 following the emergence of the global financial crisis, to include preparation of country-specific monitoring reports on a regular basis.[4] In addition to that, on 24 March 2020, the WTO Director-General encouraged Members to provide the WTO Secretariat with information on any measure or support programme which has been taken in the context of the COVID-19 crisis.[5] Such efforts undertaken by the WTO have encouraged transparency among Member States and key economic agents, and enabled cooperative actions amongst them.

As of 19 June 2020, the WTO had registered a total of 203 trade measures relating to COVID-19.[6] The WTO report on 'Export Prohibitions and Restrictions' mentioned that, by April 2020, 80 out of 164 Members had introduced export prohibitions or restrictions in response to the pandemic.[7] Members had adopted different types of export constraints on medical products, such as export bans, non-automatic licensing requirements and exporting restrictions of various kinds. These measures have raised major concerns, in particular when adopted by the relatively large exporters of medical products.[8]

Although such restrictions may help increase domestic supply and reduce domestic prices in the short run, they may also lower global production and supply and hence increase the world prices of these basic goods in the longer run.

[3] ibid.

[4] The TPRM was introduced in the GATT Council Decision on 12 April 1989. In 1994, the TPRM was confirmed as an integral part of the WTO under Annex 3 of the Marrakesh Agreement. See Trade Policy Review Mechanism (TPRM), Marrakesh Agreement Establishing the World Trade Organization, Annex 3 (Marrakesh, 15 April 1994). In 2009 the WTO has expanded its trade-monitoring role, producing wide reports every six months. For a comprehensive study on the functioning of the TPRM see M Kende, *The Trade Policy Review Mechanism. A Critical Analysis* (Oxford, Oxford University Press, 2018).

[5] 'DG Azevêdo requests WTO members to share information on trade measures related to COVID-19' (*WTO*, 25 March 2020), www.wto.org/english/news_e/news20_e/dgra_24mar20_e.htm; WTO, 'Transparency' (n 1).

[6] The list of measures published by the WTO Secretariat is the result of a compilation by the organisation from official sources. So, the list and the information are considered as 'an informal situation report and an attempt to provide transparency with respect to trade and trade-related measures taken in the context of the COVID-19 crisis'. See 'Goods measures – COVID-19: Trade and trade-related measures' (WTO), www.wto.org/english/tratop_e/covid19_e/trade_related_goods_measure_e.htm. 'COVID-19: Measures affecting trade in goods' (WTO), www.wto.org/english/tratop_e/covid19_e/trade_related_goods_measure_e.htm.

[7] 'Export Prohibitions and Restrictions' (WTO, 23 April 2020), www.wto.org/english/tratop_e/covid19_e/export_prohibitions_report_e.pdf.

[8] In February 2020, when COVID-19 hit Europe, eg, it was announced that the major European suppliers – France, Germany and the Czech Republic – started to impose export restrictions, threatening the EU principles of free trade and collaboration. See A Tsang, 'EU Seeks Solidarity as Nations Restrict Medical Exports' *New York Times* (7 March 2020), www.nytimes.com/2020/03/07/business/eu-exports-medical-equipment.html.

Recent studies have shown that such restrictions may only worsen the situation, whereas a better option would be to promote international trade through cooperation.[9]

In contrast to export restrictions and other trade barriers, a number of countries have introduced measures to further liberalise trade and facilitate access to medical supplies. Such measures have taken the form of, for example, reduction in import tariffs, exemption of anti-dumping and other remedy duties, and relaxation of regulatory barriers. Notably, the trade-facilitating measures identified by the WTO fall into four main categories: streamlining certification procedures; ensuring that medical goods are safe; making food available by relaxing technical regulations; and addressing COVID-19 risks emanating from international trade of live animals.[10]

With respect to medical goods, pharmaceutical products and medical devices are usually tightly regulated, comprising laws, product registrations, tests, mandatory regulations and conformity assessment procedures to ensure effectiveness and consumer safety. Easing and expediting those requirements in a health crisis seems a rational choice. Furthermore, some of the sanitary precautionary measures – such as social distancing guidelines – require the adaptation of certain regulatory prescriptions (for example, in loco and in-person inspections). These trade-facilitating measures can considerably ease the import and domestic production of essential products, thereby helping governments and their healthcare systems to better contain the spread of the virus.

III. The Value of Transparency and Technical Work in a Pandemic

Transparency obligations, embedded in many of the WTO Agreements, have increasingly been considered of critical importance. They have also been considered as foundational to support the recent reform proposals to the international trade system.[11] The WTO Glossary describes transparency as 'the degree to which trade policies and practices, and the process by which they are established, are open and predictable'.[12] The notion of transparency within the WTO may still

[9] R Baldwin and SJ Evenett, 'Introduction' in R Baldwin and SJ Evenett (eds), *COVID-19 and Trade Policy: Why Turning Inward Won't Work* (London, CEPR Press, 2020).

[10] 'Standards, Regulations and COVID-19 – What Actions Taken by WTO Members?' (WTO, 20 May 2020), www.wto.org/english/tratop_e/covid19_e/standards_report_e.pdf. In the case of the Group of 20 (G20) economies, the WTO's latest biannual monitoring reports significant moves to facilitate imports. During the pandemic period, from 154 new trade and trade-related measures implemented by the G20 economies, 93 were facilitating measures and linked to the COVID-19 pandemic. See 'Report on G20 trade measures' (WTO, 29 June 2020), www.wto.org/english/news_e/news20_e/report_trdev_jun20_e.pdf.

[11] For an insightful account of these proposals and overall discussion on transparency mechanisms in the WTO see LS Borlini, 'A crisis looming in the dark: Some remarks on the reform proposals on notifications and transparency' (2019) *QIL, Zoom-out* 63, 83, ssrn.com/abstract=3525423.

[12] 'WTO Glossary', www.wto.org/english/thewto_e/glossary_e/transparency_e.htm.

be understood in a wider perspective. It also encompasses rules on notification, publication, monitoring, reporting and reviewing commitments as provided in the WTO Agreements.[13] These disciplines, for example, require Members to formally notify the WTO of all laws and regulations affecting trade, so that Members can be aware of what measures their trading partners are undertaking and if they are acting accordingly to their WTO obligations.

As outlined in section II, at the outbreak of the pandemic, new trade measures, restricting or liberalising trade in medical goods, sprung each day in a rapid and somewhat reactive and chaotic manner. This made it crucial for states, exporters and importers to be aware of new requirements, restrictions, tariff modifications and overall regulations to be able to continue trading in this unprecedented scenario. Transparency and information thus represented light in the darkness.

Since the GATT 1947,[14] transparency obligations have evolved from the general obligation to publish laws affecting trade (as provided in Article X), to include monitoring and surveillance mechanisms that take place in the various WTO committees, and peer review procedures in the TPRM.[15] In addition, the emergence of the internet in 2002 facilitated the efforts towards enhancing this openness and transparency.[16] Yet, as Halle and Wolfe have observed,[17] these third generation transparency policies are yet to be applied to the functioning of the WTO itself. This involves a greater openness and effective participation of developing countries, allowing them to use the information generated by the transparency mechanisms, and reducing information asymmetries not only among governments, but also among the economic actors and citizens.[18] Hoekman has also put

[13] Just as examples, transparency is encouraged through the general transparency principles stated in Art X of the General Agreement on Tariffs and Trade (GATT), Art III of the General Agreement on Trade in Services (GATS) and Article 63 of the Agreement on Trade-Related Aspects of Intellectual Property Rights (TRIPS). Today, nearly every WTO Agreement contains provisions on transparency and WTO Members have called for enhanced transparency provisions. See Annexes 1A, 1B and 1C of the Marrakesh Agreement Establishing the World Trade Organization (Marrakesh, 15 April 1994).

[14] General Agreement on Tariffs and Trade (GATT) (Geneva, 30 October 1947).

[15] TPRM (n 4).

[16] For a broad overview of such transformations, encompassing three generations of transparency policies within the WTO, see P Mavroidis and R Wolfe, 'From Sunshine to a Common Agent: The Evolving Understanding of Transparency in the WTO' (2015) 21 *Brown Journal of World Affairs* 117, 123–29. See also S Charnovitz, 'Transparency and Participation in the World Trade Organization' (2004) 56 *Rutgers Law Review* 927. For a critical and comprehensive view on the evolution of the WTO jurisprudence on transparency see P Ala'i, 'From the Periphery to the Center? The Evolving WTO Jurisprudence on Transparency and Good Governance' (2008) 11 *Journal of International Economic Law* 779.

[17] M Halle and R Wolfe, 'A new approach to transparency and the accountability in the WTO' (2010) ENTWINED and IISD Issue brief 06, www.iisd.org/system/files/publications/IssueBrief6-2010-09-14-low.pdf.

[18] Various WTO Members have proposed new procedures to enhance transparency and notification obligations. There are two major proposals: one from Argentina, Australia, Canada, Costa Rica, the European Union (EU), Japan, New Zealand, Taiwan and the US (Communication, 'Procedures to Enhance Transparency and Strengthen Notification Requirements under WTO Agreements' (27 June 2019) JOB/GC/204/Rev.2, JOB/CTG/14/Rev.2); and another from Cuba, India, Nigeria, South Africa, Tunisia, Uganda and Zimbabwe (Communication, 'An Inclusive Approach to Transparency and Notification Requirements in the WTO' (27 June 2019) JOB/GC/218, JOB/CTG/15, JOB/SERV/292, JOB/IP/33/DEV/58, JOB/AG/158). See WA Reinsch and Jack Caporal, 'Why Does Transparency

it in a simple and straightforward way: 'transparency is a critical input into WTO processes as well as an important output of the organization'.[19]

Owing to the technical work carried out by the WTO on such monitoring and reviewing procedures through the TPRM and relevant WTO committees, the multilateral trading system has encouraged and given support to the creation of a myriad of national bureaucratic structures that are responsible for collecting information on trade-related domestic policies, sharing it with other officials and holding debates within the committees. These debates not only offer opportunities for clarifying technical issues and de-escalating trade irritants but are also a fundamental exercise in confidence building.

They also offer important opportunities for experience sharing and learning of best practices. By discussing specific policies adopted for a diverse set of public policy objectives, this under-the-radar technical cooperation has been providing a public good available for developing countries and developed economies alike, leading some to refer to it as the true 'jewel of the crown'.[20]

The WTO's transparency and notification mechanism has played a valuable role in combating the pandemic. On March 2020, the WTO Secretariat established a dedicated central information point and adapted its trade policy monitoring function to collect and report on the measures adopted in reaction to the sanitary crisis.[21] It has also issued a series of information notes seeking to provide more clarity on the intrinsic and complex relationship between trade policy and the health policy responses.

The enhanced transparency promoted by these initiatives is indispensable in the fog-of-war of a global pandemic. Without accurate and timely information on measures affecting export and imports of medical goods and foodstuff, new regulations affecting transportation or specific technical requirements, essential goods could be stuck at borders and precious time lost in misinformation and rushed, piecemeal coordination.

The connections, relationships and bureaucratic cooperative tissues developed through the years of regular committee work at the WTO, facilitated by governmental institutions mandated by the Technical Barriers to Trade (TBT) and Sanitary and Phytosanitary (SPS) Agreements[22] called 'enquiry points', should equally contribute to the exchange of information needed for trade to play its role in fighting the pandemic. The experience has also highlighted some potential

Matter, and Are Members Meeting Their Obligations?' (CSIS, 22 April 2020), www.csis.org/analysis/transparency-wto-why-does-transparency-matter-and-are-members-meeting-their-obligations.

[19] B Hoekman, 'Proposal for WTO Reform: A Synthesis and Assessment' in A Narlikar, M Dauton and RM Stern (eds), *The Oxford Handbook of the World Trade Organization* (Oxford, Oxford University Press, 2012).

[20] MB Karttunen, *Transparency in the WTO SPS and TBT Agreements: The Real Jewel in the Crown* (Cambridge, Cambridge University Press, 2020).

[21] 'Covid-19 and World Trade' (WTO), www.wto.org/english/tratop_e/covid19_e/covid19_e.htm.

[22] Agreement on Technical Barriers to Trade, Marrakesh Agreement Establishing the World Trade Organization, Annex 1A (Marrakesh, 15 April 1994); Agreement on the Application of Sanitary and Phytosanitary Measures, Marrakesh Agreement Establishing the World Trade Organization, Annex 1A (Marrakesh, 15 April 1994).

avenues for improvement, be it relating to the varying periodicity of notification requirements of different trade policies, or better clarity and improvements on the role of international and national bureaucracies with regard to transparency and cooperative efforts.

Finally, one least known functional arm of the multilateral trading system is its technical assistance work on capacity building to developing countries.[23] Such work has been growing in relevance and evolving in nature in the past few years.[24] The pandemic has exposed many of the underlying discrepancies and fragilities in terms of physical and virtual infrastructures among countries. At the WTO, developing countries can, and have constantly, asked for assistance in strengthening their trade administrative structures and building capacity of their trade officials. Training and capacity building are critical during the pandemic for the transparency arm of the multilateral system to continue to operate.

In the current context of growing nationalism, inward policy prioritisation and diminishing opportunities for multilateral collaboration, the public good provided by the regular technical work developed under the multilateral trading system has been highly important in the fight against the COVID-19 pandemic.

International organisations are described as important *locus* for cooperation, but their efficacy is dependent on the voluntary participation of Member States. With this focus on national policies, the following section assesses the case of Brazil, its trade policies and trade-related regulatory measures, and their connection with the WTO's institutional structure and its lesser known role.

IV. Brazil as a 'Case Study': Trade-Related Regulatory Measures in Support of Health Policies

Brazil is an interesting case to test the proposed hypothesis – that the coordinated work promoted by the WTO with domestic agencies may be of relevance to overcome policies of populist leaders in denial of the crisis due to two main reasons. First, the current President of Brazil, Jair Bolsonaro, has been noted as one of the main leaders denying the seriousness of the COVID-19 pandemic.[25] The national

[23] The Doha Ministerial Declaration (14 November 2001) WT/MIN(01)/DEC/1. This Ministerial Declaration explained and enhanced the WTO mandate to carry out technical cooperation activities, as provided for in various WTO Agreements and decisions. There are currently several programmes, publications and handbooks on this work carried out by the WTO to meet this mandate, see 'Building Trade Capacity' (WTO), www.wto.org/english/tratop_e/devel_e/build_tr_capa_e.htm.

[24] For an evolution of WTO capacity-building programmes and a critical assessment on competing rationales for trade-related capacity building and technical assistance, see G Shaffer, 'Can WTO Technical Assistance and Capacity-Building Serve Developing Countries?' in E Petersmann and J Harrison (eds), *Reforming the World Trading System: Legitimacy, Efficiency, and Democratic Governance* (Oxford, Oxford University Press, 2012). See also HBS Lecomte, 'Capacity-building and Technical Assistance for Developing Countries After Doha' (2002) 6 *Bridges (ICTSD)* 3.

[25] E Londoño, M Andreoni and L Casado, 'Bolsonaro, Isolated and Defiant, Dismisses Coronavirus Threat to Brazil' *New York Times* (1 April 2020), www.nytimes.com/2020/04/01/world/americas/brazil-bolsonaro-coronavirus.html; D Kirkpatrick and JML Cabrera, 'How Trump and Bolsonaro Broke Latin

politics towards the pandemic has been against the implementation of prevention measures, and the World Health Organization (WHO) protocols and recommendations. Second and paradoxically, Brazil has been the country with the largest number of notifications of trade and trade-related measures on COVID-19, being more than 95 per cent, easing the import of needed medical products to combat the virus.[26] What is the relevance of the WTO's role in this domestic context?

In contrast to other countries and its analogues, the Brazilian agencies concerned acted fast, based on a fairly embedded recognition that international expertise and cooperation is valuable to achieve national policy goals.[27] Due to that, Brazil heads the number of regulatory notifications to the WTO on matters relating to COVID-19, as per the data in the figure below.

Figure 6.1 Notifications Submitted by WTO Members on COVID-19[28]

America's COVID-19 defenses' *New York Times* (27 October 2020), www.nytimes.com/2020/10/27/world/trump-bolsonaro-coronavirus-latin-america.html.

[26] WTO, 'Report on the G20 trade measures' (n 10).

Beyond the temporary elimination of import tariffs and suspension of anti-dumping duties notified,[29] two-thirds of all notifications about Brazil's COVID-19 actions to the WTO correspond to regulatory measures. Until 20 May 2020, 27 members had submitted 85 notifications under the TBT and SPS Agreements, which set out disciplines for standards and regulatory measures to ensure product safety and protect human life, among other public policy objectives,[30] and Brazil accounts for a large part of those notifications.[31]

This Brazilian bottom-up approach translated into administrative measures taken by regulators, especially the National Institute of Metrology, Quality and Technology (INMETRO) and Brazil's Health Regulatory Agency (ANVISA),[32] and the timely notifications sent to the WTO TBT and SPS Committees. Such an approach is in sharp contrast to broader political policies at the top of the President Bolsonaro-led Executive Branch.[33]

One relevant aspect of the Brazilian measures is the focus on regulatory aspects that could potentially delay imports and distribution. Certification of products, authorisations of plants and manufacturers, inspections for good manufacturing practices, and availability of standards are essential to ensure the products are available, adequate and safe, but the regulatory enforcements may also pose as obstacles to responding with the required urgency. This is a delicate balance that Brazil's agencies, as in all countries, have been challenged to achieve in different ways, depending on the regulatory environments in which they are operating. The goal was to facilitate imports and distribution to hospitals, healthcare units, consumers and patients, without compromising the safety standards and the legitimate administrative requirements needed to comply with national laws and regulations.

The efforts taken by Brazil's regulators focused on the temporary removal or suspension of authorisations to operate mandatory certifications and streamlining

[27] 'Tackling Coronavirus (COVID-19). Contributing to a global effort. No policy maker is an island: the international regulatory co-operation response to the COVID-19 crises' (OECD, 8 June 2020), read.oecd-ilibrary.org/view/?ref=134_134311-cbjgrk3pwj&title=No-policy-maker-is-an-island-the-international-regulatory-co-operation-response-to-the-COVID-19-crisis.

[28] 'WTO members' notifications on COVID-19' (WTO, as of 4 October 2020), www.wto.org/english/tratop_e/covid19_e/notifications_e.htm.

[29] CAMEX Resolutions nº 17/2020 de 17 de março de 2020, nº 22/2020 de 25 de março de 2020, Nº 28/2020 de 1º de abril de 2020, nº 31/2020 de 7 de abril de 2020, nº 32/2020 de 16 de abril de 2020, nº 33/2020 de 29 de abril de 2020; GECEX Resolution nº 44/2020 de 14 de maio de 2020.

[30] WTO, 'Standards, Regulations and COVID-19' (n 10).

[31] WTO, 'Report on the G20 trade measures' (n 10). For an interesting comparative study on nine country cases – Brazil, Canada, Kenya, Kuwait, the EU, Namibia, Switzerland, Uganda and the US – on regulatory cooperation actions on medical products with an aim to coping with the pandemic, see D Prabhakar, S Lee, M Li and C Ngo, 'Strengthening International Regulatory Cooperation for Medical Supplies in Times of Medical Emergencies' (2020), United Nations ESCAP, www.unescap.org/sites/default/files/142%20Final-Team%20Divya%20Prabhakar-Switzerland_0.pdf.

[32] INMETRO and ANVISA are Brazil's Enquiry points to respectively the WTO TBT and SPS Agreements. See 'Brazil and the WTO' (WTO), www.wto.org/english/thewto_e/countries_e/brazil_e.htm.

[33] BQ Cunha, 'Brazil's COVID-19 Response is Caught Between Denialism and Technocratic Hubris' *The Regulatory Review* (1 June 2020), www.theregreview.org/2020/06/01/cunha-brazil-covid-19-response-caught-between-denialism-technocratic-hubris/.

or expedition of conformity assessment procedures by using remote technologies, analysis based on risk, and post-market surveillance. Examples of measures adopted by Brazil's government since the inception of the crises are the following:

a. *Exemption of registration and authorisations*: ANVISA temporarily exempted manufacturers and importers of several PPE and medical devices from the requirements relating to registration, company operating licence (*Autorização de Funcionamento de Empresa*), and other health authorisations (RDC 356/20).[34] However, the manufacturer and importer must remain compliant with all technical standards and regulations applicable to post-market controls. This exceptional regulation has also consolidated PPE product requirements and applicable Brazilian standards.
b. *Suspension of mandatory certification*: INMETRO suspended the requirement of compulsory certification of medical gloves and filter for particles (*Portaria 102/20*)[35] and made it conditional upon the supplier's records proving the fulfilment of technical requirements through tests carried out in a laboratory accredited by INMETRO or other member of the International Laboratory Accreditation Cooperation Mutual Recognition Agreement.
c. *Flexible criteria for manufacture and sale*: ANVISA established extraordinary and temporary criteria and procedures for the manufacture and sale of sanitisers and antiseptics (RDC 347/20[36] and RDC 350/20).[37]
d. *Expedited registration*: ANVISA defined extraordinary and temporary criteria and procedures for expedited registration and post-registration of medicines, biological products and products for *in vitro* diagnosis indicated for COVID-19 (RDC 348/2020).[38] The main criteria for conditional approval are based on imminent or existing shortages of the medicines or active

[34] ANVISA. RDC n 356, as of 23 March 2020, www.in.gov.br/en/web/dou/-/resolucao-rdc-n-379-de-30-de-abril-de-2020-254764712. Provides, on an extraordinary and temporary basis, the requirements for the manufacture, import and acquisition of medical devices identified as a priority for use in health services, due to the international public health emergency related to SARS-CoV-2. RDC n 356 was altered by RDC n 379, as of 30 April 2020.

[35] INMETRO, Portaria n 102 as of 20 March 2020, www.inmetro.gov.br/legislacao/rtac/pdf/RTAC002627.pdf. It suspends the compulsory certification of medical and hospital supplies for coping with the coronavirus epidemic (COVID-19).

[36] ANVISA. RDC n 347 as of 17 March 2020, www.in.gov.br/en/web/dou/-/resolucao-rdc-n-347-de-17-de-marco-de-2020-*-250404851. It defines the extraordinary and temporary criteria and procedures for exposure to the sale of antiseptic preparations or officinal sanitisers, due to the emergence of international public health related to SARS-CoV-2.

[37] ANVISA. RDC n 350, as of 20 March 2020, www.in.gov.br/en/web/dou/-/resolucao-rdc-n-350-de-19-de-marco-de-2020-249028045. It defines the extraordinary and temporary criteria and procedures for the manufacture and commercialisation of antiseptic preparations or officinal sanitisers without prior authorisation from Anvisa and takes other measures, due to the emergence of international public health related to SARS-CoV-2.

[38] ANVISA. RDC n 348, as of 17 March 2020, www.in.gov.br/en/web/dou/-/resolucao-rdc-n-348-de-17-de-marco-de-2020-248564332. It defines the extraordinary and temporary criteria and procedures for handling applications for registration of medicines, biological products and products for in vitro diagnosis and post-registration change of medicines and biological products due to the international public health emergency arising from the new Coronavirus.

pharmaceutical ingredients essential to the treatment of COVID-19 in the national market.

e. *Extraordinary criteria for conformity assessment procedures and good manufacturing practices*: Both INMETRO (*Portaria 79/20*[39] and *Portaria 99/20*)[40] and ANVISA (RDC 346/20[41] and RDC 349/20)[42] introduced changes and extraordinary criteria for conformity assessment procedures and good manufacturing practices with respect to medicines and medical devices indicated for the treatment of COVID-19. These measures temporarily allow remote inspections through videoconference, transmission of data, tests in laboratories of manufacturers, and acceptance of documentary risk-analysis based on the records of the latest internal audits and analysis of the company's management.

In addition to the above-mentioned unilateral measures, Brazil's regulatory agencies have also relied on coordinated measures, dubbed by the WTO and the Organisation for Economic Co-operation and Development (OECD) as International Regulatory Cooperation mechanisms.[43] Such mechanisms are aimed at facilitating trade, based on good regulatory practices, mutual recognition agreements, harmonisation with international standards and practices, and different forms of cooperation among regulators.[44] ANVISA's rules for expedited registration and exemption of good manufacturing practices certification leverage on the Medical Device Single Audit Program (MDSAP)[45] and on the Pharmaceutical Inspection Co-operation Scheme,[46] are examples of such coordinated measures.

[39] INMETRO, Portaria n 79, as of 4 March 2020, www.inmetro.gov.br/legislacao/rtac/pdf/RTAC002625.pdf. It approves extraordinary conditions for realisation of conformity assessment activities in countries affected by the coronavirus epidemic (COVID-19).

[40] INMETRO, Portaria n 99, as of 20 March 2020, www.in.gov.br/en/web/dou/-/portaria-n-99-de-20-de-marco-de-2020-249243964. It approves extraordinary conditions for regulated services, in the area of conformity assessment, which depend on the performance of delegated bodies that make up Brazil's Network of Legal Metrology and Quality – RBMLQ-I, due to the coronavirus epidemic (COVID-19).

[41] ANVISA, RDC n 346, as of 12 March 2020, www.in.gov.br/en/web/dou/-/resolucao-de-diretoria-colegiada-rdc-n-346-de-12-de-marco-de-2020-247801951. It defines the extraordinary and temporary criteria and procedures for the certification of good manufacturing practices for the purposes of registration and post-registration changes to active pharmaceutical ingredients, medicines and health products due to the international public health emergency of the new Coronavirus.

[42] ANVISA.RDC, n 349, as of 20 March 2020, www.in.gov.br/en/web/dou/-/resolucao-rdc-n-349-de-19-de-marco-de-2020-249028270. It defines the extraordinary and temporary criteria and procedures for handling requests for regularisation of personal protective equipment, 'of the ventilator type' and other medical devices identified as strategic by Anvisa, due to the emergence of international public health resulting from the new Coronavirus and other measures.

[43] 'International Regulatory Co-operation' (OECD), www.oecd.org/gov/regulatory-policy/irc.htm.

[44] 'Facilitating Trade Through Regulatory Cooperation: The Case of WTO's TBT/SPS Agreements and Committees' (WTO, 2019), www.wto.org/english/res_e/booksp_e/tbtsps19_e.pdf.

[45] The MDSAP is a harmonised approach to auditing and monitoring the quality management systems of medical device manufacturers on an international scale, based on audits conducted by Auditing Organisations authorised by participating regulatory authorities. See IMDRF, www.imdrf.org/workitems/wi-mdsap.asp.

[46] The Pharmaceutical Inspection Convention and the Pharmaceutical Inspection Co-operation Scheme (jointly referred to as PIC/S) is an international cooperation between pharmaceutical inspection authorities in the field of good manufacturing practices. See PICSCHEME, picscheme.org.

This implies the acceptance of information provided directly from regulators of other countries that participate in these coordinated schemes. Under such rules, Brazil could directly accept certification of ventilators and other medical devices under MDSAP, as well as novel medical devices and PPE not regulated in Brazil but already authorised in jurisdictions of other members of the International Medical Devices Regulators Forum (IMDRF).[47]

Normally, Brazil applies its own set of good manufacturing practices requirements.[48] Although the country joined MDSAP in 2014 and recognises that a single audit satisfies requirements for all MDSAP countries' regulators, the MDSAP certificate does not replace the Brazilian good manufacturing practices certificate issued by ANVISA. The importation of medical devices in Brazil is subject to several technical regulations provided by INMETRO and ANVISA, as well as from Brazil's Association of Technical Standards. Both INMETRO and ANVISA have taken important steps to adapt their regulation in the last five years. ANVISA has been leading the construction and employment of good regulatory practices and International Regulatory Cooperation among Brazilian regulatory agencies and is considered to be the regulatory agency most attuned to international regulatory practices. A recent study on Brazilian general regulatory responses evaluates that ANVISA took measures to confront COVID-19 even before the disease became a serious threat to national public health and well before other agencies started to take similar action.[49] INMETRO had also taken relevant steps before the crisis, launching and submitting to public consultation a new regulatory model based on post-market surveillance, a mechanism that has been tested on a temporary basis during the pandemic.[50]

Countries around the world have different regulatory approaches, and even when harmonised, the implementation of guidelines and recognition of inspection outcomes vary domestically. The COVID-19 pandemic has accelerated other coordination efforts and schemes, calling for more harmonised global drug regulation, consortium and crowdsourcing solutions[51] to accelerate research and development processes, production and equitable access to diagnostics, therapeutics and vaccines for the virus.[52]

[47] IMDRF is a worldwide voluntary group of medical device regulators, created in 2011, to build on an international medical device regulatory harmonisation and convergence through a Global Harmonisation Task Force on Medical Devices.

[48] Manufacturers of medicines and medical devices are required to obtain a Certificate of Good Manufacturing Practices, a document issued by ANVISA certifying that a particular establishment complies with good manufacturing practices in the sanitary legislation in force.

[49] S Guerra, NSC Salinas and LT Gomes, 'Regulatory agencies in response to the COVID-19 crisis' (2020) 54 *Brazilian Journal of Public Administration* 874.

[50] For more information, see INMETRO: www4.inmetro.gov.br/novo-modelo-regulatorio.

[51] C Simone Fishburn, 'COVID R&D: Pharmas Aligned Behind Crowdsourcing solution' *Biocentury* (23 April 2020), www.biocentury.com/article/304928/covid-r-d-pharmas-align-behind-crowdsourcing-solution.

[52] 'Access to COVID-19 Tools (ACT) Accelerator' (WHO): www.who.int/initiatives/act-accelerator.

These domestic and administrative initial responses from Brazilian regulators, relying on international cooperative approaches, demonstrate how this path taken by the regulatory agencies towards the adoption of international standards and 'good regulatory practices' are relevant for trade liberalisation in line with the WTO's policies. However, most importantly, they evidence the technical work carried out by the enquiry points to the WTO's TBT and SPS Agreements and Committees. In a time of crisis, these actions may have the potential to directly impact access to critical medical products, especially considering Brazil's status as a net importer of such goods.

Additionally, the relevance of the legal disciplines of these WTO multilateral agreements (TBT/SPS) and their implementation through their respective committees, highlights a relatively 'hidden world, related to sites of non-judicial governance within the WTO'.[53] This relates to the role of the WTO, specifically performed by the committees, in promoting processes of information exchange and norm elaboration, and acting as 'facilitators of technical assistance and regulatory learning' in the words of Lang and Scott.[54] By looking at the role of these relatively unnoticed administrative and technical bodies of the WTO, which operate in day-to-day activities, eschewing matters of high politics, these authors have somewhat advanced a shift in the role of this organisation, from a forum for the creation and enforcement of binding legal commitments to an institution for the supervision, monitoring and management of the international trade system. The setback suffered by the Dispute Settlement System from 2018 to 2019, and the pandemic, may accelerate this shift.

Moreover, the transparency provisions and the requirements for notification present both in the TBT and SPS WTO Agreements, implemented by their respective Committees, can also be understood as instruments to promote cooperation among members.[55] A feature of these Agreements rests on their need to be implemented through the sharing of information on domestic trade policies among members, the raising of specific trade concerns, and coordination among members on various aspects including assistance on capacity building.[56] An outcome of these practices can be envisioned, at least in part, in relation to the expertise acquired by the Brazilian regulatory agencies acting before these WTO committees as enquiry points. This may also be reflected in their timely actions reacting to the health crisis and sending prompt notifications to the WTO.

[53] A Lang and J Scott, 'The Hidden World of WTO Governance' (2009) 20 *European Journal of International Law*, academic.oup.com/ejil/article/20/3/575/402393. The work of Lang and Scott analyses specifically the Services Council and the Committee on Sanitary and Phytosanitary Measures (SPS Committee).

[54] ibid 576.

[55] PC Mavroidis, 'Regulatory Cooperation: Lessons from the WTO and the World Trade Regime' (2016) ICTSD and World Economic Forum, e15initiative.org/publications/regulatory-cooperation-lessons-wto-world-trade-regime/.

[56] Lang and Scott (n 53).

It is interesting to note that these actions came in sharp distinction from other policies taken by Brazil's federal government. At the time of writing, Brazil's coronavirus cases hit 1.5 million people, becoming the second country in the world, after the US, to register more than 59,000 deaths from COVID-19 and a new epicentre of the pandemic.[57] In addition to the health and economic crisis that all countries are facing, Brazil also faced an escalating political crisis.

In some ways, the contradiction seen at the international sphere between nationalist policies on one side and efforts for international cooperation to facilitate trade and to harmonise the production of drugs and vaccines on the other, replicates the divergences that have happened at the national level in Brazil. While a federal law was amended to restrict exports on all medical products,[58] in line with nationalistic and populist movements, the several administrative measures mentioned above to facilitate and harmonise trade were based on cooperative efforts with other countries and regulatory networks. It is fair to recognise that, in a federal law enacted on February 2020,[59] the Brazil's Congress had already provided for a broad, exceptional and temporary authorisation for the import and distribution of any materials, medicines, equipment and supplies without registration with ANVISA. However, this temporary waiver was based solely on the discretionary power of the Health Minister. As such, later on, this provision became subject to a fierce political dispute within the Brazilian institutional context on which authority was responsible to authorise the imports without the regular agency registration.[60]

As a result, the case of Brazil illustrates the combination of a two-fold system: a politically driven one with high level authorities; and a technically driven one led by bureaucrats and lower-level policymakers. The first is coordinated by Brazil's executive, currently under Bolsonaro's administration, which contests multilateral organisations' values and principles in promoting coordinated actions at the global level. In the case of the WTO, such criticism is mainly targeted at the most notorious negotiating function of the organisation. However, at the second – mostly hidden and technical – level of the WTO, the articulation of the lower Brazilian domestic bureaucracy with the international bureaucracy around shared ideas has remained preserved and strives to resist. The case of Brazil lays out that, although the President and a minor group of ministerial level authorities push forward

[57] K Watson, 'Coronavirus: Brazil becomes second country to pass 50,000 deaths' *BBC News* (22 June 2020), www.bbc.com/news/world-latin-america-53132225.

[58] Lei n 13.993, as of 23 April 2020. See A Verdélio, 'Bolsonaro sanciona lei que proíbe exportação de produtos médicos e EPI' *Agência Brasil* (24 April 2020), agenciabrasil.ebc.com.br/saude/noticia/2020-04/bolsonaro-sanciona-lei-que-proibe-exportacao-de-produtos-medicos-e-epi.

[59] Lei n 13.979, as of 6 February 2020.

[60] On May 2020, a project for amending Law 13,979/2020 (PL 864/2020), coming from the Chamber of Deputies, transferred back the prerogative to authorise the import of foreign medicines and medical supplies to a previous authorisation of ANVISA, to be given in 72 hours after request, as long as they have been registered for commercial distribution by competent agencies of the US, EU, Japan or China. The project was approved as Law 14,006/2020. However, President Jair Bolsonaro vetoed the power given to ANVISA on the grounds that the transferring of this authority to the agency was unconstitutional. On 19 August 2020 the National Congress overturned the partial veto of Law 14,006.

anti-globalist views and voices along with discretionary measures to respond with urgency, this approach left behind the implementation of more adequate policies to control the pandemic, at least on trade matters. It is the hidden world of trade policies that keeps its movement towards measures favouring access to medical goods, along with promoting trade facilitation and transparency of domestic policies at the global level. To put it in metaphorical terms, this can be described as a four-wheel drive system for automobiles, in which one of the wheels is stuck, while others keep pushing forward.

Table 6.1 The Four-Wheel Drive System

Moving Wheel **'Front Axle'** WTO high level meetings	**The Stuck Wheel** **'Front Axle'** Brazilian high level authorities (presidency and foreign policy representatives)
Moving Wheel **'Rear Axle'** WTO Committees	**Moving Wheel** **'Rear Axle'** Brazilian federal agencies

The analysis does not ignore the limitations of each system. Therefore, the question is posed as to what extent the WTO system can push for resilience of the 'rear axle' of Brazilian agencies to keep the wheels moving in periods of turmoil and institutional change.[61] However, in the current political and sanitary scenario in Brazil, it does considerably support the implementation of the second-best option of public policy. If central government is not developing and implementing a national policy of combating the COVID-19 pandemic, the regional and local governments, on the other hand, are promoting their own policies that are much more aligned to international recommendations. In this case, the measures taken and notified by the technical federal agencies to the WTO, easing the imports of medical goods – of which Brazil is a net importer – may make a visible difference at the end of the day.

V. Final Remarks

The analysis of trade policy responses to COVID-19 is still based on a moving target. Therefore, it is not possible to adequately gauge the outcomes of those measures – no matter whether from a nationalistic type or from an international cooperative type of trade measure to fight the pandemic. Nevertheless, the purpose of this chapter was to identify the forces influencing the current trade and trade-related measures, and to assess the role of the WTO and its extensions

[61] We thank Professor L Alan Winters for this sharp perception and comments about the resilience of national agencies and their technical work under periods of political crisis.

in contributing to them, not only during the crisis but looking back at solid and steady work prior to the pandemic.

In elucidating the hidden works of the WTO, at the technical committee – especially the TBT and the SPS Committees – the coordinated work promoted by the WTO with domestic agencies is relevant in responding to the ongoing crisis. Such coordination has eased and facilitated imports of essential goods to deal with the pandemic, not on purely discretionary basis, but grounded on efforts of scientific and technical cooperation. In addition to that, such coordination also favours transparency of trade policies, even in times of emergency.

It should be recognised that the multilateral trading system managed to avoid the widespread use of beggar-thy-neighbour restrictive policies during the 2008–09 financial crises and thus played its role to prevent a repeat of the afflictions that wrecked the world economy during the 1930s.[62] While it might still be premature to determine whether the WTO system will perform equally well during this sanitary and increasingly deep social and economic crisis, there are hints pointing towards a similar path.

[62] B Ruddy, 'The Critical Success of the WTO: Trade Policies of the Current Economic Crisis' (2010) 13 *Journal of International Economic Law* 475.

PART II

Repackaging World Trade Law and Sustainable Development

7

Trade and UN SDGs 2030: The Interplay between Public International Law and Contract Law

LORENZA MOLA AND CRISTINA PONCIBÒ

I. Setting the Scene

The 2030 Agenda for Sustainable Development recognises international trade as a vector for delivering the Sustainable Development Goals (SDGs).[1] To pursue the achievement of these goals in trade regulation and trade transactions, each separate legal regime engages different subjects and uses different sources. This chapter seeks to bring to light the intermingling and interaction between domestic and international law, and between public and private law, when it comes to achieving sustainability through international trade.

Socio-environmental interests can be incorporated in the regulation of trade through international treaties. In addition, international soft law including principles, guidelines and codes of conduct – mainly developed by international organisations – attempts to direct the behaviour of both states and traders, encouraging voluntary compliance or inspiring business conduct. In implementing their international obligations, states may adopt internal regulations to shape the business environment; some unilateral regulations are able to reach activities that are outside a state's territorial jurisdiction. Traders, whose transnational activities specifically affect the achievement of non-economic interests, while not being legal subjects of international trade law, are the principal subjects of domestic legal

[1] 'Transforming our world: the 2030 Agenda for Sustainable Development', UNGA Res 70/1 (25 September 2015); United Nations Commission on Trade and Development (UNCTAD), 'Report on Trading into Sustainable Development: Trade, Market Access and Sustainable Development' (2016) UNCTAD/DITC/TAB/2015/3. This Report analyses the interactions between trade policy and factors underpinning sustainable development. On the role of the WTO in delivering the SDGs, see WTO, 'Mainstreaming trade to attain the Sustainable Development Goals' (2018), www.wto.org/english/res_e/publications_e/sdg_e.htm. On trade as a means for gender justice, see A Bahri, 'Gender Mainstreaming in Free Trade Agreements: What have we Achieved, and what More is Needed for Inclusive Post-Pandemic Recovery?', ch 10 in this book.

orders under which they may be held liable. Traders' interactions are governed by contract law. Economic operators have increasingly incorporated sustainability into their supply contracts; sustainability has thus reached the stage of a binding, private-to-private legal source – the contract – although this contractualisation of sustainability presents enforcement issues.

Conceptualising the dynamics involving subjects and sources across different legal regimes may assist in understanding how to improve the delivery of SDGs in global trade. Public international law and comparative private law, as different fields of scholarship, offer separate analyses.[2] Arguably, the legal solutions they envisage within their respective regimes can be considered complementary to each other or may suggest that innovative repackaging of public and private law is needed to accommodate environmental and trade interests within the perspective of sustainability. In these brief reflections, the chapter attempts to address the interplay between public international law and private law on trade and sustainability. Sections II and III analyse how public international law and private law currently accommodate sustainable development goals. Section IV discusses the extent to which contractual, domestic and international legal sources interact and shape each other in this respect.[3]

II. Trade and Sustainability from the Perspective of Public International Law

A. Treaties

States are bound by international treaties in various fields relating to SDG areas, including trade, environment, human rights and labour. As a result, they face

[2] In the field of public international law, a typical strand of analysis deals with the 'relations between international law and multi-national enterprises (MNEs)'. See M Karavias, 'Shared Responsibility and Multinational Enterprises' (2015) 62 *Netherlands International Law Review* 91. With respect to the private legal dimension of sustainability, see KP Mitkidis, *Sustainability Clauses in International Business Contracts* (Haag, Eleven Publishing, 2015). In C Beverelli, J Kurtz and D Raess (eds), *International Trade, Investment, and the Sustainable Development Goals* (Cambridge, Cambridge University Press, 2020) the contributions of the various authors are structured in two distinct parts according to whether they adopt a top-down (ie, through public bodies) or a bottom-up (ie, through private initiatives) approach.

[3] In the vein of legal analysis cross-cutting public (international) law and contract law, see P Paiement and S Melchers, 'Finding International Law in Private Governance: How Codes of Conduct in the Apparel Industry Refer to International Instruments' (2020) 27 *Indiana Journal of Global Legal Studies* 303; K Mccall-Smith and A Ruhmkorf, 'From international law to national law: The opportunities and limits of contractual CSR supply chain governance' in V Ulfbeck, A Andhov and K Mitkidis (eds), *Law and Responsible Supply Chain. Contract and Tort Interplay and Overlap* (London, Routledge, 2019) 37; KW Abbott, 'Engaging the Public and the Private in Global Sustainability Governance' (30 November 2011), ssrn.com/abstract=1966730. See also JA van Zanten and R van Tulder, 'Multinational Enterprises and the Sustainable Development Goals: An Institutional Approach to Corporate Engagement' (2018) 1 *Journal of International Business Policy* 208.

multiple and separate obligations that may at times contradict each other. At the same time, to pursue non-trade goals they may use trade tools, and this may be done in a way that is prima facie incompatible with their trade obligations. A typical scenario illustrating this contrast is the relationship between international environmental law and law of the World Trade Organization (WTO) concerning climate change, as illustrated in the following two chapters of this book.[4]

Unless states include sustainable development clauses in their trade agreements,[5] some devices pertaining to the relations between treaties – such as the *lex posterior* and *lex specialis* criteria to solve conflicts of norms between the same parties, coordination clauses and the principle of systemic integration among the general principles of treaty interpretation[6] – may act as gateways for incorporating environmental and social interests into the trade law. Reconciliation of non-trade and trade interests may also be ensured under exception clauses included in trade agreements. Such clauses are a gateway for striking a compromise between contrasting interests as they define legitimate non-trade goals and set other conditions to identify non-precluded domestic measures. This is notably the case of the General Agreement on Tariffs and Trade (GATT) Article XX on 'General exceptions', which allows the incorporation of SDG-related interests into the GATT regime through the objectives that are identified therein.[7]

These gateways at the same time differ and intersect in a number of directions. Coordination clauses are legal solutions that identify directly and establish ex ante which of the contrasting obligations stemming from two different treaties applies in the relationship between states that are bound by both. As general exceptions clauses, they are not necessarily open-ended as regards the interests which can prevail over the interest(s) pursued through the agreements that contain them. Conversely, the principle of systemic integration allows for the incorporation into the trade law of non-trade interests that are not determined in advance; it therefore adapts to the evolution of non-trade interests expressed at the international level. According to this principle and Article 31(3)(c) of the Vienna Convention on the Law of Treaties (VCLT),[8] the interpretation of the provisions of a treaty must also

[4] The debate in literature and case law is too vast and well known to be covered here. See D Boklan, 'Combating Climate Change under the WTO: Exploring the Relevance of Process and Production Methods', ch 8; and L Almeida, 'The EU Green Deal and International Trade Law: Bringing Trade and Sustainability Together', ch 9 in this book, and the references found therein.

[5] This aspect will not be addressed here. On the insertion of sustainable development chapters into trade agreements, with reference to the practice of one specific actor, the European Union (EU), see G Adinolfi, 'A Cross-Cutting Legal Analysis of the European Union Preferential Trade Agreements' Chapters on Sustainable Development' in C Beverelli, J Kurtz and D Raess (eds), *International Trade, Investment, and the Sustainable Development Goals* (Cambridge, Cambridge University Press, 2020).

[6] C McLachlan 'The Principle of Systemic Integration and Article 31(3)(C) of the Vienna Convention' (2005) 54 *International & Comparative Law Quarterly* 279.

[7] Art XX of the General Agreement on Tariffs and Trade (GATT), Marrakesh Agreement Establishing the World Trade Organization, Annex 1A (Marrakesh, 15 April 1994); PC Mavroidis, *The Regulation of International Trade: GATT* (Cambridge, Cambridge University Press, 2016) 414 ff.

[8] Art 31(3)(c) of the Vienna Convention on the Law of Treaties (VCLT) (Vienna, 23 May 1969) states: '3. There shall be taken into account, together with the context: … (c) any relevant rules of international law applicable in the relations between the parties'.

consider their outer context, consisting of international rules applicable between the parties at the moment when the interpretation is being made. Thus, with regard to exception clauses of trade agreements, the principle of systemic integration allows for the interpretation of the terms that specify legitimate non-trade objectives in light of the related international rules. While the WTO Appellate Body has shown restraint from even looking at other treaties,[9] the practice of international courts especially in the field of human rights shows a much more generous attitude towards binding and non-binding international legal sources and international documents.[10] It is also notable that, differently from coordination clauses and the principle of systemic integration, the gateway of general exceptions in trade agreements operates in such a way as to allow for the consideration, at the international level within the sphere of trade law, of not only the non-trade interests that find expression at the international level but also domestic preferences of a state which are unilaterally implemented.

With a focus on the last point, an example may help identify the dynamics involving international and municipal laws, including private law, on the basis of domestic preferences and private actors' preferences. Under the GATT, WTO jurisprudence has specified consumer tastes and habits as one of the criteria to assess the 'likeness' of products under non-discrimination clauses.[11] Were this criterion construed as incorporating product and production methods (PPMs), WTO Members would be able to distinguish lawfully between foreign products or penalise foreign products in favour of domestic products due to the detrimental impact of such products from a non-economic perspective.[12] Legal analyses of this type usually consider the potential inward impact of unilateral regulations as a means of disguised protection. At the same time, domestic regulations, as well as private choices and habits of consumers that are sensitive to environmental and social issues have an outward impact. Domestic approaches can indirectly influence the PPMs of products abroad. In addition, general exceptions provided in Article XX of the GATT, as they have been intended since the *Shrimps* case by the

[9] Art 3.2 of the Understanding on Rules and Procedures Governing the Settlement of Disputes (DSU), Marrakesh Agreement Establishing the World Trade Organization, Annex 2 (Marrakesh, 15 April 1994) provides that the meaning of WTO agreements must be clarified 'in accordance with customary rules of interpretation of public international law'. The Appellate Body has said that those customary rules of interpretation are found in the VCLT. On the WTO Appellate Body's jurisprudence on Art 31(3)(c) VCLT, see H Andersen, 'Protection of Non-Trade Values in WTO Appellate Body Jurisprudence: Exceptions, Economic Arguments, and Eluding Questions' (2015) 18 *Journal of International Economic Law* 383, 391 ff.

[10] R Gardiner, *Treaty Interpretation*, 2nd edn (Oxford, Oxford University Press, 2015) 308 ff.

[11] Arts I and III of the GATT (n 7); *European Communities–Measures Affecting Asbestos and Asbestos-Containing Products*, Report of the Appellate Body (5 April 2001) WT/DS135/AB/R, para 101.

[12] See ch 8 by D Boklan in this book. *cf United States–Measures Concerning The Importation, Marketing And Sale Of Tuna And Tuna Products*, Report of the Panel (15 September 2011) WT/DS381/R para 7.249: 'To the extent that consumer preferences, including preferences relating to the manner in which the product has been obtained, may have an impact on the competitive relationship between these products, we consider it a priori relevant to take them into consideration in an assessment of the likeness'.

Appellate Body,[13] allow for unilateral domestic policies and private actors' preferences to influence the PPMs of foreign products.[14]

From the above discussion, the following dynamics emerge. Domestic approaches to environmental and social interests may achieve expression at the international level through a state's adhesion to treaties; at the same time, domestic approaches to such interests may be shaped by commitments made under international treaties. In order to implement their international obligations in socio-environmental fields, states may adapt or adopt domestic regulations addressing the production and placement of products in their respective markets. This may collide with the commitments they have undertaken under international trade agreements. The discussion shows how the law of treaties is able to accommodate potentially conflicting interests, ex ante or ex post, but also that it cannot impede outward effects which may override the choice of other countries not to be bound by treaties. Unilateral measures adopted by states sensitive to sustainable development may have repercussions abroad as they may affect the behaviour of private actors – producers, traders and consumers – through tariffs, restrictions, labels or other types of incentive.

However, the legal solutions thus envisaged do not exhaust the legal dynamics of the interaction between socio-environmental interests and trade interests. Individuals (traders) are not the formal direct recipients or addressees (subjects) of international trade obligations. Moreover, treaty norms, including trade agreements, very rarely have a direct effect in the domestic legal order of the State parties, in vertical and – even less so – horizontal, inter-private dimensions. Also, international conventional law does not prescribe or otherwise directly involve the domestic liability of private actors for conduct not in line with SDGs. There have been some attempts in this direction. Very recently, within the United Nations (UN) Human Rights Council, the Open-Ended Intergovernmental Working

[13] *United States–Import Prohibition of Certain Shrimp and Shrimp Products*, Report of the Appellate Body (6 November 1998) WT/DS58/AB/R, para 121: 'conditioning access to a Member's domestic market on whether exporting Members comply with, or adopt, a policy or policies unilaterally prescribed by the importing Member may, to some degree, be a common aspect of measures falling within the scope of one or another of the exceptions (a) to (j) of Article XX. Paragraphs (a) to (j) comprise measures that are recognized as *exceptions to substantive obligations* established in the GATT 1994, because the domestic policies embodied in such measures have been recognized as important and legitimate in character. It is not necessary to assume that requiring from exporting countries compliance with, or adoption of, certain policies (although covered in principle by one or another of the exceptions) prescribed by the importing country, renders a measure *a priori* incapable of justification under Article XX'.

[14] L Bartels, 'Article XX of GATT and the Problem of Extraterritorial Jurisdiction. The Case of Trade Measures for the Protection of Human Rights' (2002) 36 *Journal of World Trade* 366. The consideration paid in this chapter to the outward (or 'extraterritorial') impact of the accommodation of socio-environmental interests and trade interests through treaties is separate from the analysis of the extraterritorial application of international obligations upon State parties to environmental and human rights treaties, although the two approaches deal with interrelated and intersecting dynamics. The debate of the extraterritorial reach of states' due diligence obligations in the field of human rights is illustrative of the impact of international law of treaties on transnational business conduct. For a clear conceptual framework, see S Besson, 'Due Diligence and Extraterritorial Human Rights Obligations – Mind the Gap!' (2020) 9 *ESIL Reflections*.

Group on Transnational Corporations and Other Business Enterprises with respect to Human Rights has been discussing a 'legally binding instrument' which would regulate 'in international human rights law' the conduct of economic operators engaging in transnational activities. The revised versions of the original draft of such a 'legally binding instrument' include an obligation upon the State parties to provide for a domestic system of 'legal liability for human rights violations or abuses in the context of business activities, including those of transnational character'.[15] While the final output of this initiative is still to be determined, including whether it will be apt and able to directly engage and impose obligations on private individuals, it can be noted here that it would (only but significantly) concern human rights-related issues of the SDGs.

B. Soft Law

The behaviour of businesses carrying out transnational activities, including businesses trading internationally, has been addressed at the international level through instruments emanating from international organisations. Widely known instruments apply across the board of business activities – from the 1976 Organisation for Economic Co-operation and Development (OECD) 'Guidelines for Multinational Enterprises' (last updated for the fifth time in 2011) to the 2000 UN 'Global Compact' to the 2011 UN 'Guiding Principles on Business and Human Rights: Implementing the United Nations "Protect, Respect, and Remedy" Framework'. Other documents are sector-specific – such as the OECD's 'Due Diligence Guidance for Responsible Supply Chain of Minerals from CAHR Areas'[16] implementing the OECD Guidelines. These types of instruments recommend adhesion to the principles they provide, by states and private actors alike. Insofar as they are international legal documents which play a role as a means of governance, they can be seen as international soft law.[17]

Vis-a-vis the Member States, it could be said that these principles and standards of conduct assume the legal status of the act adopted by the international

[15] UNHRC, Open-Ended Intergovernmental Working Group on Transnational Corporations and Other Business Enterprises with Respect to Human Rights (OEIGWG), Chairman's 'Second Revised draft of the Legally Binding Instrument to Regulate, in International Human Rights Law, the Activities of Transnational Corporations and other Business Enterprises' (6 August 2020), Art 8, www.ohchr.org/Documents/HRBodies/HRCouncil/WGTransCorp/Session6/OEIGWG_Chair-Rapporteur_second_revised_draft_LBI_on_TNCs_and_OBEs_with_respect_to_Human_Rights.pdf. See also Art 9, ibid, determining criteria for 'adjudicative jurisdiction'.

[16] OECD, 'Due Diligence Guidance for Responsible Supply Chains of Minerals from Conflict-Affected and High-Risk Areas', 3rd edn (2016), www.oecd.org/daf/inv/mne/OECD-Due-Diligence-Guidance-Minerals-Edition3.pdf.

[17] Documents issued by human rights treaty bodies, particularly CESCR's General Comment 24 (10 August 2017) E/C.12/GC/24, could also be considered among soft law instruments. On the current blurred distinction between hard and soft law in the light of the role the latter has played, see, from the theoretical perspective of the function of the sources of international law, M Goldmann, 'We Need to Cut Off the Head of the King: Past, Present, and Future Approaches to International Soft Law' (2012) 25 *Leiden Journal of International Law* 335.

organisation that contains them. They are usually created in the form of a resolution or a recommendation, which do not bind Member States to implement their content in domestic regulations. However, a Member State may well decide to adhere to the contents of these instruments by adopting unilateral measures to make such contents mandatory upon private persons under its own domestic legal order.[18] The possible legal dynamics triggered by domestic regulation of business conduct in international trade have already been taken into consideration.[19] Here, it can be pointed out that soft law can be used as a supplementary means of interpretation of treaties under Article 32 of the VCLT.

As regards private actors, the international instruments under consideration certainly do not consider private actors as being the bearers of rights and obligations deriving from themselves, but rather exhort voluntary compliance by private actors or inspire the development of private standards by them. It is worth highlighting here that, although international organisations do not directly regulate business conduct, including conduct abroad, they nonetheless play an important role in launching, adopting and managing adherence to international principles and standards that shape businesses' behaviour. An example is given by the UN Secretariat's initiatives on the 'Global Compact' and on the 'Guiding Principles on Business and Human Rights', both already mentioned. Altogether, the UN initiative now appears formally engaged with the achievement of SDGs, as it is committed to influence private behaviour towards sustainable development.[20] Another example of involvement of an international organisation with the private sector is found within the International Labour Organization (ILO). In recent years, this UN agency has focused its debate on the issue of labour standards through global value chains (GVCs).[21] International labour standards have inspired the conclusion of 'transnational company agreements' (TCAs), including 'international (or global) framework agreements' since the late 1980s.[22] Alongside its role in identifying

[18] With reference to the EU, see, eg, Regulation 2017/821 laying down supply chain due diligence obligations for Union importers of tin, tantalum and tungsten, their ores, and gold originating from conflict-affected and high-risk areas, incorporating the OECD's Due Diligence Guidance for Responsible Supply Chain of Minerals from CAHR Areas (n 16). Regulation 2017/821 of the European Parliament and of the Council [2017] OJ L130/1. See S Van der Velde, 'Curbing Supply-Chain Human Rights Violations Through Trade and Due Diligence. Possible WTO Concerns Raised by the EU Conflict Minerals Regulation' (2017) 51 *Journal of World Trade* 1043. On the pervasive force of the OECD Guidelines for Multinational Enterprises, see J Klabbers, *Introduction to International Institutional Law* (Cambridge, Cambridge University Press, 2009) 193.

[19] See above, section II.A.

[20] 'United Nations Sustainable Development Goals', www.unglobalcompact.org/sdgs/.

[21] International Labour Conference (105th Session), 'Decent Work in Global Supply Chains', Report IV (2016) 2; ILO, Resolution concerning decent work in global supply chains (10 June 2016) para 23(c); ILO, Final Conclusions of the Meeting of experts on cross-border social dialogue (12–15 February 2019) Conclusion no 8, www.ilo.org/wcmsp5/groups/public/---ed_dialogue/---dialogue/documents/meetingdocument/wcms_700599.pdf.

[22] See most recently S Marassi, 'International framework agreements and management of global supply chain: Extra-judicial mechanisms to enforce international labour standards' (2020) *Questions of International Law*, www.qil-qdi.org/international-framework-agreements-and-management-of-global-supply-chain-extra-judicial-mechanisms-to-enforce-international-labour-standards/, and the references found therein. According to this author, the emergence of TCAs as 'a form of transnational

and developing international labour standards, the ILO not only welcomes such inter-private initiatives but considers that it may also play a role throughout all the phases of these agreements, including in conflict resolution or mediation of disputes.[23] Notably, the ILO sees itself as having a role in the enforcement of inter-private agreements through extra-judicial mechanisms (see below, section III).

C. The SDGs as Soft Law

The SDGs themselves arguably represent more than political objectives.[24] They may have the nature of soft law being enunciated in a non-binding legal instrument as a UN General Assembly resolution.[25] Some structural features highlight their importance. On one side, they are intended to form a holistic and integrative approach to development, making the various goals inseparable. On the other side, they are characterised by universality, requiring that change be pursued 'with a sense of the global public good'.[26] Thus, the SDGs can certainly be perceived as voicing community interests in international law, whereby 'community' refers to individuals and/or states,[27] but especially the interests of the international community as a whole.

However, it is argued here that in order for the SDGs to provide, in and of themselves, legitimate grounds for public policies that adhere to one or more of their targets and seek to meet their indicators, their legal relevance in the development of international law should be asserted, and their legal value should be enhanced in the hierarchy of international legal sources. The latter certainly occurs insofar as the SDGs replicate or find expression in specific international norms, such as in human rights treaties, environmental conventions or free trade agreements.[28]

private labour regulation is one way to address [a] "governance gap"', and 'the conclusion of these agreements displays the current shift from public, state-based forms of social regulation to private, self-regulatory initiatives'.

[23] ibid, fn 60, referring to Report of the Governance and Tripartism Department of the International Labour Office for discussion at the Meeting of Experts on Cross-border Social Dialogue, 'Cross-border social dialogue' (12–15 February 2019) 39.

[24] D French and LJ Kotzé (eds), *Sustainable Development Goals: Law, Theory and Implementation* (Cheltenham, Edward Elgar Publishing, 2018).

[25] On the literature debate on the nature of the SDGs, see M Montini, 'L'interazione tra gli SDGs ed il principio dello sviluppo sostenibile per l'attuazione del diritto internazionale dell'ambiente' (2019) 1, 4–7, 9, www.federalismi.it/nv14/articolo-documento.cfm?Artid=38580, and the references found therein.

[26] United Nations, Synthesis Report of the Secretary-General on the Post-2015 Agenda, 'The road to dignity by 2030: ending poverty, transforming all lives and protecting the planet' (December 2014) A/69/700, para 48.

[27] E Benvenisti and G Nolte, *Community Interests Across International Law* (Oxford, Oxford University Press, 2018).

[28] *cf* M Brus, 'Soft law in public international law: a pragmatic or a principled choice? Comparing the Sustainable Development Goals and the Paris Agreement' in P Westerman et al (eds), *Legal Validity and Soft Law* (Cham, Springer, 2018).

Other than this, it is difficult to establish whether SDGs could be used directly to assess the legitimacy of state (trade) measures.

From the perspective of the international law of treaties, it must be assessed in theory and verified in practice as to whether the SDGs could play a role in treaty interpretation. Indeed, they would play a significant role for coordination and incorporation of socio-environmental and trade interests. Under the rules of interpretation of the VCLT, the SDGs (or the General Assembly resolution containing them) should be characterised as internal or external 'context' to a treaty. On the former side, for example, the SDGs might be explicitly mentioned in the Preamble. On the latter side, it is difficult to assert that the SDGs can be considered as 'relevant rules of international law applicable in the relations between the parties' which interpreters of a treaty have to take into account under Article 31(3)(c) of the VCLT. With regard to this provision, it is usually excluded but still debated whether the covered 'rules' encompass non-binding legal instruments.[29] In any case, the SDGs could be considered among the supplementary means of interpretation which interpreters can have recourse to (Article 32 of the VCLT) – and moreover, of particular authoritativeness, given the features attached to them. If interpreters of trade agreements endorse an interpretative role for SDGs, this would favour the incorporation of non-trade interests into trade law in a holistic way, ie, across the whole range of sustainable development goals, and 'universally', ie, in the relationship between any two parties.

In addition, the SDGs could be referred to collectively in a 'sustainability clause' as an essential element of a trade agreement if the parties agree to a conditionality approach to the application of the treaty.[30] However, problems may arise in implementing such a clause when undertaking certain measures or suspending the agreement, due to the vagueness of the terms that any general clause on sustainability with reference to SDGs may entail, and the vague and imprecise content of some goals.

Indeed, the SDGs interact with the principle of sustainable development, and at least some SDGs could be seen as reflecting general principles of international law[31] or contributing to the formation of customary rules.[32] Their 'use' could thus extend to trade relationships with states that have not concluded international

[29] Gardiner (n 10) 307.

[30] Empirical studies exist on the number and coverage of non-trade policy objectives under conditionality clauses in EU agreements: I Borchert et al, 'Trade Conditionality in the EU and WTO legal regimes' (2018) RESPECT working paper, respect.eui.eu/wp-content/uploads/sites/6/2019/02/EU_conditionality_D2.2.pdf. The document analyses whether EU trade agreements include provisions relating to four issues: human rights, labour standards, social matters and the environment.

[31] On the role played by general principles as 'a tool for intra-systemic convergence', by promoting coherence between sub-fields of international law, see M Andenas and L Chiussi, 'Cohesion, Convergence and Coherence of International Law' in M Andenas et al (eds), *General Principles and the Coherence of International Law* (Leiden, Boston, Brill Nijhoff, 2019) 15–16.

[32] *cf* the International Court of Justice on the possibility, the conditions and the modalities of the contribution of the UN General Assembly's resolutions to the formation of customary law through state practice and *opinio juris*, in *Legal Consequences of the Separation of the Chagos Archipelago from Mauritius in 1965* (Advisory opinion) [2019] ICJ Rep 95, para 151.

agreements on the specific topic covered by the SDG at stake. One such example is the incorporation of gender equality considerations in free trade agreements.[33]

III. Trade and Sustainability from the Perspective of Contract Law

Following the above-mentioned soft law instruments, multinational enterprises (MNEs) have drafted their codes of conduct to include the SDGs and promote their compliance internally (within the company and the group) and externally (with respect to their suppliers).[34] More recently, MNEs have started to incorporate the SDGs into their supply agreements by designing contractual clauses specifically dealing with sustainability concerns. This process confirms the authors' assumption, ie, that there is an interplay between public international law and contract law in advancing the SDGs 2030.

Legal scholars in the field have studied 'contracts and regulation', 'contract governance' and contractual regulation of global supply chains extensively. Supply agreements often imply long-term contractual relationships between the parties and these contracts are often part of a larger network of relationships throughout the supply chain.[35] Such literature is very insightful for positioning sustainability contractual clauses (SCCs) in the comprehensive theoretical framework of contract governance.[36] More precisely, legal scholars have explored SCCs within the context of public procurement, investment agreements and international supply chain contracts.[37] The most frequently studied case concerns contractual provisions dealing with the goal of environmental sustainability.[38] These provisions are particularly common in managing commercial relationships between

[33] See A Bahri, Gender Mainstreaming in Free Trade Agreements: What have we Achieved, and what More is Needed for Inclusive Post-Pandemic Recovery?', ch 10 in this book.

[34] A Beckers, *Enforcing Corporate Social Responsibility Codes on Global Self-Regulation and National Private Law* (Oxford, Hart Publishing, 2015); A Beckers, 'Towards a Regulatory Private Law Approach for CSR Self-Regulation? The Effect of Private Law on Corporate CSR Strategies' (2019) 27 *European Review of Private Law* 221; A Rühmkorf, *Corporate Social Responsibility, Private Law and Global Supply Chain* (Cheltenham, Edward Elgar Publishing, 2015); AL Vytopil, *Contractual Control in the Supply Chain on Corporate Social Responsibility, Codes of Conduct, Contracts and (Avoiding) Liability* (The Hague, Eleven International Publishing, 2015).

[35] S Grundmann, F Möslein and K Riesenhuber, *Contract Governance Dimensions in Law and Interdisciplinary Research* (Oxford, Oxford University Press, 2015).

[36] R Brownsword, RAJ van Gestel and H Micklitz, *Contract and Regulation* (Cheltenham, Edward Elgar Publishing, 2017).

[37] Mitkidis, *Sustainability Clauses in International Business Contracts* (n 2); L Cotula, 'Investment contracts and sustainable development. How to make contracts for fairer and more sustainable natural resource investments' (2010) 20 *Natural Resource Issues, IIED* 1; see also, KP Mitkidis, 'Sustainability Clauses in International Supply Chain Contracts: Regulation, Enforceability and Effects of Ethical Requirements' (2004) 1 *Nordic Journal of Commercial Law* 1.

[38] C Poncibò, 'The Contractualisation of Environmental Sustainability' (2016) 4 *European Review of Contract Law* 335.

MNEs and suppliers in GVCs.[39] In this context, contract law serves regulatory goals given that many MNEs govern their global supply chains by relying on international supply contracts.[40] In this sense, it can be said that SCCs are 'legal irritants' with respect to traditional contract theory which focuses on party autonomy and freedom, namely private goals.[41] These contractual clauses concern the public values of the SDGs, while contracts generally focus on the (private) rights and obligations of the parties. In this sense, one may note that the goals of SDGs are transplanted across jurisdictions by the contracts entered into force within MNEs and with their suppliers.

The premise is that only parties to contracts should be able to sue to enforce their rights or claim damages as such. However, the doctrine has proven problematic because of its implications for contracts made for the benefit of third parties who are unable to enforce the obligations of the contracting parties.

The main question concerns the legal meaning of such clauses and, more importantly, whether such clauses are enforceable before the courts and arbitration panels. At least two scenarios must be distinguished here: first, the enforcement in respect of suppliers and sub-suppliers within the GVC; second, the enforcement on third parties to the contract, such as suppliers' employees, local communities, or consumers. The following subsections address the issue of enforceability in respect of these two scenarios.

A. The Legal Nature of Sustainability Contractual Clauses

The first issue here concerns the legal meaning of SCCs. The few empirical studies conducted in this field reveal that MNEs tend to adopt a variety of similar contractual provisions ranging from vague (non-binding) assertions to more precise contractual obligations.[42] Some SCCs contain a clear, binding and verifiable clause

[39] For a sociological perspective, see S Ponte, G Gereffi and G Raj-Reichert, *Handbook on Global Value Chains* (Cheltenham, Edward Elgar Publishing, 2019); G Gereffi, *Global Value Chains and Development: Redefining the Contours of 21st Century Capitalism* (Cambridge, Cambridge University Press, 2018); G Gereffi, J Humphrey and T Sturgeon, 'The Governance of Global Value Chains' (2005) 12 *Review of International Political Economy* 78. For a legal perspective see IGLP Law and Global Production Working Group, 'The role of law in global value chains: a research manifesto' (2016) 4 *London Review of International Law* 57. On the role of contract law in GVCs, see KH Eller and J Salminen, 'Reimagining Contract in a World of Global Value Chains' (2020) 16 *European Review of Contract Law* 1; F Cafaggi and P Iamiceli, 'Regulating Contracting in Global Value Chains: Institutional Alternatives and their Implications for Transnational Contract Law' (2020) 16 *European Review of Contract Law* 44; V Ulfbeck, A Andhov and K Mitkidis (eds), *Law and Responsible Supply Chain. Contract and Tort Interplay and Overlap* (London, Routledge, 2019).

[40] J Salminen, 'The Accord on Fire and Building Safety in Bangladesh: A New Paradigm for Limiting Buyers' Liability in Global Supply Chains?' (2018) 66 *American Journal of Comparative Law* 411.

[41] The expression is from G Teubner, 'Legal Irritants: Good Faith in British Law or How Unifying Law Ends Up in New Differences' (1998) 61 *Modern Law Review* 11.

[42] See, eg, para 1 and para 2 of the sustainability contractual clause of Pirelli Group: 'Sustainability clause', www.pirelli.com/asset/index.php?idelement=59887.

('express term model'). In this case, the issue of whether or not SCCs clauses are binding and enforceable depends on how they are drafted in the contractual text. Generally, unspecified and generic statements are not considered to be contractual terms. One important issue to consider is whether the model clause mentioned here is sufficiently detailed and precise as to create an obligation between the parties and thus be enforceable. In addition, certain SCCs refer to the company's code of conduct ('reference model'). They may also refer to the SDGs or to the national legislation implementing some of the SDGs ('reference to international standards, such as the SDGs, or to the national legislation implementing some of the SDGs').[43]

In any case, the question of whether or not SCCs are binding depends on the wording of the provision of the code of conduct or standard. Thus, in the two cases considered here, the legal nature and binding force of SCCs depends on their wording and clarity. In practice, MNEs usually frame the requirements in broad terms when drafting SCCs, particularly when adopting reference models. Although general terms might be intended to reach a broad audience and retain flexibility in relation to the rules, the terminology risks being so vague as to prevent any clear obligations intended to be extracted from the text. In such a case, SCCs may fulfil other functions that do not require enforcement. They may, for example, play an informative role. New information on the risks of a specific behaviour may alter the relevant social norms. MNEs should therefore accompany their contracts and codes of conduct with underlying clauses, as providing information can have an even greater effect on compliance among suppliers than enforcement.

Additionally, SCCs may also represent a signal or statement that is not accompanied by a great deal of intentions to enforce them. There are numerous instances where laws that aspire to announce or signal a change in social norms are nonetheless accompanied by few enforcement actions. In this case, the contractual form, even though the undertaking may not be legally enforceable, signals the seriousness of the issue for suppliers within the GVC. The increased credibility of the commitment by way of a contract may compensate for the low possibility of enforcing any non-compliance. If they fail to comply, suppliers may therefore fear adverse consequences, although these may not amount to any formal dispute resolution procedure.

B. Enforcing Sustainability Contractual Clauses between the Parties

In the case of enforcement between the parties, MNEs and suppliers seem to favour the assessment of contractual obligations by relying on a cooperative approach, ie, one in which the contracting parties are expected to cooperate, particularly in a

[43] On the relationship between SDGs and CSR, see N Schönherr, F Findler and A Martinuzzi, 'Exploring the Interface of CSR and the Sustainable Development Goals' (2017) 24 *Transnational Corporations* 33.

long-term contractual relationship.[44] One explanation for such an approach can be found in the relational contract theory.[45] In short, the theory considers the formal legal infrastructure governing the contractual relationship to be of secondary importance compared with informal norms of decency, solidarity and cooperation. According to this theory, the remedies upon breach provided by the law are not the only option deserving the attention of practitioners and scholars.

Scholarly literature on the relational theory has typically focused on extra-legal or informal devices for regulating long-term contractual relations. These include consensual adjustment of primary contractual arrangements in light of changing circumstances; informal incentives for performance and cooperation; the tendency to abstain from relying on formal rights and duties; and the frequent use of alternative dispute resolution mechanisms.[46] Indeed, an examination of SCCs confirms the prominence of informal over formal remedies. In discussing informal remedies, the chapter distinguishes between ex ante strategies (ie, before the breach of contract occurs) and ex post remedies (ie, applicable after the breach of the contractual obligation).

It should also be noted that the above-mentioned informal enforcement occurs in the shadow of formal remedies. If the supplier is in breach of SCCs, the buyer can procure a remedy. First, the breach of SCCs might constitute a fundamental violation of the agreement (see the provisions of Article 49(1) and Article 25 of the UN Convention on Contracts for the International Sale of Goods (CISG),[47] for example). However, a fundamental breach occurs when the main obligation under a contract is not fulfilled, or when the parties expressly agree about the fundamental role of certain obligations under the agreement.[48] In this respect, legal scholars and courts often struggle to ascertain if the breach of an SCC amounts to

[44] F Cafaggi and P Iamiceli, 'Contracting in global supply chains and cooperative remedies' (2015) 20 *Uniform Law Review* 135. The article focuses on food global value chains.

[45] IR Macneil, 'Reflections on Relational Contract' (1985) 141 *Journal of Institutional and Theoretical Economics* 541. The network theory of contract law may also be useful to explain the nature of SCCs. This point cannot be further developed here; see, for reference, H Collins, 'Introduction to Networks as Connected Contracts' in G Teubner and H Collins (eds), *Networks as Connected Contracts* (Oxford, Hart Publishing, 2011) 14–15.

[46] Y Adar and M Gelbard, 'The Role of Remedies in the Relational Theory of Contract: A Preliminary Inquiry' (2011) 7 *European Review of Contract Law* 399; JM Feinman, 'Relational Contract Theory in Context' (2000) 94 *Northwestern University Law Review* 737; I Macneil, 'Contracts: Adjustment of Long-Term Economic Relations under Classical, Neoclassical, and Relational Contract Law' (1978) 72 *Northwestern University Law Review* 854.

[47] Arts 49(1) and 25 of the United Nations Convention on Contracts for the International Sale of Goods (CISG) (Vienna, 11 April 1980). Art 49(1) states that: 'The buyer may declare the contract avoided: (a) if the failure by the seller to perform any of his obligations under the contract or this Convention amounts to a fundamental breach of contract; or (b) in case of non-delivery, if the seller does not deliver the goods within the additional period of time fixed by the buyer in accordance with paragraph (1) of article 47 or declares that he will not deliver within the period so fixed'. Art 25 states that: 'A breach of contract committed by one of the parties is fundamental if it results in such detriment to the other party as substantially to deprive him of what he is entitled to expect under the contract, unless the party in breach did not foresee and a reasonable person of the same kind in the same circumstances would not have foreseen such a result'.

[48] Beckers, Enforcing Corporate Social Responsibility Codes (n 34).

a 'fundamental' breach. Moreover, in other cases, the breach of SCCs may result in a non-fundamental breach. This occurs when SCCs are interpreted by courts and scholars as posing ancillary obligations on the parties. Additionally, a fundamental breach should also be 'foreseeable' by the parties according to the general rules on contract interpretation. The main aspect to examine in this respect is once again the wording of the SCCs and/or the manner in which the supplier was informed of the buyer's standards on sustainable development.

Turning to contractual damages, in order to claim damages for the breach of SCCs, the buyer has to prove the breach, the foreseeable damage and the causal relationship between the breach and damage (Articles 45(1) and 74 of the CISG).[49] More specifically, the causal relationship between the breach of an SCC and the related damage will often be a controversial matter that will be even harder to prove if a buyer claims a future loss, which must be evidenced with reasonable certainty. It may be impossible to achieve reasonable certainty, unless, for example, the buyer is subjected to litigation by third parties due to the breach in question and expects to lose the case. Interestingly, if an SCC is breached, it is more likely to result in non-pecuniary damage, usually in the form of reputational harm.

It should also be noted that, generally, the breach of SCCs does not directly influence the tangible quality of the goods. Thus, the legal consequences of their infringement do not follow the usual reasoning according to Article 35(1) of the CISG, which requires the seller to deliver 'goods which are of the quantity, quality and description required by the contract'.[50] Indeed, while Article 35(1) deals with what the contract actually requires, Article 35(2) sets out a series of objective criteria used to determine conformity. It is a subsidiary definition, which only applies to the extent that the contract does not contain any or contains only insufficient details of the requirements to be satisfied under that provision. Thus, the primary consideration is whether the contract requires the goods to be produced while safeguarding

[49] Art 45(1) of the CISG (n 47). Art 45(1) states that: 'If the seller fails to perform any of his obligations under the contract or this Convention, the buyer may: (a) exercise the rights provided in articles 46 to 52; (b) claim damages as provided in articles 74 to 77'. Art 74 (ibid) states that: 'Damages for breach of contract by one party consist of a sum equal to the loss, including loss of profit, suffered by the other party as a consequence of the breach. Such damages may not exceed the loss which the party in breach foresaw or ought to have foreseen at the time of the conclusion of the contract, in the light of the facts and matters of which he then knew or ought to have known, as a possible consequence of the breach of contract'.

[50] Art 35 of the CISG (n 47). Art 35 states as follows: '(1) The seller must deliver goods which are of the quantity, quality and description required by the contract and which are contained or packaged in the manner required by the contract. (2) Except where the parties have agreed otherwise, the goods do not conform with the contract unless they: (a) are fit for the purposes for which goods of the same description would ordinarily be used; (b) are fit for any particular purpose expressly or impliedly made known to the seller at the time of the conclusion of the contract, except where the circumstances show that the buyer did not rely, or that it was unreasonable for him to rely, on the seller's skill and judgement; (c) possess the qualities of goods which the seller has held out to the buyer as a sample or model; (d) are contained or packaged in the manner usual for such goods or, where there is no such manner, in a manner adequate to preserve and protect the goods. (3) The seller is not liable under subparagraphs (a) to (d) of the preceding paragraph for any lack of conformity of the goods if at the time of the conclusion of the contract the buyer knew or could not have been unaware of such lack of conformity'.

the goals of SDGs 2030. If these goals are not expressly required by the contract, the requirements of Article 35(2) of the CISG can then be considered. The way in which the goods are produced influences their value on the market: a buyer may be willing to pay a higher price for goods manufactured and traded in a manner that respects the environment and other values. From this perspective, it could be inferred that goods produced in conditions that violate these goals are not of the quality implicitly required under the contract (Article 35(1)–(2) of the CISG).

In view of the foregoing, it emerges that contract law remedies are not adequate to address breaches of SCCs mainly due to the peculiarities of these provisions. Yet, they concern not only the private autonomy and interests of the parties but also the shared goals and values of SDGs 2030.

C. Enforcing Sustainability Contractual Clauses by Third Parties

Enforcement of SCCs by third parties, such as suppliers' employees, local communities, or consumers, is also possible, albeit difficult. Contract law first and foremost concerns the parties. The doctrine of privity of contract provides that a contract cannot confer rights or impose obligations upon any person who is not a party to the contract. However, the recognition of the rights of a third party to enforce a contract has posed some problems in contract law theory and practice.

The notion of third-party rights to contract is generally accepted across international and European jurisdictions.[51] In this respect, Article 6:110 (Stipulation in Favour of a Third Party) of the Principles of European Contract Law (PECL) states that:

> (1) A third party may require performance of a contractual obligation when its right to do so has been expressly agreed upon between the promisor and the promisee, or when such agreement is to be inferred from the purpose of the contract or the circumstances of the case. The third party need not be identified at the time the agreement is concluded.[52]

Moreover, traditional approaches to third-party rights in contracts under civil law and common law are not easily applicable to the case of third parties to SCCs.[53]

[51] See, eg, Arts 5.2.1. and 5.2.6 of the Unidroit Principles of International Commercial Contracts (2016), www.unidroit.org/instruments/commercial-contracts/unidroit-principles-2016.

[52] Art 6:110 (Stipulation in Favour of a Third Party) of the Principles of European Contract Law (PECL) states: '(2) If the third party renounces the right to performance the right is treated as never having accrued to it. (3) The promisee may by notice to the promisor deprive the third party of the right to performance unless: (a) the third party has received notice from the promisee that the right has been made irrevocable, or (b) the promisor or the promisee has received notice from the third party that the latter accepts the right'. H Beale and O Lando (eds), *Principles of European Contract Law, Part I, Performance, Non Performance and Remedies, prepared by the Commission of the European Contract Law* (Dordrecht, Martinus Nijhoff Publishers, 1995).

[53] ME Storme, 'A Civilian Perspective on Network Contracts and Privity' (2018) 85 *George Washington Law Review* 1740. TM Yeo, 'When Do Third Party Rights Arise Under the Contracts (Rights of Third

In addition, the issue becomes increasingly difficult with respect to SCCs where the notion of third parties may not only include the employees of the suppliers, but also local communities, consumers, NGOs and supporters of SDGs. Here, the issue concerns the identification of the third party. This does not mean that the third party must be defined in the agreement, but it must be identifiable at least as a member of a specific group or class.

The point here is clear: how far can we go in redesigning the doctrine of third-party rights to contract? Private law offers many options in this respect, without the need to reform the structure of contract law.[54] There is clearly a difficulty in enlarging the boundaries of doctrine to include an indeterminate number of potential plaintiffs, as in the case of standing for sustainability. For the sake of completeness, it should also be underlined that some promising strategies to hold MNEs' parent companies and/or suppliers liable before national jurisdictions for the breach of some of the SDGs are now under discussion.[55]

IV. Concluding Thoughts: Interplay of Public International Law and Contract Law

The interaction of international trade and SDGs currently appears to be sustained by sources and subjects, ie, norms and players, within – rather than across – public international law and contract law. However, some dynamics reveal both a potential powerful impact and the need for merging public and private action. Our point follows, that the achievement of the SDGs is pursued by a hybrid regulatory system grounding on both public international law and contract law. One author has noted that the concept of hybridity refers to a system in which different forms of regulation interact, such as contract law (or private law in general), public law, and hard and soft law, relying both on standards developed by international organisations and on private regulation by and between companies.[56]

International law of treaties can accommodate trade and other SDG-related interests in trade agreements. This process is two-pronged: it is triggered by the choices of private actors which express community interests recognised at international level under the SDGs. Conversely, it has effects on private contracts which underpin trade flows. Principles of conduct in international soft law instruments,

Parties) Act 1999 (UK)?' (2001) 13 *Singapore Academy of Law Journal* 34. See also *Chudley v Clydesdale Bank* [2019] EWCA Civ 344.

[54] K Sobel-Read, G Anderson and J Salminen, 'Recalibrating Contract Law: Choses in Action, Global Value Chains and the Enforcement of Obligations Outside of Privity' (2018) 93 *Tulane Law Review* 1. See also Ulfbeck, Andhov and Mitkidis (n 39).

[55] N Bueno, 'The Swiss Popular Initiative on Responsible Business: From Responsibility to Liability' in L Enneking et al (eds), *Accountability, International Business Operations, and the Law: Providing Justice for Corporate Human Rights Violations in Global Value Chains* (Abingdon, Routledge, 2019).

[56] KH Eller, 'Private governance of global value chains from within: lessons from and for transnational law' (2017) 8 *Transnational Legal Theory* 296.

without being legally binding on states and individuals, have prompted private actors to incorporate sustainability in their contractual relations. It is becoming a common strategy to adopt contractual clauses for suppliers within the area of human rights, labour conditions, environmental protection, business ethics and sustainable development. Formulating these clauses in international supply agreements is certainly a helpful first step in communicating MNEs' values and expectations towards commercial partners, addressing societal concerns about respect for SDGs, and protecting their reputations.[57]

Indeed, reliance upon private law tools to render sustainability legally binding, on the one hand, and upon private remedies to enforce sustainable conduct, on the other, could be seen from a dual perspective. From one perspective, it could be said that businesses are called to act as either delegates or agents by international institutions setting principles and voluntary standards. From the other perspective, private tools employed in global production can be seen as pursuing public or community interests which have been identified and endorsed at international level.

An assessment of whether the current public/private interplay in pursuing sustainability in international trade operations is satisfactory from a legal point of view mainly depends on the enforceability of the obligations that bind private actors. The problem here is twofold. First, while private actors are not directly bound by international law, private law – and specifically contract law – has not been designed to assume a public, regulatory function and has proven to be ill-equipped for pursuing public goals. Second, whereas a contract often requires precision, SDG standards are usually identified vaguely and imprecisely. Moreover, the mere incorporation of SCCs into contracts does not make them formally enforceable.[58] The coordination of treaties and contracts in the global market, which could be enhanced by treaties that expressly impose on the State parties the obligation to regulate and enforce sustainable business conduct at home and abroad, has not (yet) been achieved. The authors consider that understanding the interplay of public international law and contract law on the matter will help reconcile the presence of non-binding international goals and irritant contractual provisions in terms of the environment, human rights, equality and poverty in international trade.

[57] A van Heerdenn and S Bosson, 'Private Actors and Public Goods – A new role for the Multinational Enterprises in the global supply chain' (2009) 23 *Management & Avenir* 36.

[58] V Ulfbeck and O Hansen, 'Sustainability Clauses in an unsustainable Contract Law?' (2020) 16 *European Review of Contract Law* 186.

8

Combating Climate Change under the WTO: Exploring the Relevance of Process and Production Methods

DARIA BOKLAN

I. Introduction

The COVID-19 pandemic has shown that the vast majority of emerging infectious human diseases are coming from wild animals.[1] Some of these diseases could be blamed on the human interference in wildlife habitats. This is mostly caused by anthropogenic economic activity which negatively affects and harms wildlife habitats. In addition, air pollution increases the risk of people getting sick with bacterial and viral pathogens that cause pneumonia.[2] Hence, climate change may trigger and magnify the disruptions caused by health pandemics such as COVID-19.

The year 2019 was the second warmest year on record and the end of the warmest decade (2010–19) ever recorded. Carbon dioxide (CO_2) levels and other greenhouse gases in the atmosphere rose to new records in 2019.[3] These drastic changes in climate may be a contributing factor to the current health pandemic. To address the climate emergency, post-pandemic recovery plans need to trigger long-term systemic shifts that will change the trajectory of CO_2 levels in the atmosphere.[4]

Sustainable Development Goal[5] (SDG) 13 is focused on taking urgent action to combat climate change and its impact. SDG 13 provides for the integration of

[1] N Banerjee, 'Q&A: A Harvard Expert on Environment and Health Discusses Possible Ties Between COVID and Climate' *Inside Climate News* (12 March 2020), insideclimatenews.org/news/11032020/coronavirus-harvard-doctor-climate-change-public-health.

[2] ibid.

[3] 'Goal 13: Take urgent action to combat climate change and its impact' (UN), www.un.org/sustainabledevelopment/climate-change/.

[4] ibid.

[5] The 2030 Agenda for Sustainable Development, adopted by all UN Member States in 2015, provides a shared blueprint for peace and prosperity for people and the planet, now and into the future. At its heart are the 17 Sustainable Development Goals (SDGs), which are an urgent call for action by all countries – developed and developing – in a global partnership. See 'The 17 Goals' (UN), sdgs.un.org/goals.

climate change measures into national policies, strategies and planning.[6] To implement this integration, such national policies and strategies need to focus on the process and production methods (PPMs) as they are the main contributors of greenhouse gases (GHG) emissions.

In the OECD report of 1997, the term 'PPMs' was defined as the way in which products are manufactured or processed and natural resources extracted or harvested.[7] In recent years, however, the term has been used much more broadly[8] to include all activities necessary to place the product on the market.[9] The policies aimed at combating climate change and GHG mitigation could be regarded as such activities. Indeed, climate change-related policies targeting GHG reductions often do not deal with products per se and generally address PPMs.[10] An example of this is a policy that may seek to combat 'carbon leakage'. The more a PPM is carbon-constrained, the more costly it becomes, which may lead to loss of income and economic diversification. This could lead to a situation, where

> economic activity can shift to less carbon-constrained jurisdictions and GHG emissions would not be reduced, but simply shifted to other national locations. Therefore, the more carbon-constrained countries can feel aggrieved about additional competitive pressure from the same industries in less constrained countries.[11]

This relocation to countries with less stringent environmental policies is generally referred to as 'carbon leakage'.[12] The mechanisms enshrined in the Paris Agreement[13] are aimed to prevent the carbon leakage and internalise costs for combating climate change.

Currently, as many as 190 countries have ratified the Paris Agreement.[14] Thus, even those states which have not ratified or have withdrawn from the Agreement[15]

[6] 'Transforming our World: The 2030 Agenda for Sustainable Development' (UN), sustainabledevelopment.un.org/post2015/transformingourworld.

[7] OECD, 'Process and Production Methods (PPMs): Conceptual Framework and Considerations on Use of PPMs-based Trade Measures' (1997) OECD/GD(97)137, 7, www.oecd.org/officialdocuments/publicdisplaydocumentpdf/?cote=OCDE/GD(97)137&docLanguage=En.

[8] CR Conrad, *Process and Production Methods (PPMs) in WTO Law. Interfacing Trade and Social Goals* (Cambridge, Cambridge University Press, 2011) 28, 537.

[9] RE Hudec, 'The Product–Process Doctrine in GATT/WTO Jurisprudence' in M Bronckers and R Quick (eds), *New Directions in International Economic Law: Essays in Honour of John H Jackson* (The Hague, Kluwer Law International, 2000).

[10] P Low et al, 'Interface between the Trade and Climate Change Regimes: Scoping the Issues' (2012) 46 *Journal of World Trade* 485, 486.

[11] ibid 485.

[12] C Kaufmann and RH Weber, 'Carbon-related Border Tax Adjustment: Mitigating Climate Change or Restricting International Trade?' (2011) 4 *World Trade Review* 497.

[13] Paris Agreement to the United Nations Framework Convention on Climate Change (Paris, 12 December 2015). The Paris Agreement entered into force on 4 November 2016, 30 days after the date on which at least 55 Parties to the UN Framework Convention on Climate Change accounting in total for at least an estimated 55% of the total global greenhouse gas emissions have deposited their instruments of ratification, acceptance, approval or accession with the Depositary. See 'Paris Agreement – Status of Ratification' (UNFCCC), unfccc.int/process/the-paris-agreement/status-of-ratification.

[14] 'Status of Ratification' (n 13).

[15] On 4 November 2019, the government of the United States notified the Secretary-General of its decision to withdraw from the Agreement, which shall take effect on 4 November 2020 in accordance with

may be affected by it as the signatory countries take actions to fulfil their objectives of the Agreement.

The Paris Agreement enshrines in its Preamble that Parties recognise that 'sustainable lifestyles and sustainable patterns of consumption and *production*, with developed country Parties taking the lead, play an important role in addressing climate change'.[16] Article 4 of the Agreement stipulates that 'each Party shall prepare, communicate and maintain successive nationally determined contributions' that it intends to achieve.[17] Parties shall pursue domestic mitigation measures, with the aim of achieving the objectives of their contributions.[18] Most of such domestic measures directed at the mitigation of the GHG emissions are connected with the PPMs. The purpose of including PPMs in the context of climate change policies is to incorporate the environmental cost of production in the price of products so as to give an incentive to both producers and consumers to limit the use of carbon-intensive or environmentally unfriendly products.[19]

Moreover, the Preamble (recital 1) of the Paris Agreement refers to the UN Framework Convention on Climate Change (UNFCCC), according to which, 'measures taken to combat climate change, including unilateral ones, should not constitute a means of arbitrary or unjustifiable discrimination or a disguised restriction on international trade'.[20] Hence, the UNFCCC, read together with the Paris Agreement, creates a connection between the multilateral trade rules established under the WTO and Paris Agreement.

The OECD recognises that negative impacts of PPMs can be of two sorts. A process or production method can affect the characteristics of a product so that the product itself may pollute or degrade the environment when it is consumed or used (product-related PPMs). Alternatively, a process or production method itself can have a negative impact on the environment through, for example, the release of pollutants into the air or water during the production stage (non-product related PPMs).[21]

Both kinds of PPM can be affected by various WTO law disciplines including taxes, technical regulations and standards. This chapter will assess whether these WTO disciplines are compatible with the commitments WTO Members have taken

Art 28(1) and (2) of the Agreement. See the Notification of the USA, C.N.575.2019.TREATIES-XXVII.7.d (4 November 2019), treaties.un.org/doc/Publication/CN/2019/CN.575.2019-Eng.pdf.

[16] Preamble of the Paris Agreement (n 13) 16th recital (emphasis added).

[17] Nationally determined contributions are – the global response to climate change, according to which all Parties are to undertake and communicate ambitious efforts as defined in the Paris Agreement (in particular, keeping a global temperature rise below 2 degrees Celsius above pre-industrial levels, establishing the global goal on adaptation of enhancing adaptive capacity, providing financial resources to assist developing country Parties, technology development and transfer) with the view to achieving the purpose of the Paris Agreement, which is (according to Art 2) to strengthen the global response to the threat of climate change, in the context of sustainable development.

[18] Art 4 of the Paris Agreement (n 13).

[19] Low et al (n 10) 491.

[20] Art 3, para 5 of the UN Framework Convention on Climate Change (UNFCCC) (Rio de Janeiro, 9 May 1992).

[21] OECD (n 7) 7.

under the Paris Agreement, and consequently how the WTO rulebook can help Members further the fulfilment of their obligations in accordance with SDG 13.

Section II analyses the issue of 'likeness' which is crucial for defining the legal status of the PPMs under WTO law. Section III discusses the WTO-legality of carbon taxes as a traditional instrument for internalising externalities. Section IV reflects on the possibility to justify climate change-related measures under general exceptions enshrined in Article XX of the General Agreement on Tariffs and Trade (GATT). Section V focuses on carbon labelling. Section VI concludes.

II. 'Likeness' and PPMS in the WTO Jurisprudence

This section discusses whether non-physical, unincorporated characteristics of the product such as PPMs could be taken into account for determining 'likeness' of products under the GATT.[22]

PPMs are the factual aspects that constitute the throughput stage of production and hence merely one of the many other aspects of production in a product's life-cycle.[23] However, for the purposes of environmental protection, PPMs assume more importance when the likeness of products is assessed. For instance, in *US–Shrimp*, Japan's third-party submission stated that 'in view of the increased awareness of the importance of policy objectives of environmental protection and resource conservation, it should be noted that certain cases required differential treatment according to PPMs to tackle global and transboundary environmental problems'.[24] However, it might be difficult to establish that two physically similar and competing products are nonetheless 'not like' based on their respective levels of GHG emissions, since this is not a product-related criterion, but rather related to a PPM.[25]

At the same time, the Appellate Body has stressed that

> there can be no one precise and absolute definition of what is 'like'. The concept of 'likeness' is a relative one that evokes the image of an accordion. The accordion of 'likeness' stretches and squeezes in different places as different provisions of the WTO Agreement are applied. The width of the accordion in any one of those places must be determined by the particular provision in which the term 'like' is encountered as well as by the context and the circumstances that prevail in any given case to which that provision may apply.[26]

Moreover, in each of the provisions where the term 'like products' is used, the term must be interpreted in light of the context, the object and purpose of the provision

[22] General Agreement on Tariffs and Trade (GATT), Marrakesh Agreement Establishing the World Trade Organization, Annex 1A (Marrakesh, 15 April 1994).

[23] OECD (n 7) 63.

[24] *United States–Import Prohibition of Certain Shrimp and Shrimp Products*, Report of the Panel (6 November 1998) WT/DS58/R, para 4.50 (*US–Shrimp*); *US–Shrimp*, Report of the Appellate Body (6 November 1998) WT/DS58/AB/R.

[25] Low et al (n 10) 488.

[26] *Japan–Taxes on Alcoholic Beverages*, Report of the Appellate Body (1 November 1996) WT/DS8/AB/R, WT/DS10/AB/R, WT/DS11/AB/R, 21 (*Japan–Alcoholic Beverages II*).

at issue, and the object and purpose of the covered agreement in which the provision appears.[27]

The Preamble of Marrakesh Agreement Establishing the WTO mentions sustainable development as one of its primary objectives.[28] There are three integrated and indivisible dimensions of sustainable development – the economic, social and environmental. All United Nations (UN) members 'recognise that social and economic development depends on the sustainable management of our planet's natural resources'.[29] Therefore, environmental protection in general and combating climate change in particular is the cornerstone for sustainable development. Hence, the notion of 'likeness' under each of the WTO covered agreements must be interpreted in light of the purpose of sustainable development which includes combating climate change in a way that would give 'effect to all the terms of the treaty'.[30]

In addition, Article 3.2 of the Dispute Settlement Understanding enshrines that

> the [WTO] Members recognise that [the dispute settlement system of the WTO] serves to preserve the rights and obligations of Members under the covered agreements, and to clarify the existing provisions of those agreements in accordance with customary rules of interpretation of public international law.[31]

In other words, the 'General Agreement is not to be read in clinical isolation from public international law'.[32] WTO panels and the Appellate Body have the obligation to interpret WTO provisions by taking into account the relevant rules of international law that are applicable to relations among WTO Members.[33] The vast majority of WTO Members have ratified the Paris Agreement. To date, only Turkey and Yemen have signed but not ratified and the United States (US) has withdrawn from the Paris Agreement.[34] Article 18 of the Vienna Convention on the Law of the Treaties enshrines the obligation to respect the object and purpose of a treaty, according to which a 'state is obliged to refrain from acts which would defeat the object and purpose of a treaty when it has signed the treaty […] until it

[27] *European Communities–Measures Affecting Asbestos and Asbestos-Containing Products*, Report of the Appellate Body (5 April 2001) WT/DS135/AB/R, para 88 (*EC–Asbestos*).

[28] Preamble of the Marrakesh Agreement Establishing the World Trade Organization (Marrakesh, 15 April 1994).

[29] 'Transforming our world: the 2030 Agenda for Sustainable Development', UNGA Res 70/1 (25 September 2015).

[30] *United States–Standards for Reformulated and Conventional Gasoline*, Report of the Appellate Body (29 April 1996) WT/DS2/AB/R, 23 (*US–Gasoline*); *Japan–Alcoholic Beverages II*, Report of the Appellate Body (n 12).

[31] Art 3.2 of the Understanding on Rules and Procedures Governing the Settlement of Disputes (DSU), Marrakesh Agreement Establishing the World Trade Organization, Annex 2 (Marrakesh, 15 April 1994).

[32] *US–Gasoline*, Report of the Appellate Body (n 30) 17.

[33] G Marceau, 'Conflicts of Norms of Jurisdictions: The Relationship between the WTO Agreement and MEAs and Other Treaties' (2001) 6 *Journal of World Trade* 1081, 1129.

[34] 'Status of the Paris Agreement', treaties.un.org/Pages/ViewDetails.aspx?src=TREATY&mtdsg_no=XXVII-7-d&chapter=27&clang=_en. See the Notification of the USA (n 15).

shall have made its intention clear not to become a party to the treaty'.[35] Therefore, the Paris Agreement supplemented by UN Framework Convention on Climate Change and relevant soft law instruments on climate change (such as SDG 13) could be regarded as 'relevant rules of international law' to interpret 'like products' under the WTO Agreements.

The determination of 'like products' needs to be made on a case-by-case basis, taking into account the relevant evidence.[36] In particular, the criterion of consumers' tastes and habits may provide room for consideration of non-incorporated PPMs related to GHG mitigation.[37]

Scholars have observed that not only physical aspects of products, but also non-physical aspects may influence consumers' choice and preferences; and in some circumstances, non-physical aspects may be decisive for the determination of 'likeness'.[38] Evidence has shown that consumers have increasingly considered unincorporated PPMs in their purchasing decisions.[39]

In this regard, the Appellate Body has noted that, 'evidence relating to the health risks associated with a product may be pertinent in an examination of "likeness" under Article III:4 of the GATT 1994'.[40] If the 'product' at issue contributes to pollution, then its sale and importation may be restricted on a non-discriminatory basis.[41] Hence, it is possible to argue that while the national treatment obligation of Article III of the GATT prohibits less favourable treatment of like products, it is legitimate to make regulatory distinctions in the treatment accorded to foreign products on the basis of GHG-related PPMs so long as the domestic like products with similar GHG–PPM concerns are granted the same treatment.[42] These observations and arguments show that the likeness test leaves room for the consideration of environment-related PPMs under the criterion of consumers tastes and habits.

The WTO provisions analysed in the following sections strengthen this argument even further.

[35] Art 18 of the Vienna Convention on the Law of Treaties (VCLT) (Vienna, 23 May 1969).
[36] *EC–Asbestos*, Report of the Appellate Body (n 27) para 113.
[37] ibid para 130. Specifically, the Appellate Body noted that 'in addition, even if the cement-based products were functionally interchangeable, we consider it likely that the presence of a known carcinogen in one of the products would have an influence on *consumers' tastes and habits* regarding that product. We believe this to be true irrespective of whether the consumer of the *cement-based* products is a commercial party, such as a construction company, or is an individual, for instance, a do-it-yourself ("DIY") enthusiast or someone who owns or lives or works in a building. This influence may well vary, but the possibility of such an influence should not be overlooked by a panel when considering the "likeness" of products containing chrysotile asbestos. In the absence of an examination of consumers' tastes and habits, we do not see how the Panel could reach a conclusion on the "likeness" of the cement-based products at issue'.
[38] Conrad (n 8) 173.
[39] ibid 237–38.
[40] *EC–Asbestos*, Report of the Appellate Body (n 27) para 113.
[41] Kaufmann and Weber (n 12) 496.
[42] Low et al (n 10) 496.

III. Carbon Taxes Based on PPMS

According to Article III of the GATT 'the contracting parties recognise that internal taxes ... affecting ... *processing* of products ... should not be applied to imported or domestic products so as to afford protection to domestic production'.[43] Some scholars have argued that WTO law traditionally considers a priori WTO-inconsistent taxes (and regulations) applicable to 'production processes and production methods' (including carbon emissions) that do not change the 'physical' properties of a product.[44] However, others have opined that the rule of effective treaty interpretation[45] means that the term 'processing' needs to be given a specific meaning. More specifically, one could argue that the word 'processing' refers to those aspects of production that do not affect the physical properties of a product.[46]

To support this, Joost Pauwelyn confirms that under a carbon tax, the 'nexus' between the tax and the products concerned appears to be tight enough so as to allow adjustment. Therefore, even if technically the carbon tax or charge were levied on producers based on emissions at the production site, rather than directly on products at the point of sale, such tax or charge could still be regarded as 'applied indirectly to products'.[47]

These observations confirm that carbon taxes could be subject to WTO law disciplines, in particular Article III of the GATT and its Ad Note. This means that in case WTO Members levy carbon taxes on the PPMs in order to fulfil their obligations under the Paris Agreement, they at the same time have to comply with the national treatment obligations under Article III of the GATT. This means that a state being subject to both Paris Agreement and GATT obligations may apply carbon taxes to fulfil Paris Agreement objectives as long as it complies with the national treatment obligation under Article III of the GATT.

IV. Can PPMS Relating to Combating Climate Change be Justified under GATT Article XX?

Article XX allows WTO Members to use measures that would otherwise be GATT-inconsistent to pursue certain legitimate policy objectives, such as public morals, human, animal, or plant life or health, conservation of exhaustible natural

[43] Art III of the GATT (n 22) (emphasis added).

[44] Low et al (n 10) 489.

[45] As Appellate Body noted in *EC–Chicken Cuts*, pursuant to the principle of effective treaty interpretation, it is the task of the treaty interpreter to give meaning to all the terms of the treaty. *European Communities–Customs Classification of Frozen Boneless Chicken Cuts*, Report of the Appellate Body (27 September 2005) WTO/DS269/AB/R, para 214.

[46] Conrad (n 8) 152–53.

[47] J Pauwelyn, 'Carbon Leakage Measures and Border Tax Adjustments under WTO Law' in GV Calster and D Prevost (eds), *Research Handbook on Environment, Health and the WTO* (Cheltenham, Edward Elgar Publishing, 2013) 476.

resources, subject to certain legal requirements. These legal requirements include: (1) the chosen objective falls within the objectives listed in the sub-paragraphs; (2) the measure passes the legal tests under the sub-paragraphs (ie, provisional justification); and (3) the chapeau.[48]

In relation to the first requirement, Article 5.2 of the Paris Agreement provides a relevant context. It reads:

> Parties are encouraged to take action to implement and support ... for: *policy approaches* and positive incentives for activities relating to reducing emissions from deforestation and forest degradation, and the role of conservation, sustainable management of forests and enhancement of forest carbon stocks in developing countries; and alternative policy approaches, such as joint mitigation and adaptation approaches for the integral and sustainable management of forests, while reaffirming the importance of incentivising, as appropriate, non-carbon benefits associated with such approaches.[49]

It could be reasonably inferred from the wording of Article 5.2 of the Paris Agreement that it encourages the Parties to take 'policy' measures aimed at combating climate change. Therefore, such measures, including regulations of the PPMs, could be regarded as important and legitimate policy objectives for the purposes of Article XX of the GATT. More specifically, Article XX contains an exhaustive list of public policy exceptions and two of them could be invoked to justify measures applied to combat climate change, namely exception necessary to protect human, animal or plant life or health (paragraph b) and exception relating to the conservation of exhaustible if such measures are made effective in conjunction with restrictions on domestic production or consumption natural resources (paragraph g).

According to the Panel Report in *China–Raw Materials*, the two-tier test is needed to justify a measure under Article XX(b):

> [A] panel must, first, determine whether the challenged measure falls within the range of policies designed to protect human, animal or plant life or health.[50] Second, a panel must thereafter ensure that a measure is 'necessary' to fulfil the invoked policy objective.[51]

As for the first element, in *Brazil–Tyres* the Panel noted that

> to the extent that Brazil is invoking the existence of a risk to animal or plant life or health within the meaning of Article XX(b), it has to establish the existence not just of risks to 'the environment' generally, but specifically of risks to animal or plant life or health. This is consistent with the terms of Article XX(b).[52]

[48] *US–Gasoline*, Report of the Appellate Body (n 30) 119–20.

[49] Art 5.2 of the Paris Agreement (n 13) (emphasis added).

[50] *US–Shrimp*, Report of the Appellate Body (n 24) para 165; *China–Measures Related to the Exportation of Various Raw Materials*, Report of the Appellate Body (22 February 2012) WT/DS394/AB/R, WT/DS395/AB/R, WT/DS398/AB/R, para 7.479 (*China–Raw Materials*).

[51] *China–Raw Materials*, Report of the Appellate Body (n 50) para 7.480.

[52] *Brazil–Measures Affecting Imports of Retreaded Tyres*, Report of the Panel (17 December 2007) WT/DS332/R, para 7.46 (*Brazil–Tyres*); *Brazil–Tyres*, Report of the Appellate Body (17 December 2007) WT/DS332/AB/R. This part was not reviewed by the Appellate Body.

This means that for the measure to be justified under Article XX(b), it is not enough if it is merely aimed at combating climate change; it must also be aimed at mitigating the existence of risks to animal life or health.

Regarding the second element of necessity,

> a panel must consider three relevant factors including the importance of the interests or values at stake, the extent of the contribution to the achievement of the measure's objective, and its trade restrictiveness. If this analysis yields a preliminary conclusion that the measure is necessary, this result must be confirmed by comparing the measure with possible alternatives, which may be less trade restrictive while providing an equivalent contribution to the achievement of the objective.[53]

As for the importance of the measure, 'the more vital or important the common interests or values pursued, the easier it would be to accept as "necessary" measures designed to achieve those ends'.[54] Air is a global common interest and is a globally shared natural resource. Due to its specific characteristics, air pollution has no jurisdictional limitation. As Paolo Galizzi points out,

> some emissions are only problematic upon reaching harmful concentrations in the atmosphere, as in the cases of ozone depletion and climate change, introducing the further complication of allocating how and where reductions should be made and who pay for them.[55]

Therefore, climate change is a global problem, and taking into account that most of the WTO Members are Parties to the Paris Agreement, it should not be problematic for the measure aimed at combating climate change to satisfy this criterion.

As for the extent of the contribution to the achievement of the measure's objective, the Appellate Body accepted that a measure could be considered 'necessary' even if the contribution of the measure 'is not immediately observable'.[56] This is exactly the case of the measures aimed at combating climate change; their contribution could be seen only through a long period of time. Article 14.2 of the Paris Agreement also stipulates that the 'Conference of the Parties … shall undertake its first global stocktaking in 2023 and every five years thereafter unless otherwise decided by the Conference of the Parties serving as the meeting of the Parties to this Agreement'.[57]

Moving to the criterion of trade restrictiveness and possible less trade-restrictive alternatives, this would be the obligation of the complaining party to show the existence of less trade-restrictive alternatives with the same contribution to combating climate change. For instance, technical regulations and standards with respect to the PPMs might be considered less trade-restrictive alternatives than import bans or taxes levied on goods with a high carbon footprint.

[53] *Brazil–Tyres*, Report of the Appellate Body (n 52) para 178.

[54] *EC–Asbestos*, Report of the Appellate Body (n 27) para 172.

[55] P Galizzi, 'Air, Atmosphere and Climate Change' in S Alam et al (eds), *Routledge Handbook of International Environmental Law* (Abingdon, Routledge Handbooks, 2013).

[56] *Brazil–Tyres*, Report of the Appellate Body (n 52) para 151.

[57] Art 14.2 of the Paris Agreement (n 13).

To justify measures combating climate change under Article XX(g), three requirements should be satisfied. The first is whether climate could be regarded as an exhaustible natural recourse. The notion of 'exhaustible natural resource' was examined by the Appellate Body in *US–Shrimp*. The Appellate Body noted that

> the words of Article XX(g), 'exhaustible natural resources', were actually crafted more than 50 years ago. They must be read by a treaty interpreter in the light of contemporary concerns of the community of nations about the protection and conservation of the environment ... We note that the generic term 'natural resources' in Article XX(g) is not 'static' in its content or reference but is rather 'by definition, evolutionary'.[58]

Moreover, the clean air was considered to be an 'exhaustible natural resource' by the Panel in *US–Gasoline*, where the Panel ruled that 'clean air was a resource (it had value) and it was natural. It could be depleted'. Accordingly, the Panel found that a policy to reduce the depletion of clean air was a policy to conserve a natural resource within the meaning of Article XX(g).[59]

Considering the international importance given today to the problem of climate change – and the catastrophic consequences that are linked to it for all forms of life on earth – it would be surprising if the WTO did not accept the planet's atmosphere (that is, the layer of gases around the earth that regulates the planet's climate) as an 'exhaustible natural resource'.[60] Therefore climate is likely to be considered as an exhaustible natural resource under Article XX(g) of the GATT.

The second requirement is that the measure should 'relate to' the conservation of climate. The 'relating to' criterion must be considered by looking at the challenged measure 'in light of its policy and regulatory context and not in isolation'.[61] There must be a close and genuine relationship between the ends and means.[62] However, such an assessment would not require an evaluation of the actual impact of the concerned measure.[63] There is therefore no need for the Panel to decide, in quantitative or qualitative terms, precisely what level of contribution a challenged measure has made to the objective. Instead, the Panel looks at the nature of the challenged measure to determine whether, as a matter of design, aim and architecture, they assist, support or further the goal.[64] Article XX(g) does not prescribe an empirical effects test, given the well-known problems associated with determining causation.[65] Therefore, unlike the 'necessity' test, the assessment of 'relating to' does not require the respondent to establish the contribution of the measure to its objective and the actual impact of the measure. It is sufficient to show that the

[58] *US–Shrimp*, Report of the Appellate Body (n 24) paras 128–30.

[59] *US–Gasoline*, Report of the Panel (20 May 1996) WT/DS2/R; *US–Gasoline*, Report of the Appellate Body (n 30) para 6.37. This part was not reviewed by the Appellate Body.

[60] Pauwelyn (n 47) 492.

[61] *China–Measures Related to the Exportation of Rare Earths, Tungsten and Molybdenum*, Report of the Appellate Body (29 August 2014) WT/DS431/AB/R, paras 5.108–5.109 (*China–Rare Earths*).

[62] *US–Shrimp*, Report of the Appellate Body (n 24) para 136.

[63] *China–Rare Earths*, Report of the Appellate Body (n 61) para 5.147.

[64] ibid 5.109 upholding para 7.379 of the Report of the Panel.

[65] ibid 5.112.

measure 'assists, supports or furthers the objective'. Also, there is no need to assess the trade restrictiveness of the measure. The word 'conservation', in turn, means 'the preservation of the environment, especially of natural resources'.[66] This means that a measure should obviously be aimed at the preservation of climate in accordance with the Paris Agreement obligations.

With respect to the third requirement, the Appellate Body noted that Article XX(g) permits trade measures relating to the conservation of exhaustible natural resources if such trade measures work together with restrictions on domestic production or consumption.[67] This criterion is directly connected with the PPMs, which should 'operate' to conserve climate as exhaustible natural resource. To satisfy this criterion, such measures should work together with restrictions on domestic PPMs connected with GHG emissions.

The last step in the analysis is the chapeau. The chapeau of Article XX imposes additional requirements on measures that are found to violate an obligation under GATT 1994, even though these measures are provisionally justified under one of the general exceptions. The chapeau requires that the measures shall not be 'applied in a manner which would constitute a means of arbitrary or unjustifiable discrimination between countries where the same conditions prevail, or a disguised restriction on international trade'.[68] The function of the chapeau is to prevent the abuse of general exceptions.[69] The analysis of whether the application of a measure results in arbitrary or unjustifiable discrimination should focus on the cause or rationale given for the discrimination.[70] In *US–Shrimp*, the Appellate Body clarified the meaning of 'arbitrary' or 'unjustifiable' discrimination. It viewed the US measure as arbitrary, as it was a 'rigid and unbending requirement' that required shrimp-exporting countries to adopt a regulatory programme that is essentially the same as the US programme.[71] It determined that the application of the measure amounted to unjustified discrimination because, while the US negotiated the exportation of shrimp into its territory seriously with some WTO Members for concluding international agreements for the conservation of sea turtles, it did not do so with other WTO Members.[72] It is likely that the measures aimed at combating climate change face the same difficulties that the US measure faced in *US–Shrimp*. First, the respondent might be accused of forcing other WTO Members to adopt environmental standards that are essentially the same or very similar to its own standards. Second, other WTO Members might show that they already have measures in place to promote their climate policy. Third, it would be

[66] *China–Raw Materials*, Report of the Appellate Body (n 50) para 355.

[67] ibid 360.

[68] *European Communities–Measures Prohibiting the Importation and Marketing of Seal Products*, Report of the Appellate Body (16 June 2014) WT/DS400/AB/R, WT/DS401/AB/R, para 5.296 (EC–Seal Products).

[69] *US–Gasoline*, Report of the Appellate Body (n 30) 20–21.

[70] *Brazil–Tyres*, Report of the Appellate Body (n 52) 246.

[71] *US–Shrimp*, Report of the Appellate Body (n 24) paras 163, 177.

[72] ibid, paras 166, 172.

burdensome for the respondent to multilaterally negotiate with WTO Members an agreement or understanding that aims to reduce GHG emissions.

In addition, the examination of whether a measure is applied in a manner that would constitute a means of 'arbitrary or unjustifiable discrimination between countries where the same conditions prevail' necessitates an assessment of whether the 'conditions' prevailing in the countries between which the measure allegedly discriminates are 'the same'. For this assessment, only 'conditions' that are relevant for establishing arbitrary or unjustifiable discrimination in light of the measure's specific character should be considered. The question therefore is whether the conditions prevailing in different countries are relevantly 'the same'.[73] In other words, 'conditions' relating to a particular policy objective under the applicable subparagraph are relevant for this analysis. If a respondent considers that the conditions relating to the policy objective prevailing in different countries are not 'the same', it bears the burden of proving that claim.[74] Pauwelyn notes that the following questions should be addressed to see if the requirements of the chapeau are met: does the domestic climate change legislation take account of local conditions in foreign countries or does it essentially require that foreign countries adopt domestic policies?[75] Pauwelyn also notes that 'it may force the carbon-restricting country to consider whether a foreign country already imposes emission cuts or otherwise addresses climate change'. Also 'the requirement to take into consideration different conditions which may occur in different foreign countries, may force the carbon-restricting country to consider whether developing countries should carry the same burden as other countries'.[76]

In line with these observations the Preamble of the Paris Agreement stipulates that the Parties pursue 'the principle of equity and common but differentiated responsibilities and respective capabilities, in the light of different national circumstances'.

V. Carbon Labelling and PPMS

Another effective tool to fulfil Paris Agreement obligations is to apply technical regulations with respect to PPMs as a condition for importation. While the TBT Agreement explicitly refers to PPMs,[77] it does not define this notion. Hence, the exact coverage of the Agreement with respect to PPMs, especially unincorporated PPMs, is not beyond debate.[78]

[73] *EC–Seal Products*, Report of the Appellate Body (n 68) para 5.299.
[74] ibid para 5.301.
[75] Pauwelyn (n 47) 496–98.
[76] ibid 496.
[77] See paras 1 and 2 in Annex 1 of the Agreement on Technical Barriers to Trade, Marrakesh Agreement Establishing the World Trade Organization, Annex 1A (Marrakesh, 15 April 1994) (TBT Agreement).
[78] Conrad (n 8) 375.

Annex I to the TBT Agreement defines technical regulation as follows:

> Document which lays down products characteristics or their *related process and production methods*, including the applicable administrative provisions, with which compliance is mandatory. It may also include or deal exclusively with terminology, symbols, packaging, marking or labelling requirements [as they apply to a *product, process or production method*] (emphasis added).

Standard is defined as:

> Document approved by a recognised body, that provides, for common and related use, rules, guidelines or characteristics for products or *related process and production methods*, with which compliance is not mandatory. It may also include or deal exclusively with terminology, symbols, packaging, marking or labelling requirements as they apply to a *product, process or production method*.[79]

The word 'related' is present in both first sentences of the definitions of technical regulation and standard, but it is absent in the second sentences in both definitions. This word could be interpreted to mean 'having physical impact on the product'. This interpretation means that only PPMs altering the physical characteristics of a product, so-called incorporated PPMs, are covered by the TBT Agreement.[80] Pauwelyn argues that the carbon footprint of a product could be found to be related to 'product characteristics' or 'related' PPM. Nothing in the text of the definition of 'technical regulation' requires that product characteristics or their related PPMs must be physically incorporated in the end product.[81]

The Appellate Body has clarified that 'the word "characteristic" has a number of synonyms that are helpful in understanding its ordinary meaning. Thus, the "characteristics" of a product include any objectively definable "features", "qualities", "attributes", or other "distinguishing mark" of a product'.[82] In the definition of a 'technical regulation' in Annex 1.1, the TBT Agreement itself gives certain examples of 'product characteristics', including, for example, 'terminology, symbols, packaging, marking or labelling requirements'.[83] These examples indicate that 'product characteristics' not only include the features and qualities intrinsic to the product itself, but also its related 'characteristics' such as the means of identification, the presentation and the appearance of a product. The definition of 'technical regulation' provides that such a regulation

> may also include or deal exclusively with terminology, symbols, packaging, marking or labelling requirements … The use here of the word 'exclusively' and the disjunctive word 'or' indicates that a 'technical regulation' may be confined to laying down only one or a few 'product characteristics'.[84]

[79] Annex 1 of the TBT Agreement (n 77) (emphasis added).
[80] Conrad (n 8) 378.
[81] Pauwelyn (n 47) 33.
[82] *EC–Asbestos*, Report of the Appellate Body (n 27) para 67.
[83] Annex 1 of the TBT Agreement (n 77).
[84] *EC–Asbestos*, Report of the Appellate Body (n 27) para 67.

Therefore, all technical regulations and standards in the form of labelling requirements regarding non-incorporated PPMs, including those which contain information in respect of GHG emitted in the process of production, may fall under the scope of the TBT Agreement.

Articles 2.1, 2.2 and 2.4 of the TBT Agreement are amongst the most likely provisions to be invoked for challenging a carbon labelling measure. In other words, a complainant may argue that a carbon labelling measure is discriminatory (ie, it is not consistent with MFN and national treatment (NT) obligations), creates unnecessary obstacles to trade, or is not consistent with a relevant international standard. With respect to the non-discrimination obligation (Article 2.1 of the TBT Agreement), the carbon labelling requirements that apply equally to both domestic and imported like products and are the same for all WTO Members may be de jure consistent with MFN and NT obligations. However, carbon labelling may amount to de facto discrimination against imported like products and hence could be seen as a possible violation of NT obligations.

This is because the application of the regulation can disproportionately impact foreign industries more than domestic industries, because foreign industries that would like to keep exporting need to adapt their products solely and exclusively for the markets of a particular WTO Member applying carbon labelling, even if the market of such Member represents only a fraction of its sales. This need to adapt would increase the cost of production for foreign industries, thereby increasing the price of foreign products.[85] The Appellate Body in *US–COOL* decided that such an examination 'must take account of all the relevant features of the market, which may include particular characteristics of the industry, the relative market shares in a given industry, consumer preferences, and historical trade patterns'.[86] Therefore to establish de facto discrimination, a panel should analyse the operation of the challenged carbon labelling in the particular market. Moreover, the Appellate Body has clarified that if the respondent can show that the detrimental impact on imported products exclusively stems from a legitimate regulatory distinction rather than discrimination, then the challenged measure is not inconsistent with Article 2.1 of the TBT Agreement.[87] Hence, the TBT Agreement permits a detrimental impact on 'competitive opportunities for imports in cases where such detrimental impact on imports stems exclusively from legitimate regulatory distinctions'.[88] Therefore, the country applying a carbon labelling requirement could argue that its measure has some detrimental impact but this impact stems

[85] A Bahri, 'The Mexican Front-of-Pack Labeling Reform: Is it Compatible with International Trade Law?' *Journal of World Investment and Trade* (2021, forthcoming).

[86] *United States–Certain Country of Origin Labelling (COOL) Requirements*, Report of the Appellate Body (23 July 2012) WT/DS384/AB/R, WT/DS386/AB/R, para 269 (*US–COOL*).

[87] *United States–Measures Concerning the Importation, Marketing and Sale of Tuna and Tuna Products*, Report of the Appellate Body (16 May 2012) WT/DS381/AB/R, para 21 (*US–Tuna II*).

[88] *United States–Measures Affecting the Production and Sale of Clove Cigarettes*, Report of the Appellate Body (24 April 2012) WT/DS406/AB/R, paras 174–75.

exclusively from legitimate regulatory distinction rather than discrimination against a particular group of imported products.[89]

Moving to the possible challenge of carbon labels under Article 2.2 of the TBT Agreement, the analysis of whether a measure creates unnecessary obstacles to international trade is based on examination of the following factors: the legitimate objective; the degree of contribution to the achievement of it; the trade-restrictiveness of the measure; and the risks non-fulfilment would create.[90] A 'legitimate objective' within the meaning of Article 2.2 of the TBT Agreement constitutes an aim or target that is lawful, justifiable or proper.[91] The aim or target relates to the underlying policy concern to be addressed through the measure.[92] The TBT Agreement treats environmental protection as a legitimate objective and allows WTO Members to 'tak[e] measures necessary to ensure … the protection of human, animal or plant life or health, of the environment'.[93] Article 2.2 further provides that

> technical regulations shall not be more restrictive than necessary to fulfil a legitimate objective, taking account of the risks non-fulfilment would create. Such legitimate objectives are, *inter alia*: … protection of human health and safety, animal or plant life or health, or the environment.[94]

Similar policy objectives are also recognised in other WTO Agreements such as the Preamble of the Agreement on Agriculture on 'the need to protect the environment', and the Preamble of the SPS Agreement on the 'improvement of the human and animal heath'. These provisions provide a relevant context for the interpretation of the TBT Agreement, as the Appellate Body has confirmed, 'objectives recognised in the provisions of other covered agreements may provide guidance for, or may inform, the analysis of what might be considered to be a legitimate objective under Article 2.2 of the TBT Agreement'.[95]

Therefore, the objective to combat climate change and GHG mitigation may be considered a 'legitimate objective' under the TBT Agreement.

The degree of contribution that the measure makes to the achievement of the objective is relevant to identify whether the regulation 'fulfils' the legitimate objective in the context of Article 2.2 of the TBT Agreement.[96] A contribution exists where there is a 'genuine relationship of ends and means' between the measure and

[89] Bahri (n 85).

[90] *US–Tuna II*, Report of the Appellate Body (n 87) para 318.

[91] ibid para 313.

[92] *Australia–Certain Measures Concerning Trademarks, Geographical Indication and other Plain Packaging Requirements Applicable to Tobacco Products and Pack*, Report of the Panel (28 June 2018) WT/DS435/R, WT/DS441/R, WT/DS458/R, WT/DS467/R28, para 7.198 (*Australia–Tobacco Plain Packaging*).

[93] Preamble of the TBT Agreement (n 77).

[94] ibid Art 2.2.

[95] *US–Tuna II*, Report of the Appellate Body (n 87) para 313.

[96] ibid paras 315–16.

the objective it pursues.[97] Such contribution is supposed to be significant.[98] The design, architecture and evidence of application of the technical regulation serve to guide the Panel in such as assessment.[99] For the WTO Member applying carbon labelling, it can be difficult to establish a causal link between combating climate change and carbon labelling, because measures taken to combat climate change may not show an immediate impact and that such an impact 'can only be evaluated with the benefit of time'.[100] However, a connection can be shown between the labelling regulation (the means to achieve the objective) and its influence on consumer behaviour (the intended objective).[101]

According to Article 2.2 of the TBT 'technical regulations shall not be more trade-restrictive than necessary to fulfil a legitimate objective, taking account of the risks non-fulfilment would create'. The Appellate Body noted that 'some' trade restrictiveness is allowed.[102] Analysis of this provision was developed in *Australia–Tobacco Plain Packaging*, where the Panel stated that for the purposes of the analysis under Article 2.2 of the TBT Agreement, it does not suffice that the technical regulation is trade-restrictive per se.[103] The measure must impose a limiting effect on international trade.[104] The evaluation of a limiting effect could be based on qualitative assessment of the design of the technical regulation, or on quantitative assessment of the actual trade effects it creates, or both.[105] Further this assessment was elaborated in the recent Appellate Body Report in *Australia–Tobacco Plain Packaging*, where the Appellate Body noted that 'measures are trade-restrictive, insofar as, by reducing the use of … products, they reduce the volume of imported … products on the … market, and thereby have a "limiting effect" on trade'.[106] Therefore carbon labels may or may not be considered as trade restrictive measures, depending on the extent to which they reduce the use and sale of imported products in a given market. In the majority of cases brought under Article 2.2 of the TBT Agreement, 'a "comparative analysis" of the evaluated measure and proposed alternatives is required[107] in the assessment of whether the measure is *more* trade-restrictive than necessary'.[108] Gregory Shaffer observes that 'it will be more difficult for complainants to win Article 2.2 claims because of the [Appellate Body's] focus on the "degree" to which an alternative meets a respondent's objective, which can be narrowly defined'.[109] Therefore the WTO

[97] *US–COOL*, Report of the Appellate Body (n 86) para 462.
[98] *Brazil–Tyres*, Report of the Appellate Body (n 52) para 210.
[99] *US–Tuna II*, Report of the Appellate Body (n 87) para 317.
[100] *Brazil–Tyres*, Report of the Appellate Body (n 52) para 210.
[101] *Australia–Tobacco Plain Packaging*, Report of the Panel (n 92) para 7.1034. See also Bahri (n 85).
[102] *US–COOL*, Report of the Appellate Body (n 86) para 375.
[103] *Australia–Tobacco Plain Packaging*, Report of the Panel (n 92) para 7.1166.
[104] ibid para 7.1166.
[105] ibid.
[106] ibid para 7.3.
[107] *US–Tuna II*, Report of the Appellate Body (n 87) para 322.
[108] *US–COOL*, Report of the Appellate Body (n 86) para 376.
[109] G Shaffer, 'The WTO Tuna-Dolphin II Case (United States – Measures Concerning the Importation, Marketing and Sale of Tuna and Tuna Products)' (2013) 107 *American Journal of International Law* 192.

Member applying carbon labelling may argue that even though carbon labelling restricts trade and alternatives presented by the complainant can be found to be less trade-restrictive, they may not make an equivalent contribution to the objective of combating climate change.

The assessment of risks of non-fulfilment requires a consideration of the nature of the risks at hand, and the gravity of consequences that would arise from non-fulfilment of the legitimate objective through the measure.[110] The relevant points for evaluation are '*inter alia*: available scientific and technical information related processing technology or intended end-uses of products'.[111] As was already mentioned, the mere fact that 189 states have ratified the Paris Climate Agreement shows that risk of not fulfilment of the objective of combating climate change is obvious and evident.

To assess the compatibility of a carbon labelling requirement under Article 2.4 of the TBT Agreement, it should be noted that use of labelling regarding unincorporated PPMs has increased over recent years, both in the form of mandatory labelling as a policy tool and in the form of voluntary labelling that is often used by producers for marketing purposes.[112] However, there are no international standards agreed in this respect.

According to Article 2.4 of the TBT Agreement,

> where technical regulations are required and relevant international standards exist or their completion is imminent, Members shall use them … as a basis for their technical regulations except when such international standards … would be an ineffective or inappropriate means for the fulfilment of the legitimate objectives pursued.[113]

It therefore remains unclear which climate change standards could be regarded as 'international standards' for TBT purposes.[114] This is because the issue of climate change per se is not part of the WTO's ongoing work programme and there are no WTO rules specific to climate change.[115] The International Organization for Standardization (ISO) has adopted four standards[116] that include requirements for quantification and reporting of greenhouse gas emissions and reductions. However, these standards are related to conformity assessment procedures and do not include any product-specific requirements on emission levels. Hence, it is questionable whether they could be regarded as 'relevant' international standards for technical regulations in the meaning of Article 2.4 of the TBT Agreement.[117]

[110] *US–Tuna II*, Report of the Appellate Body (n 87) para 322.
[111] ibid para 321.
[112] ibid 382. For instance, GHG labelling is used in the UK, Switzerland, Australia and Japan.
[113] Art 2.4 of the TBT Agreement (n 77).
[114] Pauwelyn (n 47) 481.
[115] 'The multilateral trading system and climate change: introduction' (WTO), www.wto.org/english/tratop_e/envir_e/climate_intro_e.htm.
[116] International Organization for Standardization (ISO), 14064-3:2006 and 14065:2007, www.iso.org/standard/38382.html, www.iso.org/standard/40685.html.
[117] United States–Measures Concerning the Importation, Marketing and Sale of Tuna and Tuna Products, Report of the Panel (15 September 2011) WT/DS381/R, para 7.701.

VI. Conclusion

Despite their different objectives, the Paris Agreement and WTO Agreement are complementary in terms of their distributional consequences of climate change policies.[118] The WTO law appears to leave room for states to take measures addressing the climate impacts of the production process.[119] Despite its many tenuous compromises and infirmities, the Paris Agreement represents a hard fought deal to achieve SDG 13. Countries made significant concessions from long-held positions in the closing hours of the conference, thus making the final agreement possible.[120]

Now it is a question of particular implementation of measures aiming at the fulfilment of Paris Agreement objectives in accordance with the WTO legal regime. Most of these measures are connected with the PPMs. They have a clear connection with the WTO legal regime, which could be seen as the most effective instrument to fulfil Paris Agreement objectives.

This complementariness calls for repackaging the WTO law to ensure that it accommodates sustainable development. Repackaging here does not entail changing the rulebook; it merely entails interpreting the rulebook in line with sustainable development goals. Today's economic development is limited not by the level of scientific or technical progress, but rather by the condition of the environment and, more importantly, the condition of climate.

We are witnessing the process of merging the environmental and economic elements of sustainable development. This approach may give rise to an ecocentric approach to economic development, as opposed to an anthropocentric approach, and this will take us a step closer to sustainable economic development.

[118] J Stephenson and S Upton, 'Competitiveness, Leakage, and Border Adjustment: Climate Policy Destructions?' (2009) OECD Round Table on Sustainable Development, SG/SD/RT, www.oecd.org/sd-roundtable/papersandpublications/43441650.pdf, 3.

[119] D Bodansky, J Brunnee and L Rajamani, *International Climate Change Law* (Oxford, Oxford University Press, 2017) 340.

[120] ibid 249.

9

The EU Green Deal and International Trade Law: Bringing Trade and Sustainability Together

LUANA ALMEIDA*

I. Introduction

In December 2019, the European Commission launched the European Green Deal[1] – the blueprint for European policy for the upcoming years. The Deal reinforces the European Union's (EU) commitment to sustainability, and it is an essential part of its strategy to implement the United Nation's 2030 Agenda and the Sustainable Development Goals (SDGs).[2] It is a comprehensive document, with proposals addressing several SDGs, such as Goal 7 (affordable and clean energy), Goal 11 (sustainable cities and communities) and Goal 12 (responsible consumption and production).

The Green Deal, however, especially reinforces the commitments concerning Goal 13 (ie, take urgent action to combat climate change and its impacts). With this document as a roadmap, the EU aims to transition to a circular economy[3] and to be climate-neutral by 2050. That means, it aims to be an economy with net-zero greenhouse gas emissions. This objective is at the core of the Green Deal and is in line with the EU's commitment to global climate action under the Paris

* This chapter represents the opinions of the author. It is not meant to represent the position or opinions of the European Commission or its Members, nor the official position of any staff members. Any errors are the fault of the author only.

[1] Commission, Communication to the European Parliament, the European Council, the Council, the European Economic and Social Committee and the Committee of the Regions 'The European Green Deal' COM (2019) 640 (Green Deal).

[2] ibid 3; 'Transforming our world: the 2030 Agenda for Sustainable Development', UNGA Res 70/1 (25 September 2015).

[3] A circular economy is an economic model based, inter alia, on sharing, leasing, reuse, repair, refurbishment and recycling, in an (almost) closed loop, which aims to retain the highest utility and value of products, components and materials at all times. See D Bourguignon, 'Closing the Loop: New circular economy package' (2016) European Parliamentary Research Service, Briefing, www.europarl.europa.eu/RegData/etudes/BRIE/2016/573899/EPRS_BRI(2016)573899_EN.pdf.

Agreement,[4] which has the goal of keeping the global temperature increase to well below 2°C and pursue efforts to keep it to 1.5°C.

Nevertheless, since its release, several actors have questioned and commented on the compatibility of the Green Deal with the existing international trade law framework. For some activists, the Green Deal is insufficient and it is necessary to redefine the rules of international trade law in order to allow for an ecological transition.[5] Political actors, on the one hand, have accused the initiative of being an instrument for disguised protectionism.[6] On the other hand, others have seen the Green Deal as giving new purpose to EU trade policy.[7] Both trade and climate experts have published policy papers on the topic, mostly on the normative perspective examining the consistency of the Green Deal with international trade law.[8]

The present chapter contributes to the debate about the Green Deal's implementation by analysing the EU's current international trade law commitments. Special emphasis is given to the World Trade Organization (WTO) framework, which aims at preventing environmental policies from being used as a protectionist tool for domestic industries.[9] Therefore, this chapter addresses the following question: to what extent is the EU Green Deal in line with the current EU's trade law framework?

Climate change is an urgent matter. Nonetheless, this fact is only being recognised now by countries. The General Agreement on Tariffs and Trade (GATT)[10] was written in a moment when most of those involved in the negotiations were unaware of the extent to which international trade impacts the environment and, subsequently, how much change is required to tackle the current climate disaster. Now, there is a growing realisation that policies and regulations focused on sustainability are necessary. Therefore, understanding how trade can contribute to tackling climate change is of paramount importance.

[4] United Nations Framework Convention on Climate Change (Rio de Janeiro, 9 May 1992) (Paris Agreement).

[5] M Dupré, 'European Trade Policy and the Green Deal' (*Green European Journal*, 17 March 2020), www.greeneuropeanjournal.eu/european-trade-policy-and-the-green-deal/.

[6] See, eg, A Beattie, 'Is the EU's green policy protecting the planet or European industry?' *Financial Times* (11 December 2019), www.ft.com/content/0432eb26-15f2-11ea-9ee4-11f260415385.

[7] See, eg, J Bjerkem, 'EU trade policy: Global enforcer for the European Green Deal' (*European Policy Centre*, 17 December 2019), www.epc.eu/en/Publications/EU-trade-policy-Global-enforcer-for-the-European-Green-Deal~2db144. See also H von der Burchard et al, 'Here comes European protectionism' *Politico* (17 December 2019), www.politico.eu/article/european-protectionism-trade-technology-defense-environment/.

[8] See, eg, M Kettunen et al, 'An EU Green Deal for trade policy and the environment: Aligning trade with climate and sustainable development objectives' (2020) Institute for European Environmental Policy Report, eu.boell.org/en/2020/02/06/eu-green-deal-trade-policy-and-environment. See also S Dröge et al, 'How EU trade policy can enhance climate action' (*CEPS*, 23 September 2019), www.ceps.eu/ceps-publications/how-eu-trade-policy-can-enhance-climate-action.

[9] See, eg, A Krenek, 'How to implement a WTO-compatible full border carbon adjustment as an important part of the European Green Deal' (2020) *ÖGfE Policy Brief*, oegfe.at/wordpress/wp-content/uploads/2020/07/OEGfE_Policy_Brief-2020.02.pdf, 2305–635.

[10] General Agreement on Tariffs and Trade (GATT) (Geneva, 30 October 1947).

Section II of this chapter presents an overview of the European Green Deal, explaining what it is and its connection to the European trade law framework. Section III focuses on three proposals aimed at increasing sustainability. These proposals also help in exploring if the commitments under this Deal can be reconciled with existing WTO case law. Finally, section IV looks at the EU's strategy of focusing on regional trade agreements (RTAs) and how it can relate to the implementation of the Green Deal.

II. Green Deal and European Trade Law Framework

The European Green Deal is a legislative proposal, launched by European Commission President Ursula von der Leyen, and submitted for further consideration to the European Parliament,[11] the Council, the Economic and Social Committee and the Committee of the Regions. It provides a roadmap with actions to be adopted by the EU in order to achieve climate neutrality by 2050. In other words, it is a commitment to reduce greenhouse gas emissions to a minimum and to offset all remaining emissions with climate protection measures. Beyond that, the Green Deal aims to promote a transition towards a circular economy by encompassing measures concerning, among others, supply of clean energy, zero pollution ambition, preservation and restoration of ecosystems, and environmentally friendly food systems.[12] Functioning as guidelines, the Green Deal is a plan to make the EU's economy sustainable by turning climate and environmental challenges into opportunities.

Between 1990 and 2018, the EU reduced greenhouse gas emissions by 23 per cent, whilst the economy grew by 61 per cent. The current EU policies aim to reduce greenhouse gas emissions by 60 per cent by 2050.[13] In order to achieve climate neutrality by 2050, the European Commission has presented a plan to increase the EU's greenhouse gas emission reductions target for 2030 to a minimum of 50 per cent and a maximum of 55 per cent as compared with 1990 levels. This means that the EU is making bolder commitments than those established in the Paris Agreement.[14]

The Green Deal, on its own, is neither binding nor enforceable. Therefore, as a strategy to achieve its sustainability objectives, the Green Deal includes the use of all policy levers: regulation and standardisation, investment and innovation, national reforms, dialogue with social partners and international cooperation. Consequently, the objective is that every EU action and policy will contribute to the European Green Deal's goals. Since its launch in December 2019, the Green

[11] Resolution of the European Parliament on the European Green Deal [2020] 2019/2956(RSP).
[12] Green Deal (n 1) 3.
[13] ibid 4.
[14] United Nations Framework Convention on Climate Change (n 4).

Deal has already unfolded in, among other strategies and policies, the proposals and formulations of three major developments: the European Climate Law Framework,[15] the Farm to Fork Strategy[16] and the Circular Economy Action Plan.[17]

By bringing the fight against climate change to the centre of European policy and by promoting a transition towards a circular economy, the Green Deal can have considerable effects on international trade. In fact, trade policy is underlined as a key element for the EU's ecological transition and as a fundamental tool in the European vision of being a global leader in sustainability.[18]

The Green Deal's commitments gain relevance due to the EU's major position in global trade. The EU is the world's largest trading bloc and the top trading partner for 80 countries, accounting for 16 per cent of global imports and exports.[19] Such a significant role in trade also means a significant international environmental spillover. That is, most EU Member States generate, among other negative externalities, large negative impacts through trade, which include greenhouse gas emissions, biodiversity loss and water scarcity.[20]

Trade policy falls exclusively under the EU's competence. This means that the EU, and not the Member States, legislates on trade matters that include negotiating international trade agreements. Currently, the EU has trade agreements in place (fully or partly) with 85 countries, and agreements either pending to enter into force or under negotiation with 46 countries. The vastness of its preferential trade relations makes the EU the most productive trade negotiating authority.[21] At the same time, the EU has been a complainant in 104 WTO disputes, a respondent in another 87 cases and a third party participant in almost 205 cases.[22] Hence, the European trade law framework, for the purpose of this chapter, comprises the

[15] Commission, 'Proposal for a Regulation of the European Parliament and of the Council establishing the framework for achieving climate neutrality and amending Regulation 2018/1999 European Climate Law' COM (2020) 80 final. This proposal aims to write into law the goal of achieving climate-neutrality by 2050.

[16] Commission, Communication to the European Parliament, the Council, the European Economic and Social Committee and the Committee of the Regions, 'A Farm to Fork Strategy for a fair, healthy and environmentally-friendly food system' COM (2020) 381 final (Farm to fork strategy). This strategy sets out both regulatory and non-regulatory initiatives aiming to enable and accelerate the transition to an environmentally-friendly food system (Farm to Fork Strategy).

[17] Commission, Communication to the European Parliament, the Council, the European Economic and Social Committee and the Committee of the Regions, 'A new Circular Economy Action Plan For a cleaner and more competitive Europe' COM (2020) 98 final. The Action Plan establishes a comprehensive body of legislative and non-legislative actions aimed to transition the European economy from a linear to a circular model.

[18] Green Deal (n 1) 18.

[19] 'EU position in world trade' (European Commission, 18 February 2019), ec.europa.eu/trade/policy/eu-position-in-world-trade/.

[20] 'The 2019 Europe Sustainable Development Report' (2019), SDSN & IEEP report, 12, sdgindex.org/reports/2019-europe-sustainable-development-report/.

[21] Kettunen et al (n 8).

[22] 'Disputes by member' (WTO, September 2020), www.wto.org/english/tratop_e/dispu_e/dispu_by_country_e.htm.

commitments arising from WTO Agreements and other bilateral or plurilateral FTAs signed by the EU.

Due to the relevance of the EU in WTO disputes and in FTAs, when assessing the compatibility of the Green Deal with the international trade framework, both sets of trade commitments need to be analysed. The following section assesses this compatibility with WTO case law.

III. Green Deal and WTO Law

As previously mentioned, the Green Deal includes all policy levers, using different strategies and consequently affecting international trade in several ways. The proposal which has probably received most attention is the carbon border adjustment mechanism,[23] directed at selected sectors to reduce the risk of carbon leakage.[24] The rationale behind this is that, in case companies transfer production to countries with less strict rules concerning emissions, the mechanism would counteract by putting a carbon price on imports of certain goods from outside the EU. It is, therefore, an attempt to ensure the reduction of global emissions.

This measure has been well debated by several authors and is discussed in a separate chapter in this book.[25] Therefore, it will not be further addressed in this chapter. The following subsections focus on other measures presented in the Green Deal which affect trade but have received less attention, although they might still generate a possible conflict with WTO law.

A. 'Farm to Fork Strategy'

The 'Farm to Fork Strategy' was first presented in the EU Green Deal and officially launched in May 2020.[26] It sets out regulatory and non-regulatory measures with the aim of balancing the food supply with respect to biodiversity. With this goal,

[23] See, eg, S Fleming and C Giles, 'EU Risks Trade Fight Over Carbon Border Tax Plans' *Financial Times* (16 October 2019), www.ft.com/content/154368c8-ef55-11e9-ad1e-4367d8281195; see also R Ismer et al, 'Border Carbon Adjustments and Alternative Measures for the EU ETS: An Evaluation' (2020) DIW Berlin discussion paper 1855, www.diw.de/de/diw_01.c.743700.de/publikationen/diskussionspapiere/2020_1855/border_carbon_adjustments_and_alternative_measures_for_the_eu_ets__an_evaluation.html.

[24] Carbon leakage refers to the situation that may occur if, for reasons of costs related to climate policies, businesses were to transfer production to other countries with laxer emission constraints. This could lead to an increase in their total emissions. See 'EU emissions trading system (EU ETS): Carbon leakage' (European Commission), ec.europa.eu/clima/policies/ets/allowances/leakage_en.

[25] ibid. See also A Nosowicz, 'EU Border Carbon Adjustment and the WTO: Hand in Hand Towards Tackling Climate Change' (2020) 15 *Global Trade and Customs Journal* 15. See D Boklan, 'Combating Climate Change under the WTO: Exploring the Relevance of Process and Production Methods', ch 8 in this book.

[26] See 'Farm to fork strategy' (n 16).

the document establishes that 'appropriate EU policies, including trade policy, will be used to support and be part of the EU's ecological transition'.[27]

The Strategy prescribes that EU trade policy will contribute to obtaining the commitment of third countries in areas such as animal welfare, the use of pesticides and the fight against antimicrobial resistance. It equally includes a legislative proposal to prevent the offering for sale of products associated with deforestation or forest degradation in the EU market.[28]

Actions taken to enforce these commitments might lead to the restriction of imported goods that do not comply with certain sanitary standards, due to the presence of pesticides, use of antibiotics, or when there is suspicion of them contributing to deforestation or disrespect of certain animal welfare standards. The trade restrictions might then raise questions about the strategy's compliance with WTO Agreements, such as the Agreement on Technical Barriers to Trade (TBT Agreement)[29] and the Agreement on the Application of Sanitary and Phytosanitary Measures (SPS Agreement)[30] in addition to the GATT 1994.

WTO Members have agreed that it is within states' rights under WTO law to set criteria for the way products are produced, if the production method leaves a trace in the final product.[31] For instance, the use of pesticides in coffee crops leave residue in the coffee bean. Among the four scenarios presented above (ie, the presence of pesticides, use of antibiotics, contribution to deforestation or disrespect for certain animal welfare standards), the presence of pesticides or antibiotics in the final product is considered as part of the process and production method (PPM). As for deforestation or animal welfare standards, they constitute what is commonly called 'non-product related PPM' (npr-PPM), meaning that the production mode does not change the final product, but might still affect how the product is perceived by consumers.

The EU's requirements relating to maximum levels of pesticides faced criticism from other WTO Members for having a negative impact on trade of a number of agricultural products.[32] Therefore, it is necessary to look at how the WTO has previously dealt with disputes concerning trade restrictions based on the presence of controversial substances, such as pesticides, antibiotics or other chemicals. The following cases entail arguments for the protection of human health and the environment on the one side, and arguments prioritising free trade on the other.

[27] ibid 18.

[28] ibid.

[29] Agreement on Technical Barriers to Trade, Marrakesh Agreement Establishing the World Trade Organization, Annex 1A (Marrakesh, 15 April 1994) (TBT Agreement).

[30] Agreement on the Application of Sanitary and Phytosanitary Measures, Marrakesh Agreement Establishing the World Trade Organization, Annex 1A (Marrakesh, 15 April 1994) (SPS Agreement).

[31] 'Environment: issues, Labelling' (WTO, 2020), www.wto.org/english/tratop_e/envir_e/labelling_e.htm.

[32] See, eg, 'Members address trade concerns, promote transparency in SPS Committee' (WTO, 19 July 2019), www.wto.org/english/news_e/news19_e/sps_22jul19_e.htm; 'Pesticide residues top of agenda of WTO food safety body' (WTO, 2 November 2017), www.wto.org/english/news_e/news17_e/sps_02nov17_e.htm.

One of the landmark examples was the *EC–Asbestos* dispute,[33] in which Canada requested consultations concerning measures imposed by France with respect to the prohibition of asbestos and products containing asbestos, including a ban on imports of such goods. Canada alleged that these measures violated Articles 2, 3 and 5 of the SPS Agreement, Article 2 of the TBT Agreement and Articles III, XI and XIII of the GATT. In this case, the Panel Report confirmed that the ban was justified on health grounds, thereby allowing the prohibition of asbestos. Canada appealed, but the Appellate Body upheld the Panel's Report. Importantly, the Appellate Body modified the reasoning, reversing the finding of the Panel that considerations of health effects and consumers' habits could not be taken into account in the analysis of whether two products are 'like' under Article III:4. The Appellate Body reports affirmed that:

> We are very much of the view that evidence relating to the health risks associated with a product may be pertinent in an examination of 'likeness' under article III:4 of the GATT … we believe that this evidence can be evaluated under the existing criteria of physical properties, and of consumers' tastes and habits.[34]

In addition, the Appellate Body affirmed that the asbestos ban protects human life and health and that 'no reasonably available alternative measure' existed, confirming the Panel's finding that the ban was justified as an exception under Article XX(b) of the GATT.

This case certainly lays down an important precedent with respect to PPMs. For in this case, the traces left in the final product played an important role in the likeness test. In *EC–Asbestos*, the health concerns and consumers' behaviour were especially relevant for the distinction between products. Thus, it can be argued that the concentration level of pesticides or antibiotics is a physical property affected by PPM and the fact that a product is organic or not shapes consumers' habits. Additionally, the Appellate Body confirms that evidence relating to health risks can be considered in the likeness test. Hence, restrictions based on these concerns can also be justified under Article XX(b) of the GATT. In other words, one can argue that it is not only possible to differentiate between products due to the presence of pesticides or antibiotics (likeness test), but that it is also a justifiable exception to accord different treatment based on health and environmental concerns. In the case of an eventual implementation of trade restrictive measures, such as the restriction of imports of goods with certain levels of pesticides or antibiotics, this interpretation could then support the argument for the non-existence of a violation of WTO rules.

Trade restrictions based on npr-PPM are analysed in subsection C below, since similar proposals are mentioned not only in the Farm to Fork Strategy but throughout the Green Deal itself.

[33] *European Communities–Measures Affecting Asbestos and Products Containing Asbestos*, Report of the Appellate Body (5 April 2001) WT/DS135/AB/R.

[34] ibid para 103.

B. Packaging and Recycling Requirement

When specifically addressing the concerns about the impact of plastic in the environment, the European Green Deal affirms that 'the Commission will develop requirements to ensure that all packaging in the EU market is reusable or recyclable in an economically viable manner by 2030'.[35]

Packaging and recycling requirements are subjects assigned to the Committee on Trade and Environment at the WTO. This demonstrates that WTO Members have been concerned about the impact on international trade of requirements governments make for products in order to protect the environment.

There have been no disputes addressing exactly the types of requirements foreseen in the Green Deal, that is, concerning packaging and recycling requirements. However, it is possible to make a parallel with the *Brazil–Tyres* case,[36] as both the Green Deal and this case refer to attempts to block the import of certain products due to the negative impact of waste on the environment. In *Brazil–Tyres*, among other measures, the EU questioned Brazil's ban on retreated and used tyres. The Panel found that the objective of the import ban was the reduction of the 'exposure to the risks to human, animal or plant life or health arising from the accumulation of waste tyres'.[37] The Appellate Body found that the MERCOSUR exemption to the ban had resulted in it being applied in a manner that constituted arbitrary or unjustifiable discrimination. Yet, the Appellate Body considered the measure to be 'necessary', within the meaning of Article XX(b) of the GATT, and thus provisionally justified under that provision.[38]

Under the necessity test of Article XX(b), it is essential to prove that there are no reasonable and WTO-consistent alternatives available for achieving the desired aim. Whether alternatives are reasonably available depends on factors such as the extent to which the alternative measure contributes to the realisation of the end pursued; the difficulty of implementation; and the trade impact of the alternative measure compared with the measure at issue in the dispute. In addition to being 'reasonably available', the alternative measure must also achieve the level of protection sought.[39]

The necessity test is relevant because it gives autonomy to the country issuing the regulation to determine the level of protection it aims to achieve. In the case of packaging requirements, the level of protection intended by the EU was already clearly stated in the Plastics Strategy from 2018.[40] Foreshadowing the Green Deal,

[35] Green Deal (n 1) 8.

[36] *Brazil–Measures Affecting Imports of Retreaded Tyres*, Report of the Appellate Body (17 December 2007) WT/DS332/AB/R (*Brazil–Tyres*).

[37] *Brazil–Measures Affecting Imports of Retreaded Tyres* Report of the Panel (17 December 2007) WT/DS332/R, para 7.102.

[38] *Brazil–Tyres*, Report of the Appellate Body (n 36) para 258.

[39] P Low et al, 'The Interface Between the Trade and Climate Change Regimes: Scoping the Issues' (2011) 46 *Journal of World Trade* 485.

[40] Commission, Communication to the European Parliament, the Council, the European Economic and Social Committee and the Committee of the Regions 'A European Strategy For Plastics in a Circular Economy COM (2018) 028 final.

the Plastics Strategy was already a step towards a circular economy and established the commitment to ensure that all plastic packaging in the EU market is recyclable by 2030, to reduce the consumption of single-use plastics and to restrict the intentional use of microplastics.

Thus, based on the necessity test applied in *Brazil–Tyres* (Article XX(b) of the GATT), in which the level of protection sought is an important component, one can argue that an eventual ban on non-reusable and non-recyclable packaging could still be justified under WTO law, even though the level of protection required by the EU may call for highly trade-restrictive measures. The severity or trade-restrictiveness of such measures may be weighed and balanced with the reasonably available less trade-restrictive alternatives.[41] In *US–Gambling*,[42] the Appellate Body stated that the complainant bears the burden of proof to identify reasonably available alternative measures. Therefore, the challenge for a complainant who may question such measures will be to come up with an alternative that can achieve the level of protection sought by the EU, which is having all plastic packaging in the internal market recyclable by 2030. In sum, if the Green Deal implementation indeed leads to a ban, even with the weighting and balancing analysis, a complainant will most likely have difficulties succeeding based on the necessity test because the standard of protection established by the EU is very high.

C. Barrier to Products from Deforestation

Although included in both the Farm to Fork Strategy and the main text of the Green Deal, the wording concerning a possible barrier to products from deforestation is softer, compared with the two measures presented above. It states that 'the Commission will take measures, both regulatory and otherwise, to promote imported products and value chains that do not involve deforestation and forest degradation'.[43] It is most likely due to the difficulties of proving the non-existence of forest degradation or deforestation in long supply chains.

Thus, it is harder to foresee bans or similar measures to products due to their connection with deforestation. One can rather think of labels or similar types of incentive for consumers to opt for products that can guarantee a sustainable origin. Yet, because distinctions based on this factor might still be seen as discriminatory by other states and thus affecting trade, an analysis of previous WTO disputes wherein npr-PPM were central remains relevant.

Several authors have analysed process and production methods and their connection to environmental issues.[44] One of the most relevant cases in this

[41] *Brazil–Tyres*, Report of the Appellate Body (n 36) para 182.

[42] *United States–Measures Affecting the Cross-Border Supply of Gambling and Betting Services*, Report of the Appellate Body (20 April 2005) WT/DS285/26, paras 309–11.

[43] Green Deal (n 1) 14.

[44] See, eg, G Marceau, 'Do PPM Concerns Have a Future?' in D Prévost et al (eds), *Restoring Trust in Trade: Liber amicorum in Honour of Peter van den Bossche* (Oxford, Hart Publishing, 2018).

respect is the *US–Tuna II* dispute,[45] in which Mexico alleged that the measures establishing the conditions for the use of a dolphin-safe label on tuna products were inconsistent with Articles I:1 and III:4 of the GATT and Articles 2.1, 2.2 and 2.4 of the TBT Agreement.

The Appellate Body affirmed that Article 2.1 of the TBT Agreement should not be read to mean that any distinctions, especially those based exclusively on particular product characteristics or on particular processes and production methods, would per se constitute less favourable treatment within the meaning of Article 2.1.[46] The Appellate Body also acknowledged that the objectives of the US dolphin-safe provisions were legitimate within the meaning of Article 2.2 of the TBT Agreement, upholding the Panel's following analysis:

> The objectives of protecting consumers from deceptive practices and contributing to protecting dolphins by discouraging certain fishing practices do not go against the object and purpose of the TBT Agreement, even in light of the existence of potentially conflicting objectives that could also be recognized as legitimate.[47]

As Gabrielle Marceau explains, the concerns over PPM-based distinctions came from the fear of protectionism, but the WTO case law has maintained the view that PPMs are generally not enough to distinguish like products if PPM-compliant and PPM non-compliant products compete for the same consumers.[48] This was the case in *US–Gasoline*,[49] in which the Panel held that it was inadmissible to differentiate between imported and domestic gasoline on the basis of the importing company's ability to provide certain statistical data on its pollution reduction obligations.[50]

Nonetheless, the WTO has also conferred on governments the right to treat like products differently on the basis of policies, including npr-PPM measures, if such regulatory distinctions are consistent with the relevant WTO provision.[51] The above-mentioned *US–Tuna II* case exemplifies this understanding. It is important to note, however, that these PPM-related cases differ from *EC–Asbestos* for, in the latter, the remaining traces in the final product and the differences in consumers' behaviour were considered enough to distinguish products based on the likeness test of Article III:4 of the GATT.

Thus, considering previous WTO case law on PPM, one can argue that an eventual label to identify products that do not contribute to deforestation is not per se discriminatory, because other factors, such as consumers' behaviour or even

[45] *United States–Measures Concerning the Importation, Marketing and Sale of Tuna and Tuna Products*, Report of the Appellate Body (13 June 2012) WT/DS381/AB/R.

[46] ibid paras 212–15.

[47] *United States–Measures Concerning the Importation, Marketing and Sale of Tuna and Tuna Products*, Report of the Panel (13 June 2012) WT/DS381/R, para 7.443.

[48] Marceau (n 44) 184.

[49] *United States–Standards for Reformulated and Conventional Gasoline*, Report of the Panel (20 May 1996) WT/DS2/R.

[50] ibid para 6.11.

[51] Marceau (n 44) 184.

justifiable policies, are equally assessed. Additionally, the reasons for such a label, that is, informing consumers and tackling deforestation by supporting sustainable practices, can be considered legitimate and therefore compliant with WTO law.

IV. Regional Agreements, WTO and the Green Deal

The Appellate Body is paralysed and struggling to come back to action, which consequently leads to major doubts about the future of the Dispute Settlement Body (DSB). The inability of appealing panel decisions could also mean that WTO Members now have the ability to block panel decisions by simply filing an appeal to a dysfunctional Appellate Body. At the same time, climate change is an urgent matter and the Green Deal includes short-term actions and deadlines. Considering these time constraints, even though it is relevant to ensure that new regulations are WTO compliant, the EU seems to strongly invest in plurilateral actions to trade policy. That is, the EU is investing in a network of trade agreements to advance its sustainability objectives.

RTAs in the WTO refer to any reciprocal trade agreement between two or more partners, not necessarily belonging to the same region, thus, including FTAs and similar ones.[52] RTAs constitute an exception to the most-favoured-nation rule.[53] The aim of both RTAs and WTO law is to facilitate trade, as long as the set of rules concerning RTA is followed.[54] Additionally, the inclusion of environmental clauses in RTAs is not a novelty. The 1994 North American Free Trade Agreement (NAFTA) included a side agreement on the environment,[55] although not specifically on climate change.

Thus, when assessing the extent to which the EU Green Deal is in line with the current European trade law framework, it is important to note that the EU has been shaping the trade law framework by signing several trade agreements and negotiating many others. The relevance of the EU in international trade, as demonstrated in the first section of this chapter, provides the required influence that the EU seeks to employ in implementing the plans comprised in the Green Deal.[56]

One of the main actions included in the Green Deal is to make the implementation of the Paris Agreement an essential element for all future EU comprehensive trade agreements.[57] This is the confirmation of a previous commitment to not sign trade agreements with countries that do not ratify the Paris Agreement.

[52] See Art XXIV and *ad* Art XXIV of the General Agreement on Tariffs and Trade (GATT), Annex 1A, Marrakesh Agreement Establishing the World Trade Organization (Marrakesh, 15 April 1994).

[53] eg, Art I of the General Agreement on Tariffs and Trade (GATT), Annex 1A, Marrakesh Agreement Establishing the World Trade Organization (Marrakesh, 15 April 1994).

[54] See Art XXIV and *ad* Art XXIV of the GATT (n 52).

[55] North American Agreement on Environmental Cooperation (Mexico City, Washington, DC and Ottawa, 8, 9, 12 and 14 September 1993).

[56] Green Deal (n 1) 2.

[57] ibid 21.

Therefore, the EU's most recent FTAs include a binding commitment of the parties to ratify and effectively implement the Paris Agreement. The EU–Japan Economic Partnership Agreement,[58] which entered into force on 1 January 2019, was the first to include a clause on the Paris Agreement.[59] However, there has been criticism that these clauses are rarely enforceable.[60] As an attempt to ensure the implementation and enforcement of sustainable development commitments, the European Commission has even created the position of a Chief Trade Enforcement Officer (CTEO), which was filled for the first time in July 2020. The actual impact of this measure is still to be seen, considering that the role of the CTEO remains unclear. Yet, their attributions do include monitoring and improvement of the compliance with EU trade agreements.[61]

The overall European plan is to form Green Alliances with like-minded countries, with the EU using its influence, expertise and financial resources to mobilise partners in this respect.[62] In this line, the agreements with Vietnam, Singapore, MERCOSUR and Mexico include reinforced commitments to effectively implement the Paris Agreement.[63] Similar clauses are also proposed in the ongoing negotiations with Australia, Chile, Indonesia and New Zealand. This demonstrates that the EU has added the Paris Agreement clause as a requirement not only for new FTAs, but also in the revision and renegotiation of existing trade agreements.

Some analyses have demonstrated that the inclusion of sustainability clauses in RTAs can contribute to climate governance.[64] Regional agreements allow for the inclusion of bolder experimental provisions among like-minded countries. These different clauses provide an intersection between trade and sustainability; these clauses could relate to trade liberalisation for climate-related products and technologies, and fossil fuel subsidies.[65] These agreements are particularly important at

[58] Agreement between the European Union and Japan for an Economic Partnership (Tokyo, 17 July 2018) (EU–Japan Agreement).

[59] ibid Art 16.4: 'The Parties recognise the importance of achieving the ultimate objective of the United Nations Framework Convention on Climate Change, done at New York on 9 May 1992 (hereinafter referred to as "UNFCCC"), in order to address the urgent threat of climate change, and the role of trade to that end. The Parties reaffirm their commitments to effectively implement the UNFCCC and the Paris Agreement, done at Paris on 12 December 2015 by the Conference of the Parties to the UNFCCC at its 21st session. The Parties shall cooperate to promote the positive contribution of trade to the transition to low greenhouse gas emissions and climate-resilient development. The Parties commit to working together to take actions to address climate change towards achieving the ultimate objective of the UNFCCC and the purpose of the Paris Agreement'.

[60] See, eg, Bjerkem (n 7).

[61] 'European Commission appoints its first Chief Trade Enforcement Officer' (European Commission, 24 July 2020), ec.europa.eu/commission/presscorner/detail/en/IP_20_1409.

[62] Green Deal (n 1) 2.

[63] 'EU trade agreements: delivering new opportunities in time of global economic uncertainties' (European Commission, 14 October 2019), trade.ec.europa.eu/doclib/press/index.cfm?id=2071.

[64] See H van Asselt, 'Climate Change and Trade Policy Interaction: Implications of Regionalism' (2017) OECD Trade and Environment Working Papers 2017/03, dx.doi.org/10.1787/c1bb521e-en.

[65] K Das et al, 'Making the International Trade System Work for Climate Change: Assessing the Options' (2018) Climate Strategies Report, climatestrategies.org/wp-content/uploads/2018/07/CS-Report-_Trade-WP4.pdf.

a time when the WTO faces major paralysis, which prevents multilateral progress in negotiations or judicial decision-making.

On the other hand, considering the urgency of the climate crisis, there is a risk that the plurilateral approach might not be broad or quick enough to enforce the changes required to tackle a climate disaster. Furthermore, the lack of enforceability of sustainability clauses in trade agreements has led to scepticism concerning their effectiveness, especially as dispute settlement provisions are seldom applicable to them.[66] One can argue that an alternative is to subject sustainability clauses to the existing dispute settlement machinery of the WTO's DSB. However, this argument becomes less convincing considering the current stand-off concerning the Appellate Body, for the lack of a functioning system would further perpetuate the lack of enforceability of sustainability clauses.

The EU acknowledged the challenge of enforceability in a reflection paper on harnessing globalisation.[67] Since then, the European approach has been to include a government-to-government dispute settlement procedure consisting of various stages, such as consultations and the creation of a panel of independent experts. This was the case in the EU–Japan Economic Partnership Agreement.[68] The mechanism has not been tested yet. Thus, the doubts about the effectiveness of a case-to-case dispute settlement procedure remain.

V. Conclusion

If the aim of sustainability has not advanced further in the WTO, it is hardly the organisation's fault. The WTO as an institution shares to a good extent the EU's concerns about sustainability.[69] The cases presented in this chapter demonstrate that well-written regulatory measures, imposed with legitimate concerns about the environment, can be WTO-consistent. Even though the WTO texts were written decades ago, exceptions contemplating environmental policies have been foreseen and panels and the Appellate Body have applied them in ways that allow for legitimate concerns to be implemented. One can still argue that relying on interpretation is too risky when dealing with problems such as a climate disaster. However, the case law analysed presents a rather consistent protection of environmental and health concerns, while at the same time addressing the threats for potential hidden protectionism.

[66] K Hradilová and O Svoboda, 'Sustainable Development Chapters in the EU Free Trade Agreements: Searching for Effectiveness' (2018) 52 *Journal of World Trade* 1019.

[67] European Commission, 'Reflection Paper on Harnessing Globalisation' (10 May 2017) 240, ec.europa.eu/commission/publications/reflection-paper-harnessing-globalisation_en.

[68] See EU–Japan Agreement (n 58).

[69] Preamble of the Marrakesh Agreement Establishing the World Trade Organization (Marrakesh, 15 April 1994).

The same level of commitment to sustainability issues does not seem to exist among certain members of the organisation. Thus, the emphasis given to Green Alliances allows the EU to build trade partnerships focused on sustainable development, especially considering the relevance of global value chains and the EU's share of global trade. Moreover, the European network of trade agreements removes to a great extent from the WTO sphere the debate about trade law compliance. This is due to the special status of RTAs in the multilateral organisation. At the same time, the RTAs allow more room to bargain and the inclusion of bolder provisions than those of multilateral agreements. Additionally, cooperation and political influence are very relevant when it comes to compliance with international regulation. Therefore, RTAs make it easier from a legal perspective to implement the ambitions described in the Green Deal and to ensure its consistency with international trade law.

In sum, the European Green Deal might seem bold from a trade and sustainability perspective. However, a more detailed analysis demonstrates that regulations aimed at prioritising sustainability concerns can be both reconciled with WTO law and with RTAs. That is what the EU has been doing. It is, therefore, possible to conciliate the Green Deal and the European trade law framework.

10

Gender Mainstreaming in Free Trade Agreements: What have We Achieved, and What More is Needed for Inclusive Post-Pandemic Recovery?

AMRITA BAHRI*

I. Introduction

The world is facing an unprecedented health pandemic. COVID-19 has upended the global economy, and with it international trade, creating enormous shocks to supply and demand. Never before has the world experienced a health contingency leading to an economic contagion of this nature – with shrinking output, massive job losses and rising hunger. This economic contagion is exacerbating the existing inequalities; be it inequality between developed and developing nations, rich and poor, or women and men. The pandemic has brought to light the vulnerabilities of women in trade as its economic and social effects have fallen disproportionately upon women.

COVID-19 has put women employees, women entrepreneurs and women consumers at the front line of this struggle.[1] A recent United Nations (UN) report explains it as follows: '[a]cross every sphere, from health to the economy, security to social protection, the impacts of COVID-19 are exacerbated for women and girls simply by virtue of their sex'.[2] This is happening for various reasons. First,

* This chapter is a revised and improved version of a working paper that was prepared and selected for inclusion at the 'Online Repository of Contributions to the Policy Hackathon on Model Provisions for Trade in Times of Crisis and Pandemic', www.unescap.org/resources/online-repository-contributions-policy-hackathon-model-provisions-trade-times-crisis-and. Thanks to Francisco Solano, Ana Cecilia Cueva and Arnav Bose for their brilliant research assistantship.

[1] For details, see T Alon et al, 'The Impact of COVID-19 on Gender Equality' (2020) NBER Working Paper No 26947, www.nber.org/system/files/working_papers/w26947/w26947.pdf; 'COVID-19: A Gender Lens, Technical Brief Protecting Sexual and Reproductive Health and Rights, and Promoting Gender Equality' (UNFPA, March 2020), www.unfpa.org/resources/covid-19-gender-lens.

[2] UN Secretary-General, 'The Impact of COVID-19 on Women' (UN, 9 April 2020) Policy Brief, www.unwomen.org/en/digital-library/publications/2020/04/policy-brief-the-impact-of-covid-19-on-women.

with 30 per cent of the female workforce employed in service-based industries, women are experiencing a serious loss of employment in pandemic-inflicted service sectors such as tourism and hospitality.[3] Second, out of two billion workers in informal employment worldwide, over 740 million are women. In South Asia, over 80 per cent of women in non-agricultural jobs are in informal employment.[4] Women working in informal sectors are either putting their lives at risk as they continue to venture out to work or they are losing their livelihood due to the continuing lockdowns.[5] Third, women own close to 10 million or more than 30 per cent of the world's small and medium-sized enterprises (SMEs).[6] The pandemic is disrupting the economic activities of women who own or work in SMEs as the pandemic is forcing many SMEs to face closure or scale down their operations.[7] Fourth, this pandemic is exacerbating the existing digital disparities between women and men.[8] This implies that working remotely or in an online-mode is either not an option for some women with no access to laptops, smart phones and internet or they have to face a steep learning curve and financial burden to switch to working online. This growing disparity also implies that women cannot take advantage of the booming digital trade transformation that provides new avenues for the economic empowerment of women. Moreover, owing to fears of contagion and loss of income, this pandemic is reducing women's access to medical services including family planning services such as abortion.[9] Difficulty and fear in approaching medical services for an abortion or accessing contraceptives could cause untimely and unwanted pregnancy to many women professionals, which in turn could take some women a step further from their professional aspirations.[10] The impact of this problem is compounded by the fact that working women often have less access to social safety nets, such as paid sick leave and maternity leave

[3] J Faus, 'This is how coronavirus could affect the travel and tourism industry' (World Economic Forum, 17 March 2020), www.weforum.org/agenda/2020/03/world-travel-coronavirus-covid19-jobs-pandemic-tourism-aviation/; 'COVID-19 Educational Disruption and Response' (UNESCO, 2020), en.unesco.org/covid19/educationresponse.

[4] 'Progress of the World's Women 2015–2016: Transforming economies, realizing rights' (*UN Women*, 2015) ch 2, 71, www.unwomen.org/en/digital-library/publications/2015/4/progress-of-the-worlds-women-2015.

[5] 'Women in informal economy' (*UN Women*), www.unwomen.org/en/news/in-focus/csw61/women-in-informal-economy.

[6] U Ahmed et al, 'Filling the Gap: How Technology Enables Access to Finance for Small- and Medium-Sized Enterprises' (2015) 10 *Innovations: Technology, Governance, Globalization* 35, 42.

[7] ibid; OECD, 'Coronavirus (COVID-19): SME Policy Responses' (2020), read.oecd-ilibrary.org/view/?ref=119_119680-di6h3qgi4x&title=Covid-19. Empirical research finds that due to COVID-19, more than half of SMEs now already face severe losses in revenues, with many having only a few months' reserves to withstand the crisis.

[8] P Mlambo-Ngcuka and A Albrectsen, 'Op-ed: We cannot allow COVID-19 to reinforce the digital gender divide' (*UN Women*, 6 May 2020), www.unwomen.org/en/news/stories/2020/5/op-ed-ed-phumzile-covid-19-and-the-digital-gender-divide.

[9] A Peterman et al, 'Pandemics and Violence Against Women and Children' (2020) Center for Global Development Working Paper 528, www.cgdev.org/sites/default/files/pandemics-and-violence-against-women-and-girls.pdf.

[10] 'COVID-19: A Gender Lens, Technical Brief' (n 1).

since such benefits usually come with formal employment. The other reasons include a massive increase in household responsibilities[11] and an increasing rate of domestic violence against women.[12] These developments depict how this pandemic has delayed the accomplishment of the UN's Sustainable Development Goal 5 that seeks to achieve gender parity by the year 2030.

This chapter is not trying to show how or why more working women than working men (in absolute numbers) are being affected; this may not be the case as more men than women are involved in economies and hence men may be impacted more in absolute terms. Sex-disaggregated industry-wise data is needed to better understand the gendered impact of this pandemic. Instead, the chapter aims to underline how the limited gains made in respect of women's empowerment over the past few decades might be lost as a result of this pandemic. The post-pandemic world will require multiple interventions to repair this harm at domestic and international levels. International trade can form an important part of this recovery. International trade law and policies can participate in this process, as they can contribute to the economic empowerment of women. This crisis presents a unique opportunity to 'build back better' and in an inclusive manner in the post-COVID-19 world and explore how trade policies can contribute in this respect through existing and future free trade agreements (FTAs).[13]

This chapter will first address the question as to whether gender considerations form part of existing FTAs. The chapter will identify and analyse several best practice examples of mainstreaming gender considerations in the existing FTAs signed by countries in North America and the European Union (EU). These two regions are chosen as the FTAs in these regions present diverse best practice examples and also provide an indication of the flaws in current gender-mainstreaming trends. Subsequently, the chapter will address the second question: how can the existing and future FTAs be better prepared to encourage women's empowerment for achieving faster and inclusive economic growth in the post-pandemic world? To respond to this question, the chapter will explore how future FTAs can take a step further in respect of strengthening women's empowerment, to enable them to better respond to the pandemic-inflicted disruptions to inclusive growth. Furthermore, the chapter will propose several policy recommendations that trade

[11] M Doepke and F Kindermann, 'Bargaining over Babies: Theory, Evidence, and Policy Implications' (2019) 109 *American Economic Review* 3264. The authors observe that women provide the majority of childcare even if both spouses are working.

[12] See Infographic: 'The Shadow Pandemic – Violence Against Women and Girls and COVID-19' (*UN Women*, 6 April 2020), www.unwomen.org/en/digital-library/multimedia/2020/4/infographic-covid19-violence-against-women-and-girls; M Mohan, 'Coronavirus: I'm in lockdown with my abuser' *BBC News* (31 March 2020), www.bbc.com/news/world-52063755; A Taub, 'A New Covid-19 Crisis: Domestic Abuse Rises Worldwide' *New York Times* (6 April 2020), www.nytimes.com/2020/04/06/world/coronavirus-domestic-violence.html?smid=fb-.

[13] The expression 'Free trade agreements' or 'FTAs' in this chapter is used to refer to all international trade agreements (except the WTO multilateral agreements) and may include regional trade agreements, plurilateral agreements, bilateral agreements, economic partnership agreements, and such others.

negotiators and policymakers can consider for negotiation of new and renegotiation of existing FTAs.

II. 'Building Back Better' after COVID-19: Can Free Trade Agreements Help?

Women's economic empowerment and international trade share an intricate and complex relationship as the former could be enhanced through an effective regulation of the latter.[14] The Addis Ababa Agenda of Action[15] and the UN's 2030 Agenda for Sustainable Development[16] recognise foreign trade as an important instrument to reach development objectives including gender equality. The Sustainable Development Goals directly address the need to achieve full and effective participation of women for furthering economic growth and sustainable development.[17] The most recent multilateral instrument that reinforces this view is the World Trade Organization's (WTO) Joint Declaration on Trade and Women's Economic Empowerment. The Declaration reaffirms that 'international trade and investment are engines of economic growth for both developing and developed countries, and that improving women's access to opportunities and removing barriers to their participation in national and international economies contributes to sustainable economic development'.[18]

FTAs can play an instrumental role in enhancing women's empowerment and hence 'building back better' in a sustainable manner in the post-COVID-19 world. Through gender mainstreaming[19] in FTAs, countries can encourage their trade partners to create laws and procedures to reduce barriers that impede women's access to trade and commerce.[20] Countries in these FTAs can bind themselves to certain minimum legal standards for improving the employment conditions for women or prohibiting sex-based discrimination. In addition, countries can also

[14] A Hutchens, 'Empowering Women through Fair Trade? Lessons from Asia' (2010) 31 *Third World Quarterly* 449.

[15] 'Third International Conference on Financing for Development (FfD3)' (UN, 13–16 July 2015), www.un.org/esa/ffd/ffd3/conference.html.

[16] 'Transforming our world: the 2030 Agenda for Sustainable Development', UNGA Res 70/1 (25 September 2015).

[17] ibid Goal 5.

[18] WTO Ministerial Declaration, 'Buenos Aires Joint Declaration on Trade and Women's Economic Empowerment' (12 December 2017), www.wto.org/english/thewto_e/minist_e/mc11_e/genderdeclarationmc11_e.pdf.

[19] Gender mainstreaming provides a tool to ensure that FTAs do not perpetuate gender inequalities but rather promote more equitable opportunities. Mainstreaming gender in FTAs entails the inclusion of gender considerations and concerns in the drafting and implementation of FTAs.

[20] A Bahri, 'Measuring the Gender-Responsiveness of Free Trade Agreements: Using a Self-Evaluation Maturity Framework' (2019) 14 *Global Trade & Customs Journal* 517; for a discussion on barriers, see International Trade Centre, 'Unlocking Markets for Women to Trade' (2015) Doc P356.E/DBIS/TS/15-XII, ch 3.

endeavour to increase women's access to health services, education and skill development. Furthermore, encouraging conditions for women's businesses to flourish can be created through FTAs, for instance by pushing for the creation of business networks and improved infrastructure in relevant sectors and industries. FTAs can also be used as an instrument to secure a commitment to increasing the representation of women in decision-making and policymaking roles.

Countries can use trade agreements as laboratories of change, where they can experiment with different legal provisions regarding gender equality. In recent years, there has been a sharp increase in this experimentation.[21] The last three years in particular have been phenomenal in this respect. In 2020, Canada, Chile and New Zealand signed the Global Trade and Gender Arrangement that seeks to 'promote mutually supportive trade and gender policies and unlock new opportunities to increase women's participation in trade as part of broader efforts to improve gender equality and women's economic empowerment'.[22] In 2019, two FTAs were enforced with a dedicated chapter on gender.[23] The EU committed itself to ensuring that trade-related aspects of gender will be adequately addressed in trade agreements.[24] In 2018, the European Parliament passed a resolution to include gender-equality consideration in all future trade agreements it would sign.[25] These recent developments show that gender mainstreaming in trade agreements is here to stay.

III. Best Practice Examples: North America and the EU

This section identifies and assesses several best practice examples of gender mainstreaming in existing FTAs signed by countries in two regions: North America and the EU. These two regions are selected for three reasons: (a) some FTAs in these regions are probably the most gender-responsive FTAs in force so far; (b) FTAs in these regions present diverse and unique ways of embracing gender considerations in trade agreements; (c) several gender-related provisions in these FTAs indicate

[21] J Monteiro, 'Gender-Related Provisions in Regional Trade Agreements' (18 December 2018) WTO Economic Research and Statistics Division, Staff Working Paper ERSD-2018-15.

[22] Global Trade and Gender Arrangement – Joint Communiqué (4 August 2020), www.international.gc.ca/trade-commerce/inclusive_trade-commerce_inclusif/itag-gaci/2020-08-04-joint-communique-commun.aspx?lang=eng.

[23] Modernized Canada–Chile Free Trade Agreement (CCFTA) (Santiago, 5 December 1996, amendments entered into force 5 February 2019); Modernized Canada–Israel Free Trade Agreement (CIFTA) (Montreal, 31 July 1996, amendments entered into force 1 September 2019).

[24] European Commission, 'Communication from the Commission to the European Parliament, the Council, the European Economic and Social Committee and the Committee of the Regions, A Union of Equality: Gender Equality Strategy 2020–2025' [2020] COM/2020/152.

[25] European Parliament Resolution, 'Gender Equality in EU Trade Agreements' [2018] 2017/2015(INI).

that the door is still half open and hence further efforts are required to make these trade instruments work for inclusive economic recovery in the post-COVID-19 world.

This section contains two subsections. Each subsection focuses on the FTAs signed by countries in a specific region. Tables 1 and 2 provide a quick glance at the gender component of FTAs signed by countries in these regions. Only gender-explicit FTAs (with one or more gender-explicit provisions) are included in these tables, while FTAs with no gender-related provisions or gender-implicit provisions are excluded in this assessment. Those provisions which use terms directly relating to 'gender', 'women', 'female', 'maternity' or a similar expression in the provision in an explicit manner are 'gender-explicit provisions'.[26] 'Gender-implicit provisions' are those provisions which address the issues of gender in an indirect and implicit manner through areas such as, but not limited to, human rights, vulnerable groups focus, labour discrimination, corporate social responsibility, intellectual property rights and SMEs.

An FTA's gender-responsiveness in this study is assessed based on three questions:

1. Does the FTA reflect parties' mere awareness or commitment to act on gender equality concerns?
2. Do parties establish any institutions, procedures, activities, or other tools to implement gender-explicit provisions?
3. If there are any commitments, are they binding or non-binding in nature?

The first question is focused on assessing the parties' state of readiness to use FTAs for achieving gender equality. The second question seeks to find if parties have provided for any means (procedures, institutions, cooperation activities, etc) to implement the provisions relating explicitly to gender concerns. The third question tests the parties' level of commitment by assessing whether the included gender-explicit commitments are drafted in a binding or non-binding fashion. In this manner, each FTA in the selected two regions is read and assessed in light of these three questions. Three colours are used in the tables to reflect three degrees of gender-responsiveness. The 'white' corresponds to 'least gender-responsive' option. The 'light grey' corresponds to something in between the least and the most gender-responsive options. The 'dark grey' corresponds to the 'most gender-responsive' option. Gender responsiveness of an agreement indicates how sensitive or informed a trade agreement is to issues relating to gender equality and whether it seeks to minimise the negative impact of FTAs and maximise its positive impact on women. In this sense, it is different from the gender impact assessment exercise, which seeks to assess the impact an agreement may have on the economic and social lives of women.

[26] Gender-explicit words used for listing products or entities are not included in this assessment.

A. North America

In North America, the following countries are covered: Canada, the United States (US) and Mexico. In total, these three countries are party to 48 agreements. Of these 48 FTAs, only 17 contain gender-explicit provisions in one form or another. Table 10.1 provides a quick glance at the gender fabric of these 17 agreements.

Table 10.1 North American FTAs with Gender-Explicit Provisions[27]

FTAs with Gender-explicit provisions	1. Does the FTA reflect parties' mere awareness or commitments to act on gender equality concerns?	2. Do parties establish any institutions, procedures, activities, or other tools to implement gender-explicit provisions?	3. If there are any commitments, are they binding or non-binding in nature?
Canada–Israel	Commit to act	Yes: Cooperation Activities, Institutions and Procedures	Mostly non-binding
Canada–Jordan	Commit to act	No	Binding and non-binding
Canada–Peru	Awareness	No	Non-binding
Canada–Ukraine	Awareness	No	Non-binding
Canada–Chile	Commit to act	Yes: Cooperation activities, institutions and procedures	Mostly non-binding
Canada–Honduras	Awareness	No	Non-binding
Canada–Panama	Awareness	No	Non-binding
Canada–Costa Rica	Commit to act	No	Binding and non-binding
Canada–Colombia	Awareness	No	Non-binding
CPTPP	Commit to act	Yes: Cooperation Activities	Mostly non-binding
EU–Canada	Commit to act	No	Binding
EU–Mexico	Commit to act	Yes: cooperation activities	Non-binding

(continued)

[27] Only FTAs with explicit gender provisions were considered for the purpose of this table. [FTAs' texts available at WTO RTA Database, rtais.wto.org/UI/PublicMaintainRTAHome.aspx].

Table 10.1 ***(Continued)***

FTAs with Gender-explicit provisions	**1. Does the FTA reflect parties' mere awareness or commitments to act on gender equality concerns?**	**2. Do parties establish any institutions, procedures, activities, or other tools to implement gender-explicit provisions?**	**3. If there are any commitments, are they binding or non-binding in nature?**
Dominican Republic–Central America	Awareness	No	Non-binding
United States–Bahrain	Awareness	No	Non-binding
United States–Colombia	Awareness	No	Non-binding
United States–Panama	Awareness	No	Non-binding
United States–Peru	Awareness	No	Non-binding

Out of 17 FTAs included in the table, only seven demonstrate their parties' commitment to act. The other 10 agreements merely show parties' awareness towards issues relating to gender inequality. This finding shows that out of a total of 48 agreements signed by countries in North America, only about seven agreements reflect the parties' commitment to take positive action in this respect. For example, US–Peru[28] merely demonstrates the parties' awareness in Article 17.6 on Labour Cooperation, as it includes elimination of employment discrimination against women as one of the many possible cooperation activities that parties may seek to work on. In contrast, in EU–Mexico[29] the parties seek to encourage dialogue and joint cooperative action on women's empowerment and enhancing women's access to productive resources (Articles 36, 37).

Out of the seven agreements with a commitment to act, four contain some kind of mechanism or means to implement these commitments. The Comprehensive and Progressive Agreement for Trans-Pacific Partnership (CPTPP)[30] can serve an example here. The highlight of its gender fabric is found in the chapter on development, which includes a provision on the economic empowerment of women and their contribution to economic growth (Article 23.4). Under this provision, the parties seek to cooperate on activities to help women entrepreneurs and workers benefit from the trade opportunities the agreement would create. These activities focus on information sharing, capacity building and increasing market access for

[28] United States–Peru Trade Promotion Agreement (Lima, 12 April 2006).

[29] Economic Partnership, Political Coordination and Cooperation Agreement between the European Community and the United Mexican States (Brussels, 8 December 1997).

[30] Comprehensive and Progressive Agreement for Trans-Pacific Partnership (CPTPP) (Santiago, 8 March 2018).

women. They include providing advice or training; exchanging information and experiences on programmes to help women build skills and capacity; improving women's access to markets, technology and financing; developing women's leadership networks; and identifying best practices relating to workplace flexibility. However, it is important to point out that the parties undertake these commitments in a rather modest and non-binding manner.

The recently modernised Canada–Israel[31] and Canada–Chile[32] accords contain several best practice examples from the perspective of the second question (ie, implementation of commitments). They are both very similar in content and scope. Both agreements have a stand-alone chapter on gender (Canada–Israel, Chapter 13; Canada–Chile, Chapter N-bis). Both enlist cooperation activities directly relating to women's empowerment and inclusive trade that see women not merely as employees or labourers, but also as entrepreneurs, leaders, decision-makers and scientists (Canada–Israel, Article 13.3; Canada–Chile, Article N bis-03). These activities focus on improving educational or skill development opportunities in fields that can translate to high-paid job opportunities for women (such as science, technology, engineering and mathematics (STEM) and information and communication technology (ICT)). These FTAs are exceptional in this respect, as most trade agreements only consider cooperation focused on traditional roles for women (such as farming, fisheries and handloom). In addition, they create specialised institutions and procedures to further ensure implementation of gender-related commitments (Canada–Israel, Article 13.4; Canada–Chile, Article N bis-04).

Finally, in the assessment of the agreements in light of the third question, it can be noted that there is only one agreement in this region in which parties have committed themselves to fully-binding gender-explicit commitments. The EU–Canada[33] FTA provides a binding gender-explicit provision in its investment chapter. Article 8.10(d) of the Agreement states that a party will breach its obligation to provide fair and equitable treatment to foreign investors if any of its measures constitute 'targeted discrimination on manifestly wrongful grounds, such as gender'. Though this is the only gender-related commitment found in the entire Agreement's text, parties subsequently have adopted a stand-alone recommendation on trade and gender.[34] In this recommendation, parties create a work plan to gather and analyse gender-disaggregated data, carry out the Agreement's gender impact assessment, add a gender lens to the implementation of this Agreement, conduct webinars on trade and gender, and report on these activities. It remains unclear whether a subsequent adoption of such a recommendation can form part

[31] Modernized Canada–Israel FTA (n 23).

[32] Modernized Canada–Chile FTA (n 23).

[33] Comprehensive Economic and Trade Agreement (CETA) between Canada, of the one part, and the European Union and its Member States, of the other part (Brussels, 30 October 2016).

[34] 'CETA Trade and Gender Recommendation: EU–Canada Work Plan 2020–2021', www.international.gc.ca/trade-commerce/trade-agreements-accords-commerciaux/agr-acc/ceta-aecg/CETA_work_plan-AECG_plan_travail-2020-2021.aspx?lang=eng.

of an FTA per se if they are not mentioned or incorporated by reference into that treaty's text; yet, such developments allow parties to work together on activities that may inform future policymaking.

In this discussion, Canada clearly emerges as the frontrunner of this approach in North America. Gender equality is part of Canada's priorities in trade policy-making and trade negotiations. In the early years, this objective was implemented by inclusion of language regarding the elimination of employment discrimination in labour cooperation agreements and labour chapters in FTAs. More recently, Canada has sought to mainstream gender considerations throughout its FTAs. This is based on a commitment made in Canada's 2018 Federal Budget that more FTAs would be subject to gender-based analysis, using Canada's analysis tool, 'Gender-based Analysis Plus' (GBA+).[35] On 5 June 2017, Canada became the first G20 country to include a trade and gender chapter in an FTA, with its modernised Canada–Chile FTA. Since then, it has mainstreamed gender in FTAs with Mexico, EU, Israel and the Trans-Pacific. The political will in Canada to mainstream gender equality considerations is the key motivator behind this approach.

Some key takeaways from these best practice examples are outlined below.

Best Practice Examples: Key Takeaways from North America

- Canada–Israel and Canada–Chile include a stand-alone chapter on gender and trade. In the absence of a stand-alone chapter, gender concerns can be incorporated in a chapter on development/sustainable development (as seen in the CPTPP).
- The most recent FTAs signed by North American countries (Canada–Israel, Canada–Chile and the CPTPP) envisage women in different roles: as business owners, employees, consumers, decision-makers and leaders. This differentiates these agreements from others in this region, as most of the others envisage women solely as employees or labour.[36]
- In cooperation activities, Canada–Israel and Canada–Chile focus on improving women's access to education and skill development in areas that can translate to high-paid job opportunities.
- Canada–Israel and Canada–Chile encourage industries and enterprises to incorporate corporate social responsibility explicitly relating to gender.
- Only two FTAs – Canada–Israel and Canada–Chile – create specialised institutions to monitor and implement gender-related commitments.
- Only Canada–Israel explicitly provides for an applicable dispute settlement mechanism for gender-related provisions, but the mechanism has binding yet non-compulsory jurisdiction.
- None of these FTAs foresee or identify how the implementation of their respective gender commitments could be financed.

[35] 'Employment and Social Development Canada 2018–2019 Departmental plan – Supplementary information – Annex 1.7: Gender-Based Analysis' (GBA+), www.canada.ca/en/employment-social-development/corporate/reports/departmental-plan/2018-2019/gender-based-analysis.html.

[36] USMCA not included in this analysis, as it is pending enforcement at the time of writing.

B. The EU

This subsection assesses 41 FTAs the EU has signed so far. Out of these, 29 contain gender-explicit provisions in one form or another. Table 2 provides a quick glance at the gender fabric of these 29 agreements.[37]

Table 10.2 EU's FTAs with Gender-Explicit Provisions[38]

FTAs with gender-explicit provisions	1. Does the FTA reflect parties' mere awareness or commitments to act on gender equality concerns?	2. Do parties establish any institutions, procedures, activities, or other tools to implement gender-explicit provisions?	3. If there are any commitments, are they binding or non-binding in nature?
EC-Treaty	Commit to act	Yes: procedures	Binding
EU-Albania	Commit to act	No	Mostly non-binding
EU–Algeria	Commit to act	Yes: procedures, cooperative activities	Mostly binding
EU–Armenia	Commit to Act	Yes: cooperative activities	Mostly non-binding
EU–Bosnia and Herzegovina	Awareness	No	Non-binding
EU–Cameroon	Awareness	No	Non-binding
EU–Canada	Commit to act	No	Binding
EU–CARIFORUM	Awareness	No	Non-binding
EU–Central America	Commit to act	Yes: cooperative activities	Mostly non-binding
EU–Chile	Commit to act	Yes: cooperative activities and procedures	Mostly non-binding

(continued)

[37] Most of these agreements, strictly speaking, are broader than FTAs. They are drafted as 'Association Agreements' (AAs), which establish association between parties in various areas including international trade. Other areas may include immigration, education and training, social cooperation, political dialogues, environment and poverty. In some of these agreements, gender issues have featured only in political dialogue, social or education related pillars of AAs. Since some of the gender-relevant provisions mentioned in this section are not located within the trade pillar of these agreements, the EU negotiators do not engage with their partner countries on gender issues within the trade policy context. However, they are considered in this section as these provisions are packaged as part of the same accord, and hence their implementation is related to the ratification of the entire agreement and implementation of provisions included in different pillars. For ease of audience, AAs are mentioned as FTAs in the chapter's text.

[38] Only FTAs with explicit gender provisions were considered for the purpose of this table. Source: WTO RTA Database (n27).

Table 10.2 ***(Continued)***

FTAs with gender-explicit provisions	1. Does the FTA reflect parties' mere awareness or commitments to act on gender equality concerns?	2. Do parties establish any institutions, procedures, activities, or other tools to implement gender-explicit provisions?	3. If there are any commitments, are they binding or non-binding in nature?
EU–Eastern and Southern African States Interim EPA	Commit to act	Yes: procedures, cooperation activities	Mostly binding
EU–Egypt	Commit to act	Yes: procedures	Mostly non-binding
EU–Georgia	Commit to act	Yes: institution	Mostly non-binding
EU–Israel	Awareness	No	Non-binding
EU–Jordan	Commit to act	Yes: procedures	Non-binding
EU–Republic of Korea	Awareness	No	Non-binding
EU–Lebanon	Commit to act	Yes: cooperative activities	Non-binding
EU–Mexico	Commit to act	No	Non-binding
EU–Republic of Moldova	Commit to act	No	Non-binding
EU–Montenegro	Awareness	No	Non-binding
EU–Morocco	Commit to act	Yes: cooperative activities	Non-binding
EU–North Macedonia	Awareness	No	Non-binding
EU–OCT	Awareness	No	Non-binding
EU–Palestinian Authority	Commit to act	Yes: cooperative activities	Non-binding
EU–Serbia	Commit to act	Yes: cooperative activities	Non-binding
EU–South Africa	Commit to act	Yes: procedures	Non-binding
EU–Tunisia	Commit to act	Yes: cooperative activities, Institution	Non-binding
EU–Ukraine	Commit to act	Yes: cooperative activities	Non-binding
EEA	Commit to act	No	Binding

Out of 29 FTAs included in the table, as many as 21 demonstrate their parties' commitment to act. The other eight agreements merely show parties' awareness towards issues relating to gender inequality. This finding shows that out of a total of 41 agreements signed by the EU so far, half of them reflect parties' commitment to take positive action in this respect. This is a reassuring number; however, the picture gets dimmer when addressing the next two questions. Out of 21 agreements demonstrating parties' commitment to act, about 16 provide for some kind of mechanism or means to implement these commitments and only about three of these FTAs frame these commitments as binding legal obligations. Some examples are discussed below.

The EU–Central America FTA[39] seems to be one of the most advanced FTAs in the region in this respect. Article 13 of the Agreement encourages the parties to hold political dialogues about social issues including gender equality. Another best practice provision is Article 32 that is focused on conflict prevention, as it includes a commitment to protect the lives of women against anti-personnel mines. Article 41 on Social Cohesion includes a commitment to combat xenophobia and discrimination on the grounds of sex (amongst other grounds). Article 47 is a stand-alone provision on gender, and it contains multiple cooperation-styled promises to work on women's equal participation in economic, social and cultural life, integration of gender perspective in public policies, development strategies and policy actions. It also seeks to equate women's and men's access to services and resources such as education, health, vocational training, political decision-making, governance structures and private undertakings. It also gives particular attention to initiating programmes that could address violence against women. Article 44 is another best practice provision which focuses on women's health as parties through this provision seek to improve maternal health, and to address health priority areas such as sexual and reproductive health and the care for and prevention of sexually transmitted diseases and unwanted pregnancies. The parties to this FTA also reaffirm the commitments they have undertaken under ILO Convention 100 (concerning Equal Remuneration for Men and Women Workers for Work of Equal Value) and Convention 111 (concerning Discrimination in Respect of Employment and Occupation). Finally, the parties to this Agreement agree to reserve a right to enforce any measure for the protection of social security, health, education and childcare. This reservation is a unique best practice example which is the only provision in this Agreement drafted with binding expressions.

In EU–Albania,[40] parties seek to cooperate on ensuring the adjustment of Albanian legislation concerning working conditions and equal opportunities for women. Such provision seems to be a minimum legal standard but drafted in a best endeavour language (Article 99). This provision can be contrasted to the European Economic Area,[41] which contains a binding obligation wherein parties commit to ensuring the application of the equal pay for equal work requirement.

[39] Agreement establishing an Association between the European Union and its Member States, on the one hand, and Central America on the other (Tegucigalpa, 29 June 2012).

[40] Stabilisation and Association Agreement between the European Communities and their Member States, of the one part, and the Republic of Albania of the other part (Luxembourg, 12 June 2006).

[41] Agreement on the European Economic Area (Porto, 2 May 1992).

Such wording implies a minimum legal standard drafted with binding expressions and is quite rare in most of the existing FTAs.

The EU–Eastern and Southern Africa States Interim EPA[42] incorporates gender considerations in a different manner. Its provision on trade in fisheries includes the parties' best endeavour promise to promote gender equality and women's capacity in fisheries. Moreover, Article 38 identifies gender mainstreaming as one of the cooperation areas for economic development. In Annex IV, the parties seek to promote female entrepreneurship and women's access to business and resources as part of their development matrix. However, nowhere in the Agreement do the parties explain how they might want to implement these activities or put these promises into action.

In EU–Egypt,[43] parties seek to enhance women's access to higher education and training (Article 42). Yet, the Article does not identify whether this education and training would focus on traditional and low-paid skills or would extend to lucrative fields of education (such as STEM and ICT) which might translate to high paid and attractive employment. This Agreement, together with the EU–Jordan FTA[44] are unique in the sense that the parties to these agreements seek to align Jordanian and Egyptian laws and policies with the objective of gender equality through effective use of education and media. The parties seek to develop family planning policies which might work in favour of women, as lack of family planning regulations could cause a barrier to their participation in trade and commerce (Article 82). This angle of women's empowerment makes this provision unique and different from most existing FTAs (except for some FTAs the EU has signed with other countries in the Middle East region with similar provisions).

In EU–CARIFORUM,[45] parties in Article 5 commit to review the operation of the Agreement to ensure that the Agreement is implemented for the benefit of men as well as women. This commitment to review the impact or operation of the Agreement is a best practice provision. However, the parties to this Agreement do not commit to any affirmative action in this respect, either in the form of cooperation or a binding commitment. They also do not identify how this review or impact assessment may be carried out and whether it would be an ex ante or an ex post assessment of the Agreement's impact.[46]

[42] Interim Agreement establishing a framework for an Economic Partnership Agreement between the Eastern and Southern Africa States, on the one part, and the European Community and its Member States, on the other part (Grand Baie, 29 August 2009).

[43] Euro-Mediterranean Agreement establishing an Association between the European Communities and their Member States, of the one part, and the Arab Republic of Egypt, of the other part (Luxembourg, 25 June 2001).

[44] Euro-Mediterranean Agreement establishing an association between the European Communities and their Member States and the Hashemite Kingdom of Jordan (Brussels, 24 November 1997).

[45] Economic Partnership Agreement between the CARIFORUM States, of the one part, and the European Community and its Member States, of the other part (Brussels, 28 October 2008).

[46] Countries can use the UNCTAD's toolbox on trade and gender for conducting these assessments. More details at UNCTAD, 'UNCTAD Trade and Gender Tool Box' (UNCTAD, 2017) unctad.org/en/pages/PublicationWebflyer.aspx?publicationid=1877.

In EU–Chile,[47] Article 45 is a stand-alone gender provision that seeks parties' cooperation on 'strengthening policies and programmes that improve, guarantee and extend the equitable participation of men and women in all sectors of political, economic, social and cultural life'. It also contains parties' unequivocal willingness to ensure that gender and gender-related issues are taken into account at every level and in all areas of cooperation including macroeconomic policy, strategy and development operations. This best practice provision reflects parties' willingness to incorporate gender perspective into their economic growth and development, policies, programmes, decision-making, policymaking and practices at the national level. However, most of these commitments are promises that the parties are not bound to fulfil.

In addition to these inclusions, the EU has also demonstrated a political commitment to use its trade instruments for fostering gender equality, as it has promised to ensure that trade-related aspects of gender would be adequately addressed in its future trade agreements.[48] The European Parliament passed a resolution in 2018 to include gender equality consideration in all future EU trade accords.[49] The implementation of this commitment can clearly be seen in its ongoing negotiations with Chile, wherein the EU is negotiating perhaps the most comprehensive chapter on gender and trade in trade agreements so far.[50] These examples demonstrate that the extent to which FTAs embrace gender concerns largely relies on the political willingness of the administrations in power. This can also be exemplified by the Chilean example, wherein gender became an explicit component of Chile's trade policy during Michelle Bachelet's second administration from 2014 to 2018.[51]

Let us consider some key takeaways from these best practice examples.

Best Practice Examples: Key Takeaways from the EU

- In EU–Eastern and Southern Africa States Interim EPA, parties seek to promote female entrepreneurship and women's access to business and resources as part of their development matrix.
- In EU–Egypt and EU–Jordan, EU giving its market access in exchange for the counterparts agreeing to bolster and develop their family planning policies and mother and child protection programmes.

[47] Agreement establishing an association between the European Community and its Member States, of the one part, and the Republic of Chile, of the other part (Brussels, 18 November 2002).

[48] European Commission, Gender Equality Strategy, ec.europa.eu/info/policies/justice-and-fundamental-rights/gender-equality/gender-equality-strategy_en.

[49] Resolution on 'Gender Equality in EU Trade Agreements' (n 25).

[50] EU proposal, 'Draft provisions on Trade and Gender Equality in the context of the Modernisation of the EU-Chile Association Agreement', trade.ec.europa.eu/doclib/html/156962.htm.

[51] D Lopez, F Munoz and J Caceres, 'Gender Inclusion in Chilean Free Trade Agreements' (Working Paper) 14 (on record with the author); Bachelet's administration is widely known for its works and accomplishments relating to gender issues. For more information, see L Stevenson, 'The Bachelet Effect on Gender-Equity Policies' (2012) 39 *Latin American Perspectives* 129.

- In EU–Ukraine, parties seek to address major health concerns of women such as maternity needs and mental healthcare.
- In EU–CARIFORUM, parties commit to review the operation and impact of the Agreement to ensure that agreement is implemented for the benefit of men as well as women.
- In EU–Central America, the focus is turned to protecting the lives of women in conflict situations and to combat xenophobia and discrimination on the grounds of sex. Also mentions programmes that could address violence against women.
- In EU–Central America, attention paid to sexual and reproductive health of women and the care for and prevention of sexually transmitted diseases and unwanted pregnancies.
- EU–Chile reflects parties' willingness to incorporate gender perspective into their economic growth and development, policies, programmes, decision-making, policymaking and practices at the national level.
- European Economic Area contains a binding minimum legal standard on equal pay for equal work.

The discussions so far show that there is a half-opened door in existing FTAs that countries need to push open further by finding different ways of implementing or enforcing their gender-related commitments. A number of existing agreements mainstream gender considerations in their own unique ways; however rarely would an FTA contemplate how gender-related commitments could be implemented, financed, or enforced. For implementation of gender-related commitments, countries in their future FTAs need to create dedicated procedures and institutions that can put their long list of commitments into action. FTAs need to spell out the functions of these specialised institutions, milestones and objectives these institutions are expected to achieve, and a time line by which to achieve these milestones. The most important in this regard is to provide for funding arrangements to finance gender-related activities if there is a genuine intent of putting these commitments into action. The Canada–Chile and Canada–Israel FTAs provide for specialised institutions (gender committees), but neither of them clarify precise procedures nor identify channels to finance these activities. Moreover, it can be noted that most of the gender-related provisions in existing FTAs are drafted as best endeavour promises and not so much as commitments and almost never as binding commitments (with very few exceptions as seen in the section above). How should the half-opened door be opened? Put differently, how can countries put these commitments into action? The next section addresses this question.

IV. Putting Gender Equality Provisions into Action

This section will put forward five policy recommendations that can help countries negotiate and craft trade agreements that can contribute to a sustainable economy.

Policymakers and trade negotiators can adopt, in part or fully, these recommendations to increase the gender-responsiveness of trade agreements they are currently negotiating or planning to renegotiate or modernise in the future. They can make these adjustments in accordance with their individual political willingness, socio-economic needs, existing domestic laws and available resources.

A. Policy Recommendation 1: Craft a Gender-Explicit Exception

It is very common to find various GATT-like exceptions in existing FTAs; they could range from protection of public morals, human health or life, to environment or national security.[52] In the same way, a new exception for gender can be designed for future FTAs. No such exception exists to date in FTAs. If countries can allow FTA-inconsistent practices and laws to operate if they harm their public morals, or animal health or life, or even plant health or life, how can countries oppose an exception that can reduce gender inequality and include humankind's half population in the journey towards economic growth and development? In this uncertain environment, more governments than ever would have to extend various support measures (including subsidies, bail-outs and other financial benefits) mainly to those industries that are most severely hit by the pandemic. A gender-specific exception can allow countries to provide such support (that may otherwise be inconsistent with their trade obligations) for industries that particularly impact women employees and entrepreneurs in the form of government bail-outs, loans and subsidies. Such an exception can also allow parties to create favourable conditions for investment and growth in sectors that are particularly relevant for women (such as agriculture, tourism, hospitality and education services).

B. Policy Recommendation 2: Cooperate on (or Commit to) Enhancing Women's Access to Education

As discussed earlier, the pandemic has made women more time-poor as it has drowned them in increased household responsibilities, taking them further away from the possibility of availing themselves of educational opportunities they might have otherwise taken. The lockdown mode of academic institutions has made this situation even worse for women, as women with no or fewer technological abilities are more poorly equipped than men to benefit from online education.[53] Hence, improving women's access to education is a crucial commitment that policymakers should consider. Efforts directed at women's access to education should entail increasing their access to technology and the internet, which is crucial to reconnect

[52] See Art 32.1 of Agreement between the United States of America, the United Mexican States, and Canada (USMCA) (Buenos Aires, 30 November 2018).

[53] ITC, 'Unlocking Markets for Women to Trade' (n 20).

women to the economy and help them reap the benefits of trade digitisation. As seen in the earlier section, many FTAs already include cooperation provisions on enhancing women's access to education and skill development. However, the fundamental problem with most of these provisions is that they either do not spell out the type of education and skill development; or the type of education or skill development mentioned in the agreement can only prepare women for traditional and low-paid jobs for example in the field of nursing, farming and knitting. Importantly, future FTAs should contain provisions that clearly spell out the kind of education and encourage women to undertake studies in the fields of STEM that can prepare them for high-paid career opportunities.[54] These new roles will enable women to move away from the traditional stereotyped jobs that societies have imposed on them such as farming, nursing or household responsibilities.

C. Policy Recommendation 3: Cooperate on (or Commit to) Enhancing Women's Access to Health

Insufficient protection of health requirements such as maternity needs, childcare and prevention of unwanted pregnancy have been an impediment to women's empowerment even before the onset of this pandemic. This pandemic has exacerbated these pre-existing concerns, as medical services worldwide are now focused on tackling virus-inflicted patients and patients with non-urgent issues are reluctant or even fearful to approach medical establishments. This situation can lead to complications in birth and higher rates of unwanted pregnancy.[55] Hence, COVID-19 has reduced women's access to crucial health services. To top it all, women who work in informal sectors mainly in developing countries are putting their lives at risk as they still have to venture out in search of their livelihood. A focus on access to health is therefore crucial in future regional trade negotiations to undo the repercussions this pandemic is having on women's health. As seen in the section before, none of the North American FTAs put a direct focus on women's access to health services. However, the EU has signed a couple of agreements with best practice provisions on health. The EU–Ukraine FTA is one such example where parties seek to cooperate on addressing major health concerns of women such as maternity needs and mental healthcare.[56] To be better prepared to operate in the post-COVID-19 world and to engage women in the economic recovery process, it is important that trade agreements embrace this focus on health requirements.

[54] This best practice can be seen in Modernized Canada–Israel FTA (n 23) and Modernized Canada–Chile FTA (n 23).

[55] 'The women who can't get an abortion in lockdown' *BBC News* (13 July 2020), www.bbc.com/news/world-asia-india-53345975.

[56] Art 427 of Ukraine–European Union Association Agreement (Brussels, 21 March 2014).

D. Policy Recommendation 4: Include Minimum Legal Standards

With increased cases of violence, loss of jobs and rising unfavourable conditions to achieve professional development in the post-COVID-19 world, it is important that policymakers consider including certain legal standards in future FTAs. Minimum legal standards require a change in a country's domestic laws and regulations. One important standard to repair or minimise the ongoing harm could be the inclusion of the 'equal pay for equal work' requirement. This obligation is mentioned in several agreements, but it is mostly framed in permissive language without any binding obligations on the negotiating members to provide for binding equal pay legislation. Eliminating or reducing the wage gap is crucial for engaging women in the economic recovery process. FTAs can provide an avenue for imposing such obligations on individual countries: a country otherwise unwilling to employ equal pay legislation in its domestic laws may be willing to consider it as part of its domestic law if it comes as a package with enhanced market access to an important trading nation. Other standards could relate to the elimination of employment discrimination on the basis of sex, provision of anti-harassment procedures at workplaces, and the protection of women against any form of violence.

E. Policy Recommendation 5: Create Institutions, Procedures and Financing Channels to Ensure Implementation

Gender commitments in FTAs would be meaningless if they cannot be implemented. To build back better and in an inclusive manner, FTAs need to have an implementation mechanism to put either binding or best endeavour into action. Such a mechanism could be institutional or procedural. In the earlier section, some very good examples of institutional mechanisms have been provided. For example, the Canada–Chile and Canada–Israel FTAs have provisions which create a Gender Committee and some operational arrangements for the Committee such as its composition, functions and meeting frequencies. Yet, these provisions fall short of clarifying how these functions or activities or Gender Committee meetings might be financed. Therefore, in addition to providing for institutions or procedures, it is important that policymakers identify funding options alongside these commitments to bring these promises a step closer to implementation. In the absence of such provisions, the resource-constrained pandemic-hit countries may not have sufficient resources to invest in the women-favouring promises they might have made in trade instruments.

Inclusion of the elements proposed above in trade agreements would help minimise the damage this pandemic is inflicting on inclusive growth and development. Yet, gender-related commitments in existing trade agreements may remain a distant reality if these commitments cannot be enforced. It cannot be ignored that almost all FTAs have explicitly and unambiguously excluded gender-related provisions and chapters from the application of their dispute settlement machineries. This fact implies that a country's failure to comply with these obligations or commitments or affirmations has no direct consequence. The only exception is the Canada–Israel FTA which provides (for the very first time) a binding dispute settlement procedure that is applicable to its chapter on trade and gender.[57] This also seems to be a cosmetic attempt to provide for an enforcement mechanism as the parties have subjected the binding jurisdiction of this mechanism to their consent, making its jurisdiction non-compulsory in nature.[58] Future trade agreements should consider going a step further by subjecting gender provisions to binding and compulsory dispute settlement provisions.

V. Conclusion

Women are bearing a disproportionate burden of the COVID-19 pandemic, in terms of health, employment, business, consumption and social protection. The limited gains made in the past decades in respect of achieving gender equality are at risk of being rolled back as the pandemic is deepening pre-existing inequalities. FTAs may play an important role in minimising this loss, as they can help restart the economy in the post-COVID-19 world. FTAs can provide the architecture for sustainable and inclusive economic growth. As seen in the chapter, FTAs can help in reducing the barriers that impede women's participation in the economy, in particular, those barriers that relate to access to education, health services, finance and productive resources, and creation of lucrative business and employment conditions. They can also create encouraging conditions for women's businesses to flourish, for example by the creation of business networks and improved infrastructure in relevant sectors and industries. FTAs can also inspire countries to carry out ex post and ex ante gender impact assessments of trade agreements that they are party to.[59] Parties to FTAs could also commit to increasing the representation of women in decision-making and policymaking roles. Therefore, countries can use trade agreements as laboratories of change where they can experiment with different legal provisions and commitments regarding gender equality.

Amidst this crisis, it is necessary to think beyond the immediate. Policy response needs to play an important role in determining the pace and nature of economic recovery. Before this crisis is over, policymakers and international organisations need to work together and prepare action plans for repairing the harm. The world economy will suffer even more if women – who account for one

[57] Ch 19 of CIFTA (n 23).
[58] ibid Art 13.6.
[59] Countries can use the UNCTAD's toolbox on trade and gender for conducting these assessments. See 'UNCTAD Trade and Gender Tool Box' (n 46).

half of the world's working-age population – are further excluded from the economy and hence impeded from contributing to economic growth and economic recovery post-COVID-19.[60] Future trade policy responses must recognise this risk and include women at the heart of the COVID-19 response. Placing women at the centre of economies will lead to a more rapid recovery; this recovery will rekindle the efforts to achieve the Sustainable Development Goals.[61]

[60] J Woetzel et al, 'The Power of Parity: How Advancing Women's Equality can Add $12 Trillion' (Mckinsey Global Institute, September 2015), www.mckinsey.com/featured-insights/employment-and-growth/how-advancing-womens-equality-can-add-12-trillion-to-global-growth#.

[61] Observed in UNCTAD, 'Making Trade Agreements Work for Gender Equality – Data and Statistics' (2020) Policy Brief No 81, unctad.org/webflyer/making-trade-agreements-work-gender-equality-data-and-statistics.

PART III

Rescuing World Trade Law and Other Fundamental Challenges

11

The Current State of Dispute Settlement at the WTO: How did We Get Here and What Next?

JAN YVES REMY*

I. Introduction

By 10 December 2019, the number of judges serving on the Appellate Body (or Appellate Body members) – the final appeal court of the World Trade Organization (WTO) – had dwindled to just one, well short of the full complement of seven envisaged under the rules establishing the Dispute Settlement Understanding (DSU)[1] or the three required to hear a given appeal. Still, by operation of a special rule of appellate procedure (Rule 15 to be precise), judges who had already commenced stayed on to complete the few remaining cases in the docket, with a bare-bones secretariat providing legal and technical support.

It was not until the final report of the Appellate Body issued on 9 June 2020[2] that the certainty of the Appellate Body's demise finally materialised, signalling the end of an era in dispute settlement that began in 1995 when the Appellate Body emerged as one of the innovations accompanying the establishment of the WTO. Less certain, however, are the consequences of the loss of the Appellate Body for dispute settlement and the legitimacy of the WTO, at a time of increasing unilateralism by WTO Members and a fragile world economy plagued by the unforeseen COVID-19 pandemic.

* This chapter has been adapted from a contribution made by the author to a Commonwealth Secretariat 'Trade Hot Topics' entry entitled 'Dispute Settlement at the WTO: How Did We Get Here and What Next for Commonwealth States?'

[1] Understanding on Rules and Procedures Governing the Settlement of Disputes (DSU), Marrakesh Agreement Establishing the World Trade Organization, Annex 2 (Marrakesh, 15 April 1994).

[2] *Australia–Tobacco Plain Packaging (Honduras)*, Report of the Appellate Body (29 June 2020) WT/DS435/AB/R; *Australia–Tobacco Plain Packaging (Dominican Republic)*, Report of the Appellate Body (29 June 2020) WT/DS441/AB/R.

This chapter begins by briefly outlining the history of the Appellate Body, highlighting its successes and the criticisms it has attracted, as well as the reasons for its demise. This is followed by a discussion on the technicalities of one proposed option to temporarily fill the void left by the Appellate Body's absence – that is, the Multiparty Interim Appeal Arbitration Agreement (MPIA) – assessing the merits of the MPIA and explaining what it might portend for participating and non-participating Members. The chapter concludes with two recommendations for WTO Members as they seek to define and promote their dispute settlement interests in the current WTO environment.

II. History and Benefits of the Appellate Body

The Appellate Body emerged at the same time as the WTO was founded, at the conclusion of the Uruguay Round in 1995.[3] In a series of recent papers, Hoekman and Mavroidis catalogue some of the motivations of the DSU's drafters when they decided to create new procedures to replace the non-automatic, consensus-based, single-tier structure for dispute settlement under the GATT (the WTO's predecessor).[4] Key participants in the discussions were the United States (US), the European Union (EU), Canada, Australia, South Korea, Japan and Brazil. Interestingly, it was the US that requested reforms to the non-binding GATT system (under which there was no right to appeal and a losing party could block adoption of a Panel Report), while the EU preferred to keep intact its diplomatic character. For the US, which had increasingly resorted to unilateralism, only a strong dispute settlement system would persuade it to give up its 'nuclear option' of unilateral enforcement through its so-called 'Section 301' legislation.[5]

Only belatedly in the negotiations did Canada first propose the concept of an appeals board, as a 'fast-track procedure' to be completed within 30 days. Although not many details had been worked out, no one objected to the proposal:

[3] General Agreement on Tariffs and Trade (GATT), Marrakesh Agreement Establishing the World Trade Organization (Marrakesh, 15 April 1994).

[4] See B Hoekman and PC Mavroidis, 'Burning Down the House? The Appellate Body in the Centre of the WTO Crisis WTO Crisis' (2019) EUI Working Papers, RSCAS 2019/56 Robert Schuman Centre for Advanced Studies Global Governance Programme-353, s 2; see also generally, B Hoekman and PC Mavroidis, 'Preventing the Bad from Getting Worse: The End of the World (Trade Organization) As We Know it?' (2020) EUI Working Papers RSCAS 2020/06 Robert Schuman Centre for Advanced Studies Global Governance Programme-381.

[5] As Hoekman and Mavroidis explain, the US was 'disappointed with the impossibility of enforcing dispute settlement outcomes in the realm of farm trade (the European Union would routinely block panel rulings that were adverse to its interests), and the lack of progress in integrating services trade and protection of intellectual property rights into the GATT framework' and therefore took justice into its own hands through 'Section 301', 'Special 301', 'Super 301', that is, legislation through which the US administration would enforce its 'rights' unilaterally, that is, without observing GATT Arts XXII and XXIII. Hoekman and Mavroidis, 'Burning Down the House?' (n 4) 5.

its acceptance would not upset the overall compromise, and some – like Japan, Korea, Australia and the EU – expressed support for the added layer of review.[6]

By the time the negotiations concluded, one solitary provision – Article 17, along with its numerous sub-paragraphs – had been inserted into the DSU, setting out parameters for the operation of the Appellate Body as well as its institutional and jurisdictional limits. Important features of the appeal system included: (i) strict timelines (including a 90-day overall time frame for appeals); (ii) delimitation of appeal issues to matters of legal interpretation and application – as opposed to factual review – arising from Panel reports; (iii) a standing body of seven part-time Appellate Body members who were to be 'broadly representative' of the WTO membership; and (iv) a legal secretariat of career lawyers to assist the judges. The first slate of judges drafted the working procedures that further elaborated the day-to-day operations of the Appellate Body.[7]

Since then, in its 25 years of operation, the Appellate Body has generated an impressive volume of case law (over 100 appeal reports adopted and an appeal rate of over 65 per cent);[8] contributed to formalising dispute settlement at the WTO; and largely brought consistency to trade law jurisprudence. The Appellate Body has also succeeded in its aims: providing an effective second-tier level of review to standardise case law and bring 'predictability and security' in international trade relations; securing the enforcement of obligations by filling in the interstices of the incomplete WTO 'contract'; and providing the necessary safeguard against governments' wanton reneging on negotiated commitments.

Yet its track record is not perfect. It is often stated that dispute settlement – and the Appellate Body – has not delivered for the smallest WTO Members, who struggle to access and effectively utilise the system given their human and financial (cost) limitations and the lack of enforceability of decisions. For example, in a 2014 study featuring the performance of small states[9] and least developed countries (LDCs) in WTO dispute settlement, it was noted that, up to that date, these states participated as complainants and defendants in under 1 per cent of cases. Sadly, little if anything has changed since the publication of that paper.[10]

[6] ibid s 2, 10.

[7] WTO, 'Working Procedures for Appellate Review' (15 February 1996) WT/AB/WP/1. They have since been revised six times.

[8] See, for instance, WTO, 'Dispute Settlement Statistics', www.wto.org/english/tratop_e/dispu_e/stats_e.htm.

[9] The small states considered were Commonwealth Small States: 'Small States' (The Commonwealth), thecommonwealth.org/our-work/small-states.

[10] eg, the Appellate Body ruled in favour of Antigua and Barbuda against the US in a case involving access to the latter's market in cross-border gambling and betting services. Despite winning on the merits, and although the WTO authorised Antigua and Barbuda to retaliate against the US through suspension of its TRIPS obligations, there has still not been a successful outcome for Antigua and Barbuda. *United States–Measures Affecting the Cross-Border Supply of Gambling and Betting Services*, Report of the Panel (20 April 2005) WT/DS285/R; *United States–Measures Affecting the Cross-Border Supply of Gambling and Betting Service*, Report of the Appellate Body (20 April 2005) WT/DS285/AB/R.

Inevitably, as time elapsed and more and more cases were decided, some questioned whether the Appellate Body was operating as intended and meeting the needs of the WTO's expanded membership.[11]

The impetus for the first set of formal reform efforts came from a 1994 Ministerial Decision, which mandated a review of the DSU (the DSU Review) to be completed by the end of 1998.[12] The discussions were not successful and were thereafter subsumed within the broader Doha negotiations, under a mandate to 'improve and clarify' the DSU by 2004. That multilateral process has continued to this day.

In the context of the DSU Review, core topics being discussed include: (i) mutually agreed solutions; (ii) third-party rights; (iii) strictly confidential information; (iv) sequencing; (v) post-retaliation; (vi) transparency and amicus curiae briefs; (vii) time frames; (viii) remand; (ix) panel composition; (x) effective compliance; (xi) developing country interests; and (xii) flexibility and member control.[13] Most DSU Review proposals do not call into question the basic architecture of the system, including the Appellate Body.

III. The US Complaints Bring Appeals to a Halt

The US has for a long time now complained of 'overreach' by the Appellate Body, with its disapproval manifested in proposals on 'flexibility and Member control' in the context of the DSU Review, and in statements at meetings of the WTO's Dispute Settlement Body (DSB) or General Council.[14]

What is new, however, is the US decision to link its long-standing concerns with the Appellate Body to the selection process for its judges, specifically using its veto at the DSB to block new appointments.[15] A confluence of factors has led to

[11] Hoekman and Mavroidis attribute some of the objections to the results of the 'zeroing' cases, involving methodologies for calculating duty margins under the Agreement on Anti-Dumping. Hoekman and Mavroidis, 'Burning Down the House?' (n 4).

[12] In 1994, the GATT Contracting Parties adopted a decision at their Ministerial Conference in Marrakesh, Morocco to complete a full review of dispute settlement rules and procedures under the newly created WTO within four years after the entry into force of the Agreement Establishing the World Trade Organization. Members were to take a decision at that time on whether to continue, modify or terminate such dispute settlement rules and procedures (see 'Negotiations to improve dispute settlement procedures' (WTO), www.wto.org/english/tratop_e/dispu_e/dispu_negs_e.htm).

[13] For a comprehensive discussion, see R McDougall, 'The Crisis in WTO Dispute Settlement: Fixing Birth Defects to Restore Balance' (2018) 52 *Journal of World Trade* 867.

[14] See, for instance, Statement of Ambassador D Shea at the WTO General Council Meeting (US Mission in Geneva, 23 July 2019), geneva.usmission.gov/2019/07/23/statements-delivered-by-ambassador-dennis-shea-wto-general-council-meeting-july-23-2019/.

[15] Under the rules of procedure of the DSB, decisions regarding appointments require consensus – or an absence of objection – among the WTO membership, failing which there can be no renewal of the judges' four-year terms or selection of new ones. See US Statements at the DSB meeting (US Mission in Geneva, 27 August 2018), geneva.usmission.gov/wp-content/uploads/sites/290/Aug27.DSB_.Stmt_.as-delivered.fin_.public.pdf.

the current recalcitrance of the US, including the 2016 election of President Trump and his appointment of Robert Lighthizer as the US Trade Representative (USTR), a known proponent of WTO dispute settlement reform.[16]

The main concerns the US has with the Appellate Body's alleged judicial 'overreach' have been represented as follows:

- Disregard for the 90-day deadline for appeals under Article 17.5 of the DSU.
- Application of Rule 15 of its Working Procedures to extend the terms of office of Appellate Body members whose terms have expired, for the purpose of completing appeals to which they were assigned.
- Issuance of 'advisory opinions' on issues unnecessary to resolve a dispute.
- Review of facts and domestic law *de novo*.
- Treatment of its prior reports as binding precedent.[17]

As an immediate response to the continued blockage of appointments, Ambassador David Walker (New Zealand) was tasked with facilitating an informal process to address these concerns and revitalise the selection process to fill vacancies at the Appellate Body. A total of 12 proposals were submitted, reviewed and discussed. A number of countries including Australia, Canada, New Zealand, India, the EU and the African Group, participated in and provided proposals for those discussions.[18]

A key outcome of the Informal 'Walker Process' was a draft General Council decision (Draft Decision) based on points of convergence identified in the informal consultations.[19] WTO Members considered the Draft Decision at the meeting of the General Council in December 2019, just in time for the expiration of the terms of two of the remaining Appellate Body members. Among the points noted in the Decision was a shared view that the Appellate Body had, in some respects,

[16] This is at least the perception that is widely held in the news media. See, for instance, A Behsudi, 'The man getting ready to take on the WTO' *Politico* (15 February 2017), www.politico.com/agenda/story/2017/02/robert-lighthizer-wto-000304/.

[17] See, for instance, Statement of Ambassador Shea (n 14).

[18] The following proposals for DSU reform were made: WTO General Council, Communication from the EU, China, Canada, India, Norway, New Zealand, Switzerland, Australia, Korea, Iceland, Singapore, Mexico, Costa Rica and Montenegro to the General Council (11 December 2018) WT/GC/W/752/Rev.2; WTO General Council, Communication from the EU, China, India and Montenegro to the General Council (11 December 2018) WT/GC/W/753/Rev.1; WTO General Council, Communication from Separate Customs Territory of Taiwan, Penghu, Kinmen and Matsu: Guideline Development Discussion (8 April 2019) WT/GC/W/763/Rev.1; WTO General Council, Communication from Brazil, Paraguay and Uruguay: Guidelines for the Work of Panels and the Appellate Body (25 April 2019) WT/GC/W/767/Rev.1; WTO General Council, Communication from Japan, Australia and Chile: Informal Process on Matters related to the Functioning of the Appellate Body (26 April 2019) WT/GC/W/768/Rev.1; WTO General Council, Communication from Thailand: General Council Decision on the Dispute Settlement System of the WTO (26 April 2019) WT/GC/W/769; WTO General Council, Communication from the African Group: Appellate Body Impasse (26 June 2019) WT/GC/W/776.

[19] See The Draft General Council decision, 'Functioning of the Appellate Body' (28 November 2019) WT/GC/W/791. This Draft decision was presented to the General Council at its 9–11 December 2019 meeting.

not been functioning as intended under the DSU.[20] In an effort to appease US concerns, the Decision was drafted in sections addressing (i) transitional rules for outgoing Appellate Body members; (ii) the 90-day time frame for appeals; (iii) the meaning of municipal law; (iv) advisory opinions; (v) precedent; and (vi) 'overreach' in the interpretation of the WTO Agreements. Also set out was a process under the DSB to establish, in consultation with the Appellate Body, a mechanism for regular dialogue between WTO Members and the Appellate Body where members could express their views on issues unrelated to specific cases.

The US objected to the adoption of the Draft Decision on the ground that it failed to address the 'fundamental question' of 'why Appellate Body [felt] free to disregard the clear text of the agreements'.[21] Consequently, the General Council could not adopt the Draft Decision, and the US has continued, as of this writing, to block the selection process.

IV. Requiem for the Appellate Body

As well intentioned as the Walker Process was, it could not prevent the fall of the Appellate Body. As of 10 December 2019, only one Appellate Body member remained; and on 9 June 2020, the Appellate Body issued its last report.[22]

This situation raises deep systemic concerns, including that WTO Members, having effectively been stripped of a right to appeal, no longer have a way to correct legal errors in Panel reports. This would also endanger consistency across panel decisions. More disturbingly, it means that panel decisions can be rendered unenforceable: a losing member can now simply 'appeal' unfavourable Panel reports under the provisions of the DSU to a non-existent Appellate Body, thereby suspending the dispute indefinitely.[23] Without a legal fix to preclude this treaty-based right that still exists under the current DSU, adoption of reports can be forestalled by a (losing) party 'appealing into the void'.

Of course, irrespective of what happens with appeals, WTO Members retain their right to use other (non-binding) dispute settlement options – that is, alternative dispute resolution (ADR) mechanisms – such as good offices, conciliation and mediation (under Article 5 of the DSU), and arbitration (under Article 25 of the DSU). These options are available in addition to or in lieu of the Panel and appeal processes and are considered by many to be a more expeditious and less costly means of resolving disputes. Nonetheless, there has been limited uptake of ADR

[20] ibid, fourth preambular recital.

[21] General Council, Minutes of Meeting (9–10 December 2019) WT/GC/M/181, para 5.103.

[22] *Australia–Tobacco Plain Packaging*, Report of the Appellate Body (n 2).

[23] This has happened, for instance, in *United States–Countervailing Measures on Certain Hot-Rolled Carbon Steel Flat Products from India*, Recourse to Article 21.5 of the DSU by India (15 November 2019) WT/DS436 (*US–Carbon Steel (India)*). See *US–Carbon Steel (India)*, Notification of an Appeal by the United States under Article 16 of the DSU (19 December 2019) WT/DS436/21.

owing to its voluntary nature (parties have to agree to use it) and the perception that it is sub-standard. Many potential DSU users seem unaware that there is a right provided to developing countries under Article 3.12 of the DSU to invoke special 1966 Procedures[24] in lieu of standard panel procedures in any dispute against a developed country and that Article 24.2 of the DSU provides that the WTO Director-General must offer good offices, conciliation and mediation in any dispute involving an LDC. Despite its under-utilisation, the track record of ADR is impressive, leading in one situation to the resolution of a 20-year-old dispute in just two years.[25]

V. MPIA as a Single Possible Solution

The real risk of panel decisions being rendered unenforceable, as well as the destruction of the two-tier system of appeal, has led a group of members to initiate a proposal first mooted by WTO practitioners,[26] and then announced as bilateral solutions,[27] to use DSU Article 25 arbitration procedures as a temporary substitute for the now defunct appeal process.[28]

The proposal was taken up by 19 WTO Members who formally announced the MPIA to the DSB on 30 April 2020.[29] Since the original announcement, five more WTO Members have signed up to the MPIA, bringing its current total membership to 24.[30]

[24] The Decision on Procedures under Article XXIII (5 April 1966) BISD 14S/18. The Decision provides for the Director-General of the WTO, in matters involving developing countries, to use his good offices to facilitate the settlement of a dispute.

[25] H Nottage, 'Commonwealth Small States and Least Developed Countries in the WTO Dispute Settlement System' (2014) Commonwealth Trade Policy Discussion Papers 2014/02, s V, 28. The author refers to the *EC–Bananas* dispute.

[26] S Andersen et al, 'Using Arbitration Under Article 25 of the DSU to Ensure the Availability of Appeals' (2017) CTEI Working Paper 2017-17, repository.graduateinstitute.ch/record/295745.

[27] In July 2019, the EU and Canada notified the DSB of the interim appeal arbitration agreement that would apply in future disputes between them, in circumstances where the Appellate Body was unable to hear appeals due to an insufficient number of ABMs. See, for instance, 'Joint Statement by the European Union and Canada on an Interim Appeal Arbitration Arrangement' (European Commission, 25 July 2019), ec.europa.eu/commission/presscorner/detail/en/STATEMENT_19_4709). A subsequent proposal between the EU and Norway was notified in October 2019.

[28] Art 25 of the DSU (n 1) – entitled 'Arbitration' – allows parties to mutually agree procedures for dispute settlement, establishes the bindingness of the awards by arbitrators, and engages the full enforcement and implementation procedures under Arts 21 and 22 of the DSU once awards are rendered.

[29] Multi-party Interim Appeal Arbitration Arrangement Pursuant to Article 25 of the DSU (27 March 2020), trade.ec.europa.eu/doclib/docs/2020/march/tradoc_158685.pdf (MPIA).

[30] As of 31 January 2021, the MPIA Members are Australia, Benin, Brazil, Canada, China, Chile, Colombia, Costa Rica, Ecuador, the EU (including the United Kingdom), Guatemala, Hong Kong (China), Iceland, Mexico, Montenegro, Macao (China), New Zealand, Nicaragua, Norway, Pakistan, Singapore, Switzerland, Ukraine and Uruguay. In total, 51 countries are members of MPIA, if the EU, its 27 Member States and the United Kingdom are counted individually.

By design, the MPIA provides an 'interim' regime for appellate proceedings for 'as long as the Appellate Body is not able to hear appeals'.[31] It is, therefore, expressly without prejudice to finding a lasting solution to the appeal crisis. Its drafters aim to safeguard two important aspects of the WTO's dispute settlement system – its binding character and the two-level adjudication process – while also ensuring independence and impartiality in appeals. Any WTO Member may join at any point.

The MPIA framework is divided into three main parts: the overarching institutional arrangement; the procedures for the conduct of MPIA appeals (Annex 1); and the system for selecting a 'pool' of arbitrators (Annex 2).

First, under the institutional arrangement section, participating members give their consent to use the MPIA as a basis for settling future appeals among themselves. This part sets out the aims of the MPIA, the procedures for joining and withdrawing from it, the duties and responsibilities of the arbitrators selected to serve under it, and how, procedurally, it will operate alongside the other aspects of the dispute settlement procedures, including panel proceedings.

Second, Annex 1 to the MPIA provides for default procedures to be used by the participating members – although parties can mutually agree to depart from these procedures in a specific dispute. In effect, the MPIA process utilises the arbitration process under Article 25 of the DSU to replicate the main features of the existing WTO appeal process. It thereby mimics the original system's time frames for completion of appeals; the scope of the appeals and the powers of arbitrators; the process for selecting the Division to settle appeals; the overall decision-making process; and the rights of third parties. The MPIA, however, includes some adjustments to ensure that the new procedures can be effectively grafted onto existing ones. For instance, participating members must notify an agreement to arbitrate under the MPIA 60 days after panels are established; and must request that panels suspend their work after they have issued their interim reports, so that an appeal arbitration can begin without the risk that the Panel Report will be adopted while the appeal is pending.[32]

As a nod to the US, the MPIA includes a number of innovations: support staff to arbitrators are 'answerable … only to appeal arbitrators'[33] which might diminish the 'power' of the Secretariat. Moreover, the MPIA provides the opportunity to simplify appeals thereby making it easier for appeals to be completed within the 90-day time frame provided for in the DSU. In this regard, arbitrators are

[31] MPIA (n 29) para 1.

[32] ibid para 20 provides that '[i]n order to render the appeal arbitration procedure operational in particular disputes, the participating Members indicate their intention to enter into the arbitration agreement (the "appeal arbitration agreement") contained in Annex 1 to this communication and to notify that agreement pursuant to Article 25.2 of the DSU within 60 days after the date of the establishment of the panel. For pending disputes where, on the date of this communication, the panel has already been established but an interim report has not yet been issued, the participating Members will enter into the appeal arbitration agreement and notify that agreement pursuant to Article 25.2 of the DSU within 30 days after the date of this communication'.

[33] ibid para 7.

permitted to 'streamline procedures', including through the imposition of page and time limits and deadlines,[34] and by making recommendations to the parties that claims questioning the objectivity of panels' factual assessments be excluded.[35] In addition, arbitrators are encouraged to confine review to matters necessary to resolve a dispute.[36]

Finally, the MPIA establishes a system for selecting the pool of arbitrators from which the division of three arbitrators per case will be composed. Each of the 22 members nominates one candidate to a pre-selection committee comprising the WTO Director-General and other chairs of relevant WTO committees (Chairperson of the DSB, and the Chairpersons of the Goods, Services, TRIPS and General Council). The pre-selection committee's job is to 'screen' the nominees for selection by the participating members, who must agree to a final list of 10 arbitrators by a process of 'consensus'. Notably, current and past Appellate Body members are exempted from the pre-selection screening process and are automatically eligible for selection. Arbitrators must possess the same qualifications and competences as the Appellate Body members. However, unlike the appellate system where seven judges are chosen for a period of four years, renewable once, on the basis of broad geographic representativeness, under the MPIA, 10 arbitrators are to be chosen on the basis of an 'appropriate overall balance'.[37]

VI. Reactions to the MPIA Proposal

Since its formal announcement, a few developments have taken place to operationalise the MPIA. For instance, the pool of 10 arbitrators has been selected and discussions on the budgetary allocation for the MPIA have also taken place.

The jury is still out on how the MPIA will fare, but there is no shortage of debate.[38] With an uptake so far of less than a quarter of the membership – excluding the US, India, South Africa, Japan and the African, Caribbean and Pacific (ACP) group of states – its proponents will have to launch a more ambitious lobbying campaign if the proposal is to enjoy widespread legitimacy.

At the moment, the criticisms seem to be of a technical and political nature. As it is an untested procedure to date, some remain doubtful about the real prospects for its use.[39] Commentators have questioned how 'representative' it will be, given

[34] ibid Annex 1, para 12.
[35] ibid Annex 1, para 13.
[36] ibid Annex 1, para 10.
[37] ibid Annex 2, para 4.
[38] For a flavour of the ongoing debate on the MPIA, see recent blog entries the International Economic Law and Policy Blog, eg, J Kreier, 'India, South Africa and the MPIA' (*International Economic Law and Policy Blog*, 23 June 2020), elp.worldtradelaw.net/2020/06/india-south-africa-and-the-mpia.html.
[39] One dispute in the pipeline that uses the MPIA to settle an appeal is *Costa Rica–Measures Concerning the Importation of Fresh Avocadoes from Mexico*, Agreed procedures for arbitration under Article 25 of the DSU (3 June 2020) WT/DS524/5.

that only the initial participating countries will have a hand in selecting arbitrators; the possibility of fragmentation of the case law and the legal status of MPIA decisions vis-a-vis future or previous WTO jurisprudence; and how the MPIA will affect the balance of rights and obligations under the DSU.[40]

The US has come out against the scheme, highlighting the MPIA's potential to entrench, rather than resolve, problems with the appeal system, and questioning whether budgetary allocations for the MPIA could be justified given its limited membership. The US has therefore made it clear that it has no intention of joining the MPIA, at least at this point in time. In addition to some of the technical issues highlighted above about the systemic impact of the MPIA on dispute settlement, at a meeting of the DSB on 29 June 2020, South Africa raised a number of issues with the MPIA including: whether the mechanism of Article 25 of the DSU is the proper vehicle for a broad multilateral effort like the MPIA; the likelihood of the MPIA becoming a default 'permanent' system, by stealth, without an express decision to do so by the broader membership; lack of attention in the MPIA to developing country concerns, including how the MPIA will affect issues of costs, access and representativeness for African countries; concern that the MPIA will distract from the energy for resolving the Appellate Body impasse (as well as the ongoing Walker Process); and a general lack of clarity – and agreement – on how the MPIA will be funded from the WTO budget.[41]

Although there have been rumblings among delegates in the corridors of the WTO, and some statements in the DSB meetings have been made on the MPIA, other non-participating members have been slower to publicly declare their hand. Their reticence is likely to derive from one or a combination of the reasons highlighted above as well as others, including: the preference for a 'wait-and-see' approach as to how the system will work before committing to it; a fear of the consequences of engagement for their relations with the US; the long-standing concerns with dispute settlement and the WTO reform more generally; and general antipathy towards fixing a system that has yielded very few tangible results for them.

VII. Conclusion: Many Questions … and a Few Answers

As it is the only option on the table, there is a real chance that the MPIA will – or may – become the default option for many countries for years to come. For this

[40] See, for instance, JY Remy, 'What the new Appeal-Arbitration System Might Mean for the Future of WTO Dispute Settlement' (*Shridath Ramphal Centre Trade Blog*, 10 April 2020), shridathramphal-centre.com/cure-or-curse-the-new-appeal-arbitration-system-in-wto-dispute-settlement/.

[41] South Africa's statement at the Meeting of the Dispute Settlement Body of 29 June 2020, Minutes of Meeting (14 October 2020) W/DSB/M/443.

reason, a country that opts not to formulate a position on the MPIA as an appeal alternative – or on dispute settlement generally – does so at its own risk. It would also be a mistake for countries with a limited participation in dispute settlement to think they can 'sit this one out'. The view that such states have little at stake is exaggerated at best, and belies the interest that all countries have in the clarification of rules and their enforcement, even when they are not directly involved in litigation, since they can 'free-ride' on the coat-tails of those with greater litigating experience, deeper pockets and more direct trade interests.

While the loss of the Appellate Body may not precipitate a descent into anarchy or a complete 'breakaway' from the rules-based system as some might fear, its impact should not be underestimated.[42] COVID-19 is exacerbating a tendency by world powers to revert to beggar-thy-neighbour measures, and the EU has even proposed that countries in a dispute with it that choose to 'appeal into the void'[43] might be subjected to EU countermeasures.[44] There is also the not inconsiderable issue of the ongoing US–China 'trade war'. The spat regarding dispute settlement only exacerbates US criticisms of Chinese participation in the WTO and makes a US compromise on the MPIA – of which China is part – even less likely.[45] Simmering trade tensions between the US and EU, the latter being another key MPIA member, also casts doubt on the political viability of the MPIA as a solution for all, at least for now.[46]

Against the current background, it is in the interests of all countries to contemplate the future of dispute settlement in the light of their individual and collective interests. In any such discussion, a fundamental point of departure must be whether members want to preserve a system of binding dispute settlement. For those that do, the current situation that tolerates the possibility of 'appealing into the void' presents a major threat. A priority would be to find a workaround to current DSU rules that would lead to automatic adoption of Panel reports. They

[42] R McDougall, 'Impasse in the WTO Dispute Settlement Body: Consequences and Responses' (2018) ECIPE Brief No 11/2018, 2.

[43] In at least one dispute, the US appealed a Panel Report to a non-existent Appellate Body. See *US–Carbon Steel (India)* (n 23). For more discussion, see S Lester, 'The US Appeal in DS436' (*International Economic Law and Policy Blog*, 19 December 2019), ielp.worldtradelaw.net/2019/12/the-us-appeal-in-ds436.html.

[44] Under this proposal, if the EU won a panel ruling but its trading counterpart refused to allow an effective appeal, the EU would calculate damages in the form of quotas and tariffs. P Blenkinsop, 'EU moves to reclaim trade authority after US cripples WTO' *BusinessDay* (12 December 2019), www.businesslive.co.za/bd/world/europe/2019-12-12-eu-moves-to-reclaim-trade-authority-after-us-cripples-wto/. See also, 'Commission reinforces tools to ensure Europe's interests in international trade' (*European Commission*, 12 December 2019), trade.ec.europa.eu/doclib/press/index.cfm?id=2091&title=Commission-reinforces-tools-to-ensure-Europes-interests-in-international-trade.

[45] The US has accused China of flouting WTO rules, whether through its alleged subsidisation of its state-owned enterprises, its self-designation as a developing country, or its alleged disregard of intellectual property rights.

[46] The US recently announced a tax on French goods in response to the digital tax imposed by France. See D Palmer, 'USTR announces duties on $1.3B in French goods in tax dispute' *Politico* (7 October 2020), www.politico.com/news/2020/07/10/french-tax-ustr-356628.

could also seriously consider joining the MPIA – which has the added advantage of retaining appeal review. Failing that, the unfair consequence of being part of the MPIA is to bind some countries to comply with decisions, while leaving many free to act unilaterally.

A second issue to confront directly is the massive elephant in the room for many WTO Members – the US. Many developing countries still rely on the largesse of, and trade relations with, the US and might fear consequences if they join the MPIA. They are unlikely to proceed with the MPIA option if they consider that it would endanger their prospects with the US under the current Trump administration, or if they are not convinced that there is some clear advantage to them to sign on.

For countries that have not yet signed up to the MPIA, all options are now on the table. One option worth pursuing is the formulation of a template that would provide for a more flexible or '*à la carte* approach' to dispute settlement that defies the one-size-fits-all approach that has typified dispute settlement to date and is adapted to the needs of the specific litigants and subject matter of the dispute. Such an approach would look anew at all the procedures available under the DSU – including ADR procedures of good faith, mediation, conciliation and arbitration, as well as the more traditional panel procedures – and use them at different stages of the dispute, even allowing for use of MPIA procedures on an ad hoc basis (that is, without formally signing up to the MPIA but adopting the procedures in Annex 1). Being dependent on the complicity of members, a tailor-made approach to disputes would minimise the legitimacy issues dogging the current system and allow countries to choose procedures more attuned to their needs and sensitive to their resource constraints. Such an approach would depend on the goodwill of the parties to follow through on any agreement made *ex ante*, and the Achilles' heel would still be enforceability.

There is also the reality – and opportunity – that COVID-19 has brought to the fore: that is, the conduct of online dispute settlement proceedings. With face-to-face meetings and interactions currently impractical, the option of moving DSB meetings and panel proceedings (including the filing of documents,[47] oral hearings of the parties and panel deliberations) to online platforms has become a real possibility. A virtual format has the ability to make the settlement of disputes a more accessible process for a wider group of stakeholders, who can now remain at home and participate in disputes. Not only does that translate to cost savings for disputing parties, but equally for the WTO since the huge amounts spent on panellists' travel to the WTO Secretariat in Geneva, and their accommodation, can be avoided. The result would undoubtedly be a shift in the centre of gravity for dispute resolution away from just Geneva since more stages of the process – consultations, ADR options, panel proceedings and even eventually meetings of

[47] The WTO online registry has been an ongoing project for many years and has become a reality in recent times.

the DSB – might be conducted online. While cybersecurity and confidentiality issues would have to be addressed, one positive outcome of COVID-19 may well be to usher in new possibilities for a more inclusive and participatory dispute settlement system.

Regardless of one's view about how precisely to formulate next steps, one thing is certain: the present moment allows WTO countries to reimagine dispute settlement in a way that meets the needs of all its members. They should take advantage of it.

12

Precedent in the MPIA: What Role for Consistency and Predictability?

MARIANA CLARA DE ANDRADE*

I. Introduction

Rescuing and repackaging the World Trade Organization (WTO) inevitably entails rethinking the functioning of its adjudicatory mechanism. The reform of WTO dispute settlement involves revising and amending provisions of the Understanding on Rules and Procedures Governing the Settlement of Disputes (DSU),[1] and has long been an object of debate in WTO negotiations. Yet, such talks have not led to any concrete results.[2] To make matters more complicated, the blocking of the appointment of the Appellate Body members by the United States (US) led to the paralysis of that organ in December 2019.

One of the US criticisms against the Appellate Body is that 'the Appellate Body claims its reports are entitled to be treated as precedent'.[3] Indeed, the value of past reports in WTO adjudication is not free of controversy. Although it is generally accepted that there is no system of binding precedent in the WTO's dispute settlement mechanism (DSM), it is also generally accepted that the reports of WTO tribunals, particularly those of the Appellate Body, have a 'de facto precedential effect'. More generally, although in international law there is no doctrine of *stare decisis*, '[j]udicial decisions work as arguments and influence the law through their

* The author wishes to thank Simon Lester and Jan Yves Remy for valuable comments on earlier versions of this work, and Amrita Bahri and Weihuan Zhou for their thorough review and editing. All errors remain my own.

[1] Understanding on Rules and Procedures Governing the Settlement of Disputes (DSU), Marrakesh Agreement Establishing the World Trade Organization, Annex 2 (Marrakesh, 15 April 1994).

[2] For a recent overview of the state of play of DSU reform, see WTO, Special Session of the Dispute Settlement Body, Report by the Chairman Ambassador Coly Seck (17 June 2019) TN/DS/31.

[3] USTR, '2018 Trade Policy Agenda and 2017 Annual Report of the President of the United States on the Trade Agreements Program' (2018), ustr.gov/sites/default/files/files/Press/Reports/2018/AR/2018%20Annual%20Report%20FINAL.PDF, 28. For a detailed account of the US criticisms on the practices of the Appellate Body, see United States Trade Representative (USTR), 'Report on the Appellate Body of the World Trade Organization' (2020), ustr.gov/about-us/policy-offices/press-office/press-releases/2020/february/ustr-issues-report-wto-appellate-body.

impact in the legal discourse'.[4] Indeed, legal certainty is a fundamental tenet in any legal system.[5] Moreover, it has been argued that the Appellate Body has taken up the role of ensuring the uniformity and correct interpretation of the law.[6] There is, thus, a blurred line between the lack of *stare decisis* and the need for a legal system which ensures legal certainty in the interpretation and application of rules.

To address the procedural and systemic issues ensuing from the demise of the Appellate Body, some WTO Members have designed the so-called 'Multiparty Interim Appeal Arbitration Arrangement' (MPIA)[7] in order to maintain the appellate function. As of this writing, 24 Members have joined the MPIA.[8] However, the MPIA differs from the Appellate Body in fundamental ways. First, it is established under an 'ad hoc', interim system pursuant to Article 25 of the DSU, a provision that allows for the possibility of arbitration within WTO adjudication. Second, it is a 'multi-party arrangement' which includes only a limited number of WTO Members. Notwithstanding the fact that MPIA participants currently include some major users of the DSM (for example, the European Union (EU), China and Brazil), the majority of WTO membership, and players like India, the US and Japan, have not subscribed to it. This also means that MPIA arbitrators are chosen by a limited number of WTO Members rather than by the Dispute Settlement Body (DSB) that represents the entire WTO membership. Finally, following Article 25.3 of the DSU, MPIA awards will not be adopted by the DSB, but merely notified.

This chapter explores how the MPIA may affect the continuity, security and predictability that the DSM is designed to protect. More specifically, it examines the following question: will the creation of the MPIA disrupt the consistency of decision-making in WTO dispute settlement, or rather will it strengthen the system and contribute to its further development?

The remainder of this chapter is divided into two parts. Section II analyses the legal framework established under the MPIA with a focus on the issue of precedent, taking into account the 'drafting history' of the MPIA. Section III then discusses the practical impacts that MPIA arbitration may bear on the issue of precedent. It examines the relevant MPIA provisions that may play a role in determining

[4] A Von Bogdandy and I Venzke, 'On the Functions of International Courts: An Appraisal in Light of their Burgeoning Public Authority' (2013) 26 *Leiden Journal of International Law* 49, 56.

[5] See, eg, EH Caminker, 'Why Must Inferior Courts Obey Superior Court Precedents?' (1994) 46 *Stanford Law Review* 817, 850 ff, arguing that 'consistent interpretation and application of law can secure several important values undergirding a government dedicated to the rule of law. To the extent the doctrine of hierarchical precedent promotes these values, the doctrine has a plausible normative foundation'.

[6] Marotti provides a thorough explanation of how the Appellate Body took up the function of '*nomofilachia*' in world trade adjudication. See L Marotti, *Il doppio grado di giudizio nel processo internazionale* (Torino, G Giappichelli Editore, 2020).

[7] WTO, 'Statement on a mechanism for developing, documenting and sharing practices and procedures in the conduct of WTO disputes' (30 April 2020) JOB/DSB/1/Add.12 (MPIA).

[8] As of 31 January 2021, the list of MPIA participants is as follows: Australia, Benin, Brazil, Canada, China, Chile, Colombia, Costa Rica, Ecuador, the EU, Guatemala, Hong Kong (China), Iceland, Macao (China), Mexico, Montenegro, New Zealand, Nicaragua, Norway, Pakistan, Singapore, Switzerland, Ukraine and Uruguay.

whether MPIA arbitration will follow the existing case law and whether MPIA awards will have an authoritative value despite being an 'interim arrangement' and a de facto separate adjudicatory organ. Granted, this analysis bears the caveats that it cannot foresee how the practice of this novel instance of adjudication will unfold. However, this contribution tries to examine the issue of precedent in the MPIA by teasing out the applicable legal framework and pointing out which elements will likely play a role in integrating MPIA awards into one consolidated WTO case law or disrupting the consistency and predictability by setting itself as a separate WTO organ. Section IV offers some concluding remarks.

II. The Text of the MPIA and the Treatment of Prior Reports

To better grasp the role given to past reports in the MPIA, it is necessary to first consider the relevant WTO rules. For example, much of the discussion around the value of past adopted reports in the WTO has relied on Article 3.2 of the DSU. This provision states:

> The dispute settlement system of the WTO is a central element in providing security and predictability to the multilateral trading system. The Members recognize that it serves to preserve the rights and obligations of Members under the covered agreements, and to clarify the existing provisions of those agreements in accordance with customary rules of interpretation of public international law. Recommendations and rulings of the DSB cannot add to or diminish the rights and obligations provided in the covered agreements.[9]

The wording shows that Article 3.2 acknowledges the value of 'security and predictability'. As put by Bacchus and Lester:

> 'Security and predictability' is just another way of referring to the certainty and the foreseeability that traders need to engage in trade. Consistent reasoning over time in the

[9] A rudimentary form of Art 3.2 of the DSU can be found in paragraph A.1 of the 'Decision of 12 April 1989 on improvements to the GATT dispute settlement rules and procedures': '1. Contracting parties recognize that the dispute settlement system of GATT serves to preserve the rights and obligations of contracting parties under the General Agreement and to clarify the existing provisions of the General Agreement. It is a central element in providing security and predictability to the multilateral trading system'. See GATT, 'Decision of 12 April 1989 on improvements to the GATT dispute settlement rules and procedures' (1989), worldtradelaw.net/misc/1989improvements.pdf. This paragraph was later incorporated in the draft text by the Chairman of the Negotiating Group on Dispute Settlement, Julio Lacarte-Muró, on a document dated 19 October 1990 (*Chairman's Text on Dispute Settlement* (19 October 1990) GATT Doc CGT/807-14 (NG13). According to Stewart and Callahan, the Chairman's Text was the result of meetings and consultations held throughout the latter half of 1990 (TB Stewart and CJ Callahan, 'Dispute Settlement Mechanisms' in *The GATT Uruguay Round: A negotiating history (1986–1992)*, vol IIb: Commentary (Deventer, Kluwer Law and Taxation Publishers, 1993) 2779, fns omitted). This early formula indicates that already in the GATT era the contracting parties seemed to place a strong emphasis on the value of dispute settlement for the clarification of GATT provisions, as well as for the 'security and predictability' of the system.

> clarification of WTO obligations through dispute settlement is a key element of ensuring this 'security and predictability'.[10]

On the other hand, this provision also states that DSB reports 'cannot add to or diminish the rights and obligations provided in the covered agreements'. In other words, they have no value as sources of law, and can 'only' serve as clarifications of the law. However, as in any other (domestic or international) forum, the line between judicial interpretation and judicial law-making in the WTO can be blurred: '[t]he act of clarifying an ambiguity in a legal provision may sometimes lead to gap-filling, and filling a gap or a grey area can be seen by critics as the act of law-making'.[11] In particular, because (WTO) treaties are drafted so as to achieve agreement amongst participating Members, often provisions are worded in an ambiguous manner.[12]

As the MPIA is based on Article 25 of the DSU, it is subject to the other relevant provisions of the DSU, including Article 3.2. Therefore, like panels and the Appellate Body, MPIA arbitrators can interpret WTO Agreements but may not create law through this exercise. Moreover, the MPIA has other provisions which are relevant to the question of precedent, as discussed below.

A. The MPIA Provisions Relevant to the Treatment of Past Reports

The MPIA is composed of three parts: the first part sets out the general framework of functioning of the interim arbitration arrangement under Article 25 of the DSU. The second part (MPIA Annex 1)[13] is a template to be submitted in each individual dispute. As explained in paragraph 10 of the MPIA, '[i]n order to render the appeal arbitration procedure operational in particular disputes, the participating Members indicate their intention to enter into the arbitration agreement (the "appeal arbitration agreement") contained in Annex 1'.[14] Annex 1 also sets out the specific procedural rules for MPIA arbitration. Finally, the third part sets out the process for the composition of the pool of MPIA arbitrators.[15] The relevant

[10] J Bacchus and S Lester, 'The Rule of precedent and the role of the Appellate Body' (2020) 54 *Journal of World Trade* 183, 188.

[11] A Bahri, 'Appellate Body Held Hostage': Is Judicial Activism at Fair Trial?' (2019) 53 *Journal of World Trade* 293, 308.

[12] Zhou and Gao thoroughly explain how the 'considerable loopholes or ambiguities in WTO rules make it extremely difficult to ascertain what the agreed rights and obligations should be'. See W Zhou and H Gao, '"Overreaching" or "Overreacting"? Reflections on the Judicial Function and Approaches of WTO Appellate Body' (2019) 53 *Journal of World Trade* 951, 958.

[13] Annex 1, 'Agreed procedures for arbitration under Article 25 of the DSU in dispute DS X' of MPIA (n 7).

[14] ibid para 10.

[15] ibid Annex 2, 'Composition of the pool of arbitrators pursuant to paragraph 4 of communication JOB/DSB/1/add.12'.

provisions for analysing the issue of precedent in MPIA arbitration are stipulated under the first two parts.

The text of the MPIA does not explicitly deal with the precedential value of adopted reports and arbitration awards. However, it lays out two relevant provisions: the Preamble which recognises the value of 'consistency and predictability'; and paragraph 5 which sets out the principle of collegiality among MPIA arbitrators.

First, the MPIA Preamble's sixth recital largely reproduces Article 3.2 of the DSU. It reaffirms that 'consistency and predictability in the interpretation of rights and obligations under the covered agreements is of significant value to Members and that arbitration awards cannot add to or diminish the rights and obligations provided in the covered agreements'.[16] This suggests the intention of the MPIA drafters to maintain one of the fundamental objectives of the DSM. It is interesting to note, however, that the MPIA uses the wording 'consistency and predictability', rather than 'security and predictability'. This difference may have arisen from the context in which the MPIA was crafted.

The MPIA was negotiated in parallel with another set of discussions which took place during the months preceding the deadlock of the Appellate Body: the informal talks facilitated by New Zealand Ambassador David Walker, which set out to 'address concerns raised by delegations with regard to the functioning of the Appellate Body and adherence with DSU provisions' and seek solutions to these concerns.[17] The concerns at the centre of the debate were those advanced by the US delegation, who, however, did not partake in those talks. These informal negotiations culminated in the proposal of a Draft Decision (the Walker Principles) put before the General Council, which directly dealt with US concerns.[18] Nonetheless, the Draft Decision was never adopted.

On the issue of precedent, the Walker Principles suggested the adoption of the following paragraphs:

> **Precedent**
>
> 15. Precedent is not created through WTO dispute settlement proceedings.
>
> 16. Consistency and predictability in the interpretation of rights and obligations under the covered agreements is of significant value to Members.
>
> 17. Panels and the Appellate Body should take previous Panel/Appellate Body reports into account to the extent they find them relevant in the dispute they have before them.[19]

Some of the current MPIA participants sent their suggestions to David Walker's informal talks, in particular the EU, China, Canada, Norway, New Zealand,

[16] ibid Preamble.

[17] WTO, General Council, 'Informal process on matters related to the functioning of the Appellate Body – Report by the Facilitator', Dr D Walker (New Zealand) (25 July 2019) JOB/GC/220.

[18] WTO, General Council, Draft Decision, 'Functioning of the Appellate Body' (28 November 2019) WT/GC/W/791 (Draft Decision).

[19] ibid.

Switzerland, Australia, Iceland, Singapore and Mexico (who, together with some other WTO Members, submitted a joint Communication at the end of 2018);[20] and Brazil and Uruguay (who, together with Paraguay, submitted a joint proposal).[21] Therefore, it can be assumed that the informal talks and the resultant Walker Principles affected the negotiations of the MPIA.

For example, the choice for the terms 'consistency and predictability' seems to draw from paragraph 16 of the Walker Principles. Moreover, the choice of MPIA negotiators of the word 'consistency' rather than 'security' arguably implies a stronger emphasis on the quest for a consistent and coherent WTO case law. While 'security' does emphasise legal certainty as a value for the WTO dispute settlement, 'consistency' goes beyond and further conveys the idea of a coherent case law, and thus of a de facto system of precedent.

The second factor relevant to the value of precedent is the principle of collegiality, introduced by paragraph 5 of the MPIA. This provision states that '[i]n order to promote consistency and coherence in decision-making, the members of the pool of arbitrators will discuss amongst themselves matters of interpretation, practice and procedure, to the extent practicable'.[22] The practice of discussing legal issues not only among the subset of arbitrators designated for the adjudication of a dispute, but with the entirety of the pool of MPIA arbitrators, enshrines the principle of collegiality in MPIA proceedings. Additionally, MPIA Annex 1, paragraph 8 states that:

> In order to give effect to paragraph 5 … the arbitrators may discuss their decisions relating to the appeal with all of the other members of the pool of arbitrators, without prejudice to the exclusive responsibility and freedom of the arbitrators with respect to such decisions and their quality. All members of the pool of arbitrators shall receive any document relating to the appeal.[23]

It has been pointed out that the principle of collegiality is a unique feature of WTO adjudication.[24] Moreover, the practice of exchange of views,[25] together with the practice of limited dissenting and separate opinions,[26] have been viewed as strong

[20] Communication from European Union, China, Canada, India, Norway, New Zealand, Switzerland, Australia, Republic of Korea, Iceland, Singapore and Mexico to the General Council (26 November 2018) WT/GC/W/752.

[21] Communication from Brazil: Guidelines for the Work of Panels and the Appellate Body (28 March 2019) WT/GC/W/767; Communication from Brazil, Paraguay And Uruguay: Guidelines for the Work of Panels and the Appellate Body (25 April 2019) WT/GC/W/767/Rev.1. The latter added Paraguay and Uruguay as co-sponsors of the Communication, originally drafted by the Brazilian delegation.

[22] MPIA (n 7).

[23] ibid.

[24] HR Fabri and J Paine, 'The Procedural Cross-Fertilization Pull' (23 August 23) MPILux Research Paper 2019(6) 10, ssrn.com/abstract=3441701.

[25] For a description of the practice of exchange of views in the Appellate Body, see DP Steger, 'The founding of the Appellate Body' in G Marceau, *A History of Law and Lawyers in the GATT/WTO: The Development of the Rule of Law in the Multilateral Trading System* (Cambridge, Cambridge University Press, 2015) 457.

[26] ibid 458.

factors behind the 'consistency' of WTO case law.[27] As explained by Steger when commenting on the practice of the Appellate Body:

> Unlike the ICJ practice of each judge writing his or her notes or opinion and then discussing the case, which encourages individual views to solidify once an individual judge has invested considerable time and effort in drafting his or her opinion, the Appellate Body practice of immediate, face-to-face exchange of views among all the Appellate Body members followed by in-person deliberations for as long as it takes among members of the division has enabled the development of an early consensus opinion in most cases.[28]

Therefore, the practice of exchange of views in the process of decision-making is a way to encourage that the findings and interpretations contained in the reports are the result of a process of discussion, and that they reflect converging views by different Appellate Body members – including those who are not part of the division assigned to the case. This ensures that, should the same legal issue arise in a different case, there will be no divergence on the interpretation of the same legal question. Consequently, different Appellate Body divisions would be less likely to decide the same legal issue in different ways. One can infer MPIA drafters envisaged a continuation of this practice by way of collegiality.

In sum, a combined reading of the MPIA Preamble sixth recital, MPIA paragraph 5 and MPIA Annex 1, paragraph 8 leads to a conclusion that the MPIA is intended to maintain a consistent application of WTO jurisprudence.

B. Distinctions between the MPIA and the Early EU Bilateral Interim Arbitration Arrangements: A Slight Shift of Approach

While the MPIA was negotiated among 19 WTO Members,[29] it built upon the EU's bilateral interim arrangements with Canada[30] and Norway,[31] now all parties to the MPIA. The verbatim for the negotiations are not publicly available, but a comparison between the early bilateral arrangements and the MPIA may shed light on how the negotiators (or at least the EU, Canada and Norway) intended the MPIA

[27] AV Ganesan, 'The Appellate Body in its formative years: a personal perspective' in G Marceau, *A History of Law and Lawyers in the GATT/WTO: The Development of the Rule of Law in the Multilateral Trading System* (Cambridge, Cambridge University Press, 2015) 529.

[28] Steger (n 25) 458.

[29] These were: Australia, Brazil, Canada, China, Chile, Colombia, Costa Rica, the EU, Guatemala, Hong Kong (China), Iceland, Mexico, New Zealand, Norway, Pakistan, Singapore, Switzerland, Ukraine and Uruguay. As of 31 August 2020, also Ecuador, Nicaragua and Benin have further notified their participation in the MPIA.

[30] WTO, 'Interim Appeal Arbitration Pursuant to Article 25 of the DSU' between Canada and the European Union (22 October 2019) JOB/DSB/1/Add.11/Rev.1 (Interim Appeal Arbitration between Canada and the EU).

[31] WTO, 'Interim Appeal Arbitration Pursuant to Article 25 of the DSU' between Norway and the European Union (21 October 2019) JOB/DSB/1/Add.11/Suppl.1.

to work. The bilateral arrangements and the MPIA differ in one important aspect: while the former would function on an ad hoc basis involving only three WTO Members, the latter is a standing, albeit interim, mechanism with an extended membership representation and open for participation to all WTO Members.

Some provisions in the original Agreement between the EU and Canada/Norway[32] hinted, to a large extent, at an attempt to make Article 25 a continuation of the Appellate Body. First, paragraph 2 provided that all substantive and procedural aspects for the functioning of appeal arbitration under Article 25 would be 'replicated as closely as possible' with respect to the functioning of the Appellate Body.[33] This provision was modified in the MPIA, and paragraph 3, much less deferential to the Appellate Body in tone, now reads:

> The appeal arbitration procedure will be based on the substantive and procedural aspects of Appellate Review pursuant to Article 17 of the DSU, in order to keep its core features, including independence and impartiality, while enhancing the procedural efficiency of appeal proceedings.[34]

Paragraph 3 of the bilateral arrangements, in turn, stated that appeals would be heard by former Appellate Body members.[35] In particular if read in conjunction with paragraph 2, paragraph 3 implied a strong effort for an implicit continuation of the Appellate Body. If the same Appellate Body members would continue to decide the disputes, arbitration under these bilateral arrangements would likely maintain the patterns of the Appellate Body decision-making process and apply the established case law.

Paragraph 8 of the Annex of the bilateral arrangements (Agreed procedures for arbitration under Article 25 of the DSU in dispute DS X) is particularly relevant for the issue of the precedential value of reports and awards. It stated that 'awards of other arbitrators under similar appeal arbitration procedures shall be deemed to constitute Appellate Body reports adopted by the DSB for the purposes of interpretation of the covered agreements'.[36] This provision could be read to mean that

[32] Given the identity between the two bilateral declarations, the interim arrangement between the EU and Canada will be used as reference.

[33] The full provision stated: '2. Under the appeal arbitration procedure Canada and the European Union intend to replicate as closely as possible all substantive and procedural aspects as well as the practice of Appellate Review pursuant to Article 17 of the DSU including the provision of appropriate administrative and legal support to the arbitrators by the Appellate Body Secretariat'. Para 2 of the Interim Appeal Arbitration between Canada and the EU (n 30).

[34] MPIA (n 7).

[35] The full provision stated: '3. In particular, Canada and the European Union envisage that, under the appeal arbitration procedure, appeals will be heard by three former members of the Appellate Body, serving as arbitrators pursuant to Article 25 of the DSU. The arbitrators will be selected by the Director-General from the pool of available former members of the Appellate Body, based on the same principles and methods that apply to form a division of the Appellate Body under Article 17.1 of the DSU and Rule 6(2) of the Working Procedures for Appellate Review. However, two nationals of the same Member may not serve on the same case'. Para 3 of the Interim Appeal Arbitration between Canada and the EU (n 30) (fns omitted).

[36] The full provision stated: '8. Unless otherwise provided for in these agreed procedures, the arbitration shall be governed, *mutatis mutandis*, by the provisions of the DSU and other rules and procedures

the EU, Canada and Norway considered Appellate Body reports as authoritative. Moreover, deeming these awards as adopted by the DSB also grants a further element of acknowledgement of the authoritative value of Appellate Body reports. However, given that this understanding operated on a bilateral basis, it meant that appeal arbitration awards under Article 25 would only be regarded as DSB-adopted Appellate Body reports for the EU, Canada and Norway. This paragraph was not included in the MPIA.

Another difference between the bilateral arrangements and the MPIA is that the former did not foresee a standing pool of arbitrators and hence did not set out the principle of collegiality in decision-making. Indeed, paragraph 7 of the Annex of the bilateral agreements, which sought to use former Appellate Body members as arbitrators, also stated that 'the exchange of views provided for in Rule 4(3) shall not apply'.[37] Conversely, as described in section II.A, the MPIA explicitly sets out the practice of collegiality and exchange of views in paragraph 5 of Annex 1.[38]

In sum, the above provisions of the bilateral arrangements suggested a strong intention to maintain the de facto system of precedent. Those provisions, particularly paragraphs 7 and 8 of the Annex of the bilateral arrangements, were not replicated in the MPIA. It can be inferred that the EU, Norway and Canada initially intended Article 25 to constitute a de facto continuation of the Appellate Body, but this approach was attenuated with the drafting of the MPIA. This change of approach may be due to the larger number of participants to the interim agreement, and presumably the preference of some in having a more nuanced language in the text of the MPIA. Moreover, because the MPIA is expressly conceived as a stopgap, provisional solution for the paralysis of the Appellate Body, the drafters may have thought it wise to weaken the idea of the multiparty arrangement as a de facto continuation of the Appellate Body.

Nonetheless, the MPIA contains explicit references to 'consistency and predictability in the interpretation of rights and obligations', as well as the introduction of the principle of collegiality into MPIA proceedings. This leads to the inference that, while the other WTO Members who negotiated the MPIA may have been more cautious in devising a mechanism as a continuation of the Appellate Body, they nonetheless did acknowledge the importance of following previously adopted reports and arbitral awards in future disputes.

applicable to Appellate Review. This includes in particular the Working Procedures for Appellate Review and the timetable for appeals provided for therein as well as the Rules of Conduct. Except for panel findings that are deemed to form an integral part of an arbitration award pursuant to paragraph 9 or are incorporated in the award pursuant to footnote 6, *awards of other arbitrators under similar appeal arbitration procedures shall be deemed to constitute Appellate Body reports adopted by the DSB for the purposes of interpretation of the covered agreements, provided that the other arbitrators were selected consistently with the provisions of paragraph 7.* The arbitrator may adapt the Working Procedures for Appellate Review and the timetable for appeals provided for therein, where justified under Rule 16 of the Working Procedures for Appellate Review, after consulting the parties and taking into account the practice of the Appellate Body' (emphasis added).

[37] ibid.

[38] See nn 22 and 23 and accompanying texts above.

III. Precedent in the MPIA: A Two-Fold Analysis

In addition to the procedural provisions and the drafting context examined in the previous section, other factors may also influence 'continuity' of WTO case law in MPIA arbitration. This section discusses whether the creation of the MPIA may disrupt or maintain the consistency of decision-making in WTO dispute settlement.

A. The Use of Adopted Panel and Appellate Body Reports in MPIA Proceedings

There are at least four relevant factors in considering whether and how MPIA arbitrators may refer to adopted Panel and Appellate Body reports in deciding disputes submitted to it. First, if the MPIA is viewed as a 'separate organ' in WTO adjudication, the arbitrators would be less inclined to refer to the existing case law. Nonetheless, there are important similarities between MPIA and Appellate Body proceedings, which could lead to consistent practices: the agreements being interpreted are the same; the Membership (or at least a sub-group) is the same; and, as examined in the previous section, the text of the MPIA stresses the importance of 'consistency and predictability' in WTO adjudication. Moreover, as put by Cohen, '[t]here is a common intuition, reflected in many theories of law, that one of the core principles or qualities of law is that it treat like situations alike', so '[i]f like cases must be treated alike, future decisions must at least make reference to prior ones'.[39] This need for legal certainty also informs the WTO legal system. Therefore, the fact that the MPIA constitutes a separate mechanism is not enough to prevent MPIA arbitrators from maintaining and developing a consistent approach in addressing issues that have already been decided by panels and the Appellate Body.

Second, to address US concerns about the Appellate Body, MPIA arbitrators may seek to avoid reinforcing a de facto system of precedent. Relatedly, to 'distinguish' themselves from the Appellate Body, arbitrators may view that less reference to previous case law and more 'interpretation from scratch' will strengthen their legitimacy within the WTO adjudication (even if their interpretation coincides with previous case law).[40] In particular, the arbitrators may feel more inclined to develop their own interpretations on issues which remain unsettled in the current case law.[41] These issues include, for example, the practice of zeroing under

[39] HG Cohen, 'Lawyers and Precedent' (2013) 46 *Vanderbilt Journal of Transnational Law* 1025, 1035–36.

[40] See S Lester, 'Can Interim Appeal Arbitration Preserve the WTO Dispute System?' (2020) 77 *Free Trade Bulletin, Herbert A Stiefel Center for Trade Policy Studies* 3.

[41] This is what Bhala calls the influence of 'legal thought' in the strength of precedent. See R Bhala, 'The Precedent Setters: De Facto Stare Decisis in WTO Adjudication (Part Two of a Trilogy)' (1999) 9 *Journal of Transnational Law & Policy* 145.

the WTO Agreement on Anti-Dumping,[42] the meaning of 'public body' in the Agreement on Subsidies and Countervailing Measures,[43] the standard for interpreting DSU Article 11,[44] etc.

At the same time, it is difficult to conceive that MPIA arbitrators will not defer to well-established interpretations of WTO rules. Examples can be found in procedural (such as the standards on burden of proof)[45] and substantive (such as the two-step analysis under Article XX of the General Agreement on Tariffs and Trade (GATT))[46] matters. Moreover, if certain interpretations are undisputed within the WTO membership more generally and MPIA disputants, there would be little reason why MPIA arbitrators should not follow previous case law. Therefore, it is expected that there will be some level of reliance on previous panels and Appellate Body reports.

The drafting of MPIA awards will also depend on the personal preferences of the arbitrators and their legal background (common law or civil law; public international lawyers or trade lawyers; academics or practitioners). This may influence whether they will strive for judicial economy and thus resort more largely to previous reports; defer more to the work of panels than the Appellate Body used to; or, instead, follow 'their own' legal interpretations, lessening the impact of prior adopted reports. These factors, moreover, are largely influenced by the claims and submissions of the parties.

Indeed, and third, disputants' claims and submissions significantly shape the outcome of WTO dispute settlement reports. For example, disputing parties often offer different interpretations of the relevant WTO rules as well as previous rulings of WTO tribunals.[47] Consequently, adjudicators are compelled by the parties' submissions to refer to past reports. Hence, whether MPIA arbitrators may refer to

[42] For an overview on the issue of zeroing in the WTO, see CP Bown and TJ Prusa, 'US Antidumping: Much Ado about Zeroing' (2010) World Bank Policy Research Working Paper Series 5352.

[43] See, for instance, the differing views of WTO Members on the issue: S Lester, 'The Appellate Body and the Meaning of "Public Body"' (*International Economic Law and Policy Blog*, 20 March 2011), worldtradelaw.typepad.com/ielpblog/2011/03/appellate-body-and-public-body.html. For an assessment of whether the Appellate Body engaged in judicial activism on the issue of 'public body, see also, J Pauwelyn, 'Treaty Interpretation or Activism? Comment on the AB Report on *United States–ADs and CVDs on Certain Products from China*' (2013) 12 *World Trade Review* 235; Bahri (n 11) 303–04.

[44] On this, see J Bohanes and N Lockhart, 'Standard of Review in WTO Law' in D Bethlehem et al, *The Oxford Handbook of International Trade Law* (Oxford, Oxford University Press, 2009) 379. It should be noted that the MPIA introduces a procedural novelty regarding Art 11 of the DSU in its Annex 1, para 13: 'If necessary in order to issue the award within the 90 day time-period, the arbitrators may also propose substantive measures to the parties, such as an exclusion of claims based on the alleged lack of an objective assessment of the facts pursuant to Article 11 of the DSU'.

[45] For an early analysis of the 'precedential impact' of the Appellate Body *US–Shirts and Blouses* report on the question of the burden of proof, see Bhala (n 41) 22 ff.

[46] See I Venze, 'Making General Exceptions: The Spell of Precedents in Developing Article XX GATT into Standards for Domestic Regulatory Policy' (2011) 12 *German Law Journal* 1111.

[47] See, eg, the US (complainant) and EU (respondent) claims on GATT Article XIX in the *EU–Additional Duties* dispute: *EU–Additional Duties on Certain Products from the United States*, First Written Submission of the United States of America (6 May 2019), ustr.gov/sites/default/files/enforcement/DS/US.Sub1.(DS559).(public).pdf; *EU–Additional Duties on Certain Products from the United States*, First Written Submission by the EU (6 June 2019), trade.ec.europa.eu/doclib/docs/2019/october/tradoc_158389.pdf.

the existing case law will depend on whether MPIA participants will maintain the practice of basing their submissions on prior Appellate Body and Panel reports. One can expect that since the parties to the MPIA do not particularly oppose the current de facto precedent system in WTO adjudication, not much will change in the practice of the MPIA.

Fourth, not only the practice and the submissions of the disputants, but also the support of a secretariat (or lack thereof) may influence the extent to which MPIA arbitrators will rely on prior reports. As Jackson pointed out, one factor that impacted the 'less legalistic' (ie, less deferential to prior reports) approach followed in the GATT era was that:

> Since there was no single body that was permanently in session, there was probably less thinking about deferring to prior cases and, certainly until GATT set up a legal unit at the beginning of the 1980s, the panels often did not have much in the way of staff assistance to point out the existence of prior relevant GATT panel reports to a panel currently considering a new measure.[48]

An empirical study conducted by Pauwelyn and Pelc also concluded that a substantive role for the Secretariat may bear an impact on an increased role for precedent.[49] They argued that the WTO Secretariat has a strong impact on the drafting of the reports, through practices such as the writing of 'issues papers' (a summary of the facts and arguments of the parties, as well as the ways in which the legal questions can be decided based on rules and past cases) and the first drafts of panels and Appellate Body reports.[50] These heavily influence the de facto reliance on precedent in WTO adjudication.

The MPIA states that arbitrators will be provided with 'appropriate administrative and legal support'.[51] It is unclear how this support will be instituted to the arbitrators. Yet, the empirical evidence that demonstrates the influence that the WTO Secretariat has on the final reports issued by panels and the Appellate Body suggests that the way in which this support will be provided to arbitrators will bear a considerable impact on the relevance of past reports in MPIA awards.

In short, different factors will influence the degree to which MPIA arbitrators will rely on previous case law, and the way in which they will do so (for example, by explicitly invoking previous reasoning or by following the same dicta but without

[48] JH Jackson, *Sovereignty, the WTO, and Changing Fundamentals of International Law* (Cambridge, Cambridge University Press, 2006) 176.

[49] J Pauwelyn and K Pelc, 'Who Writes the Rulings of the World Trade Organization? A Critical Assessment of the Role of the Secretariat in WTO Dispute Settlement' (2019) 31, papers.ssrn.com/sol3/papers.cfm?abstract_id=3458872.

[50] ibid 10.

[51] Para 7 determines that: '7. The participating Members envisage that appeal arbitrators will be provided with appropriate administrative and legal support, which will offer the necessary guarantees of quality and independence, given the nature of the responsibilities involved. The participating Members envisage that the support structure will be entirely separate from the WTO Secretariat staff and its divisions supporting the panels and be answerable, regarding the substance of their work, only to appeal arbitrators. The participating Members request the WTO Director-General to ensure the availability of a support structure meeting these criteria'.

explicit acknowledgement). However, given the significant body of case law including many well-established rulings and practices, it seems unlikely that adjudicators will completely ignore the relevant previous decisions. Combined with the MPIA provisions which reinforce the value of the 'consistency and predictability' of WTO case law, a coherent body of law seems to be ensured at least in this respect.

B. The Authoritative Value of MPIA Awards

In his magisterial work on the question of precedent, Bhala points out that different variables influence the degree of acceptability of a precedent in a legal system. One of these variables, which he places within the broader category of 'legal infrastructure', is that 'the higher the tribunal that issues a precedent sits in the judicial hierarchy, the more forceful the precedent'.[52] Just like the Appellate Body, the MPIA is a mechanism for the review of legal interpretations in reports issued by panels. Therefore, one can consider that they are 'higher' in the hierarchy of WTO adjudication and 'a precedent of a more influential or prestigious tribunal will, *ipso facto*, be more persuasive'.[53]

However, the already mentioned particularities of the MPIA (ie, the selection of the pool of arbitrators by a limited number of participants, the fact that the reports are not adopted, etc) may signify a weaker 'authoritative pull'. Marotti thoroughly argues that the 'public function' exercised by the Appellate Body (ie, its de facto role as a second instance of adjudication whose reports and interpretations are perceived as more authoritative than those of panels) is a consequence of its permanent character.[54] This permanent character is not envisaged for the MPIA. Given these particularities on the nature of the MPIA, will MPIA awards be viewed as authoritative?

Article 25.3 of the DSU, which applies to the arbitral proceedings in WTO adjudication and to the proceedings of the MPIA, states that '[a]rbitration awards shall be notified to the DSB and the Council or Committee of any relevant agreement where any Member may raise any point relating thereto'. Moreover, MPIA Annex 1, paragraph 15 states that:

> The parties agree to abide by the arbitration award, which shall be final. Pursuant to Article 25.3 of the DSU, the award shall be notified to, but not adopted by, the DSB and to the Council or Committee of any relevant agreement.[55]

From a socio-legitimacy perspective,[56] the fact that MPIA awards are not adopted and are not drafted by a more representative institutional body (ie, drafted by a

[52] Bhala (n 41) 145.
[53] ibid.
[54] Marotti (n 6) 157 ff.
[55] MPIA (n 7).
[56] As defined by Cohen et al, '[w]hile normative legitimacy is concerned with the right to rule according to predefined standards, sociological legitimacy derives from perceptions or beliefs that an institution

pool of arbitrators selected by a limited number of WTO Members) may have some impact on the legitimacy of the awards. In other words, these factors may influence how the WTO membership perceives the legitimacy and authoritative value of the awards. Whether MPIA awards are to be commented on by WTO Members in DSB meetings, as is currently the case with circulated reports, could be relevant to determining its legitimacy. Indeed, the lack of possibility for the circulation and discussion of the awards will make more of a difference in terms of its legitimacy for precedential purposes.

On the other hand, from a legal perspective, it is difficult to differentiate the legal value of adopted reports and non-adopted awards, since neither formally qualifies as a binding 'authoritative interpretation' of WTO Agreements.[57] Moreover, because of the reverse consensus rule for the adoption of reports, one can argue that in practice there is not much difference between an adopted report and a 'notified' award. Finally, Article 15 of MPIA Annex 1 states that '[t]he parties agree to abide by the arbitration award, which shall be final'. Therefore, even though MPIA awards will not be formally adopted, they will be binding and final for the parties to the dispute.

In *Japan–Alcoholic Beverages II*, the Appellate Body was asked to determine whether adopted Panel reports under the GATT and the WTO dispute settlement mechanisms constituted 'subsequent practice' in the terms of Article 31(3)(b) of the Vienna Convention on the Law of Treaties.[58] With the obvious disclaimer that MPIA awards will not be formally adopted by the DSB, the reasoning the Appellate Body provided then could be useful to understand the value that MPIA awards may have:

> Although GATT 1947 panel reports were adopted by decisions of the CONTRACTING PARTIES, a decision to adopt a panel report did not under GATT 1947 constitute agreement by the CONTRACTING PARTIES on the legal reasoning in that panel report … We do not believe that the CONTRACTING PARTIES, in deciding to adopt a panel report, intended that their decision would constitute a definitive interpretation of the relevant provisions of GATT 1947. Nor do we believe that this is contemplated under GATT 1994.[59]

has such a right to rule'. See HG Cohen et al, 'Legitimacy and International Courts – A Framework' in N Grossman et al, *Legitimacy and International Courts* (Cambridge, Cambridge University Press, 2018) 4.

[57] Art IX:2 of the WTO Agreement stipulates that '[t]he Ministerial Conference and the General Council shall have the exclusive authority to adopt interpretations of this Agreement and of the Multilateral Trade Agreements. In the case of an interpretation of a Multilateral Trade Agreement in Annex 1, they shall exercise their authority on the basis of a recommendation by the Council overseeing the functioning of that Agreement. The decision to adopt an interpretation shall be taken by a three-fourths majority of the Members'. See Art IX:2 of the Marrakesh Agreement Establishing the World Trade Organization (Marrakesh, 15 April 1994).

[58] Art 31(3)(b) on the General rule of interpretation of treaties states that '[t]here shall be taken into account, together with the context: … (b) any subsequent practice in the application of the treaty which establishes the agreement of the parties regarding its interpretation'. See Art 31(3)(b) of the Vienna Convention on the Law of Treaties (Vienna, 23 May 1969).

[59] *Japan–Taxes on Alcoholic Beverages*, Report of the Appellate Body (1 November 1996) WT/DS8/AB/R, 14, fns omitted (*Japan–Alcoholic Beverages II*).

At the same time, also in *Japan–Alcoholic Beverages II*, the Appellate Body considered the value of unadopted GATT reports, and concluded that, although unadopted Panel reports 'have no legal status in the GATT or WTO system since they have not been endorsed through decisions by the CONTRACTING PARTIES to GATT or WTO Members', '[a] panel could nevertheless find useful guidance in the reasoning of an unadopted panel report that it considered to be relevant'.[60]

This approach seems to be the most likely to apply to MPIA awards. Yet, how strongly parties and adjudicators will 'find useful guidance' in MPIA awards may vary according to whether MPIA awards (a) advance interpretations on novel legal issues (ie, issues that have not been examined in previous reports) or (b) depart from 'established' case law. The practice of MPIA arbitrators in either of these scenarios may bear an impact on the development of the case law. Moreover, the general practice of the Appellate Body of avoiding issuing separate and dissenting opinions has arguably created a rather rigid case law.[61] Therefore, diverging interpretations in MPIA awards may trigger variations on the interpretation of WTO Agreements. Conversely, if MPIA adjudication simply follows previous reports, there is little reason for adjudicators to cite MPIA awards rather than reports adopted by the DSB and issued by organs established by the entirety of the WTO membership.

Another factor which will likely influence how parties and adjudicators regard MPIA awards will be the participation of WTO Members in this appeal arrangement. The more Members decide to become participants of the MPIA, the more legitimacy the awards will gain. Finally, and relatedly, the volume of the practice of MPIA arbitration will also impact the authoritative value of MPIA awards. One can expect that the more voluminous the decision docket of the MPIA becomes, the more developed its practice and the more legitimacy it gains.

IV. Conclusions

The question of precedent in WTO adjudication constitutes one of the many facets in the process of rethinking the world trading system. The 'precedential value' of past reports was one of the factors leading to the paralysis of the Appellate Body and it is central to the WTO DSM. This chapter addressed this issue having in mind the potential for change that may ensue from the functioning of the MPIA. Based on an analysis of the relevant provisions of the MPIA and the rationale behind them, it is submitted that the drafters of the MPIA had an intent to ensure the consistency of WTO case law, even though the MPIA may be perceived as a 'separate' organ in the WTO DSM.

[60] ibid, citing the Panel Report in the same dispute, 14–15.

[61] See MK Lewis, 'The lack of dissent in WTO dispute settlement (2006) 9 *Journal of International Economic Law* 895, 927–28. The author also argues that dissent could be a useful tool to assist the negotiation and for reform of the WTO Agreement.

However, the extent to which MPIA arbitrators may refer to past Panel and Appellate Body reports will depend on a variety of factors, such as the background and personal preferences of arbitrators, the fact that it is placed under a different institutional framework than that of panels and the Appellate Body, and the uncertainties around whether it will be supported by a division of the WTO Secretariat such as the Rules, Legal Affairs and Appellate Body. Arguably, MPIA awards will have a lessened authoritative value than adopted Panel and Appellate Body reports due to its non-permanent status and its limited Member representation. Nonetheless, this does not prevent MPIA arbitrators from following the same legal interpretations already consolidated in WTO case law. Where novel legal issues arise, MPIA arbitrators may play a more active role in developing WTO jurisprudence.

All these questions will further be impacted by how long the MPIA will remain in place, and how many disputes it will adjudicate. The more disputes come before MPIA arbitration, the more 'legal material' shall have to be produced and the more 'robust' its own case law will become.

Overall, the chapter has shown that the MPIA was conceived to preserve the functions of WTO adjudication, and hence may not undermine coherence in WTO case law. Although the dispute settlement mechanism needs to be adapted to new realities, MPIA arbitrators should strive to ensure consistency and predictability in trade law, which would be essential to safeguarding the value of, and regaining the trust in, the multilateral trading system.

13

Is the Phase One Deal the Emergence of a 'New Generation' of Bilateral Trade Agreements that Challenge the WTO?

MARÍA MANUELA MOCCERO

I. Introduction

The 'Economic and Trade Agreement between the Government of the United States of America and the Government of the People's Republic of China', commonly known as the 'US–China Phase One Deal', entered into force on 14 February 2020.[1] It has generated optimism in the global business community and stock markets, as it had allowed a truce – at least on a temporary basis – in the trade and technological war between the world's two largest economies.

At first glance, the Phase One Deal may also appear to be good news for the multilateral trading system, as in its framework China has assumed obligations beyond the World Trade Organization (WTO) Agreements and has pledged to implement many commitments it made when it joined the organisation in 2001. These obligations include opening of its financial services sector;[2] decreasing barriers to trade;[3] enhancing transparency of its domestic support programmes in the agricultural sector;[4] strengthening protection and enforcement of intellectual property rights of American companies;[5] and avoiding of forcing or exercising

[1] Economic and Trade Agreement Between the Government of the United States and the Government of the People's Republic of China (Washington DC, 15 January 2020) (Phase One Deal).

[2] See ch 4 of the Phase One Deal (n 1).

[3] Mainly, barriers to trade in food and agriculture are mostly related to health standards. See ch 3 of the Phase One Deal (n 1). See also P Lunenborg, 'US–China trade deal: preliminary analysis of the text from WTO perspective' (2020) South Centre Policy Brief No 72, www.southcentre.int/wp-content/uploads/2020/02/PB72_US-China-trade-deal-preliminary-analysis-of-the-text-from-WTO-perspective_EN-1.pdf.

[4] See ch 3 and Annex 15 of the Phase One Deal (n 1).

[5] See ch 1 ibid. Ch 1 'Intellectual Property' (IP) addresses numerous United States (US) long-standing concerns in the areas of trade secrets, patents and pharmaceutical-related intellectual property,

pressure on foreign companies to transfer their technology as a condition for market access.[6]

However, does the Phase One Deal actually represent good news for the multilateral trading system or instead does it pose a new challenge to the WTO, calling for its membership to react in order to safeguard the core principles of the multilateral organisation?

Indeed, it may be argued that the Phase One Deal raises certain legal questions regarding its consistency with the WTO Agreements.

The first legal question is whether the deal is a market-oriented deal or a 'managed trade agreement' forbidden by the provisions of the WTO Agreement on Safeguards (SG Agreement).[7] This deal, hence, must be brought into conformity with the SG Agreement.

A second question is whether certain provisions of the Phase One Deal are in breach of the most-favoured nation (MFN) rule and, in the affirmative case, whether it may be characterised as a 'free trade agreement' under Article XXIV of the General Agreement on Tariffs and Trade (GATT),[8] or an 'agreement' under Article V of General Agreement on Trade in Services (GATS).[9] That is, as a legitimate exception to the non-discrimination principle, that is under multilateral scrutiny.

A last and broader concern relates to whether the relevant provisions of the WTO Agreements are sufficiently 'updated' to effectively protect the rest of the membership from the legal consequences of its dubious legal 'managed trade' approach and its lack of characterisation as a 'comprehensive agreement'.

In order to answer the above-mentioned questions, the following sections will address the legal nature of the 'managed trade approach' of its Chapter 6 'Expanding Trade' and its consistency with the SG Agreement. Additionally, the chapter will examine the consistency of the Chinese purchase commitments under the same chapter with the MFN rule and the difficulties to prevail in a claim of

geographical indications, trademarks, and enforcement against pirated and counterfeit goods, preventing piracy and counterfeiting. The IP chapter also requires China to promulgate an Action Plan that will outline the structural changes that China will take to implement its obligations under this chapter. See United States Trade Representative (USTR), 'Fact Sheet on Intellectual Property', ustr.gov/sites/default/files/files/agreements/phase%20one%20agreement/Phase_One_Agreement-IP_Fact_Sheet.pdf.

[6] See ch 2 ibid. Ch 2 'Technology Transfer' prohibits the forcing or pressuring of foreign companies to transfer their technology as a condition for market access, administrative approvals, or receipt of any advantages. It also requires that any transfer or licensing of technology be based on market terms that are voluntary and reflect mutual agreement and prohibit state-directed or supported outbound investment aimed at acquiring foreign technology in sectors and industries targeted by a party's industrial policies. See USTR, 'Fact Sheet on Technology Transfer' (15 January 2020), ustr.gov/sites/default/files/files/agreements/phase%20one%20agreement/US_China_Agreement_Fact_Sheet.pdf.

[7] Agreement on Safeguards, Marrakesh Agreement Establishing the World Trade Organization, Annex 1A (Marrakesh, 15 April 1994) (SG Agreement).

[8] Art XXIV of the General Agreement on Tariffs and Trade (GATT), Marrakesh Agreement Establishing the World Trade Organization, Annex 1A (Marrakesh, 15 April 1994).

[9] Art V of the General Agreement on Trade in Services (GATS), Marrakesh Agreement Establishing the World Trade Organization, Annex 1B (Marrakesh, 15 April 1994).

violation of Article I.1 of the GATT. The final section will be devoted to addressing the legal implications of its lack of characterisation as a 'comprehensive agreement' and the challenges that poses for WTO Members, its lack of transparency and multilateral scrutiny.

II. The 'Expanding Trade' Chapter, the Diversion of Trade and its WTO Consistency

A key aspect of the Phase One Deal is China's commitment under Chapter 6, to increase purchases of United States (US) goods and services to $200 billion above 2017 levels over 2020 and 2021.[10]

Under Chapter 6 China committed to purchase from the US (1) manufactured goods of no less than $32.9 billion in 2020 and $44.8 billion in 2021; (2) agricultural goods of no less than $12.5 billion in 2020 and $19.5 in 2021; (3) energy products of no less than $18.5 in 2020 and $33.9 billion in 2021; and (4) services of no less than $12.8 billion in calendar year 2020, and more than $25.1 billion in 2021.[11]

Given the magnitude of the purchase commitment pledged by China, that would mean that this country will need to increase its exports by 35 per cent in 2020 and by 50 per cent over the 2017 level in 2021.[12] The immediate question that arises is how that would be achieved without distorting competition and violating cornerstone principles and obligations of the multilateral trading system like the MFN rule.

At first glance, the relevant provisions of the deal and the stated objectives of Chapter 6 may give the impression that they are consistent with WTO Agreements,[13] since Article 6.2.5 suggests that China may not be required to fulfil

[10] See Art 6.2.1 of the Phase One Deal (n 1).

[11] For overall amounts and the category of US goods and services benefited see also Annex 6.1 ibid.

[12] W Zhou and H Gao, 'US–China Phase One Deal: A Brief Account' (*Kluwer Regulating for Globalization Blog*, 22 January 2020), regulatingforglobalization.com/2020/01/22/us-china-phase-one-deal-a-brief-account.

[13] Art 6.1 'Objectives' of the Phase One Deal (n 1) states as follows:

'1. The Parties acknowledge that trade and economic structural changes resulting from this Agreement and from other actions being taken by China to open up its economy and improve its trade regime should lead to improved trade flows, including significant increases in exports of goods and services to China by the United States and other countries.
2. The Parties believe that expanding trade is conducive to the improvement of their bilateral trade relationship, the optimal allocation of resources, economic restructuring, and sustainable economic development, given the high degree of complementarity in trade between them.
3. The Parties recognize that the United States produces and can supply high-quality, competitively priced goods and services, while China needs to increase the importation of quality and affordable goods and services to satisfy the increasing demand from Chinese consumers.
4. The Parties accordingly seek to work constructively and cooperatively toward an improved bilateral trade relationship and to explore appropriate steps to facilitate increased trade'.

its purchase commitments, if goods are not available in suitable quality or are not offered at market-oriented prices based on commercial considerations. Thus, leaving in principle enough space for alternative WTO suppliers.[14]

A further legal argument in support of Chapter 6 consistency with WTO Agreements is that, on its face, the legal text of the Phase One Deal does not prohibit or restrict China from purchasing the covered goods and services from other WTO Members. This would prevent a successful allegation of de jure violation of the non-discrimination principle.

However, as it remains unclear how such a massive increase in imports from the US may be guaranteed without substituting Chinese imports from other WTO Members,[15] then the question here is whether the potential diversion of trade could be reconciled with the MFN clause or other relevant WTO provisions. Indeed, in this respect, it has been noted that in order to meet the targets set forth in Chapter 6, China could shift purchases away from other WTO suppliers, several of which are traditional US allies, like Europe, Japan, Australia or South Korea.[16] Thus, the 'managed trade approach' adopted by Chapter 6 of the Phase One Deal has implications beyond the bilateral trade relationship between China and the US and may potentially affect cornerstone principles and obligations of the multilateral trading system. The potential violation of the MFN rule and other allegations of inconsistency with other WTO Agreements, like the SG Agreement, will be discussed below.

A. The Consistency of Chapter 6 of the Phase One Deal with the SG Agreement

Article 11.1(b) of the SG Agreement establishes that WTO Members shall not seek, take or maintain any voluntary export restraints (VER), orderly marketing arrangements (OMA) or 'any other similar measures on the export or the import side',[17] and prescribes that such measures shall be brought into conformity

[14] Art 6.2.5 of the Phase One Deal (n 1) specifically provides the following: 'The Parties acknowledge that purchases will be made at market prices based on commercial considerations and that market conditions, particularly in the case of agricultural goods, may dictate the timing of purchases within any given year'.

[15] According to CP Bown, 'If fulfilled, the deal would result in a 92 percent increase – a near doubling – of US exports to China of the covered products between 2017 and 2021'. See 'Unappreciated Hazards of the US–China Phase One Deal' (*PIIE, Trade and Investment Policy Watch*, 21 January 2020), www.piie.com/blogs/trade-and-investment-policy-watch/unappreciated-hazards-us-china-phase-one-deal; See also A García-Herrero, 'Why the US Trade Agreement will slow China's Economy' (18 February 2020), www.brinknews.com/why-the-us-trade-agreement-will-dampen-economic-activity-in-china/.

[16] See Bown (n 15).

[17] See Art 11 of the SG Agreement (n 7) on Prohibition and Elimination of Certain Measures. Paras 1(a) and 1(b) read as follows:

with the Agreement and phased out, in accordance with paragraph 2 of this provision.[18]

Article 11.1(a) and (b) of the SG Agreement was negotiated in large part because GATT Contracting Parties had been increasingly applying a variety of the so-called 'grey area' measures to mainly limit imports of certain products that were not subject to multilateral discipline through the GATT. In view of this, the SG Agreement now clearly prohibits such measures and has specific provisions for eliminating those that were in place in 1995.

However, while in the current legal framework these 'grey area' measures are now explicitly forbidden, the question of whether the relevant provisions of Chapter 6 of the Phase One Deal would amount to an 'orderly marketing arrangement or any other similar measure on the export or the import side' within the meaning of Article 11.1(b) is not so clear.

First, the term 'orderly marketing arrangement' is not defined in the SG Agreement. In fact, sometimes it has been used as a synonym for the term 'voluntary export restraints'.[19] While, on other occasions it has been assigned a broader connotation, that is 'as referring to total coordination of supply of a commodity in order to achieve the joint market objectives of both sellers and buyers'.[20]

Second, at least throughout the GATT era, the 'grey-area' measures have been generally described by Contracting Parties as bilateral restraint arrangements of a VER or OMA type, concluded between importing and exporting countries, or as unilateral actions limiting imports, but rarely as a measure to expand trade or imports.[21]

Third, footnote 4 to paragraph 1(b) of Article 11, that provides examples of 'similar measures on the export or the import side', does not give either a conclusive answer to the question of the precise legal nature of the Chinese purchase

'1. (a) A Member shall not take or seek any emergency action on imports of particular products as set forth in Article XIX of GATT 1994 unless such action conforms with the provisions of that Article applied in accordance with this Agreement.

(b) Furthermore, a Member shall not seek, take or maintain any voluntary export restraints, orderly marketing arrangements or any other similar measures on the export or the import side.(3),(4) These include actions taken by a single Member as well as actions under agreements, arrangements and understandings entered into by two or more Members. Any such measure in effect on the date of entry into force of the WTO Agreement shall be brought into conformity with this Agreement or phased out in accordance with paragraph 2'.

[18] Art 11 of the SG Agreement (n 7).

[19] eg, an OMA agreement has been defined as a 'Bilateral arrangement whereby an exporting country (government or industry) agrees to reduce or restrict exports without the importing country having to make use of quotas, tariffs or other import controls'. OECD, 'Glossary of statistical terms', stats.oecd.org/glossary/detail.asp?ID=4996.

[20] EU Petersmann, *The GATT/WTO Dispute Settlement System: International Law, International Organizations and Dispute Settlement* (The Hague, Kluwer Law International, 1996) ch 2.

[21] Negotiating Group on Safeguards, Background Note by the Secretariat on '"Grey-area" measures' (16 September 1987) MTN.GNG/NG9/W/6; see also, Negotiating Group on Safeguards, Background Note by the Secretariat on 'Drafting History of Article XIX and its Place in GATT' (16 September 1987) MTN.GNG/NG9/W/7.

commitment and its consistency with the SG Agreement, as all of the examples listed there seem also to refer to measures that seek to restrain rather than expand trade.[22]

Based on this narrow interpretation, it may be considered that China's purchase commitments, aiming at expanding the covered US imports, cannot be characterised as 'orderly marketing arrangements or any other similar measures on the export or the import side' within the meaning of Article 11.1(b).

The legal implications of such a narrow interpretation should not be underestimated, as it may signify that these types of commitments do not need to be brought into conformity with the SG Agreement. It may further mean that the affected WTO Members are not entitled to take any remedy or countermeasure under this Agreement.[23] Most importantly, it may weaken multilateral disciplines on safeguards and trigger a new wave of 'grey area' measures.[24]

In contrast, a broader interpretation which treats the voluntary import expansion agreements, like China's purchase commitments, as 'any other similar measures on the export or the import side' under Article 11.1(b), may also be warranted. This provision, therefore, also applies to 'any other similar measures' adopted at 'the import side' such as a voluntary import expansion arrangement.

Notably, the list of 'Examples of similar measures' provided in footnote 4 in Article 11 of the SG Agreement is not exhaustive and includes any other similar measure 'which afford protection'.[25] Therefore, a 'voluntary' import expanding agreement, like the Phase One Deal, may also qualify as a covered measure that appears to serve a similar purpose to an OMA, since just like the OMA, they reflect bilateral negotiations with respect to trade levels.

Thus, members seeking, taking or maintaining voluntary import expansion agreements will be required to notify such measures to the Committee on Safeguards to its examination pursuant to Article 12.7 and Article 13.1(d) of the SG Agreement.[26]

[22] fn 4 of the SG Agreement states that: 'Examples of similar measures include export moderation, export-price or import-price monitoring systems, export or import surveillance, compulsory import cartels and discretionary export or import licensing schemes, any of which afford protection'. See fn 4 to para 1(b) of Art 11 of the SG Agreement (n 7).

[23] See Art 14 ibid, that states that consultations and disputes arising under the Agreement are to be conducted in accordance with Arts XXII and XXIII of the GATT as elaborated by the Dispute Settlement Understanding.

[24] Indeed, in the past, Japan and the US signed an agreement in which Japan accepted that the foreign share of its semiconductor market would increase to 20 per cent, from a level of 8 per cent, over a period of five years and the US may impose retaliatory tariffs in case of non-compliance. Another agreement was signed between the US and Japan in 1992 and concerned a voluntary import expansion in automobile parts. See World Bank, 'East Asia and Pacific in the Time of COVID-19' (April 2020), openknowledge.worldbank.org/bitstream/handle/10986/33477/211565-ch04.pdf, ch II.

[25] GATT Secretariat Note on 'Inventory of Article XIX actions and other measures which appear to serve the same purpose' (17 August 1987) MTN.GNG/NG9/W/2/Rev.1 and (31 August 1987) MTN.GNG/NG9/W/2/Rev.1/Corr.1.

[26] It would further mean that any Member may notify the Committee on Safeguards of any voluntary import expanding agreement, that has not been notified by other Members that are required by this Agreement to make such notifications. See Art 12.8 of the SG Agreement (n 7).

B. The Consistency of the 'Managed Trade' Approach with the GATT

Another major issue in China's purchasing commitments under Chapter 6 concerns whether they may amount to a de jure or de facto violation of the MFN rule. To answer this legal question, we start by recalling that Article I:1 of the GATT prohibits discrimination among like imported products originating in, or destined for, different countries, as the essence of the non-discrimination obligation is that like products should be treated equally, irrespective of their origin.[27]

As explained by the Appellate Body in *EC–Seal Products*, to establish an inconsistency with the MFN clause under the GATT, the following elements must be demonstrated:

(i) that the measure at issue falls within the scope of application of Article I:1;
(ii) that the imported products at issue are 'like' products within the meaning of Article I:1;
(iii) that the measure at issue confers an 'advantage, favor, privilege, or immunity' on a product originating in the territory of any country; and
(iv) that the advantage so accorded is not extended 'immediately' and 'unconditionally' to 'like' products originating in the territory of all Members.[28]

With respect to the first element, it may be argued that the Chinese purchase commitments may amount to a 'rule' 'in connection with importation' within the meaning of Article I:1.[29]

Such a characterisation may, in principle, be warranted by the broad interpretation of that phrase made in *US–Poultry*, where the Panel observed that the phrase,

> 'in connection with importation' as used in Article I, not only encompasses measures which directly relate to the process of importation but could also include those measures … which relate to other aspects of the importation of a product or have an impact on actual importation.[30]

Alternatively, it may also be considered that China's purchase commitments may fall within the scope of application of Article I:1 as a 'matter referred to in

[27] In *EC–Seal Products*, the Appellate Body explained that 'In so doing, Article I:1 protects expectations of equal competitive opportunities for like imported products from all Members'. *European Communities–Measures Prohibiting the Importation and Marketing of Seal Products*, Report of the Appellate Body (16 June 2014), WT/DS400/AB/R, WT/DS401/AB/R, para 5.87 (*EC–Seal Products*).

[28] ibid para 5.86.

[29] As noted by the Panel in *EC–Bananas III*, 'Article I requires MFN treatment in respect of "rules and formalities" in connection with importation'. *European Communities–Regime for the Importation, Sale and Distribution of Bananas*, Report of the Panel (25 September 1997) WT/DS27/R/ECU, para 7.189 (*EC–Bananas III*).

[30] See *United States–Certain Measures Affecting Imports of Poultry from China*, Report of the Panel (25 October 2010) WT/DS392/R, para 7.410.

paragraph 4 of Article III',[31] and more specifically, as 'a law, regulation or requirement "affecting" the "internal sale, offering for sale, purchase"'.[32]

However, to show that the Chinese purchase commitments fall within the scope of application of Article I:1 may not be so straightforward, as much would depend on the actual implementation of the Agreement and on the legal nature of the internal measures to be adopted by China to ensure compliance with the import targets.[33]

Further challenges may imply to establish that Article 6.2.1 of the Phase One Deal confers an 'advantage, favor, privilege, or immunity' on a product originating in the territory of any country' within the meaning of Article I.1. In this regard, such 'advantages' have been considered by WTO tribunals as encompassing those that create 'more favourable import opportunities' or affect the commercial relationship between products of different origins.[34]

Accordingly, the affected members may in principle argue that China violates the MFN rule on the ground that the advantages granted to US imports under Chapter 6, do not extend immediately and unconditionally to their like products. However, it should also be noted that a Panel may always disregard this legal argument on the basis that the market price and commercial consideration clause does not prevent China from fulfilling its purchase commitments on a non-discriminatory basis.[35]

[31] See the *EU–Energy Package* dispute where the Panel acknowledged that Art I:1 of the GATT incorporated all matters referred to in para 4 of Art III. *European Union and its Member States–Certain Measures Relating to the Energy Sector*, Report of the Panel (circulated 10 August 2018) WT/DS476/R, para 7.829 (*EU–Energy Package*).

[32] Art III.4 of the GATT (n 8) in its relevant parts states that: '4. The products of the territory of any contracting party imported into the territory of any other contracting party shall be accorded treatment no less favourable than that accorded to like products of national origin in respect of all laws, regulations and requirements affecting their internal sale, offering for sale, purchase, transportation, distribution or use'. See also *Argentina–Financial Services*, where the Panel noted that 'the precedents accord a broad meaning to the scope of application of Article III:4 of the GATT 1994 and indicate that that provision also covers those measures which, even though their main objective is not to regulate the internal sale, offering for sale, purchase or use of the product, affect the conditions of competition of the products in question on the domestic market'. *Argentina–Measures Relating to Trade in Goods and Services*, Report of the Panel (9 May 2016) WT/DS453/R, para 7.1023 (*Argentina–Financial Services*).

[33] Example of internal measures to be adopted by China to ensure compliance with the import targets may constitute the screening and monitoring mechanism of companies imports, statutory requirement for companies to supply information on import or the imposition of penalties attached for failure to comply with that requirement by private companies.

[34] See *EC–Bananas III*, Report of the Panel (n 29) paras 7.189 and 7.239. See also *Canada–Autos*, where the Appellate Body observed that 'Article I:1 requires that "*any advantage*, favour, privilege or immunity granted by any Member to *any product* originating in or destined for any other country shall be accorded immediately and unconditionally to the like product originating in or destined for the territories of *all other Members*" (emphasis added). The words of Article I:1 refer not to some advantages granted "with respect to" the subjects that fall within the defined scope of the Article, but to "*any advantage*"; not to *some* products, but to "*any product*"; and not to like products from *some* other Members, but to like products originating in or destined for "*all other*" Members'. *Canada–Certain Measures Affecting the Automotive Industry*, Report of the Appellate Body (19 June 2000) WT/DS139/AB/R, WT/DS142/AB/R, para 79 (*Canada–Autos*).

Furthermore, it should also be recalled that, although an inconsistency with Article I:1 is not contingent upon the actual trade effects of a measure,[36] for the purposes of establishing a violation of the MFN rule, the detrimental impact of a measure on competitive opportunities for like imported products must be demonstrated.[37]

In light of the above, it may be argued that the Phase One Deal may drag the affected members into a complex litigation process, as the evidence to demonstrate the elements to establish an inconsistency with the MFN clause may not always be available.[38]

To begin with, it should be noted in this regard that the Phase One Deal is silent on the import targets for the specific products. Indeed, while Article 6.2.2 establishes that the Parties shall specify the increases in purchases and imports for the subcategories listed in Annex 6.1 as appropriate, until today neither party to the deal has published the detailed import targets for the covered products.

Second, China's fulfilment of the purchase commitments may require implementing measures that, again, may be affected by other transparency issues.[39]

Third, as will be seen in the following section, the Phase One Deal is under no surveillance or WTO scrutiny, since it has not been notified under any of the relevant WTO transparency provisions.

Therefore, despite the fact that the massive purchase commitments may likely lead to trade diversion,[40] establishing an inconsistency with the MFN rule may place an onerous burden of proof on the claimants, as the evidence required may not be available due to the lack of transparency that surrounds the legal text and the effective and concrete implementation of the Phase One Deal.

[35] As noted above, the legal text of the Phase One Deal contains a market price and commercial consideration clause, that provides that purchases will be made at market prices based on commercial considerations and that market conditions may dictate the timing of the purchases. Thus, eventually leaving enough space for other WTO suppliers, if the conditions set forth in Art 6.2.5 of the deal are not met.

[36] *EC–Seal Products*, Report of the Appellate Body (n 27) para 5.87.

[37] ibid paras 5.90–5.93.

[38] See, eg, the GATT Panel Report in *Japan–Trade in Semi-Conductors*, where the Panel examined, inter alia, measures by Japan to promote sales of certain foreign semi-conductors in Japan where the Panel 'found that the information submitted to it did not demonstrate that the Japanese measures to improve access to its market for semi-conductors favoured United States products inconsistently with Article I of the General Agreement'. *Japan–Trade in Semi-Conductors*, GATT Panel (4 May 1988) 24L/6309 – 35S/116, paras 60–62, 127.

[39] See, eg, Lunenborg (n 3) who stated: 'The product categorization in the US--China agreement does not fully correspond with the categorization of agricultural goods, as listed in Annex 1 of the WTO Agreement on Agriculture, and by implication non-agricultural goods (which are all products not classified as agriculture). For instance, mineral waters (HS2201 and HS2202) are considered "other manufactured goods" (but these are agricultural goods in the WTO context) and mixtures of odoriferous substances (HS 3302) and seafood (under HS Chapters 3 and 16) are considered "agriculture" (but considered non-agriculture in the WTO context)'.

[40] See Figures 3 and 4 in CP Bown and ME Lovely, 'Trump's Phase One Deal Relies on China's State-Owned Enterprises' (3 March 2020), www.piie.com/blogs/trade-and-investment-policy-watch/trumps-phase-one-deal-relies-chinas-state-owned-enterprises.

C. The Consistency of Chapter 6 of the Phase One Deal with Article XVII of the GATT

A further challenge that Chapter 6 may pose to affected WTO Members relates to the fact that, in order to meet the import targets, China may probably have to rely on its State Trading Enterprises and to direct them to fulfil the obligations under the deal.[41] In that case, the Phase One Deal may also lead to a violation of Article XVII of the GATT.

Article XVII requires that State Trading Enterprises in their purchases or sales involving either imports or exports, act in accordance with the general principles of non-discrimination. Article XVII further establishes that commercial considerations shall guide their decisions on imports and exports.[42]

In this regard it should be recalled that this provision seeks to make state traders behave as private competitive traders, and thus to remove the potential for trade distortion offered by government involvement in an enterprise's decisions and activities. To that end, Article XVII:1 imposes an obligation on WTO Members not to use State Trading Enterprises in order to discriminate in ways that would be prohibited if undertaken directly by members.[43]

However, due to the lack of transparency concerning China's implementation of the purchasing commitments, showing a violation of Article XVII may once again be difficult, as under this provision, the assessment of whether a State Trading Enterprise makes the purchases solely in accordance with commercial considerations will involve a careful analysis of the relevant market,[44] and the evidence needed in this regard may not always be available.

III. The Phase One Deal and the Legal Implications of Not being Characterised as a Regional Trade Agreement Pursuant to the Relevant WTO Provisions

A. The Characterisation of the Phase One Deal as a Regional Trade Agreement under Article XXIV of the GATT

Even though China's purchase commitments under the Deal may lead to an MFN breach, China may always invoke Article XXIV of the GATT to justify a finding

[41] ibid.

[42] It should be noted in this regard that the commercial considerations obligation applies only to trade in goods. See the Interpretative Note Ad Art XVII (Paragraph 2) that states that 'The term "goods" is limited to products as understood in commercial practice and is not intended to include the purchase or sale of services'. Annex I to GATT (n 8).

[43] *Canada–Measures Relating to Exports of Wheat and Treatment of Imported Grain*, Report of the Appellate Body (27 September 2004) WT/DS276/AB/R, para 97. The Appellate Body held that para 1(a) 'is an anticircumvention' provision'. ibid para 85.

[44] See ibid para 149.

of such a breach. Article XXIV allows for the establishment of customs unions and free-trade areas, as a legitimate exception to the non-discrimination principle, provided certain conditions are met.

Indeed, although regional trade agreements (RTAs), by their very nature are discriminatory as they provide preferential treatment to the parties involved, WTO Agreements recognise the contribution to the expansion of world trade that may be made by RTAs which aim at facilitating trade between its parties and do not raise trade barriers to third parties.[45]

More specifically, to be consistent with Article XXIV and qualify as a legitimate exception to the MFN rule, free-trade areas, customs unions and interim agreements leading to the formation of a customs union or free-trade area, must satisfy the provisions of paragraphs 5, 6, 7 and 8 of that Article.[46] Those paragraphs require that: the effects of the resulting trade measures and policies of the new RTA shall not be more trade restrictive, overall, than were the constituent countries previous trade policies;[47] the constituent members of a customs union shall eliminate 'duties and other restrictive regulations of commerce' with respect to 'substantially all the trade' between them; the constituent members of a customs union shall apply 'substantially the same' duties and other regulations of commerce to external trade with third countries; the external tariffs and commercial regulations applicable to non-parties shall not be higher or more restrictive than those in effect before the FTA was formed.[48]

Lastly, paragraph 7(a) of Article XXIV requires that any WTO Member deciding to enter into a customs union or free-trade area, or an interim agreement leading to the formation of such a union or area, shall promptly notify WTO

[45] According to para 4 of Art XXIV the purpose of a customs union or of a free-trade area should be to facilitate trade between the constituent territories and not to raise barriers to the trade of other contracting parties with such territories. Indeed, as found by the Panel in *US–COOL*: 'In regulating entry into preferential regional and bilateral trade agreements, Article XXIV of the GATT 1994 allows for the establishment of customs unions and free trade areas, stipulating that "[the purpose of a customs union or a free-trade area should be to facilitate trade … and not to raise barriers to … trade". Thus, the formation of regional trade agreements is not meant to undermine WTO concessions and other obligations, or to frustrate WTO market access benefits'. *United States–Certain Country of Origin Labelling (COOL) Requirements* (Article 21.5 – Canada and Mexico), Report of the Panel (29 May 2015), para 7.687. See the 'Understanding on the Interpretation of Article XXIV of the GATT 1994', www.wto.org/english/docs_e/legal_e/10-24_e.htm. In this Understanding the WTO Members reaffirm 'that in their formation or enlargement the parties to them should to the greatest possible extent avoid creating adverse effects on the trade of other Members'.

[46] See ibid para 1.

[47] See Art XXIV:5, para (a) of the GATT (n 8) that states that the duties and other regulations of commerce imposed at the institution of any such FTA shall not on the whole be higher or more restrictive than the general incidence of the duties and regulations of commerce applicable in the constituent territories prior to the formation of such union. See also *Turkey–Textiles*, where the Appellate Body stated that the test for assessing trade-restrictiveness under paragraph 5(a) is an economic one. *Turkey–Restrictions on Imports of Textile and Clothing Products*, Report of the Appellate Body (19 November 1999) WT/DS34/AB/R, para 55 (*Turkey–Textiles*).

[48] See ibid para 49. See para 8 of Art XXIV of the GATT (n 8). Art XXIV further provides that an interim agreement leading to the formation of a customs union or free-trade area must contain a plan and schedule to achieve these goals within a reasonable period of time.

Members and make available the necessary information to enable to make them the reports and recommendations they may deem appropriate.

In light of the above, the question that immediately arises here is whether the Phase One Deal can be characterised as an RTA pursuant to this provision, and hence, as a legitimate exception to the MFN rule. In the author's opinion, the correct answer to this question should be negative.

First, the Phase One Deal fails to comply with Article XXIV.8(a)(i) that requires the constituent members of a customs union to eliminate 'duties' and other restrictive regulations of commerce with respect to 'substantially all the trade' between them.[49] Indeed, the Phase One Deal not only does not contain commitments on tariff reductions, but also, beyond the Chinese purchase commitments under Chapter 6, does not encompass any provisions addressing trade in manufactured goods. Furthermore, the Phase One Deal leaves in place the trade war tariffs between the US and China, that is, the US unilaterally imposed tariffs under section 301 of the Trade Act 1974 and the Chinese retaliatory tariffs. More generally, no reference is made in the Phase One Deal to the formation of a customs union or a free-trade area between China and the US. Nor did the parties to the deal make any notification to the WTO pursuant to Article XXIV.7(a).

A Phase Two Deal, or a more comprehensive deal, does not appear to be imminent either, and Article 8.4 of the Phase One Deal on 'Further Negotiations' is also silent in this regard. Thus, in principle, it may be argued that the Deal cannot either be characterised as an interim agreement leading to the formation of a customs union or free-trade area pursuant to Article XXIV.[50]

B. The Characterisation of the Phase One Deal as an 'Agreement' Pursuant to Article V of the GATS

Just like Article I of the GATT, under Article II of the GATS, WTO Members have committed to extend immediately and unconditionally to services or services suppliers of all other members 'treatment no less favourable than that

[49] See the *Turkey–Textiles* dispute, where the Appellate Body addressed the definition in Art XXIV:8(a) for a GATT consistent customs union, finding that: 'Sub-paragraph 8(a)(i) of Article XXIV establishes the standard for the internal trade between constituent members in order to satisfy the definition of a "customs union". It requires the constituent members of a customs union to eliminate "duties and other restrictive regulations of commerce" with respect to "substantially all the trade" between them. It is clear, though, that "substantially all the trade" is not the same as all the trade, and also that "substantially all the trade" is something considerably more than merely some of the trade'. *Turkey–Textiles*, Report of the Appellate Body (n 47) para 48.

[50] Art XXIV.5(c) further provides that an interim agreement leading to the formation of a customs union or free-trade area must contain a plan and schedule to achieve these goals within a reasonable period of time.

accorded to like services and services suppliers of any other country'.[51] Likewise, Article XXIV of the GATT, under the GATS provisions derogations to the MFN rule are also possible pursuant to Article V 'Economic Integration', if certain conditions are met.

More specifically, to provide legal coverage for measures taken pursuant to economic integration agreements, which would otherwise be inconsistent with the principle of non-discrimination, in accordance with Article V of the GATS, RTAs in trade in services must (a) have a substantial sectoral coverage,[52] and (b) in the covered sectors, eliminate substantially all discrimination between or among the parties through (i) the elimination of existing discriminatory measures, and/or (ii) the prohibition of new or more discriminatory measures. Additionally, paragraph 4 of Article V.4 requires that:

> Any agreement referred to in paragraph 1 shall be designed to facilitate trade between the parties to the agreement and shall not in respect of any Member outside the agreement raise the overall level of barriers to trade in services within the respective sectors or subsectors compared to the level applicable prior to such an agreement.

In other words, Article V of the GATS permits any WTO Member to enter into an 'agreement' within the meaning of Article V, provided that the Agreement has 'substantial sectoral coverage', removes substantially all discrimination between participants, and does not raise barriers to third parties.

However, in view of this, the Phase One Deal cannot be characterised as an RTA under the GATS, and thus, as a legitimate exception to the MFN rule in Article II, as the Deal does not provide 'substantial sectoral coverage', as required by Article V.1. Indeed, leaving aside the purchase commitments in services pledged by the Chinese government under Chapter 6, Chapter 4 of the Phase One Deal is limited in scope, as it only covers six sub-sectors of financial services: banking; credit rating; electronic payment; financial asset management; insurance and securities; fund management and futures services. This is clearly contrary to the purpose of Article V of the GATS that, as noted by the Panel in *Canada–Autos* is 'to allow for ambitious liberalisation to take place at a regional level, while at the same time guarding against undermining the MFN obligation by engaging in minor preferential arrangements'.[53]

[51] Under Art II of the GATS, and with respect to any measure covered by this Agreement, each Member shall accord immediately and unconditionally to services and service suppliers of any other Member treatment no less favourable than that it accords to like services and service suppliers of any other country. Art II of the GATS (n 9). In *Canada–Autos*, the Appellate Body explained how a Panel should proceed when examining the consistency of a measure with Art II:1 of the GATS. *Canada–Autos*, Report of the Appellate Body (n 34) paras 170–71. See also *EU–Energy Package*, Report of the Panel (n 31) paras 7.227, 7.404.

[52] See fn 1 to para 1(a) of Art V that establishes that 'This condition is understood in terms of number of sectors, volume of trade affected and modes of supply'. Art V of the GATS (n 9).

[53] *Canada-Certain Measures Affecting the Automotive Industry*, Report of the Panel (19 June 2000) WT/DS139/R, WT/DS142/R, paras 10.269–10.272.

C. The Legal Implications of the Lack of Characterisation of the Phase One Deal as an RTA under Article XXIV and Article V of the GATS

The failure of the Phase One Deal to be characterised as an RTA under the relevant WTO provisions, and thus as a legitimate exception to the non-discrimination rule, would in principle imply that any concession and obligation made under the deal that is beyond the WTO Agreements, would have to be applied on an MFN basis.[54]

This multilateralisation may also, in principle, encompass China's purchase commitments not only on trade in goods, but also on trade in services, as under the GATS the MFN obligation is applicable to 'any measure' that 'affects' trade in services in any sector falling under the Agreement.[55] Yet, again, the effective multilateralisation of any obligation made under the Deal that goes beyond the relevant WTO Agreements may not be so straightforward, considering that much will depend on the actual implementation of the Deal and its transparency.

In this later respect, it should be highlighted that, maybe on the consideration that the Phase One Deal is a 'minor preferential agreement', it was not notified to the WTO pursuant to any of the relevant multilateral transparency provisions applicable to RTAs or interim agreement leading to the formation of an RTA. The Deal has not been notified in conformity with the Transparency Mechanism for Regional Trade Agreements (Transparency Mechanism) either.[56]

The Transparency Mechanism is a relevant instrument from the WTO consistency perspective of RTA with multilateral agreements, as it clarifies and strengthens the notification obligations of members and introduces new procedures to enhance the transparency of such Agreements.

[54] According to Lunenborg (n 3): 'In the area of goods, any preferential tariff, duty exemption or Tariff Rate Quota which would be more beneficial than the MFN rate would have to apply to all WTO Members. In principle, MFN treatment also applies in the case of the SPS Agreement (food safety measures). In the area of services, commitments made by China that go beyond its GATS commitments, including the treatment or approval of applications of financial services to operate in China, would have to be applied on an MFN basis'.

[55] See *EC–Bananas III*, where the Panel defined the scope of application of the GATS by observing that 'No measures are excluded a priori from the scope of the GATS as defined by its provisions' and 'encompasses any measure of a Member to the extent it affects the supply of a service regardless of whether such measure directly governs the supply of a service or whether it regulates other matters but nevertheless affects trade in services'. *EC–Bananas III*, Report of the Panel (n 29) para 7.285. In the same dispute the Appellate Body set out its interpretation of the term 'treatment no less favourable' in Art II:1 of the GATS, observing that this provision covers both de jure and de facto discrimination. *EC–Bananas III*, Report of the Appellate Body (25 September 1997) WT/DS27/AB/R, para 233.

[56] On 14 December 2006, the General Council of the WTO adopted a Transparency Mechanism for Regional Trade Agreements. Decision of the General Council, 'Transparency Mechanism for Regional Trade Agreements' (14 December 2006) WT/L/671.

Indeed, the Transparency Mechanism provides for early announcement and notifications of any RTA to the WTO,[57] and most importantly, for the consideration of the RTA by WTO Members based on a factual presentation prepared by the WTO Secretariat.[58]

None of the above will be applicable to the Phase One Deal, that until today is under no WTO scrutiny.

IV. Conclusions

Leaving aside its positive aspects, due to its 'managed trade approach' along with its lack of transparency and multilateral scrutiny, the Phase One Deal should raise several systemic concerns from the WTO perspective.

Indeed, a first concern relates to the possibility that its legal characterisation as a 'voluntary' import expanding agreement cannot be considered encompassed in the scope of Article 11.1(b). Or in other words, that it cannot be considered an 'orderly marketing arrangement or any other similar measure on the export or the import side' that is forbidden by the SG Agreement, and that then has also to be brought into conformity with this Agreement.

Given that a narrow interpretation in this regard may suppose a return to the GATT era, where the 'grey area' measures were widespread, a broader interpretation of the scope of application of Article 11.1(b) is encouraged. The latter would, at least, help enhance the transparency of this type of arrangement (like OMAs), thereby reflecting the negotiations with respect to trade levels and 'afford protection' within the meaning of footnote 4 and paragraph 1(b) of Article 11 of the SG Agreement.

Another aspect of the Phase One Deal that should raise concerns, is the WTO consistency of the Chinese purchase commitments with the MFN clause as well as the challenges that may pose to affected members to establish a violation of that rule, since that may depend on the actual implementation of the Deal and evidence, which may not always be available, due to a lack of transparency.

This last scenario, calls for the rest of the WTO membership to remain particularly vigilant, because the purchase commitments may have effects beyond 2021, as Article 6.2.3 envisages that Chinese purchase commitments may continue in calendar years 2022 to 2025.[59]

[57] See s A ibid. s A of the Transparency Mechanism that introduces the concept of an early announcement of the RTA. According to it, Members participating in new negotiations aimed at the conclusion of an RTA should inform the WTO Secretariat of such negotiations and should send to the Secretariat information on the RTA.

[58] See ibid s A para (b). See ibid s B 'Notification' and s C 'Procedures to Enhance Transparency'.

[59] See Art 6.2.3 of the Phase One Deal (n 1) that states that 'The Parties project that the trajectory of increases in the amounts of manufactured goods, agricultural goods, energy products, and services purchased and imported into China from the United States will continue in calendar years 2022 through 2025'.

A third aspect of the Phase One Deal that should raise systemic concerns relates to the fact that it cannot be characterised as an RTA, pursuant to Article XXIV of the GATT or Article V of the GATS, and to its lack of multilateral scrutiny. This may undermine the effective multilateralisation of the Phase One Deal commitments that go beyond the relevant WTO Agreements.

Then, a broader concern about the deal relates to whether the relevant WTO Agreements and the mechanisms directed to enhance transparency are sufficiently 'updated' to effectively protect the rest of the membership from this 'type of agreement'. Or alternatively, should it rather be another 'issue' on which the proposed WTO 'reform' should also focus?

In this respect, WTO Members should consider 'updating' the relevant WTO provisions, having in mind that the decision to remain silent in this regard may be interpreted as a precedent for legitimising the dubious legal aspects of this not comprehensive and managed trade agreement, that challenge core principles of the multilateral trading system.

The modernisation of the relevant WTO provisions may for example take place on the ground of the Doha Ministerial Declaration[60] or Section I (Reappraisal of the Mechanism) of the Transparency Mechanism.[61]

Finally, in the meantime, and to avoid the undermining of the MFN rule by engaging in 'minor' preferential trade agreements, a broader and more flexible interpretation of the current WTO transparency provisions, like those regarding the interim agreements in paragraph 7(a), or those related to paragraph 10 of Article XXIV,[62] should not be discarded.

[60] See para 29 of the Doha Ministerial Declaration that mandates for negotiations aimed at 'clarifying and improving disciplines and procedures under the existing WTO provisions applying to regional trade agreements'. Doha Ministerial Declaration (4 November 2001) WT/MIN(01)/DEC/1.

[61] This section provides the following: '23 Members will review, and if necessary modify this Decision, in light of the experience gained from its provisional operation, and replace it by a permanent mechanism adopted as part of the overall results of the Round, in accordance with paragraph 47 of the Doha Declaration. Members will also review the legal relationship between this Mechanism and relevant WTO provisions related to RTAs'.

[62] In the past, para 10 of Art XXIV was understood to enable the approval of the establishment of customs unions and free-trade areas which include non-Members. See Analytical index of the GATT, Art XXIV, 829, www.wto.org/english/res_e/publications_e/ai17_e/gatt1994_art24_gatt47.pdf.

14

China's Response to the 'Market-Oriented Conditions' Proposal for WTO Reform and its Implications in the (Post-) COVID-19 Era

LUYAO CHE*

I. Introduction

While the World Trade Organization (WTO) is presently undergoing a severe crisis, several WTO Members have expressed their intentions to reform the world trading system and have circulated their proposals.[1] A major proposal has been to recognise the principle of market-oriented conditions (MOCs) as fundamental guidance for further WTO reforms. On 31 May 2018, a Ministerial Statement made jointly by the United States (US), the European Union (EU) and Japan announced that MOCs 'are fundamental to a fair, mutually advantageous global trading system'.[2] Annexed to this statement was a 'Joint Statement on Market-Oriented Conditions'.[3] On 20 February 2020, the US released a proposal themed

* This research is supported by the Programme for Young Innovative Research Team in China University of Political Science and Law (19CXTD09), the National Rule of Law and Legal Theory Research Programme by Ministry of Justice of the People's Republic of China (18SFB3044), and the Institute of Governance Studies (IGS), Tsinghua University. The author expresses special acknowledgement to Dr Suresh Nanwani, Professor in Practice at Durham University for his insightful and inspiring comments and suggestion for the improvement of this chapter, as well as Emily X Han for her kind help in proofreading.

[1] eg, the trade ministers from the US, the EU and Japan have jointly released seven statements concerning WTO reforms. See 'Press releases' (USTR), ustr.gov/about-us/policy-offices/press-office/press-releases. The EU, Canada and China have respectively clarified their positions and attitudes towards WTO reforms. The European Council, 'WTO Modernisation: Introduction to Future EU Proposals' (28–29 June 2018) EU Concept Paper, trade.ec.europa.eu/doclib/docs/2018/september/tradoc_157331.pdf; Communication from Canada: Strengthening and Modernizing the WTO: Discussion Paper (24 September 2018) JOB/GC/201; Communication from China: China's Proposal on WTO Reform (13 May 2019) WT/GC/W/773.

[2] Joint Statement on Trilateral Meeting of the Trade Ministers of the United States, Japan, and the European Union (31 May 2018), trade.ec.europa.eu/doclib/docs/2018/may/tradoc_156906.pdf.

[3] ibid, Annexed Statement 3.

'the Importance of Market-Oriented Conditions to the World Trading System' in the form of a draft decision by the WTO General Council.[4] More recently, on 21 July and 2 October 2020, Brazil[5] and Japan[6] successively joined the US and made the proposal a joint statement. With the little difference[7] among the documents mentioned above, this chapter will use the phrase 'market-oriented conditions' proposal (MOC proposal) to refer to all the aforementioned documents.

The MOC proposal has two components. One is a statement of the importance of the MOCs as a principle of WTO reform. Serving as the core principle, MOCs may direct the ongoing trade negotiations, the formation of a series of WTO rules, and perhaps the interpretation of the existing WTO rules. The other component of the proposal is a set of criteria for assessing whether an economy, an industry, or the external environment of a particular enterprise is market oriented or not. Both the 'Joint Statement on Market-Oriented Conditions' and the US proposal on 20 February 2020 include a list of MOC criteria. For example, the US proposal set out eight indicators as follows:

i. Decisions of enterprises on prices, costs, inputs, purchases, and sales are freely determined and made in response to market signals.
ii. Decisions of enterprises on investments are freely determined and made in response to market signals.
iii. Prices of capital, labor, technology, and other factors are market-determined.
iv. Capital allocation decisions of or affecting enterprises are freely determined and made in response to market signals.
v. Enterprises are subject to internationally recognized accounting standards, including independent accounting.
vi. Enterprises are subject to market-oriented and effective corporation law, bankruptcy law, competition law, and private property law, and may enforce their rights through impartial legal processes, such as an independent judicial system.
vii. Enterprises are able to freely access relevant information on which to base their business decisions.
viii. There is no significant government interference in enterprise business decisions described above.[8]

[4] Communication from the United States: The Importance of Market-Oriented Conditions to the World Trading System – Draft General Council Decision (20 February 2020) WT/GC/W/796.

[5] Statement from Brazil and the United States: Importance of Market-Oriented Conditions to the World Trading System (21 July 2020) WT/GC/W/803.

[6] Statement from Brazil, Japan and the United States: Importance of Market-Oriented Conditions to the World Trading System (2 October 2020) WT/GC/W/803/Rev.1.

[7] Compared with the elements for 'market-oriented conditions' listed in the Trilateral Statement in 2018, those mentioned in the proposal by the US in 2020 include an additional element, which is 'enterprises are able to freely access relevant information on which to base their business decisions'. Besides, there are some difference in the language used between the Statement and the Proposal. Meanwhile, the Joint Statement by the US, Brazil and Japan is an exact duplication of the Proposal by the US.

[8] The Importance of Market-Oriented Conditions to the World Trading System (n 4).

The only difference in the US–EU-Japan version is the absence of item vii. It is rather obvious that the MOC proposal mainly targets China. In July 2018, the US submitted a communication entitled 'China's Disruptive Economic Model' to the General Council of the WTO, complaining that China's 'non-market-oriented conditions' have created an unfairly advantageous position for itself while resulting in detrimental effects to other WTO Members.[9] According to the US, China not only sets out the general layout for industrial development,[10] but also maintains an extensive network of state-owned enterprises (SOEs).[11] These practices ensure that commercial entities in China are in line with the purposes of the state. When the issues addressed by this communication are compared with the eight criteria of MOCs, a high degree of consistency is revealed.

Although the topic of MOCs is closely connected with China, among all publicly available documents released by the Chinese government, so far no one has directly addressed the concern of MOCs. While China has played an active role in the discussions of WTO reforms,[12] none of its statements at or submissions to the WTO has explicitly or implicitly responded to the MOC proposal.

In the absence of a direct response by China to the MOC proposal, it is often questioned whether China has even formed an answer to it. Some may argue that being passive and avoiding more in-depth discussion is perhaps the best way to prevent further accusation.[13] This argument might be seen as convincing a few years ago. Before the inception of the US–China trade war in 2017, China had consistently complied with a 'not-to-argue' strategy when dealing with any challenge regarding its institutional choice of an economic model.[14] Now, China has become increasingly vocal in defending its own economic system.

The outbreak of the COVID-19 pandemic, to some degree, has provided more moral reasons for China to advocate a rethinking of the justifiability of institutional varieties. Therefore, it can be reasonably expected that, in the foreseeable future, China may provide a formal response to the MOC proposal.

This chapter contributes to the ongoing debate about China's economic model, its compatibility with the WTO, and the relevant WTO reforms by discussing China's possible response to the MOC proposal and its potential implications in the (post-) COVID-19 era. Section II explores the core concerns behind the

[9] Communication from the United States: China's Trade-Disruptive Economic Model (26–27 July 2018) WT/GC/W/745.

[10] ibid ss 1, 2–3.

[11] ibid ss 2, 3–4.

[12] The Ministry of Commerce of the People's Republic of China, 'China's Position Paper on WTO Reform' (2018), images.mofcom.gov.cn/sms/201812/20181217184454064.docx; China's Proposal on WTO Reform (n 1).

[13] See, eg, F Godement, 'China, the Reluctant WTO Reformer' (Institut Montaigne, 2019) www.institutmontaigne.org/documents/china-trends/190311-china-trends-1.pdf.

[14] 'Not to argue' is a concept created by Deng Xiaoping and adhered to as a guiding doctrine for Chinese economic reform. Its core idea is to ensure the absence of existing theoretical ground of China's practice in forming political-economic institutions not to delay the practice. See Z Gao (高正礼) 'The thought of "to argue" and "not to argue" by Deng Xiaoping' (邓小平"争论"和"不争论"思想研究' (2013) 1 *Studies of Contemporary Chinese History (当代中国史研究)* 66.

MOC proposal. Sections III–V, respectively, discuss China's possible responses at three different levels: the supply of legal instruments that disciplines governmental intervention (section III); the institutional background of the Chinese economy (section IV); and the underlining ideology (section V). At each level, this section examines the implications of China's response in the context of COVID-19. Section VI provides some concluding remarks.

II. The Concerns behind the 'Market-Oriented Conditions' Proposal

A. Legal Instruments: The Insufficient Supply of Relevant Rules

Controversy arises when it comes to the question as to how the MOC proposal would contribute to the reform of WTO rules. The US has explicitly shown its frustration about the insufficient supply of legal instruments that are provided to WTO Members to deal with 'non-market-oriented' practices. The area of trade remedy provides a good illustration of US concerns. One example concerns the law on the determination of 'public bodies', which is crucial in determining whether a subsidy exists. The US sought to treat all Chinese SOEs as public bodies so as to facilitate a finding of subsidies. In two WTO disputes, however, the Appellate Body unveiled a jurisprudence that a public body should be empowered with governmental authority.[15] Thus, a careful examination about whether such empowerment exists becomes a necessary step in anti-subsidy investigations. The US vigorously criticised this approach stating that it blurs the boundary between public and private entities.[16] This has contributed to the US view that the Agreement on Subsidies and Countervailing Measures (SCM Agreement) does not provide sufficient rules for Members to deal with the 'non-marker-oriented' practice, ie, using SOEs to grant 'hidden' subsidies.

Another example is the use of out-of-country benchmarks in the calculation of benefits transferred through a subsidy. To the US, where in-country benchmarks are distorted, the use of out-of-country benchmarks should be permitted under WTO rules. However, as suggested by the Appellate Body, the SCM Agreement provides relatively limited room for the use of out-of-country benchmarks: to apply out-of-country benchmarks, the investigating authority should not rely

[15] *United States–Definitive Anti-Dumping and Countervailing Duties on Certain Products from China*, Report of the Appellate Body (11 March 2011) WT/DS379/AB/R, para 317; *United States–Countervailing Measures on Certain Hot-Rolled Carbon Steel Flat Products from India*, Report of the Appellate Body (19 December 2014) WT/DS436/AB/R, para 4.29.

[16] United States Trade Representative (USTR), 'Report on the Appellate Body of the World Trade Organization' (February 2020), ustr.gov/sites/default/files/Report_on_the_Appellate_Body_of_the_World_Trade_Organization.pdf, 88.

solely on the existence of government price but also on a demonstration why the price is distorted.[17] The US questioned the preconditions for the application of out-of-country benchmarks as interpreted by the Appellate Body, holding that an investigating authority should preserve more discretion in dealing with market distortion.[18] It is highly likely that the satisfaction of the criteria of MOCs will be set to be the preconditions for the application of out-of-country benchmarks in future proposals by the US.

B. Institutions of Political Economy: The Need to Counter the State-Directed Economic Model

More fundamentally, there are deeper concerns regarding the setting of economic institutions behind the demand for reforming specific rules and norms. This chapter uses the term 'institutions' to refer to a series of political-economic settings that underpin the roles of the state in the economy, which are distinguishable from specific measures made by particular governmental authorities. Accordingly, Chinese institutions could be characterised as a distinctive market–state relationship, in which the state is integral to the market.[19] The strategies adopted by the US have witnessed a shift from a largely cooperative approach to a unilateral approach targeting China's economic model.

Over the past four decades, the US had expected China to achieve a transition towards the free-market capitalist economy, together with liberalist democracy.[20] For a majority of this period, the US government's trade policies had consistently been to maintain a cooperative relationship while imposing certain pressure and restrictions to help achieve the expected changes.[21]

Since 2017, however, the US has changed its cooperative approach to a confrontational and unilateral one. For example, the US Ambassador Dennis Shea made the following statement in the General Council of the WTO:

> Contrary to Members' expectations, China has not been moving toward a fuller embrace of market-based policies and practices since it joined the WTO in 2001. In fact, the opposite is true. The state's role in China's economy has been increasing.[22]

[17] *United States–Countervailing Duty Measures on Certain Products from China (Recourse to Article 21.5 of the DSU)*, Report of the Appellate Body (15 August 2019) WT/DS437/AB/RW, para 5.161.

[18] ibid para 105.

[19] L Che, *China's State-Directed Economy and the International Order* (Singapore, Springer, 2017) ch 2.

[20] F Fukuyama, *The End of History and the Last Man* (Free Press, 2006) 177–78; M Du, 'China's State Capitalism and World Trade Law' (2014) 63 *International & Comparative Law Quarterly* 409, 409.

[21] JA Bader, 'US–China Challenges: Time for China to Step Up' (*Brookings*, 2017), www.brookings.edu/research/u-s-china-challenges-time-for-china-to-step-up/.

[22] See statement by Ambassador D Shea, 'Views on China's Trade-Disruptive Economic Model and Implications for the WTO' (US Mission in Geneva, 26 July 2018), geneva.usmission.gov/2018/07/27/55299.

This statement sent a clear signal that underpins the change of the US approach towards China. In the meantime, the US currently upholds a policy of ensuring all non-market economies to bear the costs of their own non-market practices. The US has abandoned its traditional efforts to indoctrinate Chinese officials and the public. Various US documents have focused on the unbalanced trade relationship between China and the US, arguing that the economic model has created 'unfair advantages' for its own competitor while negatively impacted US industries and businesses.[23]

In short, the transition of the US approach results from an awareness that China's so-called non-market practices are not merely individual and separate trade measures, but a series of phenomenon underlined by a highly institutionalised political-economic system. Therefore, not only should relevant legal instruments be explored, but the institutions behind them must also be addressed properly.

C. Ideology: Challenges to the Traditional Free-Market Consensus

Differentiated from countries like the US, China's gradually deepening involvement in the international economic order is not accompanied by strong ideological demand.[24] In the legal instruments, including contracts, memoranda, statements and treaties, concluded between China and its partners, an ideological ally is not required for economic cooperation. However, this does not mean that China is not regarded as an ideological challenge by the traditional free-market camp.

After the collapse of the Union of Socialist Soviet Republics (USSR), there had been a predominant belief that free-market capitalism, combined with political democracy, should be the ultimate form of the development of socioeconomic institutions.[25] However, such a conviction was frustrated by an unexpected development approach adopted by China, which seems capable enough of achieving economic success without the accommodation of the Washington Consensus (ie, a set of recommendations for the 'best practice' of economic policies under the idea of free-market capitalism).[26] Meanwhile, the financial crisis in 2008 and the resultant global economic recession resulted in scepticism towards the idea of free-market capitalism and its promotion as a worldwide movement. All the factors above constitute a strong motivation jointly for countries like the US to form a more concrete conception for the preservation of the free-market belief.

[23] See, eg, China's Trade-Disruptive Economic Model (n 9) ss 3–4.

[24] A Dreher et al, 'Apples and Dragon Fruits: The Determinants of Aid and Other Forms of State Financing from China to Africa' (2018) 62 *International Studies Quarterly* 182, 182–94.

[25] Du (n 20) 409.

[26] See, eg, N Birdsall, A Torre and VC Felipe, 'The Washington Consensus: Assessing a Damaged Brand' (2010) the World Bank Policy Research Paper, documents1.worldbank.org/curated/en/848411468156560921/pdf/WPS5316.pdf.

This is why MOCs are not considered as merely a set of recommendations but normative pursuance.

As will be shown below, albeit the absence of an integral document concerning the MOC proposal, China has already formed a relatively mature attitude in response to the proposal at each of the levels, namely, specific measures of governmental intervention, the institutions of political economy and the underlining ideology.

III. The Response at the Level of Specific Legal Instruments

A. Promoting the Revival of the Green-Light Subsidy Category

At the legal instruments level, China has suggested the revival of the category of green-light subsidies, also known as non-actionable subsidies. These subsidies are permissible under the WTO and are not subject to countervailing measures. As stated in China's WTO Reform Proposal, 'non-actionable subsidies should be reinstated, and their coverage expanded' to provide a solid legal basis for Members to pursue public interests.[27]

A popular view of China's proposal regarding the revival of green-light subsidies is that such a proposal constitutes a bargaining power to counter the proposals of the expansion of the category of prohibited subsidies and the creation of a rebuttable presumption for adverse effects on certain types of subsidies, both proposed jointly by the US, Japan and the EU.[28] It is worth noting that the category of green-light subsidies once had its solid legal basis under Article 8 of the SCM Agreement,[29] but elapsed on 31 December 1999 pursuant to Article 31 of the SCM Agreement owing to the failure of WTO Members to reach a consensus for its continuation.[30] What elapsed at the same time for the same reason was exactly the category of subsidies with a rebuttable presumption for adverse effects under Article 6.1, which is also addressed as 'dark-amber-light' subsidies.[31]

[27] China's Proposal on WTO Reform (n 1) 4–5.

[28] Joint Statement on Trilateral Meeting of the Trade Ministers of the United States, Japan and the European Union, Annexed Statement 1: EU-Japan-US Scoping Paper to Define the Basis for the Development of Stronger Rules on Industrial Subsidies (31 May 2018), trade.ec.europa.eu/doclib/docs/2018/may/tradoc_156906.pdf; Joint Statement of the Trilateral Meeting of the Trade Ministers of Japan, the United States and the European Union (14 January 2020), trade.ec.europa.eu/doclib/docs/2020/january/tradoc_158567.pdf.

[29] Art 8 of the Agreement on Subsidies and Countervailing Measures, Marrakesh Agreement Establishing the World Trade Organization, Annex 1A (Marrakesh, 15 April 1994) (SCM Agreement),

[30] Committee on Subsidies and Countervailing Measures, Minutes of the Regular Meeting Held on 1–2 November 1999 (26 April 2000) G/SCM/M/24.

[31] ibid.

Under Article 6.1, if a subsidy meets certain conditions, such as being set for the purpose of covering operating losses sustained by an industry or an enterprise, serious prejudice, which represents one kind of adverse effect, can be deemed to exist.[32] This means that the investigating authority bears no obligation to demonstrate the existence of any adverse effect, while the enterprises under investigation bear the burden to prove that such effect does not exist. For China, the joint proposal by the US, Japan and the EU to restart and revise the dark-amber-light subsidy category is a practical strategy for buffering the impact of the trilateral statement.

However, after the outbreak of COVID-19, the importance of green-light subsidies has increased incredibly. It is no longer merely a means to augment China's bargaining power in trade negotiations. Instead, it becomes the actual demand from not only China but also all countries to reallocate its medical and research and development resources. Therefore, for China, the proposal to reinstate and expand the green-light subsidies becomes a substantive claim for concrete development interests, rather than purely accumulating its bargaining chips.

B. Defying the Idea of Applying 'Market-Oriented Conditions' as a Precondition for Non-Discriminative Treatment

China's proposal repeatedly stated that the principle of non-discrimination is core to the world trading system and should be firmly continued. It states that 'the reform shall preserve such core values of the multilateral trading system as non-discrimination and openness, to create a stable and predictable environment for international trade'.[33]

According to China's position, in two scenarios, universal non-discrimination would be significantly undermined. The first scenario is the circumstance in which some laws and regulations provide a presumption that all industries or businesses from one particular country are non-market-oriented, thereby shifting the burden to producers and exporters of that country to rebut that presumption. For example, this used to be the approach of the EU[34] until it introduced a country-neutral system based on a test of 'significant market distortions' in 2017. Under the new regulation, the EU investigating authority is tasked to produce and publish a country-specific report regarding the existence of market

[32] Art 6.1 of the SCM Agreement (n 29).
[33] China's Proposal on WTO Reform (n 1) 2.
[34] Art 2.7(a) of Regulation (EU) 2016/1036 of the European Parliament and of the Council on protection against dumped imports from countries not members of the European Union [2016] OJ L176.

distortions in a particular country.[35] Such a report would establish a prima facie case of market distortions. In this sense, the new approach is comparable to the previous approach given the existence of the non-market assumption and hence the burden on foreign producers and exporters to prove otherwise. To date, the EU has published two country-specific reports, one on China and the other on Russia.[36] Accordingly, the new mechanism is likely to lead to the same discrimination as under the old system.

Moreover, some MOC criteria might be particularly designed for certain countries, making it difficult for them to pass the MOC test. This selective approach is problematic. It is generally acknowledged that, in different economic systems, the state has developed various ways to intervene in the market. A more traditional way of state intervention is either through creating trade barriers, such as the imposition of tariffs, or through granting advantageous positions for its own nationals, such as subsidisation.[37] In a central planning system, the state may directly negate the legality of the market mechanism, while maintaining state-trading enterprises and settling prices for all actors in the economy. Alternatively, the state may respect market forces, while actively participating in market activities, as the Chinese state presently does. Admittedly, some kinds of state intervention may be more trade- or market-distortive than others. The actual impacts from different types of state intervention, however, can hardly be ascertained in the absence of empirical evidence. Therefore, it would be unjustified to target certain types of state intervention while leaving others unaddressed.

For instance, the EU's new anti-dumping regulation introduced two indicators that target China's economic model, namely: governmental ownership, control, supervision or guidance; state presence in the enterprise.[38] These two indicators are more China-specific because China's economic model is characterised by an extensive network of SOEs and their significant role in the market. If such a mechanism were adopted by the WTO, then it will create not only origin-specific discrimination but also a fundamental issue of treating different types of state interventions and market distortions in different ways without justification.

[35] Art 2.6(a)(c) of Regulation (EU) 2017/2321 of the European Parliament and of the Council of 12 December 2017 amending Regulation (EU) 2016/1036 on protection against dumped imports from countries not members of the European Union and Regulation (EU) 2016/1037 on protection against subsidised imports from countries not members of the European Union [2017] OJ L338.

[36] European Commission, Commission Staff Working Document, 'Significant Distortions in the Economy of the People's Republic of China for the Purposes of Trade Defence Investigations', SWD(2017) 483 final/2 (20 December 2017), trade.ec.europa.eu/doclib/docs/2017/december/tradoc_156474.pdf. See also European Commission, Commission Staff Working Document, 'Significant Distortions in the Economy of the Russian Federation for the Purposes of Trade Defence Investigations', SWD(2020) 242 final (22 October 2020), trade.ec.europa.eu/doclib/docs/2020/october/tradoc_158997.pdf.

[37] This categorisation has been adopted by several scholars. For example, see RD Atkinson, 'Enough is Enough: Confronting Chinese Innovation Mercantilism' Information Technology and Innovation Foundation (ITIF, 28 February 2012), itif.org/publications/2012/02/28/enough-enough-confronting-chinese-innovation-mercantilism.

[38] Art 2.6(a)(b) of Regulation 2017/2321 (n 35).

C. Restraining the Unilateral Capacity in Establishing the 'Market-Oriented Conditions' Test

China's WTO Reform Proposal stated that 'misuse and abusive application of trade remedy measures abound'.[39] This suggests that China is concerned that the principle and criteria in the proposals will continue to provide unfettered discretion for investigating authorities in determining whether specific practices and policies applied by a WTO Member are 'market-oriented' or not. Any measure taken in order to deal with so-called 'market-oriented' practices or policies may deteriorate into a de facto selective safeguard.

As mentioned, the criteria for the determination of whether a market economy status (MES) exists vary among countries and regions. One major criterion concerns the existence and maintenance of a private law system that underpins market conditions for enterprises to undertake commercial activities for their own sake. This criterion may be used to show how such criteria may be abused. In response to China's request for its MES under the EU anti-dumping law in 2003, the EU authority made a preliminary assessment in 2004 about whether an MES should be granted to China.[40] The finding by the EU authority suggested that, although China had achieved economic progress, its MES would not be granted unless China met a set of conditions.[41] Among the examined conditions, one is whether all companies are treated equally in terms of the implementation of private law, especially property and bankruptcy law.[42] What is emphasised here, clearly, is equal treatment provided to all companies. In its progress report on China's MES in 2008, however, the European Commission slightly changed the criterion by requiring a market economy to ensure: [t]he existence and implementation of a coherent, effective and transparent set of laws which ensure the respect of property rights and the operation of a functioning bankruptcy regime'.[43] According to this text, equal treatment is no longer the sole indicator. Rather, the laws that constitute the private legal system should be 'coherent, effective and transparent'. The EU's new regulation maintained the criterion of whether a 'significant market distortion' exists. The regulation states that a distorted market situation may be found if there exists a 'lack, discriminatory application or inadequate enforcement of bankruptcy, corporate or property laws'.[44] The wording 'inadequate enforcement' leaves even more flexibility for the investigating authority to use this criterion against China.

[39] China's Proposal on WTO Reform (n 1) para 2.14.

[40] See European Commission, 'China – Market Economy Status in Trade Defence Investigations' (28 June 2004) MEMO/04/163 1.

[41] ibid 2. These conditions are categorised into four divisions: (1) state influence; (2) corporate governance; (3) property and bankruptcy law; and (4) financial sector.

[42] ibid 3.

[43] Commission of the European Communities, Commission Staff Working Document, 'Progress by the People's Republic of China Towards Graduation to Market Economy Status in Trade Defence Investigations', SEC(2008) 2503 (19 September 2008).

[44] Art 2.6(a)(b) of Regulation 2017/2321 (n 35).

It is noted that, although not proposed by the EU, the expression of the US proposal on the 'Importance of Market-Oriented Conditions to the World Trading System' seems to follow the trend of increasing flexibility. The relevant indicator reads: '[e]nterprises are subject to market-oriented and effective corporation law, bankruptcy law, competition law, and private property law, and may enforce their rights through impartial legal processes, such as an independent judicial system'.[45] Undeniably, a stable and transparent legal environment that applies equally to all market actors, may minimise the influence of the governmental authority while making enterprises more responsive to their own decisions. As illustrated below in the table, however, the most recent version of the private law criterion has arguably created greater uncertainties and ambiguities and hence even more flexibility for investigating authorities.

Table 14.1 An Evolution Towards Further Ambiguity of Expression in the Criteria Systems for the Market Economy Test

Criteria systems	**Requirements for private law**	**The phrases that leave flexibility**
Preliminary Assessment in 2004 by the EU	Equal treatment (non-discrimination)	none
Progress Report in 2008 by the EU	coherence, effectiveness, and transparency	none
Regulation (EU) 2017/2321	non-discrimination	'inadequate'
US Proposal 2020	Market-orientation and effectiveness	'market-oriented', 'effective', 'such as'

IV. The Response at the Level of Institutions of Political Economy

A. Ceasing the Inherent Incompatibility between the State and the Market

China's economic model has long been criticised as being irreconcilable with the WTO. On 19 December 2018, US Ambassador Shea blamed China for 'maintaining a regime that is fundamentally incompatible with the rules and principles' of the WTO system.[46] The conclusion of the 'incompatibility' is based on the ground that Chinese economic institutions, which permit the extensive use of

[45] The Importance of Market-Oriented Conditions to the World Trading System (n 4) 2.

[46] 'Ambassador Shea's Statement at the WTO Trade Policy Review of the United States – Day 2' (USTR, 19 December 2018), ustr.gov/about-us/policy-offices/press-office/press-releases/2018/december/ambassador-shea%E2%80%99s-statement-wto.

SOEs, industrial policies and the use of subsidies, have created significant state-led distortions in the economy.[47]

A rationale underlying this argument is an alleged incompatibility between the state and the market. Under a long-held discourse developed by some traditional capitalist countries in the West, SOEs could be naturally equated to an extension of the government. However, it can also be argued that the purpose of examining the adherence to the market of an SOE is not the same as assessing the degree of the enterprise's subordination with the government. Existing literature suggests that a non-market economy does not mean a high degree of state participation, but a situation in which actors in an economy do not fully play according to market forces.[48]

In response to the MOC proposal, China made it clear that an enterprise should not be subject to discriminatory measures only because of ownership.[49] This is actually a way to advocate a conception of compatibility between the state and the market: the fact that the state holds ownership or shares in an entity would not necessarily mean that the entity's behaviour and activities are not market-oriented.

The question whether the conception of compatibility is acceptable is highly relevant to a core problem of the WTO system, which is whether the state's conduct of running businesses should be presumed as a form of state intervention that necessarily results in a non-market economy. In this regard, it must be noted that, even for the US, government entities may operate based on purely commercial terms and conditions. For example, the USTR report on the Appellate Body released in February 2020 explained how the Appellate Body has erred in its interpretation of the applicability of out-of-country benchmarks in countervailing investigations. In this regard, the Appellate Body has clarified that in order to show in-country prices are distorted and hence should be disregarded for the determination of 'the conferral of benefit', an investigating authority must consider not only evidence of private market prices, but also 'government prices' unless government prices are also distorted.[50] This suggests that 'government prices' must not be deemed to be distorted and such distortion must be proved by evidence. Surely, the USTR objects to this approach. However, the reason addressed by the USTR is not that government prices are always non-market, but that it is not necessary for an investigating authority to demonstrate that the government prices are not non-market.[51] Accordingly, the US does not challenge the Appellate Body's view

[47] ibid.

[48] P Hall and D Soskice, *An Introduction to Varieties of Capitalism, in Varieties of Capitalism: The Institutional Foundations of Comparative Advantage* (Oxford, Oxford University Press, 2001) 1–68.

[49] China's Proposal on WTO Reform (n 1) paras 2.35–2.37.

[50] *United States–Countervailing Measures on Certain Hot-Rolled Carbon Steel Flat Products from India*, Report of the Appellate Body (19 December 2014) WT/DS436/AB/R; *United States–Countervailing Duty Measures on Certain Products from China*, Report of the Appellate Body (18 December 2014) WT/DS437/AB/R.

[51] USTR, Appellate Body Report (n 16) 106.

that a governmental price could either be market-oriented or market-distorted. The difference exists in how to set out a presumption, which essentially is about the allocation of the burden of proof. In the US view, government prices should be presumed as non-market, whereas the Appellate Body tends to presume that such prices per se are market-based.

By advocating the concept of compatibility,[52] China understandably favours the approach of the Appellate Body. To justify this presumption, China may suggest a paradigm shift in rethinking the relationship between the market and the state. Through economic reforms, SOEs are corporatised under private law, gradually gaining their independent role in making business decisions, and exercising independent property rights. Accordingly, although the state still maintains its representation in the economy, the ways for the state to be involved in the economy have diversified: directly limiting the functioning of the market mechanism is no longer the only way for the state to intervene in the economy, and the state is capable of positively utilising the market mechanism to advance its economic purposes by investing in corporatised SOEs. In short, under the paradigm of market–state compatibility conceived by China, the state's guiding role in the economy would no longer be premised on the nullification of market power. Therefore, under the paradigm, the existence of several factors of state representation, such as public ownership or governmental guidance, would not on its own amount to the non-existence of a market economy.[53]

In the era of the (post-) COVID-19 pandemic, such a rethinking is potentially implicative, for it indicates the possibility that state intervention can take a more market-oriented form. Such a proposition may make the market economy more tolerant of some factors of state involvement, including the extensive network of SOEs. This will also encourage the state to introduce more market-oriented ways to guide the markets that are crucial to public health and security by, for example, investing in SOEs and their subsidiaries to operate in the fields of medical and pharmaceutical products.

B. Respecting the Diversification of Economic Institutions

The cancellation of the state–market dichotomy, as discussed above, implicates that a state is more integrated into a market mechanism. Various institutions should be introduced to underpin its diversified roles. How can the WTO system accommodate these diversified economic institutions, as well as its Members that adopt distinctive economic models?

Before China became a major player in global trade, the question regarding the multilateral trading system and diversified economic institutions had already

[52] China's Proposal on WTO Reform (n 1) paras 2.35–2.37.
[53] Che (n 19) ch 7.

been subject to heated debate.[54] The question is two-fold: first, whether the GATT/WTO system should be inclusive enough so as to welcome Members that are not in a traditional free-market capitalist model; and second, whether the GATT/WTO system should introduce specific instruments to accommodate these Members with diversified institutions or merely rely on the general rules that apply to all Members. The first question seems less controversial since the accession of several Members that were once in a centrally planned system, including Poland, Romania and Hungary. However, the second question has attracted continuous attention, especially in the past decade, while China has intensively released signals that it would not see the traditional free-market model as the ultimate purpose of its economic transition.

The position of China is simple: the multilateral trading system should respect various economic institutions and should not maintain any special treatments merely because of the institutional background of Members. At a normative level, as stated by the Chinese Ambassador Zhang Xiangchen, the creation of the WTO system was driven by a wish by various negotiating parties to strike a balance between their industrial policies and trade liberalisation, rather than unifying trade policies.[55] According to Ambassador Zhang, the extent to which WTO Members agreed to discipline their industrial policies and to achieve trade liberalisation is strictly defined by existing WTO rules. Once the idea that Members are committed to pursue liberalisation has been incarnated by specific rules, then the legality of Members' behaviour and conduct should be assessed strictly based on the rules as opposed to the overarching idea.[56]

At a practical level, as stated by Ambassador Zhang, the WTO rules provide no basis to discriminate against Members in terms of their institutional setting:

> There is no one-size-fits-all 'market economy' standard in the world. The WTO rules never authorize any Member to use its own economic model as the template of 'market economy', and to accuse any other Member who would not copy it as a 'non-market economy'.[57]

This argument may be interpreted as a response by China: a practical question should be resolved at a practical level rather than at a normative level. Practical claims should only be raised based on breaches of rules or the actual nullification or impairment of trade interests that a Member could legitimately expect under the rules.

[54] D Wallace, 'Preface' in D Wallace et al (eds), *Interface One: Conference Proceedings on the Application of US Antidumping and Countervailing Duty Laws to Imports from State-controlled Economies and State-owned Enterprises* (Washington DC, Institute for International and Foreign Trade Law, 1980) vii.

[55] 'Statement by HE Ambassador Zhang Xiangchen at the WTO General Council Meeting, Geneva' (Permanent Mission of the People's Republic of China to the WTO, 26 July 2018), wto2.mofcom.gov.cn/article/chinaviewpoins/201807/20180702770676.shtml.

[56] ibid.

[57] ibid.

C. Distinguishing 'Market-Oriented Conditions' as a Status with 'Market Orientation' as a Principle

China's response repeatedly emphasised that there is no consensus among WTO Members on the definition of the term 'market economy', nor its potential legal implications. The interpretation of this statement should take into account the fact that China has never alienated itself from the concept of market orientation. In its recent statement, the Central Committee of the Communist Party of China maintained the position on further deepening market-oriented reforms.[58] Specifically, it mentioned that not only the market should be further liberalised, but the legal environment should be more open and predictable.

It may be argued that China has never denied the consensus of market orientation as an important principle for multilateral cooperation. The true intention of China is to differentiate the term MOCs as a status of a particular country or economy, which is usually used as a justification for discriminatory measures, from the 'market orientation' principle, which could be pursued as a value but not as a legal basis for specific claims. Indeed, there is a gap between the principle and the status, and to fill the gap, it is also necessary to obtain more empirical evidence.

V. The Response at the Level of Underlying Ideology

A. Development Essentialism and Market Instrumentalism

When discussing the underlying ideology, China reaffirms the goal of promoting economic development as the essential principle of the WTO. As stated in the US proposal, the MOCs have consistently served as the basic principle of the WTO system since its creation. The US has resorted to the Preamble of the Marrakesh Declaration of 15 April 1994, where WTO Members commit that 'the participation of their economies in the world trading system [will be] based on open, market-oriented policies'.[59] To respond to this argument, merely focusing on legal or institutional issues is far from sufficient. There is a need for China to invoke a similarly strong justification at an ideological level, and the answer from China is the 'principle of development'.

As an ideological principle, development implies a de-essentialisation of marketisation. While advancing economic development becomes the purpose, adopting a market mechanism then becomes an instrument serving the purpose of

[58] 'Decisions on Speeding Up the Reform Process of Marketization in the New Era by the CCCPC' (中共中央 国务院关于新时代加快完善社会主义市场经济体制的意见) (CCCPC, 11 May 2020), cpc.people.com.cn/n1/2020/0518/c419242-31713779.html.

[59] Marrakesh Ministerial Declaration (15 April 1994), the fifth preambular para.

development. Accordingly, the creation or reservation of MOCs regains the nature of instrumentality.[60]

To manage the pace of market-oriented transformation and economic liberalisation, China has taken an experimental and incremental approach to economic reforms. For instance, China has transformed its administration regime of the market entry of foreign investors from ex ante control to ex post supervision by gradually introducing the pre-establishment national treatment principle together with a 'negative list' management system.[61] Foreign investors were required to obtain approval but, after the transformation, only have to perform an information-reporting obligation.[62] This information-reporting approach was first introduced in the Shanghai Free Trade Zone, which is a pilot for China to advance its economic reform.[63] Recently in March 2019, the formally promulgated Foreign Investment Law finally established the system as one unified law for application within Mainland China's territory.[64] A trial-and-error approach is clearly shown from the gradual adoption of the ex post supervision regime.

B. The Inclusiveness of the Multilateral Trading System

In its WTO Reform Proposal, China reintroduces the conception of the inclusiveness of the multilateral trading system.[65] First, inclusiveness is considered necessary in reforming the pattern of trade negotiations, as the traditional approach for introducing new rules is largely under the direction of several more influential Members.[66]

Second, regarding substantive issues, China demonstrates a rationale that, the greater the disparity between Members' positions, the more inclusiveness is required. For example, in the negotiations of rules on e-commerce, China, by noting the diversified concerns and initiatives held by various negotiating groups, advocates that these rules need to be more inclusive so as to accommodate different needs and interests.[67]

Third, inclusiveness itself should become a value of the multilateral trading system. China appreciates the efforts that 'will be conducive to bolstering

[60] C Herrmann-Pillath, *China's Economic Culture: The Ritual Order of State and Markets* (Abingdon, Routledge, 2017) 401.

[61] Art 4 of the Foreign Investment Law of the People's Republic of China (中华人民共和国外商年投资法) (2019).

[62] ibid Art 34.

[63] Art 3 of the Regulations on the Administration of the Record-Keeping of the Foreign Investment in the Shanghai Free Trade Zone (Trial) (自由贸易试验区外商投资备案管理办法（试行) (2015), www.mofcom.gov.cn/article/ae/ai/201504/20150400947673.shtml.

[64] Art 34 of the Foreign Investment Law (n 61).

[65] The term 'inclusiveness' appears eight times in the main text. See China's Proposal on WTO Reform (n 1).

[66] ibid para 1.11.

[67] ibid para 2.21.

inclusive trade'.[68] From such an expression, it may be reasonably argued that an 'inclusive trade' itself is regarded as an independent doctrine that must be complied with. Inclusiveness does not serve the purpose of advancing negotiations or a political compromise. Rather, inclusiveness embodies a value, which should be as important as other values, including open, free and transparent.

VI. Conclusion

This chapter has reviewed the major claims under the MOC proposal and discussed China's possible responses in three aspects: the supply of legal instruments that discipline governmental intervention; the institutions of political economy; and the underlining ideology. The table below provides a summary of China's responses.

Table 14.2 A Framework for the Analysis of China's Response to the MOC Proposal

Levels	**Topic 1: on the limitation of market power**	**Topic 2: on the role of the WTO system in underpinning the market mechanism**	**Topic 3: on the application of the principle of market orientation**
Legal instruments	Legal instruments that support the use of green-light subsidies should be revived	The grant of non-discriminative treatment should not be conditional on a successful establishment of 'market-oriented conditions'	A single Member should not enjoy the capacity to decide the 'market-oriented' nature of others
Institutional backgrounds	Governmental intervention can be either market-distorting or market-enabling, and thus it is not inherently incompatible with the market	The system should provide an interface for trade cooperation but not differentiate Members in terms of whether 'market-oriented conditions' exist	A distinction exists between market-oriented conditions and the principle of market orientation
Underlying ideologies	A market is instrumental to the development goal	The system should maintain a certain degree of inclusiveness	The conception should not be accepted as a priori

These findings have significant implications for the ongoing discussions of WTO reforms in the (post-) COVID-19 era. First, China has demonstrated its efforts to

[68] ibid.

address the limitation or the boundary of market power without rejecting the idea of market orientation. As opposed to the approach that assumes a one-size-fits-all criterion to assess and decide the quality of market orientation, China would take the approach that helps craft and formulate more detailed doctrines and rules in response to the characteristics of different subject matters under the WTO system.

Second, China strives to deliberate on the role of the WTO, which is not a promoter of free-market capitalism but a mediator or interface between diversified institutions.

Third, China focuses on specific issues such as how to apply the market-orientated principle in practice. The practical application of the MOC proposal must avoid the (ab)use of unilateral measures which can only undermine multilateral cooperation. It could be anticipated that, in the (post-) COVID-19 era, the concerns of market orientation may be extended from a China-related issue to a global one. China's responses to the MOC proposal may provide some guidance for how to resolve these concerns, which would in turn contribute to facilitating multilateral cooperation which is the only way to rescue the world trading system.

15

Winning Strategy or Own Goal? Reflections on the United States Exiting the Trans-Pacific Partnership

MEREDITH KOLSKY LEWIS

I. Introduction

Participating in the Trans-Pacific Partnership (TPP), a free trade agreement (FTA) comprising 12 countries on both sides of the Pacific, was a central objective of United States (US) trade policy for close to 10 years, beginning in the George W Bush administration and continuing throughout President Barack Obama's two terms in office. Notwithstanding the strategic and economic rationales for participating in the TPP and the leadership role the US played throughout the negotiations, candidate and then President-elect Donald Trump consistently expressed hostility towards the TPP. President Bush and President Obama saw the TPP as providing an opportunity to put the US at the head of the table to negotiate new rules that would likely be incorporated into many other agreements; to assume a leadership role in the Asia-Pacific; and to open important markets for US exporters. In contrast, then candidate Trump viewed the TPP as a 'disaster' and bad for US workers and US companies. Trump vowed that as soon as his presidency began, he would withdraw the US from the Agreement, and he proceeded to do just that.

Although US participation in the TPP attracted many of its current members to the negotiating table, the withdrawal of the US has not spelled the end for the initiative. The remaining 11 countries could not operationalise the TPP as drafted due to the nature of its entry into force criteria,[1] but they did not let this detract

[1] Trans-Pacific Partnership (Auckland, 4 February 2016) (TPP). The TPP provided that it would enter into force either (1) 60 days after all twelve signatories ratified the agreement domestically (Art 30.5(1), or (2) if 1) is not satisfied within two years after signature, it would enter into force 60 days after the expiry of the two-year period, if at least six of the original signatories, which together account for at least 85 per cent of the combined gross domestic product of the original signatories in 2013, ratified the agreement (Art 30.5(2); or, if neither (1) or (2) were satisfied, it would enter into force

from their desire to proceed with a linkage. The 'TPP-11' quickly worked to negotiate the Comprehensive and Progressive Agreement for Trans-Pacific Partnership (CPTPP), which is nearly identical to the TPP. The CPTPP has now come into force for seven of its signatories.[2]

The differences between the original TPP and the CPTPP mainly lie in provisions the US had wanted in the TPP having been placed on indefinite hold within the CPTPP.[3] By leaving these largely unpopular provisions in the CPTPP but without giving them effect as yet, the CPTPP countries have figured out a way to have their cake and eat it too. The Agreement as it stands does not require the CPTPP-11 to provide heightened intellectual property (IP) protections and other measures favoured solely by the US, but the participating countries nonetheless are now enjoying all the benefits of the TPP that they found favourable, or at least not as objectionable. At the same time, by including the US-focused provisions in the CPTPP and freezing their application, the CPTPP countries have left the door open for the US to join the TPP replacement relatively easily, should it wish to do so in the future.

Similar to the Multi-Party Interim Appeal Arrangement (MPIA) various WTO Members have created to work around the current inoperability of the Appellate Body,[4] the CPTPP countries have not accepted defeat in the face of a change in the US policy approach. In this way, the US decision to withdraw from the TPP can be seen as a move that impacted the US in various ways, but also provided an inflection point for its previous TPP brethren. The remaining countries could have walked away from the entire TPP endeavour, reasoning that without the US a significant part of its raison d'etre had evaporated. But they did not do this; instead, the other 11 countries regrouped and rescued their agreement, remoulding it into a pragmatic new text that allowed them to reap benefits, while still preserving the possibility of the union with the US they had anticipated. The CPTPP may therefore serve as an example (alongside the MPIA and other initiatives) that with creativity and resolve, WTO Members may be able to create workarounds to seemingly existential obstacles that are threatening the existing of multilateralism.

Section II of this chapter provides a brief background of the TPP and examines the motivations underlying President Bush and President Obama's decisions to pursue the multiparty trade agreement. Section III looks at the response to the TPP post-signature, and the anti-trade sentiment that permeated the 2016

60 days after the date on which at least six of the original signatories, which together account for at least 85 per cent of the combined gross domestic product of the original signatories in 2013, have ratified the agreement domestically (Art 30.5(3)). With the US withdrawal, none of these three alternatives could be satisfied.

[2] Comprehensive and Progressive Agreement for Trans-Pacific Partnership (Santiago, 8 March 2018) (CPTPP). The CPTPP entered into force on 30 December 2018 for Australia, Canada, Japan, Mexico, New Zealand and Singapore, and on 14 January 2019 for Vietnam.

[3] See, eg, 'CPTPP vs TPP' (New Zealand Ministry of Foreign Affairs and Trade), www.mfat.govt.nz/en/trade/free-trade-agreements/free-trade-agreements-in-force/cptpp/understanding-cptpp/tpp-and-cptpp-the-differences-explained.

[4] See 'Precedent in the MPIA: What Role for Consistency and Predictability?', ch 12 in this book.

US presidential campaign season. It goes on to identify President Trump's stated rationales for disliking, and ultimately withdrawing from, the Agreement. Section IV examines criticism of the TPP by candidates running for president during the 2016 campaign, revealing the official antipathy towards trade on both sides of the political spectrum. Sections V and VI assess the strategic and economic ramifications for the US of the remaining 11 TPP parties continuing to work together without the US and signing a slightly revised version of the TPP known now as the CPTPP. After making the case that the US did not advance its interests by withdrawing from the TPP, section VII concludes with a consideration of possible future directions for the CPTPP and whether the US may yet have a role to play. It also provides an assessment of the CPTPP as an exemplar for how WTO Members can rescue their trade liberalisation objectives, even in an era of populism, pandemic and other challenges.

II. From P-4 to TPP

Over the several years of TPP negotiations, the possible agreement became more and more widely known and discussed. However, its origins began much earlier, long before the TPP negotiations even started. The idea for a high-standards multiparty FTA that would include Asia Pacific Economic Cooperation (APEC) countries seems to have originated at least as early as 1997, when the US, Singapore, Chile, Australia and New Zealand contemplated forming a 'Pacific Five' FTA.[5] The Pacific Five talks did not advance; however, New Zealand and Singapore proceeded to negotiate an FTA known as the New Zealand Singapore Closer Economic Partnership in 1999 and 2000, which came into force on 1 January 2001.[6] A further step occurred at the 2002 APEC Leaders' Summit, at which leaders from New Zealand, Singapore and Chile launched talks to create the Pacific Three Closer Economic Partnership, an FTA that was envisioned as being a launching pad for additional widening within the Asia-Pacific.[7] This concept was embraced by APEC; in 2004, the APEC Leaders formally referred to a Free Trade Agreement of the Asia-Pacific (FTAAP) as a long-term objective.[8] Soon thereafter, Brunei asked to join in negotiations with the Pacific Three Closer Economic Partnership countries, and the four countries signed the Trans-Pacific Strategic Economic Partnership, more commonly referred to as the P-4 Agreement or simply as the P-4, in 2005. The P-4 came into force in 2006 with provision for negotiations

[5] Japan External Trade Organization (JETRO), 'Prospects for Free Trade Agreements in East Asia' (2003), www.jetro.go.jp/en/reports/survey/epa/pdf/2003_01_epa.pdf, 1.

[6] 'From the CEP to CPTPP' (New Zealand Ministry of Foreign Affairs and Trade), www.mfat.govt.nz/en/trade/free-trade-agreements/free-trade-agreements-in-force/nz-singapore-closer-economic-partnership/from-the-cep-to-cptpp/.

[7] ibid.

[8] 'APEC Achievements' (APEC), www.apecchile2019.cl/apec/about-apec/apec-achievements.

to commence two years later to expand the coverage of the Agreement to include investment and financial services.[9] The P-4 countries included an open accession clause in their Agreement to facilitate discussions with like-minded countries that might wish to join the Agreement in the future.[10]

Although these early Asia-Pacific FTAs did not include the US, the US had previously explored several different FTAs with APEC partners, even prior to the emergence of the Pacific Five concept. Examples include a 1980s US proposal for an agreement with Australia; the US Ambassador to Japan (Mike Mansfield) suggesting in 1987 a study into a possible Japan–US FTA; and a 1989 recommendation for an ASEAN-US FTA arising from a joint study.[11] This backdrop helps contextualise the US decision to participate in the 2008 negotiations to broaden the P-4 scope. The US saw these negotiations as a testing ground to determine whether it wished to negotiate to become a fellow member of the trade agreement.[12] In particular, then US Trade Representative Susan Schwab explained US interests in participating in the 2008 negotiations as follows:

> We see these investment and financial services negotiations as an opportunity to further our engagement with countries committed to high-standard trade agreements … This initiative also will provide another opportunity for the United States to participate in the regional trade architecture that is emerging in the vitally important Asia-Pacific region.[13]

Ambassador Schwab appears to have recognised the potential for the P-4 to be an avenue to place the US within an agreement that could ultimately form the basis for an FTAAP. Indeed, the US Trade Representative (USTR) press release announcing US participation in the P-4 financial services and investment talks states that:

> Participation could provide a pathway to broader Asia-Pacific regional economic integration with like-minded countries committed to high-standard agreements. The United States is already pursuing further regional economic integration in the Asia Pacific Economic Cooperation forum (APEC) through intensive exploration of the prospect of a Free Trade Area of the Asia- Pacific (FTAAP), as well as through bilateral FTAs, such as the pending agreement with South Korea.[14]

[9] 'From the CEP to CPTPP' (n 6). See also MK Lewis, 'Expanding the P-4 Trade Agreement into a Broader Trans-Pacific Partnership: Implications, Risks and Opportunities' (2009) 4 *Asian Journal of WTO & International Health Law* 401, 403–04.

[10] For a discussion of open accession provisions in FTAs, see Lewis, 'Expanding the P-4 Trade Agreement' (n 9) 406.

[11] 'Prospects for Free Trade Agreements in East Asia' (n 5) 1.

[12] 'United States to Join Sectoral Negotiations with Four Asia-pacific Countries Will Explore Participation in Broader Strategic Partnership Agreement' (United States Trade Representative, 4 February 2008), www.ustr.gov/sites/default/files/uploads/pdfs/press_release/2008/asset_upload_file806_14451.pdf.

[13] ibid.

[14] ibid.

While the US initially indicated that its participation in the financial services and investment negotiations would be a precursor to deciding whether to seek to join the P-4, its subsequent participation was almost immediately positioned as engaging in negotiations towards forming a new trade agreement, the TPP, rather than as a move to expand the existing P-4 Agreement.

III. The TPP Negotiations and US Politics

As noted above, at the outset the US saw an agreement with the P-4 countries as, among other things, an avenue towards achieving, in Susan Schwab's words, 'broader Asia-Pacific regional economic integration'.[15] Thus, the US wanted and expected that other countries would also join in the TPP negotiations. Indeed, the US already had FTAs with Chile and Singapore, and had long rebuffed New Zealand's FTA overtures, and the prize in mind was surely not simply market access to tiny Brunei.

Furthermore, officials in the USTR likely saw the P-4 as an opportunity not only to partner with like-minded countries, but to position the US as a central player in expanding that Agreement. By being at the table at the outset of any expansion, the US would not only cement its place within a broader Asia-Pacific agreement, it would also be in a position to steer the pact in directions consistent with US objectives. At the same time, it was becoming increasingly unlikely that those US objectives would be realised any time soon within the multilateral system. The US overture towards the P-4 countries occurred in the midst of a series of collapses in the Doha Round negotiations. While GATT negotiating rounds had revolved substantially around the desires of the quad countries (the EU, US, Japan and Canada), the Doha Development Round was supposed to focus on the developing country members. Notwithstanding this objective, the developed countries still had their own priorities, and common ground amongst the new G-4 of the US, EU, Brazil and India, was proving elusive.[16] In this context, US trade officials may have calculated that plurilateral negotiations with like-minded countries could yield significant benefits without the unattractive compromises that resolving the Doha Round would likely require.[17]

The US entry into negotiations with the P-4 countries occurred at the tail-end of President George W Bush's administration. When Barack Obama, a Democrat,

[15] See 'NZ Welcomes US Entering Trade Talks' (*Stuff*, 31 January 2009), www.stuff.co.nz/business/253540/NZ-welcomes-US-entering-P4-trade-talks, quoting Schwab.

[16] See, eg, D Palmer and L MacInnis, 'G4 Talks Collapse, Throw Trade Round into Doubt' *Reuters* (21 June 2007), www.reuters.com/article/us-trade-wto/g4-talks-collapse-throw-trade-round-into-doubt-idUSL2179513320070621.

[17] Indeed, once the TPP negotiations began in earnest, USTR seemed to be singularly focused on the plurilateral arrangement and not on the WTO. See MK Lewis, 'The Trans-Pacific Partnership: New Paradigm or Wolf in Sheep's Clothing?' (2011) 34 *Boston College International and Comparative Law Review* 27, 35.

came into office in January 2009, his administration took some time to assess US trade policy and to determine whether to continue with or diverge from the priorities of the (Republican) Bush White House. In November 2009, President Obama announced in a speech in Japan that the US would continue with the negotiations, and in December 2009, he formally notified Congress of this intention.[18]

From the start of US involvement, other countries from both sides of the Pacific took notice. Australia, Peru and Vietnam were the first to join the negotiations, and Malaysia joined in a bit later, towards the end of 2010. It seemed clear that the TPP would expand further, and APEC referred to the TPP as a possible path towards an FTAAP at its November 2010 summit.[19] Significantly, from the US perspective, Mexico and Canada entered the talks in late 2012, which provided the US with the potential to fix some of the perceived problems with the North American FTA (NAFTA) without needing to reopen that treaty. But the most important development was the entry of Japan in 2013. If a deal could be reached, two of the largest economies in the world would be linked together for the first time in an FTA, and Japan's participation would seem to be necessary (though not on its own sufficient) for the TPP to ultimately expand into an FTAAP. It would be hard to imagine that an agreement lacking China, Japan and Korea could be seen as an FTA covering the Asia-Pacific. With Japan in, however, the TPP would feature the world's first and third largest economies by GDP,[20] and it was anticipated that Korea would be one of the first new countries to accede to the TPP after its initial entry into force.

Once Japan joined the negotiations, the participants determined that the focus should be on concluding the TPP amongst the 12 parties, deferring any further expansion of membership to a 'TPP 2.0', to follow after completing and ratifying an initial agreement. The parties recognised that with upcoming elections and possible changes in governments, it was particularly important to try to conclude the negotiations sooner rather than later, and in particular well before the 2016 US election. In this regard, it would have been optimal to conclude the negotiations by mid-2015, so that Congress could have voted on the agreement before the 2016 presidential campaign took centre stage in the US. Notwithstanding this dynamic, the negotiators were unable to reach a final agreement until early February 2016.[21]

Following the signing of the TPP, the USTR released a fact sheet identifying various anticipated benefits for the US of the TPP, including the removal of tariffs on thousands of US-made products, and the anticipation that the Agreement

[18] IF Fergusson et al, 'The Trans-Pacific Partnership Negotiations and Issues for Congress' (Congressional Research Service, 20 March 2015), fas.org/sgp/crs/row/R42694.pdf, 3.

[19] 'Pathways to FTAAP' (APEC, 14 November 2010), www.apec.org/Meeting-Papers/Leaders-Declarations/2010/2010_aelm/pathways-to-ftaap.aspx.

[20] The US is the world's largest economy by GDP, and Japan is the third-largest. See, eg, 'GDP Ranking' (World Bank, as of July 2020), datacatalog.worldbank.org/dataset/gdp-ranking.

[21] See 'Trans-Pacific Partnership Ministers' Statement' (United States Trade Representative, 4 February 2016), ustr.gov/about-us/policy-offices/press-office/press-releases/2016/February/TPP-Ministers-Statement.

would lead to increased US exports of manufactured goods, agricultural products and services.[22] In addition to these market access opportunities, President Obama highlighted some of the strategic implications of the Agreement; in his official statement announcing the signing of the TPP, he stated that 'TPP allows America – and not countries like China – to write the rules of the road in the 21st century, which is especially important in a region as dynamic as the Asia-Pacific'.[23]

Notwithstanding the TPP's selling points, the Agreement was on shaky ground within the US due to the complexities of a Republican Congress not wanting to give a Democratic president – and by extension, the Democratic presidential nominee Hillary Clinton – a win in the lead-up to the 2016 US presidential election.[24] Had the Agreement been signed six or eight months earlier, there would have been a better likelihood of Republicans being willing to overtly support the Agreement, and of some Democrats, albeit likely a minority, also signing on. However, in the year or so prior to a US election, both major political parties are wary of working with the other, and without a significant majority in both the House and Senate, it is very difficult to get any meaningful legislation passed, and even less so when that legislation is favoured by a president whose party is not in control of both houses of Congress. To add to the challenges, the presidential candidates who obtained any traction during the campaigns had all spoken out in opposition to the TPP. The TPP had become a radioactive topic, and Senate Majority Leader Mitch McConnell made clear in August 2016 that he would not bring the TPP to a vote in the Senate prior to the November presidential election.[25]

IV. Criticism of the TPP

Amongst the candidates for president, the most unequivocal support for the TPP came from Republicans Jeb Bush and John Kasich, while others, including Republicans Marco Rubio and Ben Carson, positioned themselves as being pro-free trade and in support in principle, but with concerns about the details of the Agreement.[26] However, none of these individuals received much traction during

[22] 'TPP Benefits Fact Sheet' (United States Trade Representative), ustr.gov/sites/default/files/TPP-Overall-US-Benefits-Fact-Sheet.pdf.

[23] 'Statement by the President on the Signing of the Trans-Pacific Partnership' (The White House, 3 February 2016), obamawhitehouse.archives.gov/the-press-office/2016/02/03/statement-president-signing-trans-pacific-partnership.

[24] See generally, MK Lewis, 'The United States' Path to Concluding the Trans-Pacific Partnership: Will TPA + TAA = TPP?' in M Bungenberg et al (eds.), *European Yearbook of International Economic Law*, vol 7 (Switzerland, Springer, 2016).

[25] D Lawder, 'Obama's TPP deal won't get Senate vote this year: McConnell' *Reuters* (25 August 2016), www.reuters.com/article/us-usa-trade-tpp-mcconnell-idUSKCN1102CM.

[26] See E Rosenfeld, 'Trans-Pacific Partnership: GOP candidates split on deal' *CNBC* (21 October 2015), www.cnbc.com/2015/10/21/trans-pacific-partnership-gop-candidates-split-on-deal.html.

the primary season. Indeed, the TPP faced criticism from all the most successful candidates in the 2016 election cycle, including Hillary Clinton, Bernie Sanders and Donald Trump, as well as from other prominent politicians such as Elizabeth Warren.

While some candidates such as Trump and Sanders expressed consistent opposition to the TPP, several candidates disavowed their previous support for the TPP and became naysayers during the election season. For example, both Vice Presidential candidates, Senator Mike Pence and Senator Tim Kaine, had spoken in favour of the Agreement prior to joining presidential tickets. In April 2015, Senator Pence wrote a letter to the Indiana congressional delegation stating, 'I encourage your support for Trade Promotion Authority, the Trans-Pacific Partnership, the Trans-Atlantic Trade and Investment Partnership and any other trade-related measures when they are brought before the Congress for consideration'.[27] Similarly, although Senator Kaine rejected the notion that he had changed his position on the TPP upon joining the Democratic presidential ticket, he too had voted in favour of Trade Promotion Authority (which President Obama needed to be able to call for an up or down vote on the TPP rather than subjecting the proposed deal to Congressional line editing) and had spoken favourably about the agreement: 'I see much in it to like … I think it's an upgrade of labour standards, I think it's an upgrade of environmental standards. I think it's an upgrade of intellectual property protections'.[28] Most notably, candidate Hillary Clinton stated she would not support the deal, despite having strongly promoted the TPP while serving as President Obama's Secretary of State.[29]

When candidates for office in the US express populist anti-trade positions during their political campaigns, such messages may or may not be consistent with their true views or intentions. In some cases, the prospective officeholders are expressing positions that align with their actual views. Bernie Sanders, for example, has been consistently opposed to FTAs. In other instances, the candidates likely are pro-trade (for example, Hillary Clinton) and therefore hedge their statements, for example by saying the TPP as drafted isn't acceptable, to leave room to embrace a different position post-election.[30] But why would candidates hide their true views on trade? In the context of US elections, it appears that many would-be voters respond favourably to messages that blame economic struggles

[27] '2016 presidential candidates on the Trans-Pacific Partnership trade deal' (*Ballotopedia*), ballotpedia.org/2016_presidential_candidates_on_the_Trans-Pacific_Partnership_trade_deal.

[28] S Min Kim and B Everett, 'Kaine praised TPP as recently as Thursday' *Politico* (22 July 2016), www.politico.com/story/2016/07/tim-kaine-trade-tpp-226054.

[29] D Palmer, 'Clinton raved about Trans-Pacific Partnership before she rejected it' *Politico* (8 October 2016), www.politico.com/story/2016/10/hillary-clinton-trade-deal-229381.

[30] ibid. 'As I understand her position, she is against TPP in its current form but is open to moving forward with TPP if it is restructured in some way' (quoting Jeffrey Schott); '[Clinton] hasn't disavowed trade or trade agreements altogether, but has expressed her opposition to 'this' TPP … Opposing "this" TPP …. provides Clinton with enormous latitude to flip-flop again' (quoting Dan Ikenson).

on international trade. Candidates' promises of 'America first', and bringing back US manufacturing are bolstered with claims that opening US markets has helped outside actors at the expense of Americans. Furthermore, while the US has a sizeable domestic economy and as such is less reliant on international trade than many other countries, amongst the workers who have been displaced, many believe that their plight could have been avoided had protectionist trade policies been applied.[31] Although the losses from trade are less than the gains, those who are disadvantaged experience their hardships intensely, whereas those who gain, although more numerous, experience their benefits in a more diffuse manner. Furthermore, while Kaldor–Hicks efficiency justifies trade on the basis that the winners could compensate the losers and still be better off than pre-trade, in reality the losers in the US (as elsewhere) generally are not compensated to the level of their losses, if at all.[32] In the case of Donald Trump, he sometimes levied his critiques while maintaining that he was a free-trader.[33] Thus, initially it was unclear whether his anti-TPP rhetoric reflected his own views or whether he was instead tapping into populist sentiments; trying to woo Bernie Sanders supporters; and/or seeking to tie Clinton to President Obama and to differentiate himself from both.

Notwithstanding uncertainty as to the authenticity of Trump's professed views, he spoke out against the TPP regularly and fervently. He often relied upon messaging similar to that of anti-trade Democrats, stating that the TPP would lead to lost jobs and be bad for US manufacturing. At a campaign rally, Trump analogised the TPP to rape, professing that '[t]he Trans-Pacific Partnership is another disaster done and pushed by special interests who want to rape our country, just a continuing rape of our country … That's what it is, too. It's a harsh word: It's a rape of our country'.[34] Following his election in November 2016, Trump pledged to withdraw from the TPP on 'day one' of his presidency.[35]

[31] J Mason and M Solis, 'Order from Chaos: Globalization on the Cheap: Why the US Lost its Way on Trade' (*Brookings*, 28 August 2017), www.brookings.edu/blog/order-from-chaos/2017/08/28/globalization-on-the-cheap-why-the-u-s-lost-its-way-on-trade/. The authors note that 'Americans are more skeptical about the impact of trade on jobs than publics in other industrialized nations … 50 percent of respondents in the United States believe that trade destroys jobs, whereas the average elsewhere is 19 percent'.

[32] This is sometimes referred to as the potential Pareto principle. See, eg, MK Lewis, 'WTO Winners and Losers: The Trade and Development Disconnect' (2007) 39 *Georgetown Journal of International Law* 165, 167–68.

[33] 'Here's Donald Trump's Presidential Announcement Speech' *Time* (16 June 2015), time.com/3923128/donald-trump-announcement-speech/.

[34] C Lima, 'Trump calls trade deal 'a rape of our country'' *Politico* (28 June 2016), www.politico.com/story/2016/06/donald-trump-trans-pacific-partnership-224916.

[35] 'Trump just announced he'd abandon the TPP on day one. This is what happens next' *Washington Post* (22 November 2016), www.washingtonpost.com/news/wonk/wp/2016/11/22/trump-just-announced-hed-abandon-the-tpp-on-day-one-this-is-what-happens-next/?noredirect=on&utm_term=.2d5fc7d540e5.

V. Withdrawal from the TPP: Time did not Stand Still

President Trump followed through with his campaign promise (albeit on day four rather than day one) to withdraw the US from the TPP. Trump contended that he did so because the TPP 'would have been a disastrous deal for our workers' and that he intended instead to negotiate bilateral trade agreements 'that protect American workers'.[36]

Within the US, reaction to Trump's action ranged from pleased to concerned. Pro-labour Democratic lawmakers, who have often been cool towards international trade agreements and likely would have voted against the TPP had President Obama put it to a vote, applauded the measure,[37] while many Republican leaders, who have generally been more favourably inclined towards trade agreements, expressed concerns.[38] The US business community had mixed views, with unions generally supporting the move and exporters more likely to oppose President Trump's decision.[39] Amongst academics, think tanks and policymakers, those who have generally opposed trade largely approved, but the reaction otherwise was mostly critical. Critiques raised a number of concerns, including that the US had been the driver of the negotiations and largely stood to benefit without making many concessions itself,[40] and that the US had also stood to benefit geopolitically by establishing itself more firmly in Asia, whereas withdrawal would create uncertainty in the Asia-Pacific and elsewhere about US reliability as an ally and partner.[41]

VI. From TPP to CPTPP

Following the US withdrawal, the remaining 11 TPP countries could not simply continue with the original agreement because without the US, it was impossible for the TPP, as drafted, to enter into force. Article 30.5 of the TPP identified

[36] 'President Trump's First Weekly Address' (The White House, 28 January 2017), www.whitehouse.gov/briefings-statements/president-trumps-first-weekly-address/.

[37] eg, Democratic Senator Sherrod Brown stated: 'Throwing out TPP is the first necessary step in overhauling our trade policy to put American workers first'. See 'Brown Applauds Executive Action on TPP after Decades Fighting for Fair Trade' (*S Brown*, 23 January 2017), www.brown.senate.gov/newsroom/press/release/brown-applauds-executive-action-on-tpp-after-decades-fighting-for-fair-trade.

[38] See, eg, J Devaey, 'McCain: Withdrawal from TPP a Mistake, Opening for China' *Newsmax* (23 January 2017), www.newsmax.com/Politics/john-mccain-tpp-withdrawal-mistake/2017/01/23/id/770046/.

[39] See, eg, MS Mahaskey, 'Trump's Trade Pullout Roils Rural America' *Politico* (7 August 2017), www.politico.com/magazine/story/2017/08/07/trump-tpp-deal-withdrawal-trade-effects-215459.

[40] See, eg, J Schott, 'Safety in Numbers: Despite the US Pullout, a Trans-Pacific Trade Partnership Still Has Legs' (*Milliken Institute Review*, July 2018), www.milkenreview.org/articles/safety-in-numbers.

[41] See, eg, M Solis, 'Trump Withdrawing from the Trans-Pacific Partnership' (*Brookings*, 24 March 2017), www.brookings.edu/blog/unpacked/2017/03/24/trump-withdrawing-from-the-trans-pacific-partnership/.

three paths to operationalising the Agreement. The TPP could come into effect either: (1) sixty days after all 12 signatories had ratified the agreement; (2) if two years after signature all 12 had not ratified, the TPP would come into force 60 days after the two-year mark if by that time at least six signatories had ratified, comprising at least 85 per cent of the collective GDP of the 12 signatories; or (3) if neither option 1 or 2 were satisfied, 60 days after ratification by six signatories comprising at least 85 per cent of the collective GDP.[42] With the US out, none of these options could be satisfied: all 12 could not ratify, and the US accounted for about 60 per cent of the collective GDP of the TPP members – thus the 85 per cent threshold could not be achieved.

The TPP-11 therefore had to decide whether to form a new agreement or to abandon the TPP project. Shortly after Trump's election but before the beginning of his presidency, Japan's Prime Minister Shinzo Abe said the other 11 countries had not discussed moving forward without the US if Trump followed through with withdrawing from the TPP, because '[t]he TPP would be meaningless without the United States'.[43] However, Prime Minister Abe changed his mind and ultimately all 11 countries participated in discussions to conclude a new agreement. The TPP-11 could have tried to renegotiate the provisions that existed primarily at the demand of the US, such as TRIPS-plus protections for pharmaceuticals manufacturers, and could have reopened discussions on the most sensitive market access issues. However, the 11 took a pragmatic approach, and decided to proceed in a fashion that would make it as seamless as possible for the US to slot back into the original 12-country grouping. To accomplish this, the TPP-11 renegotiated the TPP text very slightly. They left unchanged the vast majority of the TPP's 30 chapters, while putting on hold several provisions, primarily involving investment and intellectual property commitments, upon which the US had insisted but the other parties had not favoured. The TPP-11 ultimately signed a very similar agreement to the TPP, now called the Comprehensive and Progressive TPP (CPTPP), in March 2018.[44]

Some of the provisions put on hold related to aspects of the TPP about which Trump had complained, such as the inclusion of investor–state dispute settlement,[45] and Trump initially even teased the possibility of joining the new pact.[46] However, Trump appears not to have been serious, having made no effort to initiate such a step. The CPTPP went into force on 30 December 2018 for the first six countries to ratify (Australia, Canada, Japan, Mexico, New Zealand and Singapore), and on

[42] Art 30.5 of the TPP (n 1).

[43] See 'Japan's Prime Minister Says the TPP is "Meaningless Without the US"' *Reuters* (22 November 2016), fortune.com/2016/11/22/donald-trump-tpp-japan-trade/.

[44] CPTPP (n 2).

[45] For a comparison of the TPP and CPTPP texts, see MP Goodman, 'From TPP to CPTPP' (Center for Strategic and International Studies, 8 March 2018), www.csis.org/analysis/tpp-cptpp.

[46] 'Return of the TPP: Trump realizing trade deal aligns with goals on China' *The Hill* (16 April 2018), thehill.com/opinion/finance/383327-return-of-the-tpp-trump-realizing-trade-deal-aligns-with-goals-on-china.

14 January 2019 for Vietnam. Brunei, Chile, Malaysia and Peru have yet to ratify the Agreement.[47]

VII. A CPTPP without the US: Good Call or Missed Opportunity?

Although the CPTPP has not been in force long enough to measure the full effects of the US withdrawal from the pact, this section offers a preliminary assessment of whether the US strategy of withdrawal was a successful one, or whether it was instead an unwise decision. There may be multiple true answers to this question, depending on the perspective from which the question is approached.

It is likely that President Trump remains pleased with his decision to withdraw from the TPP and views it as having been a successful move. Part of Trump's overall approach to trade has been to seek to negotiate bilaterally rather than in larger groups, consistent with his view that the US can obtain more of its objectives in a bilateral context than in a larger plurilateral (as in TPP) or multilateral (as in the WTO) setting. From this perspective, Trump's move was a good strategy. It is often the case that an actor such as the US with substantial bargaining power will be in a position to negotiate from a greater position of strength in the bilateral context than in the WTO or a plurilateral negotiation such as the TPP.[48] For example, in the renegotiation of the NAFTA, which has led to a new agreement called the US–Mexico–Canada Agreement or USMCA, the US, inter alia, obtained more stringent rules of origin concessions on autos than it had in its TPP negotiations with Canada and Mexico.[49] Likewise, the US has recently negotiated the US–Japan Trade Agreement, which provides the US with some, but not all, of the market access to which it would have been entitled under the TPP.[50] Viewed through a narrow lens, one could see this as evidence that leaving the TPP was successful. However, from other perspectives, leaving the TPP can be seen as having been counterproductive for the US.

First, now that the CPTPP has come into force, the US has started to experience some negative trade impacts. Tariffs have begun to come down within the Partnership, which has led some US exporters to feel the impacts of the Trump

[47] This information is current as of 14 November 2020.

[48] See, eg, A Bahri and M Lugo, 'Trumping Capacity Gap with Negotiation Strategies: the Mexican USMCA Negotiation Experience' (2020) 23 *Journal of International Economic Law* 1, raising a similar point in the context of the USMCA negotiations.

[49] Ch 4 of the USMCA addresses rules of origin in general. Annex 4-B contains product-specific rules of origin, and as reflected in Art 4.10, the appendix to Annex 4-B contains additional provisions specific to automotive goods. Art 4.10 indicates that for automotive goods. See United States–Mexico–Canada Agreement (USMCA) (Buenos Aires, 30 November 2018, revised 10 December 2019).

[50] See, eg, D Lawder, 'US–Japan Trade Deal Versus TPP: Where it Falls Short, Where it Exceeds' *Reuters* (7 October 2019), www.reuters.com/article/us-usa-trade-japan-idUSKBN1WM0A3.

administration's decision to abandon the TPP.[51] Analysts initially projected that the US will lose 0.5 per cent of GDP as a consequence of leaving the Agreement.[52] As an example, Japan will lower its tariffs on beef over the next 15 years down to 9 per cent.[53] This has enabled CPTPP partners, particularly Australia, to make new inroads into the Japanese market. At the same time, American beef producers, who had anticipated taking advantage of these lower tariffs, were not in an immediate a position to do so. The US withdrawal from the TPP meant that the applicable Japanese tariff on US beef remained at 38.5 per cent, while dropping for TPP partners.[54] The US has now, via the US–Japan Trade Agreement, obtained market access commitments from Japan on beef, pork and wine in line with those provided to CPTPP members;[55] however, there was a period of time in which Japanese consumers had the opportunity to experience Australian beef at significantly lower prices than American beef, which may have locked in a degree of preference for the Australian product In addition, the US–Japan Agreement does not provide US exporters with all the market access that would have been provided had the US remained in the TPP. Excluded areas include any access to the agricultural quotas CPTPP members are receiving, and tariff concessions on items such as US semiconductor manufacturing equipment.[56] There will likely be further negative economic consequences due to supply chains deciding to use CPTPP-based suppliers instead of American suppliers for certain products. In the context of the coronavirus, many countries are rethinking their dependence on supply chains that rely upon China. The CPTPP countries are well positioned to develop their own supply chains that will insulate the members from the uncertainties of relying on either China or the US.[57]

Second, US participation in the TPP was touted in part as an opportunity to contain China's influence in the economic sphere in the Asia-Pacific. By withdrawing, the US has instead provided an opening for China to solidify its strategic

[51] 'US Farmers Being Cut out of Japan After TPP Withdrawal' *Financial Times* (18 March 2019), www.ft.com/content/07d14730-4831-11e9-bbc9-6917dce3dc62.

[52] JJ Schott, 'The TPP: Origins and outcomes' in RE Looney (ed), *Handbook of International Trade Agreements: Country, Regional and Global Approaches* (Abingdon, Routledge 2018) 409; PA Petri et al, 'Going it alone in the Asia-Pacific: Regional Trade Agreements without the United States' (2017) Peterson Institute for International Economics Working Paper 17-10, piie.com/publications/working-papers/going-it-alone-asia-pacific-regional-trade-agreements-without-united. See also, 'What the Death of the TPP Means for America' *The New Yorker* (24 January 2017), www.newyorker.com/business/adam-davidson/what-the-death-of-the-t-p-p-means-for-america.

[53] MP Goodman and A Listerud, 'US–Japan Trade Talks: What to Expect' (Center for Strategic and International Studies, 23 January 2019), www.csis.org/analysis/us-japan-trade-talks-what-expect; 'CPTPP outcomes: Goods market access' (Australian Government Department of Foreign Affairs and Trade, January 2019), dfat.gov.au/trade/agreements/in-force/cptpp/outcomes-documents/Pages/cptpp-goods.aspx.

[54] Goodman and Listerud (n 53).

[55] See Lawder, 'US–Japan Deal Versus TPP' (n 50).

[56] ibid.

[57] See generally, S Olson, 'Post COVID-19: More Regional Trade and Shorter Supply Chains?' (Hinrich Foundation, 24 April 2020), www.hinrichfoundation.com/research/article/protectionism/post-covid-19-trade/.

strength in the region. China has been participating in the Regional Comprehensive Economic Partnership (RCEP), a separate megaregional trade negotiation featuring 15 countries, seven of which are also in the CPTPP, which was signed on 15 November 2020.[58] Without the US in the CPTPP to counterbalance China, China has had less to lose for not being in CPTPP and has been able to negotiate with the overlapping countries from a position of strength without being constrained by unpopular US provisions already having been locked into place. While the Trump administration has touted the US–China Phase One Deal as a way to keep China in check while obtaining more sales for American exporters, this deal has been subject to significant criticism. Not only does the deal appear to violate the WTO's most-favoured nation (MFN) principle by providing market access commitments not offered to other WTO Members (and not being a comprehensive enough deal to qualify as an FTA under Article XXIV of the GATT and therefore be treated as an exception to the MFN rule), but thus far China has not been purchasing the volumes of US products to which it committed.[59] As with many of President Trump's manoeuvres, the US–China Phase One Deal has provided better soundbites than results.

Beyond China, the US had positioned itself as a rule-setter in the Asia-Pacific, and an active geostrategic force. Both of these roles are now called into question. If RCEP and CPTPP largely align on issues such as heightened intellectual property protections that fall short of what the US would like, it will be more difficult for the US to convince Asia-Pacific FTA partners to agree to its preferred protections in the future. With the WTO largely stalled, rules are increasingly being made in FTAs – a dynamic President Trump had been keen to perpetuate – yet the US now sits outside a very large FTA that is likely to expand further. And finally, the US withdrawal from the TPP likely will have geopolitical implications; it will become more difficult to exert political influence in a region that is going to become more heavily integrated economically.

While it is unlikely that President Trump will ever regret his decision to remove the US from the TPP, many others already view this choice as unwise. The US voluntarily went from a position of being able to obtain trade concessions without having to give much in return, and of strengthening its role in the critically important Asia-Pacific region, to ceding control over the regional international trade agenda and sitting on the outside of a club that is likely to expand in numbers and influence. For these reasons, amongst others, withdrawing from the TPP appears to have been a short-sighted move that is having more negative than positive repercussions. The CPTPP countries had the foresight, however, to envision that a later US administration might see the error of its ways and wish to re-join, and elected to structure the CPTPP in a way to facilitate that move. However, even if

[58] The seven overlapping countries are Australia, Brunei, Japan, Malaysia, New Zealand, Singapore and Vietnam.

[59] See, eg, D Ikenson, 'Why Bother Assessing the US–China Phase One Deal Anyway?' (*Cato Institute*, 30 October 2020), www.cato.org/blog/why-bother-assessing-us-china-phase-one-trade-deal-anyway.

the US does seek to enter the CPTPP at a later date, which President-elect Biden appears open to, it is not guaranteed that the US Congress would approve such a move. Even if the US does join the CPTPP at some point, it will still have lost the bargaining power which it once held, and the impacts on supply chains will not reverse overnight. As such, it is hard to view the US withdrawal as a winning strategy rather than an 'own goal'.[60]

The US trade strategy during the Trump administration was to eschew multilateral and plurilateral arrangements in favour of bilateral (and in the case of USMCA, trilateral) negotiations that would allow the US to exploit its bargaining power to full effect. The limits of this strategy are already evident. First, the countries the US has spurned have not retreated into the shadows. To the contrary, they are finding new ways to engage with each other. The remaining TPP-11 formed the CPTPP and took the opportunity to freeze the provisions of the original agreement that they had not been in favour of and had only included at US insistence. Although many countries would undoubtedly prefer for the US to be in the agreement, the CPTPP has numerous countries keen to accede, notwithstanding the US absence. Thus, the CPTPP is not only surviving, it is thriving and poised to expand. Similarly, many WTO Members are unwilling to deem WTO dispute settlement dead just because the US has thwarted the current operation of the Appellate Body, and have developed their own workaround, in the form of the MPIA, to ensure their disputes can still be appealed.

Second, with the CPTPP in force and the RCEP now having been signed, the Asia-Pacific region is growing ever more integrated, limiting the ability of the US to dictate the terms of future agreements with countries within the region. Not too long ago, the US had a template for its FTAs that it was able to impose on its negotiating partners. The ability to utilise that template going forward has likely been impeded by the US withdrawal from the TPP, and the impending growth of the CPTPP on the basis of a revised, less US-centric, text. The US is about to usher in a new administration, and President-elect Biden is likely to approach trade differently from the Trump administration. The US is likely to re-engage with the WTO going forward and may seek to join the CPTPP. The CPTPP members may find that the Biden administration will not insist on reclaiming all the stalled provisions from the TPP, and the WTO membership may find that the new US administration is open to discussing the various proposals for Appellate Body reform that the Trump administration refused to entertain. The CPTPP members on the one hand, and the WTO membership on the other, have focused on their own objectives, and in so doing have fortified their bonds. At the same time, they have been wise to leave open the opportunity for the US to re-engage. This may lead to a win-win in the future, in which the US returns to its TPP partners, but without having dominated the CPTPP terms, and the Appellate Body is ultimately restored, but with some addressing of the concerns raised by the US and others.

[60] An 'own goal' is a football/soccer reference to kicking the ball into your own net, thus scoring for the opposing team against yourself.

VIII. Conclusion

While the US withdrawal from the TPP may have served President Trump's purposes, those purposes were narrow – perhaps even myopic – and did not represent the best interests of the US. By leaving the TPP, the US ceded the opportunity to place itself squarely within the most ambitious effort at Asia-Pacific regional integration to date, and to embed many of its policy objectives into that project. Now, instead of having set the rules for an agreement that is likely to expand, the US sits on the side lines of not only the CPTPP, but also the recently concluded RCEP, neither of which feature the heightened IP protections the US had succeeded in inserting into the TPP. As a result, even if the US does seek to join the CPTPP in the future, it has become less likely that the CPTPP countries will feel obliged to recommit themselves to unpopular IP provisions.

Although the US presence in the TPP talks was the catalyst for the negotiation's expansion, that expansion brought substantial potential benefits for the other participants, as the US withdrawal did not trigger a parallel unwinding. Instead, the remaining parties developed a pragmatic solution to move forward. In December 2016, aware of Trump's threats to pull the US out of the TPP, former New Zealand TPP negotiator Tracey Epps proposed that the remaining 11 enter into a 'TPP 2.0' that would allow a deal to come into force, while providing a path for the US to re-enter easily in the future.[61] This idea quickly gained traction – but would Japan, the largest player (by GDP) remaining, get on board? When faced with the hypothetical possibility of the US withdrawing from the TPP, Prime Minister Abe had expressed scepticism that there would be any point in the parties continuing on without the US.[62] However, when the hypothetical became reality, Abe did not hesitate to pursue TPP-11. While it is unclear what lay behind Abe's earlier remarks, it was evident that there was more in the Agreement for Japan than just an FTA with the US. Even if a deal with the US would have been preferable, Abe likely saw its role in the pact as still providing an opportunity to strengthen its bargaining power in the parallel RCEP negotiations.[63] In addition, the TPP had already been integrated into Abe's growth and reform strategy for Japan.[64] Japan therefore did not retreat upon the US withdrawal, and instead took a leading role in overcoming obstacles and bringing TPP-11 to fruition.[65]

The decision of the TPP-11 to conclude a new agreement also had implications for China, impelling it to push the RCEP negotiations to a conclusion. Had the

[61] T Epps, 'TPP: Is TPP dead – or not?' (*Trade Working Blog*, 19 December 2016), tradeworks.org.nz/guest-post-is-tpp-dead-or-not/.

[62] See 'Japan's Prime Minister Says the TPP is "Meaningless Without the US"' (n 43).

[63] See, eg, 'Why Japan Must Join the TPP' *The Diplomat* (5 June 2013), thediplomat.com/2013/06/why-japan-must-join-the-tpp/.

[64] 'Japan Chair Platform: Moving Forward with TPP 11' (Center for Strategic and International Studies, 12 May 2017), www.csis.org/analysis/japan-chair-platform-moving-forward-tpp-11.

[65] See, eg, 'TPP Deal Came Down to Convincing Canada' *The Mainichi* (24 January 2018), mainichi.jp/english/articles/20180124/p2a/00m/0na/018000c.

US withdrawal led to the dissolution of any agreement amongst the remaining TPP-11, the RCEP negotiations may have continued to meander. However, the conclusion of a CPTPP which the US could easily slot into likely heightened China's desire to finalise an RCEP deal. Supply chains that may have anchored themselves within CPTPP countries may now be more favourably drawn to the RCEP, given its larger concentration of global GDP and the presence of China, Japan and Korea. This alone should raise concerns within the incoming Biden administration.[66] To further complicate matters, now that the RCEP has been signed, China is signalling that it may seek to capitalise on US absence by seeking to join the CPTPP itself.[67]

If the US withdrawal from the TPP leads solely to its absence from either of the possible contenders to expand into an FTA of the Asia-Pacific and from their new market access opportunities, this would constitute a clear 'own goal'. But if China ends up being in both agreements, the implications for the US economy magnify further.

There are a few lessons to be learned from these shifting dynamics. First, as has been clear since the collapse of the Doha Round negotiations in the mid-2000s, when countries want to liberalise, they are not being deterred by obstacles, but are instead finding new pathways to achieve what they want to achieve. The TPP-11 did not simply hang their heads and go home when the US withdrew from the agreement; they regrouped in a clever way that both created an attractive agreement that is likely to expand further, while also leaving a pathway for their original cornerstone partner to join them anew. Second, power politics can be disruptive, but coalitions of the willing have their own power. The Trump administration did exactly what it set out to do, but it likely did not expect WTO Members to create an Appellate Body workaround, nor for the TPP-11 to form a new agreement without it. These developments demonstrate that even in an era of populism, by working together, those still invested in multilateralism can forge a way forward. And finally, much can be accomplished by pursuing one's objectives while retaining a degree of pragmatism. Extrapolating beyond the TPP, we need to recognise that universal coalitions are extremely difficult to maintain. The WTO's reliance on consensus has long held the organisation back in various ways, but it should now be evident that this decision-making approach is not sustainable. This should not be seen as a failure, but rather an opportunity to rescue the multilateral trading system by surrounding the core mandatory obligations with a looser, more flexible and pragmatic outer layer of commitments that can appeal to most, even if not to all.

[66] See H Hung, 'After RCEP's Launch, the US Needs to Urgently Rejoin the TPP' *The Diplomat* (18 November 2020), thediplomat.com/2020/11/after-rceps-launch-the-us-urgently-needs-to-rejoin-the-tpp/.

[67] 'China to "Favorably Consider" Joining TPP' *Global Times* (21 November 2020), www.globaltimes.cn/content/1207536.shtml.

INDEX

www.ingramcontent.com/pod-product-compliance
Lightning Source LLC
Chambersburg PA
CBHW071301180926
51613CB00001B/99

Edition KWV

Die „Edition KWV" beinhaltet hochwertige Werke aus dem Bereich der Wirtschaftswissenschaften. Alle Werke in der Reihe erschienen ursprünglich im Kölner Wissenschaftsverlag, dessen Programm Springer Gabler 2018 übernommen hat.

Weitere Bände in der Reihe http://www.springer.com/series/16033

Ralf Günther

Impact of Aircraft Sourcing & Financing on Financial Success

A strategic view on basic aircraft sourcing & financing characteristics and their impact on stock market and long term financial performance of aircraft operating and holding companies

Springer Gabler

Ralf Günther
Wiesbaden, Germany

Bis 2018 erschien der Titel im Kölner Wissenschaftsverlag, Köln
Dissertation, Wirtschafts- und Sozialwissenschaftliche Fakultät der Universität zu Köln, 2013

Edition KWV
ISBN 978-3-658-24093-6 ISBN 978-3-658-24094-3 (eBook)
https://doi.org/10.1007/978-3-658-24094-3

Library of Congress Control Number: 2019933395

Springer Gabler

This Springer Gabler imprint is published by the registered company Springer Fachmedien Wiesbaden GmbH part of Springer Nature
The registered company address is: Abraham-Lincoln-Str. 46, 65189 Wiesbaden, Germany

To my parents
& my wife

Preface

In the view of current developments in the airline market the present thesis investigates the question, whether fundamental characteristics of an aircraft fleet have a (statistically significant) correlation to the financial accomplishments of an airline or to a corresponding holding company, respectively. For this, an empirical analysis is carried out to examine the influence of elementary decisions concerning aircraft acquisition and financial structures upon the development of stock values and of selected performance figures of airlines. Hereby a strategic viewpoint of investors and of top decision-makers of airlines is chosen, which directly results in the choice of the empirical method of multivariate regression analysis with abnormal gains or losses of stocks as well as with key indicators of profitability, efficiency and sales increase of companies.

In addition to this perspective and methodical extension, the present dissertation complements previous studies with till now not examined aircraft fleet characteristics and their influence on the financial success of airlines. These features include the relation of own to leasing, the ratio of already planned aircraft acquisitions compared to the size of the existing fleet and the proportion of prolonged parked or temporarily not used aircraft in comparison with those operatively in use. For all these variables the analyses of this study prove a statistical relevance in reference to abnormal returns in stock prices, to profitability and to sales growth of airlines. Additional new knowledge is gained relating to the financial variables equity ratio, ratio of net debt over earnings before interest, taxes, depreciation and amortization (EBITDA) as well as to interest coverage and their correlation with long-term growth in turnover and high profit margins.

Analyses of the development of stock prices of airlines during economic cycles or following industry-wide or company-specific incidents already exist repeatedly in the literature. Examples for this are among others the events of 9/11, the reaction of stock markets to airplane crashes and the cyclical industrial development over several years. In addition, the present thesis analyzes the consequences of the financial crisis 2008 for the performance of airline stocks. By supplementing this research period, the effects of two shock-events and the resulting global crises (referring to the airline industry) can for the first time be compared with each other.

Altogether, the present dissertation explores – in examining the connection between strategic aircraft fleet decisions and short- or long-term stock price development or key performance indicators, respectively – a theoretically demanding and a practically contemporary and relevant subject area. The undertaking to present a differentiated empirical research to this topic bears considerable potential. The study imparts very informative and innovative results. I wish this thesis a lively discussion in science and in practicc.

Werner Delfmann

Acknowledgement

The dissertation project took more than five years from the first thought till publication. Although a doctoral thesis is a lonely undertaking for many hours, it does not succeed without supporting inspiration, trust, and motivation from others to discuss content and to stay focused on the objectives.

My thanks go to Professor Dr. Dr. h.c. Werner Delfmann, Department of Business Policies and Logistics at the University of Cologne, for the scientific support as my doctoral father and guidance throughout the time of my research, as well as to his team members with whom I enjoyed discussing and laughing over the last years,
to Charles Graham, former CEO Global Aviation at DHL Express and former CEO of AWAS, for inspiration, trust in the idea of my thesis, and for immediate commitment of sponsorship by DHL Express,
to Charlie Dobbie, EVP Global Network Operations at DHL Express, for continuous business sponsorship, as well as to my DHL colleagues who supported me in the early stage to shape the topic.

I highly appreciate the time and insights that were shared in 2009 at the start of my thesis project by William Flynn (President and CEO Atlas Air Worldwide Holdings), Harry Forsythe (EVP Marketing and at that time SVP Sales and Marketing Macquarie AirFinance), Jason Grant (at that time SVP and CFO Atlas Air Worldwide Holdings), Stephan Sayre (Managing Director and at that time Investment Adviser at Deucalion Aviation Funds, DVB Bank SE), Crispin Maunder (Executive Chairman and at that time CEO Lease Corporation International), Jaspal Jandu (CFO Lease Corporation International), Ray Sisson (CEO of AWAS and at that time CEO Titan Aviation Leasing Ltd.), and Carter White (Head of and at that time SVP Aircraft Trading at AWAS), who confirmed the interest of the industry in the research topic and encouraged me to continue this project.

Further, I would like to thank Sabine Mueller (EVP) and Olaf Hermanni (Partner) from Deutsche Post DHL Inhouse Consulting for providing me with a stable and still flexible working environment to pursue my thesis and for supporting my personal development.

I would like to thank my parents and my wife for their support, understanding, and encouragement throughout the years of my study.

Ralf Günther

Abstract

Aircraft operating and holding companies apply different strategies to source and finance aircraft. The basic sourcing decision is to acquire air capacity on demand or to plan future capacity by committing to aircraft firm orders and purchase options. The general financing choice is between buying (via direct purchase or capital lease) and operating lease of aircraft.

This study takes the perspective of investors and evaluates the correlation of basic sourcing and financing strategies with a company's financial success in shocks and crises, company specific isolated positive and negative events, and over long term business cycles.

Multivariate regression methodology is used to analyze abnormal returns in stock market's reaction to the terrorist attacks on September 11, 2001, the Financial Crisis 2008, and to aircraft accidents and aircraft orders 1994-2009. In further regressions the relationship of basic aircraft fleet and fleet planning variables to a company's long term revenue growth and profitability is examined.

The findings show a positive correlation of aircraft ownership (buy or capital lease) and of future oriented aircraft acquisition (firm orders and purchase options) with a company's long term average EBITDA and EBIT margins. Merely in times of strong business growth, operating lease is the right measure to quickly supply capacity, beside firm orders and purchase options. The findings further support the theory of rational pricing and the assumption that the stock market distinguishes between different basic aircraft sourcing and financing strategies. A high portion of owned or capital leased aircraft in the fleet, long term orders, and purchase options proved to positively influence also a company's stock return in times of crises. Exception to this is found when governmental financial aid actions influenced stock market's behavior. The analysis of stock market reaction on aircraft accidents and aircraft firm orders is of low explanatory power; hence, the results allow for speculation but not for reliable conclusions on the influence of basic fleet characteristics.

The findings of this study suggest to companies, which historically have been relying on operating lease and purchasing capacity ad hoc, to review their aircraft sourcing and financing strategy. This is stated under the assumption that demand of air transport grows as currently predicted by the aviation industry and anticipating an increasing shortage of capacity and price increase caused by ongoing carrier consolidation, insolvencies among airlines, decommissioning programs for aging aircraft, shortage in production slots for new aircraft, and an insufficient number of passenger-to-cargo conversions.

Table of content

Index of figures

Index of tables

List of abbreviations & symbols

*	Statistically significant at the ten percent level
**	Statistically significant at the five percent level
***	Statistically significant at the one percent level
=	equals
<	is less than
≤	is less than or equal to
>	is greater than
≥	is greater than or equal to
#	number (count)
%	percent
∑	sum
1YROPTION	Explanatory variable: number of purchase options with execution day in the next calendar year over total number of aircraft in the fleet
3PL	Third-party logistics
9/11	September 11, 2001
α	Alpha (residual risk)
α’	Change in alpha
β	Beta (systematic risk)
β’	Change in beta
Δ	Delta
ε	Epsilon (random disturbance term)
σ	Sigma (standard deviation)
A	Airbus (e.g. A320 Airbus 320)
A/C	Aircraft
A/L	Airline
AAGR	Average annual growth rate
AARG	Average annual revenue growth (average annual rate of net sales or revenue growth with one year equal to a full calendar year ending December 31)
AB	Aktiebolag [Swedish for: stock company]
ABX/ABX Air	Airborne Express
ACMI	Aircraft, Crew, Maintenance, and Insurance
ACPORDER	Explanatory variable: aircraft per order (number of aircraft per single firm order)
add.	additional

AG	Aktiengesellschaft [German for: stock company]
AIG	American International Group
AMR	American Airlines
AMR/UAL	Explanatory variable: American Airlines or United Airlines
ANA	All Nippon Airways
AOC	Air Operator Certificate
APAC	Asia Pacific
AR	Abnormal return
ARG	Annual revenue growth (year-on-year revenue growth with one year equal to a full calendar year ending December 31)
ATA	Air Transport Association (not to confuse with ATA Holdings)
ATI	Air Transport International
ATK	Available Ton Kilometer
AVAC	Aircraft Value Analysis Company
AVGAGE	Explanatory variable: average age of total number of existing aircraft in service or stored
AVGEBITDAMAR	Average margin of annual earnings before interest, taxes, depreciation and amortization
AVGEBITMAR	Average margin of annual earnings before interest, taxes, depreciation and amortization
B	Boeing (e.g. B737 Boeing 737)
bn	billion
C	Consumption
CAGR	Cumulated Annual Growth Rate
CAR	Cumulative Abnormal Return
CASM	Cost per Available Seat Mile
CEO	Chief Executive Officer
CFO	Chief Financial Officer
cf.	confer (compare)
Co. (or comp.)	Company
Corp.	Corporation
OYJ	Osakeyhtiö [Norwegian for: stock company]
CRSP	Center of Research in Security Prices
D_s	Dummy variable representing a shift in stock risk after an event
DEA	Data Envelopment Analysis
e.g.	exempli gratia [Latin for: for example]
EBIT	Earnings before interest and taxes (operating income)
EBITDA	Earnings before interest, taxes, depreciation and amortization

EBITDAFY	Total earnings before interest, taxes, depreciation and amortization in a company's fiscal year
EBITDAMAR	EBITDA margin (earnings before interest, taxes, depreciation and amortization over total operating revenue)
EBITFY	Total earnings before interest and taxes in a company's fiscal year
EBITMAR	EBIT margin (earnings before interest and taxes over total operating revenue)
EMEA	Europe, Middle East and Africa
EQUITRAT	Explanatory variable: equity ratio (owners' equity over total assets)
EUR	Euro
excl.	excluding
f	risk free rate
F-stat.	F-statistics
FAA	Federal Aviation Administration
FATALITY	Explanatory variable: on-board fatality (number of passengers and crew killed in an aircraft accident over total number of passengers and crew on board)
FedEx	Federal Express
Fin. (or fin.)	Financial (or financial)
FLYI	Independence Air (former Atlantic Coast Airlines)
FREIGHT(ER)	Freight carrier
FTK (or RTK)	Freight Ton Kilometer (or Revenue Ton Kilometer)
FTKMKTSHR	Explanatory variable: Freight Ton Kilometer Market Share
G	Government spending
G7	Group of seven (industrial nations)
GDP	Gross Domestic Product
GWP	Gross World Product
Hlg.	Holdings
H.R. (or HR)	(U.S. Congress) House Bill
I	Investment
i	Individual company stock
ICAO	International Civil Aviation Organization
i.e.	id est [Latin for: that is to say]
Inc.	Incorporated
incl.	including
INJURY	Explanatory variable: on-board injury (number of passengers and crew injured in an aircraft accident over total number of passengers and crew on board)

INTRSTCOVRG	Explanatory variable: interest coverage (interest expenses for debt over earnings before interest and taxes)
IR	Interest rate
IT	Information Technology
JAR(s)	Joint Aviation Requirement(s)
JAR-OPS	Joint Aviation Requirement for the operation of commercial air transport (aeroplanes)
JIT	Just in time
JP	Japan
KLM	Koninklijke Luchtvaart Maatschappij (Royal Dutch Airlines)
LAN	Línea Aérea Nacional (de Chile)
LATAM	Latin America
LCC	Low Cost Carrier
LIQUIDITY	Explanatory variable: cash & cash equivalents over current liabilities
LN	Natural logarithm
LOSTVALUE	Explanatory variable: lost value (book value of the aircraft before hull loss)
Ltd.	Limited (company)
M	Import
m	market (benchmark)
mYTFYE	Number of months from calendar year start to end of a company's fiscal year
MAIR	Mesaba Holdings
Mesa	Mesa Air Group
MFSC	Major Full Service Carrier (or major network carrier)
mn	million
MSCI	Morgan Stanley Capital International
MTOW	Maximum Takeoff Weight
MVRM	Multivariate Regression Methodology
n	(total) number of something (1, 2, …, n)
N/A (or n/a)	not applicable or not available
NASDAQ	National Association of Securities Dealers Automated Quotations
NDTEBITDA	Explanatory variable: net debt over earnings before interest, taxes, depreciation and amortization
NFSC	Non-major Full Service Carrier (or non-major network or regional carrier)
NORAM	North America
Nov	November

nYROPTION	Explanatory variable: total number of purchase options total number of aircraft in the fleet count
nYRORDER	Explanatory variable: total number of jet aircraft orders to existing fleet count
NYSE	New York Stock Exchange
O&D	Origin & Destination
Oct	October
OECD	Organisation for Economic Co-operation and Development
OEM	Original Equipment Manufacturer
OPSLEASE	Explanatory variable: operating lease (ratio of aircraft on operating lease to total number of aircraft)
p. (pp.)	page(s)
p.a.	per annum
PFREIGHT	Explanatory variable: portion of freight business (revenue of express, cargo and mail over total operating revenue)
PINT	Explanatory variable: portion of international business (non-intra-regional revenue over total operating revenue)
PINT1	Explanatory variable: portion of international business (non-narrow home market revenue over total operating revenue)
PLC	Public limited company
Q	Quarter
r	Excess return
R	Revenue (full calendar year net sales or revenue)
R^2	Coefficient of determination of the proportion of variability; in this thesis R^2 refers always to adjusted R^2 (adjusting for the number of explanatory terms in a model)
RFY	Revenue of fiscal year (full fiscal year net sales or revenue)
RI	Return index
RoW	Rest of world
RPK	Revenue Passenger Kilometer
RPKMKTSHR	Explanatory variable: Revenue Passenger Kilometer Market Share
RTK (or FTK)	Revenue Ton Kilometer (or Freight Ton Kilometer)
S.A. (SA)	Sociedad Anónima (or Société Anonyme)
SARS	Severe Acute Respiratory Syndrome
SAS	Scandinavian Airline Systems
SEC	(U.S.) Security and Exchange Commission
Sep	September
SIZE	Explanatory variable: natural logarithm of total assets
SPC	Special purpose company

STORAC	Explanatory variable: stored aircraft (ratio of aircraft on storage to total number of aircraft)
t (or T)	time (referring to a day t in the MVRM)
T-bill	Treasury bill
T-stat.	T-statistic
TAM	TAM (Táxi Aéreo Marília) Linhas Aéreas
TOTALAC	Explanatory variable: total aircraft (sum of all jet aircraft in a fleet)
U.S. (or US)	United States
UAL	United Airlines
UPS	United Parcel Service
USD	United States Dollar
WaMu	Washington Mutual
X	Export
y	Daily abnormal return
Ye	Year end

1. Introduction

The strategies according to which airlines and other air transport companies manage their aircraft portfolios are as multifarious as the number of firms in the industry. Some buy aircraft, others trust in leasing. Some order aircraft many years ahead and deal with options, others procure capacity ad hoc. Some fancy to operate a very young fleet, others prefer older aircraft or simply care less about average fleet age. What all these companies have in common is that they have to plan and secure air capacity in one or the other way to stay competitive in the market. This has become more difficult in the past two decades. Not only had the industry to deal with the typical economic cycles, but also a number of external events caused or still cause severe impact on the business. This thesis is based on the assumption that actual standard fleet planning is not sufficient to face future business challenges and that aircraft portfolios and fleet plans should be optimized on a higher strategic level regarding basic aircraft sourcing and financing decisions. It is further believed that this adjustment has a positive impact on a company's financial performance throughout normal business cycles, in times of crises, and potentially also in company specific isolated positive and negative events, such as aircraft acquisition or loss.

1.1 Research background and motivation

The world of aircraft sourcing and financing has been in a status of uncertainty since the end of the year 2008. The global financial crisis has increasingly influenced demand and supply of aircraft and respectively its price, and has been changing the risk perception of airlines, aircraft leasing companies and the capital market. Once again, after the terrorist attacks on September 11, 2001, the Severe Acute Respiratory Syndrome (SARS), and the Iraq war, the air transport industry has to face a severe business challenge and in parallel has to plan and secure the future need of air capacity.

Despite the aftermath of the recent crisis, air traffic and respectively air capacity demand are growing again and the interaction of different trends in the industry might easily cause a capacity shortage in the future. Recent economic forecasts predict an annual growth of global trade of 3.3% until 2031 based on the world's real gross domestic product (Federal Aviation Administration, 2009 and 2011). Traditionally, the aviation industry has developed relatively synchronically to the world gross domestic product (Federal Aviation Administration, 2008) and popular forecasts of the aviation business usually build upon this key influencing factor. Hence, an increasing demand in sufficient air capacity can be expected while companies have to focus more than before on profitability and maximizing shareholders' value. The two major airframe manufacturers Airbus (2011) and Boeing

R. Günther, *Impact of Aircraft Sourcing & Financing on Financial Success*,
Edition KWV, https://doi.org/10.1007/978-3-658-24094-3_1

(2011) predict an average positive annual growth trend in global air transport until 2030 of 4.8% based on passenger traffic, 5.1% based on revenue passenger kilometers[1] and 5.6% and freight ton kilometers[2] (positively adjusting their earlier predictions in 2009 of 4.6% to 5.2% until 2028; in Airbus, 2009 and Boeing, 2009). Naturally, the manufacturers see this positive trend as significant sales opportunity but do not provide details to the question whether they will be able to serve this high demand in terms of timely production and deliveries. A decrease in available capacity relative to demand is expected by an increasing number of industry experts (Expert interviews with Atlas Air, AWAS, DVB Bank, LCI Aviation, Macquarie AirFinance, and Titan Aviation Leasing, 2009). Reasons mentioned for the anticipated capacity shortage are ongoing consolidation and insolvencies among the airlines. Recent examples for the latter are Frontier Airlines and Air Midwest in the passenger sector and Ocean Airlines, Transmile, Kitty Hawk, Tradewind and Gemini in the air cargo business. In addition, most airlines run decommissioning programs for their aging aircraft and the market already faces today – impacting cargo and passenger business – a shortage in production slots for new aircraft and – specific to the cargo business – an insufficient number of passenger-to-cargo conversions. Production slots for new aircraft have mainly been blocked by some future oriented well established airlines with respective options at the manufacturers (Interview with Macquarie AirFinance, 2009). Conversion slots are lacking because of the small capacity of the conversion service providers. Considering all of the above, not all suppliers of air transport will be able to serve their customer's demand in the future.

Based on current expectations regarding both the financial and the capacity market, all air transport dependent business models face the same questions: How to secure future competitiveness in terms of air capacity and simultaneously prepare best for demand fluctuation in the normal business cycle and with regard to unexpected events? And, how do the different ways of planning and managing an aircraft portfolio influence the company's financial and stock performance?

The state of scientific literature can only partly be used to answer the question regarding the right strategy to secure air capacity for different business models. Most literature focuses on established passenger airlines reflecting the state of knowledge ex ante or ex post 9/11[3]. Current theories and models, of which some will be mentioned in more detail in the following, just start to consider the impact of the financial and economic crisis 2008. The air transport industry has not been evaluated holistically although, whenever it comes to air capacity and aircraft fleet planning, the key to a successful business seems to lie somewhere

1 Revenue Passenger Kilometers (RPK): "The sum of the products obtained by multiplying the number of revenue passengers carried on each flight leg by the flight leg distance (one fare-paying passenger transported one kilometer)." (Butler & Keller, 2000, p. 671)

2 Freight Ton Kilometers (FTK): also called Revenue Ton Kilometers (RTK); "the number of tones carried multiplied by the number of kilometres flown." (Butler & Keller, 2000, p. 671)

3 9/11: Terroristic attacks in the United States of America on September 11, 2001

between or in a balance of aircraft financing decisions, successful sourcing of capacity and other factors that can influence an air transport company to react flexibly on demand fluctuation.

The following paragraphs summarize trend statements in the air transport industry and describe why these statements are believed to be insufficient and how this thesis is planned to add further insights into the topic of high level financing, sourcing of aircraft, and fleet planning.

Regarding aircraft financing, Abeyratne (2001) describes in his publication *Aviation Trends in the New Millennium* aircraft leasing, especially operating leasing, as "strategic commercial manoeuvre" of airlines in the past 20 years to acquire air capacity without high capital impact. Abeyratne details the benefits of operating leasing and emphasizes risk allocation (between lessor and lessee), tax advantages and immediate operational flexibility. Nevertheless, the long term impact of operating leases in comparison to ownership on a company's financial performance is not considered and its behavior in times of crisis is covered neither by Abeyratne nor in other empirical studies. The theoretical basis for quantitative evaluation of decisions in aircraft acquisition and financing are so far mainly based on Morrell (2007) and Littlejohns & McGairl (2003). Models of both authors include primarily discounted cash flow analyses, capital value analyses, residual value analyses and special tax models and were already tested in practice by e.g. Gibson & Morrell (2004). Yet, all methods focus on concrete buy versus lease decisions on a single aircraft basis and purely consider monetary comparison of the two options. This thesis lifts the decision of buy versus lease to a strategic level and tests whether high level financing structure in an aircraft portfolio has a positive or negative impact on a company's performance in normal business cycles, in times of crisis, and in times of aircraft acquisition or loss. In other words, this thesis tries to find evidence for the hypothesis that the simple ratio of owned versus leased aircraft has an impact on a company's business success.

In terms of aircraft sourcing, Clark's (2007) second edition of *Buying the Big Jets* is probably one of the most elaborated works on aircraft fleet planning. Clark lists precisely the requirements of both long term fleet planning and capacity planning and explains the various possibilities of aircraft acquisition (e.g. purchase options, firm orders, operating leasing). Additional topics touched are airlines' behavior in the business cycle and factors such as life cycles of aircraft types and flexibility in capacity adjustment. Clark's elaborations on the interaction of company profit, firm orders and aircraft deliveries are of special interest for this thesis. Astonishingly, the correlation shows that the majority of companies place firm orders when the market is in an up-cycle or even at peak. Vice versa, aircraft are delivered when capacity demand has declined. Consequently, this lack of synchronization has to be compensated by the airlines with higher flexibility in the overall fleet composition and short to mid term grounding of aircraft. Logically, there is an advantage of synchronizing market development and companies' decisions regarding aircraft acquisition. On the other hand it is understandable that top management is reluctant to approve major capital investments in times of economic downturn. This thesis tries to find quantitative evidence of the advantage of future oriented capacity acquisition in form of firm orders and purchase options and its effect on companies' financial performance and investors.

In daily business, the focus of fleet planning is on calibrating capacity demand versus aircraft size and optimizing total cost in the airline's network. Fleet rationalization plays a major role. Button & Kilpi (2007) further developed the "Fleet Standardization Index" introduced by Pan & Santo (2004) to numerically analyze the correlation of fleet size and harmonization of aircraft types in airlines between 1952 and 2005. The results show that though fleet size constantly increased, the degree of uniformity declined. This is mainly triggered by capacity expansions in economic booms. During such periods, airlines pay less attention to additional costs connected with non-standardized fleets. On the other hand, fleet harmonization increases with growing cost pressure in times of economic downturns. This finding is of interest for this thesis, showing that airlines tend to make changes in their aircraft portfolios regularly, giving the possibility to also strategically improve the fleet composition in terms of aircraft acquisition and financing. This finding also provides an argument for the lack of consequent strategic optimization of aircraft portfolios. It gives room for speculation that the same airlines treat decisions on aircraft acquisition and financing or other opportunities to improve fleet composition with the similar carelessness when not facing cost pressure. This thesis considers the introduction of a new step ahead of actual investment planning and aircraft acquisition in a company's overall fleet planning process. In this step the aircraft portfolio is reviewed from a strategic aircraft sourcing and financing perspective.

A recent work by Merkert & Hensher (2011, p. 686) makes a further step towards the evaluation of "the impact of strategic management and fleet planning on airline efficiency". Merkert & Hensher start with a similar question: "what survival and cost management strategies should airlines choose in order to remain in the market or to grow and perform well under current market conditions?" Their approach is to determine the impact of several fleet mix characteristics, such as aircraft size, aircraft family diversity in the fleet, and age of fleet on "three types of airlines efficiency: technical, allocative and [...] cost efficiency." The method used is DEA[4] efficiency scoring with bootstrap approach. The global sample consists of 56 passenger airlines with data from the years 2007-2009. Some of the findings support hypotheses formulated for this thesis that fleet planning and some fleet

[4] Data Envelopment Analysis

characteristics have a statistically significant influence; however, the measurement of impact on efficiency remains under a strongly operational view. In order not to replicate previous studies and literature in testing operational factors on operational efficiency level, the topic of the influence of basic fleet characteristics is viewed from an even stronger strategic and management oriented level. This is tried by focusing on the ultimate financial performance, i.e. on stock returns, revenue growth, and profit margin.

Trying to change the decision making process of top managers is challenging and requires compelling arguments. It is important to realize that a manager's decision is not only dependent on individual business cases, whether they are compelling or not. Key influencing factors are always the manager's incentive scheme and his or her belief in the impact of a decision in his or her area of responsibility in the company. A simplified example: The global fleet planning manager might have a target agreement regarding the minimization of the overall fleet costs, therefore proposes to buy an old aircraft and to convert it to fit the operational purpose. The chief financial officer (CFO) is incentivized to run the company asset light, therefore prefers operating leases in shorter intervals. The head of sales and marketing has a target on yield and sales numbers; he or she sees a valuable sales argument in a young fleet, therefore wants to acquire a newly built aircraft but does not care how it is financed. The chief executive officer (CEO), who most likely decides finally on investments of this value, will consider all opinions as fair as possible and to his or her best knowledge, but ultimately has to decide what he or she thinks is optimal for the company's shareholders.

If we assume that deciding in favor of shareholders is equal to the long term success of the company, most prominently reflected in the company's financial results and stock price, it is important to provide the final decision maker in an air transport company with detailed information on how aircraft portfolio and fleet plan decisions influence investors and the key financial measures they consider in their own decisions.

This thesis incorporates elements of previous research of Carter & Simkins in 2004 in which the impact of the September 11 attacks, 2001, on U.S. airline stocks was analyzed. Carter & Simkins focused on the difference between passenger and cargo airlines and identified some further financial and non-financial key influencing factors. This thesis extends the scope of Carter & Simkins' research first geographically by including not only U.S. airlines but a wider sample of stock listed global airlines and airline holding companies. Secondly, more time windows are included by also observing stock market's reaction and companies' financial performance in a second external shock (the Financial Crisis 2008), in company specific isolated positive and negative events, and in the normal business cycle. Thirdly,

content is added by testing the influence of basic aircraft portfolio and fleet plan compositions on companies' financial results and stock prices.
In addition, this thesis enriches the recent study of Merkert & Hensher (2011) by significantly expanding the observation period, including specialized freight aircraft, and adding three additional fleet mix characteristics: owned versus leased aircraft, existing versus future planned aircraft, and active versus stored aircraft. Besides that, the different choice of methodology supplements Merkert & Hensher's technical, allocative, and cost efficiency focused analysis with stock market's and financial statements' viewpoints.

The thesis project was started in February 2009 with first interviews of top managers and decision makers from a sample of airlines, aircraft leasing companies, and capital market investors. This group of people expressed a high interest of the aviation industry in the impact of strategic aircraft fleet and fleet planning decisions on stock performance and on financial success of aircraft operating and holding companies. Further, the missing elaboration of the topic in economic and scientific literature was confirmed. (Interviews: Atlas Air, AWAS, LCI Aviation, Macquarie AirFinance, Titan Aviation Leasing, and DVB Bank, 2009).

1.2 Research aim and objectives

Overall aim of this research paper is to prove or disprove the following statement:

Basic aircraft sourcing and financing decisions have a statistically significant influence on a company's financial results and stock price during normal business cycles and in times of crisis, potentially also in times of aircraft acquisitions and losses.

Objectives are to (a) keep the analysis independent from detailed fleet planning decisions such as individual aircraft costs and fleet harmonization, (b) concentrate on the basic acquisition and financing structure buy versus lease and on the basic sourcing decisions of long term firm orders and use of purchase options versus ad hoc planning and (c) further test (or re-test, if already evaluated in earlier research) other high level structural means, such as fleet size, the ratio of stored to active aircraft, or the age composition of a fleet, that might have a statistically relevant effect on the operational flexibility of a company and consequently on its business performance.

Beside the interest of the airline industry in such findings, the results shall also support companies such as global logistics and express service providers. The latter have historically focused on entering new markets and increasing customer share rather than managing capacity like an airline. In future the global logistics and express service providers will have to defend their air transport competitiveness against established airlines in a situation of growing world trade and increasing shortage of air transport capacity.

1.3 Research questions

The key research question of this thesis is based on the unsecure future supply of air capacity in the current competitive situation of global air transport providers and their long term obligations to shareholders:

How should aircraft operating and holding companies strategically source and finance future air capacity in an environment oriented towards financial success and shareholder benefit?

The comprehensive analysis of this key question requires a breakdown of the research scope into the following sub-questions:

1. Which air capacity alternatives and financing options exist?
2. How does the air capacity market develop and is there a need to change the general strategy of how aircraft capacity is sourced and financed?
3. What is the financial situation of aircraft operating and holding companies and do they differ in financial success?
4. Combining aircraft sourcing and financing with financial success: which companies took retrospectively the right decisions with regard to times of crisis, company specific events, and in the normal business cycles and why?
    a. Does the stock market react to different aircraft fleet management and fleet planning in the short and mid term, and if so: how?
    b. What aircraft fleet and fleet planning factors influence a company's financial success positively (negatively) in the long term?

1.4 Research structure and thesis layout

Chapter 1 introduces to the study and details the research background and motivation in light of the latest scientific literature relating to the topic. It further presents aim and objectives of this dissertation and summarizes the research questions. Finally a layout of the research structure and the thesis is given.

Chapter 2 gives an overview on air capacity alternatives and basic financial structures. It describes the players in the air capacity market, elaborates on strategic constraints and requirements for aircraft acquisition and puts the research scope in the perspective of fleet planning.

Chapter 3 provides an outline on the development of the air capacity market from 1993 to the beginning of 2010. It portrays air traffic growth and respective air capacity development in different periods: 1993-2000 (before September 11, 2001), between the two crises (September 11, 2001, and the Financial Crisis 2008), as well as from the Financial Crisis 2008 onwards. Additionally, it gives an overview on industry forecasts and highlights the need for change in behavior regarding fleet optimization and planning.

Chapter 4 introduces to the financial performance of airlines and airline holding companies. Choosing two different perspectives – the view on the stock market and the view on key operating figures in the financial statements – the chapter portrays the financial situation of different companies in the airline and airline holding industry relative to each other.

Chapter 5 summarizes the key statements of the previous chapters. It builds a bridge from the information given on air capacity alternatives and basic financial structures, development of the air capacity market, and financial performance of airlines and airline holding companies, to the research hypotheses and scope described in the next chapter.

Chapter 6 explains research hypotheses and scope. It describes the investor's perspective taken and the choice of the right performance indicators for the subsequent analysis. The key research hypothesis is broken down to testable null and alternative hypotheses and their rationale is outlined in consideration of the current state of literature. Further, the company sample is listed and the observation periods are described superficially.

Chapter 7 constitutes the heart of the thesis. It analyzes the relevance of key financial and non-financial influencing factors on companies' stock performance (stock market's reaction) and financial success. Factors tested include high level aircraft portfolio and fleet plan characteristics in terms of financing and sourcing. Apart from a thorough description of the empirical methodology, the observation periods are defined in more detail. The chapter supplies an exhaustive description of the findings and concludes with a summary of success factors in times of crisis, company specific events and in normal economic cycles.

Chapter 8 provides a discussion of the results of the analysis in comparison with the consulted literature and hypotheses stated in Chapter 6.

Chapter 9 concludes the thesis and recommends on how to use the findings.

Please refer to Figure 1 for a consolidated overview on research structure and thesis layout.

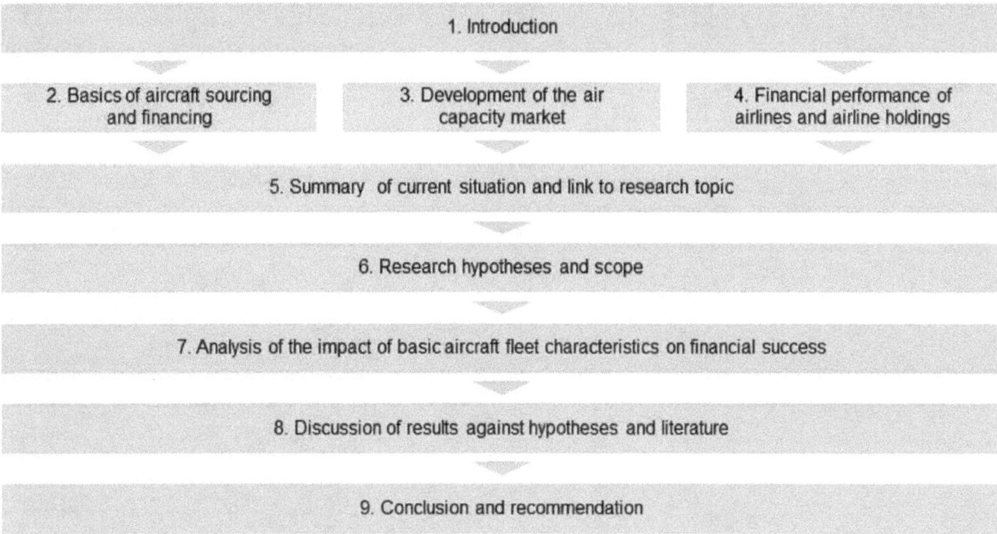

Figure 1: *Overview on research structure and thesis layout*

This figure presents the nine chapters into which both research and thesis are structured:
1. Introduction into research background and motivation, aim and objectives, summary of research questions, overview on research structure & thesis layout, 2. Overview on air capacity alternatives and basic financial structures, players in the market, and research scope in perspective of fleet planning, 3. Summary of the development of the air capacity market 1993-2010, air traffic growth and development 1993-2000 (pre 9/1), between the two crises, and post Financial Crisis 2008, 4. Introduction to the financial performance of airlines and airline holding companies with a view on stock market performance and on key operating figures from financial statements, 5. Summary of key statements and the open topic for research in subsequent chapters, 6. Research hypotheses and scope, 7. Description of the analysis in terms of empirical methodology, data selection, observation periods, and findings, 8. Discussion of the findings against consulted literature and research hypotheses, and 9. Conclusion and recommendation on how to use the findings.

2. Basics of aircraft sourcing and financing

Basis for any analysis and optimization of aircraft portfolios and fleet plans is a profound understanding of the game. Which capacity options exist? Who are the players? The more expertise a company has with regard to market environment and behavior, the better it can prepare for future business. Therefore it is interesting to see how the different types of capacity are handled by the different players.

According to data published by Ascend Worldwide Ltd. (2009), the typical ratio of operating leases to total number of aircraft in passenger and cargo airlines between 1993 and 2008 ranged on average between 10% and 25% with medians of 5%-15% for passenger and 3%-25% for cargo carriers. Future fleet planning is quite divers. Although almost all companies including freight carriers such as UPS and FedEx deposit long term firm orders, purchase options or issue letters of intent to the manufacturer, the extent to which they do so deviates significantly. For example the total commitment in airlines' order books 2009 for new aircraft with deliveries planned up to 2020, varies between 0 and 156 aircraft. Similarly, some companies have as many as 453 options outstanding until 2025, whereas others have none.

This chapter lists the different types of capacity that air transport companies can choose from and restricts the focus of subsequent research to what is called dedicated capacity, i.e. the capacity that a company has most control over and that is usually the most cost sensitive choice in the long term. It further provides an overview on the different players in the aircraft market, describes their basic role and activities and their behavior with regard to aircraft sourcing and financing. The chapter ends with a snapshot on how fleet planning is executed today and how the research topic integrates into the ideal planning process.

2.1 Overview on air capacity alternatives and basic financial structures

There is a variety of different air capacity options companies can choose from to transport passengers and/or cargo. Which alternative or mix of options the companies opt for depends on availability, the individual characteristics of the capacity, and the circumstances under which it is needed. Rationally, key differencing factors of air capacity are (1) schedule control, i.e. the operator's power to control where and when the capacity is available (including legal, regulatory, and safety issues), and (2) time frame, i.e. the anticipated time for which the capacity is used (DHL Express Global Aviation, 2007). Both, schedule control and time frame finally influence the cost of capacity or relative unit cost (e.g. cost in USD

R. Günther, *Impact of Aircraft Sourcing & Financing on Financial Success*,
Edition KWV, https://doi.org/10.1007/978-3-658-24094-3_2

per kilogram transported). Other actuating aspects could be supplier diversification or for some governmental owned airlines even national pride.

Capacity options can be allocated to two major clusters: dedicated capacity and commercial capacity. There is no common definition of the two clusters, but "dedicated" generally refers to capacity over which the operator has full schedule control, "commercial" refers to capacity that is operated and schedule-controlled by a 3rd party. Time frame and certainty of demand play a role, too. Airlines have to handle "the short term assignment problem, when actual demand is known, as well as the long term capacity decision in the face of uncertain demand" (Netessine et al., 2002, p. 375). The first might require the use of commercial capacity as it can be acquired ad hoc, while the latter leads to dedicated capacity, especially when there is a correlation within the demand and capacity substitution is possible in the service of an airline (Netessine et al., 2002).

For an overview on operational air capacity alternatives and key differentiators please refer to Figure 2. In the following, the individual air capacity options are described in more detail. The focus will lie on dedicated capacity. Commercial capacity will only be mentioned briefly as the objective of this thesis is to enable air transport companies to better secure and control their future capacity need, i.e. being less dependent on commercial capacity.

	Dedicated capacity				**Commercial capacity**	
Capacity option	**Purchase**	**Dry lease**	**Wet lease/ ACMI**	**Charter or block space agreement**	**Allotment**	**Spot/ contingency**
Description	Full acquisition of aircraft under operator's own Air Operator Certificate (AOC)	Finance or operating lease of aircraft under lessee's AOC	Lease of aircraft, crew, maintenance and insurance (ACMI) under lessor's AOC	Firmly committed capacity on a specific flight or full flight charter operated by 3rd party air carrier	Reserved capacity on a specific flight operated by 3rd party with cancellation possibility	Ad hoc purchased capacity
Key differentiators						
Schedule control	Yes	Yes	Yes	Yes / no	No	No
Typical time frame	Long-term (>10 years)	Medium-term (2-10 years)	Short-term (< 2 years)	Short-term or low capacity need (< 2 years)	Short-term or low capacity need (seasonal to 1 year)	Ad hoc (< 1 month)
Relative unit cost	Low					

Figure 2: *Overview on operational air capacity alternatives and key differentiators*

This figure presents basic air transport capacity alternatives incl. high level financial structure allocated to one of the two major clusters dedicate capacity and commercial capacity with a description of their three key differentiators schedule control, typical time frame and relative unit cost. For analyses, dedicated capacity was defined as capacity the operator has schedule control over and which is used for a minimum of 3 continuous months (i.e. very short term wet leases or charters are not considered dedicated capacity, also because they are usually utilized ad hoc and with a very high cost). Source is DHL Express Global Aviation (2007).

Purchase

Purchase refers to the full acquisition of the asset under the buyers own Air Operator Certificate (AOC)[5]. The price depends fully on type and age of the aircraft. In 2008, the sticker price[6] for a new commercial commodity jet from the Airbus family ranged approximately from USD 60mn for an A318 with 59 tons Maximum Takeoff Weight (MTOW)[7] to USD 250mn for a A340-600 with 368 tons MTOW (Airbus, 2008a and Airbus, 2008b). In the same year, Boeing listed its new aircraft with sticker prices from USD 55mn for a B737-600 with 66 tons MTOW to USD 300mn for a B747-8 with 442 tons MTOW (Boeing, 2008). Of course, the actual sales prices deviate from the sticker prices based on the individual negotiations between manufacturer and customer.

Used aircraft of the same type bought from manufacturers, leasing companies, or airlines could be acquired for a significantly lower price, completely dependent of course on the physical condition of the aircraft and its life cycle in terms of technology and regulatory condition. For freighters, additionally the option exists to convert passenger aircraft to cargo aircraft. As cargo airlines do not have to serve passengers' thinking that flight safety is linked to the age of aircraft, they can buy older passenger aircraft and convert them into freighters for their own purposes. The overall package is cheaper than buying new freighters, but the issue lies in the availability of conversion slots on the market. Cargo airlines might face a situation where used aircraft would be available, but the missing conversion slot makes the option unfeasible.

From an accounting perspective, purchased aircraft are fully shown on the owner's balance sheet and depreciated over time. In recent years, airlines were sometimes not able to generate savings from their earnings, hence did not have sufficient cash to finance aircraft acquisitions. In these cases, airlines tend to convert their assets, i.e. they sell and lease back the aircraft to/from financial or operating lessors. The transaction "allows airlines to use the generally appreciated value of aircraft to finance additional aircraft, to remove older aircraft from balance sheets while values are still high, to finance investment in other airlines, or to finance their own internal operations (in case of undercapitalized airlines)." (Wensveen, 2007, p. 430)

---

[5] Air Operator Certificate (AOC) in Europe or Air Carrier's Operating Certificate in the United States: document issued to an aeroplane operator by its national safety regulator to officially authorize the ability to conduct safe aeroplane operations. The AOC is based on the terms and conditions of the Joint Aviation Authority under JAR-OPS 1, 1.175 General Rules for Air Operator Certificate (Joint Aviation Authority, 2007)

[6] Sticker price refers to the retail price suggested by the manufacturer for a new aircraft. It is sometimes also called list price and is usually subject to further negotiation for discounts.

[7] The Maximum Takeoff Weight (MTOW) is stated in the aircraft's airworthiness requirements and refers to the absolute maximum weight at which the aircraft is allowed to take off given its structural limits.

Dry lease

A dry lease is the lease of an aircraft excluding ("dry") additional services such as maintenance, insurance or crew, under the lessee's AOC. Dry lease is typically used for time periods starting from two years onwards. The lessee takes the operational risks and rewards from the aircraft during this time. From a financial perspective, dry lease can be further split in finance lease and operating lease (Littlejohns & McGairl, 2003).

Finance lease

Finance lease or capital lease is defined as a dry lease in which one of the three following conditions is met compared to operating lease (Littlejohns & McGairl, 2003):

1. The lessee has the option to purchase the aircraft at an agreed price at the end of the lease term
2. The lease payments account for more than 90%of the aircraft's market value
3. The lease period covers more than 75% of the aircraft's usable life

Financial leases are fully amortized. "This means the lessor receives rental payments that are equal to the cost of the equipment plus a return on the investment" (Kaps, 2000, p. 131). According to Littlejohns & McGairl (2003), from an accounting perspective a finance or capital lease is treated the same as a purchase. The lessee takes most of the risks and rewards of ownership and the aircraft appears on its balance sheet. The lessor on the other hand considers the predefined credit of a single lessee as return on the aircraft rather than the value of the asset.
Cancellation of a financial lease agreement is basically not possible, but the lessee has full operational control over the asset. Hence, the lessee has the obligation to pay the lessor, but has the right to apply other cost reduction measures if needed. These might include subleasing, grounding or transferring the asset to another region, similar to the flexibility associated with owned (purchased) aircraft.

Operating lease

Operating (or service) lease refers to the dry lease of an aircraft with a lease period (from the lessee's perspective) generally significantly shorter compared to the aircraft's usable life. The lease price is set by the market, i.e. it is dependent on a normal supply-demand-relationship like any commercial product and reflects less the actual purchase price of the aircraft. The cost of an operating lease is typically more expensive than owning the aircraft over the same period of time. This is due to the fact that operating leases are usually not fully amortized. "In other words, the payments required under the lease agreement are not sufficient to recover the full cost of the equipment. However, the lease contract is written for a period considerably shorter than the expected economic life of the equipment, and the lessor expects to recover all investment costs through subsequent renewal payments, through subsequent lease contract with other lessors, or by selling the equipment outright" (Kaps, 2000, p. 131). From an accounting perspective, operating leases do not occur on the lessee's balance sheet but as operating expenses in the profit and loss statement (Morrell, 2007).

Operating lease periods usually range from two to ten years, seldom up to 15 years, depending on when the conditions of a finance lease start to apply for the individual aircraft (Frost & Sullivan, 2005). The contract might contain a termination or cancellation clause. This clause gives the lessee the right to cancel the contract before the actual expiration date, which results in high flexibility to react on capacity surplus (Kaps, 2000). However, often the lease agreement does not contain special clauses or only very restricted, which might cause the lessee to face a significant overcapacity when business declines, without the possibility to return, sublease, or transfer the aircraft in the short to mid term. (Crans, 2004)

ACMI

The abbreviation ACMI stands for Aircraft, Crew, Maintenance and Insurance. In an ACMI, the lessor provides not only the basic aircraft but also crew, all necessary maintenance and insurance associated with the asset.

According to Good (2000, p. 371) ACMI is the airlines' answer to the constantly changing and increasingly complex world of aircraft operations. "[…] airlines must now adjust on a more continuous basis to changes in market demand, fleet composition, training, staffing requirements, unscheduled maintenance, and regulatory uncertainties […]". Airlines buffer these uncertainties by using ACMI rather than building up the capacity and resources in-house.

Some companies in the last two decades, most prominent the cargo airline Atlas Air, Inc[8], have specialized in global ACMI outsourcing to other airlines and turned this service into a quite successful business model. The lessee pays per block hour usually with a minimum agreed number of block hours in the contract. The charge typically includes aircraft acquisition costs, crew salaries and expenses, all necessary maintenance effort and the

[8] In the early 1990s demand for air freight services started to grow. Trigger for this were the facts that passenger traffic had been scared by Gulf War related terrorism and that freight was shipped more and more in bulk which did not fit in the belly space of passenger aircraft. Consequently there was a growing demand for freight carriers which not all airlines could meet. The visionary Michael Chowdry, CEO of Atlas Air, Inc. at that time saw in this situation a chance for a new business model: outsourcing of aircraft including the major cost drivers, called ACMI (Aircraft Crew Maintenance, Insurance). The ACMI business turned into a fast-growing sub-segment of the air cargo transport market and Atlas Air became market leader with the world's biggest fleet of Boeing 747 freighters. Atlas Air quickly built a critical market mass and reputation that enabled it to maintain its dominant position with this unique niche product. (Neidl, 2000)

insurance broken down to one hour of aircraft utilization. Further, the lessee carries all other costs or fees (e.g. fuel, ground-handling and landing fees, marketing costs) for operating the aircraft under its own flight number and schedule control (Neidl, 2000).
ACMI is a typical lever to "obtain extra lift capacity without having to make large investments in capital, maintenance, personnel, and other operating costs" (Butler & Keller, 2000, p. 659). The time period typically covered by an ACMI is between one month and two years (in some cases even up to 5 years depending on the individual situation of the lessee and then often connected to legal or regulatory restrictions that the lessee could not meet with owned aircraft).

Wet lease

For the difference between wet lease and ACMI various descriptions exist. Basically, wet lease is similar to ACMI, but does not necessarily include maintenances or insurance. Butler & Keller (2000, p. 673) define wet lease as "a contractual agreement whereby the lessor provides at least an aircraft and a cockpit crew [...]. The lessor maintains operational control of the aircraft while operating the aircraft for the commercial benefit of the lessee."

Charter or block space agreement

Charter or block space agreements refer to firmly committed capacity on a specific flight or full flight charter operated by 3rd party air carrier. Charters and block space agreements can be offered ad hoc by airlines as an on-demand service to a destination without a published time schedule. Other charter types are the typical leisure-oriented passenger charter flights offered to summer destinations. What all charter types usually have in common is that they operate by a non-published schedule and often on seasonal basis. (Wensveen, 2007)

Allotment

Reserved capacity on a specific flight operated by 3rd party with cancellation possibility.

Spot and contingency

Ad hoc purchased capacity on a flight operated by 3rd party air carrier.

Ideally, the different capacity alternatives would be compared and tested according to their interdependencies and effects on a company in terms of operational flexibility and financial impact. However, data from the commercial capacity market are rarely available and even wet leases, ACMIs, and charters, are often not sufficiently made transparent in the annual statements of the airlines. In all three capacity types the aircraft operates under the Air Operator Certificate of the lessor and it is mostly impossible to trace back who leased the aircraft and when. Therefore, the subsequent chapters and the analyses conducted for this thesis focus on the two dedicated capacity alternatives purchase and dry lease, i.e. on the capacity the operator has schedule control over and that has a typical operational time horizon of minimum 2 years (cf. Figure 2). Research can thus focus on those capacity alternatives that can be planned long term and – compared to the other alternatives – operate at the lowest unit price. The capacity alternatives wet lease and charter are usually employed ad hoc or based on legal restrictions with a very high cost, and commercial capacity is commonly known as the most expensive way of ensuring air transport, hence should be avoided whenever possible. With purchase and dry lease, the analysis eventually compares the two remaining "best" options. In any case, the research focuses on the capacity decision in uncertain demand which leads to dedicated capacity as described with the words of Netessine et al. (2002) in the beginning of the chapter.

2.2 Players in the air capacity market

The air transport business is a multiple player industry and the basic activities are clustered around the industry's most important equipment, the aircraft. This chapter gives a brief outline of the two major company clusters represented in the industry: (1) aircraft manufacturers and (2) aircraft operating and holding companies (airlines, leasing companies, logistics companies & integrators), and describes their relationship and interaction.

2.2.1 Aircraft manufacturers

The global airframe supplier market for big commercial jets is almost a duopoly. Figure 3 clearly illustrates this power of the two major manufacturers by showing the deliveries of commercial long-haul and regional jets per manufacturer in the years 1993 to 2008.

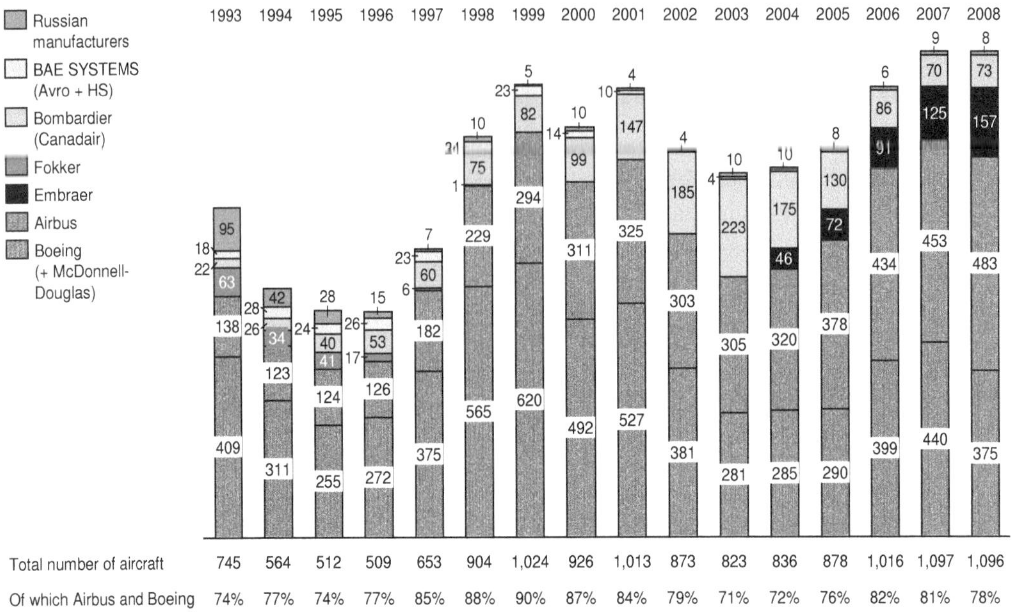

Figure 3: *Deliveries of commercial long-haul and regional jets per manufacturer 1993-2008*

This figure presents aircraft deliveries made by airframe suppliers to their customers (airlines, leasing companies, etc.) based on data retrieved from Ascend Worldwide Ltd. (2009) for the individual years 1993 to 2008. The count of aircraft refers to commercial long-haul and regional jets with a seat capacity of more than 50 seats or freighter equivalent size. Excluded are non-commercial (e.g. military) jets, business and executive jets with a size of equal to or less than 50 seats (or freighter equivalent size) and turboprops. The cluster "Russian manufacturers" includes the air frame suppliers Antonov, Ilyushin, Tupolev and Yakovlev. Boeing includes McDonnell-Douglas.

The two manufacturers Airbus and Boeing produced 74-90% of all aircraft delivered in the years 1993-2008 (Ascend Worldwide Ltd., 2009). Other players such as Russian aircraft suppliers are still regionally focused and despite their capabilities and (still) ongoing consolidation in the regional aircraft industry (Holloway, 1998) have not yet made their way up to the leading airframe manufacturers in the recent years. Only the Brazilian manufacturer of regional jets, Embraer, has significantly increased its deliveries since 2004, ranking number three among the world's airframe suppliers in 2008. The Chinese commercial aircraft manufacturer COMAC[9] started in 2009/10 to produce aircraft in competition to regional jets of Bombardier and Embraer with first deliveries planned in 2011 and 2014, respectively (COMAC, 2010). At the current point in time it is not possible to predict whether COMAC will find its way to the top 7 of the airframe manufacturers displayed in Figure 3.

[9] The Commercial Aircraft Corporation of China, Ltc. (COMAC) was founded May 11, 2008, and started its production of the aircraft COMAC (former ACAC) ARJ21 and C919 in 2009/10. At the time of this research no aircraft had yet been delivered. (COMAC, 2012)

2.2.2 Aircraft operating and holding companies

Airlines

The airline business has gone through extreme times in the last two decades. Starting with the early 1990s recession and an economic upturn between 1994 and 2000 (Morrell, 2007), the airlines had to face the consequences of the terrorist attacks in the United States on September 11, 2001, the Golf War, the SARS epidemic and rising fuel prices in the twenty-first century. In addition, permanently changing regulatory, operational, and technological constraints as well as developments like privatization, global alliances, and electronic commerce have made the airline industry inherently unstable (Liehr et al, 2001).

Most literature about the airline business accentuates its character of marginal long term profitability and cyclical development. Times of rising profits follow periods of declining profits. But, the latter was clearly dominating the industry in the last years. Doganis (2006, p. 1) even described this time as the "deepest crisis the airline industry has ever faced." Figure 4 illustrates the airline industry's cyclical movement based on operating and net profit of the International Civil Aviation Organization (ICAO) scheduled airlines in the years 1989 to 2010.

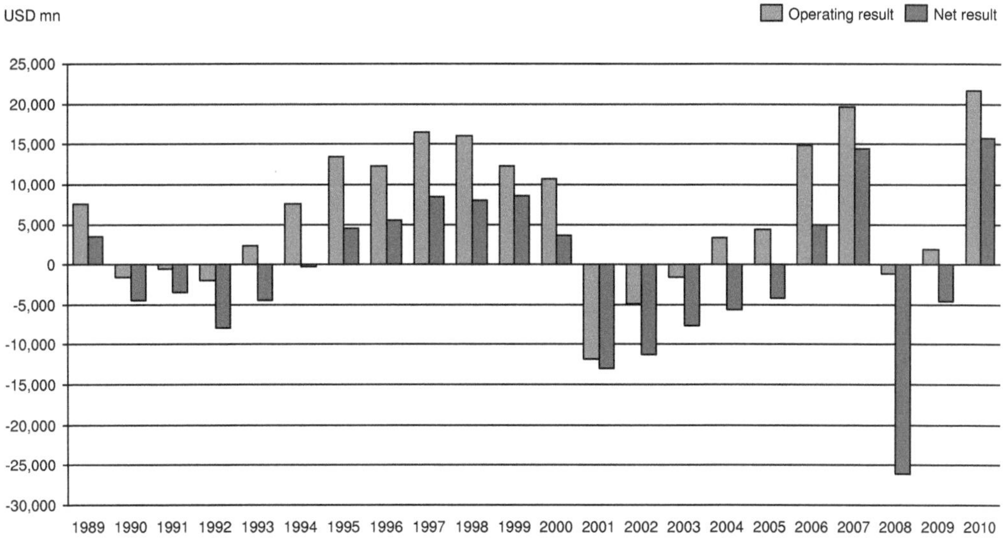

***Figure 4:** Operating and net results of ICAO scheduled airlines 1989-2010*

This figure presents operating and net profit in USD of ICAO scheduled airlines for the years 1989 to 2010. Source is Morrell (2007) for data 1989-2000, based on data from the International Civil Aviation Organization (ICAO). For the years 2001-2010 the corresponding data is based directly on ICAO (2010). The difference between operating and net results can be explained mainly by "net interest paid [but also by] gains or losses on asset sales, taxes and subsidies, and provisions for restructuring" (Morrell, 2007, p. 2).

Many airlines suffered from severe losses since the start of the crisis in 2000, which was accelerated by 9/11 but, as many experts believe, also without shock event, would have caused the same harm just slower to the aviation industry. Some airlines went bankrupt; some found remedy in their government. Merely the U.S. Courts unofficially counted 37 airlines that filed for liquidation (chapter 7) or (often more than once) for reorganization (chapter 11) under the U.S. Bankruptcy Code[10] since the year 2000. The most familiar passenger airlines that filed for chapter 11 were US Airways (for the first time in August 2002), United Airlines (for the first time in December 2002), Delta Air Lines and Northwest Airlines (both September 2005). Freight carriers were significantly less affected by the crisis, though still some of them can be found on the list, e.g. Atlas Air/Polar Air Cargo (January 2004). For a complete list of these airlines, please refer to Appendix 1[11].

Today, the market still comprises of hundreds of commercial airlines, including passenger and cargo. Regardless of progressing consolidation in the airline industry, the market is highly fragmented. Figure 5 and Figure 6 illustrate the market share distribution of the top 250 passenger and freight operators, respectively, based on their actual passengers and cargo transported in the year 2008.

[10] "[U.S.] Bankruptcy laws [...] protect troubled businesses and provide for orderly distributions to business creditors through reorganization or liquidation. [...] The vast majority of [airline] cases are filed under [two of] the three main chapters of the Bankruptcy Code": Chapter 7 and Chapter 11. Chapter 7 is "providing for 'liquidation,' i.e., the sale of a debtor's nonexempt property and the distribution of the proceeds to the creditors." "Chapter 11 is "providing (generally) for reorganization, usually involving a corporation or partnership. A chapter 11 debtor usually proposes a plan of reorganization to keep its business alive and pay creditors over time." (U.S. Courts, 2009)

[11] The information provided on U.S. airlines that filed for liquidation or reorganization under the U.S. Bankruptcy Code between 2000 and 2008 is taken from Air Transport Association (2008) and is based on an unofficial compilation of research. ATA states that the information should not be considered as from an authoritative source as its accuracy is not validated.

Market share of total Revenue Passenger Kilometers (RPK) 2008

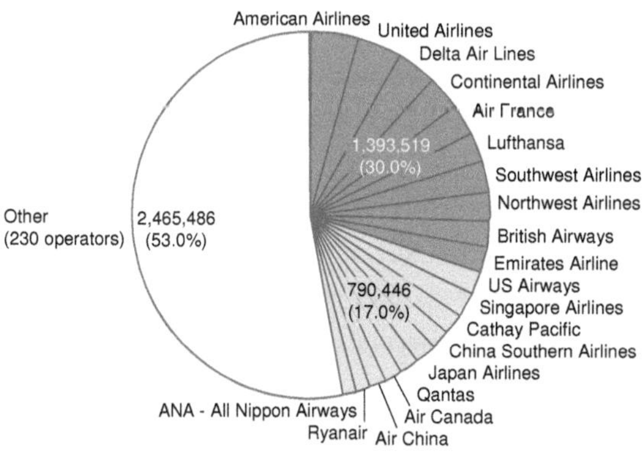

#	Operator	RPK mn	Market share
1	American Airlines	212,037	4.6%
2	United Airlines	177,171	3.8%
3	Delta Air Lines	170,147	3.7%
4	Continental Airlines	133,299	2.9%
5	Air France	129,712	2.8%
6	Lufthansa	126,014	2.7%
7	Southwest Airlines	118,304	2.5%
8	Northwest Airlines	115,332	2.5%
9	British Airways	110,831	2.4%
10	Emirates Airline	100,672	2.2%
	Subtotal top 10	1,393,519	30.0%

#	Operator	RPK mn	Market share
11	US Airways	97,503	2.1%
12	Singapore Airlines	93,626	2.0%
13	Cathay Pacific	90,975	2.0%
14	China Southern Airlines	83,184	1.8%
15	Japan Airlines	82,122	1.8%
16	Qantas	81,438	1.8%
17	Air Canada	74,718	1.6%
18	Air China	66,013	1.4%
19	Ryanair	62,000	1.3%
20	ANA - All Nippon Airways	58,866	1.3%
	Subtotal next 10	790,446	17.0%
Σ	**Total top 20**	**2,183,964**	**47.0%**

Figure 5: *Airlines' market share of total revenue passenger kilometers (RPK) 2008*

This figure presents market share of the top 20 operators of air freight versus the total market based on revenue passenger kilometers (RPK) 2008. Data source is Ascend Worldwide Ltd. (2009). The operator list is not exhaustive. The total market is defined as the total RPKs of the top 250 operators which are represented with RPK figures in the database. For some smaller operators no data are available; nevertheless the big players are included in the source.

Market share of total Freight Ton Kilometers (FTK) 2008

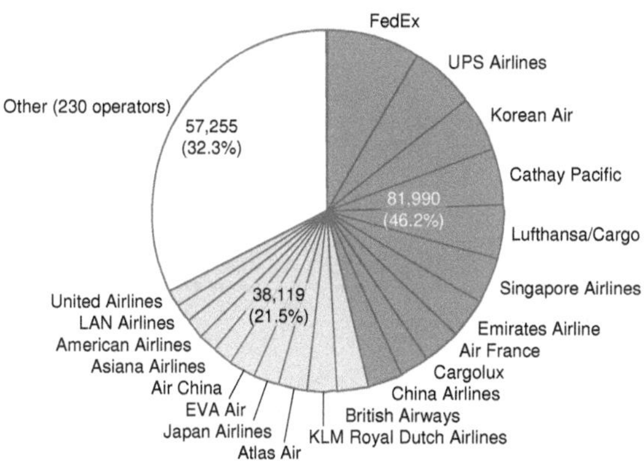

#	Operator	FTK mn	Market share
1	FedEx	15,463	8.7%
2	UPS Airlines	10,024	5.7%
3	Korean Air	9,006	5.1%
4	Cathay Pacific	8,842	5.0%
5	Lufthansa/Lufthansa Cargo	8,283	4.7%
6	Singapore Airlines	7,590	4.3%
7	Emirates Airline	6,156	3.5%
8	Air France	5,831	3.3%
9	Cargolux	5,411	3.1%
10	China Airlines	5,384	3.0%
	Subtotal top 10	81,990	46.2%

#	Operator	FTK mn	Market share
11	British Airways	4,837	2.7%
12	KLM Royal Dutch Airlines	4,787	2.7%
13	Atlas Air	4,718	2.7%
14	Japan Airlines	4,307	2.4%
15	EVA Air	4,077	2.3%
16	Air China	3,487	2.0%
17	Asiana Airlines	3,267	1.8%
18	American Airlines	2,928	1.7%
19	LAN Airlines	2,907	1.6%
20	United Airlines	2,805	1.6%
	Subtotal next 10	38,120	21.5%
Σ	**Total top 20**	**120,109**	**67.7%**

Figure 6: *Airlines' market share of total freight ton kilometers (FTK) 2008*

This figure presents market share of the top 20 operators of air freight versus the total market based on freight ton kilometers (FTK) 2008. Data source is Ascend Worldwide Ltd. (2009). The operator list is not exhaustive. The total market is defined as the total FTKs of the top 250 operators which are represented with FTK figures in the database. For some smaller operators no data are available; nevertheless the big players are included in the source with the exception of DHL. As this company makes use of a variety of different operators its FTK cannot be easily consolidated and are spread over several smaller operators not listed in the top 20.

Looking at the top 250 airlines in terms of revenue passenger kilometers (RPK)[12], no operator has a market share larger than 4.6% (American Airlines). The top 10 passenger airlines own approximately 30% of the market, the top 20 together merely 47% in maximum. This estimate can be considered upper limit as the real number of passenger airlines is more around 800-1000 operators and including them would downsize the market share of the major airlines to some even more.

The freight market appears only slightly different. Based on freight ton kilometers (FTK)[13], and a peer group of the top 250 freight carriers in the market, the operator with the biggest share of 8.7% is FedEx. The top 10 freighters own 46.2%, the top 20 in total approximately 67.7% of the market. Again, this numbers show upper market share limits. One exception among the freight carriers is DHL. This company makes use of a variety of different operators and its FTKs cannot be consolidated as they are spread over several smaller operators. In sum DHL would certainly rank among the top 10 freight carriers. Some companies appear in both illustrations as some operators are playing equally good in both passenger and cargo markets.

Airlines naturally operate almost all commercial aircraft, but they are also yet the biggest single owner of air capacity in form of aircraft (cf. Figure 7). Though the ownership share of commercial airlines and airline holding companies of all Airbus and Boeing aircraft decreased from 52% to 47% between 1993 and 2009, they still lead the market ahead of banks, special purpose companies, and financial lessors with 38% and operating lease companies with 15%.

[12] Revenue passenger kilometers (RPK); "the sum of the products obtained by multiplying the number of revenue passengers carried on each flight leg by the flight leg distance (one fare-paying passenger transported one kilometer)". (Butler & Keller, 2000, p. 671)

[13] Freight ton kilometers (FTK); is the equivalent measure of RPK for freight, i.e. one FTK is equal to one metric tonne of revenue load transported for one kilometer in distance. An airline's total FTKs over time is the sum of all FTKs on all flights in the same period.

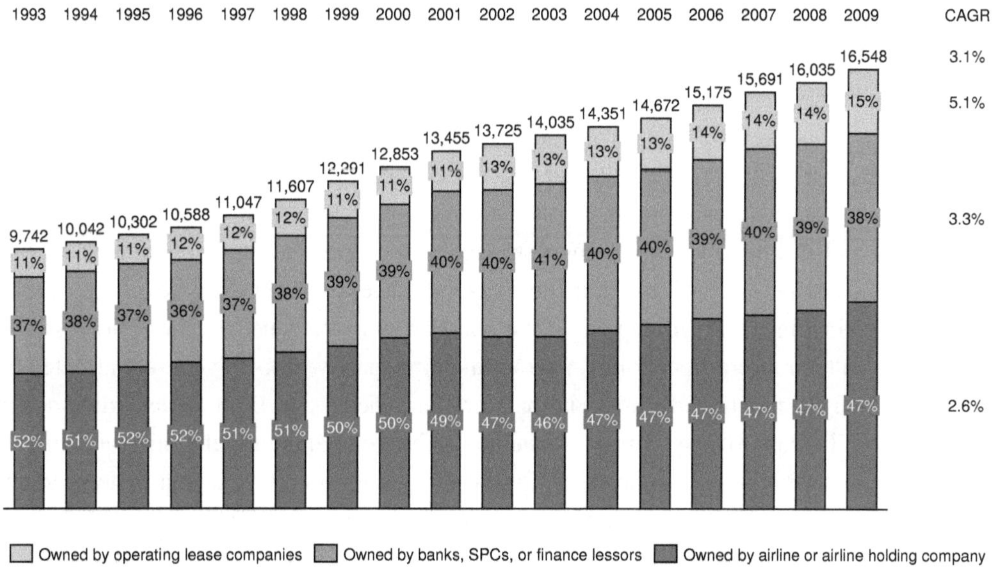

Figure 7: *Ownership share of the three major owner categories in Airbus and Boeing aircraft 1993-2009*

This figure presents the percentage share and respective compounded annual growth rates of the three major owner categories 1) airlines and airline holding companies, 2) banks, special purpose companies (SPCs), or financial lessors, and 3) operating lease companies in total number of aircraft from Airbus and Boeing in the years 1993 to 2009. Boeing includes McDonnell-Douglas. Excluded are non-commercial owner categories: air taxi operators/executive charters, military airlines, government or military operators, and private or corporate operators. Further, the following owner categories were neglected because of size: broker/dealer/ferry companies, fractional operators, manufacturers, trust companies, and unknown owners. Data source is Ascend Worldwide Ltd. (2009).

Nevertheless, these other owner categories together already possess more than half of all Airbus and Boeing aircraft worldwide and both financial owners and operating lease companies show with 3.3% and 5.1% a higher compound annual growth rate (CAGR) between 1993 and 2009 than airlines and airline holding companies (2.6%). Thus, if we believe in a similar constant growth (3.1%) of aircraft numbers in the future, it can be expected that the ownership share of airlines in their most important equipment will further decrease. The question yet remains open whether this will in the long term restrict or positively or negatively influence the performances of airlines.

What are the challenges airlines will have to face in the twenty-first century? Doganis (2006) elaborated on several topics, the most critical of which can be summarized in a few keywords: increasing open skies and abandonment of the nationality rule[14], consolidation[15],

[14] With increasing liberalization in the air transport industry and further opening up of access to foreign markets, national airlines will face increasing international competition. The progressive abandonment of the nationality rule will escalate this trend. "Hitherto, this has required governments to designate airlines to operate their country's traffic rights only if they were 'substantially owned and effectively controlled' by nationals of their own country." (Doganis, 2006, p. 20)

cutting costs at declining yield[16], and impact of environmental regulations. On top of the major future challenges, many airlines struggled with the short term survival of the 9/11 crisis the industry had just experienced. Independent of future growth forecast, many airlines were hit so severely that survival became the major objective in the years 2004-2007. Therefore, it is almost sarcastic that just as the market seemed to show mercy with the airline industry a new economic and financial crisis burst in at end of 2008. Once more, airlines had and still have to rethink their strategies and make essential adjustments to stay profitable and competitive. All in all, the airlines will have to trigger every lever they can to guarantee their long term competitiveness in the market. One of these levers will definitively be their aircraft portfolio. Aircraft and air capacity, respectively, are affected by all the challenges mentioned above in one or the other way. Both, consolidation and bankruptcy will lead to less capacity available. Environmental regulations will further trigger decommissioning and renewal programs for aging aircraft, causing a demand for new aircraft and conversions which airframe manufacturers will most likely not be able to supply.

Leasing Companies

Abeyratne (2001, p. 14) states that "[...] a lease at law is essentially a commercial arrangement whereby a lessor (or equipment owner) conveys to the lessee (or operator of the equipment) for valuable consideration in the form of rentals, over a period of time specified in the lease agreement, the right to use the equipment. The lessee is legally obligated to return to the lessor the equipment he leases at the expiration of the term of the lease, in reasonably good order, leaving a margin for wear and tear of normal usage."

Nowadays, leasing is well known in many industries. One can lease real estate, a car or even smaller equipment, in terms of size and value, such as a printer. The principle of leasing is always the same. Possession is transferred without ownership from the lessor to the lessee with the benefits of spreading the financial risk and increasing flexibility (at least in the short term and depending on the characteristics of the asset). The lessor buys the land or equipment and leases it to another party for a rental charge higher than its own amortization of the capital costs, herewith earning a profit over the life of the asset. On the other side, the lessee can choose the asset, e.g. based on its ad hoc or seasonal demand, and pays the rental charges from its operating cash without having to take the burden of a loan or mortgage or touch its cash reserves to purchase the asset outright.

---

[15] According to Doganis (2006, p. 21-22) there will be "two parallel developments: growing consolidation into larger operating companies and, at the same time, growing concentration of these and other airlines into multinational alliances. [...] A period of instability will occur as soon as the nationality and ownership constraints are relaxed and cross-border acquisitions and mergers become possible."

[16] Resulting from an ongoing downward trend in real fare levels which will escalate with open skies, further growth of low-cost airlines, and the shift from a supplier to a consumer market in times of online purchase (not only in the passenger but also in the freight market). (Doganis, 2006)

Aircraft leasing emerged in the 1970s and developed throughout the 1980s and 1990s mainly because of three fundamental economic situations. Firstly, the commercial aviation boom in the 1980s which caused a tremendous need for capacity when especially smaller airlines could not take the financial risk of owning aircraft. Secondly, the economic downturn and the ensuing financial crisis in the 1990s in which raising funds to finance aircraft became even more challenging. Thirdly, the increasing globalization of airline operations with the deregulation of air transportation in which airlines newly obtained traffic rights to operate into and within specific countries but their aircraft did not meet the legal and regulatory requirements to actually execute the operations. (Abeyratne, 2001)[17]

Beside these three fundamental reasons, acting as an aircraft lessor becomes further attractive because of the relationship between aircraft price and lease rate. Aircraft values change significantly over the aviation industry cycle. Gorjidooz & Vasigh (2010, p. 1) support this statement with their recent study of Aircraft Valuation in Dynamic Air Transport Industry in which they evaluate the factors influencing the value of Boeing 737 and 767 as well as Airbus 320 and 330. They summarize that "external factors, such as market demand and its elasticity, fuel cost, and environmental regulations" are even more important than "internal factors directly related to the aircraft", such as age, size, fuel efficiency, etc. "The external factors are extremely important because they indicate where in the aviation industry cycle the aircraft is and this, in turn, has the greatest impact on the aircraft value."

As described before, the typical rental system charges a mark up over the normal amortization over the aircraft's life time. Hence, one would agree that changes in the underlying price of an aircraft should also be reflected in the lease rate. But although lease rates on short term basis (daily and weekly) are very volatile, they fluctuate in the long term (annually) significantly less than prices for new aircraft. This gives leasing companies room for opportunistic buying and consequently even higher profits, because aircraft are bought for a relatively lower price than actually translated into a lease rate. This becomes clearer by looking at the development of purchase price versus annual lease rate of two exemplary commodity aircraft, Boeing's 747 and Airbus' 320, over the last decade (cf. Figure 8).

[17] Bi- and multi-lateral agreements between countries grant airlines the right to operate in other countries' territory. A group of generalized agreements are commonly referred to as the "freedoms of the air" (Schwenk & Giemulla, 2005 and Bartlik, 2007):

1st freedom:	The right to overfly the territory of another state other than the state of registration/of the operator
2nd freedom:	The right to make technical stops in another state than the state of registration/of the operator
3rd freedom:	The right to carry passengers, cargo, mail from the state of the operator into another state
4th freedom:	The right to carry passengers etc. from another state into the state of the operator
5th freedom:	The right to carry passengers etc. from another state into a third country
6th freedom:	The right to carry passengers etc from another country via the state of the operator into a third country
7th freedom:	The right to carry passengers etc. into another country and from there into a third country
8th freedom:	The right to fly cabotage, which means to fly domestically into another country

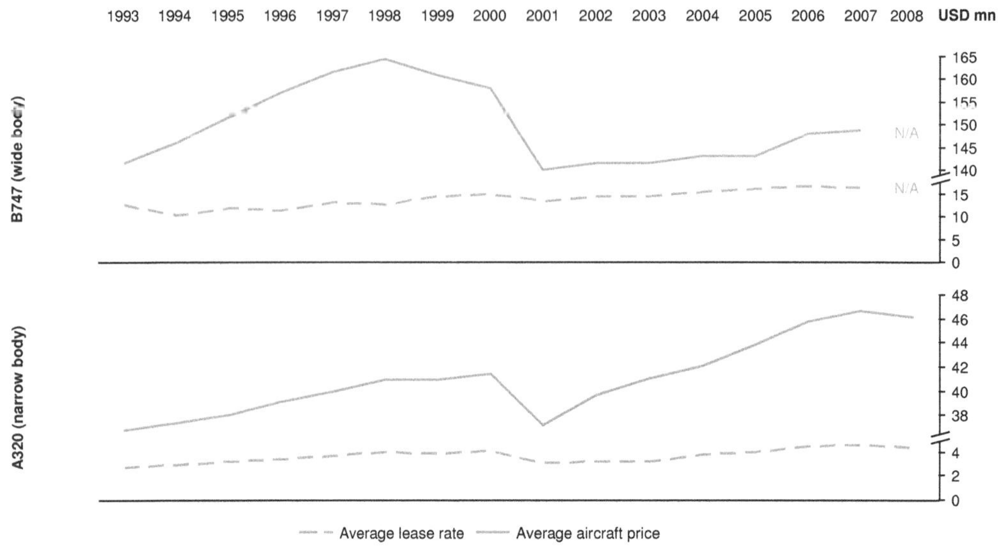

Figure 8: *Development of aircraft prices versus annual lease rates 1993-2008 (examples: B747 and A320)*

This figure presents the development of average aircraft prices versus average annual lease rates in million USD from the year 1993 to 2008 at the example of one wide body and one narrow body commodity aircraft. The wide body aircraft is represented by a Boeing 747-400F, the narrow body by an Airbus 320-200. Prices refer to the purchase value of a new aircraft in the respective year. Likewise, annual lease rates were calculated based on monthly rentals of a new aircraft in the same year. Raw data for calculations were provided by the Aircraft Value Analysis Company (AVAC), 2008.

All this laid the ground for the successful business model of aircraft leasing companies. The number of orders placed by financial and operating lessors (incl. banks and special purpose companies) over the last years was growing relative to the market cycles. In 2008, the number of orders equaled with 581 aircraft 34% of all commercial aircraft orders placed (Ascend Worldwide Ltd., 2009). Figure 9 illustrates aircraft orders placed by financial and operating lease companies vs. total orders placed in the years from 1993 to 2008.

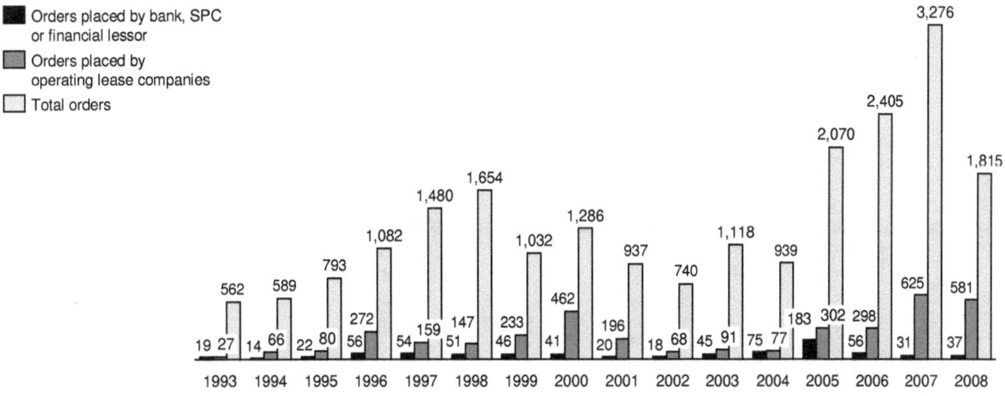

Orders by bank, SPC or financial lessor as % of total	3.1%	2.1%	2.5%	4.0%	3.2%	2.8%	3.5%	2.3%	1.7%	2.2%	3.6%	6.9%	7.2%	2.0%	0.8%	1.5%
Orders by operating lease companies as % of total	4.4%	9.9%	8.9%	19.3%	9.4%	7.9%	17.8%	25.8%	17.0%	8.2%	7.3%	7.1%	11.8%	10.8%	15.9%	23.9%
Orders by both as % of total	8.2%	13.6%	12.9%	30.3%	14.4%	12.0%	27.0%	39.1%	23.1%	11.6%	12.2%	16.2%	23.4%	14.7%	20.0%	34.0%

Figure 9: *Aircraft orders placed by financial and operating leasing companies vs. total orders placed 1993-2008*

This figure presents aircraft orders placed by banks, special purpose companies (SPCs) and financial lessors as well as operating lease companies versus total number of "commercial" orders placed in the years from 1993 to 2008. Total orders exclude "non-commercial" operator categories such as Air Taxi Operator/Executive Charter, Military Airline, Government or Military Operator (Military Aircraft), Private, Government or Corporate Operator. All raw data were retrieved from Ascend Worldwide Ltd. (2009).

Aircraft leasing companies are generally classified into two clusters: independent service providers and original equipment manufacturers (OEMs). According to Frost & Sullivan (2005) the industry is already somewhat consolidated with the top 20 players owning 95% of market share. The independent service providers are dominating the OEMs and the top two players in this cluster of independent service providers own even more than 50% of the total market share. Still, it is not surprising that manufacturers have entered the leasing business to gain a share of the good positioning of leasing companies, first of all Boeing Capital. Figure 10 illustrates the distribution of the aircraft leasing market over the top 20 participants (Frost & Sullivan, 2005).

Market share of global asset portfolio 2004

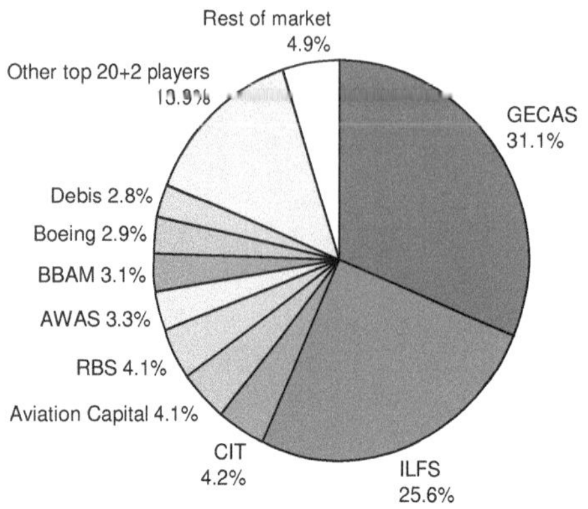

Company (top 20 players)	Cluster
GE Commercial Aviation Service (GECAS)	Independent
International Lease Finance Corporation (ILFC)	Independent
Aircraft Leasing CIT Group (CIT)	Independent
Aviation Capital / Boullioun	Independent
RBS Aviation Capital	Independent
AWAS (a Morgan Stanley company)	Independent
Babcock & Brown Aircraft Management (BBAM)	Independent
debis AirFinance	Independent
Singapore Aircraft Leasing Enterprise (SALE)	Independent
GATX Corporation	Independent
Pegasus Aviation	Independent
Pembroke Group	Independent
Willis Lease Finance	Independent
Bavaria International Aircraft Leasing	Independent
Boeing Capital	OEM
Cessna Finance (a Textron company)	OEM
United Technologies	OEM
BAE Systems Capital	OEM
ECC Leasing Co. Ltd. (an Embraer company)	OEM
Bombardier Capital	OEM

***Figure 10:** Aircraft leasing companies and their share of global asset portfolio 2004*

This figure presents participants in the aircraft leasing market and their market share of the global asset portfolio 2004. Leasing companies are allocated to one of the two major clusters, independent service providers (Independent) and original equipment manufacturers (OEMs). The category "other top 20 players" in the illustration of the market shares includes Singapore Aircraft Leasing Enterprise, GATX Corporation, Pegasus Aviation, Pembroke Group, Willis Lease Finance, Bavaria International Aircraft Leasing, United Technologies, BAE Systems Capital, ECC Leasing Co. Ltd., as well as (not listed in the top 20 players) World Star Aviation and Aviation Group. All figures are rounded. Source of the information is Frost & Sullivan (2005); no more recent market share data were available.

Within the aviation industry, timely availability of aircraft is of high importance. Most leasing companies see aircraft as an investment and secure aircraft early in the process to be able to lease the capacity to the airlines whenever they need it. According to Clark (2007, p. 231) "more than one quarter of future production by the leading airframe manufacturers Boeing and Airbus are destined for the leasing companies". Evidence for this can also be found in the aircraft fleet database of Ascend Worldwide Ltd. (2009). Here, approximately 20% of all firm orders at Boeing and Airbus for the years 2010 to 2020 have been placed by finance and operating lessors (cf. Figure 11).

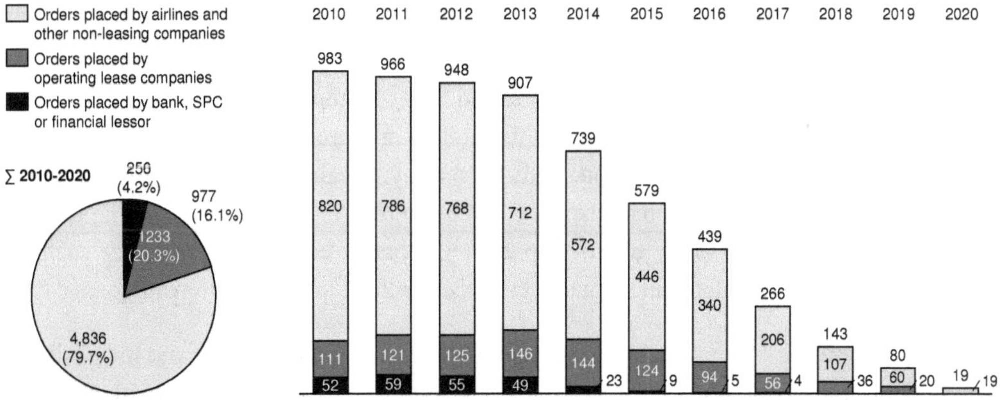

	2010	2011	2012	2013	2014	2015	2016	2017	2018	2019	2020
Share of bank, SPC or financial lessor as % of total	5.3%	6.1%	5.8%	5.4%	3.1%	1.6%	1.1%	1.5%	0.0%	0.0%	0.0%
Share of operating lease companies as % of total	11.3%	12.5%	13.2%	16.1%	19.5%	21.4%	21.4%	21.1%	25.2%	25.0%	0.0%
Total share as % of total	16.6%	18.6%	19.0%	21.5%	22.6%	23.0%	22.6%	22.6%	25.2%	25.0%	0.0%

Figure 11: *Orders placed at Airbus and Boeing by owner category 2010-2020*

This figure presents aircraft orders at Boeing and Airbus for the years 2010 to 2020 by 1. banks, special purpose companies (SPCs) and financial lessors as well as 2. operating lease companies versus 3. total number of "commercial" orders including orders by airlines, airline holding companies and other smaller non-leasing companies. Total orders exclude "non-commercial" owner categories Air Taxi Operator/Executive Charter, Military Airline, Government or Military Operator (Military Aircraft), Private, Government or Corporate Operator. All raw data were retrieved from Ascend Worldwide Ltd. (2009).

Manufacturers face a constant challenge to find the right balance of handling leasing companies as customers versus competitors, i.e. "the manufacturer has an interest in regulating how many aircraft are in the hands of the leasing companies. Too many, and the manufacturer may risk competing with the lessors to place aircraft. Too few, and opportunities to place aircraft may be less evident. One important function of the leasing companies is to place capacity in airlines that would not otherwise be in a position to purchase. Thus the market coverage of aircraft types is broadened, perhaps paving the way [for] direct purchase at a later stage." (Clark, 2007, p. 231)

The airlines' perspective is summarized by Frost & Sullivan (2005, p. 1-1) as follows: "today, with a structured aircraft leasing industry, airlines no more fancy nor can afford to own all the aircraft in their fleet." Although it cannot be denied that leasing aircraft is very compelling for especially small airlines, the question that remains unanswered is whether some airlines already rely too much on the aircraft leasing industry and whether avoiding the financial risk anticipated with the ownership of aircraft really outweighs higher costs per unit and less flexibility in the long term.

Forwarders, logistics providers, and integrators

Freight forwarders, logistics service providers, and also – except UPS and FedEx which are usually listed among the air cargo airlines – integrators are rarely mentioned when it comes to air capacity and aircraft utilization. This is mainly because these companies follow business models which include air transportation but do not "require" thinking as an airline. Most of the firms do not manage own capacity, i.e. prefer commercial capacity such as block space agreements, allotment, spot and contingency to ship their customers' goods.

The air freight business is naturally an international business because short and increasingly also medium range intra-continental transport focuses on cost efficient road and rail transport. Looking at the inter-continental market, the air cargo supply side can be characterized as an oligopoly in which freight forwarders act as strong intermediaries between the cargo airlines which actually transport the goods and the end customer whose goods are transported. The shippers' or forwarders' market share is as high as approximately 90% compared to direct sales by cargo airlines of 10% (Aberle, 2003).

Air freight, which started as a niche product, developed throughout past decades and today plays what is described by Chiavi (2005, p. 490 and p. 499) as "a vital role in supporting the globalization of production and distribution processes driven from international business opportunities." He argues that the reaction of air freight demand and supply on economic, regulatory and institutional developments in the past 40-50 years shaped what we call nowadays logistics service. Primarily, "the trends of liberalization, the attractiveness of low cost countries and enforced JIT [just in time] strategies empowered a new process of global relocation of production and distribution, as well as an enhancement of logistics concepts." Logistics companies are, simply speaking, nothing else than former forwarders with new value adding services. With increasing competition and in light of an easily substitutable product, some forwarders integrated into or were acquired by logistics service providers in order to create a new competitive advantage. Precondition for a successful integration are logistics know-how, significant investments in assets, equipment and IT as well as high service quality, i.e. the entry barriers to the logistics market are high and not many companies manage to make the step (Aberle, 2003). However, the market segment of logistics providers is increasing and the outsourcing trend of logistics over the past 20 years accelerated the growth of so called third-party logistics (3PL)[18]. "Much of the burgeoning 3PL business is carried out by major freight forwarders [...]. These firms leverage the volume of the shipments they control, their warehouse space [...], their expertise in state-of-the-art logistics practice and their advanced IT systems to lower the cost of portions of the customer's supply chain" (Leinbach & Capineri, 2007, p. 9).

[18] First party is the shipper, second party is the recipient, third party is the service provider that takes over logistics functions that were previously performed by either the shipper or the recipient. (Leinbach & Capineri, 2007)

Integrators are another group of air freight transport companies. In distinction to normal cargo airlines, "integrators do not leave the air cargo transportation chain as a sequence of independent, single activities, but integrate it into a holistic, comprehensive concept, covering the transportation from door to door – from the shipper up to the consignee" (Koch & Kraus, 2005, p. 518). In other words, "A critical difference between integrators and other air freight carriers is that the former deal directly with customers rather than working through forwarders." (Bowen & Slack, 2007, p. 44) The key element of an integrator's business is its transportation network, which is subject to regular changes and high fluctuation based on the permanent need to adapt their products to changing customer expectations and market regulatory environment. The integrator defines a transportation network door-to-door which then is being filled with respective transport mode needed, including air transport. Koch & Kraus (2005, p. 524) further state that in the general decision process of network design, airport choice and aircraft fleet selection, the latter takes most time and contains a major element of financial risk evaluation. "In order to avoid the financial risks involved in developing an own aircraft fleet and to maintain a certain flexibility regarding aircraft types and numbers utilized, some express carriers have decided to have parts of their network operated by partner or full-charter airlines." Of course, this risk averseness has different degrees in the industry, i.e. not every integrator does avoid managing an own fleet.

The integrator industry is dominated by the four major players FedEx, UPS, DHL and TNT. The two U.S. based integrators Federal Express (FedEx) and United Parcel Service (UPS) for example have historically managed their fleet similar to an airline and usually appear as one in annual cargo reports and statistics. In 2009, FedEx operated a fleet of 379 aircraft of which 96% was owned or finance leased and UPS operated 266 all fully owned or finance leased aircraft[19] (Ascend Worldwide Ltd., 2009).

On the other extreme, the European integrator TNT has only recently started to invest in own aircraft and nowadays owns 48 aircraft (22 owned, 10 leased, 16 chartered) next to a variety of different partners that operate the rest of TNT's required air capacity (TNT, 2009).

DHL's air capacity management is probably the most interesting or "odd" or simply the one that is most intransparent for outsiders. Founded in 1969, DHL expanded quickly in the international market as an independent air express courier. Parallel to its fast growth, DHL invested in own aircraft and operated several freight airline subsidiaries worldwide. In 2002,

[19] The total number of aircraft and percentage of owned and capital leased aircraft was retrieved from Ascend Worldwide Ltd. as the information stated in the annual reports of FedEx and UPS is insufficient in the required breakdown of financial versus operating lease and is not providing full transparency on the consolidation of short term operating leased aircraft and potentially different considerations of small feeder aircraft. Information on supplemental aircraft under agreements with cancellation terms of less than 30 days notice – not considered dedicated aircraft in this thesis (cf. Chapter 2.1) – is only partly disclosed.

DHL was fully acquired by the German postal service provider, Deutsche Post World Net (today Deutsche Post DHL), and got integrated into a multi-national and multi-business group providing integrated mail, express and logistics services. The original express sector became a separate division in a company that slowly but surely adopted the thinking of a logistics service provider. Investment in own aircraft became rare and the portion of partners and 3rd party operators increased significantly. Most recently (2010/2011), the company decided to purchase some more aircraft in view of its re-fleeting programs. Today, DHL's overall dedicated fleet in terms of aircraft numbers (including own aircraft and those operating under DHL schedule control) would easily rank among the world's largest cargo airlines together with FedEx and UPS. However, the intransparent network of operators flying for DHL only allows insiders to judge on the exact number of aircraft.

What most of these firms – independent from whether they run under the business model of forwarders, logistics companies or integrators – have in common is that transport is only one aspect out of many playing a role in their business models (Chiavi, 2005). Further, air transport is just one transportation mode these companies choose from and it is "usually a derivative or consequence of decisions taken on higher level. These decisions yield a set of transportation service requirements, such as lead time, reliability, and so on, which are later translated in transport decisions. In other words: [these companies] generally do not specifically demand a special transportation mode but rather a transport performance." (Henstra, Ruijgrok and Tavasszy, 2007, p. 135) As a consequence, forwarders, logistics companies or integrators mostly opt for a solution which from their perspective appears the easiest to acquire air transport capacity. This solution is not seen in managing own capacity but rather in taking it from the commercial market. Managing air capacity is simply seen as non-core element of the business and therefore is handled similar to any other service that would underlie an outsourcing decision. With changing capacity supply and demand, and assuming that logistics providers and definitively express service providers cannot fully dispense of air transport, a rethinking of the strategy to acquire and secure future air capacity might be required.

2.3 Fleet Planning

"There is an old joke that in the early years of airlines, it was the pilots who bought aircraft. Then we went through a phase in which fleet planning was driven by engineers. After that, the marketing people got their hands on the process […]. Life is not, of course, that simple any more. […] So the focus has shifted away from the engineer to other players: the commercial teams, who determine route structures, fare policies and brands; the financial controllers, who determine investment levels, sources of funds and whether any money can be spent at all" (Clark, 2007, p. 3).

Fleet planning today is a recurring sequence of consecutive steps in which an airline determines the capacity need at present and for a variety of periods of time into the future (short-, mid-, and long term planning) and based on this procures aircraft by different means of financing. "The airlines choose their network structures and construct capacities while demands are unknown." "[Only] after uncertainty is resolved, they determine the [concrete capacity] to offer in each leg constrained by their capacities built earlier." (Hu, 2010, p. 98) Key decision criteria for any planning should always be long term profitability.

Figure 12 summarizes the ideal aircraft fleet planning process and integrates a new step "review of strategic sourcing and financing" to position the research focus of this paper in the regular planning sequence.

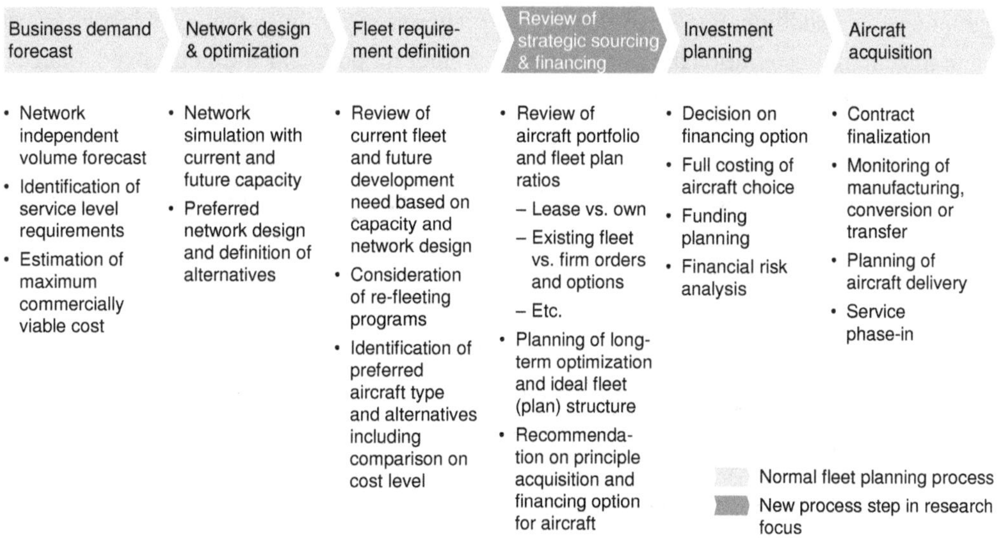

Figure 12: *Review of strategic sourcing & financing in the ideal aircraft fleet planning process*

This figure presents a summary of the ideal aircraft fleet planning process from business demand forecast to aircraft acquisition and delivery, including the new process step "review of strategic sourcing & financing". This step is in focus of this thesis. Strategic sourcing and financing is defined as the process step in which an aircraft operating company reviews its existing aircraft portfolio and fleet plan to find the right mix of e.g. owned versus leased or existing fleet to firm orders and options that enables to flexibly react on capacity changes and minimize long term risk associated with the capacity. This evaluation and optimization should ideally take place imbedded between the definition of fleet requirements and investment planning. Source of the information is DHL Express Global Aviation (2007).

The ideal process starts with the business forecast of the commercial department. It predicts sales volume on different origin and destination (O&D) pairs – in the best case unrestricted by the currently existing network of the company – to then enhance it with requirements regarding service level and maximum commercially viable costs, the latter linked to the company's fare policy and yield competition on O&Ds. Based on this information the network planning team can in the next step run network simulations with current and future capacity requirements and define the preferred network design and possible phasing over the next years. Within the optimal network, capacity demand is calibrated versus aircraft size and number and routing defined in a way that total costs in the network are minimized. Like every single step in this process, so network planning also is mostly an annually recurring activity to refine the future network design with the latest information available. Once the preferred network and routing are designed, the actual definition of the aircraft fleet can begin. At this step, the existing fleet is reviewed to identify whether it fits to the adjusted network. Here, a first fleet assignment takes place as described in various studies by Jarrah (2000), Rexing, Barnhart & Kniker (2000), Bard, Yu & Argüello (2001), and Smith & Johnson (2006). For new capacity needed, alternative aircraft types are identified and rationally compared with regard to availability, technical status, operational cost, and regulations. Additionally, re-fleeting programs with the objective to standardize/harmonize/rationalize and renew the aircraft portfolio are considered (Pan & Santo, 2004). Finally, a decision is made on how many of which aircraft type are needed over the next years.

When the aircraft is selected, it is usually time for concrete investment planning and funding of the individual aircraft, but it is not yet clear whether the fleet can, from a strategic perspective, be further balanced to better secure long term capacity and to positively influence financial performance measures and anticipated stock market's behavior. Airlines still seem to be quite ad hoc driven. A real long term strategic view on their fleet portfolio is often missing. One argument for a missing consequent strategic optimization of aircraft portfolios can be drawn from the way airlines handle their fleet rationalization programs. The results of a study conducted by Button & Kilpi (2007)[20] show that exactly in those times when airlines expand their aircraft fleet (in an economic upswing), they pay less attention to additional costs from non-standardized fleets. These findings are of interest for this thesis as they give room for speculation that the same airlines, with the same carelessness when not facing cost pressure, treat possibilities to strategically improve the fleet composition in terms of aircraft acquisition and financing or age of the fleet. Since evidence for this still has to be provided in the remaining chapters, it shall be allowed at this stage to continue with the normal fleet planning process (cf. Figure 12).

Investment planning includes the decision for one of the basic dedicated capacity types and respective financing options – purchase, dry lease, wet lease, or ACMI (cf. Figure 2) – and of course does not remain on this level but dives deeply into the latest state-of-the-art financial, legal, and tax optimized structures of aircraft acquisition and funding. In this

[20] Button & Kilpi (2007) further developed in their research the "Fleet Standardization Index" introduced by Pan & Santo in 2004 to numerically analyze the correlation of fleet size and harmonization of aircraft types in airlines between 1952 and 2005. The outcome was that though fleet size constantly increased, the degree of uniformity declined. This is mainly triggered by capacity expansions in economic booms. On the other hand, fleet harmonization increases with growing cost pressure in times of economic downturns.

phase the full costs of the aircraft choice (funding and operating costs) and the financial risk associated with the asset are calculated. This is usually also the phase where the responsible department of a company confronts the board of management (or the respective decision making body) with request for approval of the business case. According to Clark (2007), acquisition and management activities are more and more separated and more emphasis is put on market orientation and financials as opposed to the technical evaluation of aircraft. Opportunistic acquisitions, of course mainly by big airlines and leasing companies[21], become more frequent. This is especially true for airlines with high liquidity. These "unconstrained airlines significantly increase buying activity when aircraft prices are depressed […]" (Pulvino, 1998, p. 939). These purely speculative activities include firm orders[22] way ahead of any precise market forecast (an overview on orders by owner category is provided in Chapter 2.2.2, Figure 11). Where and how the capacity will be employed is of secondary importance. It is essential to secure the capacity whenever the price is right. To make the right judgment it becomes again important to look not only at the individual aircraft but also at the effect on the overall aircraft portfolio.

When the decision for acquiring an aircraft under specified terms and conditions has been made, the negotiations with the supplier are finalized and, depending on the form of acquisition, the manufacturing, conversion or transfer of the asset is monitored. Simultaneously aircraft delivery and phase-in into operations are planned.
In reality, not all steps follow a strict consecutive order, but the different departments involved interact on a frequent basis to adjust and align information in the actual planning process from volume forecast to aircraft phase-in.

[21] For leasing companies, the definition of fleet planning could adopt the following meaning: "The acquisition of a fleet of aircraft is a means to provide a portfolio or opportunity to profitably rent to organizations requiring flexible solutions to their aircraft capacity needs." (Clark, 2007, p. 2)

[22] "A firmly-ordered aircraft is contractually committed, whereas an optioned aircraft is subject to a future and separate negotiation." (Clark, 2007, p. 12)

3. Development of the air capacity market

Market development is commonly defined by the interaction of demand and supply over time resulting in a price for the goods and services sold. Furthermore, industries are often linked to one major economic indicator. In the aviation industry, this economic indicator is the world's gross domestic product (GDP)[23]. This chapter will firstly outline the correlation between air traffic and global GDP and secondly describe the development of air capacity in terms of aircraft deliveries and orders in the normal business cycle as well as pre and post external economic shock events.

3.1 Air traffic growth

The correlation between air traffic growth and world gross domestic product (GDP) has been described many times in the literature. The fluctuation of the world gross domestic product shows the classical sequence of recession, depression (or bust), recovery, prosperity and boom[24]. The dynamic of this so called business cycle is the economy's internal, self-regulated, periodic movement, sometimes changed in direction or influenced by external events such as wars. An economy does not necessarily run through all stages of the cycle every time. Depression and boom, the most extreme scenarios in the cycle, appear infrequently and less often than recession and prosperity. (Kaps, 2000)

The aviation industry, i.e. air traffic, developed relatively synchronically to the world gross domestic product over the last 15 year. Figure 13 illustrates the annual growth of world revenue passenger kilometers (RPKs) and world revenue ton kilometers (RTKs) versus world GDP real growth rates. It becomes visible that air traffic performs the same movements as the world economy over time, but on a significantly wider scale. This means that for any percentage point change in the world GDP annual growth rate, the aviation industry reacts with a factor of 2-10.

[23] The gross domestic product (GDP) of a country is the sum of the four different expenditures consumption (C), investment (I), government spending (G), and net imports [exports (X) minus imports (M)] of the country, i.e. GDP (country) = C + I + G + (X-M); the world GDP or gross world product (GWP) is the sum of all countries' GDPs worldwide. (Kaps, 2000)

[24] Definition of the different stages of the economic cycle: recession = two consecutive quarters of declining gross domestic product (severity graded by the degree of unemployment); depression (or bust) = "severe decrease in business activity, leading to high unemployment, low income, and low corporate profits; recovery"; prosperity = upswing in production, employment, wages, profits, and increasing investment in new equipment; boom = "a period of rapidly rising prices and increased demand for goods and services, usually accompanied by full employment" (Knaps, 2000, pp. 60-63).

R. Günther, *Impact of Aircraft Sourcing & Financing on Financial Success*,
Edition KWV, https://doi.org/10.1007/978-3-658-24094-3_3

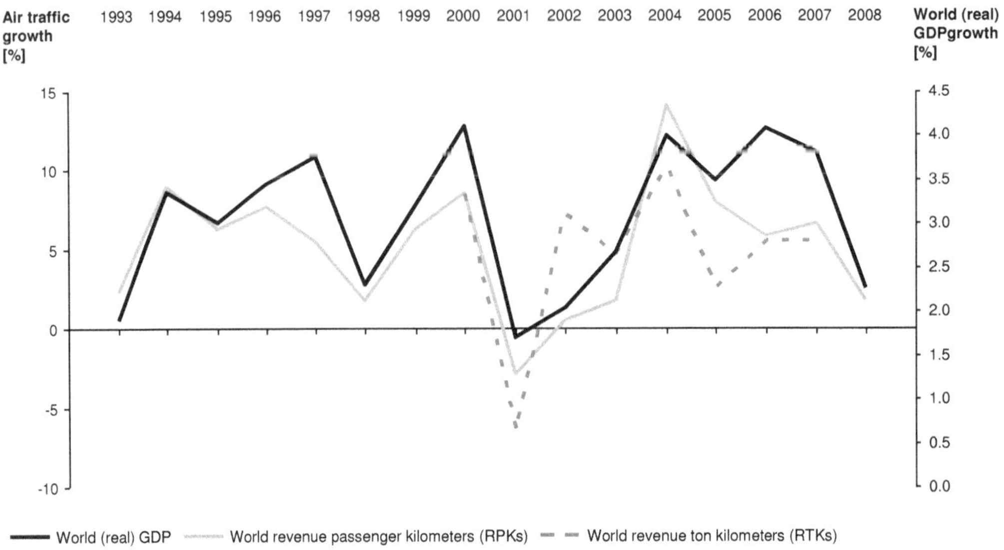

Figure 13: *Percentage growth of air traffic versus world (real) GDP growth 1993-2008*

This figure presents percentage growth of air traffic (year on year) based on world revenue passenger kilometers (RPKs) and world revenue ton kilometers (RTKs) versus real world gross domestic product (GDP) growth rates for the years 1993 to 2008. Data source for years 2000-2008 is Federal Aviation Administration (2008 and 2009) based on ICAO. Information pre 2000 is retrieved from Airbus (2009), based on Global Insight and ICAO, and could not be validated with other sources. For the years 1993-1999 and 2008 no reliable world RTK data were available.

For example, from the year 1997 to 1998 (two normal years in the business cycle when no external events occurred) the world GDP growth rate dropped by 1.5 percentage points from 3.8% to 2.3%. In the same time, the world RPK growth decreased by 3.7 percentage points from 5.5% to 1.8% (factor 2.6). In times of recovery such in the years 2003 to 2004 after 9/11, the world GDP growth gained 1.3 percentage points from 2.7% to 4.0% whereas the world RPK growth increased by 12.3 percentage points from 1.8% to 14.1% (factor 9.3) and the world RTK growth went up by 5.5 percentage points from 4.7% to 10.2% (factor 4.2 compared to the change in GDP). A difference with a factor of 40 is observed from 2001 to 2002 between the change in the world GDP growth rate (+0.3 percentage points) and the world ATK growth rate (+13.7 percentage points) can be considered abnormal. This situation is ascribable to the fast recovery of the air freight market after the terrorist attacks in the United States and the effects of substitution of passenger flights, i.e. a significant number of people decided to rather ship documents and packages than to take the safety risk of flying in person.

In sum, the strong reaction of the air traffic on changes in the world GDP appears in both directions, positive and negative, making the aviation industry a highly unstable environment. This environment requires to either very accurately forecast long term capacity demand, which is almost impossible, or to structure current and future capacity in a way that quick and also relatively big adjustments are possible if needed.

3.2 Air capacity development 1993 to 2000

In the years 1993 to 2000, after the end of the early 1990s recession and Golf War II, the aviation industry was shaped by a world economic upswing. The world GDP showed significant positive growth rates of approximately 3-4% p.a. in five out of the eight years. The years 1995 and 1998 experienced slightly lower growth rates, but still more than 2.5% (cf. Figure 13). Consequently, air traffic grew and airlines and other air capacity operating companies had to ramp up their fleet in order to follow demand.

Figure 14 illustrates total deliveries and net orders of Airbus and Boeing aircraft versus air traffic growth rates from 1993 to 2000 (please refer to Appendix 2 for an overview 1993-2009). Air traffic in this chart is purely based on world RPK as no reliable world RTK data were available for that time. The graph indicates that aircraft deliveries were limping behind market growth. It seems like airlines either had enough spare capacity in their fleet to serve the first years of significantly increasing air traffic 1993-1996 or could not ramp up their capacity fast enough. The latter would mean that actual air traffic growth could have been even higher but was restricted by a capacity shortage. This scenario is unlikely because the development of net orders somehow supports the argument that airlines had enough capacity available in the first years of the economic upswing. The number of net orders per year increased only hesitantly, but became stronger when the market remained growing.

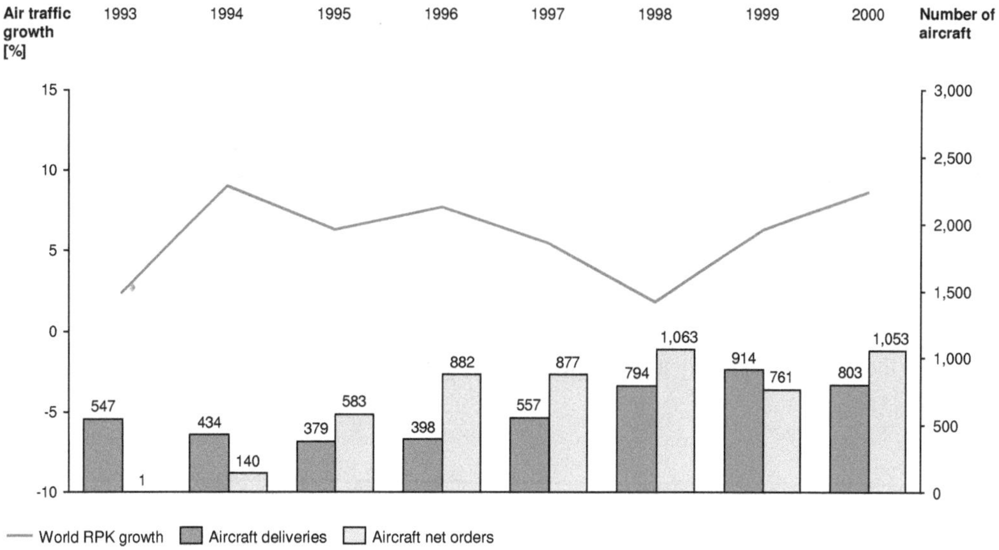

Figure 14: Deliveries and net orders of Airbus and Boeing aircraft versus air traffic growth 1993-2000

This figure presents deliveries and net orders (total gross orders minus total cancellations) of Airbus and Boeing aircraft in the years 1993 to 2000 in comparison to the percentage growth of air traffic (year on year) based on world revenue passenger kilometers (RPKs). Boeing includes McDonnell-Douglas. Source of aircraft data is Ascend Worldwide Ltd. (2009). Information on RPK growth rates is obtained from Airbus (2009), based on Global Insight and ICAO.

At the end of the year 2000, the aviation market was at a peak. Airbus and Boeing (incl. McDonnell-Douglas) had delivered more than 4800 aircraft over 8 years. Although in the year 2000, the leading manufacturers of airframes received 1,053 firm orders, yet the financial results of the airline industry already started to diminish. Decreasing operating and net profits defined the turning point in the economic cycle, signaling the beginning of a recession (cf. Figure 4).

3.3 The aftermath of 9/11 – Crisis and recovery until Q3 2008

The world was hit hard by the terrorist attack on September 11, 2001 in the United States. One of the industries that suffered most from the resulting crisis was the aviation industry. Air traffic, both passenger and freight, dropped dramatically until the end of 2001. Passenger traffic growth (world RPK) decreased by 11.5 percentage points from 8.6% to -2.9%, showing a negative growth rate for the first time. Freight traffic got struck even harder. World RTK growth lost 15.0 percentage points from 8.5% to -6.5% within a few months.

Still, the airlines were facing obligation of aircraft they had ordered in the years before the shock. Figure 15 shows the aircraft deliveries and net orders compared to air traffic growth development for the years 2001 to 2008 (for a full overview 1993-2009 please refer to Appendix 2). Boeing and Airbus continued to deliver a relatively high number of aircraft per year (compare Figure 14) and recorded approximately between 500-700 firm orders (net of cancellations) per annum in the first years of the crisis. However, although the air traffic market seemed to grow with high rates again (freight traffic already in 2002, passenger traffic with some more caution), confidence into a positive future was not back until the year 2005. Compared to previous years, aircraft net orders more than tripled. Growth rates began to stabilize around 5.0% in the three consecutive years 2005-2007 in both freight and passenger traffic.

Nevertheless, the world economy was again heading towards the next crisis the effects of which on the aviation industry are detailed in the next chapter.

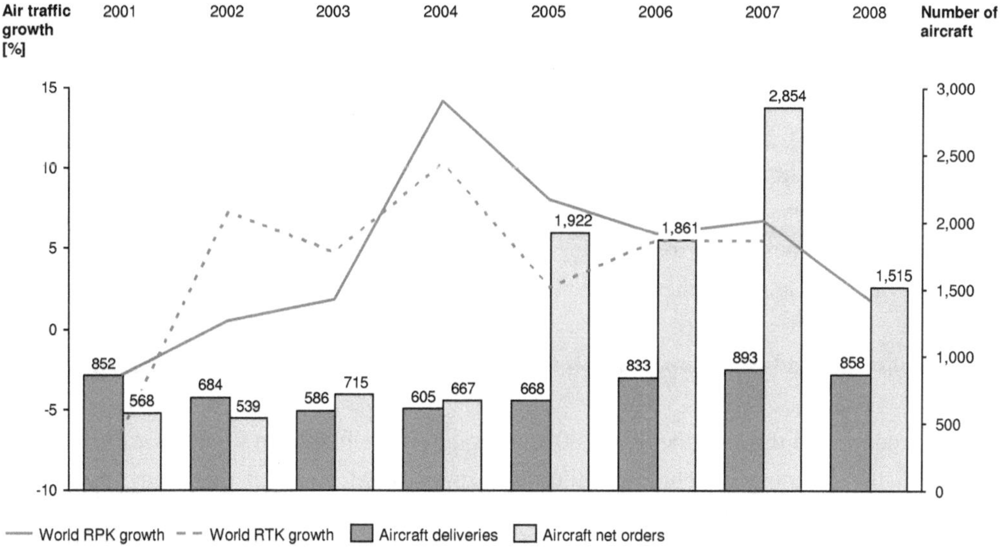

Figure 15: *Deliveries and net orders of Airbus and Boeing aircraft versus air traffic growth 2001-2008*

This figure presents deliveries and net orders (total gross orders minus total cancellations) of Airbus and Boeing aircraft in the years 2001 to 2008 in comparison to the percentage growth of air traffic (year on year) based on world revenue passenger kilometers (RPKs) and world revenue ton kilometers (RTKs). Boeing includes McDonnell-Douglas. Source of aircraft data is Ascend Worldwide Ltd. (2009). Information on RPK growth rates is the Federal Aviation Administration (2008 and 2009), based on ICAO. For the year 2008 no reliable world RTK data were available.

3.4 Financial Crisis Q4 2008 to Q1 2010

Starting with the collapse of the U.S. real estate and subprime mortgage market in the beginning of 2007 the crisis affected the global banking sector within the remaining year and slowly but surely build up to its final escalation point in September 2008. At this time, when Lehman Brothers collapsed, nobody could refuse to say that the world economy was facing a dramatic situation (more details of the event will be outlined in Chapter 7.2.2.1).

According to the World Economic Outlook of International Monetary Fund (2009), the advanced economies experienced a 7.5% decline in real GDP in the final quarter of 2008 and equally negative growth rates in the first quarter of 2009. This effect was visible not only in the U.S. (although the region probably suffered most) but also clearly in Europe, Asia and even in the emerging markets.

In sum, the failure of the financial structure behind the real estate industry affected the financial service sector in a way that the latter functioned similar to a chemical catalyst, starting a plethora of trouble in world economy. The immediate effect of the events was a lack of confidence in the financial system by private persons, financial institutes, literally everyone. This resulted mainly in a reluctance of banks to lend money, neither amongst themselves nor to anyone else. Sufferers of this change in risk awareness were mainly capital intensive industries, such as the aviation industry, which is dependent on loans and mortgages to finance aircraft. With the escalation of the Financial Crisis 2008, this industry was facing the possibility of businesses shutting down for want of funding. Additionally, with the development of the situation from a financial into a global economic crisis, world trade diminished, causing further decline in transport volume (both passenger and freight) and shrinking yield and revenues, respectively. (Interview with DVB Bank, 2009)

3.5 Forecast and industry expert expectations – The need for change in behavior

Problems continued through the year 2009. Although there had been a variety of initiatives to "stanch the bleeding", including bailout packages, public capital injections, and other liquidity facilities, the trust in the financial markets was low. Institutional investors (banks, pension funds, hedge funds, insurance companies, etc.) did not have the time to fully write down their assets and banks were still restrictive in granting credits.

Expectations for the mid term were overall slightly positive. The International Monetary Fund (2009) believed that the recession could be turned around in 2010 and that world economy would find back in all regions to a slow but positive average growth of 1.9%. The OECD (2009) predicted a similar scenario. It expected both inflation and unemployment to fall in 2010 and gave a careful but positive outlook for the world economy in the mid term, although not all regions would recover with the same speed (Europe was expected to take longer than the U.S. and Asia). 2010 would be an equally hard year for the real economy as 2009 and everybody is looking forward to better times, most likely from the year 2011 on. But does this solve the challenges? "It is natural to believe that periods of booming economic growth present no major problems. Unfortunately, this is not true. [...] Rapid growth can cause demand to outrun supply. Any economic system that is experiencing an excess of demand relative to supply is also experiencing an increase in the general level of prices (inflation). [...] Unstable price inflation causes problems that lead to inequities among individuals and groups and thus to less than optimal allocations of resources" (Kaps, 2000, p. 60).

From 2011 to 2030 world real GDP is estimated to grow with an average annual growth rate (AAGR) of 3.3% (Federal Aviation Administration, 2011). For the same period manufacturers forecast AAGRs for air passenger traffic (based on RPK) of 5.1% and for air freight traffic (based on FTK) of 5.6% (Boeing, 2011). In other words, air traffic is believed to approximately double in the next 15 years. The average net growth in number of Airbus and Boeing aircraft in the past five years (2005-2009) was around 570 frames per year (Ascend Worldwide Ltd., 2010). For this, the two major manufacturers had to deliver 670-

890 aircraft per year (cf. Figure 15). Assuming that aircraft size does not increase significantly over the next two decades and assuming that flight operations (load factor, schedule, etc.) cannot be optimized much further, the number of aircraft would have to nearly double as well. This matches statements in Boeing's Current Market Outlook 2009-2028 which predicts the average demand of aircraft (passenger plus freighters) to be 1,450 per year and 29,000 aircraft in the next 20 years, respectively. Airbus' latest Global Market Forecast is generally in line with these high numbers. They predict demand for only passenger aircraft of approximately 27,000 in the period 2011-2030[25]. Although both Airbus and Boeing enjoy high order backlogs and see this as a positive trend, critical voices fear that this might lead to a capacity shortage in the future since decommissioning programs of airlines continue and the gap between gross deliveries and demanded net increase in number of aircraft widens (Expert Interviews, 2009). The cargo business might be able to make use of passenger-to-freighter conversions, but conversion slots are rare (restricted by the low capacity at the manufacturers or service providers) and the total number of 40-90 conversions in 1993-2009 is relatively low (Ascend Worldwide Ltd., 2010).

First come, first serve? Some companies have already started to secure future capacity in form of firm orders and options at the manufacturers. Interestingly not every airline makes use of speculative acquisition of aircraft ahead of the market. And even more surprising, not every airline that does chooses the right moment in time.

Hence, Kaps' words about a supply-demand-problem describe perfectly the situation the aviation industry is going to face during the next market prosperity. Supply of aircraft in form of new productions, conversions or simply the availability of aircraft in compliance to environmental regulations will most likely not be sufficient to meet demand. Those individuals and groups of aircraft operators that secure capacity early in time will have significant advantage over their competitors when prices and respectively cost of operations increase with capacity shortage. Liehr et al. (2001, p. 321) find similar words: "[...] the intense competition for regional and global market share is mainly decided by capacity management. With the underlying structure of the market, this leads to the emergence of capacity surplus".

Additionally, nobody knows how long the restrictive credit behavior of banks will hold on. The OECD (2009, p. 213) is confident that "the decline in capital intensity may continue over the medium term in response to an increase in capital costs associated with a permanent increase in risk aversion." This would mean that air transport companies not only have to think about how much capacity to secure for the future but also how to fund it. Developing this thought, any company should try to find the optimal mix of different ownership models (owner versus lessee), ratio of existing versus planned aircraft, ratio of

[25] Demand for passenger aircraft with equal to or more than 100 seats

aircraft stored versus in service, etc. … "simply" the ideal aircraft portfolio and fleet plan that are most beneficial for the business' long term success and ultimately (at this point of the thesis still hypothetically) most rewarded by investors.

4. Financial performance of airlines and airline holdings

The previous chapters described basic aircraft sourcing and financing options that air passenger and freight transport companies can choose of, how the different players in the market have so far planned and acquired capacity, and that control over the asset aircraft seems to play an increasingly critical role. The illustration of operating and net results of ICAO scheduled airlines (cf. Figure 4) and of growth of air traffic in line with global GDP (cf. Figure 13) gave a first glance on the business performance of the air transport industry. The financial performance of airlines and airline holding companies – as key element of this thesis – has yet not been looked at. This chapter provides a view over the historical financial situation of selected airlines and airline holding companies from two perspectives, the stock market performance and the key operating figures from the financial statements.

4.1 Stock market performance

One way to look at financial performance of airlines is to observe stock market development of either industry stock indices compared to global cross-industry indices or of individual companies' stocks compared to the industry or global market. Figure 16 and Figure 17 show the development of Morgan Stanley Capital International's stock return indices[26] (1) MSCI World, (2) MSCI World Air Freight/Logistics, and (3) MSCI World Airlines from 1995 to 2010, firstly undisrupted and secondly in three series Q1 1995 to Q2 2001, Q3 2001 to Q2 2008, and Q3 2008 to Q4 2010, separating the times before and after terrorist attacks on 9/11, 2001, and the collapse of Lehman Brothers in September 2008. The graphs clearly display the growth of the overall market and industries, twice interrupted by the shocks. The air freight and logistics industry outperformed the market most of the time, while – depending on the time horizon – the airlines underperformed or developed near the cross-industry benchmark. Interestingly, it seems like the gap between the different indices shrank after each shock, bringing air freight and logistics as well as the airlines closer to the world market index.

[26] The MSCI World Index is a market-capitalization weighted free float adjusted index consisting of 24 (before May 26, 2010, only 23) developed market country indices (MSCI, 2010). The composition of the indices MSCI World Air Freight/Logistics and MSCI World Airlines is not disclosed by Morgan Stanley Capital International.

R. Günther, *Impact of Aircraft Sourcing & Financing on Financial Success*,
Edition KWV, https://doi.org/10.1007/978-3-658-24094-3_4

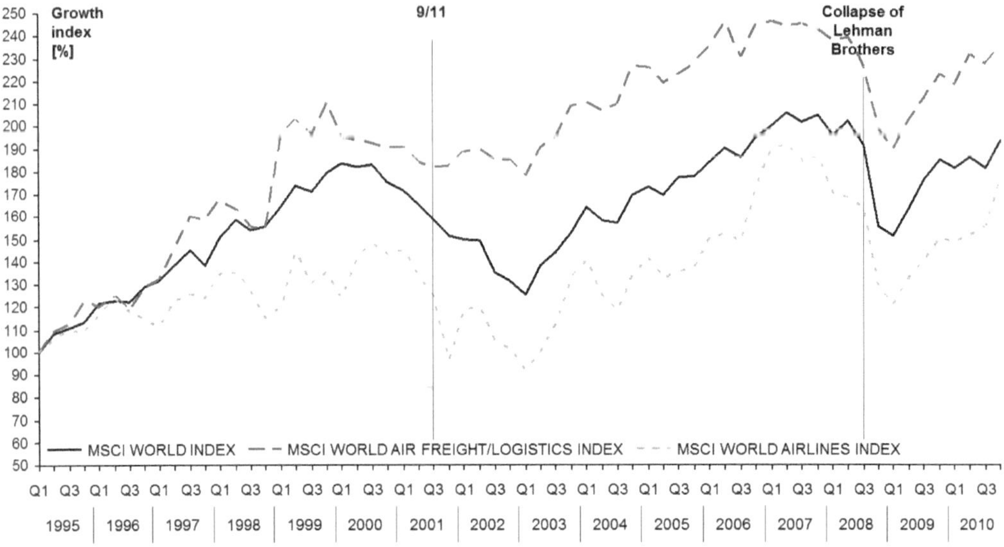

Figure 16: *MSCI stock indices 1995-2010 – World vs. Air Freight/Logistics vs. Airlines*

This figure presents the quarterly development of the two sector price indices MSCI World Air Freight/Logistics and MSCI World Airlines versus the sector-unspecific, broader MSCI World Index from 1995 to 2010. The time period includes the impact of the terrorist attacks on September 11, 2011, and the collapse of Lehman Brothers in September 2008. All data were obtained from Thomson Reuters Datastream (2011).

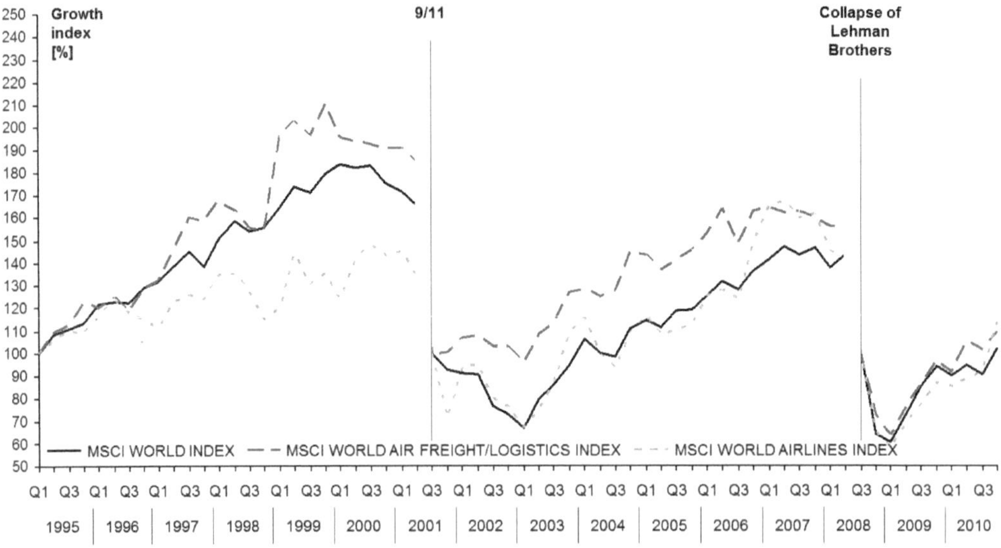

Figure 17: *MSCI stock indices time series Q1 1995 to Q2 2001, Q3 2001 to Q2 2008, Q3 2008 to Q4 2010*

This figure presents the quarterly development of the two sector price indices MSCI World Air Freight/Logistics and MSCI World Airlines versus the sector-unspecific, broader MSCI World Index from Q1 1995 to Q2 2001, Q3 2001 to Q2 2008 and Q3 2008 to Q4 2010, separating the times before and after 9/11 and the collapse of Lehman Brothers. All data were obtained from Thomson Reuters Datastream (2011).

Now, did all airlines in the industries experience the same movements and performed all companies equally successful or unsuccessful? The following figures show the quarterly development of stock returns in the four basic categories of aircraft operating and holding companies (1) major full service carriers (cf. Figure 18), (2) non-major full service carriers (cf. Figure 19), (3) low cost carriers (cf. Figure 20), and freight carriers (cf. Figure 21).[27] The purpose of the figures is not to give a comprehensive picture of stock return index performance of individual companies, but rather to display the trend of some selected airline and airline holding companies relative to each other to understand (of course only from a graphical point of view) whether their stocks performed equally successful or not. All data were obtained from Thomson Reuters Datastream (2010).

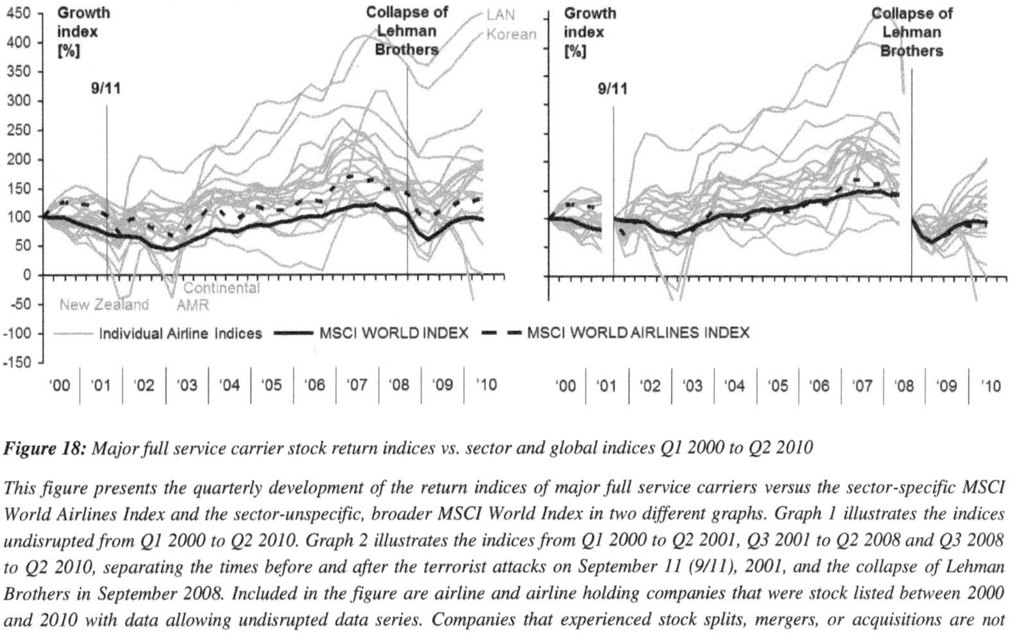

Figure 18: *Major full service carrier stock return indices vs. sector and global indices Q1 2000 to Q2 2010*

This figure presents the quarterly development of the return indices of major full service carriers versus the sector-specific MSCI World Airlines Index and the sector-unspecific, broader MSCI World Index in two different graphs. Graph 1 illustrates the indices undisrupted from Q1 2000 to Q2 2010. Graph 2 illustrates the indices from Q1 2000 to Q2 2001, Q3 2001 to Q2 2008 and Q3 2008 to Q2 2010, separating the times before and after the terrorist attacks on September 11 (9/11), 2001, and the collapse of Lehman Brothers in September 2008. Included in the figure are airline and airline holding companies that were stock listed between 2000 and 2010 with data allowing undisrupted data series. Companies that experienced stock splits, mergers, or acquisitions are not shown in the graphs. The highest and lowest performers are displayed by name. The abbreviation "AMR" refers to AMR Corporation, "Continental" refers to Continental Airlines Inc., "Korean" refers to Korean Air Lines Company Limited, "LAN" refers to LAN Airlines SA, and "New Zealand" refers to Air New Zealand Limited. All data were obtained from Thomson Reuters Datastream (2010).

[27] A more detailed description of the different clusters of aircraft operating and holding companies is provided in Chapter 6.4 together with the full list of sample companies included in the analyses.

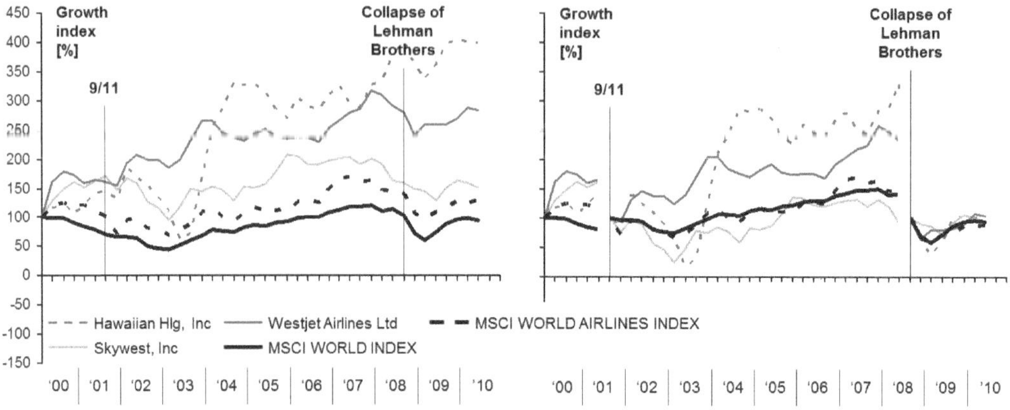

Figure 19: *Non-major full service carrier return indices vs. sector and global indices Q1 2000 to Q2 2010*

This figure presents the quarterly development of the return indices of selected non-major full service carriers versus the sector-specific MSCI World Airlines Index and the sector-unspecific, broader MSCI World Index in two different graphs. Graph 1 illustrates the indices undisrupted from Q1 2000 to Q2 2010. Graph 2 illustrates the indices from Q1 2000 to Q2 2001, Q3 2001 to Q2 2008 and Q3 2008 to Q2 2010, separating the times before and after the terrorist attacks on September 11 (9/11), 2001, and the collapse of Lehman Brothers in September 2008. Included in the figure are airline and airline holding companies that were stock listed between 2000 and 2010 with data allowing undisrupted data series. Companies that experienced stock splits, mergers, or acquisitions are not shown in the graphs. All data were obtained from Thomson Reuters Datastream (2010).

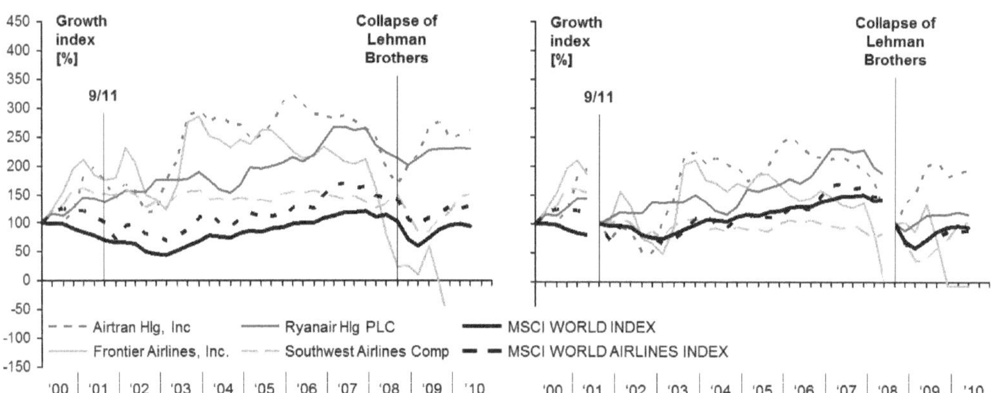

Figure 20: *Low cost carrier stock return indices vs. sector and global indices Q1 2000 to Q2 2010*

This figure presents the quarterly development of the return indices of selected low cost carriers versus the sector-specific MSCI World Airlines Index and the sector-unspecific, broader MSCI World Index in two different graphs. Graph 1 illustrates the indices undisrupted from Q1 2000 to Q2 2010. Graph 2 illustrates the indices from Q1 2000 to Q2 2001, Q3 2001 to Q2 2008 and Q3 2008 to Q2 2010, separating the times before and after the terrorist attacks on September 11 (9/11), 2001, and the collapse of Lehman Brothers in September 2008. Included in the figure are airline and airline holding companies that were stock listed between 2000 and 2010 with data allowing undisrupted data series. Companies that experienced stock splits, mergers, or acquisitions are not shown in the graphs. All data were obtained from Thomson Reuters Datastream (2010).

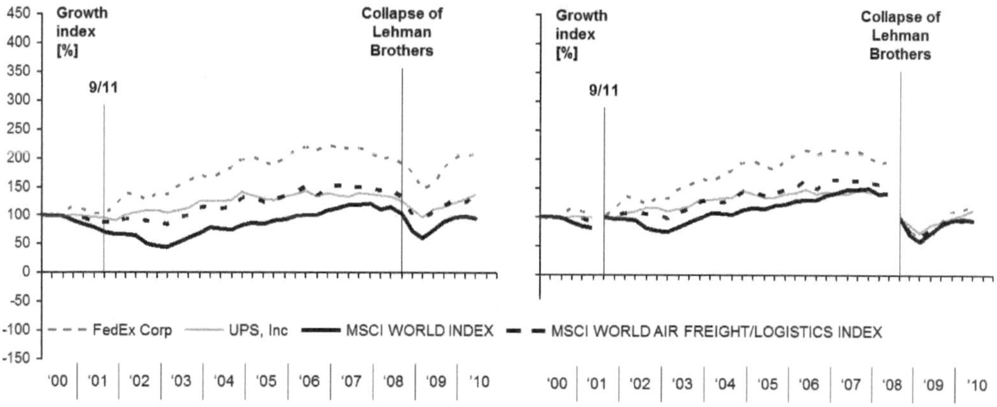

Figure 21: *Freight carrier stock return indices vs. sector and global indices Q1 2000 to Q2 2010*

This figure presents the quarterly development of the return indices of selected freight carriers versus the sector-specific MSCI World Air Freight/Logistics Index and the sector-unspecific, broader MSCI World Index in two different graphs. Graph 1 illustrates the indices undisrupted from Q1 2000 to Q2 2010. Graph 2 illustrates the indices from Q1 2000 to Q2 2001, Q3 2001 to Q2 2008 and Q3 2008 to Q2 2010, separating the times before and after the terrorist attacks on September 11 (9/11), 2001, and the collapse of Lehman Brothers in September 2008. Included in the figure are airline and airline holding companies that were stock listed between 2000 and 2010 with data allowing undisrupted data series. Companies that experienced stock splits, mergers, or acquisitions are not shown in the graphs. All data were obtained from Thomson Reuters Datastream (2010).

Among the full service carriers, the majority of the companies moved close to the market while, especially after the shock event, some started to significantly under- or overperform. Air New Zealand Ltd experienced the worst drop of -40% in Q4 2001, but also AMR Corporation (-38% in Q1 2003) and Continental Airlines Inc. (-11% in Q1 2003) had to face declining stock returns in the interim. On the other hand, LAN Airlines SA and Korean Air Lines Company Limited strongly moved above the 400% mark in the aftermath of 9/11. In the other carrier clusters similar patterns can be observed. Though fewer companies underperformed the market (Skywest Inc. in the non-major full service cluster and Southwest Airlines Company in the low cost carrier cluster after 9/11), in all four clusters, there are companies that clearly overperformed both the sector-specific and the sector-unspecific benchmark.

In essence, not all company stocks performed equally when looking at the development of the indices. There are some companies that were better off in the long term as well as in the short and mid term after the crises and others that performed significantly worse. The differences might be explained by the business models, the companies' individual financial and market situation, and – as assumed in this thesis – also in the different aircraft sourcing and financing strategies.

4.2 Key operating figures from the financial statements

Another way to look at the financial performance of airline and airline holding companies is to take the perspective of an analyst and review the companies' financial statements. From all accounting data that can be retrieved from a company's profit & loss statement, three performance indicators are commonly used by financial analysts to show information on a company's profitability, independent from tax and financing structure, and on a company's growth path: (1) earnings before interest, taxes, depreciation and amortization (EBITDA) margin, (2) earnings before interest and taxes (EBIT) margin, and (3) average annual revenue growth (AARG).[28] (Lie & Lie, 2002, Ross et al., 2005, Brealey et al., 2007) Based on these three indicators, Figure 22, Figure 23, and Figure 24 provide an overview on the financial performance of airline and airline holding companies clustered in the four previously introduced carrier categories. The information displayed covers the time period 2002 to 2007, i.e. the average performance over the "normal" business cycle after September 11, 2001, and the single year 2009, i.e. the performance in the first calendar year after the collapse of Lehman Brothers in September 2008. As not all companies have the same financial year, income statements were "annualized" to the full calendar year to enable comparison.[29] The figures are meant to give a snapshot of the industry to observe similarities and differences in the financial performance and to compliment the stock market's view in the previous section. All data were obtained from Thomson Reuters Datastream (2011).

[28] The above mentioned financial performance indicators as well as other financial control variables used in the analyses are explained in more detail in Chapter 6 together with the research hypotheses and scope.

[29] Details on the "annualization" of income statements are provided in Chapter 7.1.1.2

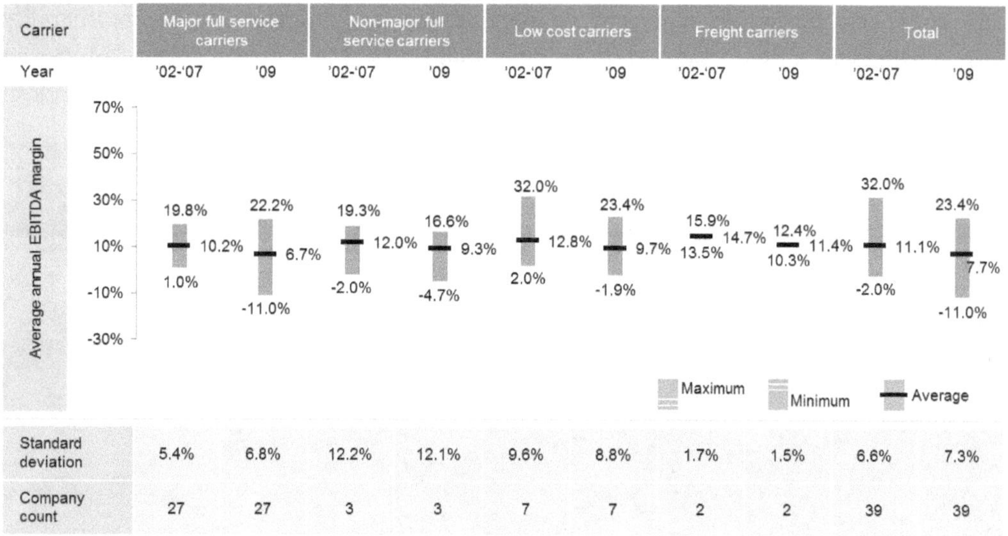

Figure 22: *Average annual EBITDA margins of airlines and airline holding companies 2002-2007 and 2009*

This figure presents average annual EBITDA margins, with maximum, average, and minimum of 39 airlines and airline holding companies clustered into four carrier categories: major full service carriers, non-major full service carriers, low cost carriers, and freight carriers. Included in the statistics are all airlines and airline holding companies that were stock listed between 2000 and 2009, for which complete accounting data were available, and that did not experience mergers or acquisitions during the observation periods. These time periods cover the years 2002-2007 and 2009. For comparison, the income statements were "annualized" to the full calendar year if required. All data were obtained from Thomson Reuters Datastream (2010).

Average annual EBITDA margins 2002-2007 ranked between 32% (max) and -2% (min) with relatively high means of 10.2% to 14.7%. With the Financial Crisis starting 2008, all carrier clusters experienced a drop. The average margin decreased from its 6-year average of 11.1% to 7.7% in 2009 with a new minimum of -11.0% in the category of major full service carriers.

Average annual EBIT margins show a similar picture. Based on margins of 24.1% to -6.0% in the years 2002-2007 all carrier clusters decreased by 1.7 to 3.6 percentage points in 2009. The new mean of the sample went down to 0.4% with a maximum at 15.6% and a minimum of -15.2%.

Comparing the different carrier clusters and observation periods, for both EBITDA and EBIT margins a pattern can be observed. In order of average profitability, freight carriers rank first followed by low cost carriers and non-major full service carriers. Major full service carriers run on the lowest average margins. The highest chances to outperform seem to lie in the low cost business. This pattern does not change with the overall drop in profitability in 2009.

The ranges and standard deviations of the margins show a significant spread in profitability of the individual airlines and airline holding companies. Merely the category of freight carriers, in which only two companies fulfill the selection criteria, operate at relatively close margins compared to the other clusters.

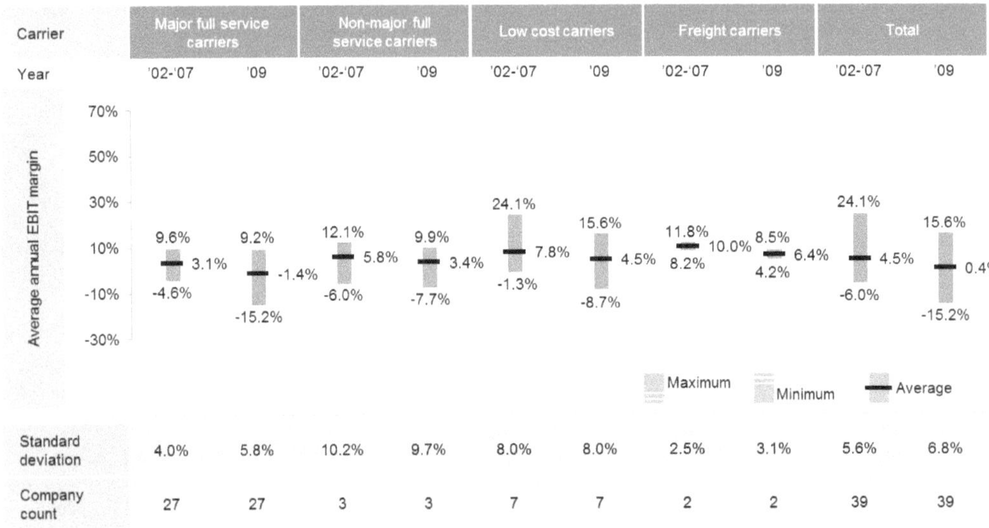

Figure 23: *Average annual EBIT margins of airlines and airline holding companies 2002-2007 and 2009*

This figure presents average annual EBIT margins, with maximum, average, and minimum of 39 airlines and airline holding companies clustered into four carrier categories: major full service carriers, non-major full service carriers, low cost carriers, and freight carriers. Included in the statistics are all airlines and airline holding companies that were stock listed between 2000 and 2009, for which complete accounting data were available, and that did not experience mergers or acquisitions during the observation periods. These time periods cover the years 2002-2007 and 2009. For comparison, the income statements were "annualized" to the full calendar year if required. All data were obtained from Thomson Reuters Datastream (2010).

When it comes to average annual revenue growth (AARG), the spread is even wider. The company with the highest average annual growth rate of 46.0% between 2002 and 2007 was among the low cost carries – which many would have expected placed first. Interestingly, the carrier cluster with the highest average growth rate in this time was non-major full service. In the aftermath of 9/11 all companies in the sample grew on average 15.6% in revenue per year. For many of them, these enormous positive growth rates ended or at least were slowed down by the Financial Crisis. In 2009, the average annual growth rate of the industry was down to dramatic -14.3% with maximum of 23.6% and minimum of -30.7% based on the previous year 2008. Again, the two freight carriers show relatively similar financial results before and after the collapse of Lehman Brothers, but all the other carrier clusters show a high variety of possible growth rates.

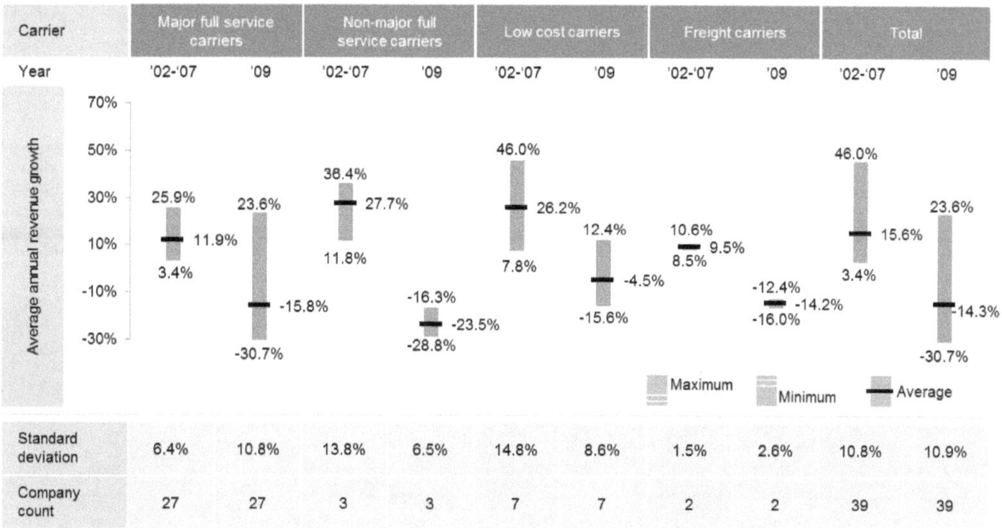

Figure 24: *Average annual revenue growth of airlines and airline holding companies 2002-2007 and 2009*

This figure presents average annual revenue growth, with maximum, average, and minimum of 39 airlines and airline holding companies clustered into four carrier categories: major full service carriers, non-major full service carriers, low cost carriers, and freight carriers. Included in the statistics are all airlines and airline holding companies that were stock listed between 2000 and 2009, for which complete accounting data were available, and that did not experience mergers or acquisitions during the observation periods. These time periods cover the years 2002-2007 and 2009. For comparison, the income statements were "annualized" to the full calendar year if required. All data were obtained from Thomson Reuters Datastream (2010).

The three financial performance indicators EBITDA margin, EBIT margin, and AARG show that not all airlines and airline holding companies are able to achieve the same profitability or growth rates. Indeed, the differences between the individual companies are significant in most carrier clusters. Subsequent analyses in this thesis will try to reveal the differences in financial success.

5. Summary of current situation and link to research topic

This section builds a bridge between the information given in the previous chapters and the research hypotheses and scope described in the next chapter. It summarizes the key statements and need for the analyses conducted in this thesis.

Chapter 2 explained the basic air capacity alternatives, the key players in the market, and the individual steps of the fleet planning process. It showed that there is a variety of different capacity options air passenger or freight transporting companies can choose from and that dedicated capacity in form of purchased or dry leased aircraft is the most cost sensitive choice (compared to wet lease, ACMI, other commercial capacity) when planning over a longer time horizon. It further highlighted the cyclical and fragmented market in which airlines and airline holding companies slowly but surely lost their majority share – and continue to lose share – in aircraft ownership to operating lease companies, banks, special purpose companies, and financial lessors, herewith reducing the level of control over their most important asset and allowing a highly supplier-controlled aircraft leasing market with high lease prices. Looking at the ideal fleet planning process, evidence was found in the literature that airlines still seem to be quite ad hoc driven and that they miss a consequent long term optimization of their fleet strategy.

Chapter 3 gave on overview on the air traffic growth and air capacity development before, in between, and after the terrorist attack on September 11, 2001, and the Financial Crisis 2008. It illustrated that despite the high correlation of air traffic growth and global GDP, synchronizing the delivery of ordered aircraft with capacity demand is difficult, especially when unexpected events such as the terrorist attack on 9/11 or the Financial Crisis 2008 interrupt the business cycle. Passenger and freight transporting companies naturally face some uncertainty in the market which results in a need for flexibility. On the one hand, airlines should quickly reduce overcapacity, e.g. by storing (grounding) aircraft, when demand suddenly drops. On the other hand, they have to plan for expected average annual growth in air traffic of 5-6% and secure sufficient capacity ahead of the market. However, the current production capabilities of the leading manufacturers are probably not sufficient to supply all airlines. Already today, manufacturers have built up a production backlog for passenger aircraft, passenger-to-freighter conversion slots are rare, and decommissioning programs of airlines continue. Industry experts predict a capacity shortage in the future, giving those airlines advantages that have secured future capacity in form of firm orders and options at the manufacturers, i.e. investing in own aircraft and optimizing the mix of different ownership models: owner versus lessor.

R. Günther, *Impact of Aircraft Sourcing & Financing on Financial Success*,
Edition KWV, https://doi.org/10.1007/978-3-658-24094-3_5

Chapter 4 introduced into the financial performance of air transport companies, looking at the stock market and at key operating figures from financial statements. It became clear that some companies perform better than others in the category of stock return as well as in terms of profitability and growth rates.

Beside the different business models often discussed in the literature, one open topic arises when combining the information of companies' capacity options, market development, and financial performance: the influence of basic aircraft sourcing and financing options on a company's financial results and stock price is yet unknown. This paper expects – based on the situation described above – that the basic fleet characteristics (1) owned versus leased, and (2) the ratio of existing versus planned aircraft, affect the overall financial performance of a company. Further, the lever (3) active (in service) versus inactive (stored) is tested as well as two variables that are included in the study of Merker & Henser (2011), (4) fleet size and (5) old versus new aircraft. The next chapter describes the research hypotheses and scope in more detail.

6. Research hypotheses and scope

The last chapters introduced to the thesis and provided an overview of the history of aircraft sourcing and financing as well as of the development of the air capacity market and of the historical financial performance of airlines and airline holding companies. In Chapter 5, the current situation of the industry was summarized together with the need for further research whether, and if so, how basic aircraft sourcing and financing decisions influence a company's financial success and whether a more strategic financial view on capacity management is beneficial. Before the next chapters describe in detail the methodology used and the analyses conducted, it is necessary to outline the research hypotheses and scope that define the basis for the analyses.

6.1 Key research hypothesis

The key research hypothesis was formulated based on (1) the key research question of "how aircraft operating and holding companies should strategically source and finance air capacity in an environment oriented towards financial success and shareholder benefit" (cf. Chapter 1.3) and (2) the open research topic that arose when consulting the literature and first data sources with regards to the various capacity alternatives and ways to acquiring aircraft, combined with the development of the capacity market, and the companies' diverse financial performances over the last years.

[Key Hypothesis]

Basic aircraft sourcing and financing decisions have a statistically significant impact on the financial performance of airlines.

To validate or reject the key hypothesis, firstly the terms "basic aircraft sourcing and financing options" and "financial performance" had to be detailed, secondly the key hypothesis had to be reformulated in several testable sub-hypotheses, and thirdly the scope of the analysis in terms of sample, geography, and observation periods needed to be defined.

R. Günther, *Impact of Aircraft Sourcing & Financing on Financial Success*,
Edition KWV, https://doi.org/10.1007/978-3-658-24094-3_6

6.2 Definition of fleet variables and financial performance measures

6.2.1 Basic aircraft financing and sourcing characteristics in focus

As previously described, airlines and other air transport companies use manifold strategies to manage their aircraft portfolio with major differences when it comes to aircraft ownership (buy versus lease) and the fleet planning horizon (placing aircraft purchase options or firm orders ahead of demand versus ad hoc capacity procurement). And, they differ in their financial performance. Objective of the analysis is to test whether the high level composition of a company's aircraft portfolio and fleet plan in terms of (1) ownership type and (2) ratio of planned to existing aircraft has significant influence on the company's stock performance in times of crisis and in times of company specific positive and negative events, as well as significant impact on a company's long term financial success during the normal business cycle. Minor fleet variables in the test include (3) aircraft activity status (stored or operating), and the by Merkert & Hensher (2004) already tested (4) total fleet size and (5) age of aircraft. Beside these fleet-based explanatory variables, a series of financial- and market-based control measures are tested. As the focus of the thesis lies on the basic strategic fleet composition only, other more detailed fleet composition factors often used in concrete dynamic capacity allocations and scheduling, such as aircraft type, size, noise restrictions, etc. (Listes & Dekker, 2005, and Merkert & Hensher, 2011), are neglected. For a detailed description of the individual variables, please refer to Chapter 7.1.2.

6.2.2 Taking the right perspective – Choosing the right measures & methodology

When striving for an analysis of company performance, the first questions to be answered are "what exactly is company performance" and "how can it be measured"? Only then, the right methodology can be selected.
Depending on the perspective taken, company performance can be expressed in different ways, e.g. operational efficiency, market share, financial success or reputation. Every one of these indicators can itself be expressed by a variety of measures. One could take the optimal use of resources in the production process, costs, profit, degree of internationalization, or air safety measures, all of these either in absolute terms or in percentage (growth) rates. Each measure may give a different indication on how successful or unsuccessful a company's performance is and lead to different conclusions and decisions.

In academic literature, there are a number of different measures and methods applied to evaluate airlines and airline holding companies. Some of them can be used to determine the influence of strategic aircraft sourcing and financing decisions on a company's performance.

Barbot et al. (2008) analyze airlines' efficiency and productivity with the total factor productivity (TFP) approach using e.g. number of employees, capital and fuel as inputs and revenue passenger kilometers (RPKs) and revenue ton kilometers (RTKs) as outputs. Assaf (2009) employs a stochastic frontier approach (SFA) in his study of technical efficiency of U.S. airlines. Later, Assaf & Josiassen (2011, p. 7) use data enveloping approach (DEA), the limitations[30] of which they account for by applying the bootstrap approach, to analyze operational performance in terms of technical efficiency of UK airlines 2002-2007. The same method is applied by Merkert & Hensher (2011) in their already mentioned evaluation of the influence of strategic fleet planning on airlines' technical, allocative, and cost efficiency.

The key to choose the right performance indicator and the right methodology for the analysis is to take the perspective of the target group that is supposed to use the results in its decision making process. In this thesis, company performance and measurement of its success refer to a company's financial performance and more specifically to the performance of this company's stock as well as to long term revenue growth rates and profit margins. With stock performance, the perspective of the shareholders is taken. One could argue that shareholders are not actively making decisions in a company but ultimately their goodwill and belief in a company determine its success. Therefore, a company's top management will always attempt to maximize shareholders value so that shareholder perspective becomes top management perspective. Operating revenue growth, EBITDA margin, and EBIT margin[31] are the long term drivers of a company's financial success and are frequently used by financial and investment analysts to determine the value of a company. (Lie & Lie, 2002, Brealey et al, 2007, Ross et al., 2005) Top managers look at these three performance indicators when optimizing their business. Often these are even included in managers' incentive schemes. Of course it can again be argued that business is not as simple as three basic financial indicators and that a variety of other financial ratios is needed to retrieve conclusions, e.g. from a company's financial statements. But, in the end it all comes down to the aspiration of sustainable long-term growth and profit and the continuous prosperity of the investors.

To measure stock performance, the above described measures and methodologies (TFP, SFA, or DEA with or without bootstrap approach) are not applicable. Here, the analysis of

---

[30] Assaf & Josiassen (2001, p.7) summarize the limitations of SFA and DEA as follows: "The main limitation of DEA is that it is a non-statistical technique and thus treats all measurement error as sources of inefficiency, while the main limitation of SFA is that it requires a pre-specification of the functional form in the estimation of cost or production frontier technologies."

[31] EBIT margin = Earnings before interest and taxes over total operating revenue; EBITDA margin = Earnings before interest, taxes, depreciation and amortization over total operating revenue

stock price changes or – more sophisticated – the analysis of abnormal stock returns compared to the market is appropriate.

Much research exists on markets' and companies' reactions to different internal and external events. When it comes to the evaluation of short to mid term effects – not exhaustive and not restricted to the aviation industry – of mergers & acquisitions (Duso et al., 2010), post-earnings announcements (Livnat & Mendenhall, 2006, Hirshleifer et al., 2008, Liu et al., 2008, Dellavigna & Pollet, 2009), industry booms and busts (Hoberg & Phillips, 2010) – the analysis of abnormal stock returns is frequently applied.[32]

The standard event-study method developed in the 1970s is often used in this respect and broadly accepted (Duso et al., 2010). But the most appropriate technique to investigate companies' stock performance or market reaction is the multivariate regression model (MVRM) methodology with abnormal returns (Belsley, Kuh, & Welsch, 2004, and Kedem & Fokianos, 2002). Among others, Carter & Simkins (2004) used this method to investigate stock market's reaction on the terrorist attacks September 11, 2001, and in the aftermath, focusing on a U.S. national airline sample and on the differences and cross-sectional differences in abnormal returns of full service passenger versus freight airlines. According to Carter & Simkins (2004, p. 542), this method "[…] is frequently employed to examine events that simultaneously affect firms in the same industry. In these cases, stock return residuals will not be independently and identically distributed. For this reason, the MVRM approach is preferred to the standard event-study method first employed by Fama, Fisher, Jensen, and Roll (1969)".

Still, the topic of sustainability remains, i.e. the question whether it is possible to draw arguments for top management decisions from shareholder reaction which might be short term return oriented. Is a shareholder reaction to a shock event such as the terrorist attacks on September 11, 2001, triggered by the effort to minimize loss and maximize value in the short term or by the belief that the event will have a sustainable positive or negative impact on the company? In order not to draw the wrong conclusions for a decision making process, which by nature of the asset aircraft can have major financial impact on a firm, abnormal returns are used only to evaluate short and mid term stock market reaction in different observation periods, including global shock events and special company specific events. The analysis of a company's long term financial success over the business cycles is based on the accounting data factors long term average revenue growth, EBITDA margin, and EBIT margin.

---

[32] The references listed to explain the diversity of research using abnormal returns to evaluate the impact of company-internal, industry-specific, or general market events is not even near to be exhaustive and only meant to be exemplary.

6.3 Testable hypotheses

Based on the definition of "basic aircraft financing and sourcing options" and "the choice for the right financial performance measures and methodology" the key research hypothesis was broken down to five null [$H_0$1 - $H_0$5] and several alternative [H_A1 – H_C5] hypotheses for subsequent validation or rejection in the analysis. The hypotheses reflect the anticipated impact of basic aircraft financing and sourcing compositions in an airline's aircraft fleet on its financial performance as defined before. All null hypotheses are expected to be rejected. All alternative hypotheses are expected to be validated or not rejected. To reject or not reject a null or alternative hypothesis in a test, strong statistical evidence against the hypothesis is needed (Bowerman & O'Connell, 2003). Test statistics used in this thesis are explained in the methodology chapter later on. In the following sections, the testable hypotheses are described one by one, each with a more detailed explanation of the rationale.

Table 1 summarizes the hypotheses and expected impact of the basic fleet variables. Assumed effects of non-fleet variables are illustrated in Chapter 7.1.2., Table 4.

Event			Times of crisis	Firm specific isolated event		Long term business cycle		
				A/C acquisition	A/C loss			
Impact on / correlation with			*Abnormal stock return*	*Abnormal stock return*		*Revenue growth*	*EBITDA margin*	*EBIT margin*
Variable			Rationale	Rationale	Rationale	Rationale	Rationale	Rationale
Major fleet variables	[H1] Ratio of leased to total A/C	High	↘ No asset value; less operational flexibility	→ No correlation expected	→ No correlation expected	↗ ops lease = short term capacity for growth	↘ Less assets = relatively lower EBITDA	↘ Higher cost of leasing
		Low	↗ Asset value; asset/operational flexibility	→ No correlation expected	→ No correlation expected	↘ Owned A/C = stable revenue	↗ More assets = relatively higher EBITDA	↗ Asset risk pays off; lower cost of asset
	[H2] Ratio of planned to total A/C – Orders – Options	High	↗ Positive growth expectation; strategic mgmt strength	→ No correlation expected	↗ Capacity cover already triggered	↗ Many A/C planned = high growth	→ No correlation expected	→ No correlation expected
		Low	↘ No growth indication or mgmt signal	→ No correlation expected	↘ No capacity cover planned yet	↘ No/few A/C planned = low growth	→ No correlation expected	→ No correlation expected
Minor fleet variables	[H3] Total number of A/C	High	↗ Big companies have better chances to survive	→ No correlation expected	↗ Big fleet can compensate loss	↘ Mature A/L; big market share = less growth	→ No correlation expected	→ No correlation expected
		Low	↘ Small businesses suffer relatively more	→ No correlation expected	↘ Relatively higher impact at small fleet	↗ Small A/L = growth (potential)	→ No correlation expected	→ No correlation expected
	[H4] Ratio of stored to total A/C	High	↗ Stored A/C = overcapacity at min. costs; quick re-activ. possible	→ No correlation expected	↗ Quick activation of capacity possible	↘ Capacity surplus = no growth	↗ Cost saving by flexibility in aircraft planning	↗ Cost saving by flexibility in aircraft planning
		Low	↘ All redundant capacity at full cost	→ No correlation expected	↘ No ad-hoc substitute	↗ Capacity shortage = high growth	↘ No flexibility in aircraft planning or at high cost	↘ No flexibility in aircraft planning or at high cost
	[H5] Average age of A/C	High	↗ Flexibility to decommission overcapacity in old A/C	→ No correlation expected	→ No correlation expected	→ No correlation expected	→ No correlation expected	↗ Old A/C = already/ mostly depreciated
		Low	↘ Young A/C = high loss if grounded	→ No correlation expected	→ No correlation expected	→ No correlation expected	→ No correlation expected	↘ Young A/C = high depre-ciation

↗ *Expected positive impact/correlation* → *Expected neutral (no) impact/correlation* ↘ *Expected negative impact/correlation*

***Table 1:** Expected impact of basic aircraft fleet and fleet planning variables*

This table summarizes the testable research hypotheses. It displays the anticipated impact and correlation of basic aircraft (A/C) financing and sourcing options and other fleet variables on the financial performance of air transport companies with a consolidated rationale. Major fleet variables, i.e. basic aircraft financing and sourcing options, include the high level composition of a company's aircraft portfolio and fleet plan in terms of ownership type (ratio of leased to total A/C), and the degree of future oriented fleet planning (ratio of planned, i.e. optioned or ordered, to existing aircraft). Further, three minor fleet variables are included: total fleet size (total number of A/C), activity status (ratio of stored to total A/C), and age of aircraft (average age of A/C). The financial performance refers to short- and mid term abnormal stock returns in times of crisis, aircraft acquisition, and aircraft loss as well as to average revenue growth, EBITDA margin, and EBIT margin over the long term business cycle.

The major fleet variables are [1] ratio of leased to total number of aircraft in the fleet and [2] the ratio of planned (future oriented firm-orders or options) to total number of aircraft in the fleet.

[Hypothesis 1]

[$H_0$1] The ratio of leased to total aircraft in a fleet is independent from a company's financial performance.

Alternatively, the higher the ratio of leased (owned) to total aircraft in the fleet,

[H_A1] the less (more) positive or more (less) negative the stock market reacts in times of crisis,

[H_B1] the higher (lower) the company's revenue growth, and

[H_C1] the lower (higher) the company's EBIDTA margin and EBIT margin.

(Intuitively, no correlation is expected between the ratio of leased to total aircraft and stock market's reaction on aircraft acquisitions or losses.)

Rationales for the hypotheses [H_A1] – [H_C1] are:

A) *Asset value and more important the asset or aircraft assignment flexibility the stock market would be looking for in times of crisis.*
Generally, the stock market prefers asset-heavy airlines, i.e. high book value, in an economic crisis (Charter & Simkins, 2003). Although a positive correlation of the number of owned aircraft in a fleet to the company's asset position on the balance sheet is likely, a low ratio of leased to total aircraft in a fleet does not necessarily mean a high asset value. Airlines could operate old aircraft with low book value or simply only few aircraft. Hence, asset value cannot be the only factor behind the anticipated significant impact of aircraft ownership. To encounter asset value, a separate financial variable will be built into the analysis and described at a later stage. The number of aircraft in the fleet is reflected in hypothesis [3].
The factor aircraft assignment flexibility and the underlying theory of asset liquidity (Shleifer & Vishny, 1992 and Gavazza, 2010) are believed to play a more important role. In this theory, assets with higher liquidity are better re-employable and less specific. An aircraft is an asset that can be handled more flexibly than immobile property, e.g. a building, to react on unforeseen demand shifts (Liehr et al., 2001). If owned, it can potentially be operated on another route, transferred to another region, send to maintenance check ahead of schedule, sold, leased to another party, or grounded to fix costs. Some of these options can be used in airline fleet assignment optimizations

(Rexing, Barnhart & Kniker, 2000, Bard, Yu & Argüello, 2001, and Smith & Johnson, 2006) which are widely used to help the company to either employ the aircraft revenue-generating or reduce operating costs, both to maximize profit (Barnhart et al., 2009). If operating leased, these possibilities are often contractually restricted and companies are tied to their liabilities without the chance to reduce operating costs with declining capacity demand. Operating lease generally provides airlines with flexibility in capacity management (Oum, Zhang & Zhang, 2000), but only in case enough time for planning and adjustment is given. In an economic shock and crisis, where dramatic ad hoc capacity reduction is required, contractual obligations are hindering. A rational stock market investor would prefer owned aircraft over operating leased aircraft in a shock event and crisis.

B) *Short-term access to capacity through operating leasing in order to grow in revenue.*
A strongly growing company is expected to make significantly more use of operating leases to quickly access additional capacity compared to companies where revenue has stabilized or grows only moderately. Basic arguments for the hypothesis can be found in Butler & Keller (2000) and Gavazza (2011, p. 325) provides further support: He evaluated commercial aircraft transactions in the primary and secondary leasing markets with the objective to understand differences in trade frequency of owned and leased aircraft. In his elaborations he states that "high volatility firms are more likely to lease than low-volatility firms."

C) *Higher costs of leasing and the payoff for the asset risk.*
An operating lease is charged with a premium by the lessor reflecting shorter time of use, asset risk, and supplier power of the lessor caused by shortage of leasing aircraft in the market and the often ad hoc driven capacity need of the lessee (Oum et al., 2000 and Abeyratne, 2001). Also, the leasing price does not consider the actual volatility in the aircraft purchase price and is rather linked to a high price (Aircraft Value Analysis Company, 2008, cf. Chapter 2.2.2). Therefore, costs of operating leasing are assumed to be usually higher than costs of operating an own aircraft. Of course the opposite might be true under specific circumstances such as that the airline bought the aircraft at the highest market price and interest rate (debt financed) which offsets the premium charged by a lessor. In the EBITDA margin the depreciation of the aircraft is not yet considered, therefore the EBITDA margin of a company with more owned aircraft is by definition relatively higher than the margin of a company with more operating leased aircraft. Under normal circumstances the EBIT margin of a company with proportionally few operating leases is assumed to be higher than the EBIT margin of a company with many operating leases.

[Hypothesis 2]

[$H_0$2] The ratio of planned to total aircraft in a fleet is independent from a company's financial performance.

Alternatively, the higher (lower) the ratio of planned aircraft, i.e. firm orders or options, to total aircraft in the fleet,

[H_A2] the more (less) positive or less (more) negative the stock market reacts in times of crisis,

[H_B2] the more (less) positive or less (more) negative the stock market reacts on aircraft losses, and

[H_C2] the high (lower) the company's revenue growth

(No correlation is expected between the ratio of planned to total aircraft and stock market's reaction on aircraft acquisitions, EBITDA margin, and EBIT margin)

Rationales for the hypotheses [H_A2] – [H_C2] are:

A) *Positive growth expectation combined with the trust in a sophisticated strategic management.*
A company's management that plans and acquires future capacity by placing aircraft firm orders or buying options ahead of the market sends three strong signals to the investors: (1) The company follows a long term fleet strategy (including aircraft replacement programs) and understands the industry cycle, (2) growth in revenue is expected for which additional capacity is needed, and (3) even with the uncertainty in forecast, the management has the trust that it can handle any unforeseen event that influences capacity demand and supply. These signals are believed to have a significant effect on the trust of rational investors in times of crisis. Supporting statements can be found in Liehr et al. (2001, p.312): "given the requirement of the global capital markets, it is necessary for airlines to be able to show substantial growth in order to attract capital [...]. The business cycles, which have impact on the profitability of the industry, are a subject of growing interest to the companies' management, since the cycles are also observed by the professional investors." With the knowledge of the industry cycle and the forecast of growth, long term fleet planning and aircraft order become essential elements of successful airline management.

B) The prospective to cover for the lost capacity with ordered or optioned new aircraft.
Empirical studies show that aircraft accidents lead to price drops in the stocks of implicated airlines and manufacturers and the effect of several independent variables such as firm size or fatality of the accident were tested (Chalk, 1987, Walker et al., 2005). The impact of future fleet plans, i.e. the ratio of ordered and optioned to total aircraft, yet has to be evaluated. As a loss of an aircraft is equal to the loss of revenue-generating capacity, it is believed that the possibility to substitute the lost capacity with a recently ordered or optioned new aircraft creates a positive outlook for the stock market. Vice versa, no planned aircraft means that no substitute (other than expensive leases) will be available in near future; therefore the stock market is expected to penalize these airlines more.

C) Correlation of capacity demand and revenue growth.
Whoever wants to grow in the air transport industry needs capacity, i.e. similar to the rationale under [H_A2] based on Liehr et al., a strong positive correlation of revenue growth and future oriented fleet planning is expected as it is in essence the only way to realize long term sustainable growth and to attract investors. Further, with purchase and production options, the airlines have the possibility to postpone or swap delivery slots with other airlines, enabling a more flexible capacity management when demand becomes certain.

There is no correlation of future aircraft planning expected with EBITDA and EBIT margins. Future-oriented orders give airlines the opportunity to acquire capacity when prices are low; however, this effect is only visible on the companies' balance sheets and not in the profit & loss statement.

The expectations regarding the impact of the minor fleet variables, [3] total number of aircraft (fleet size), [4] ratio of stored aircraft to total number of aircraft in the fleet (activity status), and [5] average aircraft age in the fleet are also formulated in null [$H_0$3] – [$H_0$5] and alternative hypotheses [H_A3] – [H_{C5}].

[Hypothesis 3]

[$H_0$3] The total number of aircraft in the fleet is independent from a company's financial performance.

Alternatively, the higher (lower) the number of aircraft in the fleet,

[H_A3] the more (less) positive or less (more) negative the stock market reacts in times of crisis,

[H_B3] the more (less) positive or less (more) negative the stock market reacts on aircraft losses, and

[H_C3] the lower (higher) the company's revenue growth.

(No correlation is expected between number of aircraft in the fleet and stock market's reaction on aircraft acquisitions, EBITDA margin, and EBIT margin.)

Rationales for the hypotheses [H_A3] – [H_C3] are:

A) The probability of survival increases with a company's size.

The stock market believes that bigger airlines have a higher chance to survive a crisis; on the other hand small businesses suffer relatively more and have a higher chance for bankruptcy. Supporting facts for this hypothesis can be found in various analyses of abnormal returns in times of crisis, including those of Chalk (1987), Carter & Simkins (2004), and Walker et al. (2005). Size often refers to the natural logarithm of assets or market capitalization. As described in the rationale of [H_A1], a positive correlation of the number of aircraft in a fleet to the company's asset position in its balance sheet is expected. The natural logarithm of asset value is included as a financial control variable later in the analysis. Another supporting argument is provided by the recent work of Merkert & Hensher (2011, p.686). They evaluated key determinants of passenger airline efficiency, including the impact of fleet planning on airline efficiency, with DEA[33] efficiency scores. Their findings "show that airline size and key fleet mix characteristics, such as aircraft size and number of different aircraft families in the fleet, are more relevant to successful cost management of airlines since they have significant impact on all three types of airline efficiency: technical, allocative and, ultimately cost efficiency. With this thesis, the variables size and number of aircraft are tested not with the focus on bottom-line efficiency but with regard to overall financial performance from an investor's point of view, i.e. stock price, revenue, and profit margin.

B) The magnitude of the loss relative to the fleet.

Rationale for the anticipated positive correlation of fleet size to abnormal stock reaction on aircraft losses is simply based on the assumption that, given that the stocks react on accidents (Chalk, 1987, Walker et al., 2005), the market will acknowledge that a company with many aircraft in its fleet realizes a relatively smaller and can easier compensate the lost capacity than airlines with few aircraft.

[33] DEA: Data Envelopment Analysis

C) The maturity of the airline and its position in the market.

The logical assumption is that the bigger the fleet of an airline the more mature is the airline's business. This means that the airline's operations in terms of market share, global footprint, etc. are likely to be higher and more stable than in smaller businesses that still have "room to grow". Hence, a negative correlation is expected between fleet size and revenue growth.

Regarding EBITDA margin and EBIT margin a positive correlation of fleet size sounds logical as one would expect synergy effects in the fleet. However, as already described in Chapter 1.1, Pan & Santo (2004) found empirical evidence of a negative correlation of fleet size and degree of uniformity or harmonization. On the other hand, the number of aircraft could be another measure of a company's size (expected to have a positive correlation). As two contradicting arguments are found that might neutralize in their effect, a neutral or no correlation is anticipated.

[Hypothesis 4]

[$H_0$4] The ratio of stored to total aircraft in the fleet is independent from a company's financial performance.

Alternatively, the higher (lower) the ratio of stored aircraft to total number of aircraft in the fleet (of course with a limit before profit is diminishing),

[H_A4] the more (less) positive or less (more) negative the stock market reacts in times of crisis,

[H_B4] the more (less) positive or less (more) negative the stock market reacts on aircraft losses,

[H_C4] the lower (higher) will be the company's revenue growth and the higher (lower) the company's EBITDA margin and EBIT margin.

(No correlation is expected between the ratio of stored to total aircraft and stock market's reaction on aircraft acquisitions.)

Rationales for the hypotheses [H_A4] – [H_C4] are:

The idea is based on the description of Liehr et al.'s discussion with Lufthansa (2001, 322). They belief in the need for flexibility in existing capacity and that "the strategy is to keep a certain percentage (10-15%) of the older aircraft in the fleet, which are operated in case of a shortage in deliveries or seats offered; in downturns this part of the fleet is quickly retired, at low costs. This policy opens margins and flexibility for fleet planning." In this thesis, merely the ratio of stored to total aircraft in the fleet is tested with the expectation that the higher the ratio A) the better in times of crisis, B) the better in times of aircraft loss, and C) the higher the EBITDA and EBIT margins of a company. Of course, the ratio has a natural threshold before it diminishes profit. Based on the data pulled from Ascend Worldwide Ltd. for the time periods and sample airlines evaluated in this thesis, the average percentage of stored aircraft is between 2-3% with maximum of ~20%.

[Hypothesis 5]

[$H_0$5] The average age of aircraft in the fleet is independent from a company's financial performance.

Alternatively, the higher (lower) the average age of aircraft in the fleet,

[H_A5] the more (less) positive or less (more) negative the stock market reacts in times of crisis, and

[H_B5] the higher (lower) will be the company's EBIT margin.

(No arguments were found for a correlation between average aircraft age and stock market's reaction on aircraft acquisitions or losses, revenue growth, and EBITDA margin[34].)

Rationales for the hypotheses [H_A5] – [H_B5] are:

A) *The flexibility to decommission overcapacity in old aircraft at low cost.*
This rationale is also closely linked to the discussion of Liehr et al. (2001) described before. Active old aircraft can be grounded and decommissioned at low costs when capacity demand drops. Besides, old aircraft are low-cost capacity surplus when stored for unexpected demand.

B) *No (or low) depreciation.*
Old aircraft are often likely to be fully or almost fully depreciated, i.e. they do not appear in the financial statements of the airlines with costs other than the regular fixed and variable maintenance and repair costs. According to Morrell (2007), straight line depreciation is used by almost all airlines since 1993 with different underlying life time and residual value assumptions for aircraft. Morrell looked at various airlines and regions and found, based on the airline's annual reports between 2001 and 2006 and mostly in line with a study by KPMG and IATA of 1992, depreciations along with

[34] Merkert & Hensher (2011, p. 692) assumed a correlation of fleet age and fuel efficiency and expected airlines with younger fleet to be more efficient. However, their findings are contrary to their prediction: "[...] fleet age has no significant impact on technical efficiency, and a small but very significant positive impact on allocative and cost efficiency." This result could provide an argument for a positive effect of old aircraft on EBITDA margin. However, the conclusions drawn by Merkert & Hensher are not solid enough to support such an argument.

aircraft life time mainly between 10-25 years and with residual values of 10-15% (depending on aircraft type and the airline's depreciation policy). Given these facts and given that some airlines in the sample operate aircraft that were build as early as 1962 and some fleets even have an average age of aircraft up to 32 years, the chances to operate fully depreciated aircraft are high. An old, fully depreciated aircraft should operate at lower total expense (incl. depreciation) compared to a new aircraft of the same size, if maintenance and repair do not offset this effect. Likewise, leasing old aircraft should be cheaper than leasing a new model. Hence, old aircraft are assumed to generate higher profits than their younger brothers.

6.4 Sample – Aircraft operating and holding companies in scope

The sample used for the analysis of companies' stock performance and market's reaction comprises a total of 56 companies, including passenger and cargo transporting companies, the latter including the subcategory of integrators. A "company" refers to a stock listed enterprise, i.e. it can refer to either an isolated airline or a holding company which consolidates several carriers. For example, Singapore Airlines Limited includes Singapore Airlines Cargo and Silk Air. This is because stock listing was chosen as common nominator, i.e. a sample company has to represent a stock listed company in order to be able to retrieve the necessary share price information and financial statements. Although many companies explicitly report the financial results of their subsidiaries, the effects of the subsidiaries in the company's stock price cannot be isolated.

Companies were selected based on the following criteria: within the period of observation, the company (1) was an active aircraft operating or holding company, listed and traded at the stock exchange and (2) operated an aircraft fleet of a minimum of one commercial jet with a capacity of more than 50 seats (or freight equivalent). Knock-out criteria were unavailability of information in terms of stock return, financial, market, and fleet data.

The companies considered are divided into four basic categories to allow for inter-cluster comparison: major full service carriers, non-major full service carriers, low cost carriers and freight carriers including integrators. The criteria used to allocate each firm to one of the four clusters are based on qualitative and quantitative factors obtained from Sterzenbach et al. (2009)[35] and the Aviation Week Business Intelligence Service (2002 and 2003)[36].

[35] Sterzenbach et al. (2009) distinguishes air carriers by their business model. Generally, four main business models are defined based on the criteria geographic scope and target group: (1) network carrier, (2) regional carrier, (3) leisure carrier, (4) low cost carrier. All four carrier clusters provide scheduled services. Taking into consideration on demand services, the list of business models can be expanded by (5) business aviation, (6) aircraft charter, and (7) day jet. Network carriers are further split into major and non major.

[36] The Aviation Week Intelligence Service further uses annual revenue as common criterion to differentiate major from non-major carriers.

All companies were assigned to one of the four clusters. As mentioned before, company refers to the stock listed unit rather than to an individual enterprise, i.e. a company can include more than one airline as long as the financials are consolidated in the statements of the traded company. For example, if subsidiaries were owned with more than 50% in 2007 but with 10% in 2000, the fleet of the affiliated company was included only in 2007. Subsidiaries, in which the mother company holds less than 50%, are usually not consolidated in the financial statements of a company.[37] In case the stock traded company consolidates not only one but several business models, the dominant business model is decisive for the allocation to one of the four carrier clusters.[38]

Table 2 provides an overview on the companies included in the analysis of shocks and crises (9/11 and the Financial Crisis 2008), company specific special events (aircraft accidents and aircraft firm orders), and the long term business cycle (2002-2007 and 1995-2009). Within the sample, major full service carriers count 33, the cluster of non-major full service carriers includes 7 companies;low cost carriers are represented by 11 and freighters by 5 companies.

---

[37] Examples and remarks: (1) Airborne became ABX Air in August 2003; Since November 2007 the Air Transport Service Group (ATSG) consolidates the three subsidiary airlines ABX Air, Air Transport International Inc. (ATI), and Capital Cargo International Airlines Inc; (2) All Nippon equals ANA All Nippon Airways, but does not include Nippon Cargo Airlines in which ANA had a minority share prior to 2004. Further, ANA All Nippon Airways does not include ANA & JP Express; although ANA & JP Express has used All Nippon Airways aircraft, it has merged with Air Japan (the latter being the surviving company); (3) ATA Holdings, formerly known as American Trans Air, includes ATA Airlines and was renamed in Global Aero Logistics Inc. in April 2007 but is presented under the former name of ATA Holdings in the sample; (4) Cathay Pacific includes Dragonair as wholly owned subsidiary since September 28, 2006; (5) China Airlines includes Mandarin Airlines; (6) China Eastern Airlines includes China Cargo Airlines; (7) FLYI Inc. (or Independence Air) was formerly known as Atlantic Coast Airlines Holdings Inc and filed for chapter 11 bankruptcy in March 2007; (8) Deutsche Lufthansa AG includes Lufthansa Cargo, Lufthansa CityLine, Air Dolomiti since July 2003, and Swiss International Air Lines as of July 1, 2007; (9) Northwest Airlines' fleet is not included in Delta Air Lines fleet in 2008 but in 2009, as the airline operated as an independent carrier throughout the year 2008 and the merger officially closed not until October 29, 2008; (10) Qantas includes the subsidiaries Jetstar Airways (established in 2003) and Jetconnect (established July 2002); (11) Singapore Airlines includes Singapore Airlines Cargo and Silk Air; (12) LAN Airlines includes affiliated airlines such as LAN Argentina and LAN Peru (operating aircraft with Chilean registration), as well as the cargo subsidiaries LAN Cargo; (13) US Airways includes America West Airlines' fleet after the merger in 2005; before America West Airlines is treated as a separate company; US Airways was acquired by America West in 2005 but the company decided to keep running operations under the better known name of US Airways.

[38] For example: Deutsche Lufthansa AG includes the major full service (or major network) carriers Lufthansa Cargo and Swiss International Air Lines (as of July 1, 2007) as well as the non-major full service (or regional) carriers and Lufthansa CityLine and Air Dolomiti (since July 2003); nevertheless, the dominant business model in the consolidated business of Deutsche Lufthansa AG is that of a major full service or major network carrier.

Company	Region	Company included in analysis of:			
		9/11	Financial Crisis	Special events	Business cycle
Major full service carriers					
1 Air Canada Inc	NORAM	●	●	●	●
2 Air China Limited	APAC	○	●	●	●
3 Air France/Air France-KLM	EMEA	●	●	●	●
4 Air New Zealand Limited	APAC	●	●	●	●
5 Alaska Air Group Inc	NORAM	●	●	●	●
6 All Nippon Airways Company Limited	APAC	●	●	●	●
7 AMR Corporation	NORAM	●	●	●	●
8 Austrian Airlines AG	EMEA	●	●	○	●
9 British Airways PLC	EMEA	●	●	●	●
10 Cathay Pacific Airways Limited	APAC	●	●	●	●
11 China Airlines Limited	APAC	●	●	●	●
12 China Eastern Airlines Corporation Limited	APAC	●	●	●	●
13 China Southern Airlines Company Limited	APAC	○	●	●	●
14 Continental Airlines Inc	NORAM	●	●	●	●
15 Delta Air Lines Inc	NORAM	●	●	●	●
16 Deutsche Lufthansa AG	EMEA	●	●	●	●
17 El Al Israel Airlines Limited	EMEA	○	●	●	○
18 EVA Airways Corporation	APAC	●	●	●	●
19 Finnair OYJ	EMEA	●	●	●	●
20 Iberia SA	EMEA	●	●	●	●
21 Japan Airlines Corporation	APAC	●	●	●	●
22 KLM Royal Dutch Airlines	EMEA	●	○	○	○
23 Korean Air Lines Company Limited	APAC	●	●	●	●
24 Lan Airlines SA	LATAM	●	●	●	●
25 Malaysian Airline Limited	APAC	●	●	●	○
26 Northwest Airlines Corporation	NORAM	●	●	●	●
27 Qantas Airways Limited	APAC	●	●	●	●
28 SAS AB	EMEA	●	●	●	●
29 Singapore Airlines Limited	APAC	●	●	●	●
30 TAM SA	LATAM	●	●	●	●
31 Thai Airways International Public Company	APAC	●	●	●	○
32 UAL Corporation	NORAM	●	●	●	●
33 US Airways Group Inc	NORAM	●	●	●	●
Non-major full service carriers					
1 FLYi Inc	NORAM	●	○	●	○
2 Hawaiian Holdings Inc	NORAM	●	●	●	○
3 Mesa Air Group Inc	NORAM	●	●	○	○
4 Mesaba Holdings/MAIR Holdings Inc.	NORAM	●	○	○	●
5 Midwest Express Holdings	NORAM	●	○	●	○
6 Skywest Inc	NORAM	●	●	○	●
7 Westjet Airlines Limited	NORAM	●	●	●	●

• In scope ○ ***Out of scope***

***Table 2**: Overview on sample companies and match to observation periods*

(Table continued on next page)

Low cost carriers					
1 AER Lingus Group PLC	EMEA	○	•	•	•
2 Air Berlin PLC	EMEA	○	•	•	○
3 Airtran Holdings Inc	NORAM	•	•	•	•
4 America West Holdings	NORAM	•	○	•	○
5 ATA Holdings	NORAM	•	○	•	○
6 Easyjet PLC	EMEA	•	•	○	•
7 Frontier Airlines, Inc.	NORAM	•	•	•	•
8 Jetblue Airways Corporation	NORAM	○	•	•	•
9 Ryanair Holdings PLC	EMEA	•	•	•	•
10 Southwest Airlines Company	NORAM	•	•	•	•
11 Virgin Blue Holdings Limited	APAC	○	•	•	○
Freight carriers					
1 Airborne Express	NORAM	•	○	○	○
2 Air Transport Service Group	NORAM	○	•	○	○
3 Atlas Air Worldwide Holdings Inc	NORAM	•	•	•	○
4 FedEx Corporation	NORAM	•	•	•	•
5 United Parcel Service Inc	NORAM	•	•	•	•
∑ 56		48	49	48	41

• In scope ***○ Out of scope***

Table 2 (continued): *Overview on sample companies and match to observation periods*

This table presents the companies included in the analysis of shock and crises (9/11 and Financial Crisis 2008), company specific special events (aircraft accidents and aircraft firm orders), and/or the long term business cycle (2002-2007 and 1995-2009). Companies were selected by the following criteria for a specific observation period: (1) the company was an active aircraft operating or holding company, listed and traded at the stock exchange, (2) the company operated an aircraft fleet of a minimum of one commercial jet with a capacity of more than 50 seats (or freight equivalent), excluding small business jets and turbo props, and (3) stock return, financial, market, and fleet data were fully available in Thomson Reuters Datastream and Ascend Worldwide Ltd. Worldwide Ltd.. Companies are separated in four basic categories to allow for inter-cluster comparison: major full service carriers, non-major full service carriers, low cost carriers and freight carriers (including integrators).

Major full service carriers (MFSC)

Major full service carriers (major network carriers) are defined as companies predominantly carrying passengers, or passengers and cargo, in a hub and spoke network not restricted to intra- or intercontinental routes, with a high yield positioning and an average revenue greater than USD 1 bn per annum over the past 15 years[39].

Non-major full service carriers (NFSC)

Non-major full service carriers (regional carriers) are defined as companies that predominantly carry passengers, or passengers and cargo, in either hub and spoke or point-to-point regional network, with a high yield positioning and average revenue less than USD 1 bn per annum over the past 15 years.

[39] In case a company was not operating and stock listed over the full period of 15 years, only the active years were taken into account.

Low cost carriers (LCC)

Some define low cost carriers as passenger airlines with extremely low operating costs compared to FSC, but a general threshold for costs does not exist. Others classify LCCs as airlines which operate only point-to-point networks, which are regionally focused, combine only secondary airports, and/or offer no service on board. The problem is that these characteristics may be applicable to some LCCs but not to others. Therefore, defining LCCs is difficult and sometimes not completely straight forward.

The example of the best-known LCC in the U.S., Southwest Airlines, shows that a LCC can operate a nationwide network, earn annual revenue as high as major full service carriers, and run at very low costs. Besides that, the global trend of LCCs is to expand their network from short-haul to medium haul, respectively from regional to national and recently even to international service. What all LCCs have in common is the low-price structure. For this paper, LCCs are defined as passenger airlines which position themselves with low fares. The criterion is that an airline stated a low-fare strategy as corporate objective in its annual report of the respective year in range of this analysis or earlier.

Freight carriers and integrators (FREIGHTER)

Freighters are all carriers which transport only cargo, freight, and/or mail, independent from their service levels. Pure cargo airlines which transport big-size freight shipments more or less without a specified delivery are represented as well as integrators which mainly transport light day-defined express shipments.

6.5 Summary of analysis scope

Two external shocks were selected representative for crises. Both affected the aviation industry collectively rather than individual firms: The terrorist attacks on September 11, 2001, and the recent Financial Crisis 2008. Company specific events refer to the evaluation of short term stock reactions to isolated positive or negative event days such as aircraft hull losses or aircraft firm orders. To evaluate stock performance throughout the business cycles two time windows were chosen: (1) companies' long term stock performance over several years including both crises and (2) a "business-as-usual" time window excluding crises.

The company sample includes aircraft operating and holding companies clustered in four different carrier categories: major full service carriers, non-major full service carriers, low cost carriers and freight carriers. Further, a dominant portion of the sample consists of United States based companies. To identify possible differences in reaction of the U.S. stock market compared to the rest of the world in initially U.S. focused shocks, the sample in the analysis of the terrorist attacks on 9/11 (not exclusively but possibly stronger impacting the

U.S.) was further split up in U.S. and non-U.S. based companies. For an illustration of the analysis structure, please refer to Figure 25.

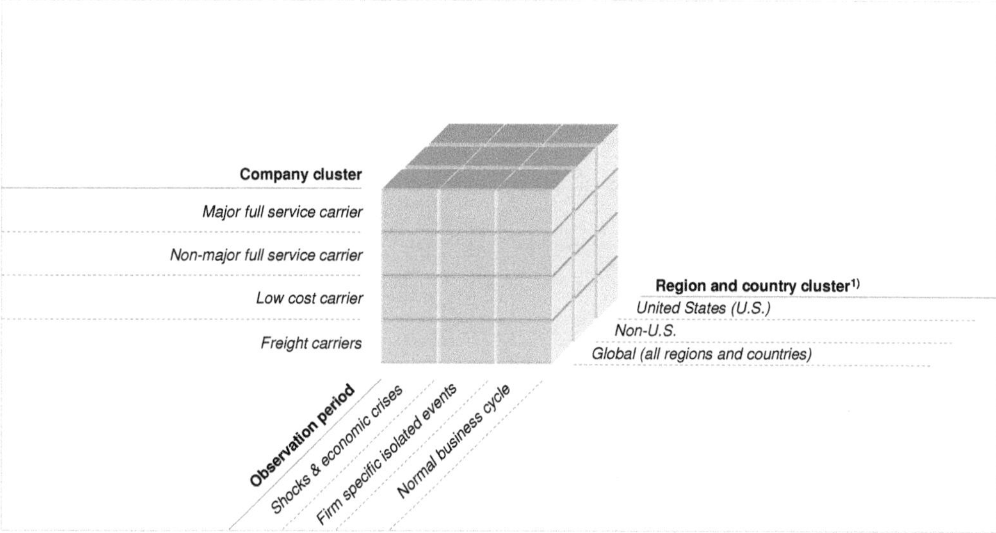

[1] *In the analysis of stock market's reaction on the terrorist attacks on September 11, 2001 possible different reaction of U.S. and non U.S. markets were tested in separate regressions.*

Figure 25: *Analysis cube – Slices of the evaluation of companies' stock market and financial performance*

This figure presents the different slices into which the analysis of aircraft operating and holding companies' stock performance was broken down. The x-axis represents the three different observations periods: (x1) Shocks or crises (terrorist attacks on September 11, 2001, and the recent Financial Crisis 2008), (x2) company specific isolated positive and negative events (aircraft hull losses and aircraft firm orders), and (x3) the normal business cycles (companies' long term financial performance over several years including crises, and mid term "business-as-usual" time window excluding crises). The y-axis represents the four company clusters: (y1) major full service carriers, (y2) non-major full service carriers, (y3) low cost carriers, and (y4) freight carriers. The z-axis – only applicable for the analysis of the terrorist attacks on September 11, 2001 – represents the three region and country clusters: (z1) United States (U.S.) based companies, (z2) Non-U.S. (i.e. in the rest of the world) based companies, and (z3) Global, i.e. all companies of all regions/countries.

7. Analysis of fleet planning decisions and financial success

The following sections describe in more detail the empirical methodology, the observation periods, and the results retrieved from this analysis.

7.1 Empirical methodology

7.1.1 Multivariate regression model (MVRM) and test statistics

Chapter 6.2.2 explained the general choice for performance indicators and methodology used in this thesis. In financial literature, MVRM mostly refers to Gibbons' advancement of Fama et al.'s (1969) standard event study methodology in 1980 to measure the influence of new information on stock prices (Binder, 1998). Binder (1985) tested the use of multivariate regression models in event studies and saw its advantage in the possibility to test joint hypotheses. There is caveat concerning the right selection of test statistics. The best of these is the F test with supporting probability value (p-value), which is consequently used throughout the analyses in this thesis. Beside the F test, adjusted R^2 and t-statistics are used in this thesis to test the null and alternative hypotheses and to determine the statistical significance of independent variables in regressions. Based on Bowerman & O'Connell (2003), the test statistics are described to give the readers a synopsis of the underlying statistical theory.

R^2 refers to the coefficient of determination of the proportion of variability. It basically measures how useful the regression model and how accurate the prediction of the independent variables in the model are. The multiple coefficient of determination R^2 is computed by dividing the explained variation by the total variation. The range of R^2 is between 0 and 1 with 1 representing a regression model that provides the most accurate predictions. R^2 can also be explained as the "proportion of the total variation in the n observed values of the dependent variable that is explained by the overall regression model (Bowerman & O'Connell, 2003, p. 541)." In this thesis R^2 always refers to adjusted R^2, i.e. R^2 adjusted for the number of explanatory terms in a model, thus avoiding that the influence of independent variables is overestimated.
The F test is another test statistic to estimate the adequacy of a regression model. If illustrated, it displays an F distribution curve over the null hypothesis with the common probability type I error range under the ends of the curve.[40] The more aggressive the

[40] Probability type I error = the null hypothesis was true and rejected; probability type II error = the null hypothesis was false and not rejected (Bowerman & O'Connell, 2003)

R. Günther, *Impact of Aircraft Sourcing & Financing on Financial Success*,
Edition KWV, https://doi.org/10.1007/978-3-658-24094-3_7

rejection point of the null hypothesis is set, the stronger the evidence to reject the hypothesis needs to be. The test can be supported by p-value, a measure of the likelihood of a true null hypothesis. Setting the rejection point at a level of significance α, the null hypothesis is rejected when the p-value is less than α. For this thesis the significance levels for p-value are – in line with other empirical studies – set at .10, .05, and .01 (in other words at the 10%, 5%, and 1% level).

The t-statistics is used to determine the significance of independent variables in alternative hypotheses. The advantage is that is does not require any knowledge of the population mean and standard deviation. First, the regression coefficient of the independent variable is determined. Secondly, the t-statistics for this coefficient is estimated by determining the ratio of the coefficient to its standard error. Based on a t-distribution and predefined level of significance of α (probability type I error), the hypothesis is tested. Also in t-statistics, the p-value is supportive in determining whether the hypothesis is rejected or not rejected. In this thesis the same significance levels are used in F and t statistics.

The words "multivariate regression" refer to the analysis of multiple explanatory or control variables in comparison to "univariate regression" in which one assumes that the dependent variable is only affected by one factor. Hence, it is not restricted to the evaluation of abnormal stock returns (to which it often refers), but can be used with any dependent variable. In this thesis, multivariate regressions are modeled with stock market as well as accounting data, depending on the time window addressed.

7.1.1.1 MVRM with abnormal returns in stock prices

Introduction to the use of abnormal returns in MVRM

To measure stock performance, the analysis of abnormal returns is preferred compared to the evaluation of simple stock return or stock price changes, because it sets stock development in relation to market development. "The abnormal return (AR) of a given stock for a particular day can be calculated by subtracting the market's return on the same day [...] from the actual return on the stock for that day." (Ross, Westerfield & Jaffe, 2005). The efficient-market hypothesis (Shleifer, 2000) implies that (1) existence of rationality, (2) independent deviations from rationality, and (3) arbitrage, each by itself leads to efficiency. In a semi-strong form the efficient-market hypothesis implies that stock prices fully reflect all available information. To test this, MVRM with abnormal returns, which is superior to standard event studies (Belsley, Kuh, & Welsch, 2004, and Kedem & Fokianos, 2002, Carter & Simkins, 2004), is often used to evaluate whether information released at time t-1, t, or t+1 is reflected in the abnormal returns AR_{t-1}, AR_t, and AR_{t+1}, respectively, or whether the information has an influence on returns of other days.

Comparison of single and multi-factor models to calculate abnormal returns

Essential for the use of abnormal returns in multivariate regressions is the choice of the right model to estimate the excess returns. The roots of risk-adjusted stock performance evaluations lie in the ambition to actively manage stock portfolios. The value of this had been heatedly discussed for decades as many well-known studies document either significant average underperformance of indices by managed mutual fund portfolios or – contrarily – significant overperformance. "This led to the emergence of extended models that control for several stock market anomalies. [...] Because of the relatively large number of mutual fund performance models this creates a problem for both academics and practitioners: what model to use for performance measurement?" (Otten & Bams, 2004, p. 203, 204)

Today, mainly three models are commonly used, which differ in the number of factors they contain and build on each other: (1) the Jensen's Adjusted Single Factor Capital Asset Pricing Model (Jensen, 1968), (2) the Fama French Three Factor Model (Fama & French, 1993), and (3) the Carhart Four Factor Model (Carhart, 1997).

Additionally, the models can be enriched (A) by using time-varying conditional instead of the unconditional expected returns, alphas, and betas (Chen & Knez, 1996, and Christopherson et al., 1998) and (B) by including a control for monetary conditions. However, the latter has some caveat regarding the multi-factor models: average returns estimated with Fama French's and Carhart's factors significantly change in restrictive versus expansive monetary policy periods (Jensen & Johnson, 1995, Jensen et al., 1996, Jensen and Mercer, 2002, and Becher et al., 2008).

In line with the comparative research conducted by Otten & Bams (2004) and the original studies of Jensen, Fama & French, Carhart, Chen & Knez, and Christopherson et al., in the following all three models and the use of time-varying conditional alphas and betas are described with their advantages and disadvantages. Subsequently, the caveat in the impact of monetary policy periods is considered to eventually make the choice for the model most suitable for this thesis.

(1) Jensen's Adjusted Capital Asset Pricing Model (CAPM)

The relationship of the expected return on a security and its beta (systematic risk relative to the market) was first presented in form of the capital asset pricing model by W. F. Sharpe and J. Lintner (independently) in the years 1964-1965, based on the preceding work of H. Markowitz. The CAPM sets the expected return equal to the sum of the risk-free rate and the product of the beta of the security and the difference between the expected return on the

market and the risk free rate. With the average market return being higher than the average risk-free rate, this implies a linear positive relationship of the expected return and its beta. (Ross et al., 2005)
Based on the CAPM, Jensen (1968) formulated the following model that contains a serially independent random disturbance term and the alpha coefficient, a measure that captures the over- or underperformance of portfolios in excess of the risk adjusted return.

$$R_{i,t} - R_{f,t} = \alpha_i + \beta_i (R_{m,t} - R_{f,t}) + \varepsilon_{i,t} \qquad \textbf{[Jensen's Adjusted CAPM]}$$

where $R_{i,t}$ is the return of individual stock or portfolio i at the time t (one day or month, etc.), $R_{f,t}$ is the return on the risk free rate (often referring to a one- or three-month treasury bill) at the same time t, $R_{m,t}$ is the return of the market-relevant benchmark at time t, $\varepsilon_{i,t}$ is the random disturbance term, β is regression estimate of the systematic risk of the stock or portfolio relative to the benchmark, and α is above mentioned intercept measuring incremental return.

Advantage of Jensen's adjusted CAPM is that it is a relatively simple model for which mostly data are available. Its disadvantage is the underlying assumption that investment behavior can be estimated using a single market index. In other words, the model assumes that all non-normal returns can be filtered out by using a single benchmark, which can result in a bias (pricing error) if the benchmark does not fit the portfolio of stocks, e.g. in terms of spread in market capitalization, and the expected return of the stock or portfolio is not cleaned completely by normal returns (Otten & Bams, 2004).

(2) Fama French Three-Factor Model

Fama & French (1993) expanded the CAPM by two additional factors which they proved to lead to significant statistical enhancement of the pricing errors compared to the single-factor model. They observed that stocks of small-cap companies and those with high book-to-market equity ratio perform better than the rest of the market. Therefore, the one proxy they add to the CAPM is "size" in terms of Small-Minus-Big (SMB) market capitalization (the product of stock price and number of shares issued), i.e. the difference in return of small and large cap stocks or portfolios. The other proxy is High-Minus-Low (HML) book-to-market equity ratio, i.e. the difference between the return of high-book-to-market equity and low-book-to-market equity stock portfolios.[41] (Fama & French, 1996) The Fama French Three Factor Model is given by the following equation.

---

[41] To include these risk factors, Fama & French constructed six portfolios and calculated value-weighted returns to be included in the test of their model. "Size – [...] SMB (small minus big), meant to mimic the risk factor in returns related to size, is the difference, [at each time], between the simple average of the returns on the three small-stock portfolios (S/L, S/M, and S/H) and the simple average of the returns on the three big-stock portfolios (B/L, B/M,, and

$$R_{i,t} - R_{f,t} = \alpha_i + \beta_{0i}(R_{m,t} - R_{f,t}) + \beta_{1i} SMB_t + \beta_{2i} HML_t + \varepsilon_{i,t} \qquad \textbf{[Fama French Model]}$$

The benefit of the Fama French Model is that combining the two variables SMB and HML improves the explanation of average returns compared to the CAPM and can generally be used in any analysis that requires estimates of abnormal returns. Also, the model seems to capture the reversal of long term returns in the SMB and HML variables, i.e. long term losers are likely to experience higher future returns and have positive SMB and HML slopes while long term winners tend to face lower future returns and have negative SMB and HML slopes. With regards to availability: These factors are continuously updated and can be easily accessed via the webpage of Kenneth R. French at Tuck School of Business at Dartmouth.

However, the model cannot capture all cross-sectional variations in average stock portfolio and industry returns, e.g. the continuation of returns of short and mid term winners or losers remains unexplained. With this drawback, pricing errors are still possible. (Fama & French, 1996)

(3) Carhart Four-Factor Model

The topic of short term winners and losers was addressed by Carhart (1997) and Carhart et al. (2002). They extended the Fama French model by another factor: PR1YR – the momentum factor in returns. The idea is based on Jegadeesh & Titman (1993, p.65), who evaluated the one year momentum anomaly in their study of *Returns to Buying Winners and Selling Losers* to find "[…] that strategies which buy stocks that have performed well in the past and sell stocks that have performed poorly in the past generate significant positive returns over 3- to 12- month holding periods." [And,] that the profitability of these strategies [is] not due to their systematic risk […]." This finding is contrary to the reversal of winners and losers in the long term as found by Fama & French. In subsequent work on momentum strategies, Chan, Jedadeesh & Lakonishok (1996) showed with more direct evidence that Fama French's three factor model cannot explain the profitability of momentum strategies or alternatively that the market responds gradually to new information such as earnings announcements. Given these findings, Carhart saw the need to compliment the Fama French Model by the momentum variable. PR1YR captures the risk factor that is imbedded in the difference in returns of short to mid term past winners and losers.[42] The following equation shows the Carhart Model.

B/H). Thus, SMB is the difference between the returns on small- and big-stock portfolios with about the same weighted-average book-to-market equity. […] The portfolio HML (high minus low), meant to mimic the risk factor in returns related to book-to-market equity, is defined similarly." (Fama & French, 1993, p. 9)

[42] The momentum strategy tries to take advantage of the momentum of past winners and past losers, i.e. it is expected that a stock or portfolio with positive returns continues generating positive returns (past winners) at least for some

$$R_{i,t} - R_{f,t} = \alpha_i + \beta_{0i}(R_{m,t} - R_{f,t}) + \beta_{1i}SMB_t + \beta_{2i}HML_t + \beta_{3i}PR1YR_t + \varepsilon_{i,t}$$ **[Carhart Model]**

The advantage of Carhart's model is clear: with the additional momentum variable it is able to offset the limitations of the Fama French model and to further enhance the explanation of the spread in returns. However, several studies show that SMB, HML, as well as PR1YR lack explanatory power when it comes to cross-sectional variation in returns (Mazouz et al., 2009). A further disadvantage will be explained together with the relationship of the three factors with monetary conditions later on.

(A) Time-varying conditional models

"Traditionally performance is measured using unconditional expected returns, assuming that both the investor and manager use no information about the state of the economy to form expectations. However, if managers trade on publicly available information, and employ dynamic strategies, unconditional models may produce inferior results." (Otten & Bams, 2004, p. 206) As risk changes over time, Chen & Knez (1996) and Christopherson et al. (1998) raise their concerns with using unconditional fixed alphas and betas and recommend applying dynamic, time-varying conditional, coefficients modeled as linear functions of lagged predictor variables. Chen & Knez (1996) take a single index model and include conditional betas to capture changes in systematic risk over time. In Christopherson et al. (1998) the same time-varying conditional logic is applied also to alphas. With this a single factor model translates into the following equation.

[Conditional Single Factor Model]

$$R_{i,t+1} - R_{f,t+1} = \alpha_{i0} + \alpha'_i Z_t + \beta_{i0}(R_{m,t+1} - R_{f,t+1}) + \beta'_i Z_t(R_{m,t+1} - R_{f,t+1}) + \varepsilon_{i,t+1}$$

where Z_t is a lagged predictor variable of information, and the elements α'_i and β'_i measure the response of the conditional beta to the information variable. In other words, the alpha and beta used to estimate the average return of an individual stock or portfolio over the risk free rate vary over time. This can apply anytime when new public information is injected into the market.

All listed models can be used with or without time-varying conditional alphas and betas independent of the number of factors included. Otten & Bams (2004) compared all models unconditional and conditional based on statistical and economic relevance. Starting with the unconditional models, they found evidence for the added value of all three additional

time and vice versa for stocks with negative returns (past losers). The momentum factor of Carhart considers this effect. The factor is the equal-weight average of the returns for the winner portfolios minus the average of the returns for the loser portfolios. Also this factor is continuously computed and can be accessed via the webpage of Kenneth R. French at Tuck School of Business at Dartmouth.

factors, size, book-to-market, and momentum. For time-varying alphas only little evidence is found, while "[...] conditioning betas on publicly available information proves to be a considerable improvement [...]. All conditional models are superior to their unconditioned peers." (Otten & Bams, 2004, p. 221)

(B) Impact of monetary conditions

There has been a strong discussion on the influence of monetary conditions on the three and four factor models. Jensen & Johnson (1995) investigated the long term impact of U.S. federal discount rate changes on security returns and found significant greater returns in the stock market following discount rate decreases, and vice versa. Further, Jensen et al. (1996) re-examined a study of Fama & French from 1989 to test the impact of monetary conditions on three business condition proxies (dividend yield, default spread, and term spread). They showed that results differ significantly across monetary environments and that monetary conditions influence the relation of business conditions and stock returns. Particularly in times of expansive monetary environment, business conditions have a significant explanatory effect on stock returns. Jensen & Mercer (2002) and test Fama French's with monetary conditions influencing the three factors and the average stock returns. They found that all three factors are strongly influenced by the monetary environment. Looking at the single factor model, they conclude that it needs to be enhanced, either by monetary policy – if available – or at least by considering the changing monetary conditions in risk premium, which underlines for time-varying conditional models. Becher et al. (2008) support the general findings, but cannot find a superior monetary indicator to capture the changes of monetary policy.

Choice of the most suitable model to estimate abnormal returns

Eventually, the choice for the most suitable model for this thesis has to be made. Under "normal" monetary circumstances, a time-varying conditional Carhart's Four Factor Model, enhanced with monetary conditions, would probably be the best choice. However, with the two shock events in scope, the terrorist attacks on September 11, 2001, and the Financial Crisis 2008, two of the most extreme monetary environments in time are analyzed. Both events triggered severe short to mid term changes in the monetary policy including changes in interest rates and support with governmental bail out packages (the latter including some fiscal policy elements). Information on monetary conditions of the two events is – given the narrow time windows in each shock – not fully accessible and not reliable enough to reflect changes from one trading day to another. The challenge is that not all companies were affected equally by the changes in monetary conditions, e.g. not every airline was granted financial aid after 9/11. Further, the international sample of companies would require access to information of monetary policies of all affected countries. The same is true for the analysis of stock markets reaction to aircraft losses or new acquisition. Considering monetary conditions is therefore not possible.

We know from the studies of Jensen & Johnson (1995), Jensen et al. (1996), Jensen & Mercer (2002), and Becher et al. (2008), that the factors in the Fama French and Carhart model are significantly influenced by the monetary environment. But, if the impact of monetary policy stances, taken by governments and central banks (predominantly those of the U.S.), cannot be included in the model, there is a high risk that including the additional factors of Fama French and Carhart will create random disturbances which outweighs its likely advantage over a single factor model.

So, if exclusion of monetary conditions for reasons of data availability and reliability leads to the elimination of SMB, HML, and PR1YR due to the high risk of creating noise that biases the planned regressions with abnormal returns, what option remains?

Time-varying conditional alphas and betas are still valid and, when applied to Jensens's Adjusted CAPM, are significantly superior to the unconditional Jensen Model (Otten & Bams, 2004). With the time-variation, the changing monetary conditions are at least included in the risk premium (Jensen & Mercer, 2002).

The above described selection of a time-varying conditional single index model is supported by the choice of the same model by Carter & Simkins (2004) in their study on U.S. airline stocks reaction to the terrorist attacks September 11, 2001, though Carter & Simkins did not name reasons for their choice.

Equations used in this thesis to estimate abnormal returns

The underlying mathematical equation of this thesis shows the stock returns of the sample companies as follows:

$$r_{i,t} = \alpha_i + \alpha_i^{'} D_S + \beta_i r_{m,t} + \beta_i^{'} D_S r_{m,t} + \sum_{j=1}^{k} y_{i,j} D_j + \varepsilon_{i,t} \qquad \textbf{Equation 1}$$

where:

$r_{i,t}$ = excess return of firm/portfolio i on day t over the risk-free rate

α_i = least square model parameter reflecting the risk prior to the event

$\alpha_i^{'}$ = least square model parameter reflecting a risk shift resulting from the event

D_S = dummy variable representing a risk shift (1 = risk shift after the event, 0 = otherwise)

β_i = least square model parameter reflecting risk prior to the event

$\beta_i^{'}$ = least square model parameter reflecting a risk shift resulting from the event

$r_{m,t}$ = excess return of the benchmark at day t over the risk-free rate

$y_{i,j}$ = abnormal return of firm/portfolio i on event day j out of the total event days k

D_j = dummy variable representing an event day (1 = event day, 0 = otherwise)

$\varepsilon_{i,t}$ = random disturbance term

Alpha represents the difference between the stock's actual and expected returns given a specific level of systematic risk. This level of systematic risk[43] is measured by beta, which represents the stock's sensitivity to market movements[44].
Especially for the MVRM one has to consider the shift in risk resulting from the terrorist attacks. This is taken into account by additionally including the parameters α' and β' which represent the change in the underlying standard market model parameters resulting from the event.

The formula can be rearranged to compute the abnormal returns for each individual sample firm and any day within the observation time ($y_{i,t}$):

$$y_{i,t} = r_{i,t} - \alpha_i - \alpha_i' D_S - \beta_i r_{m,t} - \beta_i' D_S r_{m,t} - \varepsilon_{i,t} \qquad \textbf{Equation 2}$$

Hence, cumulated abnormal returns can be calculated for any period of time ($CAR_{t,t+n}$) by summing up the daily abnormal returns:

$$CAR_{t,t+n} = \sum_{t=1}^{t+n} y_{i,t} \qquad \textbf{Equation 3}$$

Total stock returns for all listed companies in the sample were obtained from Datastream (2010). The actual daily excess stock returns of each company were computed as the natural logarithm of the total return index of stock i at day t divided by the total return index of stock i at day t-1 minus the daily risk-free interest. The actual excess return of the benchmark m was computed similarly:

$$r_{i,t} = LN\left(\frac{RI_{i,t}}{RI_{i,t-1}}\right) - r_{f,t} \qquad \textbf{Equation 4}$$

$$r_{m,t} = LN\left(\frac{RI_{m,t}}{RI_{m,t-1}}\right) - r_{f,t} \qquad \textbf{Equation 5}$$

[43] The historical alpha is the average realized residual return over a specific period of time as estimated using the least square model $r_{i,t} = \alpha_i + \beta_i \cdot r_{m,t} + \varepsilon_{i,t}$, where $r_{i,t}$ are the firm i's excess returns over the risk free rate in periods t = 1,2, … T, $r_{m,t}$ are the market's excess returns over the risk free rate in the same periods, and $\varepsilon_{i,t}$ is the standard error of firm i in the periods t = 1,2, … T (Grinhold & Kahn, 2000).

[44] The historical beta is a measure of systematic risk that reflects the sensitivity of a security's return to movements in an underlying factor, here: the market. For every 1 percent change in the market the security's return is expected to change by β percent. Beta is estimated by dividing the covariance of the security i's returns and the market's returns by the variance of the market, both over the same period of time (Ross et al., 2005).

where:

$r_{i,t}$ = the actual return of stock i at day t over the risk free rate at day t

LN = the function of the natural logarithm

$RI_{i,t}$ = the total return index of stock i at day t

$RI_{i,t-1}$ = the total return index of stock i at day t-1

$r_{m,t}$ = the actual return of the benchmark m at day t

$RI_{m,t}$ = the total return index of the benchmark m at day t

$RI_{m,t-1}$ = the total return index of the benchmark m at day t-1

$r_{f,t}$ = the daily risk-free rate on day t (rf,t)

As benchmark (market return), the *MSCI World* Index was chosen. This index consists of 24 (before May 26, 2010, only 23) developed market country indices[45] and is market-capitalization weighted as well as free float adjusted (MSCI, 2010). The *MSCI World Index* was chosen because it is a broad index which is traded in all main financial markets worldwide. Being market-capitalization weighted, the index gives the largest firms highest impact on the index's value and avoids biases related to equally-weighted indices (Canina et al., 1998). Comparable studies use the value-weighed market index CRSP (Carter & Simkins, 2004, or Flouris & Walker, 2005) or the market-capitalization weighted Russell 3000 Index (Guenther, 2005). Both, CRSP and Russell 3000 were chosen for the same reasons as the *MSCI World Index*, but they merely include the U.S. market; therefore are not applicable for comparison with a global sample of companies.

A three-month United States treasury bill was chosen as the risk-free rate. Reason for this was the high portion of U.S. based companies in the sample and the short time horizon of the bill (the shorter the investment horizon, the lower the amount of risk). As Datastream gives the annual rate of the T-bill on a daily basis, the daily risk-free rate on day t ($r_{f,t}$) was calculated by dividing the annual interest rate of the Treasury bill ($IR_{f,t}$) by the average number of trading days per year:

$$r_{f,t} = \frac{IR_{f,t}}{260}$$ **Equation 6**

The formulas can be used for any event and time and are adjusted accordingly in α_i, $\alpha_i^{'}$, β_i, and $\beta_i^{'}$. The modifications of the equations' risk components for the respective observation periods, i.e. for the two different shock events, 9/11 and Financial Crisis 2008, as well as for the company specific events are described together with the course of events and the analyses of companies' performance and market's reaction in Chapter 7.2.1.2, Chapter 7.2.2.2, and Chapter 7.3.2, respectively.

---

[45] Australia, Austria, Belgium, Canada, Denmark, Finland, France, Germany, Greece, Hong Kong, Ireland, Israel, Italy, Japan, Netherlands, New Zealand, Norway, Portugal, Singapore, Spain, Sweden, Switzerland, the United Kingdom, and the United States

7.1.1.2 MVRM with long term avg. revenue growth, EBITDA and EBIT margins

Why not use long term abnormal stock returns? To test a company's long term financial performance, abnormal returns are considered inappropriate. When looking at observation periods of several years, the stock of each firm underlies not only the normal external influences that impact all firms in the aviation industry simultaneously, such as GDP development, regulatory changes, and shocks & crises, but also company specific events, the noise of which cannot easily be filtered, e.g. stock splits, changes in dividend policies and mergers & acquisitions. Further, the market portfolio (benchmark) used to calculate abnormal returns could be biased. Barber & Lyon (1997, p. 342) evaluated these challenges in the use of long term abnormal stock returns and argue that "many of the common methods used to calculate long-run abnormal stock returns are conceptually flawed and/or lead to biased test statistics". They analyzed the calculation of the abnormal returns and the test statistics used to determine the explanatory power with focus on one- to five-year returns of NASDAQ listed companies. Their empirical results reveal the following insights: Test statistics of cumulative abnormal returns are positively biased and test statistics of buy-and-hold abnormal returns[46] are negatively biased. Reason for this is that determining long term abnormal returns using market portfolios (benchmarks) "yield test statistics that are misspecificed (empirical rejection rates exceed theoretical rejection rates)."[47]

Other (partly earlier) studies including Blume & Stambaugh (1983), Conrad & Kaul (1993) and Cowan & Sergeant (2001) also report on the faultiness of regressions with long term abnormal returns. As correcting measures to account for the biases are not considered fully reliable or only effective in computing unbiased returns in short horizons (Fisher et al, 2010), it was decided to use other financial indicators to investigate the impact of fleet and fleet planning variables on companies' long-run financial performance: average revenue growth, EBITDA margin, and EBIT margin.

However, a change of the financial performance indicator from stock market to accounting data comprises risks and further challenges. Various researchers, especially with focus on post-merger effects, including Fisher & McGowan (1983), Caves (1989) and Andrade et al. (2001), describe their skepticism in using accounting data as a measure of performance. Nevertheless, Gugler et al. (2003) elaborate on the studies and successfully use profit as a

[46] Buy-and-hold abnormal returns: "the compound return on a sample firm less the compound return on a reference portfolio" (Barber & Lyon, 1997, p. 343)

[47] Barber & Lyon (1997, p. 342) identified three biases: [1] "new listing bias, which arises because in event studies of long-run abnormal returns, sampled firms generally have a long post-event history of returns, while firms that constitute the index (or reference portfolio) typically include new firms that begin trading subsequent to the event month; [2] rebalancing bias, which arises because the compound returns of a reference portfolio, such as an equally weighted market index, are typically calculated assuming periodic (generally monthly) rebalancing, while the returns of sample firms are compounded without rebalancing; and [3] skewness bias, which arises because long-run abnormal returns are positively skewed."

performance measure. Also, Duso et al. (2010) tests stock market data based on event studies versus accounting data. They find that when using long time windows abnormal returns and profitability (and assumed for this thesis also revenue growth) positively and significantly correlate.

When looking at stock listed companies in the aviation industry, it is important to choose an earnings or profitability measure that – unlike net income – is independent from and unbiased by capital structure. This is true for earnings before interest, taxes, depreciation and amortization (EBITDA) and earnings before interest and taxes (EBIT). EBITDA and EBIT are measures often used by financial analysts and generally considered adequate in multiple estimations to determine corporate value. (Lie & Lie, 2002, Brealey et al., 2007, Ross et al., 2005)

Hence, it was decided to test accounting data in form of average revenue growth, EBITDA margin, and EBIT margin as dependent variables in this thesis and hope for meaningful and statistically significant results when used in the subsequent multivariate regressions.

Average annual revenue growth

The annual revenue of the individual companies in the sample was calculated as described in Equation 7. The formula implies the "annualization" of the income statement to the full calendar year in order to compare companies with different fiscal year ends like for like.

$$R_{i,t} = \left(RFY_{i,t} \frac{mYTFYE_{i,t}}{12} \right) + \left(RFY_{i,t+1} \frac{12 - mYTFYE_{i,t}}{12} \right) \qquad \textbf{Equation 7}$$

where:

$R_{i,t}$ = the full calendar year net sales or revenue of stock listed company i in calendar year t with year ending on December 31

$RFY_{i,t}$ = the full fiscal year net sales or revenue of stock listed company i with the company's fiscal year ending during calendar year t

$mYTFYE_{i,t}$ = the number of months from calendar year start to the end of the company's fiscal year for company i in calendar year t

$RFY_{i,t+1}$ = the full fiscal year net sales or revenue of stock listed company i with the company's fiscal year ending during calendar year t+1

The annual revenue growth of each company was computed as follows:

$$ARG_{i,t} = \frac{R_{i,t}}{R_{i,t-1}} - 1 \qquad \textbf{Equation 8}$$

where:

$ARG_{i,t}$ = the year-on-year revenue growth of stock listed company i in year t, with one year equal to a full calendar year ending on December 31

$R_{i,t}$ = the full calendar year net sales or revenue of stock listed company i in calendar year t

$R_{i,t-1}$ = the full calendar year net sales or revenue of stock listed company i in calendar year t-1

The average annual revenue growth of each company was calculated with the ordinary formula for the mean. The arithmetic average of the distribution – in comparison to the median or geometric mean – is preferred and in line with the return statistics in Ross et al. (2005).

$$AARG_{i,t+n} = \frac{ARG_{i,t=1} + ARG_{i,t=2} + ... + ARG_{i,t=n}}{n}$$ **Equation 9**

where:

$AARG_{i,t+n}$ = the average annual rate of net sales or revenue growth of stock listed company i over the observation period from year t to year n

$ARG_{i,t}$ = the year-on-year revenue growth of stock listed company i in year t, with one year equal to a full calendar year ending on December 31

n = the number of calendar years in the observation period

Average annual EBITDA margin and EBIT margin

Beside revenue growth, two earnings measures are included in order to test against efficiency and not only general turnover performance. As argued before (based on Lie & Lie, 2002, Brealey et al., 2007, Ross et al., 2005), earnings before interest, taxes, depreciation and amortization (EBITDA) and earnings before interest and taxes (EBIT) are independent from and unbiased by capital structure, thus preferred over net income.

EBITDA margin and EBIT margin, i.e. earnings in relation to turnover, describe a company's efficiency and allow for benchmarking in the sample. In this thesis both measures are included to see the effect on earnings and earnings efficiency caused by aircraft ownership versus operating lease. Also EBITDA and EBIT are derived by the "annualization" of the income statement to the full calendar year.

Equation 10

$$EBITDA_{i,t} = \left(EBITDAFY_{i,t} \frac{mYTFYE_{i,t}}{12} \right) + \left(EBITDAFY_{i,t+1} \frac{12 - mYTFYE_{i,t}}{12} \right)$$

Equation 11

$$EBIT_{i,t} = \left(EBITFY_{i,t} \frac{mYTFYE_{i,t}}{12} \right) + \left(EBITFY_{i,t+1} \frac{12 - mYTFYE_{i,t}}{12} \right)$$

where:

$EBIT[DA]_{i,t}$ = the full calendar year earnings before interest and taxes [and before depreciation and amortization] of stock listed company i in calendar year t with year ending on December 31

$EBIT[DA]FY_{i,t}$ = the full fiscal year earnings before interest and taxes [and before depreciation and amortization] of stock listed company i with the company's fiscal year ending during calendar year t

$mYTFYE_{i,t}$ = the number of months from calendar year start to the end of the company's fiscal year for company i in calendar year t

$EBIT[DA]FY_{i,t+1}$ = the full fiscal year earnings before interest and taxes [and before depreciation and amortization] of stock listed company i with the company's fiscal year ending during calendar year t+1

The computation of the annual EBITDA and EBIT margins is displayed in Equations 12 and 13. The respective revenue is obtained from Equation 7.

$$EBITDAMAR_{i,t} = \frac{EBITDA_{i,t}}{R_{i,t}}$$ **Equation 12**

$$EBITMAR_{i,t} = \frac{EBIT_{i,t}}{R_{i,t}}$$ **Equation 13**

where:

$EBIT[DA]MAR_{i,t}$ = the margin of annual earnings before interest and taxes [and before depreciation and amortization] of stock listed company i in calendar year t with year ending on December 31

$EBIT[DA]_{i,t}$ = the full calendar year earnings before interest and taxes [and before depreciation and amortization] of stock listed company i in calendar year t with year ending on December 31

$R_{i,t}$ = the full calendar year net sales or revenue of stock listed company i in calendar year t with year ending on December 31

The average annual EBITDA margin and EBIT margin of each company was calculated over the observation periods:

Equation 14

$$AVGEBITDAMAR_{i,t+n} = \frac{EBITDAMAR_{i,t=1} + EBITDAMAR_{i,t=2} + \ldots + EBITDAMAR_{i,t=n}}{n}$$

Equation 15

$$AVGEBITMAR_{i,t+n} = \frac{EBITMAR_{i,t=1} + EBITMAR_{i,t=2} + \ldots + EBITMAR_{i,t=n}}{n}$$

where:

$AVGEBIT[DA]MAR_{i,t+n}$ = the average margin of annual earnings before interest and taxes [and before depreciation and amortization] of stock listed company i over the observation period from year t to year n

$EBIT[DA]MAR_{i,t}$ = the margin of annual earnings before interest and taxes [and before depreciation and amortization] of stock listed company i in calendar year t with year ending on December 31

n = the number of calendar years in the observation period

7.1.2 Definition of explanatory and control variables

Explanatory and control variables, which are supposed to explain the differences in abnormal returns between the companies, are clustered in six categories: (1) Financial variables, (2) Market variables, (3) Aircraft fleet and fleet planning variables, (4) Carrier types, (5) Region variables, and (6) Special event day variables. Within each category several quantitative key factors were included[48]. Aircraft fleet and fleet planning variables are already discussed in Chapter 6 when describing the research hypotheses. Here they are further detailed in terms of data included and how they are calculated. Table 3 gives an overview on all explanatory and control variables with formulas and description of information contained. Table 4 illustrates the expected effects of all non-fleet or fleet planning variables.

[48] Some explanatory variables were considered but ultimately not included in the analysis because no consistent and reliable data were available for all observation periods in scope: Passenger complaints over thousand passengers transported and capital expenditures over depreciation.

Financial variables

Financial variables include measures of company size, liquidity, debt payback period, profit margin, equity ratio, and interest coverage.
SIZE is determined by the natural logarithm of total assets. LIQUIDITY is calculated as cash & equivalents over current liabilities, NDTEBITDA is computed as net debt over EBITDA. EBITDAMAR is the margin on earnings before interest, taxes, depreciation and amortization, i.e. EBITDA over total operating revenue. EQITYRAT is equity ratio of owner's equity over total assets. INTRSTCOVRG is interest coverage with interest expenses for debt over EBIT.

Market variables

Market and region variables include measures of market share, dependency on international business, dependency on cargo and mail business, and a company's home region.
RPKMKTSHR and FTKMKTSHR are market shares based on revenue passenger kilometers and freight ton kilometers, respectively.
PINT is the portion of the international revenue in total revenue calculated by subtracting all regional business of total revenue. Because airlines report differently on their geographic areas and sometimes domestic business is not only defined as the home country's share of revenue but also the business in neighbor countries, the definition of domestic business was adjusted commonly to the intra-regional business generally stated by all companies. As regions were defined: APAC (Asia Pacific), EMEA (Europe Middle East and Africa), LATAM (Latin America), NORAM (North America). Emerging markets are allocated accordingly into the four regions.
In order to test the sensitivity of the variable to a narrow definition of domestic business, a second variable with a different regional split was tested: PINT1 is the portion of the international revenue in total revenue calculated by subtracting the company's narrow home market business, i.e. the business generated in the home country and typically included neighbor countries. All data were retrieved from Datastream (2010) for the respective years if not stated otherwise. For example, the domestic business of U.S. Airways includes all business within the U.S. as well as Canada and Mexico; the domestic business of British Airways includes all business in United Kingdom, Ireland and mainland Europe. Domestic business for China or Hong Kong based airlines is defined as business in mainland China, Hong Kong and Macau. Domestic business for New Zealand or Australia based airlines is defined as business in New Zealand, Tasmania, Australia and the connecting Pacific region (excl. Asia). Domestic business of Taiwan based airlines is limited to Taiwan. Japan airlines include Japan only in domestic business. Domestic business of Chilean and Brazil airlines includes intra-country business only. Domestic business of Sweden and Finland include all intra-Scandinavia business.

PFREIGHT is the portion of freight business in total operating revenue with freight including cargo, integrator (express) and mail business.

Source of all financial and market data was Thomson Reuters Datastream (2010), cross-checked and completed with the annual reports of the respective companies when available.

Cluster Variable	Description	Formula (and alternatives)
Financial Variables		
SIZE	Company's size represented by its total assets	Natural logarithm of total assets
LIQUIDITY	Company's liquidity and ability to meet short term obligations	Cash & cash equivalents over current liabilities
NDTEBITDA	Company's debt payback period	Net debt over earnings before interest, taxes, depreciation, and amortization (net debt over EBITDA)
EBITDAMAR	Company's profitability margin on an asset neutral basis	Earnings before interest, taxes, depreciation, and amortization (EBITDA) over total operating revenue
EQITYRAT	Company's capitalization	Owners equity over total assets (equity ratio)
INTRSTCOVRG	Company's interest coverage and ease to pay back debt	Interest expenses for debt over earnings before interest and taxes
Market Variables		
RPKMKTSHR	Company's revenue passenger kilometer market share	Revenue passenger kilometers over total market's RPKs defined as the sum of the top 250 companies' RPKs
FTKMKTSHR	Company's freight ton kilometer market share	Freight ton kilometers over total market's FTKs defined as the sum of the top 250 companies' FTKs
PINT	Company's dependency on (portion of) international (non-home region) business	Non-intra-regional revenue over total operating revenue (regions are APAC, EMEA, LATAM, and NORAM)
PINT 1	Company's dependency on (portion of) international (non-domestic) business	Non-narrow home market revenue over total operating revenue (can include home and neighbor countries)
PFREIGHT	Company's dependency on freight (express, cargo and mail) business	Revenue of express, cargo and mail over total operating revenue
Aircraft Fleet and Fleet Planning Variables		
TOTALAC	Company's total fleet count	Sum of jet aircraft in the fleet of a group, i.e. the mother company and all financial consolidated subsidiaries
OPSLEASE	Company's high-level aircraft financing structure represented by the portion of operating leased aircraft	Ratio of aircraft on operating lease to total number of aircraft
STORAC	Company's short term flexibility to increase capacity in terms of portion of stored (in-active) aircraft	Ratio of aircraft on storage to total number of aircraft
nYRORDER	Company's long-term secured future capacity represented by the total number of firm ordered aircraft	Total number of firm jet aircraft orders to existing fleet count
nYROPTION	Company's long-term strategic capacity planning visible in the total number of aircraft purchase options	Total number of aircraft purchase options over existing fleet count
1YROPTION	Company's 1 year strategic capacity planning visible in the number of aircraft purchase options	Number of aircraft purchase options with execution day in the next calendar year over existing fleet count
AVGAGE	Company's technological modernity represented by the average age of its fleet	Average age of total number of existing aircraft in service or stored at year end
Carrier Type Variables		
AMR/UAL	Company is American Airlines or United Airlines (directly involved in 9/11)	Dummy variable, with 1 equal to the company allocated to this category and 0 otherwise
MFSC	Company is a Major Full Service Carrier	Dummy variable, with 1 equal to the company allocated to this category and 0 otherwise
NFSC	Company is a Non-major Full Service Carrier	Dummy variable, with 1 equal to the company allocated to this category and 0 otherwise
LCC	Company is a Low Cost Carrier	Dummy variable, with 1 equal to the company allocated to this category and 0 otherwise
FREIGHT	Company is a Freight Carrier	Dummy variable, with 1 equal to the company allocated to this category and 0 otherwise
Region Variables		
APAC	Company's base/home region is Asia Pacific	Dummy variable, with 1 equal to the company allocated to this category and 0 otherwise
EMEA	Company's base/home region is Europe, Middle East and Africa	Dummy variable, with 1 equal to the company allocated to this category and 0 otherwise
LATAM	Company's base/home region is Latin America	Dummy variable, with 1 equal to the company allocated to this category and 0 otherwise
NORAM	Company's base/home region is North America	Dummy variable, with 1 equal to the company allocated to this category and 0 otherwise
Special event day variables		
FATALITY	Company's severity of involvement in on-board fatality	Number of passengers & crew killed in an aircraft accident over total number of passengers & crew on board
INJURY	Company's severity of involvement in on-board injury	Number of passengers & crew killed in an aircraft accident over total number of passengers & crew on board
LOSTVALUE	Company's monetary loss in asset value	Book value of the aircraft before hull loss
ACPORDER	Company's capacity commitment per order	Number of aircraft per single firm order

***Table 3:** Overview on explanatory and control variables for MVRM analyses*

This table presents six clusters of explanatory and control variables for the multivariate regression model analyses: (1) Financial variables, (2) Market variables, (3) Aircraft fleet and fleet planning variables, (4) Carrier type variables, (5) Region variables, and (6) Special event day variables. It further includes a general description of each variable and how it can be interpreted, and the formula how it is computed.

Aircraft fleet and fleet planning variables

Aircraft fleet and fleet planning variables include measures of a company's total existing fleet size, activity status, funding composition and average age as well as measures reflecting a company's future fleet planning.
TOTALAC is the total number of aircraft, OPSLEASE is the ratio of aircraft on operating lease to total number of aircraft, and STORAC is the ratio of aircraft on storage to total number of aircraft. AVGAGE is the average age of the total number of existing aircraft in service or stored. nYRORDER is the number of aircraft firm orders not yet delivered for all (n) years over the total existing fleet count. nYROPTION is the number of aircraft options and letters of intent for aircraft purchase not yet executed for all (n) years over the total existing fleet count. nYROPTION was calculated also for a more narrow time horizon to test for time sensitivity of the market[49]. 1YROPTION represents the number of options placed with planned execution within the next calendar year. All variables are calculated with data at calendar year end and refer to primary market data consolidated by Ascend Worldwide Ltd. Due to incompleteness of data, used aircraft market information as applied in the aircraft transaction study by Pulvino (1998) was excluded. The following section describes the data selection in more detail.
All data were taken from Ascend Worldwide Ltd. at year ending December 31 and might differ from the fleet information given in the companies' annual reports. Only companies' dedicated aircraft were included in the analysis, i.e. owned, financial or operating leased aircraft. Seasonal and short term wet leases and charters were excluded (cf. Chapter 2.1). The aircraft count was focused to include long-haul and regional jets but to exclude turbo props of any size, business jets and any other small aircraft. Further, (sub-)leases to 3rd parties are included in the 3rd party's fleet count and not in the fleet count of the initial lessee. Fleet count of the listed companies include, beside the parental airline, also the respective cargo division (or subsidiary airline) and affiliated airlines if consolidated in the annual report of the years in scope (i.e. majority share in the subsidiary). Fleet data were available through Ascend Worldwide Ltd. for the respective years. An overview on the sample companies is provided in Chapter 6.4.

Carrier type variables

Carrier type variables include binary dummy variables with 1 being equal to the airline's allocation to one out of four company clusters major full service carrier (MFSC), non-major full service carrier (NFSC), low cost carrier (LCC), freight carrier (FREIGHT), and 0 being the others.

---

[49] Initially, also 1YRORDER was considered, but excluded because too few companies in the sample had aircraft orders with planned delivery date within the next year (Ascend Worldwide Ltd., 2010).

Region variables

To further analyze whether the market generally differentiated between companies based in different geographic regions, binary dummy variables were introduced with 1 being equal to the company's home region APAC, EMA, LATAM, or NORAM, and 0 being the others.

Special event day variables

For the analysis of stock market's reaction to company specific isolated negative and positive events – aircraft accidents and aircraft firm orders – four additional variables are included that might explain differences in abnormal returns. FATALITY and INJURY refer to the percentage of passengers and crew killed and injured in an aircraft accident. LOSTVALUE is the actual book value of the lost aircraft. ACPORDER refers to the number of aircraft per firm order.

To complete the testable hypotheses of the influence of explanatory and control variables on stock market reaction, long term revenue growth, and profitability (cf. expected impact of basic aircraft fleet and fleet planning variables, Chapter 6.3, Table 1), Table 4 summarizes the assumed effect of the non-fleet variables. Some but not all of these non-fleet variables were already tested in previous researches. The rationales are based upon supporting statements found in the literature consulted for this thesis. As the focus of this research is on fleet and fleet planning characteristics, it shall be allowed to let it be done with an overview and not to expatiate on the hypotheses and rationales in lengthy texts.

	Event		Times of crisis	Firm specific isolated event		Long term business cycle		
				A/C acquisition	A/C loss			
	Impact on / correlation with		*Abnormal stock return*	*Abnormal stock return*		*Revenue growth*	*EBITDA margin*	*EBIT margin*
	Variable		Rationale	Rationale	Rationale	Rationale	Rationale	Rationale
Financial variables	SIZE	High	↗ Big companies = more likely to survive	→ No correlation expected	→ No correlation expected	↘ Big/mature company = less growth	→ Unclear effect of synergies[1]	→ Unclear effect of synergies[1]
		Low	↘ Small firm = higher chance of bankruptcy	→ No correlation expected	→ No correlation expected	↗ Small firm = high growth (potential)	→ Unclear effect of synergies[1]	→ Unclear effect of synergies[1]
	LIQUIDITY	High	↗ Liabilities can be paid independent of add. funds	→ No correlation expected	→ No correlation expected	↘ Liquidity = no growth or investment	→ No correlation expected	→ No correlation expected
		Low	↘ No flexibility to invest or pay liabilities	→ No correlation expected	→ No correlation expected	↗ Low liquidity = potentially high invest.	→ No correlation expected	→ No correlation expected
	NDTEBIT-DA	High	↘ Bankruptcy risk if debt cannot be paid back[2]	→ No correlation expected	→ No correlation expected	→ No correlation expected	→ No correlation expected	→ No correlation expected
		Low	↗ Lower risk that debt obligations cannot be met[2]	→ No correlation expected	→ No correlation expected	→ No correlation expected	→ No correlation expected	→ No correlation expected
	EBITDA-MAR	High	↗ High margin = efficient business	→ No correlation expected	→ No correlation expected	→ Unclear effect of synergies[1]	n/a Not tested	n/a Not tested
		Low	↘ Low margin = low efficiency/ cost pressure	→ No correlation expected	→ No correlation expected	→ Unclear effect of synergies[1]	n/a Not tested	n/a Not tested
	EQUITRAT	High	↗ Less debt = lower risk of bankruptcy	→ No correlation expected	→ No correlation expected	↗ Higher changes to be granted new debt to invest/grow	→ No correlation expected	→ No correlation expected
		Low	↘ More debt = higher risk of bankruptcy	→ No correlation expected	→ No correlation expected	↘ Banks are reluctant to lend more	→ No correlation expected	→ No correlation expected
	INTRST-COVRG	High	↘ Difficulties to pay interest; risk of bankruptcy	→ No correlation expected	→ No correlation expected	→ No correlation expected	→ No correlation expected	→ No correlation expected
		Low	↗ Lower risk that interest obligations are not met	→ No correlation expected	→ No correlation expected	→ No correlation expected	→ No correlation expected	→ No correlation expected

The table is split into four pages. For more information and the legend please refer to the table description on the last table page.

↗ *Expected positive impact/correlation* → *Expected neutral (no) impact/correlation* ↘ *Expected negative impact/correlation*

[1] *Some uncertainty remains regarding the correlation of SIZE (natural logarithm of total assets) and EBITDA margin and EBIT margin as the effect of a company's underlying business model and the relationship of SIZE to cost synergies and bargaining power is unclear. A similar doubt remains in the expected relationship of EBITDA margin and revenue growth. Investment and growth is supposed to be a lever to create synergies, but the ultimate proof of the synergies is not certain.*

[2] *Net debt over EBITDA ratio is a measure banks often refer to when they consider to lend further money to a company. Above a certain "healthy" ratio, the bank will not issue further debt as the risk increases that the EBITDA of the company is not sufficient to pay back the debt. If the company is significantly below the "healthy" ratio, the tax benefits of debt financing are not leveraged*

Table 4 (1/4): *Expected effect of non-fleet and fleet planning explanatory and control variables*

	Event		Times of crisis		Firm specific isolated event				Long term business cycle					
					A/C acquisition		A/C loss							
	Impact on / correlation with			*Abnormal stock return*	*Abnormal stock return*				*Revenue growth*		*EBITDA margin*		*EBIT margin*	
	Variable			Rationale		Rationale		Rationale		Rationale		Rationale		Rationale
Market variables	RPKMKT-SHR	High	↘ ↗ →	9/11: full impact by passenger emotions; 2008: general downturn but passenger business better off	n/a	Not tested	n/a	Not tested	n/a	Not tested	n/a	Not tested	n/a	Not tested
		Low	↗ → ↘	9/11: smaller share in effected business 2008: general downturn but cargo business worse off	n/a	Not tested	n/a	Not tested	n/a	Not tested	n/a	Not tested	n/a	Not tested
	FTKMKT-SHR	High	↗ ↘	9/11: less impact by passenger emotions; 2008: world trade drops	n/a	Not tested	n/a	Not tested	n/a	Not tested	n/a	Not tested	n/a	Not tested
		Low	↘ ↗ →	9/11: smaller share in less effected cargo 2008: smaller share in more effected cargo	n/a	Not tested	n/a	Not tested	n/a	Not tested	n/a	Not tested	n/a	Not tested
	PINT (PINT1)	High	↗ ↘	Depending on time in crisis and geographic spread[3]	n/a	Not tested	n/a	Not tested	n/a	Not tested	n/a	Not tested	n/a	Not tested
		Low	↗ ↘	Depending on time in crisis and geographic spread[3]	n/a	Not tested	n/a	Not tested	n/a	Not tested	n/a	Not tested	n/a	Not tested
	PFREIGHT	High	↗ ↘	9/11: Less impacted by passenger emotions; 2008: world trade drops	n/a	Not tested	n/a	Not tested	n/a	Not tested	n/a	Not tested	n/a	Not tested
		Low	↘ ↗ →	9/11: passenger business dependency 2008: general downturn but passenger business better off than cargo	n/a	Not tested	n/a	Not tested	n/a	Not tested	n/a	Not tested	n/a	Not tested

The table is split into four pages. For more information and the legend please refer to the table description on the last table page.

↗ *Expected positive impact/correlation* → *Expected neutral (no) impact/correlation* ↘ *Expected negative impact/correlation*

[3] *The portion of international business (non-home region and non-domestic) in total revenue is expected to significantly impact stock market reaction. However, a positive or negative effect depends on the time during crisis and geographic spread of the airline, e.g. during flight ban within and into the U.S. at 9/11, U.S. airlines with high portions of international business are expected to generate more positive or less negative abnormal returns because they could keep operating outside of the U.S. On the other hand, a high portion of international business is expected to be negative when bailout packages influence market's reaction. A wider geographic spread and independence from the U.S. market (both crises started here) are assumed to be of benefit*

Table 4 (continued 2/4): *Expected effect of non-fleet and fleet planning explanatory and control variables*

	Event	Times of crisis	Firm specific isolated event: A/C acquisition	Firm specific isolated event: A/C loss	Long term business cycle		
	Impact on / correlation with	*Abnormal stock return*	*Abnormal stock return*	*Abnormal stock return*	*Revenue growth*	*EBITDA margin*	*EBIT margin*
	Variable	Rationale	Rationale	Rationale	Rationale	Rationale	Rationale
Carrier type variables	AMR/UAL	↘ ↗ 9/11: initially negative impact due to direct involvement; later profiting from financial aid	n/a Not tested	n/a Not tested	n/a Not tested	n/a Not tested	n/a Not tested
Carrier type variables	MFSC	↗ Bigger airline = higher chance of survival	→ No correlation expected	→ No correlation expected	↘ Big/mature airline = less growth	→ No correlation expected	→ No correlation expected
Carrier type variables	NFSC	↘ Smaller airline = higher chance of bankruptcy	→ No correlation expected	→ No correlation expected	↗ Low market share = growth potential	→ No correlation expected	→ No correlation expected
Carrier type variables	LCC	→ 9/11: no correlation expected ↘ 2008: LCC = highly cost sensitive customers that stop flying first	→ No correlation expected	→ No correlation expected	↗ → New business model = strong growth[4]	→ No correlation expected	→ No correlation expected
Carrier type variables	FREIGHT	↗ 9/11: No impact by passenger emotions; ↘ 2008: world trade drops	→ No correlation expected	→ No correlation expected	→ No correlation expected	↗ Higher margin compared to passenger	↗ Higher margin compared to passenger
Region variables	APAC	↗ → Initially better off; relatively less negative when crisis reaches APAC in the mid term	→ No correlation expected	→ No correlation expected	↗ Strong growth market	↗ Significantly lower costs (especially personnel) than other regions	↗ Significantly lower costs (especially personnel) than other regions
Region variables	EMEA	↗ ↘ Initially better off; negative when crisis reaches EMEA in the mid term	→ No correlation expected	→ No correlation expected	→ Growth of Middle East, Africa offset by mature Europe	→ No correlation expected	→ No correlation expected
Region variables	LATAM	→ ↘ No correlation or negative due to vicinity to USD/NORAM region	→ No correlation expected	→ No correlation expected	→ Not yet a growth market as APAC	→ No correlation expected	→ No correlation expected
Region variables	NORAM	↘ Origin of both crises, 9/11 and fin. crisis 2008	→ No correlation expected	→ No correlation expected	↘ Mature market	→ No correlation expected	→ No correlation expected

The table is split into four pages. For more information and the legend please refer to the table description on the last table page.

↗ *Expected positive impact/correlation* → *Expected neutral (no) impact/correlation* ↘ *Expected negative impact/correlation*

[4] *The correlation of LCC to revenue growth is assumed to be dependent on the observation period. In the late 1990s low cost can be still classified as a "new" business model for which strong revenue growth is expected; therefore a positive correlation is expected for the observation period 1995-2009. In the period 2002-2007, the low cost business model was well established*

Table 4 (continued 3/4): *Expected effect of non-fleet and fleet planning explanatory and control variables*

Specific event day variables

Event		Times of crisis		Firm specific isolated event				Long term business cycle					
				A/C acquisition		A/C loss							
Impact on / correlation with		*Abnormal stock return*		*Abnormal stock return*				*Revenue growth*		*EBITDA margin*		*EBIT margin*	
Variable			Rationale		Rationale		Rationale		Rationale		Rationale		Rationale
FATALITY	High	n/a	Not tested	n/a	Not tested	↘	Liability stretched by lawsuits and claims; loss of reputation = perhaps sustainable revenue decrease	n/a	Not tested	n/a	Not tested	n/a	Not tested
	Low	n/a	Not tested	n/a	Not tested	↗	Potentially seen as less severe incident[5]	n/a	Not tested	n/a	Not tested	n/a	Not tested
INJURY	High	n/a	Not tested	n/a	Not tested	↘	Liability stretched by lawsuits and claims; loss of reputation = perhaps sustainable revenue decrease	n/a	Not tested	n/a	Not tested	n/a	Not tested
	Low	n/a	Not tested	n/a	Not tested	↗	Potentially seen as less severe incident[5]	n/a	Not tested	n/a	Not tested	n/a	Not tested
LOST-VALUE	High	n/a	Not tested	n/a	Not tested	↘	High financial loss	n/a	Not tested	n/a	Not tested	n/a	Not tested
	Low	n/a	Not tested	n/a	Not tested	↗	Potentially seen as less severe incident[5]	n/a	Not tested	n/a	Not tested	n/a	Not tested
AC-PORDER	High	n/a	Not tested	↗	Extreme growth expectation	n/a	Not tested	n/a	Not tested	n/a	Not tested	n/a	Not tested
	Low	n/a	Not tested	→	No correlation expected	n/a	Not tested	n/a	Not tested	n/a	Not tested	n/a	Not tested

The table is split into four pages. For more information and the legend please refer to the table description on the last table page.

↗ Expected positive impact/correlation *→ Expected neutral (no) impact/correlation* *↘ Expected negative impact/correlation*

[6] *FATALITY, INJURY and LOSTVALUE could isolated be seen as less severe by the stock market; however, in combination these factors might still cause significant market reaction.*

Table 4 (continued 4/4): *Expected effect of non-fleet and fleet planning explanatory and control variables*

This table is split over four pages and summarizes the anticipated impact and correlation of non-fleet and fleet planning explanatory and control variables on the financial performance of air transport companies with consolidated rationales. The variable clusters include: Financial variables, market variables, carrier type variables, region variables, and special event day variables. For a detailed description of the individual measure, please refer to Table 3 in Chapter 7.1.2). The rationales are built on supporting statements found in the literature consulted for this thesis. The financial performance refers to short- and mid term abnormal stock returns in times of crisis, aircraft acquisition, and aircraft loss as well as to average revenue growth, EBITDA margin, and EBIT margin over the long term business cycle. For a complementary synopsis on expected impact/correlation of basic aircraft fleet and fleet planning variables please refer to Chapter 6.3, Table 1

7.1.3 Analysis process – Flow of multivariate regressions

Regressions were conducted in several steps and following a structured top-down process.
In a first step, the three different categories of variables, a) financial variables, b) market variables, and c) aircraft fleet variables were tested separately to see whether one category of variables has singular significant explanatory power and whether specific variables within the categories have a higher statistical significance than others.
In a second step, the model started with all independent variables. Variables for which alternatives with high statistical multicollinearity exist (PINT/PINT1, nYRORDER/ 1YRORDER, nYROPTION/1YROPTION) were replaced to see whether the substitute shows a change in test significance. One by one, the number of variables was reduced until the model showed statistical significance measured by adjusted R^2 and the F-statistics; herewith finding the most explanatory mix of independent variables.
In a third step, the number of independent variables was further reduced to evaluate the change in explanatory power. By consequently eliminating the variables that become statistically insignificant until all variables in the model remain significant, the model's F-statistic is optimized and ultimately shows the combination of variables with the highest statistical significance.
In a fourth step, those variables identified as not statistically significant were consolidated in one model and reduced step by step to evaluate whether some variables have a less strong explanatory power which nevertheless becomes visible when tested against other weak variables.
With these four steps, statements can be made about the explanatory power of the individual variables.
In a fifth step, variables were randomly combined in terms of the number of variables in the model and the mix of variables. Sole restriction: from highly correlating variables (alternative variables) only one representative was included in the model. With the results of this final and random regression analysis step, the validity of the conclusions drawn from the previous five steps was tested.
Figure 26 summarizes the flow of the regression analyses.

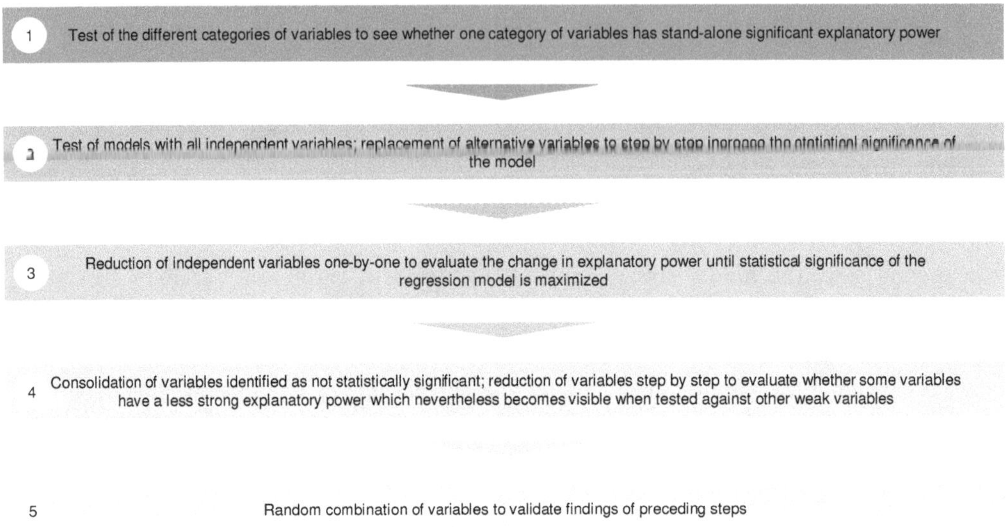

Figure 26: *Regression analysis process*

This figure presents the flow of the regression analyses in five steps. The analysis was conducted top-down starting with a model which includes all explanatory and control variables and which was subsequently reduced step-by-step in variables to test the change in explanatory power. Further, variables identified as statistically not significant were evaluated separately to test whether their explanatory power becomes statistically significant in an environment of weak variables. The validity of conclusions drawn from the top-down approach was tested against random combinations of variables.

7.2 Stock performance in times of crises – Analysis of shocks

After having detailed the analysis' objective, methodology and evaluation flow, this chapter will describe the outcome of the multivariate regression analysis focusing on shocks. Shocks are classified as unexpected events with severe impact on whole industries or even the world economy. Within the last ten years the world has been going through two of these shocks: the terrorist attacks on the World Trade Center on September 11, 2001 and the Financial Crisis 2008. In the following both shocks are evaluated in detail, each starting with the course of events, then explaining the shift of risk in investing in aircraft operating and holding companies, and eventually illustrating the differences in market's reaction with regard to individual companies, i.e. answering the questions why not all company stocks showed the same reaction and what made the difference.

	9/11 only	9/11 and Financial Crisis 2008	Financial Crisis 2008 only	
MFSC	KLM Royal Dutch	Air Canada Air France(-KLM) Air New Zealand Alaska Air Group All Nippon American Airlines Austrian Airlines British Airways Cathay Pacific China Airlines China Eastern Airlines Continental Airlines Delta Air lines Deutsche Lufthansa AG Eva Airways Finnair Iberia Japan Airlines Korean Airlines LAN Airlines Malaysia Airlines Northwest Airlines Qantas Airways SAS Singapore Airlines TAM Thai Airways United Airways US Airways	Air China China Southern Airlines El Al	Σ 32
NFSC	FLY Mesaba/MAIR Holdings Midwest Express	Hawaiian Holdings Mesa Air Group Skywest Westjet Airlines		Σ 7
LCC	ATA Holding America West Holding	Airtran Holding Easyjet PLC Ryanair Frontier Airlines Southwest Airlines	AER Lingus Air Berlin Jetblue Airways Virgin Blue	Σ 11
FREIGHT	Airborne Express	Atlas Air/Atlas Air World Wide Holdings Fedex/Federal Express UPS/United Parcel Service	Air Transport Service Group	Σ 5
	Σ 7	Σ 41	Σ 8	Σ 56
	Σ 48 (9/11)		Σ 49 (Financial Crisis 2008)	

***Table 5:** Aircraft operating and holding companies in scope of the analysis of shocks and economic crises*

This table presents the total of 56 aircraft operating and holding companies in scope of the analysis of stock market's reaction of the two shocks and economic crises the terrorist attacks on September 11, 2001 and the Financial Crisis 2008. Selection criteria were: the firm was (1) active a minimum of 6 months prior and post either one or both events, (2) listed and traded at the stock exchange, and (3) operated an aircraft fleet of a minimum of one commercial jet with a capacity of more than 50 seats (or freight equivalent), excluding small business jets and turbo props. The firms are clustered into four different categories: major full service carriers, non-major full service carriers, low cost carriers, and freighters.

The sample of companies used for the evaluation of the two shocks slightly differs. Not all companies match the sample requirements at both events, e.g. some airlines not yet existed on 9/11, filed for bankruptcy in its aftermath or merged with other companies. Table 5 presents an overview on the sample, separated into the four carrier clusters as well as into their activity status at the terrorist attacks on September 11, 2001 and/or the Financial Crisis 2008.

7.2.1 Terrorist attack on September 11, 2001

7.2.1.1 September 11, 2001 – Observation periods and course of events

It was the morning of September 11, 2001, when four commercial airliners yawed from their regular routes over U.S. territory to induce what is nowadays known by two numbers: 9/11. All four aircraft were high-jacked by terrorists who – for the first time in civil aviation – followed the brutal plan to use aircraft as weapons in a suicidal mission. The first two aircraft crashed into the towers of the World Trade Center in New York City. Shortly after, the third exploded into the Pentagon. The fourth aircraft fell southeast of Pittsburgh,

Pennsylvania into the countryside. According to several media reports more than 3,000 people died (crews, passengers and a majority of approximately 2,600 people in and around the affected buildings). The world changed drastically by what happened on this one day. Looking back over the decades, no external shock hit the world and its economy as unforeseen and strongly as the terrorist attacks on September 11, 2001 in the United States. It was different from other unexpected, catastrophic events such as earth quakes or epidemics in so far as it created an enormous emotional reaction.

Undoubtedly, 9/11 "and the images running for weeks on all types of media are forever etched in our memories. Many people remember where they were standing and what they were doing when they first heard of the attacks. But, only few will remember the detailed course of events on 9/11 and the following days" (Guenther, 2005, p. 1). Yet, the chronology of the event is important for the evaluation of stock price reaction and thus is outlined thoroughly in the following with focus on aviation relevant facts and figures (Rhoades, 2003, Federal Aviation Administration, 2001a and 2001b, Guenther, 2005):

September 11, 2001

- American Airlines Flight 11 from Boston to Los Angeles and United Airlines Flight 175 from Boston to Los Angeles crash into the two towers of the World Trade Center in New York City. Both towers collapsed shortly afterwards.
- American Airlines Flight 77 from Washington, D.C. to Los Angeles crashes into the Pentagon, United Flight 93 crashes southeast of Pittsburgh.
- A national ground stop is ordered for all aircraft in U.S. airspace and all airports close.
- The U.S. stock exchange closes.

September 13, 2001

- U.S. airspace reopens to domestic commercial and private aviation (except Boston's Logan airport and Washington, D.C.'s Reagan airport). No international carriers are allowed to enter U.S. air territory.
- U.S. bond markets open.
- September 17 is set as the reopening day of U.S. stock exchanges (on September 13).

September 14, 2001

- President Bush signs the Declaration of National Emergency by Reason of Certain Terrorist Attacks.

- General aviation aircraft operating under Instrumental Flight Rules are allowed resuming operations.
- The U.S. Security and Exchange Commission (SEC) relaxes rules on company buybacks.

September 17, 2001
- Major U.S. stock exchanges reopen.
- U.S. Federal Reserve cuts interest rates.
- Dow Jones Industrials index closing at 8920.70, down 684.82 points, or 7.1%.
- NASDAQ Composite index closing at 1579.28, down 116.02 points, or 6.8%.

September 18, 2001
- United Airlines announces to cut 20,000 jobs.
- Secretary of Transportation, Norman Mineta, meets with airline executives and discusses financial aid to the airlines.

September 21, 2001
- The Air Transportation Safety and System Stabilization Act is passed. [50]

September 23, 2001
- The Federal Aviation Administration (FAA) begins issuing government-backed insurance.

October 8, 2001
- The FAA announces new security measures for U.S. airlines and airports.

[50] The Air Transportation Safety and System Stabilization Act (H.R. 2926) was a bailout package enacted by the Senate and the House of Representatives of the United States of America as Public Law 107-42 on September 21, 2001, to prevent bankruptcy in the airline industry (Sunshine & Woodward, 2001). The package was signed into law after a first high-level analysis by the U.S.' Government Accounting Office (2001a, p. 1) which revealed that "the temporary shutdown of the nation's airspace and the severe drop in passenger traffic since the attacks" could possibly cause losses for the passenger carrier business of USD 6.5-10.5 billion through December 31, 2001. The findings were confirmed by the Air Transport Association (ATA) which estimated minimum losses of USD 10.1 billion by the end of the calendar year 2001. The Air Transportation Safety and System Stabilization Act included compensation for victims of the aircraft crashes, limits of liability of the airlines involved in the attacks, assistance through grants, federal credits, extended deadlines for tax payments, and reimbursements for increasing insurance premiums (U.S. Congress, 2001). The total financial support for the airline industry should have summed up to more than USD 15.0 billion, but to meet the requirements (especially regarding cost reduction) for approval of loan guarantees was so difficult for some airlines that only few had received help by the end of 2001 (Government Accounting Office, 2001b). "Nevertheless, immediately after September 11 the Air Transportation Safety and System Stabilization Act promised all U.S. carriers support in facing the substantial economic loss resulting from the attacks. Therefore it is expected to have an influence on investors' expectation of the airlines' future performance, reflected by the stocks' movements." (Guenther, 2005, p. 18)

November 5, 2001

- FAA administrator Jane F. Garvey announces the hiring of additional security employees to supplement the FAA's security agent forces and to increase security at U.S. airports.

Subsequent analysis will concentrate on stock market's reaction on the six trading days following the terrorist attacks. From United States perspective this means September 17, the first trading day on which the U.S. stock exchange reopened, and September 18-24, the five trading days in which the Air Transportation Safety and System Stabilization Act was enacted. Additionally, the time between September 25 and November 5 is evaluated, in which the Federal Aviation Administration announced the implementation of new security standards for airlines and airports.

A complicating factor with respect to the observation period is that United States stock exchanges reacted upon the terrorist attacks by closing from September 11 to 16, reopening September 17, while the rest of the world (RoW) kept trading during these days. Hence, companies might have experienced a market reaction including a time shift depending on where their stock was traded.

Always considering the home stock exchange for each company and ignoring secondary trading markets, U.S. based firms are restricted by the opening hours of U.S. stock exchanges with September 17 as the first trading day after the attacks. Assuming that generally all stock markets worldwide reacted to the event, two basic options exist for non-U.S. based firms, primarily traded at non-U.S. stock exchanges: (1) the market reacted immediately on September 11 and the "new" risk was priced-in before U.S. stock exchanges reopened, or (2) the RoW market "waited" for the reaction of the U.S. market and the impact of the event on non-U.S. based companies was delayed till September 17.

This situation becomes even more complicated when a sample containing all U.S. and non-U.S. based companies is investigated. Here, the first trading day in the U.S. is equal to the fifth trading day for the rest of the world. As it is still not clear when the Rest of World reacted to 9/11, the different trading start days might lead to a biased result in the regression analyses when abnormal returns are delinked in time. To cross-check for possible biases, "trading day matching" is introduced in additional analyses beside the evaluation of abnormal returns with the actual calendar dates. In "trading day matching", the first trading day for non-U.S. based companies is set equal to the first trading day for U.S. based firms, i.e. abnormal returns of September 11 at non-U.S. (Rest of World) stock markets and abnormal returns of September 17 at the U.S. market are treated as if they happened on the same day. In comparison to the actual timing (first trading day in the U.S. is equal to the fifth trading day in the RoW) conclusions can be drawn regarding the parallelism of markets' reaction.[51]

Table 6 summarizes the different compositions of home stock markets (U.S. or non-U.S.) and time windows (actual trading days or trading day matching). In a first step, market's reaction for U.S. based companies is evaluated stand-alone. In a second step, non-U.S. based companies are analyzed in two time windows starting with (a) September 11, and (b) September 17 as first trading day. In a third step, markets' reaction for all companies are tested again in two time windows considering (a) the actual trading days (e.g. y_1 U.S. = y_5 RoW), and (b) trading day matching (e.g. y_1 U.S. = y_1 RoW).

Sample		Event Day	Short Term	Mid Term
U.S. Companies	1	17.09.2001 1 trading day y_1 (U.S.)	18.-24.09.2001 5 trading days y_{2-6} (U.S.)	25.09 - 05.11.2001 30 trading days y_{7-36} (U.S.)
Non-U.S. Companies	2a	11.09.2001 1 trading day y_1 (RoW)	12.-18.09.2001 5 trading days y_{2-6} (RoW)	19.09. - 30.10.2001 30 trading days y_{7-36} (RoW)
	2b	17.09.2001 1 trading day y_5 (RoW) [= y_1 (U.S.)]	18.-24.09.2001 5 trading days y_{6-10} (RoW) [=y_{2-6} (U.S.)]	25.09. - 05.11.2001 30 trading days Y_{11-40} (RoW) [=Y_{7-36} (U.S.)]
All Companies	3a	17.09.2001 1 trading day y_1 (U.S.) = y_5 (RoW)	18.-24.09.2001 5 trading days y_{2-6} (U.S.) = y_{6-10} (RoW)	25.09. - 05.11.2001 30 trading days y_{7-36} (U.S.) = y_{11-40} (RoW)
	3b	17.09.2001 = 11.09.2001 1 trading day y_1 (U.S.) = y_1 (RoW)	18.-24.09.2001 = 12.-18.09.2001 5 trading days y_{2-6} (U.S.) = y_{2-6} (RoW)	25.09. - 05.11. = 19.09. - 30.10. 30 trading days y_{7-36} (U.S.) = y_{7-36} (RoW)

Table 6: *Overview on time windows for 9/11 regressions – Actual trading days and trading day matching*

This table presents the different compositions of home stock markets and trading time windows in the multivariate regression analyses of the terrorist attacks on September 11, 2001. The sample refers to the home market the companies' stocks are traded in: the United States (U.S.) stock market and the stock market of the rest of world (RoW) or non-U.S. market. y_i *(stock market) refers to the trading day(s) in scope of the analysis, e.g.* y_1 *(U.S) represents the first trading day at the United States stock market,* y_{2-6} *(RoW) represents the trading days 2-6 in the rest of world's stock markets (non-U.S.). The trading time windows include the event day, the short term (5 trading days) and the mid term (30 trading days). Compositions 2b and 3b are based on "trading day matching"* y_i *(U.S.) =* y_i *(RoW), i.e. trading day i of U.S. based companies is set equal to trading day i of non-U.S. based firms.*

[51] No other academic literature was found that considered a similar approach. In stock trading history, the situation of 9/11, in which the U.S. stock exchanges closed, but the stock exchanges in the rest of the world remained open, is quite unique. So far, studies using abnormal returns to explain the impact of 9/11 on airline stocks concentrated on samples of airlines within the same region. With the international sample in this thesis, the risk of creating random noise in treating abnormal stock returns on the same calendar day "like-for-like" was too high. Therefore, "trading day matching" was introduced to better understand the difference in statistical significance of abnormal returns in the use of calendar days versus the use of the actual trading days.

7.2.1.2 September 11, 2001 – Alpha, beta, and the shift in risk

Alpha and beta coefficients and their role in multivariate regression models with abnormal returns are generally described in Chapter 7.1.1.1. In order to analyze specific events, both risk components need to be adapted for the respective observation periods. Further specified: when evaluating stock market's reaction on the terrorist attacks of September 11, 2001, alpha and beta of each stock have to be modified to reflect the stock's risk prior to (α, β) and the shift in risk after 9/11 (α', β'). For better comparison to previous studies the time horizons for alpha and beta calculations were aligned with Carter & Simkins, 2004, and Guenther, 2005.

Calculation of α and β risk components for 9/11[52]:

α_i = least square model parameter reflecting the risk prior to 9/11; calculated over a period of 112 trading days starting April 1 and ending September 10, 2001

α_i' = least square model parameter reflecting a risk shift resulting from 9/11; calculated as the difference between α_i and the alpha for the same i determined over a period of 137 trading days starting September 11, 2001 and ending March 31, 2002

β_i = least square model parameter reflecting the risk prior to 9/11; calculated over a period of 112 trading days starting April 1 and ending September 10, 2001.

β_i' = least square model parameter reflecting a risk shift resulting from 9/11; calculated as the difference between β_i and the beta for the same i determined over a period of 137 trading days starting September 11, 2001 and ending March 31, 2002

Table 7 shows alpha and beta coefficients and the shift in risk for all firms in scope of the analysis, calculated using the least square market model. It further includes alphas and betas estimates for equally weighted portfolios based on the four carrier clusters and regions introduced in Chapter 6.4.

[52] The number of trading days mentioned is exemplary and refers to the trading days of the New York Stock Exchange (NYSE). Saturdays and Sundays are excluded as well as NYSE trading holidays, i.e. days with full closure of the exchange. For companies listed at other stock exchanges the actual number of trading days might vary; nevertheless, risk components were calculated for all companies from April 1 – September 10, 2001 and from September 11, 2001 – March 31, 2002.

Company	Region	α_i		α_i'		β_i		β_i'	
Major full service carriers									
1 Air Canada Inc	NORAM	-0.0013	(0.0024)	0.0007	(0.0055)	0.7984 ***	(0.2562)	0.4258 *	(0.5400)
2 Air France	EMEA	-0.0011	(0.0020)	0.0022	(0.0030)	0.6298 ***	(0.2117)	1.0403 ***	(0.2940)
3 Air New Zealand Limited	APAC	-0.0019	(0.0029)	-0.0030	(0.0080)	0.8537 ***	(0.3101)	0.0465	(0.7847)
4 Alaska Air Group Inc	NORAM	0.0020	(0.0013)	-0.0018	(0.0031)	0.7809 ***	(0.1452)	1.3898 ***	(0.3064)
5 All Nippon Airways Company Limited	APAC	-0.0001	(0.0019)	-0.0016	(0.0020)	0.4008 *	(0.2068)	0.3715 ***	(0.1988)
6 AMR Corp.	NORAM	-0.0006	(0.0017)	-0.0008	(0.0039)	1.1030 ***	(0.1806)	1.3373 ***	(0.3892)
7 Austrian Airlines AG	EMEA	-0.0006	(0.0019)	-0.0009	(0.0029)	0.0306	(0.2015)	0.4271	(0.2875)
8 British Airways PLC	EMEA	-0.0003	(0.0019)	-0.0009	(0.0038)	0.8736 ***	(0.2053)	1.1929 ***	(0.3713)
9 Cathay Pacific Airways Limited	APAC	-0.0018	(0.0016)	0.0039	(0.0028)	0.3167 *	(0.1760)	0.3319 **	(0.2777)
10 China Airlines Limited	APAC	-0.0011	(0.0025)	0.0007	(0.0029)	-0.0661	(0.2663)	-0.1057	(0.2811)
11 China Eastern Airlines Corp. Limited	APAC	-0.0010	(0.0015)	0.0000	(0.0018)	-0.0212	(0.1586)	0.1077	(0.1779)
12 Continental Airlines Inc	NORAM	-0.0005	(0.0019)	-0.0024	(0.0063)	0.0780	(0.2061)	0.6668	(0.6207)
13 Delta Air Lines Inc	NORAM	0.0005	(0.0016)	-0.0019	(0.0045)	1.1689 ***	(0.1703)	1.5840 ***	(0.4428)
14 Deutsche Lufthansa AG	EMEA	0.0000	(0.0006)	-0.0002	(0.0005)	-0.0614	(0.0697)	0.0065	(0.0444)
15 EVA Airways Corp.	APAC	-0.0020	(0.0027)	0.0028	(0.0032)	-0.2329	(0.2965)	0.1889	(0.3136)
16 Finnair OYJ	EMEA	-0.0001	(0.0017)	0.0000	(0.0015)	-0.0251	(0.1889)	0.3350 *	(0.1493)
17 Iberia SA	EMEA	0.0000	(0.0012)	0.0022	(0.0026)	0.1396	(0.1346)	1.0705 ***	(0.2548)
18 Japan Airlines Corp.	APAC	-0.0024	(0.0020)	0.0020	(0.0025)	0.5769 ***	(0.2119)	0.2425 ***	(0.2446)
19 KLM Royal Dutch Airlines	EMEA	-0.0033	(0.0020)	0.0045	(0.0036)	0.6348 ***	(0.2181)	0.5010 ***	(0.3587)
20 Korean Air Lines Company Limited	APAC	0.0012	(0.0024)	0.0053	(0.0041)	0.4106	(0.2643)	0.5111 **	(0.4017)
21 Lan Airlines SA	LATAM	-0.0003	(0.0015)	-0.0015	(0.0017)	0.0685	(0.1596)	0.6759 ***	(0.1665)
22 Malaysian Airline	APAC	-0.0001	(0.0032)	0.0005	(0.0027)	0.0992	(0.3500)	0.7154 ***	(0.2651)
23 Northwest Airlines Corporation	NORAM	-0.0003	(0.0021)	-0.0004	(0.0037)	1.1120 ***	(0.2223)	1.7179 ***	(0.3651)
24 Qantas Airways Limited	APAC	0.0032	(0.0030)	-0.0001	(0.0026)	0.9073 ***	(0.3233)	-0.2056 ***	(0.2521)
25 SAS AB	EMEA	-0.0013	(0.0022)	0.0011	(0.0025)	0.4437 *	(0.2398)	0.4387 ***	(0.2461)
26 Singapore Airlines Limited	APAC	-0.0010	(0.0020)	0.0024	(0.0024)	0.2692	(0.2129)	0.7163 ***	(0.2365)
27 TAM SA	LATAM	-0.0015	(0.0011)	0.0022	(0.0007)	0.2021	(0.1223)	0.0248 ***	(0.0700)
28 Thai Airways International Public Company	APAC	-0.0001	(0.0025)	0.0005	(0.0036)	-0.1511	(0.2714)	0.5042	(0.3508)
29 UAL Corporation	NORAM	0.0002	(0.0018)	-0.0052	(0.0052)	0.9516 ***	(0.1973)	1.7379 ***	(0.5081)
30 US Airways Group Inc	NORAM	-0.0094 ***	(0.0029)	0.0045	(0.0067)	0.3743	(0.3131)	3.5686 ***	(0.6564)
Non-major full service carriers									
1 FLYi, Inc.	NORAM	0.0022	(0.0026)	-0.0035	(0.0048)	0.2982	(0.2807)	2.7460 ***	(0.4725)
2 Hawaiian Holdings Inc	NORAM	-0.0007	(0.0028)	0.0010	(0.0044)	0.6700 **	(0.3023)	-0.3114	(0.4308)
3 Mesa Air Group Inc	NORAM	0.0058 **	(0.0027)	-0.0087	(0.0080)	1.0693 ***	(0.2972)	3.6053 ***	(0.7915)
4 Mesaba Holdings/MAIR Holdings, Inc.	NORAM	-0.0017	(0.0024)	0.0013	(0.0031)	0.2559	(0.2649)	1.2156 ***	(0.3012)
5 Midwest Express Holdings	NORAM	0.0002	(0.0020)	0.0003	(0.0040)	0.3544 *	(0.2132)	2.0816 ***	(0.3935)
6 Skywest Inc	NORAM	0.0039 *	(0.0020)	-0.0062	(0.0043)	1.4263 ***	(0.2205)	2.2674 ***	(0.4228)
7 Westjet Airlines Limited	NORAM	-0.0006	(0.0021)	0.0040	(0.0025)	-0.0075	(0.2298)	0.3464	(0.2488)
Low cost carriers									
1 Airtran Holdings Inc	NORAM	-0.0020	(0.0035)	0.0015	(0.0044)	0.4895	(0.3827)	2.4089 ***	(0.4367)
2 America West Holdings	NORAM	-0.0001	(0.0018)	-0.0036	(0.0101)	1.0880 ***	(0.1953)	2.5511 ***	(0.9958)
3 ATA Holdings	NORAM	0.0079 *	(0.0045)	-0.0118	(0.0057)	0.8034	(0.4869)	1.6593 ***	(0.5608)
4 Easyjet PLC	EMEA	0.0017	(0.0015)	-0.0001	(0.0028)	0.4206 **	(0.1626)	0.6809 ***	(0.2756)
5 Frontier Airlines, Inc.	NORAM	0.0008	(0.0032)	0.0015	(0.0037)	1.0571 ***	(0.3499)	1.5075 ***	(0.3642)
6 Ryanair Holdings PLC	EMEA	0.0008	(0.0017)	0.0005	(0.0027)	0.6810 ***	(0.1787)	0.3612 ***	(0.2620)
7 Southwest Airlines Company	NORAM	0.0005	(0.0017)	0.0000	(0.0025)	1.0314 ***	(0.1838)	0.3194 ***	(0.2422)

** Statistically significant at the 10% level*
*** Statistically significant at the 5% level*
**** Statistically significant at the 1% level*

Table 7: *Alpha, beta and the shift in risk with 9/11 for all sample firms and portfolios*

(Table continued on next page)

Freight carriers									
1 Airborne Express	NORAM	0.0023	(0.0022)	-0.0002	(0.0022)	0.8990 ***	(0.2371)	1.3920 ***	(0.2143)
2 Atlas Air Worldwide Holdings Inc	NORAM	-0.0065 **	(0.0028)	0.0066	(0.0032)	0.9960 ***	(0.2981)	1.1612 ***	(0.3154)
3 Federal Express/FedEx Corp	NORAM	0.0005	(0.0014)	0.0019	(0.0014)	1.0324 ***	(0.1516)	0.0469 ***	(0.1428)
4 United Parcel Service, Inc	NORAM	-0.0001	(0.0008)	0.0009	(0.0009)	0.6084 ***	(0.0888)	-0.0984 ***	(0.0925)
Carrier portfolios									
Major full service carriers	∑30	-0.0009	(0.0005)	0.0006	(0.0015)	0.4220 ***	(0.0575)	0.7191 ***	(0.1516)
Non-major full service carriers	∑7	0.0013	(0.0011)	-0.0016	(0.0031)	0.5808 ***	(0.1140)	1.7075 ***	(0.3103)
Low cost carriers	∑7	0.0014	(0.0012)	-0.0017	(0.0030)	0.7959 ***	(0.1281)	1.3555 ***	(0.3005)
Freight carriers	∑4	-0.0010	(0.0012)	0.0023	(0.0013)	0.8839 ***	(0.1263)	0.6254 ***	(0.1247)
Region portfolios									
APAC	∑12	-0.0006	(0.0008)	0.0013	(0.0016)	0.2468 ***	(0.0894)	0.2545 ***	(0.1580)
EMEA	∑10	-0.0004	(0.0008)	0.0008	(0.0015)	0.3767 ***	(0.0877)	0.6054 ***	(0.1437)
LATAM	∑2	-0.0009	(0.0011)	0.0003	(0.0010)	0.1353	(0.1142)	0.3504 ***	(0.0993)
NORAM	∑24	0.0001	(0.0008)	-0.0009	(0.0028)	0.7683 ***	(0.0916)	1.4720 ***	(0.2791)

* *Statistically significant at the 10% level*
** *Statistically significant at the 5% level*
*** *Statistically significant at the 1% level*

Table 7 (continued): *Alpha, beta and the shift in risk with 9/11 for all sample firms and portfolios*

This table presents the standard market model parameters α and β and standard errors (in parentheses) for each firm and equally-weighted carrier cluster and region portfolios, estimated over a period of 112 trading days starting April 1 and ending September 10, 2001. It also presents α′ and β′ which reflect a risk shift after September 11, 2001. α′ [β′] is calculated as the difference between the firm's α [β] before the event and the firm's α [β] after the event, estimated over a period of 137 trading days starting September 11, 2001, and ending March 31, 2002. Underlying daily stock data were obtained from Thomson Reuters Datastream (2009). Benchmark is the MSCI World Index. The number of trading days is indicatively and refers to the trading days of the New York Stock Exchange (NYSE). Statistical significance is based on t-statistics.

Merely a few United States based companies from all carrier clusters show significant alphas before 9/11: US Airways (-0.0094***), Mesa Air (0.0058**), Skywest (0.0039*), ATA Holding (0.0079*), and Atlas Air (-0.0065*). Also, looking at α‘, none of the companies or portfolios in the sample experiences a significant shift in alpha risk within the first half year after 9/11. These results are in line with the findings of Carter & Simkins (2004).

However, betas before 9/11 and definitively the shift in beta after 9/11 show highest statistical significance for most companies and portfolios. Although the benchmark MSCI World is a broad and diversified index, most aircraft operating and holding firms turn out to have a significant smaller beta than the market (1.0) before the event, ranging from 0.3167* (Cathay Pacific) to 0.9960*** (Atlas Air). Again some U.S. based companies stand out and present beta that are higher than the market between 1.0314*** for Southwest Airlines and 1.4263*** for Skywest.

The equally-weighted portfolios give a consolidated view on the beta. All carrier portfolios show significantly lower betas before 9/11 than the market, with major full service carriers bearing the lowest (0.4220***) and freight carriers the highest (0.8839***) systematic risk. Nevertheless, this result might be geographically biased, because the carrier clusters of non-major full service carriers, low cost carriers, and freight carriers include mainly or even purely U.S. based companies. As mentioned before, this is due to the fact that within these clusters no non-U.S. aircraft operating and holding companies are stock listed. The cluster of major full service carriers on the other hand is more geographically diversified. (cf. Chapter 6.4)

To better understand possible geographic influences on a company's beta coefficient, equally-weighted portfolios were defined based on the companies' home region APAC, EMEA, LATAM, or NORAM. From a regional perspective, the Asia Pacific (APAC) portfolio has the lowest significant beta of 0.2468*** (the LATAM portfolio undercut this with 0.1353, but no valid statement can be made regarding this coefficient as its t-statistics does not show any statistical significance). NORAM companies on average have the highest beta of 0.7683***.

This means that investing in a portfolio of aircraft operating and holding companies was always less risky than investing into the broad market before 9/11, and that the geographic scope clearly makes a difference with the Asia Pacific region bearing the lowest risk compared to the market.
Now, how did the risk of investing in aircraft operating and holding companies change compared to the market in the first half year after the terrorist attacks on September 11, 2001?

Table 7 shows that almost all stocks in the sample experience a shift in beta risk (β') that is significant at the 1% level. Overall, the significant risk shifts range from -0.2056*** (Qantas) to 3.6053*** (Mesa Air), with an increase in risk for the majority of the sample (more than 90% of the stocks).

Again, looking at the portfolios the picture becomes clearer. NFSCs (1.7075***) on average experience the highest increase in beta, followed by LCCs (1.3555***), MFSCs (0.7191***), and finally FREIGHTERS (0.6254***). Compared to the regional portfolios where NORAM clearly shows the highest beta increase of 1.4720***, the change in risk for the four U.S. based freight carriers is interestingly low. Without anticipating the results of the regression analyses, it seems as if the market distinguished between passenger and non-passenger carriers, having more confidence in the latter after 9/11.

The APAC portfolio, which already showed the smallest beta before the event, also experiences the smallest change in risk (0.2545***), followed by LATAM (0.3502***), and EMEA (0.6054***). It seems natural that NORAM reflects the highest shift in beta, because the United States and its companies were most affected by the terrorist attacks, but companies in other regions might be dependent on business in or out of NORAM. Eventually, the results of the regression analyses will give more insights into the impact of regional differences and the market's reaction to a companies' dependency cross-regional business.

7.2.1.3 September 11, 2001 – Analysis results: Stock market's reaction

This section describes the results of the evaluation of stock market's reaction to 9/11 in several steps. Starting with the time before 9/11, the industries stock performance is compared to general market development, before the abnormal returns caused by the shock are estimated. In following, multivariate regressions are conducted to analyze the root cause of market's behavior and distinguishing factors between the companies at the first trading day, in the short term, and in the mid term after the event. Following a high level illustration of the industries stock performance in the long term after the event, the chapter closes with a summary of the findings on stock market's reaction to the terrorist attacks.

Airline stocks before 9/11

How did stocks of aircraft operating and holding companies generally perform before the terrorist attacks on September 11, 2001, and is there any visible impact of 9/11?

Figure 27 gives a view on the quarterly development of the MSCI World Air Freight & Logistics[53] and on the MSCI World Airline[54] Indices versus the sector unspecific and broader MSCI World Index between Q2 1997 and Q4 2002, i.e. over a five year period including the first year after the shock.

In the first year displayed, all three indices develop relatively parallel. This changes in the fourth quarter of 1998 and for the following years. The sector of air freight and logistics clearly outperformed while airlines performed under the general market. This trend did not change with the terrorist attacks. Looking at the graph it is obvious that (passenger) airlines suffered significantly more than air freight and logistics providers. The latter even managed to encounter a drop of business and stay above the benchmark in the three months following the shock. Interestingly, the sector indices show upward trends in Q1 and Q2 2002 before another downward trend begins.

[53] MSCI World Air Freight & Logistics Index = free float weighted equity index (Bloomberg, 2011)

[54] MSCI World Airline Index = free float weighted equity index (Bloomberg, 2011); in July 2006 the index included ACE Aviation, Air China, Air France-KLM, Air Asia, All Nippon, Asiana, British Airways, Cathay Pacific, China Airlines, China Eastern, Malaysia Airlines, Qantas, Ryanair, SAS, Singapore, Southwest, TAM, Thai Airways, and Tukish (Morrell, 2007)

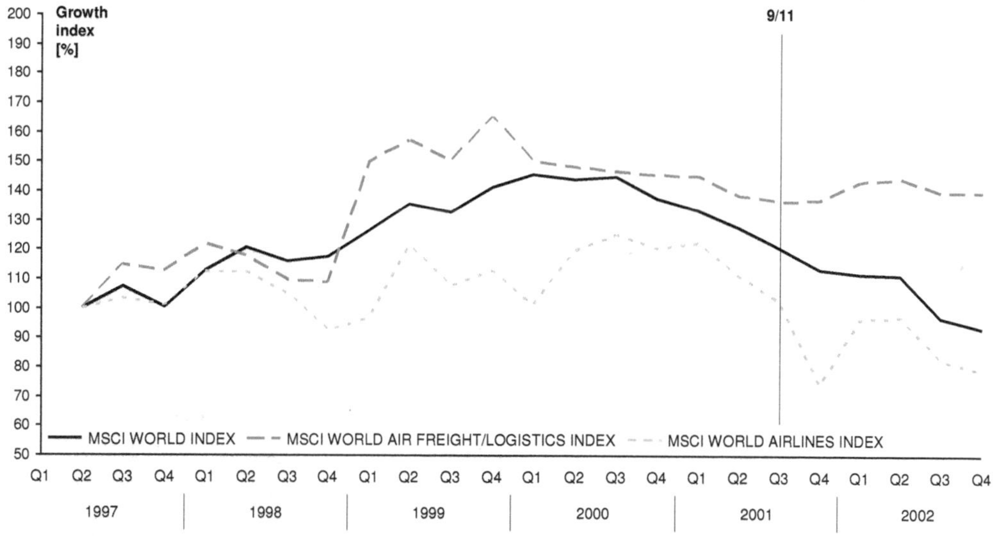

Figure 27: *Stock market development 1997 to 2002 – Sector indices versus the general market*

This figure presents the quarterly development of the two sector price indices MSCI World Air Freight/Logistics and MSCI World Airlines versus the sector-unspecific, broader MSCI World Index from Q2 1997 to Q4 2002. The time period includes the impact of the terrorist attacks on September 11, 2001. All data were obtained from Thomson Reuters Datastream (2010).

Abnormal return as a reaction upon 9/11

The reaction of the stock market to 9/11 was clearly significant. But, was the reaction of aircraft operating and holding companies' stocks significantly different from the general market, i.e. did considerable abnormal returns occur? Just by looking at the graph in Figure 27 this question could be answered with "yes". Yet, this section will finally provide statistical evidence for this statement.

Using the equations 2 introduced in Chapter 7.1.1.1, and based on the observation period defined in Chapter 7.2.1.1, daily abnormal returns were calculated for each sample firm and respective portfolio of firms for the period September 11 to 24 as well as cumulated abnormal returns for the periods (1) September 12-14, (2) September 12-18, (3) September 19 to October 30, (4) September 18-24, and (5) September 25 to November 5 (cf. Table 6). Based on the fact that U.S. stock exchanges were closed September 11-16, the daily abnormal returns for September 11-14 and the cumulated abnormal returns (1)-(3) for carrier portfolios and region portfolios do not include U.S. based companies. Table 8 shows the abnormal returns in the stock market's reaction upon 9/11.

The significance of abnormal returns and the respective F-statistics of the regressions illustrate that stocks of aircraft operating and holding companies indeed reacted stronger than the general stock market.

Between September 11 and 16, most non-U.S. based companies' stocks already showed a reaction to 9/11, before U.S. stock exchanges reopened on September 17. Only two firms, China Eastern Airlines and Finnair OYJ did not respond. The reaction of all other stocks in scope was not focused on a specific day but was rather spread over the four days. The portfolio of stocks primarily traded at EMEA stock exchanges experienced abnormal returns of -0.898 statistically significant at the 1% level from September 11 onwards, whereas the APAC portfolios mainly started to react on September 12. Reason for this is most likely the opening hours of the stock exchanges in the different time zones. When the first plane crashed in the morning of the September 11 in New York, and the world came to realize that this was not a "normal" aircraft accident but rather a terrorist attack, European and Middle East stock exchanges were still open for at least three hours, while stock exchanges further east had already closed. As soon as the new trading day started on September 12, the other markets started to react.

Generally, September 12 shows the strongest market reaction in the period September 11-14. The carrier portfolios of major full service carriers and of low cost carriers show highly significant negative abnormal returns on September 12 of -0.0590 and -0.1261, respectively. The trend remains for major full service carriers also for September 13 (-0.0398) and September 14 (-0.0525), while the returns of the low cost carrier portfolio are non-significant. Also on September 12, the sum of abnormal return for the region portfolios is highest.

Company	Region	y_1 (RoW) /a (U.S.)		y_2 (RoW) n/a (U.S.)		y_3 (RoW) n/a (U.S.)		y_4 (RoW) n/a (U.S.)		y_5 (RoW) y_1 (U.S.)		y_6 (RoW) y_2 (U.S.)		y_7 (RoW) y_3 (U.S.)		y_8 (RoW) y_4 (U.S.)		y_9 (RoW) y_5 (U.S.)		y_{10} (RoW) y_6 (U.S.)		R^2	F-stat.	$\sum^{3}_{y2\text{-}4\,(RoW)} y_j$ = n/a (U.S.)	$\sum^{5}_{y2\text{-}6\,(RoW)} y_j$ = n/a (U.S.)	$\sum^{30}_{y7\text{-}36\,(RoW)} y_j$ = n/a (U.S.)	$\sum^{5}_{y6\text{-}10\,(RoW)} y_j$ = $\sum^{5}_{y2\text{-}6\,(U.S.)} y_j$	$\sum^{30}_{y11\text{-}40\,(RoW)} y_j$ = $\sum^{30}_{y7\text{-}36\,(U.S.)} y_j$
Major full service carriers																												
1 Air Canada Inc	NORAM	-0.0334	(0.0477)	0.0145	(0.0475)	-0.2194 ***	(0.0475)	-0.2095 ***	(0.0476)	0.0903 *	(0.0483)	0.0090	(0.0684)	-0.0350	(0.0476)	0.0159	(0.0486)	-0.1336 ***	(0.0483)	-0.0906 *	(0.0490)	0.15	5.29 ***	-0.4144	-0.3151	-0.6264	-0.2343	-0.4016
2 Air France	EMEA	-0.1444 ***	(0.0261)	-0.1058 ***	(0.0260)	0.0132	(0.0260)	-0.0828 ***	(0.0260)	-0.0309 *	(0.0264)	0.0261 ***	(0.0374)	0.0454	(0.0260)	-0.0520 **	(0.0266)	-0.0087	(0.0264)	0.1213 ***	(0.0268)	0.25	8.85 ***	-0.1753	-0.1801	0.1606	0.1321	-0.0270
3 Air New Zealand Limited	APAC	0.0090	(0.0511)	-0.2232 ***	(0.0509)	0.2140 ***	(0.0509)	-0.3196 ***	(0.0509)	-0.4962 ***	(0.0517)	0.1238 ***	(0.0732)	0.0995 *	(0.0510)	-0.1680 ***	(0.0520)	-0.0570	(0.0517)	-0.5065 ***	(0.0525)	0.53	27.05 ***	-0.3288	-0.7012	-0.0525	-0.5083	0.5353
4 Alaska Air Group Inc	NORAM		—		—		—		—	-0.2776 ***	(0.0241)	-0.0131	(0.0341)	-0.0035	(0.0238)	-0.0101	(0.0243)	0.0022	(0.0241)	-0.0382	(0.0245)	0.34	13.40 ***	—	—	—	-0.0627	0.0887
5 All Nippon Airways Company Limited	APAC	0.0392 **	(0.0196)	-0.0999 ***	(0.0195)	-0.0227	(0.0195)	0.0227	(0.0195)	-0.1416 ***	(0.0198)	0.0050	(0.0281)	0.0362 *	(0.0195)	0.0390 *	(0.0200)	0.0155	(0.0198)	-0.0366 *	(0.0201)	0.25	8.91 ***	-0.1000	-0.2366	0.1054	0.0591	0.0368
6 AMR Corp.	NORAM		—		—		—		—	-0.4331 ***	(0.0245)	0.1173 ***	(0.0346)	0.0267	(0.0241)	-0.0023	(0.0246)	0.0354	(0.0244)	-0.0662 **	(0.0248)	0.58	33.58 ***	—	—	—	0.1110	-0.1460
7 Austrian Airlines AG	EMEA	0.0085	(0.0283)	-0.0937 ***	(0.0282)	-0.0213	(0.0282)	-0.0847 ***	(0.0282)	-0.0139	(0.0287)	-0.0313	(0.0406)	0.0282	(0.0282)	-0.0560 **	(0.0288)	-0.0121	(0.0286)	0.0260	(0.0291)	0.07	2.71 ***	-0.1997	-0.2450	-0.2593	-0.0452	-0.2981
8 British Airways PLC	EMEA	-0.1983 ***	(0.0311)	0.0067	(0.0309)	-0.0659 **	(0.0309)	-0.1530 ***	(0.0309)	0.1196 ***	(0.0314)	-0.0038	(0.0445)	-0.0387	(0.0310)	-0.0661 **	(0.0316)	0.1110 ***	(0.0314)	0.0421	(0.0319)	0.27	9.75 ***	-0.2122	-0.0964	-0.1533	0.0445	-0.2465
9 Cathay Pacific Airways Limited	APAC	-0.0160	(0.0235)	-0.2117 ***	(0.0234)	0.0446 *	(0.0234)	-0.0180	(0.0234)	-0.0906 ***	(0.0238)	-0.0319	(0.0336)	0.0372	(0.0234)	0.0577 **	(0.0239)	-0.0164	(0.0238)	-0.0102	(0.0241)	0.29	10.40 ***	-0.1851	-0.3076	0.1268	0.0364	0.0629
10 China Airlines Limited	APAC	0.0077	(0.0304)	0.0094	(0.0302)	-0.0706 **	(0.0302)	-0.0786 ***	(0.0303)	-0.0044	(0.0308)	-0.0004	(0.0435)	-0.0306	(0.0303)	-0.0413	(0.0310)	-0.0354	(0.0307)	-0.0656 **	(0.0312)	0.04	1.99 **	-0.1397	-0.1446	-0.2107	-0.1733	-0.0241
11 China Eastern Airlines Corp. Limited	APAC	-0.0024	(0.0191)	-0.0174	(0.0190)	-0.0079	(0.0191)	-0.0055	(0.0191)	-0.0497 **	(0.0194)	0.0151 **	(0.0274)	0.0080	(0.0191)	-0.0088	(0.0195)	0.0020	(0.0194)	-0.0433 **	(0.0197)	0.01	1.30	-0.0308	-0.0653	-0.0295	-0.0270	0.0587
12 Continental Airlines Inc	NORAM		—		—		—		—	-0.2014 ***	(0.0361)	0.0557 ***	(0.0510)	0.0670 *	(0.0355)	0.0224	(0.0363)	-0.0239	(0.0360)	-0.1508 ***	(0.0366)	0.62	39.83 ***	—	—	—	-0.0296	0.3526
13 Delta Air Lines Inc	NORAM		—		—		—		—	-0.5142 ***	(0.0247)	0.1187 ***	(0.0349)	0.0614 **	(0.0243)	0.0088	(0.0248)	0.1021 ***	(0.0247)	-0.0342	(0.0250)	0.66	46.46 ***	—	—	—	0.2568	-0.1767
14 Deutsche Lufthansa AG	EMEA	0.0081	(0.0061)	-0.0021	(0.0061)	0.0035	(0.0061)	0.0132 **	(0.0061)	-0.0027	(0.0062)	0.0025	(0.0087)	0.0079	(0.0061)	-0.0040	(0.0062)	-0.0134 **	(0.0062)	0.0012	(0.0062)	0.01	1.34	0.0145	0.0143	-0.0071	-0.0058	-0.0096
15 EVA Airways Corp.	APAC	-0.0016	(0.0342)	0.0043	(0.0340)	-0.0748 **	(0.0340)	-0.0686 **	(0.0341)	-0.0021	(0.0346)	-0.0011	(0.0490)	-0.0401	(0.0341)	-0.0358	(0.0348)	-0.0297	(0.0346)	-0.0718 **	(0.0351)	0.02	1.55	-0.1391	-0.1423	-0.4640	-0.1784	-0.2226
16 Finnair OYJ	EMEA	-0.0162	(0.0182)	-0.0051	(0.0181)	-0.0151	(0.0181)	-0.0102	(0.0181)	-0.0077	(0.0184)	0.0065	(0.0260)	0.0116	(0.0181)	-0.0641 ***	(0.0185)	-0.0254	(0.0184)	0.0039	(0.0186)	0.03	1.73 *	-0.0305	-0.0316	-0.1655	-0.0676	-0.0858
17 Iberia SA	EMEA	-0.0875 ***	(0.0209)	-0.0811 ***	(0.0208)	-0.0726 ***	(0.0208)	-0.1135 ***	(0.0208)	0.0678 ***	(0.0211)	0.0788	(0.0299)	0.0417 *	(0.0208)	-0.0136	(0.0212)	-0.0575 ***	(0.0211)	0.0394 **	(0.0214)	0.29	10.73 ***	-0.2673	-0.1207	-0.1036	0.0888	-0.1854
18 Japan Airlines Corp.	APAC	0.0886 ***	(0.0236)	-0.1278 ***	(0.0235)	-0.0171	(0.0235)	0.0519 **	(0.0235)	-0.0890 ***	(0.0239)	0.0381 **	(0.0338)	0.0419 *	(0.0235)	0.0197	(0.0240)	-0.0112	(0.0238)	-0.0365	(0.0242)	0.19	6.67 ***	-0.0929	-0.1438	-0.0038	0.0520	-0.0484
19 KLM Royal Dutch Airlines	EMEA	-0.2298 ***	(0.0299)	0.0508 *	(0.0298)	-0.0434	(0.0298)	-0.0713 **	(0.0298)	0.1015 ***	(0.0303)	-0.1462 ***	(0.0428)	0.0980 ***	(0.0298)	0.0158	(0.0305)	-0.0287	(0.0302)	-0.0211	(0.0307)	0.30	10.88 ***	-0.0639	-0.1086	0.0814	-0.0823	-0.0885
20 Korean Air Lines Company Limited	APAC	0.0074	(0.0384)	-0.1434 ***	(0.0382)	-0.0425	(0.0382)	-0.0632 *	(0.0383)	-0.1639 ***	(0.0389)	0.0366	(0.0550)	0.0030	(0.0383)	0.0225	(0.0391)	-0.0215	(0.0388)	-0.0012	(0.0394)	0.10	3.59 ***	-0.2491	-0.3763	-0.1485	0.0394	-0.2063
21 Lan Airlines SA	LATAM	-0.0214	(0.0174)	-0.0439 ***	(0.0173)	-0.0479 ***	(0.0174)	-0.0374 **	(0.0174)	-0.0438 ***	(0.0176)	0.0118 **	(0.0250)	0.0095	(0.0174)	-0.0398 **	(0.0178)	-0.0078	(0.0176)	-0.0481 ***	(0.0179)	0.11	3.81 ***	-0.1293	-0.1612	-0.0651	-0.0744	0.0273
22 Malaysian Airline	APAC	0.0119	(0.0315)	0.0033	(0.0313)	-0.1369 ***	(0.0313)	-0.0240	(0.0313)	-0.1075 ***	(0.0318)	-0.0289	(0.0451)	-0.0165	(0.0314)	-0.0483 *	(0.0320)	-0.0779 ***	(0.0318)	-0.0203	(0.0323)	0.11	4.02 ***	-0.1575	-0.2940	-0.3097	-0.1920	-0.1684
23 Northwest Airlines Corporation	NORAM		—		—		—		—	-0.3795 ***	(0.0274)	0.0518 **	(0.0387)	-0.0371	(0.0270)	-0.0018	(0.0276)	0.0232	(0.0274)	-0.0509	(0.0278)	0.44	19.80 ***	—	—	—	-0.0147	-0.0312
24 Qantas Airways Limited	APAC	0.1604 ***	(0.0277)	-0.1039 ***	(0.0276)	-0.0016	(0.0276)	0.0535 **	(0.0276)	-0.1520 ***	(0.0281)	0.0007	(0.0397)	0.0050	(0.0276)	-0.0094	(0.0282)	-0.0005	(0.0280)	-0.0005	(0.0285)	0.22	7.54 ***	-0.0521	-0.2034	0.2120	-0.0047	0.2011
25 SAS AB	EMEA	-0.0897 ***	(0.0238)	-0.1673 ***	(0.0237)	-0.0550 **	(0.0237)	0.0266	(0.0238)	-0.0856 ***	(0.0241)	0.0010	(0.0342)	0.0473 *	(0.0238)	0.0380	(0.0243)	0.0417	(0.0241)	-0.0048	(0.0245)	0.24	8.57 ***	-0.1957	-0.2803	0.2574	0.1233	0.0320
26 Singapore Airlines Limited	APAC	0.0229	(0.0245)	-0.0856 ***	(0.0244)	-0.0422 *	(0.0244)	-0.0762 ***	(0.0244)	-0.0518 **	(0.0248)	0.0137	(0.0351)	0.0062	(0.0244)	-0.0108	(0.0250)	-0.0451 **	(0.0248)	0.0093	(0.0252)	0.09	3.30 ***	-0.2039	-0.2420	-0.1097	-0.0267	-0.1056
27 TAM SA	LATAM	-0.0187 *	(0.0102)	-0.0046	(0.0101)	-0.0237 **	(0.0101)	0.0078	(0.0101)	0.0195 *	(0.0103)	-0.0044	(0.0146)	-0.0103	(0.0102)	-0.0044	(0.0104)	-0.0115	(0.0103)	0.0034	(0.0105)	0.02	1.49	-0.0205	-0.0054	-0.0425	-0.0273	0.0082
28 Thai Airways International Public Compar	APAC	0.0215	(0.0319)	0.0093	(0.0318)	-0.1718 ***	(0.0318)	-0.0679 **	(0.0318)	-0.2115 ***	(0.0323)	0.0516 **	(0.0457)	0.0746 **	(0.0318)	-0.0127	(0.0325)	-0.0272	(0.0323)	-0.0508	(0.0328)	0.24	8.35 ***	-0.2304	-0.3903	-0.1163	0.0356	-0.1270
29 UAL Corporation	NORAM		—		—		—		—	-0.4880 ***	(0.0369)	0.0985 **	(0.0523)	0.0207	(0.0364)	0.0048	(0.0372)	0.0701	(0.0369)	-0.0409	(0.0375)	0.42	18.12 ***	—	—	—	0.1532	-0.4909
30 US Airways Group Inc	NORAM		—		—		—		—	-0.6232 ***	(0.0492)	0.0643	(0.0696)	0.0178	(0.0484)	-0.1093 ***	(0.0495)	0.1312 **	(0.0491)	0.0015	(0.0499)	0.41	17.23 ***	—	—	—	0.1055	-0.2438
Non-major full service carriers																												
1 FLYi, Inc.	NORAM		—		—		—		—	-0.3595 ***	(0.0359)	-0.1843 ***	(0.0507)	-0.0315	(0.0353)	-0.1680 ***	(0.0361)	0.2149 ***	(0.0358)	0.0497 *	(0.0364)	0.43	18.48 ***	—	—	—	-0.1192	0.1503
2 Hawaiian Holdings Inc	NORAM		—		—		—		—	-0.2236 ***	(0.0425)	0.0361	(0.0602)	-0.0097	(0.0419)	0.0410	(0.0428)	-0.0746 *	(0.0425)	-0.0275	(0.0431)	0.09	3.20 ***	—	—	—	-0.0348	0.0312
3 Mesa Air Group Inc	NORAM		—		—		—		—	-0.8450 ***	(0.0491)	0.1961 ***	(0.0695)	-0.0898 **	(0.0484)	-0.1626 ***	(0.0494)	0.0605	(0.0490)	-0.1487 **	(0.0498)	0.58	33.07 ***	—	—	—	-0.1445	-0.0099
4 Mesaba Holdings/MAIR Holdings, Inc.	NORAM		—		—		—		—	-0.2001 ***	(0.0301)	-0.0647 *	(0.0427)	-0.0728 ***	(0.0297)	-0.0040	(0.0303)	-0.0107	(0.0301)	-0.0020	(0.0306)	0.16	5.49 ***	—	—	—	-0.1541	-0.0391
5 Midwest Express Holdings	NORAM		—		—		—		—	-0.3768 ***	(0.0306)	0.0325	(0.0432)	-0.0145	(0.0301)	-0.0380 *	(0.0307)	0.0547	(0.0305)	-0.0105	(0.0310)	0.38	15.59 ***	—	—	—	0.0241	-0.0951
6 Skywest Inc	NORAM		—		—		—		—	-0.3997 ***	(0.0286)	-0.0340 ***	(0.0404)	-0.0587 **	(0.0281)	-0.1692 ***	(0.0287)	0.0082	(0.0285)	0.1308 ***	(0.0290)	0.53	27.37 ***	—	—	—	-0.1228	0.0475
7 Westjet Airlines Limited	NORAM		—		—		—		—	-0.0728 ***	(0.0245)	0.0490	(0.0347)	0.0661 ***	(0.0242)	-0.0976 ***	(0.0247)	0.0890 ***	(0.0245)	-0.0081	(0.0249)	0.21	7.20 ***	—	—	—	0.0985	0.0087

** Statistically significant at the 10% level*

*** Statistically significant at the 5% level*

**** Statistically significant at the 1% level*

Table 8: *Abnormal returns Sep 11-24 and cumulated abnormal returns Sep 12 - Nov 5, 2001*

(Table continued on next page)

Low cost carriers																		
1 Airtran Holdings Inc	NORAM	—	—	—	—	-0.4260 *** (0.0387)	-0.0235 (0.0547)	0.0045 (0.0381)	-0.0231 (0.0389)	0.0999 ** (0.0386)	-0.1059 ** (0.0392)	0.34	13.20 ***	—	—	—	-0.0480	0.0249
2 America West Holdings	NORAM	—	—	—	—	-0.9508 *** (0.0588)	0.1152 (0.0831)	-0.0541 (0.0579)	-0.3979 *** (0.0591)	0.4343 *** (0.0587)	-0.0023 (0.0596)	0.60	35.80 ***	—	—	—	0.0953	-0.6198
3 ATA Holdings	NORAM	—	—	—	—	-0.5806 *** (0.0442)	-0.1670 *** (0.0625)	0.1449 *** (0.0435)	-0.2182 *** (0.0445)	0.0723 (0.0442)	0.0012 (0.0448)	0.48	22.32 ***	—	—	—	-0.1668	-0.5113
4 Easyjet PLC	EMEA	-0.0991 *** (0.0239)	-0.1205 *** (0.0237)	-0.0370 (0.0237)	-0.0687 *** (0.0238)	-0.0798 *** (0.0241)	0.0641 *** (0.0342)	0.0493 * (0.0238)	-0.0278 (0.0243)	-0.0413 ** (0.0241)	-0.0571 ** (0.0245)	0.23	8.19 ***	-0.2262	-0.2420	0.22[illegible]	-0.0128	0.3106
5 Frontier Airlines, Inc.	NORAM	—	—	—	—	-0.3197 *** (0.0350)	0.0688 * (0.0495)	0.0047 (0.0345)	0.0013 (0.0352)	-0.0953 *** (0.0350)	-0.0433 (0.0355)	0.27	9.57 ***	—	—	—	-0.0638	0.2089
6 Ryanair Holdings PLC	EMEA	-0.0493 ** (0.0222)	-0.1497 *** (0.0221)	-0.0284 (0.0221)	-0.0462 ** (0.0221)	0.1137 *** (0.0225)	0.0366 ** (0.0318)	0.0511 ** (0.0221)	-0.0065 (0.0226)	-0.1158 *** (0.0224)	-0.0392 * (0.0228)	0.30	11.23 ***	-0.2243	-0.0739	0.07[illegible]	-0.0738	0.2755
7 Southwest Airlines Company	NORAM	—	—	—	—	-0.2392 *** (0.0196)	0.0045 (0.0277)	0.0011 (0.0193)	0.0421 ** (0.0197)	0.0933 *** (0.0195)	-0.0392 * (0.0198)	0.41	17.28 ***	—	—	—	0.1018	0.0760
Freight carriers																		
1 Airborne Express	NORAM	—	—	—	—	-0.1255 *** (0.0239)	-0.0356 ** (0.0338)	-0.0045 (0.0236)	-0.0325 * (0.0241)	0.0285 (0.0239)	0.0389 * (0.0243)	0.11	3.82 ***	—	—	—	-0.0051	-0.0612
2 Atlas Air Worldwide Holdings Inc	NORAM	—	—	—	—	-0.0321 (0.0354)	0.0192 (0.0501)	0.0330 (0.0349)	-0.0442 (0.0356)	0.0237 (0.0354)	-0.0572 * (0.0359)	-0.01	0.76	—	—	—	-0.0256	0.0583
3 Federal Express/FedEx Corp	NORAM	—	—	—	—	-0.0160 (0.0162)	-0.0624 ** (0.0229)	-0.0214 (0.0159)	0.0352 ** (0.0163)	0.0117 (0.0161)	-0.0055 (0.0164)	0.05	2.32 **	—	—	—	-0.0425	0.0268
4 United Parcel Service, Inc	NORAM	—	—	—	—	-0.0398 *** (0.0093)	-0.0030 (0.0131)	-0.0405 *** (0.0092)	0.0480 *** (0.0093)	0.0156 * (0.0093)	-0.0172 ** (0.0094)	0.20	6.83 ***	—	—	—	0.0029	-0.0356
Carrier portfolios																		
Major full service carriers	∑30	-0.0134 (0.0093)	-0.0590 *** (0.0092)	-0.0398 *** (0.0092)	-0.0525 *** (0.0092)	-0.1421 *** (0.0094)	0.0222 *** (0.0133)	0.0194 * (0.0092)	-0.0171 ** (0.0094)	-0.0037 (0.0094)	-0.0380 *** (0.0095)	0.58	33.29 ***	-0.1512	-0.2706	-0.07[illegible]	-0.0162	-0.0620
Non-major full service carriers	∑7	—	—	—	—	-0.3539 *** (0.0175)	0.0044 (0.0248)	-0.0301 ** (0.0173)	-0.0855 *** (0.0176)	0.0489 * (0.0175)	-0.0023 (0.0178)	0.65	44.21 ***	—	—	—	-0.0658	0.0079
Low cost carriers	∑7	-0.0526 (0.0159)	-0.1261 ** (0.0158)	-0.0359 (0.0158)	-0.0437 (0.0159)	-0.3546 *** (0.0161)	0.0141 (0.0228)	0.0288 (0.0159)	-0.0900 *** (0.0162)	0.0639 *** (0.0161)	-0.0408 (0.0163)	0.69	53.30 ***	-0.2057	-0.5392	-0.02[illegible]	-0.0117	0.0038
Freight carriers	∑4	—	—	—	—	-0.0533 *** (0.0139)	-0.0205 (0.0196)	-0.0084 (0.0137)	0.0016 (0.0140)	0.0199 (0.0139)	-0.0102 (0.0141)	0.05	2.24 **	—	—	—	-0.0176	-0.0030
Region portfolios																		
APAC	∑12	0.0258 ** (0.0113)	-0.0739 *** (0.0113)	-0.0256 ** (0.0113)	-0.0513 *** (0.0113)	-0.1182 *** (0.0115)	0.0181 *** (0.0162)	0.0157 (0.0113)	-0.0196 ** (0.0115)	-0.0267 *** (0.0115)	-0.0664 *** (0.0116)	0.47	21.65 ***	-0.1508	-0.2509	-0.09[illegible]	-0.0789	-0.0037
EMEA	∑10	-0.0898 *** (0.0115)	-0.0668 *** (0.0114)	-0.0322 *** (0.0114)	-0.0591 *** (0.0114)	0.0182 (0.0116)	0.0034 (0.0164)	0.0342 *** (0.0114)	-0.0236 ** (0.0117)	-0.0150 * (0.0116)	0.0112 (0.0118)	0.36	14.10 ***	-0.1581	-0.1364	0.01[illegible]	0.0101	-0.0323
LATAM	∑2	-0.0200 * (0.0113)	-0.0242 ** (0.0113)	-0.0358 *** (0.0113)	-0.0148 (0.0113)	-0.0121 (0.0115)	0.0037 (0.0163)	-0.0004 (0.0113)	-0.0221 ** (0.0116)	-0.0097 (0.0115)	-0.0223 * (0.0116)	0.07	2.77 ***	-0.0749	-0.0833	-0.05[illegible]	-0.0508	0.0177
NORAM	∑24	—	—	—	—	-0.3347 *** (0.0143)	0.0187 (0.0203)	-0.0011 (0.0141)	-0.0525 *** (0.0144)	0.0514 *** (0.0143)	-0.0299 (0.0145)	0.70	57.11 ***	—	—	—	-0.0133	-0.0745

** Statistically significant at the 10% level*

*** Statistically significant at the 5% level*

**** Statistically significant at the 1% level*

Table 8 (continued): *Abnormal returns Sep 11-24 and cumulated abnormal returns Sep 12 - Nov 5, 2001*

*This table presents the abnormal returns of all firms and portfolios with standard errors (in parentheses) estimated using equation 2 (cf. section 7.1.1) for the trading days September 11-24. Standard market model parameters α, α′, β, and β′ used for the **MVRM** were estimated as presented in table 7. This table also presents R^2 and F-statistics illustrating the explanatory power of the regression model as well as cumulative abnormal returns for the period (1) Sep 12-14, (2) Sep 12-18, (3) Sep 19 - Oct 30, (4) Sep 18-24, and (5) Sep 25 - Nov 5. Cumulated abnormal returns (1)-(3) include non-U.S. companies only, (4)-(5) include all sample firms.*

Estimates of significance are based on t-statistics.

On September 17 the U.S. stock exchanges reopened with the effect that 88% (42 out of 48) company stocks in the sample responded with significant abnormal returns between 0.1137 (Ryanair Holding PLC) and -0.9508 (America West Holding).
The majority of reactions were negative, while six non-U.S. companies (Air Canada Inc., British Airways PLC, Iberia SA, KLM Royal Dutch Airlines, TAM SA, Ryanair Holdings PLC) reacted with significant positive abnormal returns. Independent from their pre-reaction September 11-14, also the non-U.S. companies' stocks experienced downturns on September 17, except some few European and Asian firms. Looking at the company portfolios, all passenger carrier portfolios experienced significant negative abnormal returns between -0.1421 for major full service carriers and -0.3546 for low cost carriers. Freight-only carriers also responded with significant negative returns but the market's reaction was with -0.0533 clearly smaller. From a regional perspective, APAC and NORAM portfolios dropped with a coefficient of -0.1181 and -0.3347, while EMEA and LATAM did not realize significant abnormal returns.

In the following five trading days, September 18-14, still significant positive and negative abnormal returns occur, but no clear pattern can be identified why the market differentiated between the companies. The cumulated abnormal returns for the time after September 24 show that the overall market reaction mostly remains negative also for the period of six weeks after the shock, but again trends are difficult to read from the table. Here, the results from the multivariate regression analyses will give more insights later on.

The information displayed in Table 8 can be summarized in the following concluding statements:

(1) The stock market reacted on 9/11with abnormal returns for aircraft operating and holding companies, which are jointly non-zero
(2) The non-U.S. stock markets significantly reacted prior to the U.S. market in the period September 11-14 throughout all carrier clusters and regions with September 12 being the trading day with the highest significant cumulated abnormal returns
(3) On September 17, 88% of all companies in the sample reacted with abnormal returns mostly statistically significant at the 1% level
(4) The market penalized freight-only carriers on average significantly less than passenger carriers
(5) The market differentiated between the companies' home region with APAC and NORAM experiencing on average significant negative abnormal returns while EMEA and LATAM companies on average show no abnormal returns
(6) In the short- and mid term after the shock, a mostly significant negative trend in abnormal returns continues; conclusions on differencing factors cannot be drawn from the table and require further analyses

Stock market's reaction on the first trading day

The overview of abnormal returns as a reaction on 9/11 (cf. Table 8) gave some first insights into the market's reaction and possible differencing factors. To retrieve further details the multivariate regression method was employed as described in Chapter 7.1.1. The upcoming section describes the results of the regressions focusing on the first trading day following the event, i.e. September 11 for non-U.S. based companies and September 17 for U.S. based firms. As explained in Chapter 7.2.1.1, five different combinations of observation period and sample firms are tested to identify possible time shifts in reaction to the opening hours of the individual stock exchanges: Model A investigates September 11 with a sample of 25 non-U.S. companies only, Model B and C focus on September 17 with either a sample of 23 U.S. companies or 25 non-U.S. companies. Model D and E include all 48 companies in scope of the 9/11 analysis with Model D evaluating the market's reaction on September 17 and Model E applying "trading day matching", i.e. artificially setting the first trading day outside the U.S. equal to the first trading day in the U.S. (September 11 = September 17).

Table 9 gives a consolidated overview on the results from the multivariate regression model analysis for y_1, the first trading day after the terrorist attacks. In the following, the individual models (A)-(E) are described. Details in form of the underlying regression models are illustrated in Appendix 4 to Appendix 8. For initial hypotheses please refer to Chapter 6.3, Table 1 and 7.1.2, Table 4.

		Model A	Model B	Model C	Model D	Model E
Observation period		y1 (RoW)	y1 (U.S.)	y5 (RoW)	y1 (U.S.) = y5 (RoW)	y1 (U.S.) = y1 (RoW)
Date		Sep 11, 2001	Sep 17, 2001	Sep 17, 2001	Sep 17, 2001	Sep 17 = Sep 11, 2001
Sample		Non-U.S.	U.S.	Non-U.S.	All companies	All companies
Sample size		25	23	25	48	48
Cluster	Variable					
Financial	SIZE					
	LIQUIDITY	-	++			
	NDTEBITDA		-			
	EBITDAMAR		+++	++	++	+++
	EQITYRAT	++				
	INTRSTCOVRG			-	-	-
Market	RPKMKTSHR	---	---		---	---
	FTKMKTSHR	---	+++	+++		
	PINT		++	--		++
	PINT 1					++
	PFREIGHT			++		++
Aircraft fleet	TOTALAC	+			-	-
	OPSLEASE	--	--	--	--	--
	STORAC	--	+++	++	+++	
	nYRORDER					
	nYROPTION			++		
	1YROPTION					
	AVGAGE	+	+	+		+
Carrier	AMR/UAL	n/a		n/a	--	--
	MFSC	++	++	++	++	++
	NFSC	n/a		n/a	--	--
	LCC				--	--
	FREIGHT	n/a	++	n/a	++	++
Region	APAC	++	n/a	--	--	
	EMEA	--	n/a	++	++	
	LATAM		n/a	++		
	NORAM	--	n/a	++	--	--
	R^2 (adjusted)	≤ 0.63	≤ 0.83	≤ 0.62	≤ 0.70	≤ 0.68
	F-statistic	2.77* - 15.88***	2.50* - 14.09***	3.24** - 9.71***	3.44*** - 12.16***	4.01*** - 16.19***

+/- Positive/negative impact on abnormal returns < 0.1/>-0.1
++/-- Positive/negative impact on abnormal returns ≥ 0.1/≤ -0.1
+++/--- Positive/negative impact on abnormal returns ≥ 1.0/≤ -1.0

xxx Statistically significant at the 10% level
xxx Statistically significant at the 5% level
xxx Statistically significant at the 1% level

Table 9: *Overview on regression results for stock market's reaction on the first trading day after 9/11 (y_1)*

This table presents a consolidated overview of cross-sectional regression results for abnormal returns of aircraft operating and holding companies for the first trading days September 11 (for non-U.S. markets) and September 17 (for the U.S. market) after the terrorist attacks on September 11, 2001. SIZE is the natural logarithm of total assets, LIQUIDITY is cash & equivalents over current liabilities, NDTEBITDA is net debt over EBITDA, EBITDAMAR is EBITDA over total operating revenue, EQITYRAT is owners equity over total assets, INTRSTCOVRG is interest expenses for debt over EBIT, RPKMKTSHR and FTKMKTSHR are revenue passenger and freight ton kilometer market shares, PINT and PINT1 are the portions of international (non-home region and non-domestic) business in total operating revenue, PFREIGHT is the portion of freight business in total operating revenue, TOTALAC is the total number of jet aircraft, OPSLEASE is the ratio of operating leased aircraft over total aircraft count, STORAC is the ratio of stored aircraft to total aircraft count, nYRORDER and nYROPTION/1YROPTION are the number of aircraft orders and purchase options to existing fleet in the next n (all) years or 1 year, and AVGAGE is the average age of existing aircraft. Nine dummy variables are included which are equal to one if the firm meets the requirements and equal to zero otherwise: MFSC if the firm is a major full service carrier, NFSC if the firm is a non-major full service carrier, LCC if the firm is a low cost carrier, FREIGHT if the firm is a freight only carrier, UAL/AMR if the firm is either United Airlines (UAL) or American Airlines (AMR), APAC, if the firm is Asia Pacific based, EMEA if the firm is based in Europe Middle East or Africa, LATAM if the firm is Latin America based, and NORAM if the firm is North American based. The magnitude of the positive and negative influence of the variables on abnormal returns refers to the regression coefficient. Statistical significance is based on t-statistics.

Within the cluster of financial variables, EBITDAMAR (EBITDA margin) has the highest significant positive impact on a first trading day after a shock, indicating that the market believed in a less severe impact of 9/11 on companies with a higher profitability. EBITDA is an important financial indicator for analysts and investors (cf. Chapter 4.2 and Chapter 6.2.2). It measures a company's efficiency and is used when comparing several companies in the same peer group. The negative impact of a higher interest coverage rate (INTRSTCOVRG) and net debt over EBITDA ratio (NDTEBITDA) – although less significant – is in favor of a rational market behavior as the shock will most likely lead to an economic downturn for the industry and companies with higher debt or interest and/or comparatively lower EBIT(DA) will have more difficulties to pay back there liabilities, herewith facing a higher risk for bankruptcy. Especially a company's NDTEBITDA ratio is a typical factor evaluated by investors when assessing a company's risk. In Model A, other variables overlap the significance of the three variables EBITDAMAR, EQUITRAT, and INTRESTCOVRG which generally show the same pattern in the detailed regression results in Appendix 4.
LIQUIDITY seems to play a less but still significant positive role. Interestingly, for non-U.S. companies in Model A, liquidity ratio show counterintuitive signs. The interpretation that the market penalized firms with higher liquidity is not rational. Usually, the market is known for the opposite reaction. Considering the low statistical significance in t-statistics, this finding is assumed to be data noise. The positive correlation of EQITYRAT (although only visible in Model A) is in line with the hypothesized effect.

The market variables show a mostly consistent picture. A higher share of the revenue passenger kilometer market (RPKMKTSHR) had the strongest negative influence and a higher share of the freight ton kilometer market (FTKMKTSHR) the strongest positive influence on a company's stock (the latter except for non-U.S. companies on September 11). 9/11 led to a fear of flying and therefore resulted mainly in a decrease in passenger business rather than a decline in freight business. This conclusion is supported by the positive affect of PFREIGHT which underlines that the higher the portion of freight in a firm's operating revenue was, the better the market saw the firm handling the crisis. A bigger portion of non-home-regional business in total operating revenue of a firm (PINT) led to a positive impact for U.S. airlines on September 17 as well as for the complete sample of 48 U.S. firms in Model E; non-U.S. firms were influenced negatively in Model C, offsetting the positive effect for U.S. firms in Model D. However, the findings of this analysis could lead to the conclusion that U.S. firms were better off when they had a higher portion of business operating outside the U.S. and therefore being less impacted by the flight bans in the U.S. On the other hand, the market possibly believed that non-U.S. firms with a high portion of international business naturally would have a higher portion of business into and from the U.S., which then would had been restricted by flight stops, leading to a negative influence on the non-U.S. firms' stock performance.

The cluster of aircraft fleet variables and fleet planning variables are the focus of this paper. Given that the impact of most individual variables was so far merely based on hypotheses and had not been evaluated by previous studies, it is already exciting to see that all variables show impact on abnormal returns even though at different levels of statistical significance.
OPSLEASE, i.e. operating leased aircraft in the fleet (rather than owned or finance leased aircraft) has a negative influence on a firm's stock performance of ≥ 0.1 with a statistical significance at the 5% level. Reason for this could be that the market sees operating leases as less flexible, i.e. operating leases are usually tied into fixed contracts, often including maintenance and other variable costs, that restrict the lessee in the decision to ground the aircraft ad hoc in order to minimize expenses to fixed costs and save variable costs (cf. definition of different aircraft lease options in Chapter 2.1). The findings for STORAC and AVGAGE support this hypothesis. The more aircraft were already stored and the older the fleet the better. One could argue again with a firm's flexibility and cost saving potential in responding to the event. Old aircraft usually run on low fixed costs and might even be written off completely, hence can be grounded more effectively. Aircraft that were already stored (grounded) at the time the shock occurred, reduced the company's total active fleet and reduced the number of aircraft that still needed to be grounded when facing overcapacity. This argument is biased by the fact that a company would not have stored aircraft before the shock if it had had enough demand to employ the aircraft, so that overcapacity resulting from the shock still needed to be reduced. The bigger a company's aircraft fleet the more overcapacity a company will face, e.g. assuming that the business to the U.S. drops to zero, an European carrier that daily operates one of its ten aircraft on the Europe-U.S. trade lane is better off than another European carrier that operates ten of its hundred aircraft on the same trade lane and has to carry the costs of reducing ten times more capacity than its competitor. The relative costs stay the same, but the absolute costs amount to more.
The total number of aircraft does not provide a consistent picture. The bigger the fleet the worse it was for the individual company (looking at the complete sample); however, only considering non-U.S. companies on September 11 the correlation is positive.
Further, nYROPTION had a positive impact on a firm's stock performance (though just statistically significant and only for the sample of non-U.S. firms in Model C). The more aircraft purchase options a firm held at manufacturers the more confident the market reacted. This can be interpreted in two ways: Either, the market believed that purchase options can just expire without any liabilities when the capacity is not required (but then a significant negative impact of firm orders should be found balancing this affect), or the market believed that a firm with sufficient number of purchasing options can easily raise its capacity when demand picks up again after the crisis. If so, the positive affect of purchase options should be also found in subsequent analyses of short- and mid term post 9/11.

From a carrier perspective, being a major full service or freight-only company was of clear advantage on the first trading day after the attacks compared to non-major full service and low cost companies. The two firms directly involved in the event, United Airlines (UAL) and American Airlines (AMR), both lost aircraft, passenger, and crew in the terrorist attacks and suffered additionally in abnormal returns although being major full service carriers.

From a region perspective, stocks of companies based in NORAM and APAC reacted negatively while those based in EMEA and (with less explanatory power) also in LATAM reacted positively.

Although at a first glance Model A seems to show a different reaction for non-U.S. based airlines on September 11, the comparison of Models B with C as well as of Models D with E supports the conclusions drawn from the table of daily abnormal returns in the previous chapter and can be summarized as follows:

(1) The market's reaction was not the same for the individual companies
(2) In all clusters, significant explanatory variables can be found
(3) All types of aircraft fleet and fleet planning variables influence a company's stock performance on the first trading day after a shock
(4) Clear positive effect on a stock's abnormal returns on a first trading day after 9/11 show (though at different statistical significance): EBITDARMAR, FTKMKTSHR, PFREIGHT, STORAC, nYROPTION, AVGAGE, MFSC, FREIGHT, and EMEA
(5) Clear negative influence on a stock's abnormal return on the same day have (though at different statistical significance): INTRSTCOVRG, RPKMKTSHR, OPSLEASE, NFSC, LCC, and NORAM

This section focused on the first single trading day after the terrorist attacks. For the detailed results of the multivariate regression models please refer to Appendix 4 to Appendix 8. In the next section, the market's short term reaction is investigated, i.e. the period of the second to sixth trading day.

Stock markets' short term reaction on 9/11

After a first rough interpretation of the abnormal returns resulting from 9/11 (cf. Table 8) and the multivariate regression analysis focusing on the first trading day after the terrorist attacks (cf. Table 9), this section evaluates the differentiating factors and explanatory power in stock market's reaction in the short term after the shock. More concretely the analysis focuses on trading days $y_{2\text{-}6}$, i.e. September 12-18 for non-U.S. markets and September 18-24 for the U.S. market. The period September 18-24 is heavily shaped by the actions of the Senate and the House of Representatives of the United States to enact the Air Transportation

Safety and System Stabilization Act (H.R. 2926, effective September 21, 2001) as a bailout package to prevent bankruptcy of U.S. airlines (Sunshine & Woodward, 2001).

Similar to the previous section, five compositions of sample and observation periods are tested: Model F analyzes the non-U.S. markets' reaction September 12-18, Models G and H evaluate the influencing factors on abnormal returns September 18-24 for U.S. and non-U.S. companies, respectively. Further, Models I and J include again the full sample of 48 companies, with Model I concentrating on September 18-24 ($y_{2\text{-}6}$ U.S. = $y_{6\text{-}10}$ for the rest of the world) and Model J matching the trading days for U.S. and non-U.S. companies, i.e. the five U.S. trading days $y_{2\text{-}6}$ September 18-24 are set equal to the five trading days $y_{2\text{-}6}$ for non-U.S. markets.

		Model F	Model G	Model H	Model I	Model J
Observation period		y2-6 (RoW)	y2-6 (U.S.)	y6-10 (RoW)	y2-6 (U.S.) = y6-10 (RoW)	y2-6 (U.S.) = y2-6 (RoW)
Date		Sep 12-18, 2001	Sep 18-24, 2001	Sep 18-24, 2001	Sep 18-24, 2001	Sep 18-24 = Sep 12-18, 2001
Sample		Non-U.S.	U.S.	Non-U.S.	All companies	All companies
Sample size		25	23	25	48	48
Cluster	Variable					
Financial	SIZE		I	I		
	LIQUIDITY	--	-			
	NDTEBITDA			-	-	-
	EBITDAMAR	++		+++	++	
	EQITYRAT		++	--		
	INTRSTCOVRG	--	-	--		
Market	RPKMKTSHR		+++		+++	+++
	FTKMKTSHR					
	PINT	--	--	--	--	
	PINT 1					
	PFREIGHT		+			--
Aircraft fleet	TOTALAC	+	+		+	+
	OPSLEASE	--	++			+
	STORAC		++		++	
	nYRORDER			++		
	nYROPTION		+			+
	1YROPTION					
	AVGAGE		+	+		
Carrier	AMR/UAL	n/a		n/a	++	+
	MFSC		++			
	NFSC	n/a		n/a		
	LCC			--		
	FREIGHT	n/a	-	n/a		
Region	APAC	--	n/a	++		--
	EMEA	--	n/a	++		--
	LATAM		n/a		++	++
	NORAM	--	n/a	--	-	++
	R^2 (adjusted)	≤ 0.42	≤ 0.90	≤ 0.56	≤ 0.47	≤ 0.53
	F-statistic	2.31* - 4.48**	2.72* - 22.63***	2.26* - 7.02***	3.61*** - 11.42***	4.19*** - 16.84***

+/- Positive/negative impact on abnormal returns < 0.1/>-0.1
++/-- Positive/negative impact on abnormal returns ≥ 0.1/≤ -0.1
+++/--- Positive/negative impact on abnormal returns ≥ 1.0/≤ -1.0

xxx Statistically significant at the 10% level
xxx Statistically significant at the 5% level
xxx Statistically significant at the 1% level

Table 10: *Overview on MVRM results for stock market's reaction in the short term after 9/11 (y_{2-6})*

This table presents a consolidated overview of cross-sectional regression results for cumulated abnormal returns of aircraft operating and holding companies for the second to sixth trading day: September 12-18 (for non-U.S. markets) and September 18-24 (for the U.S. market) after the terrorist attacks on September 11, 2001. SIZE is the natural logarithm of total assets, LIQUIDITY is cash & equivalents over current liabilities, NDTEBITDA is net debt over EBITDA, EBITDAMAR is EBITDA over total operating revenue, EQITYRAT is owners equity over total assets, INTRSTCOVRG is interest expenses for debt over EBIT, RPKMKTSHR and FTKMKTSHR are revenue passenger and freight ton kilometer market shares, PINT and PINT1 are the portions of international (non-home region and non-domestic) business in total operating revenue, PFREIGHT is the portion of freight business in total operating revenue, TOTALAC is the total number of jet aircraft, OPSLEASE is the ratio of operating leased aircraft over total aircraft count, STORAC is the ratio of stored aircraft to total aircraft count, nYRORDER and nYROPTION/1YROPTION are the number of aircraft orders and purchase options to existing fleet in the next n (all) years or 1 year, and AVGAGE is the average age of existing aircraft. Also, nine dummy variables are included which are equal to one if the firm meets the requirements and equal to zero otherwise: MFSC if the firm is a major full service carrier, NFSC if the firm is a non-major full service carrier, LCC if the firm is a low cost carrier, FREIGHT if the firm is a freight only carrier, AMR/UAL if the firm is either American Airlines (AMR) or United Airlines (UAL), APAC, if the firm is Asia Pacific based, EMEA if the firm is based in Europe Middle East or Africa, LATAM if the firm is Latin America based, and NORAM if the firm is North American based. The magnitude of the positive and negative influence of the variables on abnormal returns refers to the regression coefficient. Statistical significance is based on t-statistics.

Table 10 summarizes the findings of the multivariate regression models for the short term abnormal returns after 9/11. In the interpretation of the table it is probably the easiest to start with the commonalities to the analysis of the first trading day (cf. Table 9) and subsequently describe new insights or changes.

The variables EBITDAMAR, STORAC, nYROPTION, AVGAGE, MFSC, EMEA, and LATAM still have a significant positive impact on abnormal returns. Likewise, the variables NDTEBITDA, INTRSTCOVRG, and LCC remain having a negative influence on market's reaction.

New is that the financial variable SIZE shows highly significant positive impact on abnormal returns. Because this effect does not only apply to U.S. based, but also to the sample of non-U.S. based companies, the reason is likely not to lie in the U.S. bailout package (as concluded by Carter & Simkins, 2004), but rather in the general belief of the market that big companies in terms of their asset base will go better through the crisis compared to smaller players. The same applies for the variables RPKMKTSHR and TOTALAC which both turned positive in comparison to their effects on the first trading day. The change in RPKMTKSHR and TOTALAC could be interpreted similar to the variable SIZE, i.e. the market might have seen a company's overall market share and its total fleet count as an indicator for size or importance and eventually for survival.

New is also that nYRORDER, representing the total number of firm orders into the future in relation to existing fleet count, becomes a positively influencing factor for non-U.S. based companies. However, as demand started to drop, any aircraft delivery resulting from a previous firm order would only increase a company's capacity surplus. Would that mean that the market reacted irrationally? A reason for market's response could be the trust in a company which strategically plans its capacity into the future and is willing to place firm orders without knowing the upcoming economic situation when the aircraft is going to be delivered. If so, investors and the overall market, respectively, would not separate an aircraft operating and holding company's aircraft fleet strategy from its overall business strategy. In conjunction with the significant impact of purchase options – another lever of strategic future capacity securing – strategic fleet planning would become an important factor to consider when trying to convince stockholders. At this point in the analysis no final conclusion can yet be drawn. Full results from the evaluation of abnormal returns in shock crises, in company specific events as well as over the long term business cycle are needed in order not to form misleading conclusions.

Some explanatory variables stayed significant but switched their algebraic sign from positive to negative or vice versa. LIQUIDITY and PINT turned negative in the sample of U.S. based companies. This finding is in line with the results from previous studies (Carter & Simkins, 2004; Guenther, 2005). In the Air Transportation Safety and System Stabilization Act especially companies with low liquidity were offered financial help. In reverse, liquidity-strong companies had no advantage from the bailout package, independent from whether they were facing other operational problems caused by the shock. The market priced the effect of the bailout package into stocks with a positive impact for companies with low liquidity and a negative impact for companies with high liquidity. Further the Act was in favor of large players but the money should naturally stay in the country rather than being used abroad. Therefore, the market believed that companies with a higher market share in revenue passenger kilometer and lower share in international business were to benefit more from the bailout package. As a further effect of the Act, AMR/UAL turned positive; the market probably believed that American Airlines and United Airlines would find special help in the System Stabilization Act to cover their direct losses.

EQUITYRT and OPSLEASE became positive for the U.S. based companies in Model G, with OPSLEASE positively influencing also Model J but staying negative in the non-U.S. sample in Model F. In light of the bailout package, the switches in sign of both EQUITRAT and OPSLEASE could be interpreted as the market's belief that firms with higher liability towards stockholders (higher owner's equity leverage) and higher liabilities to third parties (aircraft lessors) would benefit from the Act. Similar to the variables PFREIGHT, APAC, and NORAM, for which the market is at odds, no final conclusion can yet be drawn for these variables from the regression models in this section.

To summarize the findings of the multivariate regressions on abnormal returns in the short term (trading days $y_{2\text{-}6}$) after 9/11, the following concluding statements can be made:

(1) Market's reaction is in favor of rational pricing
(2) The variables EBITDAMAR, STORAC, nYROPTION, AVGAGE, MFSC, EMEA, and LATAM remain with positive impact
(3) The variables NDTEBITDA, INTRSTCOVRG, and LCC remain with negative impact
(4) The variables SIZE and nYRORDER show new statistically significant positive effect on abnormal returns; the market's trust in a company's survival by size or importance is supported by the change to a positive effect of RPKMKTSHR and TOTALAC
(5) The Air Transportation Safety and System Stabilization Act had a significant influence on abnormal returns for U.S. based companies, changing some variables for the U.S. sample from positive to negative or vice versa, incl. LIQUIDITY, PINT, and AMR/UAL
(6) The effect of Air Transportation Safety and System Stabilization Act on turning the variables EQUITYRAT and OPSLEASE positive for the U.S. sample is likely but can yet not be finally concluded

After the initial (y_1) and the short term ($_{y2\text{-}6}$) reaction of the stock market on 9/11 were analyzed, the picture of what has made a difference in the abnormal returns becomes clearer. A third time window remains for analysis: The next section will focus on the mid term reaction of the stock market after 9/11.

Stock markets' mid term reaction to 9/11

The third time window of the multivariate regression analysis for 9/11 concentrates on $y_{7\text{-}36}$, i.e. September 19 to October 30 for non-U.S. based companies and September 25 to November 30 for U.S. based companies. According to the media screening described in Chapter 7.2.1.1, this mid term time span after 9/11 is characterized by the effort to implement new security standards in the aviation industry, mainly for airlines and at airports. For example, the United States' Federal Aviation Administration (FAA) started to issue government-backed insurances and to hire additional security employees at airports. Also, non-U.S. institutions started to raise their security standards. At almost all international airports worldwide new baggage security policies were introduced, manufacturers began to developed new cockpit doors against potential hijackers, and flights were accompanied by an increasing number of sky marshals.

In Table 11, five different models provide a synopsis on the explanatory power of the different variables tested on abnormal returns in the mid term after 9/11: Model K illustrates the time September 19 to October 30 for non-U.S. based companies only, Model L and M concentrate on the same time span September 25 to November 5 with Model L including U.S. based firms and Model M non-U.S. based companies. Model N and O both include the full sample of 48 firms. Model N focuses on the trading days September 25 to November 5, whereas Model O includes again trading day matching, i.e. the trading days $y_{7\text{-}36}$ for U.S. based companies (September 25 – November 5) are set equal to the $y_{7\text{-}36}$ trading days for non-U.S. based firms (September 19 – October 30).
As a reminder: trading day matching was introduced (cf. Table 6) to cross-check whether the results of the regression analysis are biased by a trading time shift caused by the different opening days of the different stock exchanges. U.S. stock exchanges closed on September 11 not to reopen before September 17 while non-U.S. stock exchanges stayed open, generally giving the primary stock markets of non-U.S. companies the possibility to react early.

The interpretation of Table 11 is not as obvious as for the two previous analyses of y_1 (cf. Table 9) and $y_{2\text{-}6}$ (cf. Table 10). Especially Models K, L, M, all including either the U.S. sample or the non-U.S. sample only, seem to give quite diverse pictures. Some variables are positive in the one but negative in the other. Some show statistical significance, others do not. One restriction of this third multivariate regression analysis of the mid term is that $y_{7\text{-}36}$ for non-U.S. companies (September 21 – October 25) overlaps with the time in which the Air Transportation and System Stabilization Act was enacted (September 21, 2001). This might lead to biased market reaction; therefore, Model K should play a subordinate role in the interpretation of the regression results of the mid term after 9/11. The assumption that the model is biased is underlined by conflicting results of FTKMKTSHR and PFREIGHT.

		Model K	Model L	Model M	Model N	Model O
Observation period		y7-36 (RoW)	y7-36 (U.S.)	y11-40 (RoW)	y7-36 (U.S.) = y11-40 (RoW)	y7-36 (U.S.) = y7-36 (RoW)
Date		Sep 19 - Oct 30, 2001	Sep 25 - Nov 5, 2001	Sep 25 - Nov 5, 2001	Sep 25 - Nov 5, 2001	Sep 25 - Nov 5 = Sep 19 - Oct
Sample		Non-U.S.		Non-U.S.	All companies	All companies
Sample size		25	23	25	48	48
Cluster	Variable					
Financial	SIZE	++			--	
	LIQUIDITY		--			
	NDTEBITDA	-	-	-	-	-
	EBITDAMAR		+++		++	++
	EQITYRAT					
	INTRSTCOVRG		-	++	-	-
Market	RPKMKTSHR		---			
	FTKMKTSHR	+++				
	PINT			++		
	PINT 1					
	PFREIGHT	--		--		
Aircraft fleet	TOTALAC		-			
	OPSLEASE	++		++		
	STORAC			---		
	nYRORDER					
	nYROPTION					
	1YROPTION				+++	+++
	AVGAGE		-			
Carrier	AMR/UAL		--		--	--
	MFSC		++	--		
	NFSC					
	LCC	++		++		--
	FREIGHT				++	
Region	APAC	++		++		
	EMEA	++		++		
	LATAM	++		--		
	NORAM	--		--		--
	R^2 (adjusted)	≤ 0.57	≤ 0.63	≤ 0.77	≤ 0.23	≤ 0.39
	F-statistic	3.00** - 11.57***	4.51*** - 6.36***	3.12** - 9.82***	1.81* - 6.36***	3.39*** - 8.50***

+/- Positive/negative impact on abnormal returns < 0.1/>-0.1
++/-- Positive/negative impact on abnormal returns ≥ 0.1/≤ -0.1
+++/--- Positive/negative impact on abnormal returns ≥ 1.0/≤ -1.0

xxx Statistically significant at the 10% level
xxx Statistically significant at the 5% level
xxx Statistically significant at the 1% level

Table 11: *Overview on MVRM results for stock market's reaction in the mid term after 9/11 ($y_{7\text{-}36}$)*

This table presents a consolidated overview of cross-sectional regression results for cumulated abnormal returns of aircraft operating and holding companies for the seventh to thirty sixth trading day: September 19 – October 30 (for non-U.S. markets) and September 25 – November 5 (for the U.S. market) after the terrorist attacks on September 11, 2001. SIZE is the natural logarithm of total assets, LIQUIDITY is cash & equivalents over current liabilities, NDTEBITDA is net debt over EBITDA, EBITDAMAR is EBITDA over total operating revenue, EQITYRAT is owners equity over total assets, INTRSTCOVRG is interest expenses for debt over EBIT, RPKMKTSHR and FTKMKTSHR are revenue passenger and freight ton kilometer market shares, PINT and PINT1 are the portions of international (non-home region and non-domestic) business in total operating revenue, PFREIGHT is the portion of freight business in total operating revenue, TOTALAC is the total number of jet aircraft, OPSLEASE is the ratio of operating leased aircraft over total aircraft count, STORAC is the ratio of stored aircraft to total aircraft count, nYRORDER and nYROPTION/1YROPTION are the number of aircraft orders and purchase options to existing fleet in the next n (all) years or 1 year, and AVGAGE is the average age of existing aircraft. Also, nine dummy variables are included which are equal to one if the firm meets the requirements and equal to zero otherwise: MFSC if the firm is a major full service carrier, NFSC if the firm is a non-major full service carrier, LCC if the firm is a low cost carrier, FREIGHT if the firm is a freight only carrier, UAL/AMR if the firm is either United Airlines (UAL) or American Airlines (AMR), APAC, if the firm is Asia Pacific based, EMEA if the firm is based in Europe Middle East or Africa, LATAM if the firm is Latin America based, and NORAM if the firm is North American based. The magnitude of the positive and negative influence of the variables on abnormal returns refers to the regression coefficient. Statistical significance is based on t-statistics.

Further, the time span of several weeks is wide enough to have company specific events influencing the findings. In order not to draw wrong conclusions from the table, the interpretation of the results will focus first on the Models N and O only, i.e. those models that include all 48 sample companies and give the possibility to directly observe a possible effect of the individual stock exchanges' opening days on the markets' reaction.

Model N and O are very much consistent in their results. EBITDAMAR continues to be a strong positively influencing factor; NDTEBITDA and INTRESTCOVRG remain negatively impacting abnormal returns.

New is that 1YROPTION becomes a highly significant factor that positively influences market's reaction. In the two previous sections, the variable nYROPTION showed the same positive influence, but became non-significant in the mid term. The shift of statistical significance of aircraft purchase options from nYROPTION to 1YROPTION indicates that the market was aware of the option window, i.e. the time in which the option could be executed. While nYROPTION includes all purchase options of a company into the future, 1YROPTION only takes into account the options within the year after the event. Rationale for this trend could be that after a first stock crash – especially for airline stocks – the market slightly picked up growth again in the fourth quarter of 2001. Not knowing at that time whether this was a consistent recovery trend or (as it finally turned out end of the second quarter 2002) only a rearing up of the aviation market before stocks began to fall again, a certain flexibility in increasing capacity by executing purchase options was probably awarded by the market. With the general downward trend in the aviation industry right after 9/11, not only airlines' economic situation was affected, but also that of the manufacturers. This led to decreasing aircraft prices giving those airlines holding purchase options to be executed in the next months an opportunity for buying cheap capacity ahead of the market.

After the short term positive impact for AMR/UAL (cf. Table 10) during the time the U.S. bailout package was issued, the market fell back into its initial reaction of penalizing especially these two airlines: American Airlines and United Airlines. The involvement of their planes in the terrorist attacks had an at least mid term impact on the companies.

The variables LCC, FREIGHT, and NORAM are statistically significant only at the 10% level and only represented in either Model N or O. Nevertheless the general trend remains: being a North American company or a low cost carrier bears a disadvantage for the market; freight-only carriers are believed to manage the crisis better, which has a positive effect on their abnormal returns. The influence of a company's SIZE cannot be interpreted because it shows a positive sign in Model K but becomes a negatively influencing factor in Model N.

Model L and M clearly show two different pictures of explanatory factors for the U.S. and the non-U.S. based companies over the same period September 25 to November 5, 2001.

What they have in common is that NDTEBITDA has a negative impact on abnormal returns in both samples. The only clear difference is MFSC which has a positive influence in the U.S. market and a negative impact on abnormal returns in the non-U.S. markets. All other variables are either significant in one model or the other: While in Model L the U.S. market sees EBITDAMAR positive and LIQUIDITY, RPKMKTSHR, TOTALAC, and AMR/UAL as negative, the non-U.S. markets in Model M prefer high PINT, OPSLEASE, LCC, APAC, and EMEA and penalize PFREIGHT, STORAC, LATAM, and NORAM. The variables LIQUIDITY in Model L and INTRESTCOVRG in Model M show non-rational signs and cannot be interpreted. In the other models, high INTRESTCOVRG appears with the expected negative correlation.

In order not to speculate too much on the differences between Model L and M, only two variables of Model M shall be discussed: OPSLEASE and STORAC. OPSLEASE was in the previous sections seen by the non-U.S. markets as being negative (cf. Table 9 Models A and C as well as Table10 Model F). This view has changed, now seeing OPSLEASE as beneficial in the mid term. STORAC was seen as positive and changed negative. Reason for this could again lie in the upward trend of the stock and underlying economic market in Q4 2001. As described before, operating leased aircraft are less flexible when an ad hoc reduction in capacity supply is needed. Some lease agreements can potentially be changed or canceled, but others not. Tied into lease contracts, carriers have to rely on decommissioning or grounding their owned aircraft and keep flying their leased aircraft. Depending on what portion of the fleet is operating leased, some carriers might even have to carry a certain overcapacity simply because they are not able to reduce it further. When the market turns into growth, these companies have an advantage because they can immediately sell their capacity without delay for re-activating grounded aircraft or having to buy new capacity. Probably for the same reason of ad hoc capacity boost, stored aircraft were seen as negative by the market.

Focusing only on the facts, the findings of the third multivariate regression analysis, which concentrates on the mid term abnormal returns after 9/11, can be summarized in three statements:

(1) When analyzed separately, the U.S. and the non-U.S. markets highlighted different explanatory variables in the mid term, indicating different believes of the stock markets in the different regions

(2) Models including the full company sample show a more consistent picture and clearly allot a positive influence on abnormal returns to EBITDAMAR and 1YROPTION, while believing that NDTEBITDA, INTRSTCOVRG and AMR/UAL have negative influence

(3) The results of the regressions leave room for speculation that in the mid term after 9/11 the market believed in a recovery of the economic situation, hence awarding those companies that could quickly re-activate or gain additional capacity

So far, the evaluation of companies' stock performance in the crisis triggered by 9/11 covered the following sections: *Airline stocks before 9/11, Abnormal return as a reaction on 9/11, Stock market's reaction on the first trading day, Stock market's short term reaction on 9/11, and Stock markets' mid term reaction on 9/11.* Before finally concluding on the differencing factors (statistically significant explanatory variables) between the aircraft operating and holding companies in scope, the next section will offer an overview on the companies' long term stock performance after 9/11.

Airline stocks' long term performance after 9/11

After intensive regression analyses to find out what factors have the explanatory power to describe differences in abnormal returns between individual companies of the same aviation industry, it shall be allowed to have again a look at a simple graph.

Figure 28 illustrates the development of the air transport industry – represented by the MSCI World Air Freight/Logistics Index and MSCI World Airlines Index – in comparison to the MSCI World Index over a period of six years starting with the terrorist attacks on September 11, 2001.

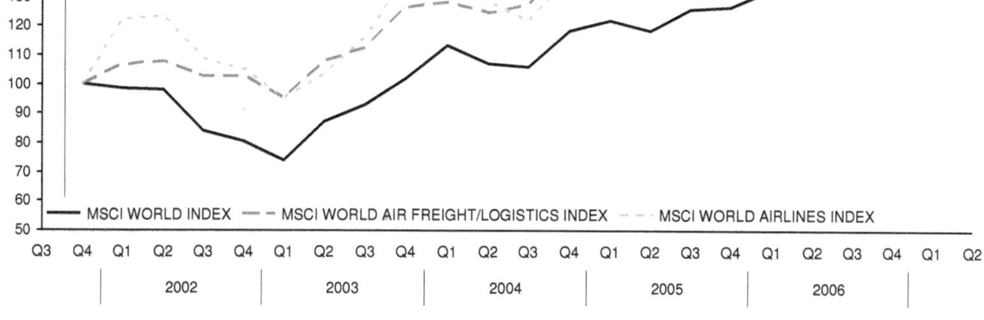

Figure 28: *Stock market development post 9/11 – Sector indices versus general market Q4 2001 to Q2 2007*

This figure presents the quarterly development of the two sector price indices MSCI World Air Freight/Logistics and MSCI World Airlines versus the sector unspecific broader MSCI World Index from Q4 2001 to Q2 2007. The time period starts with the first quarter after the terrorist attacks on September 11, 2001. All data were obtained from Thomson Reuters Datastream (2010).

Unexpectedly, the air transport industry took an advantage of the crisis, of course only in relation to the broad market, but still both, air freight and logistics providers as well as (passenger) airlines, experienced an upswing in Q1 and Q2 2002. Over the following years, the sector grew parallel to the general market; the volatility of the three indices assimilated.

7.2.2 Financial crisis 2008

As described in the last chapter, the terrorist attacks on September 11, 2001 were the first shock the world went through within the last ten years. The second shock in scope of this paper is the Financial Crisis 2008. Equal to the evaluation of 9/11, the analysis of the stock market's reaction to the Financial Crisis 2008 starts with the course of events, then illustrates the shift of risk in investing in aircraft operating and holding companies, and subsequently provides the results of the multivariate regression models that explain the differences in market's reaction with regard to individual companies and explanatory variables.

7.2.2.1 Financial Crisis – Observation periods and course of events

Almost exactly seven years after 9/11, the world experienced and still experiences the aftermath of the "worst financial crisis since the Great Depression" in the 1930s (Reuters, 2009). Of course it cannot be said that the financial crisis appeared out of a sudden like a terrorist attack. Its root cause is found in the collapse of the real estate bubble, which had built up since the 1990s in the United States.[55] Nevertheless, the immediate impact to the world economy when the crisis jumped from the real estate industry to the financial sector can be set equal to an unexpected shock. The following is an extract of financial and market news displayed in the media since the beginning of the financial crisis[56]:

First indications for an unhealthy financial status and a beginning crisis can be found early 2007. For the first time in 15 years, Q1 2007 experienced a year-on-year decline in U.S. house prices. The subprime mortgage market collapses first in February to March, spreading

---

[55] "Asset bubbles occur when an asset price rises above the underlying fundamental value. Asset bubbles can occur for any financial or real asset but recent experience shows they are pervasive in equity markets and in housing and real estate markets. The perverse interaction between easy money, asset bubbles, credit growth and leveraging that feeds asset bubbles has been observed in many episodes." Examples include all world regions: (1) the Latin American sovereign debt crisis started in 1982 (followed by a decade of lost growth), (2) the U.S. real estate bubble in the mid 1980s, (3) the Japanese real estate and equity bubble of the 1980s and its burst in 1990 (followed by a banking and corporate crisis), (4) the Scandinavian banking crises of the early 1990s, (5) the tech and Internet bubble in the 1990s, (6) "a variety of financial crises in emerging market economies: East Asia (Thailand, Indonesia, Malaysia, Korea) in 1997–98; Russia in 1998; Brazil in 1999; Ecuador, Pakistan, and Ukraine in 1999–2000; and Turkey and Argentina in 2001 [..., and (7)] the housing and credit bubble of the 2000s, followed by the housing bust and credit crunch of 2007." (World Economic Forum, 2008, p. 7)

[56] As there was no scientific chronological description of the Financial Crisis 2008 available at the beginning of this thesis, the course of events builds on a summary of news statements retrieved from providers with high reputation such as Reuters, Financial Times, Handelsblatt, New York Times, etc.

quickly to the prime lenders. Within a few months several mortgage firms announced severe financial problems or even filed for bankruptcy.

In August 2007, the problem jumped over to the global banking sector in a global credit squeeze when subprime mortgage backed securities are found in the investment portfolios of banks and hedge funds world-wide. For the first time since 9/11, the world's central banks had to align their efforts to increase liquidity. Biggest injections include USD 43 billion by the U.S. Federal Reserve Bank, USD 214.6 billion by the European Central Bank (ECB), and USD 8.4 billion by the Bank of Japan. With the end of the year 2007, the world's central banks' effort to abandon or mitigate the crisis amounts hundreds of USD 350 billion.

The downturn of the market continued through the first three quarters of the year 2008. But, even though the stock market went down, banks started to announce significant cost cutting plans, and first acquisitions took place to avoid bankruptcy in the financial service sector, the world media yet did not call it a "global financial crisis". So far, it was mainly the real estate industry's problem and that of banks which were trapped in their own investment structures. Only few voices were heard that warned openly against a probable worsening of the situation affecting the world economy.

In September 2008 the financial crisis ultimately escalated. With the nationalization of the two U.S. mortgage firms Fannie Mae and Freddie Mac on September 7[57], the sale of Merrill Lynch to Bank of America and the collapse of Lehman Brothers, both on September 14, the confidence in the financial system was finally lost. In addition, the money market mutual "Reserve Primary fund", which had held approximately USD 800 million in Lehman Brothers notes and commercial papers, fell under the USD 1 mark. The panic led to a run on the money market in which more than USD 140 billion was withdrawn, compared to USD 7 billion the week before. This in turn led to problems for the commercial paper market and subsequently to problems in funding for corporations. Funds became unavailable or only at much higher interest rates. The following weeks were characterized by the efforts of the U.S. Federal Reserve Bank and the U.S. Treasury Secretary to setup and align a national bailout plan which passed the U.S. Senate October 1 and was announced by U.S. President George W. Bush October 3 as the Emergency Economic Stabilization Act. Shortly after the shock in the United States, the crisis made its way to Europe and other continents.

Similar to 9/11, the course of the recent Financial Crisis 2008 can be broken down into few single event days important for the analysis of market's reaction. The course of events is built on a summary of news statements retrieved from providers with high reputation such

[57] Fannie Mae and Freddie Mac owned or guaranteed at that point of time approximately half of the United States' USD 12 trillion mortgage market

as Reuters, Financial Times, Handelsblatt, New York Times, etc., as no reliable scientific chronological description of the Financial Crisis 2008 was available at the beginning of this thesis.

September 7, 2008	▪ The U.S. government announces the nationalization of the two firms, Fannie Mae and Freddie Mac to ensure financial stability.
September 14, 2008	▪ After being denied support by the Federal Reserve Bank, the financial service company Lehman Brothers signals to file for bankruptcy. ▪ The Bank of America states that it would be purchasing Merrill Lynch. ▪ The Reserve Primary fund (a money market mutual fund) falls under the USD 1 mark.
September 15, 2008	▪ Lehman Brothers officially files for bankruptcy. ▪ A run on money market funds starts in which over USD 140 billion is withdrawn. ▪ Funds become unavailable or only at a much higher interest. ▪ Market value starts to drop and continues falling for three consecutive days September 15-17.
September 16, 2008	▪ The U.S. Federal Reserve Bank grants a USD 85 billion credit facility to the American International Group (AIG), which was troubled by its reduced credit rating.
September 18, 2008	▪ U.S. Treasury Secretary Henry Paulson and Fed Chairman Ben Bernanke propose USD 700 billion emergency bailout through the purchase of toxic assets to key legislatives (bypassing in the first instance the House of Representatives).
September 19, 2008	▪ The proposed USD 700 billion emergency bailout plan is unveiled.
September 21, 2008	▪ U.S. President George W. Bush and the Secretary of the Treasury announce the USD 700 billion financial aid package.

September 25, 2008

- The Federal Office of Thrift Supervision shuts the bank Washington Mutual (WaMu) because of unsound finances, after a run on WaMu's deposits in which USD 16.7 billion were withdrawn by panicked customers.
- JP Morgan steps in to purchase the majority of WaMu's assets for USD 1.9 billion.

September 28, 2008

- The banking and finance firm Fortis is announced to be semi-nationalized with Luxembourg, Belgium and the Netherlands investing over USD 16 billion (EUR 11 billion)[58].

September 29, 2008

- Citigroup intends to buy up the US Wachovia (finally bought by Wells Fargo October 2008).
- Iceland nationalizes the Icelandic lender Glitnir.

September 30, 2008

- U.S. Treasury adapts tax law to allow banks to acquire another bank and write off the acquired bank's losses.
- France, Belgium and Luxembourg make USD 13 billion (EUR 9 billion) available for the bank Dexia.

October 1, 2008

- The U.S. Senate passes the USD 700 billion bailout (HR1424).
- The financial crisis reaches Europe.

October 3, 2008

- U.S. President George W. Bush signs the Emergency Economic Stabilization Act.

October 6, 2008

- The U.S. Federal Reserve Bank announces USD 900 billion short term cash loans to banks.

October 7, 2008

- The U.S. Federal Reserve Bank makes direct emergency lending of USD 1.3 trillion to non-financial companies.

[58] Converted with two trading days average European Central Bank conversion rate of EUR 1 to USD of 1.44945 as of September 26-29, 2008 retrieved from Thomson Datastream (2009)

October 8, 2008

- Central banks world-wide cut interest rates (incl. United States, England, China, Canada, Sweden, Switzerland and the European Central Bank).
- The U.S. Federal Reserve Bank decreases its emergency lending interest rate to banks.
- U.S. President George W. Bush considers equity shares in banks in tradeoff for the bailout bill.

October 10, 2008

- The Dow Jones closes with a 22.1% loss in one week (worst week in 75 years; down 40.3% since record high of 14,164.53 on October 9, 2007.
- The Standard & Poor's 500 loses 18.2% (worst week since 1933; down 42.5% since record high October 9, 2007).

October 11, 2008

- Central bankers and finance ministers of the seven leading economies (G7) align on coordinated actions to prevent a world depression, but do not agree on concrete plans.

October 14, 2008

- USD 250 billion out of the USD 700 in the Emergency Economic Stabilization Act is announced to be injected into the U.S. banking system in tradeoff for equity shares and restrictions in executive compensation.
- The program is immediately accepted by Bank of America, Bank of New York Mellon, Citigroup, Goldman Sachs, JPMorgan Chase, Merrill Lynch, Morgan Stanley, State Street, and Wells Fargo.

October 21, 2008

- The U.S. Federal Reserve Bank announces a spend of USD 540 billion to purchase short term debt from money market mutual funds, hoping to unblock the lending markets enabling businesses and banks to obtain credits.

The evaluation of market's reaction on the Financial Crisis is split into several observation periods focusing on single event days, the short term and the mid term following the shock. Because the shock did not hit all industries right on the first trading day, September 15, after the escalation of the crisis on Sunday, September 14, 2008, the first four trading days September 15-18 are examined as single event days to identify the exact day when the

Financial Crisis reached the aviation industry (aircraft operating and holding companies), eventually reflected in the abnormal returns of the company's stocks. Additionally, four multi-trading day time windows are analyzed: The first period are the 11 trading days following September 15, i.e. September 16-30, in which several banks shut down or were taken over and different options of stabilization actions were discussed. This period represents the short term.

The second time period under investigation is October 1-8 (6 trading days), in which the U.S. authorities passed the first bailout packages and signed the Emergency Economic Stabilization Act. This was also the week in which the crisis reached Europe.

The third time window is October 9-16 (6 trading days), in which the most important stock index, the Dow Jones, made its biggest per-week losses during the crisis and the financial ministers of the G7 coordinated their actions. Finally, the full mid term period October 1-30 is examined to evaluate the conglomerate impact of all bailout packages, stabilization actions and further activities to unfreeze the credit markets to enable new lending to businesses and banks.

7.2.2.2 Financial Crisis – Alpha, beta, and the shift in risk

Similar to the general description of alpha and beta calculations in Chapter 7.1.1.1 and to the adjustment to the terrorist attacks on September 11, 2001 (cf. Chapter 7.2.1.2), the least square model parameters can be derived for the Financial Crisis 2008. For this observation period, alpha (α) and beta (β) are computed for a period of 116 trading day horizon starting April 1 and ending September 14, 2001. The shift in risk (α′, β′) is calculated as the difference between the stock's α and β before the event and α and β after the event. The latter was estimated over a period of 137 trading days starting September 11, 2001, and ending March 31, 2002.

Calculation of α and β risk components for the Financial Crisis 2008[59]:

α_i = least square model parameter reflecting the risk prior to the Financial Crisis 2008; calculated over a period of 116 trading days starting April 1 and ending September 14, 2008

α_i' = least square model parameter reflecting a risk shift resulting from the Financial Crisis 2008; calculated as the difference between α_i and the alpha for the same i

[59] The number of trading days mentioned is exemplary and refers to the trading days of the New York Stock Exchange (NYSE). Saturdays and Sundays are excluded as well as NYSE trading holidays, i.e. days with full closure of the exchange. For companies listed at other stock exchanges the actual number of trading days might vary; nevertheless, risk components were calculated for all companies from April 1 – September 14, 2008 and from September 15, 2008 – March 31, 2009.

determined over a period of 137 trading days starting September 15, 2008 and ending March 31, 2009

β_i = least square model parameter reflecting the risk prior to the Financial Crisis; calculated over a period of 116 trading days starting April 1 and ending September 14, 2008

$\beta_i^{'}$ = least square model parameter reflecting a risk shift resulting from the Financial Crisis; calculated as the difference between β_i and the beta for the same i determined over a period of 137 trading days starting September 15, 2008 and ending March 31, 2009

Company	Region	α_i		α_i'		β_i		β_i'	
Major full service carriers									
1 Air Canada Inc	NORAM	-0.0049	(0.0041)	-0.0045	(0.0066)	1.7579 ***	(0.4489)	-0.7217 ***	(0.2289)
2 Air China Limited	APAC	-0.0097 **	(0.0043)	0.0122	(0.0034)	-0.0899	(0.4701)	0.3662 **	(0.1163)
3 Air France-KLM	EMEA	0.0010	(0.0026)	-0.0049	(0.0028)	1.7086 ***	(0.2844)	-0.6783 ***	(0.0980)
4 Air New Zealand Limited	APAC	-0.0021	(0.0021)	0.0018	(0.0027)	0.4543 *	(0.2326)	0.1123 ***	(0.0931)
5 Alaska Air Group Inc	NORAM	0.0040	(0.0046)	-0.0031	(0.0051)	2.5703 ***	(0.5085)	-1.7154 ***	(0.1752)
6 All Nippon Airways Company Limited	APAC	-0.0019	(0.0012)	0.0029	(0.0019)	0.1056	(0.1266)	-0.0219	(0.0643)
7 AMR Corp.	NORAM	0.0047	(0.0067)	-0.0099	(0.0065)	3.5559 ***	(0.7311)	-2.5802 ***	(0.2264)
8 Austrian Airlines AG	EMEA	0.0030	(0.0043)	-0.0041	(0.0056)	1.6357 ***	(0.4703)	-0.7215 ***	(0.1935)
9 British Airways PLC	EMEA	0.0024	(0.0030)	-0.0038	(0.0035)	2.3194 ***	(0.3337)	-0.9772 ***	(0.1203)
10 Cathay Pacific Airways Limited	APAC	0.0007	(0.0021)	-0.0031	(0.0035)	0.8005 ***	(0.2262)	-0.1397 ***	(0.1224)
11 China Airlines Limited	APAC	-0.0047	(0.0029)	0.0047	(0.0029)	0.9173 ***	(0.3212)	-0.5117 ***	(0.1022)
12 China Eastern Airlines Corp. Limited	APAC	-0.0094 **	(0.0043)	0.0124	(0.0038)	-0.1510	(0.4685)	0.3609	(0.1328)
13 China Southern Airlines Company Limited	APAC	-0.0085 *	(0.0043)	0.0125	(0.0033)	-0.0054	(0.4722)	0.2706 **	(0.1148)
14 Continental Airlines Inc	NORAM	-0.0009	(0.0078)	-0.0026	(0.0063)	0.2248	(0.8503)	-0.0500	(0.2168)
15 Delta Air Lines Inc	NORAM	0.0020	(0.0066)	-0.0004	(0.0057)	2.4948 ***	(0.7202)	-1.2236 ***	(0.1963)
16 Deutsche Lufthansa AG	EMEA	-0.0010 *	(0.0006)	0.0012	(0.0009)	-0.0394	(0.0636)	0.2328 ***	(0.0326)
17 El Al Israel Airlines Limited	EMEA	-0.0031	(0.0028)	0.0013	(0.0030)	1.0552 ***	(0.3026)	-0.4970 ***	(0.1050)
18 EVA Airways Corp.	APAC	-0.0042	(0.0032)	0.0036	(0.0030)	0.9502 ***	(0.3489)	-0.5018 ***	(0.1053)
19 Finnair OYJ	EMEA	-0.0042 *	(0.0025)	0.0043	(0.0028)	0.6576 **	(0.2723)	-0.0300 ***	(0.0955)
20 Iberia SA	EMEA	-0.0007	(0.0029)	0.0013	(0.0030)	1.9099 ***	(0.3169)	-1.0277 ***	(0.1025)
21 Japan Airlines Corp.	APAC	-0.0018	(0.0015)	0.0019	(0.0020)	0.0261	(0.1696)	0.0762	(0.0687)
22 Korean Air Lines Company Limited	APAC	-0.0017	(0.0035)	0.0018	(0.0048)	1.1195 ***	(0.3848)	-0.1484 ***	(0.1655)
23 Lan Airlines SA	LATAM	-0.0003	(0.0020)	0.0009	(0.0021)	1.1410 ***	(0.2227)	-0.2777 ***	(0.0727)
24 Malaysian Airline	APAC	0.0002	(0.0022)	-0.0017	(0.0024)	0.3483	(0.2407)	-0.0887 ***	(0.0822)
25 Northwest Airlines Corporation	NORAM	0.0035	(0.0075)	-0.0019	(0.0037)	2.7695 ***	(0.8208)	-2.2910 ***	(0.1267)
26 Qantas Airways Limited	APAC	-0.0007	(0.0024)	-0.0024	(0.0041)	0.8117 ***	(0.2602)	-0.0394 ***	(0.1405)
27 SAS AB	EMEA	0.0013	(0.0037)	-0.0041	(0.0057)	2.3328 ***	(0.4048)	-1.1441 ***	(0.1975)
28 Singapore Airlines Limited	APAC	0.0006	(0.0013)	-0.0024	(0.0024)	0.5917 ***	(0.1458)	-0.1403 ***	(0.0816)
29 TAM SA	LATAM	0.0027	(0.0027)	-0.0078	(0.0037)	1.6904 ***	(0.2965)	-0.3178 ***	(0.1271)
30 Thai Airways International Public Company	APAC	-0.0060 **	(0.0024)	0.0042	(0.0030)	0.3905	(0.2677)	0.0544 ***	(0.1035)
31 UAL Corporation	NORAM	-0.0012	(0.0098)	-0.0003	(0.0076)	4.1371 ***	(1.0676)	-2.6114 ***	(0.2647)
32 US Airways Group Inc	NORAM	0.0035	(0.0082)	-0.0058	(0.0075)	4.4860 ***	(0.8945)	-2.7637 ***	(0.2609)
Non-major full service carriers									
1 Hawaiian Holdings Inc	NORAM	0.0063 *	(0.0034)	-0.0097	(0.0048)	1.3783 ***	(0.3766)	-0.1141 ***	(0.1672)
2 Mesa Air Group Inc	NORAM	-0.0116	(0.0093)	0.0029	(0.0120)	1.9505 *	(1.0214)	-1.8037	(0.4169)
3 Skywest Inc	NORAM	0.0009	(0.0034)	-0.0006	(0.0040)	1.8089 ***	(0.3703)	-0.8095 ***	(0.1371)
4 Westjet Airlines Limited	NORAM	-0.0012	(0.0024)	0.0013	(0.0030)	1.1861 ***	(0.2681)	-0.3300 ***	(0.1053)

** Statistically significant at the 10% level*
*** Statistically significant at the 5% level*
**** Statistically significant at the 1% level*

Table 12: *Alpha, beta and the shift in risk with the Financial Crisis 2008 for all sample firms and portfolios*

(Table continued on next page)

Low cost carriers									
1 AER Lingus Group PLC	EMEA	-0.0014	(0.0030)	-0.0049	(0.0041)	1.4666 ***	(0.3331)	-1.1050 **	(0.1430)
2 Air Berlin PLC	EMEA	-0.0046	(0.0039)	0.0048	(0.0037)	1.5563 ***	(0.4274)	-0.8130 ***	(0.1291)
3 Airtran Holdings Inc	NORAM	-0.0049	(0.0072)	0.0122	(0.0057)	2.6254 ***	(0.7903)	-1.5359 ***	(0.1970)
4 Easyjet PLC	EMEA	0.0005	(0.0035)	-0.0006	(0.0034)	2.2074 ***	(0.3830)	-1.3404 ***	(0.1187)
5 Frontier Airlines, Inc.	NORAM	-0.0182	(0.0141)	0.0181	(0.0071)	0.3837	(1.5455)	0.0669 *	(0.2466)
6 Jetblue Airways Corp.	NORAM	0.0023	(0.0039)	-0.0019	(0.0048)	2.0691 ***	(0.4226)	-0.8588 ***	(0.1664)
7 Ryanair Holdings PLC	EMEA	0.0011	(0.0040)	0.0014	(0.0029)	2.2184 ***	(0.4369)	-1.4354 ***	(0.0990)
8 Southwest Airlines Company	NORAM	0.0034	(0.0022)	-0.0071	(0.0031)	1.1917 ***	(0.2407)	-0.3083 ***	(0.1087)
9 Virgin Blue Holdings Limited	APAC	-0.0075	(0.0064)	0.0036	(0.0055)	0.6318	(0.7052)	0.0924 ***	(0.1900)
Freight carriers									
1 Air Transport Service Group	NORAM	-0.0083	(0.0062)	0.0079	(0.0115)	1.3395 *	(0.6810)	-0.9872	(0.3991)
2 Atlas Air Worldwide Holdings Inc	NORAM	0.0008	(0.0019)	-0.0014	(0.0052)	1.4143 ***	(0.2041)	0.7284 ***	(0.1805)
3 Federal Express/FedEx Corp	NORAM	0.0012	(0.0017)	-0.0028	(0.0027)	1.3431 ***	(0.1862)	-0.3349 ***	(0.0919)
4 United Parcel Service, Inc	NORAM	0.0006	(0.0014)	0.0001	(0.0018)	1.0379 ***	(0.1554)	-0.1443 ***	(0.0623)
Carrier portfolios									
Major full service carriers	∑32	-0.0012	(0.0016)	0.0001	(0.0013)	1.3337 ***	(0.1739)	-0.6171 ***	(0.0443)
Non-major full service carriers	∑4	-0.0014	(0.0033)	-0.0015	(0.0038)	1.5810 ***	(0.3648)	-0.7643 ***	(0.1319)
Low cost carriers	∑9	-0.0033	(0.0029)	0.0029	(0.0020)	1.5945 ***	(0.3121)	-0.8042 ***	(0.0692)
Freight carriers	∑4	-0.0014	(0.0018)	0.0010	(0.0034)	1.2837 ***	(0.1997)	-0.1845 ***	(0.1176)
Region portfolios									
APAC	∑15	-0.0038 **	(0.0016)	0.0035	(0.0017)	0.4601 ***	(0.1709)	-0.0173 ***	(0.0574)
EMEA	∑12	-0.0005	(0.0017)	-0.0007	(0.0017)	1.5857 ***	(0.1915)	-0.7947 ***	(0.0590)
LATAM	∑2	0.0012	(0.0019)	-0.0034	(0.0022)	1.4157 ***	(0.2109)	-0.2977 ***	(0.0775)
NORAM	∑20	-0.0009	(0.0034)	-0.0005	(0.0029)	1.9862 ***	(0.3697)	-1.0194 ***	(0.0992)

** Statistically significant at the 10% level*
*** Statistically significant at the 5% level*
**** Statistically significant at the 1% level*

Table 12 (continued): *Alpha, beta and the shift in risk with the Financial Crisis 2008 for all sample firms and portfolios*

This table presents the standard market model parameters α and β and standard errors (in parentheses) for each firm and equally-weighted carrier cluster and region portfolios, estimated over a period of 116 trading days starting April 1 and ending September 14, 2008. It also presents the market model parameters α′ and β′ which reflect a risk shift after September 15, 2008. α′ [β′] is calculated as the difference between a firm's α [β] before the event and the firm's α [β] after the event, estimated over a period of 137 trading days starting September 15, 2008, and ending March 31, 2009. Underlying daily stock data were retrieved from Thomson Reuters Datastream (2009). Benchmark is the MSCI World Index. The number of trading days refers to the trading days of the New York Stock Exchange (NYSE). Statistical significance is based on t-statistics.

Table 12 shows alpha and beta coefficients before the Financial Crisis and the shift thereafter for all sample firms in scope of the analysis. It further includes alpha and beta estimates for equally weighted portfolios based on the four carrier clusters and regions introduced in Chapter 6.4.

The sample stocks show prior to the Financial Crisis – similar to the Table 7 for 9/11 – only few significant alphas. In difference to 9/11 these few significant alphas appear not only with North American but mainly with companies from Asia Pacific and Europe. Again, the shift in alpha risk in the first half year after the event is not significant for any of the companies in scope. Therefore, alpha coefficients are not further described.

The stocks' risk compared to the market (MSCI World Index) is of more interest. On average, the beta of aircraft operating and holding companies is, over a period of six months from April to September prior to the Financial Crisis 2008, with 1.3977 higher than the market's beta. This is converse to the industry's risk before 9/11. Significant beta before the crisis 2008 range from 0.4543* (Air New Zealand) up to 4.4860*** (US Airways Group).

With the start of the global economic crisis the risk of the industry changes significantly. Generally, all carrier clusters and regions experience a drop in beta. Only few individual carriers record an increase in risk compared to the market. In descending order, LCC changes by -0.8042***, NFSC by -0.7643***, and MFSC by -0.6171***, bringing all passenger carrying clusters below the market threshold of 1.0. Only FREIGHTERS stay with a smaller beta decrease of -0.1845 above market risk. From a regional perspective, aircraft operating and holding companies' beta show a clear downward adjustment, the biggest of which within NORAM (-1.0194***), the smallest within APAC (-0.0173). This leads to a situation where all regions except LATAM fall back below the market risk.
Please refer to Table 13 for an overview of betas and shifts in betas of carrier and region portfolios before and after the two crises 2001 and 2008.

		Terrorist Attacks September 11, 2001					Financial Crisis 2008				
	Ranking	Before		Δ	After		Before		Δ	After	
Carrier Cluster	1	MFSC	0.4220	+0.7191	*Market*	*1.0000*	*Market*	*1.0000*	-0.6171	MFSC	0.7166
	2	NFSC	0.5808	+1.7075	MFSC	1.1411	FREIGHT	1.2837		LCC	0.7903
	3	LCC	0.7959	+1.3555	FREIGHT	1.5094	MFSC	1.3337		NFSC	0.8167
	4	FREIGHT	0.8839	+0.7191	LCC	2.1513	NFSC	1.5810	-0.7643, -0.1845	*Market*	*1.0000*
	5	*Market*	*1.0000*		NFSC	2.2882	LCC	1.5945	-0.8042	FREIGHT	1.0992
Region Cluster	1	LATAM[1]	0.1353	+0.2545	LATAM	0.4856	APAC	0.4601	-0.0173	APAC	0.4428
	2	APAC	0.2468	+0.3504	APAC	0.5013	*Market*	*1.0000*		EMEA	0.7910
	3	EMEA	0.3767	+0.6054	EMEA	0.9821	LATAM	1.4157	-0.7947	NORAM	0.9668
	4	NORAM	0.7683	+1.4720	*Market*	*1.0000*	EMEA	1.5857		*Market*	*1.0000*
	5	*Market*	*1.0000*		NORAM	2.2402	NORAM	1.9862	-1.0194, -0.1845	LATAM	1.1180

[1] *All figures are statistical significance at the 1% level (based on t-statistics), except the beta of the LATAM portfolio prior to the terrorist attacks September 11, 2001, which does not show any statistical significance.*

Table 13: *Alpha, beta and the change in risk with 9/11 and the Financial Crisis 2008*

This table presents beta coefficients and respective change in risk for equally-weighted carrier clusters and region portfolios compared to the market prior to and after two shock events: 1) terrorist attacks on September 11 (9/11), 2001, and 2) Financial Crisis 2008. Beta before 9/11 [Financial Crisis] are estimated over a period of 112 [116] trading days starting April 1, 2001 [2008] and ending September 10 [14], 2001 [2008]. Beta after 9/11 [Financial Crisis] are estimated over a period of 137 [137] trading days starting September 11 [15], 2001 [2008], and ending March 29 [31], 2002 [2009]. Underlying daily stock data were retrieved from Thomson Reuters Datastream (2009). Benchmark (Market) is the MSCI World Index. The number of trading days refers to the trading days of the New York Stock Exchange (NYSE). Portfolio abbreviations are: major full service carriers (MFSC), non-major full service carriers (NFSC), low cost carriers (LCC), freight carriers (FREIGHT), as well as Asia Pacific (APAC), Europe Middle East & Africa (EMEA), Latin America (LATAM), and North America (NORAM).

7.2.2.3 Financial Crisis – Analysis results: Stock market's reaction

Airline stocks before the Financial Crisis

As described in the cause of events that led to the collapse of Lehman Brothers (cf. Chapter 7.2.2.1), the crisis actually started in the first half of the year 2007 when the problems in the real estate sector reached the financial market. After several years of growth, the general market started to shake in Q2 2007 – as displayed in Figure 29 – and the cyclical downturn between Q2 2007 and Q3 2008 showed impact also on the air transport industry. When the crisis escalated with the collapse of Lehman Brothers the equity market dropped drastically. The shock hit the air transport industry equally strong. The downward trend Q4 2008 and Q1 2009 as well as the upward trend from Q2 2009 on followed the same path for all three indices illustrated.

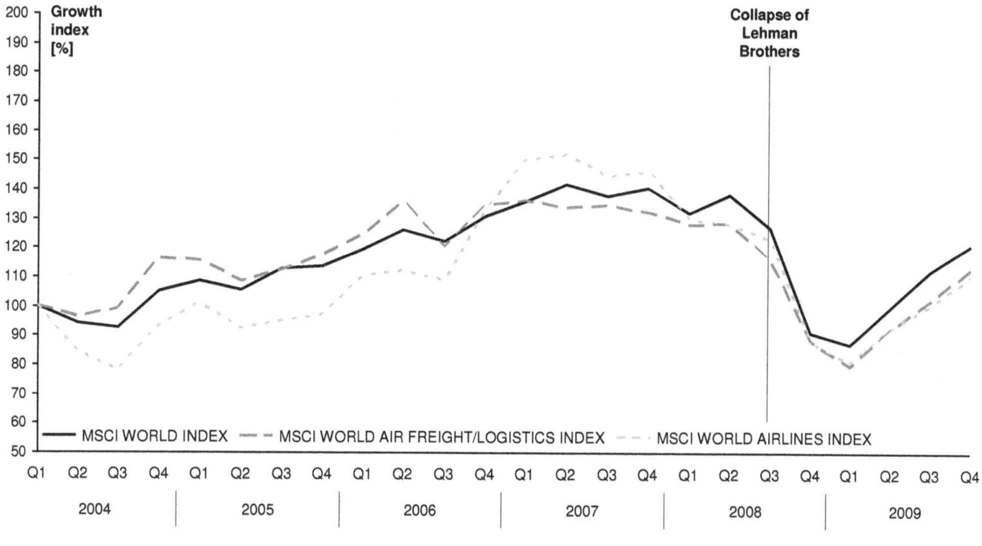

Figure 29: *Stock market development Q1 2004 to Q4 2009 – Sector indices versus general market*

This figure presents the quarterly development of the two sector price indices MSCI World Air Freight/Logistics and MSCI World Airlines versus the sector unspecific broader MSCI World Index from Q1 2004 to Q4 2009. All data were obtained from Thomson Reuters Datastream (2010).

Based on the graph, neither air freight and logistics providers nor airlines did react abnormal compared to the general market movement. If that is the case, the abnormal returns estimate in the subsequent paragraph will be statistically insignificant, therewith impeding the planned multivariate regression analyses or at least weakening their results.

Abnormal return as a reaction to the Financial Crisis

Did the Financial Crisis create significant abnormal returns for aircraft operating and holding companies just as 9/11? To answer this question with statistical evidence, abnormal returns for a global sample of 49 individual firms were calculated using equation 2 in Chapter 7.1.1.1, including the risk components as described in Chapter 7.2.2.2. Further, abnormal returns were estimated for equally weighted carrier and region portfolios.

Table 14 presents the daily abnormal returns for all firms and portfolios for the first twelve trading days September 15-30 ($y_{1\text{-}12}$), with the respective statistical relevance indicated by t-statistics behind the coefficients and F-statistics of the related regression model. The table further shows cumulated abnormal returns for the periods September 16-30 ($y_{2\text{-}12}$), October 1-8 ($y_{13\text{-}18}$), October 9-16 ($y_{19\text{-}24}$) and October 1-30 ($y_{13\text{-}36}$).

Looking at the table, it becomes obvious that abnormal returns generally occurred after the Financial Crisis began to escalate, but the picture is much more scattered than for 9/11 (cf. Table 8) and not all companies experienced abnormal returns. Within the first twelve trading days, 33 out of 49 firms reacted with abnormal returns on at least one of the trading days. 20 firms showed abnormal returns even within the first four days while others responded during the trading days $y_{5\text{-}12}$. Most companies actually reacted on the days y_2, y_4, y_5, and y_{12}. But, is there any pattern?

Company	Region	y_1	y_2	y_3	y_4	y_5	y_6	y_7	y_8	y_9	y_{10}	y_{11}	y_{12}	R^2	F-stat.	$\sum^{11}_{y2\text{-}12} y_j = 0$	$\sum^{10}_{y3\text{-}12} y_j = 0$	$\sum^{6}_{y13\text{-}18} y_j = 0$	$\sum^{6}_{y19\text{-}24} y_j = 0$	$\sum^{23}_{y13\text{-}35} y_j = 0$
Major full service carriers																				
1 Air Canada Inc	NORAM	0.0174 (0.0655)	0.0719 (0.0652)	-0.0077 (0.0654)	0.0386 (0.0653)	-0.0176 (0.0661)	-0.0401 (0.0652)	-0.0153 (0.0652)	0.0413 (0.0652)	0.1281 ** (0.0652)	0.1025 (0.0652)	0.0586 (0.0665)	-0.0125 (0.0653)	-0.01	0.76	0.3477	0.2758	-0.0180	0.0705	0.2710
2 Air China Limited	APAC	0.0076 (0.0432)	0.0027 (0.0429)	0.0018 (0.0431)	-0.0557 (0.0430)	0.0770 * (0.0435)	0.0830 * (0.0430)	-0.0424 (0.0430)	-0.0010 (0.0429)	0.0416 (0.0430)	0.0320 (0.0429)	0.0173 (0.0438)	-0.0070 (0.0430)	-0.01	0.88	0.1496	0.1469	-0.0404	-0.1886	-0.5470
3 Air France-KLM	EMEA	0.0276 (0.0316)	0.0004 (0.0315)	-0.0225 (0.0316)	-0.0361 (0.0315)	-0.0041 (0.0319)	0.0092 (0.0315)	-0.0183 (0.0315)	0.0300 (0.0315)	-0.0074 (0.0315)	-0.0054 (0.0315)	0.0455 (0.0321)	0.0044 (0.0315)	-0.03	0.49	-0.0042	-0.0046	-0.0298	0.1512	-0.1481
4 Air New Zealand Limited	APAC	0.0071 (0.0275)	-0.0422 (0.0273)	0.0687 ** (0.0274)	-0.0291 (0.0274)	-0.0026 (0.0277)	0.0403 (0.0273)	-0.0500 * (0.0273)	0.0229 (0.0273)	-0.0303 (0.0274)	-0.0126 (0.0273)	0.0222 (0.0279)	-0.0773 *** (0.0274)	0.05	2.07 **	-0.0899	-0.0477	-0.0450	-0.0681	-0.0559
5 Alaska Air Group Inc	NORAM	-0.0136 (0.0565)	0.0652 (0.0562)	-0.0389 (0.0564)	0.0083 (0.0563)	-0.0903 (0.0570)	-0.0573 (0.0563)	-0.0009 (0.0562)	0.0005 (0.0562)	0.0057 (0.0563)	0.0094 (0.0562)	-0.0144 (0.0574)	0.0570 (0.0563)	-0.02	0.51	-0.0555	-0.1207	-0.1392	0.4854	0.3528
6 All Nippon Airways Company Limited	APAC	0.0111 (0.0185)	-0.0004 (0.0184)	-0.0098 (0.0184)	0.0242 (0.0184)	0.0119 (0.0186)	-0.0084 (0.0184)	0.0109 (0.0184)	-0.0138 (0.0184)	-0.0066 (0.0184)	0.0085 (0.0184)	0.0072 (0.0187)	-0.0381 ** (0.0184)	-0.02	0.68	-0.0144	-0.0140	-0.0131	0.0647	0.0663
7 AMR Corp.	NORAM	0.1249 * (0.0750)	0.1522 ** (0.0747)	-0.1197 (0.0749)	0.0589 (0.0748)	0.0262 (0.0757)	-0.1219 (0.0747)	0.0494 (0.0747)	-0.0602 (0.0746)	-0.0027 (0.0747)	0.0135 (0.0747)	-0.0152 (0.0762)	-0.0208 (0.0748)	0.00	1.10	-0.0402	-0.1925	-0.2298	0.6132	0.3627
8 Austrian Airlines AG	EMEA	0.0502 (0.0581)	-0.0050 (0.0578)	0.0195 (0.0580)	-0.0918 (0.0579)	-0.0026 (0.0586)	0.0408 (0.0578)	-0.0710 (0.0578)	-0.0043 (0.0578)	0.0446 (0.0578)	-0.0254 (0.0578)	-0.1453 ** (0.0590)	-0.0387 (0.0579)	0.00	1.01	-0.2792	-0.2742	0.0762	-0.0603	-0.3698
9 British Airways PLC	EMEA	0.0694 * (0.0367)	-0.0093 (0.0365)	-0.0077 (0.0367)	-0.1281 *** (0.0366)	-0.0579 * (0.0371)	0.0292 (0.0366)	-0.0137 (0.0366)	-0.0083 (0.0365)	-0.0632 * (0.0366)	-0.0162 (0.0366)	-0.0530 (0.0373)	-0.0423 (0.0366)	0.05	2.05 **	-0.3706	-0.3613	-0.1299	0.0678	0.0058
10 Cathay Pacific Airways Limited	APAC	0.0271 (0.0349)	-0.0252 (0.0347)	-0.0226 (0.0348)	-0.0457 (0.0348)	-0.0057 (0.0352)	-0.0127 (0.0347)	-0.0163 (0.0347)	0.0258 (0.0347)	0.0085 (0.0347)	-0.0115 (0.0347)	0.0443 (0.0354)	0.0013 (0.0347)	-0.03	0.48	-0.0598	-0.0346	-0.0619	-0.0071	-0.1434
11 China Airlines Limited	APAC	-0.0225 (0.0329)	-0.0416 (0.0327)	0.0236 (0.0328)	-0.0844 *** (0.0328)	0.0131 (0.0331)	-0.0228 (0.0327)	-0.0319 (0.0327)	0.0143 (0.0327)	-0.0433 (0.0327)	-0.0696 ** (0.0327)	0.0292 (0.0334)	-0.0780 ** (0.0327)	0.04	1.88 **	-0.2915	-0.2499	-0.1475	0.0370	0.1976
12 China Eastern Airlines Corp. Limited	APAC	0.0046 (0.0462)	-0.0219 (0.0459)	-0.0027 (0.0461)	-0.0651 (0.0460)	0.0798 * (0.0466)	0.0541 (0.0460)	-0.0779 * (0.0459)	0.0181 (0.0459)	0.0219 (0.0460)	-0.0059 (0.0459)	0.0120 (0.0469)	-0.0065 (0.0460)	-0.01	0.78	0.0060	0.0279	0.0432	-0.2121	-0.4096
13 China Southern Airlines Company Limitec	APAC	0.0057 (0.0429)	-0.0254 (0.0427)	-0.0145 (0.0429)	-0.0731 * (0.0428)	0.0771 * (0.0433)	0.0782 * (0.0428)	-0.0531 (0.0427)	-0.0097 (0.0427)	0.0236 (0.0428)	-0.0008 (0.0427)	0.0151 (0.0436)	-0.0083 (0.0428)	0.00	0.93	0.0091	0.0345	0.0214	-0.1632	-0.2966
14 Continental Airlines Inc	NORAM	0.0251 (0.0800)	-0.0007 (0.0796)	-0.0816 (0.0799)	0.0279 (0.0798)	-0.0097 (0.0807)	0.0282 (0.0797)	0.0118 (0.0796)	-0.1085 (0.0796)	0.0533 (0.0797)	0.0587 (0.0796)	-0.0276 (0.0812)	-0.1031 (0.0797)	-0.03	0.47	-0.1513	-0.1506	-0.1156	0.3364	0.2009
15 Delta Air Lines Inc	NORAM	0.0352 (0.0688)	0.2186 *** (0.0684)	-0.0625 (0.0686)	0.0205 (0.0686)	-0.0495 (0.0694)	-0.0859 (0.0685)	0.0310 (0.0684)	-0.0931 (0.0684)	-0.0150 (0.0685)	-0.0046 (0.0684)	0.0087 (0.0698)	-0.0057 (0.0685)	0.01	1.21	-0.0375	-0.2561	-0.0794	0.5271	0.6201
16 Deutsche Lufthansa AG	EMEA	0.0079 (0.0091)	-0.0036 (0.0091)	0.0108 (0.0091)	0.0085 (0.0091)	-0.0088 (0.0092)	0.0189 ** (0.0091)	0.0082 (0.0091)	-0.0035 (0.0091)	-0.0026 (0.0091)	-0.0028 (0.0091)	0.0019 (0.0092)	-0.0306 *** (0.0091)	0.03	1.66 *	-0.0036	0.0001	0.0017	-0.0055	-0.0657
17 El Al Israel Airlines Limited	EMEA	0.0061 (0.0331)	-0.0244 (0.0330)	-0.0012 (0.0331)	-0.0502 (0.0331)	0.0367 (0.0334)	-0.0125 (0.0330)	-0.0170 (0.0330)	-0.0041 (0.0330)	0.0978 *** (0.0330)	-0.0454 (0.0330)	0.0314 (0.0337)	-0.0098 (0.0330)	0.01	1.25	0.0014	0.0259	-0.1171	-0.0412	-0.2172
18 EVA Airways Corp.	APAC	0.0170 (0.0343)	-0.0668 ** (0.0341)	0.0544 (0.0342)	-0.0864 ** (0.0342)	0.0353 (0.0346)	-0.0191 (0.0342)	-0.0126 (0.0341)	0.0165 (0.0341)	-0.0577 * (0.0342)	-0.0712 ** (0.0341)	0.0328 (0.0348)	-0.0828 ** (0.0342)	0.06	2.26 ***	-0.2576	-0.1908	-0.1367	-0.0017	0.0780
19 Finnair OYJ	EMEA	-0.0161 (0.0297)	0.0041 (0.0295)	-0.0151 (0.0296)	-0.0268 (0.0296)	0.0725 ** (0.0299)	0.0133 (0.0295)	-0.0642 ** (0.0295)	0.0428 (0.0295)	0.0164 (0.0295)	-0.0774 *** (0.0295)	-0.0186 (0.0301)	-0.0149 (0.0295)	0.04	1.76 **	-0.0680	-0.0721	-0.0009	0.0616	0.0064
20 Iberia SA	EMEA	0.0473 (0.0337)	0.0010 (0.0335)	-0.0125 (0.0337)	-0.0419 (0.0336)	-0.0220 (0.0340)	-0.0004 (0.0336)	0.0006 (0.0336)	0.0045 (0.0335)	0.0084 (0.0336)	-0.0390 (0.0335)	-0.0267 (0.0342)	-0.0537 (0.0336)	-0.02	0.68	-0.1818	-0.1828	-0.1239	0.0831	0.1452
21 Japan Airlines Corp.	APAC	0.0113 (0.0208)	-0.0225 (0.0207)	0.0186 (0.0208)	0.0131 (0.0207)	-0.0134 (0.0210)	-0.0138 (0.0207)	0.0089 (0.0207)	0.0004 (0.0207)	-0.0092 (0.0207)	0.0085 (0.0207)	0.0226 (0.0211)	-0.0483 ** (0.0207)	-0.01	0.85	-0.0351	-0.0126	-0.0242	0.0707	0.1253
22 Korean Air Lines Company Limited	APAC	0.0356 (0.0489)	-0.0850 * (0.0487)	0.0764 (0.0488)	-0.1132 ** (0.0488)	0.0018 (0.0494)	-0.0289 (0.0487)	0.0363 (0.0487)	0.0043 (0.0487)	-0.0274 (0.0487)	-0.0131 (0.0487)	0.0106 (0.0497)	-0.0546 (0.0488)	0.01	1.11	-0.1928	-0.1078	-0.1449	0.2387	0.1034
23 Lan Airlines SA	LATAM	0.0415 * (0.0232)	-0.0087 (0.0231)	-0.0318 (0.0232)	-0.0222 (0.0232)	-0.0487 ** (0.0234)	0.0711 *** (0.0231)	0.0097 (0.0231)	-0.0174 (0.0231)	0.0060 (0.0231)	-0.0074 (0.0231)	-0.0188 (0.0236)	0.0199 (0.0231)	0.04	1.74 *	-0.0483	-0.0396	-0.1060	0.0124	-0.0249
24 Malaysian Airline	APAC	-0.0113 (0.0265)	0.0083 (0.0264)	0.0099 (0.0265)	-0.0640 ** (0.0264)	0.0119 (0.0268)	0.0127 (0.0264)	-0.0043 (0.0264)	-0.0009 (0.0264)	0.0134 (0.0264)	-0.0214 (0.0264)	-0.0005 (0.0269)	-0.0014 (0.0264)	-0.02	0.59	-0.0365	-0.0448	-0.0062	-0.0509	-0.1351
25 Northwest Airlines Corporation	NORAM	0.0099 (0.0628)	0.1790 *** (0.0625)	-0.0897 (0.0627)	0.0229 (0.0626)	0.0259 (0.0634)	-0.1329 ** (0.0626)	0.0547 (0.0625)	-0.0539 (0.0625)	-0.0193 (0.0626)	-0.0055 (0.0625)	-0.0840 (0.0638)	0.0256 (0.0626)	0.02	1.47	-0.0771	-0.2562	-0.2448	0.5083	0.1559
26 Qantas Airways Limited	APAC	0.0110 (0.0397)	-0.0228 (0.0395)	0.0436 (0.0397)	-0.0559 (0.0396)	-0.0132 (0.0401)	0.0380 (0.0396)	-0.0172 (0.0396)	0.0014 (0.0395)	-0.0035 (0.0396)	-0.0066 (0.0395)	0.0438 (0.0404)	-0.0725 * (0.0396)	-0.01	0.76	-0.0649	-0.0422	-0.0971	-0.0601	-0.1908
27 SAS AB	EMEA	0.1344 ** (0.0563)	-0.0065 (0.0560)	-0.0687 (0.0562)	-0.0688 (0.0562)	0.0735 (0.0568)	0.0394 (0.0561)	-0.0743 (0.0561)	0.0268 (0.0560)	-0.0030 (0.0561)	-0.0259 (0.0560)	-0.0244 (0.0572)	-0.1019 * (0.0561)	0.01	1.29	-0.2338	-0.2273	-0.0164	0.1095	0.0809
28 Singapore Airlines Limited	APAC	-0.0003 (0.0232)	-0.0089 (0.0231)	0.0122 (0.0232)	-0.0146 (0.0231)	-0.0152 (0.0234)	0.0056 (0.0231)	-0.0027 (0.0231)	0.0126 (0.0231)	-0.0119 (0.0231)	-0.0133 (0.0231)	0.0219 (0.0236)	-0.0069 (0.0231)	-0.04	0.26	-0.0210	-0.0122	-0.0842	0.0376	-0.1486
29 TAM SA	LATAM	0.0399 (0.0379)	0.0580 (0.0377)	-0.0683 * (0.0378)	-0.0404 (0.0378)	-0.0048 (0.0382)	-0.0060 (0.0377)	-0.0172 (0.0377)	0.0071 (0.0377)	0.0163 (0.0377)	-0.0231 (0.0377)	0.0304 (0.0385)	0.0381 (0.0378)	-0.01	0.81	-0.0098	-0.0679	-0.1338	0.0840	-0.1389
30 Thai Airways International Public Compar	APAC	0.0086 (0.0322)	-0.0243 (0.0321)	-0.0148 (0.0322)	-0.0178 (0.0321)	-0.0438 (0.0325)	-0.0013 (0.0321)	-0.0252 (0.0321)	-0.0072 (0.0320)	0.0068 (0.0321)	0.0056 (0.0321)	-0.0111 (0.0327)	-0.0169 (0.0321)	-0.03	0.33	-0.1502	-0.1259	-0.0802	-0.0594	-0.3486
31 UAL Corporation	NORAM	0.1420 (0.0987)	0.1383 (0.0982)	-0.0643 (0.0985)	-0.0010 (0.0984)	-0.0580 (0.0996)	-0.0877 (0.0983)	0.0200 (0.0982)	-0.1227 (0.0982)	-0.0581 (0.0983)	-0.0702 (0.0982)	0.0177 (0.1002)	0.0309 (0.0983)	-0.02	0.64	-0.2549	-0.3932	-0.2279	0.7595	0.8626
32 US Airways Group Inc	NORAM	0.0604 (0.0894)	0.1638 ** (0.0889)	-0.1073 (0.0892)	-0.0072 (0.0891)	-0.0986 (0.0902)	-0.1110 (0.0890)	0.0521 (0.0890)	-0.1084 (0.0889)	-0.0293 (0.0890)	0.0009 (0.0890)	0.0377 (0.0908)	0.0483 (0.0891)	-0.01	0.82	-0.1590	-0.3228	-0.0819	0.6280	0.9380
Non-major full service carriers																				
1 Hawaiian Holdings Inc	NORAM	-0.0275 (0.0498)	0.0805 (0.0495)	-0.0484 (0.0497)	-0.0314 (0.0497)	-0.0448 (0.0503)	-0.0078 (0.0496)	0.0249 (0.0496)	-0.0158 (0.0495)	-0.0087 (0.0496)	0.0122 (0.0496)	0.0260 (0.0506)	0.0249 (0.0496)	-0.03	0.48	0.0117	-0.0689	-0.1871	0.0706	0.0634
2 Mesa Air Group Inc	NORAM	-0.0750 (0.1277)	-0.0382 (0.1270)	-0.0112 (0.1275)	0.0056 (0.1273)	0.0729 (0.1288)	-0.0368 (0.1271)	-0.0113 (0.1271)	0.0266 (0.1270)	-0.1757 (0.1272)	0.0945 (0.1270)	-0.0954 (0.1297)	0.0063 (0.1272)	-0.04	0.31	-0.1627	-0.1245	-0.0526	0.3321	0.3458
3 Skywest Inc	NORAM	0.0097 (0.0423)	0.1152 *** (0.0421)	-0.0176 (0.0422)	-0.0513 (0.0421)	-0.0841 ** (0.0426)	-0.0543 (0.0421)	0.0054 (0.0421)	-0.0247 (0.0420)	-0.0075 (0.0421)	0.0195 (0.0421)	0.0215 (0.0429)	-0.0264 (0.0421)	0.01	1.27	-0.1045	-0.2197	-0.0983	0.2184	0.1670
4 Westjet Airlines Limited	NORAM	-0.0097 (0.0324)	0.0029 (0.0322)	-0.0053 (0.0323)	-0.0291 (0.0323)	-0.0257 (0.0327)	-0.0712 ** (0.0323)	-0.0010 (0.0322)	-0.0007 (0.0322)	0.0182 (0.0323)	-0.0275 (0.0322)	0.0018 (0.0329)	-0.0140 (0.0323)	-0.02	0.60	-0.1515	-0.1544	-0.0993	0.0675	-0.0604

***Table14:** Abnormal returns Sep 15-30 and cumulated abnormal returns Sep 16 - Oct 31, 2008*

(Table continued on next page)

Low cost carriers																																
1 AER Lingus Group PLC	EMEA	-0.0351	(0.0431)	0.0160	(0.0429)	0.0341	(0.0431)	0.0128	(0.0430)	0.0183	(0.0435)	0.0301	(0.0429)	-0.0283	(0.0429)	0.0104	(0.0429)	0.0081	(0.0429)	-0.0014	(0.0429)	-0.0332	(0.0438)	-0.0478	(0.0430)	-0.03	0.36	0.0192	0.0032	-0.1128	0.0365	-0.1594
2 Air Berlin PLC	EMEA	-0.0308	(0.0429)	0.0593	(0.0426)	-0.0106	(0.0428)	-0.0891 **	(0.0427)	0.0336	(0.0433)	-0.0036	(0.0427)	0.0013	(0.0427)	-0.0037	(0.0426)	0.0197	(0.0427)	-0.0360	(0.0427)	-0.1330 ***	(0.0435)	-0.0040	(0.0427)	0.02	1.45	-0.1662	-0.2255	0.0329	0.0187	0.1786
3 Airtran Holdings Inc	NORAM	0.1216 *	(0.0732)	0.0503	(0.0728)	-0.1091	(0.0731)	-0.0340	(0.0730)	-0.0458	(0.0739)	-0.0803	(0.0729)	0.0256	(0.0729)	-0.0141	(0.0728)	-0.0066	(0.0729)	-0.0096	(0.0728)	-0.0502	(0.0744)	0.0522	(0.0729)	-0.02	0.66	-0.2215	-0.2717	-0.2283	0.7243	0.5835
4 Easyjet PLC	EMEA	0.0688 *	(0.0395)	0.0188	(0.0393)	0.0151	(0.0394)	0.0326	(0.0394)	0.0448	(0.0399)	-0.0661 *	(0.0393)	-0.0505	(0.0393)	0.0040	(0.0393)	-0.0176	(0.0393)	-0.0080	(0.0393)	-0.0508	(0.0401)	0.0058	(0.0394)	0.00	0.93	-0.0719	-0.0907	0.0722	0.0680	0.0638
5 Frontier Airlines, Inc.	NORAM	-0.0385	(0.1198)	-0.0158	(0.1192)	-0.2239 *	(0.1196)	-0.2573 **	(0.1194)	0.0057	(0.1209)	0.2000 *	(0.1193)	0.0055	(0.1192)	-0.0492	(0.1192)	0.1630	(0.1193)	0.0259	(0.1192)	0.0750	(0.1217)	0.2159 *	(0.1193)	0.02	1.31	0.1449	0.1607	0.1387	-0.0004	0.1610
6 Jetblue Airways Corp.	NORAM	0.0253	(0.0509)	0.0611	(0.0507)	-0.0251	(0.0508)	-0.0970 *	(0.0508)	-0.0072	(0.0514)	-0.0687	(0.0507)	0.0104	(0.0507)	-0.0316	(0.0507)	-0.0113	(0.0507)	-0.0340	(0.0507)	0.0213	(0.0517)	0.0576	(0.0507)	-0.01	0.77	-0.1245	-0.1856	-0.0928	0.3789	0.3594
7 Ryanair Holdings PLC	EMEA	0.0236	(0.0389)	-0.0109	(0.0387)	-0.0288	(0.0388)	-0.0220	(0.0387)	0.0324	(0.0392)	-0.0380	(0.0387)	-0.0148	(0.0387)	-0.0112	(0.0387)	0.0111	(0.0387)	-0.0079	(0.0387)	-0.0696 *	(0.0395)	-0.0318	(0.0387)	-0.02	0.59	-0.1914	-0.1805	-0.0155	0.0235	0.2020
8 Southwest Airlines Company	NORAM	0.0274	(0.0320)	0.0322	(0.0318)	-0.0195	(0.0319)	-0.0156	(0.0319)	-0.0404	(0.0322)	-0.0418	(0.0318)	0.0458	(0.0318)	-0.0250	(0.0318)	0.0064	(0.0318)	-0.0151	(0.0318)	0.0373	(0.0325)	0.0153	(0.0318)	-0.01	0.81	-0.0203	-0.0526	-0.0577	0.1577	0.0634
9 Virgin Blue Holdings Limited	APAC	-0.0073	(0.0665)	0.0022	(0.0662)	-0.0359	(0.0664)	-0.1142 *	(0.0663)	-0.0045	(0.0671)	0.0411	(0.0663)	-0.0886	(0.0662)	0.0417	(0.0662)	0.0148	(0.0663)	-0.0574	(0.0662)	-0.0138	(0.0676)	-0.2275 ***	(0.0663)	0.02	1.45	-0.4421	-0.4443	0.1348	-0.1938	0.1548
Freight carriers																																
1 Air Transport Service Group	NORAM	-0.0192	(0.1129)	-0.0082	(0.1123)	-0.0462	(0.1127)	-0.0189	(0.1126)	0.0386	(0.1139)	-0.0636	(0.1124)	-0.0835	(0.1124)	0.0657	(0.1123)	-0.0045	(0.1125)	-0.0870	(0.1124)	-0.0017	(0.1147)	0.0220	(0.1125)	-0.04	0.17	-0.1873	-0.1791	-0.5808	0.1050	-0.7408
2 Atlas Air Worldwide Holdings Inc	NORAM	0.0350	(0.0484)	-0.0055	(0.0481)	0.0209	(0.0483)	0.0127	(0.0482)	-0.0604	(0.0488)	0.0057	(0.0482)	-0.0203	(0.0482)	-0.0339	(0.0481)	-0.0231	(0.0482)	-0.0323	(0.0481)	0.0160	(0.0491)	0.0267	(0.0482)	-0.03	0.33	-0.0933	-0.0878	-0.0615	0.1634	-0.2685
3 Federal Express/FedEx Corp	NORAM	0.0349	(0.0261)	0.0253	(0.0260)	-0.0114	(0.0260)	0.0146	(0.0260)	-0.0660 ***	(0.0263)	-0.0314	(0.0260)	0.0035	(0.0260)	-0.0211	(0.0259)	-0.0197	(0.0260)	0.0065	(0.0260)	0.0501 **	(0.0265)	-0.0218	(0.0260)	0.02	1.38	-0.0715	-0.0968	0.0677	0.0103	0.0618
4 United Parcel Service, Inc	NORAM	0.0181	(0.0186)	0.0228	(0.0185)	-0.0221	(0.0186)	-0.0056	(0.0186)	-0.0323 *	(0.0188)	-0.0129	(0.0185)	-0.0066	(0.0185)	-0.0185	(0.0185)	-0.0070	(0.0185)	0.0167	(0.0185)	0.0506 ***	(0.0189)	-0.0257	(0.0185)	0.03	1.54	-0.0407	-0.0635	0.0594	-0.0575	-0.0032
Carrier portfolios																																
Major full service carriers	∑32	0.0288 *	(0.0161)	0.0193	(0.0161)	-0.0164	(0.0161)	-0.0311 *	(0.0161)	-0.0007	(0.0163)	-0.0063	(0.0161)	-0.0104	(0.0161)	-0.0109	(0.0161)	0.0032	(0.0161)	-0.0104	(0.0161)	0.0022	(0.0164)	-0.0221	(0.0161)	0.00	1.01	-0.0836	-0.1029	-0.0792	0.1259	0.0416
Non-major full service carriers	∑4	-0.0256	(0.0420)	0.0401	(0.0417)	-0.0206	(0.0419)	-0.0266	(0.0418)	-0.0204	(0.0423)	-0.0425	(0.0418)	0.0045	(0.0418)	-0.0037	(0.0417)	-0.0434	(0.0418)	0.0247	(0.0417)	-0.0115	(0.0426)	-0.0023	(0.0418)	-0.03	0.37	-0.1018	-0.1419	-0.1093	0.1722	0.1289
Low cost carriers	∑9	0.0172	(0.0273)	0.0237	(0.0272)	-0.0449 *	(0.0272)	-0.0649 **	(0.0272)	0.0041	(0.0275)	-0.0030	(0.0272)	-0.0104	(0.0272)	-0.0087	(0.0272)	0.0208	(0.0272)	-0.0159	(0.0272)	-0.0241	(0.0277)	0.0040	(0.0272)	0.00	0.91	-0.1193	-0.1430	-0.0143	0.1348	0.1786
Freight carriers	∑4	0.0172	(0.0331)	0.0086	(0.0329)	-0.0147	(0.0331)	0.0007	(0.0330)	-0.0300	(0.0334)	-0.0255	(0.0330)	-0.0267	(0.0330)	-0.0020	(0.0329)	-0.0136	(0.0330)	-0.0241	(0.0329)	0.0288	(0.0336)	0.0003	(0.0330)	-0.03	0.33	-0.0982	-0.1068	-0.1288	0.0553	-0.2377
Region portfolios																																
APAC	∑15	0.0070	(0.0181)	-0.0249	(0.0180)	0.0139	(0.0180)	-0.0521 ***	(0.0180)	0.0140	(0.0182)	0.0164	(0.0180)	-0.0244	(0.0180)	0.0084	(0.0180)	-0.0040	(0.0180)	-0.0152	(0.0180)	0.0169	(0.0184)	-0.0483 ***	(0.0180)	0.04	1.84 **	-0.0994	-0.0745	-0.0455	-0.0371	-0.1033
EMEA	∑12	0.0294	(0.0194)	0.0033	(0.0193)	-0.0073	(0.0194)	-0.0417 **	(0.0194)	0.0180	(0.0196)	0.0050	(0.0193)	-0.0285	(0.0193)	0.0070	(0.0193)	0.0094	(0.0193)	-0.0242	(0.0193)	-0.0397 ***	(0.0197)	-0.0304	(0.0193)	0.02	1.48	-0.1292	-0.1325	-0.0303	0.0427	-0.0231
LATAM	∑2	0.0407 *	(0.0240)	0.0247	(0.0239)	-0.0500 **	(0.0240)	-0.0313	(0.0239)	-0.0267	(0.0242)	0.0325	(0.0239)	-0.0038	(0.0239)	-0.0051	(0.0239)	0.0112	(0.0239)	-0.0152	(0.0239)	0.0058	(0.0244)	0.0290	(0.0239)	0.01	1.20	-0.0291	-0.0537	-0.1199	0.0482	-0.0819
NORAM	∑20	0.0252	(0.0354)	0.0655 *	(0.0352)	-0.0545	(0.0353)	-0.0169	(0.0353)	-0.0281	(0.0357)	-0.0436	(0.0352)	0.0101	(0.0352)	-0.0324	(0.0352)	-0.0007	(0.0352)	0.0037	(0.0352)	0.0067	(0.0359)	0.0176	(0.0353)	-0.01	0.77	-0.0725	-0.1380	-0.1165	0.3049	0.2248

** Statistically significant at the 10% level*

*** Statistically significant at the 5% level*

**** Statistically significant at the 1% level*

Table 14 (continued): *Abnormal returns Sep 15-30 and cumulated abnormal returns Sep 16 - Oct 31, 2008*

This table presents the abnormal returns of all firms and portfolios with standard errors (in parentheses) estimated using equation 2 (cf. section 7.1.1) for the trading days September 15-30, 2008. Standard market model parameters α, α′, β, and β′ used for the MVRM were estimated as presented in Table 12. This table also presents adjusted R^2 and F-statistics illustrating the explanatory power of the regression model as well as cumulative abnormal returns for the period (1) Sep 16-30, (2) Sep 17-30, (3) Oct 1-8, (4) Oct 9-16, and (5) Oct 1-31. Estimates of significance are based on t-statistics.

On the first two trading days y_1 (September 15) and y_2 (September 16) most abnormal returns were positive. On the two following trading days, y_3 (September 17) and y_4 (September 18), the algebraic sign before the abnormal return coefficients became negative. Likewise, the carrier and region portfolios mainly show positive average returns on y_1 and y_2, and negative average returns on y_3 and y_4, though not all statistically significant. MFSC reacted significantly positive on y_1 and negative on y_4. LATAM shows a similar trend for the days y_1 and y_3. NORAM carriers reacted significantly positively on y_2, while most APAC and EMEA companies reacted negatively on y_4. LCC show significant negative abnormal returns y_3 and y_4.

Overall, it seems like the market initially trusted in the aviation stocks before the downward trend kicked in on September 17 and 18, 2008 (y_3 and y_4), and continued for most following trading days y_{5-10} and companies or portfolios. On the trading days y_{11} (September 29), and y_{12} (September 30), the negative trade accelerates significantly for the region portfolios EMEA and APAC, respectively.
The cumulated abnormal returns y_{2-12} and y_{13-18} show a negative trend for the aircraft operating and holding industry, while y_{19-24} becomes positive. This shift balances the cumulated abnormal returns over the full mid term range y_{13-36}.

Some few concluding statements can be made in the interpretation of abnormal returns in the Financial Crisis 2008:

(1) Most aircraft operating and holding companies experienced statistically significant abnormal returns in the beginning of the Financial Crisis 2008, but no single starting date for the beginning crisis in the aviation industry sticks out
(2) The market reacted with positive abnormal returns for the company sample on the first two trading days September 15 and 16 (y_{1-2}) after the Financial Crisis escalated with the collapse of Lehman Brothers on September 14
(3) On trading days September 17 and 18 (y_{3-4}), the negative trend of abnormal returns began for aircraft operating and holding companies
(4) Cumulated abnormal returns for the short term September 16-30 (y_{2-12}) were significantly negative as well as for the beginning mid term October 1-8 (y_{13-18})
(5) The subsequent mid term October 9-16 (y_{19-24}) shows a strong positive trend of abnormal returns of the industry which balances the total view on the mid term October 1-30 (y_{13-36})

More insights on statistical significance of the market's reaction to the Financial Crisis and the factors differentiating between the companies will be given in the results of the multivariate regression analyses on abnormal returns in the next sections. Nevertheless, the regression models are expected to have lower explanatory power than in the regressions of 9/11, because the air transport industry reacted more in line with the general market.

Market's reaction on the first trading days of the Financial Crisis

As described in Chapter 7.2.2.1, the multivariate regression analysis of abnormal returns for aircraft operating and holding companies in the Financial Crisis starts with the evaluation of the market's reaction on the first four trading days after Lehman Brothers filed for bankruptcy on September 15, 2008. The overview on abnormal returns in Table 14 has shown that no single first shock day can be identified, but rather that company stocks reacted at different days with statistically significant abnormal returns. This leads to the assumption that variables with enough explanatory power must exist that can explain the different firms' stock performance.

Table 15 illustrates the findings of the multivariate regressions of the daily abnormal returns on the four consecutive trading days September 15-18 (y_1-y_4) based on a global sample of 49 firms. More details of the results can be found in the overview of the individual regression models in Appendix 20 to Appendix 23.

On all four trading days statistically significant explanatory variables can be found that describe the market's diverse reaction with respect to the different firms' stocks.

		Model P	Model Q	Model R	Model S
Observation period		y1	y2	y3	y4
Date		September 15, 2008	September 16, 2008	September 17, 2008	September 18, 2008
Sample		All companies	All companies	All companies	All companies
Sample size		49	49	49	49
Cluster	Variable				
Financial	SIZE	+		+	+
	LIQUIDITY		--		+
	NDTEBITDA				+
	EBITDAMAR				
	EQITYRAT		++		++
	INTRSTCOVRG				
Market	RPKMKTSHR	+++	+++	---	++
	FTKMKTSHR		--		--
	PINT			+	++
	PFREIGHT		--	++	
Aircraft fleet	TOTALAC	+	+	-	+
	OPSLEASE			--	
	STORAC			--	
	nYRORDER			+	
	nYROPTION		+	+	
	AVGAGE		+		+
Carrier	AMR/UAL				
	MFSC		-	-	-
	NFSC	-		+	
	LCC			-	-
	FREIGHT				
Region	APAC	-	-	+	-
	EMEA		-	+	
	LATAM			-	
	NORAM		+	-	
	R^2 (adjusted)	≤ 0.25	≤ 0.60	≤ 0.50	≤ 0.38
	F-statistic	2.06* - 7.71***	3.44*** - 18.17***	5.47*** - 12.31***	2.40** - 5.96***

+/- Positive/negative impact on abnormal returns < 0.1/>-0.1
++/-- Positive/negative impact on abnormal returns ≥ 0.1/≤ -0.1
+++/--- Positive/negative impact on abnormal returns ≥ 1.0/≤ -1.0

xxx Statistically significant at the 10% level
xxx Statistically significant at the 5% level
xxx Statistically significant at the 1% level

Table 15: *Overview on MVRM results for stock market's initial reaction in the Financial Crisis 2008 (y_{1-4})*

This table presents a consolidation of cross-sectional regression results for daily abnormal returns of aircraft operating and holding companies for the first four trading days after the escalation of the Financial Crisis with the bankruptcy of Lehman Brothers on September 14, 2008: September 15-18 (Model P-S). SIZE is the natural logarithm of total assets, LIQUIDITY is cash & equivalents over current liabilities, NDTEBITDA is net debt over EBITDA, EBITDAMAR is EBITDA over total operating revenue, EQITYRAT is owners equity over total assets, INTRSTCOVRG is interest expenses for debt over EBIT, RPKMKTSHR and FTKMKTSHR are revenue passenger and freight ton kilometer market shares, PINT and PFREIGHT are the portions of international business and freight business in total operating revenue, TOTALAC is the total number of jet aircraft, OPSLEASE is the ratio of operating leased aircraft over total aircraft count, STORAC is the ratio of stored aircraft to total aircraft count, nYRORDER and nYROPTION are the number of aircraft orders and purchase options to existing fleet in the next n (all) years, and AVGAGE is the average age of existing aircraft. Also, nine dummy variables are included which are equal to one if the firm meets the requirements and equal to zero otherwise: MFSC if the firm is a major full service carrier, NFSC if the firm is a non-major full service carrier, LCC if the firm is a low cost carrier, FREIGHT if the firm is a freight only carrier, APAC, if the firm is Asia Pacific based, EMEA if the firm is based in Europe Middle East or Africa, LATAM if the firm is Latin America based, and NORAM if the firm is North American based. The magnitude of the positive and negative influence of the variables on abnormal returns refers to the regression coefficient. Statistical significance is based on t-statistics.

Among the financial variables tested, especially SIZE and EQUITYRAT show a positive impact on abnormal returns. The market believed that companies with a strong asset base are likely to better withstand the beginning crisis. This is typical for times of crisis in which

investors prefer asset-heavy balance sheets much more than during the normal business cycle. To award a high equity ratio, i.e. a higher ratio of equity to debt financed assets, is likewise not the investor's reaction in times of business as usual, because as long as a company generates a return on assets (ROA) that exceeds all interest paid on debt, the market would prefer a low equity ratio. However, in a beginning crisis, where profits and consequently ROA decline while debt obligations remain, a higher equity ratio becomes beneficial.
The more astonishing it is that NDTEBITDA also shows a positive impact in Model S for September 18. Investors would usually look at a lower net debt to EBITDA ratio indicating a shorter debt payback period, i.e. less risk that the company cannot meet its debt obligations. Also, in a situation in which funding becomes difficult to procure, because financial institutions became highly averse to risks, one would expect the NDTEBITDA variable to show a significant negative impact on abnormal returns. A company with high liquidity was negatively received by the market in Model Q on September 16, but awarded in Model S on September 18. The first is not rational. Liquidity is supposed to only negatively influence abnormal returns when bailout packages – including liquidity boosts for companies with low liquidity – influence investors. In other times, a positive effect is expected. Why these to coefficients in Model S and Q do not show the rational direction is up for speculation.

In the cluster of market factors, the variables RPKMKTSHR and FTKMKTSHR show the expected positive and negative impact, respectively. Different to 9/11 which had a clear impact on the passenger business, the market believed in the beginning of the Financial Crisis that with decreasing economy naturally trade would decline, eventually influencing the freight and cargo industry's revenues. Only PFREIGHT, which shows the anticipated negative effect in Model Q, somehow undercuts a clear conclusion with its positive impact on abnormal returns in Model R. A high portion of international business in a company's operating revenue (PINT) was beneficial, i.e. a higher spread of risk in terms of business scope was awarded.

For the aircraft fleet and fleet planning variables, the conclusion seems more obvious. TOTALAC, indicating in one or the other way a company's business magnitude or importance (similar to SIZE), mainly shows a highly significant positive impact on abnormal returns.
Similar to the findings of the regressions of abnormal returns at 9/11, companies benefit from a higher number of aircraft firm orders (yYRORDER) and purchase options (nYROPTION), as well as from a generally higher average age in their aircraft fleet.
OPSLEASE and STORAC, on the other hand, have again significant negative impact on abnormal returns.

Further, the regressions underline the interpretation of the abnormal returns that all carrier and region portfolios somehow reacted within the first four trading days.

The findings of the multivariate regression analysis for abnormal returns in the first four trading days (y_{1-4}) after the escalation of the Financial Crisis on September 14, 2008 (cf. Table 15), can be summarized in five statements:

(1) Stocks of individual aircraft operating and holding companies varied in their reaction
(2) All variable clusters contain exponents with significant explanatory power
(3) All types of aircraft fleet and fleet planning variables show significant effect on abnormal returns
(4) Clear positive impact on abnormal returns on the first four trading days after Lehman Brothers filed for bankruptcy have (though at different statistical significance): SIZE, EQUITYRT, PINT, nYRORDER, nYROPTION, and AVGAGE
(5) Clear negative impact on abnormal returns on the same day have (though at different statistical significance): FTKMKTSHR, OPSLEASE, STORAC, and MFSC

For all other variables the reaction of the market on the individual days does not allow a concluding statement.

Market's short and mid term reaction in the Financial Crisis

The analysis of cumulated abnormal returns in the short and mid term of the Financial Crisis concentrates on four different models and observations periods, respectively. As previously described in Chapter 7.2.2.1, the short term is defined as the 11 trading days following the day when Lehman Brothers filed for bankruptcy, September 16 to 30 (y_{2-12}). The mid term was split into three time windows October 1-8 (y_{13-18}), October 9-16 (y_{19-24}), and the full mid term period of October 1-31 (y_{13-35}). Again, multivariate regressions were conducted to better understand the stock market's reaction and to identify the variables with statistically significant explanatory power.

The results of the regressions are consolidated in Table 16. For more details and the actual regression models please refer to Appendix 24 to Appendix 27.

Interestingly, Model P, focusing on the stock market's short term reaction between September 16 and 30, does not reveal any explanatory variables. Although daily abnormal returns occurred (cf. Table 14) either the cumulated abnormal returns were not significant enough to allow for a meaningful regression or the market's reaction did not depend on any of the tested factors. The latter is relatively unlikely as common financial decision factors, included as control variables, do not show any explanatory power. Therefore, it can be concluded that in the short term of the Financial Crisis the sample firms did not experience enough significant cumulated abnormal returns.

In the mid term of the Financial Crisis several observations can be made. As a reminder: in the time period of Model Q, October 1-8, the market reacted with mostly negative abnormal returns, in the time period of Model R, October 9-16, the stocks of the sample firms experiences mostly positive abnormal returns (cf. Table 14).

Variables that consistently show significant positive impact on abnormal returns in more than one model are SIZE, FTKMKTSHR, nYRORDER, and NORAM. The same consistencies with negative impact have PFREIGHT, STORAC, APAC, EMEA, and LATAM.

		Model P	Model Q	Model R	Model S
Observation period		y2-12	y13-18	y19-24	y13-35
Date		September 16-30, 2008	October 1-8, 2008	October 9-16, 2008	October 1-31, 2008
Sample		All companies	All companies	All companies	All companies
Sample size		49	49	49	49
Cluster	Variable				
Financial	SIZE		+		++
	LIQUIDITY		-	++	
	NDTEBITDA				
	EBITDAMAR		--		
	EQITYRAT		++		
	INTRSTCOVRG		-		
Market	RPKMKTSHR		---	+++	
	FTKMKTSHR		++		+++
	PINT				++
	PFREIGHT		--		--
Aircraft fleet	TOTALAC		+		
	OPSLEASE				++
	STORAC		---		---
	nYRORDER		+		++
	nYROPTION				
	AVGAGE		-		
Carrier	AMR/UAL				
	MFSC		-	++	
	NFSC				--
	LCC			++	
	FREIGHT		++		--
Region	APAC			--	--
	EMEA			--	--
	LATAM			--	--
	NORAM			++	++
	R^2 (adjusted)	n/a	≤ 0.63	≤ 0.61	≤ 0.48
	F-statistic	n/a	3.51*** - 10.15***	2.47*** - 10.15***	2.40** - 11.31***

+/- Positive/negative impact on abnormal returns < 0.1/>-0.1
++/-- Positive/negative impact on abnormal returns ≥ 0.1/≤ -0.1
+++/--- Positive/negative impact on abnormal returns ≥ 1.0/≤ -1.0

xxx Statistically significant at the 10% level
xxx Statistically significant at the 5% level
xxx Statistically significant at the 1% level

Table 16: *Overview on MVRM results for stock market's short-/mid term reaction in the Financial Crisis 2008*

This table presents a consolidated overview of cross-sectional regression results for cumulative abnormal returns of aircraft operating and holding companies for the short and mid term in the Financial Crisis 2008: September 16-30 (y2-12), October 1-8 (y13-18), October 9-16 (y19-24), and October 1-31 (y13-35). SIZE is the natural logarithm of total assets, LIQUIDITY is cash & equivalents over current liabilities, NDTEBITDA is net debt over EBITDA, EBITDAMAR is EBITDA over total operating revenue, EQITYRAT is owners equity over total assets, INTRSTCOVRG is interest expenses for debt over EBIT, RPKMKTSHR and FTKMKTSHR are revenue passenger and freight ton kilometer market shares, PINT and PFREIGHT are the portions of international business and freight business in total operating revenue, TOTALAC is the total number of jet aircraft, OPSLEASE is the ratio of operating leased aircraft over total aircraft count, STORAC is the ratio of stored aircraft to total aircraft count, nYRORDER and nYROPTION are the number of aircraft orders and purchase options to existing fleet in the next n (all) years, and AVGAGE is the average age of existing aircraft. Also, nine dummy variables are included which are equal to one if the firm meets the requirements and equal to zero otherwise: MFSC if the firm is a major full service carrier, NFSC if the firm is a non-major full service carrier, LCC if the firm is a low cost carrier, FREIGHT if the firm is a freight only carrier, APAC, if the firm is Asia Pacific based, EMEA if the firm is based in Europe Middle East or Africa, LATAM if the firm is Latin America based, and NORAM if the firm is North American based. The magnitude of the positive and negative influence of the variables on abnormal returns refers to the regression coefficient. Statistical significance is based on t-statistics.

Further, there are some variables that show a positive or negative affect, but were only significant in one out of three of the Models Q-S. Positively influencing variables include

EQUITYRT, PINT, TOTALAC, OPSLEASE, LCC, and FREIGHT. Negatively influencing factors are EBITDAMAR, INTRSTCOVRG, AVGAGE, and NFSC.

For all other variables the market reacted differently, i.e. the variable might cause a positive effect on abnormal returns in Model Q, but a negative impact on returns in Model R, and vice versa. Most of these variables naturally balance over the full mid term period and disappear in Model S, except PFREIGTH for which the market is equally odd as within the first four trading days of the Financial Crisis. The negative sign of LIQUIDITY in Model Q cannot be explained because LIQUIDITY generally positively correlates (+0.51) with EQITYRAT (cf. Appendix 19), the latter showing the expected positive impact on abnormal returns. Hence, LIQUIDITY should have a positive sign, too. EBITDAMAR's negative sign is counterintuitive as well; also here, no rational explanation can be found; high profit margin is always of benefit, especially in times of crisis.

Summarizing the regressions for cumulated abnormal returns in the short and mid term of the Financial Crisis brings the following conclusions:

(1) For the short term of the Financial Crisis the analysis does not reveal any significant explanatory variables that account for abnormal returns; most likely, the significance of abnormal returns was not high enough to generate meaningful regressions
(2) In the mid term, the variables SIZE, FTKMKTSHR, nYRORDER and NORAM show significant and consistent positive impact on the abnormal returns of the sample firms
(3) In the mid term the variables PFREIGHT, STORAC, APAC, EMEA, and LATAM have significant and consistent negative influence on abnormal returns

Before a final summary of the stock market's reaction to the Financial Crisis, the next section will illustrate the development of the stocks of aircraft operating and holding companies compared to the general stock market development in the recent years.

Stocks' long term performance in the Financial Crisis

Already in the second quarter of the year 2009, the market picked up confidence (cf. Figure 30). The equity indices MSCI World, MSCI World Air Freight/Logistics and MSCI World Airline experienced growth rates of 8-13% from Q1 to Q2 and of 12-14% from Q2 to Q3 2009. And, after a faint setback in 2010 the overall positive economic tendency continued, though no difference is recognizable between the general market and the air transport industry, except of a recent drop of the Airline index in Q4 2011. Similar to the aftermath of 9/11, the world puts high efforts into a fast recovery of the economic situation. The development of the equity market over the upcoming years is up to speculation but the current movement is promising. (Reinhart & Rogoff, 2008)

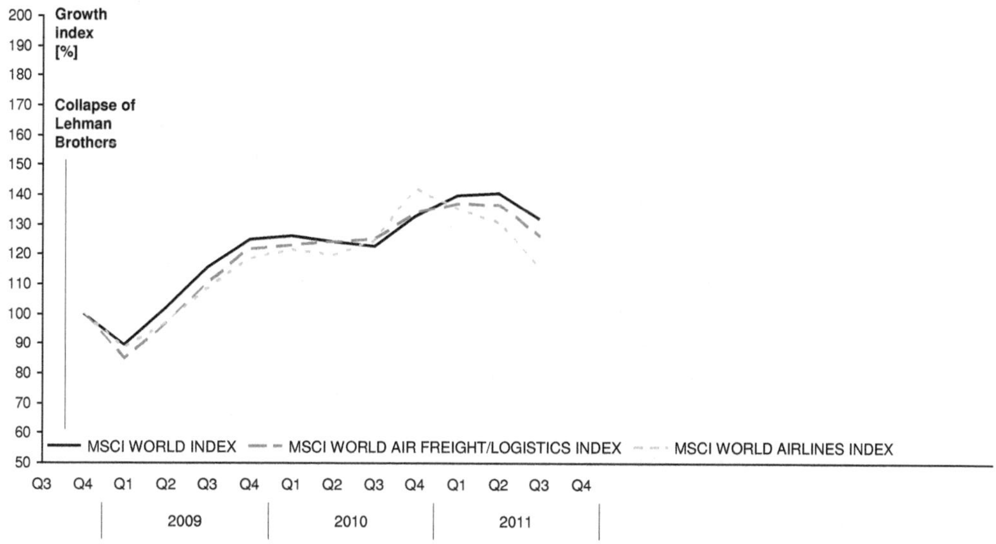

Figure 30: *Stock market development post Financial Crisis 2008 – Sector indices versus general market*

This figure presents the quarterly development of the two sector price indices MSCI World Air Freight/Logistics and MSCI World Airlines versus the sector unspecific broader MSCI World Index from Q4 2008 to Q3 2011. The time period starts with the first full quarter after the terrorist attacks on September 11, 2001. All data were obtained from Thomson Reuters Datastream (2011).

7.2.3 Summary of stock market's reaction to shocks & crises

The analysis of the reaction of aircraft operating and holding companies' stocks in times of crisis was based on the two most extreme shocks in the past years: the terrorist attacks on September 11, 2001 and the Financial Crisis 2008. For both events, the alpha and beta risks in the individual companies' stocks and stock portfolios were calculated for a period of six months preceding as well as after the shocks. Subsequently, abnormal returns were estimated compared to the development of the MSCI World Index and tested for significance with t-statistics and F-statistics. In multivariate regressions, different clusters of explanatory and control variables were evaluated to identify those variables with enough statistical explanatory power to explain the different reaction of the sample stocks to the events. Table 17 aggregates the findings of the analyses of stock market's reaction to shocks & crises.

9/11 clearly was the more extreme shock for aircraft operating and holding companies as it directly impacted the aviation industry. The Financial Crisis, on the other hand, affected the world economy in general rather than isolated sectors.
The residual risk (alpha) in the sample stocks and its shift after the events were generally of no statistical significance in contrast to the systematic risk (beta) and its respective changes.

Before 9/11 most sample stocks had a beta below market (1.0) and experienced a strong upward shift with the event, i.e. after 9/11 most aircraft operating and holding companies had betas above the market.
Preceding the Financial Crisis, no pattern can be observed in betas, but with the event the coefficients clearly adjusted towards 1.0, i.e. the crisis equally affected most companies diminishing the individual systematic risks.
Nevertheless, both events caused abnormal returns which together were non-zero and non-equal for the different stocks in the sample. Differences can be explained by some but not all explanatory and control variables tested.

The financial variables show the expected effect on abnormal returns. A company's stock is the more positively affected the higher the assets' book value, the EBITDA margin, and the equity ratio, but the lower the net debt over EBITDA ratio and the interest coverage are.

Shock/crisis	Terrorist Attacks 2001	Financial Crisis 2008
Risk in aircraft operating and holding companies' stocks and shift in risk with the shock/crisis		
Alpha	• Mainly no significant alphas prior to the shock	• Mainly no significant alphas prior to the shock
Shift in alpha	• Mainly no significant change in alpha with the shock	• Mainly no significant change in alpha with the shock
Beta	• Significant betas < 1.0 in almost all stocks prior to the	• Significant betas in almost all stocks prior to the shock
Shift in beta	• Positive shift in betas mostly significant at the 1% level	• Shift in betas towards the market beta (1.0) mostly significant at the 1% level
Abnormal returns in stocks caused by the shock/crisis		
Daily abnormal returns	• Strongest reaction of almost all companies on Sept 17; pre-reaction of non-U.S. firms' stocks Sept 11-14	• Significant daily abnormal returns for some but not all firms; no strongest reaction day stands out
Cumulated abnormal returns	• Significant cumulated abnormal returns for all periods until Nov 5, 2001	• Cumulated abormal returns signficant enough to analyze the mid term Oct 1-31, 2001, but not the short term Sept 16-30

Table 17: *Summary of stock market's reaction to shock events & crises*

(Table continued on next page)

Variables explaining the differences in abnormal returns

		Event day	Short term	Mid term	Event day	Short term	Mid term
Financial	SIZE		+		+		+
	LIQUIDITY		-				
	NDTEBITDA		-	-			
	EBITDAMAR	+	+	+			
	EQITYRAT				+		
	INTRSTCOVRG	-	-				
Market	RPKMKTSHR	-	+		+		
	FTKMKTSHR	+			-		
	PINT	+	-		+		
	PINT 1						
	PFREIGHT	+					
Aircraft fleet	TOTALAC		+		+		
	OPSLEASE	-	+	+	-		
	STORAC	+	+		-		-
	nYRORDER		+				+
	nYROPTION	+	+	+	+		
	1YROPTION						
	AVGAGE	+	+		+		
Carrier	AMR/UAL	-	+	-			
	MFSC	+	+		-		
	NFSC	-					
	LCC	-	-		-		
	FREIGHT	+					
Region	APAC			+			
	EMEA	+		+			-
	LATAM						-
	NORAM	-		-			+

Table 17 (continued): *Summary of stock market's reaction to shock events & crises*

This table presents the consolidated findings of the evaluation of stock market's reaction to the two shock events (or crises) of the terrorist attacks on September 11, 2001 and the Financial Crisis 2008. The analyses were based on multivariate regression methodology with a sample of 56 aircraft operating and holding companies' stocks. The risk components alpha and beta and the shift in risk with the shock were estimated to calculate abnormal returns of the stocks compared to the MSCI World Index. Daily and cumulated abnormal returns were calculated for the day of event (or the first trading day after) as well as for the short and mid term following the event. Explanatory and control variables tested include financial, market, aircraft fleet, carrier, and region variables. Positive and negative impact of the variables is displayed in the table when observed as a clear trend in the regression models (significant F-statistics; evidence in more than one model) and with coefficients statistically significant a minimum at the 10% level (based on t-statistics). SIZE is the natural logarithm of total assets, LIQUIDITY is cash & equivalents over current liabilities, NDTEBITDA is net debt over EBITDA, EBITDAMAR is EBITDA over total operating revenue, EQITYRAT is owners equity over total assets, INTRSTCOVRG is interest expenses for debt over EBIT, RPKMKTSHR and FTKMKTSHR are revenue passenger and freight ton kilometer market shares, PINT and PINT1 are the portions of international (non-home region and non-domestic) business in total operating revenue, PFREIGHT is the portion of freight business in total operating revenue, TOTALAC is the total number of jet aircraft, OPSLEASE is the ratio of operating leased aircraft over total aircraft count, STORAC is the ratio of stored aircraft to total aircraft count, nYRORDER and nYROPTION [1YROPTION] are the number of aircraft orders and purchase options to existing fleet in the next years [in the upcoming year], and AVGAGE is the average age of existing aircraft. Also, eight dummy variables are included which are equal to one if the firm meets the requirements and equal to zero otherwise: MFSC if the firm is a major full service carrier, NFSC if the firm is a non-major full service carrier, LCC if the firm is a low cost carrier, FREIGHT if the firm is a freight only carrier, APAC, if the firm is Asia Pacific based, EMEA if the firm is based in Europe, Middle East or Africa, LATAM if the firm is Latin America based, and NORAM if the firm is North American based.

New is the finding, that aircraft fleet and fleet planning factors play a statistically significant role in stock market's reaction to shocks and crises. A high number of aircraft in the fleet, independent from the value of the aircraft but positively correlated with the book value of a company, positively influenced abnormal returns. Likewise, the higher the number of aircraft firm orders and purchase options, the higher was the trust of the stock market into a company. Operating leases were perceived as negative in crises, except when the conditions of the Air Transportation Safety and System Stabilization Act in 9/11 influenced stock market's behavior or when operating lease enabled new growth in the mid term of the crisis. Old aircraft were of benefit on the first trading day and in the short term. Further, the stock market noticed how many inactive aircraft a company held and either penalized or awarded the company depending on the time in the crisis. In flight bans during 9/11 a company's stock was positively influenced the more aircraft were classified as stored, hence generating only fixed costs. In the Financial Crisis 2008, stored aircraft were seen by the stock market as non-revenue generating assets thus negatively influencing abnormal returns.

The influence of market, carrier, or region variables depended on the nature of the event. Air freight business, for example, was clearly less affected by the terrorist attacks on September 11, 2001 compared to the obvious emotional impact of the shock upon passengers. On the other hand, the Financial Crisis 2008 strongly influenced world trade. Consequently, companies with a high air cargo market share suffered most.

7.3 Special events – Company specific positive and negative event days

When trying to convince decision making managers that one way of managing and planning an aircraft fleet is better than another for the company's stock performance, it is not enough to just look at the market's reaction in shock events. The managers might nod in agreement to the findings for the times of crisis, but immediately question whether the market's reaction would be the same in times of normal business or when company specific events occur. In order to retrieve the full picture from this research and to build up a solid line of arguments with regard to effects of aircraft fleet and fleet planning decisions on an company's stock performance, all three time periods are observed as described in Chapter 6.5, Figure 25: Shocks, company specific positive and negative events, and the normal business cycle.

This chapter will describe the analysis of stock market's reaction to special company specific negative and positive events. For this thesis, two kinds of events were chosen that have a direct link to the firms' aircraft fleet:

(1) Aircraft accidents with hull loss represent a negative company specific event
(2) Aircraft firm orders represent a positive company specific event

Again, the multivariate regression methodology (cf. Chapter 7.1.1.1) is used to identify whether aircraft fleet and fleet planning variables – or any of the other explanatory and control variables in the analysis – influence the stock market's reaction to aircraft accidents or aircraft orders with statistical significance.

7.3.1 Special events – Observation periods

The two company specific event types in scope of this study are aircraft accidents and aircraft firm orders. Both will be described in more detail in this chapter.

Aircraft accidents

Aircraft accidents are defined as "an occurrence associated with the operations of an aircraft which takes place between the time any person boards the aircraft with the intention of flight until such time as all such persons have disembarked, in which: a) a person is fatally or seriously injured as a result of: being in the aircraft, or direct contact with any part of the aircraft, including parts which have become detached from the aircraft, or direct exposure to jet blast [...[60]]; or b) the aircraft sustains damage or structural failure which: adversely affects the structural strength, performance or flight characteristics of the aircraft, and would normally require major repair or replacement of the affected components [...[61]]; or c) the aircraft is missing or is completely inaccessible."[62] (ICAO, 2001, p. 1-1)

Under this definition a huge variety of different accidents is combined: Accidents with minor, major, or total damage of the aircraft; accidents during scheduled international or domestic flights, training, or test flights; accidents during taxing, take off, mid air, or during landing; and, accidents with different degrees of damage to passengers and crew on board of the aircraft. One would agree that the most severe accident is that of a hull loss of the aircraft with injuries or fatalities. Hence, it can be assumed that the stock market reacts stronger to these accidents than to others.

---

60 "[...] except when the injuries are from natural causes, self-inflicted or inflicted by other persons, or when the injuries are to stowaways hiding outside the areas normally available to the passengers and crew [...]" (ICAO, 2001, p. 1-1)

61 "[...] except for engine failure or damage, when the damage is limited to the engine, its cowlings or accessories,; or for damage limited to propellers, wing tips, antennas, tires, brakes, fairings, small dents or puncture holes in the aircraft skin [...]" (ICAO, 2001, p. 1-1)

62 "Note 1. – For statistical uniformity only, an injury resulting in death within thirty days of the date of the accident is classified as a fatal injury by ICAO. Note 2. – An aircraft is considered to be missing when the official search has been terminated and the wreckage has not been located." (ICAO, 2001, p. 1-1)

Aircraft accidents in scope of the analysis where chosen to match all of the following criteria:

- Accident date: between January 1, 1994 and December 31, 2009
- Company: stock listed when the accident occurred, with at least six months of stock return data before and after the accident as well as the full set of data for the explanatory and control variables used in the multivariate regressions
- Aircraft type: commercial jets only (excluding all turbo props and small business jets)
- Loss type: hull loss (100% damage)
- Service type: domestic and international scheduled and non-scheduled operations (excluding aircraft in test, training or non-operational)
- Flight phase: aircraft in take-off, in flight, or landing (excluding aircraft ground parked or ground taxi)
- Special restriction: the four aircraft crashes of American Airlines and United Airlines on September 11, 2001 are excluded from the sample; although matching the criteria these incidents cannot be isolated from the overall effect of the shock

No restrictions were made with regard to the company's carrier cluster (major full service carrier, non-major full service carrier, low cost carrier, or freight carrier), the regional origin (Asia Pacific, Europe Middle East and Africa, Latin America, or North America), the usage (passenger or freight), nor to the number of injuries and fatalities on board.

Filtering historical aircraft accidents by these criteria brings up a total number of 45 incidents for subsequent analysis. Table 18 gives an overview on all accidents in scope. Data are based on information published by Ascend Worldwide Ltd. (2010). The list contains aircraft accidents of 20 different companies from all regions and of all carrier types (except non-major full service carriers) and a minimum one accident for each of the 16 years 1994-2009. Table 19 gives additional statistics on the individual companies.

Count	Accident Date	Company	Company Cluster	Region	Operator	Aicraft type	Aircraft usage	LossType	Pax & Crew on Board	Fatalities	Injuries
1	July 2, 1994	US Airways Group Inc	MFSC	NORAM	US Airways	Boeing (McDonnell-Douglas) DC-9	Passenger	Hull loss	57	65%	28%
2	August 10, 1994	Korean Air Lines Company Limited	MFSC	APAC	Korean Air	Airbus A300	Passenger	Hull loss	160	0%	0%
3	September 8, 1994	US Airways Group Inc	MFSC	NORAM	US Airways	Boeing B737 (CFMI)	Passenger	Hull loss	132	100%	0%
4	December 20, 1995	AMR Corp.	MFSC	NORAM	American Airlines	Boeing B757	Passenger	Hull loss	164	98%	2%
5	September 5, 1996	Federal Express/FedEx Corp	FREIGHTER	NORAM	FedEx	Boeing (McDonnell-Douglas) DC-10	Passenger	Hull loss	5	0%	0%
6	July 6, 1997	Delta Air Lines Inc	MFSC	NORAM	Delta Air Lines	Boeing B727	Passenger	Hull loss	154	0%	0%
7	July 31, 1997	Federal Express/FedEx Corp	FREIGHTER	NORAM	FedEx	Boeing (McDonnell-Douglas) MD-11	Passenger	Hull loss	5	0%	0%
8	August 6, 1997	Korean Air Lines Company Limited	MFSC	APAC	Korean Air	Boeing B747	Passenger	Hull loss	254	90%	10%
9	December 16, 1997	Air Canada Inc	MFSC	NORAM	Air Canada	Bombardier (Canadair) CRJ Regional Jet	Passenger	Hull loss	42	0%	21%
10	December 19, 1997	Singapore Airlines Limited	MFSC	APAC	SilkAir	Boeing B737	Passenger	Hull loss	104	100%	0%
11	February 9, 1998	AMR Corp.	MFSC	NORAM	American Airlines	Boeing B727	Passenger	Hull loss	121	0%	0%
12	February 16, 1998	China Airlines Limited	MFSC	APAC	China Airlines	Airbus A300	Passenger	Hull loss	196	100%	0%
13	August 5, 1998	Korean Air Lines Company Limited	MFSC	APAC	Korean Air	Boeing B747	Passenger	Hull loss	379	0%	0%
14	December 11, 1998	Thai Airways International Public Company	MFSC	APAC	Thai Airways International	Airbus A310	Passenger	Hull loss	146	70%	0%
15	March 4, 1999	Air France	MFSC	EMEA	Air France	Boeing B737	Passenger	Hull loss	97	0%	0%
16	March 5, 1999	Air France	MFSC	EMEA	Air France	Boeing B747	Freight	Hull loss	5	0%	0%
17	March 15, 1999	Korean Air Lines Company Limited	MFSC	APAC	Korean Air	Boeing (McDonnell-Douglas) MD-80	Passenger	Hull loss	156	0%	1%
18	April 15, 1999	Korean Air Lines Company Limited	MFSC	APAC	Korean Air	Boeing (McDonnell-Douglas) MD-11	Freight	Hull loss	3	100%	0%
19	June 1, 1999	AMR Corporation	MFSC	NORAM	American Airlines	Boeing (McDonnell-Douglas) MD-80	Passenger	Hull loss	145	8%	31%
20	August 22, 1999	China Airlines Limited	MFSC	APAC	China Airlines	Boeing (McDonnell-Douglas) MD-11	Passenger	Hull loss	315	1%	16%
21	October 17, 1999	Federal Express/FedEx Corp	FREIGHTER	NORAM	FedEx	Boeing (McDonnell-Douglas) MD-11	Freight	Hull loss	2	0%	0%
22	December 22, 1999	Korean Air Lines Company Limited	MFSC	APAC	Korean Air	Boeing B747	Freight	Hull loss	4	100%	0%
23	January 31, 2000	Alaska Air Group Inc	MFSC	NORAM	Alaska Airlines	Boeing (McDonnell-Douglas) MD-80	Passenger	Hull loss	88	100%	0%
24	March 5, 2000	Southwest Airlines Company	LCC	NORAM	Southwest Airlines	Boeing B737	Passenger	Hull loss	142	0%	1%
25	July 25, 2000	Air France	MFSC	EMEA	Air France	Aerospatiale Concorde	Passenger	Hull loss	109	100%	0%
26	October 31, 2000	Singapore Airlines Limited	MFSC	APAC	Singapore Airlines	Boeing B747	Passenger	Hull loss	179	46%	22%
27	October 8, 2001	SAS AB	MFSC	EMEA	SAS	Boeing (McDonnell-Douglas) MD-80	Passenger	Hull loss	110	100%	0%
28	November 12, 2001	AMR Corp.	MFSC	NORAM	American Airlines	Airbus A300	Passenger	Hull loss	260	100%	0%
29	May 25, 2002	China Airlines Limited	MFSC	APAC	China Airlines	Boeing B747	Passenger	Hull loss	225	100%	0%
30	July 26, 2002	Federal Express/FedEx Corp	FREIGHTER	NORAM	FedEx	Boeing B727	Freight	Hull loss	3	0%	100%
31	August 30, 2002	TAM SA	MFSC	LATAM	TAM Linhas Aereas	Fokker 100	Passenger	Hull loss	29	0%	0%
32	December 18, 2003	Federal Express/FedEx Corp	FREIGHTER	NORAM	FedEx	Boeing (McDonnell-Douglas) DC-10	Passenger	Hull loss	7	0%	0%
33	November 7, 2004	Deutsche Lufthansa AG	MFSC	EMEA	Lufthansa Cargo	Boeing B747	Freight	Hull loss	4	0%	0%
34	August 2, 2005	Air France-KLM	MFSC	EMEA	Air France	Airbus A340	Passenger	Hull loss	309	0%	4%
35	February 7, 2006	United Parcel Service, Inc	FREIGHTER	NORAM	UPS Airlines	Boeing (McDonnell-Douglas) DC-8	Freight	Hull loss	3	0%	0%
36	July 28, 2006	Federal Express/FedEx Corp	FREIGHTER	NORAM	FedEx	Boeing (McDonnell-Douglas) DC-10	Freight	Hull loss	3	0%	0%
37	July 17, 2007	TAM SA	MFSC	LATAM	TAM Linhas Aereas	Airbus A320	Passenger	Hull loss	187	100%	0%
38	November 9, 2007	Iberia SA	MFSC	EMEA	Iberia	Airbus A340	Passenger	Hull loss	349	0%	0%
39	January 17, 2008	British Airways PLC	MFSC	EMEA	British Airways	Boeing B777	Passenger	Hull loss	152	0%	1%
40	February 2, 2008	Atlas Air/Atlas Air Worldwide Holdings Inc	FREIGHTER	NORAM	Atlas Air	Boeing B747	Freight	Hull loss	2	0%	n/a
41	December 20, 2008	Continental Airlines Inc	MFSC	NORAM	Continental Airlines	Boeing B737	Passenger	Hull loss	115	0%	4%
42	January 15, 2009	US Airways Group Inc	MFSC	NORAM	US Airways	Airbus A320	Passenger	Hull loss	155	0%	1%
43	March 23, 2009	Federal Express/FedEx Corp	FREIGHTER	NORAM	FedEx	Boeing (McDonnell-Douglas) MD-11	Freight	Hull loss	2	100%	0%
44	June 1, 2009	Air France-KLM	MFSC	EMEA	Air France	Airbus A330	Passenger	Hull loss	228	100%	0%
45	December 22, 2009	AMR Corp.	MFSC	NORAM	American Airlines	Boeing B737	Passenger	Hull loss	154	0%	3%

Table 18: *Overview on aircraft accidents 1994-2009 in scope of the analysis of company specific events*

This table presents aircraft accidents selected for the analysis of stock market's reaction on isolated company specific negative events. Historical accidents were filtered to match the following criteria: (a) Accident date between January 1, 1994, and December 31, 2009, (b) affected companies stock listed when the accident occurred, with at least six months of stock return data before and after the accident as well as the full set of data for the explanatory and control variables used in the multivariate regressions, (c) aircraft was a commercial jet, (d) type of loss was classified as hull loss (100% damage), (e) aircraft was in domestic or international scheduled or non-scheduled operations, (f) flight phase was either in take-off, en route, or landing, and (g) accident was not an incident of September 11, 2001. Data were retrieved from Ascend Worldwide Ltd. (2010).

Company	Accident Count	Lost Value [USD m]	Passengers & Crew on Board	Fatalities	Injuries
Federal Express/FedEx Corp	7	220.1	27	2	3
Korean Air Lines Company Limited	6	360.9	956	236	27
Air France-KLM	5	191.7	748	337	11
AMR Corp.	5	94.0	844	431	53
China Airlines Limited	3	117.7	736	424	50
US Airways Group Inc	3	45.6	344	169	17
Singapore Airlines Limited	2	128.8	283	187	39
TAM SA	2	32.5	216	187	0
Air Canada Inc	1	17.0	42	0	9
Alaska Air Group Inc	1	19.1	88	88	0
Atlas Air/Atlas Air Worldwide Holdings Inc	1	8.4	0	0	0
British Airways PLC	1	83.3	152	0	1
Continental Airlines Inc	1	8.8	115	0	5
Delta Air Lines Inc	1	1.9	154	0	0
Deutsche Lufthansa AG	1	18.0	4	0	0
Iberia SA	1	116.8	349	0	0
SAS AB	1	8.3	110	110	0
Southwest Airlines Company	1	13.6	142	0	2
Thai Airways International Public Compan	1	15.0	146	102	0
United Parcel Service, Inc	1	5.0	3	0	0
Grand Total	45	1506.1	5459	2273	217

Table 19: *Aircraft accident statistics of companies with aircraft hull losses 1994-2009*

This table presents the 20 companies in scope of the analysis that experienced aircraft hull losses between 1994 and 2009, sorted by the total number of hull losses. Per company the table further shows the total lost value in million United States Dollars, total number of passengers and crew on board, as well as total number of passenger and crew fatalities and injuries. All data were retrieved from Ascend Worldwide Ltd. (2010).

Although most companies are represented with only one accident, some firms had significantly more accidents. In order of descending number of hull losses, FedEx leads the unlucky ranking with 7 accidents, followed by Korean Air Lines with 6 accidents. Third rank share Air France, American Airlines, each carrying 5 accidents. United Airlines (3), China Airlines (3), Singapore Airlines (2) and TAM (2) follow on fourth and fifth rank. The ranking of the five companies in terms of most passengers and crew killed in the listed accidents starts with American Airlines (431) followed by China Airlines (424), Air France (337), Korean Airlines (236), and Singapore Airlines and TAM (both 187). Overall, in 67% of the accidents at least one passenger or crew member was injured or killed, and 13 out of the 48 accidents (27%) caused 100% fatalities. Whether the degree of injuries or fatalities in the accident had a significant impact on the stock market will be examined at a later stage.

Aircraft firm orders

Positive events in the analysis of stock market's reaction upon isolated company specific events are aircraft firm orders. As described in Chapters 0 and 2.3 some companies order aircraft when demand requires, others seem to order capacity ahead of the market by buying opportunistically when prices are low. According to Ascend Worldwide Ltd. (2010), the 56 companies in view of this thesis ordered a total of more than 8000 aircraft in around 900 order placements during the last 20 years. The number of aircraft confirmed in one order differs. Some companies are presented in the data from Ascend Worldwide Ltd. (2010) with as much as 120 aircraft in one order.

For the analysis of market's reaction, the observations were filtered to match the following criteria:

- Date of order announcement: between January 1, 1994 and December 31, 2009
- Company: acted as the direct order customer for the manufacturer and was stock listed when the order was placed, with at least six months of stock return data before and after the announcement as well as the full set of data for the explanatory and control variables used in the multivariate regressions
- Order type: initial firm orders (no purchase swaps)
- Aircraft type: commercial jets only (excluding all turbo props and small business jets)
- Order-to-order time: minimum of eight consecutive days, i.e. the order does not overlap with another order of the same company within a period of 7 days[63]

No restriction was made with respect to the aircraft manufacturer or the number of different aircraft types in one order at the same manufacturer.

Considering the above criteria, the general distribution curve for aircraft numbers per order is displayed in Figure 31. The sum of aircraft and orders amounts to 6057 and 616, respectively. The descriptive statistics show a mean of 9.8, a standard deviation of 15.2, and a median of 4 aircraft per order.

---

[63] The analysis of stock market's reaction on single-day multiple aircraft order announcements focuses on short term abnormal returns in the period of six trading days starting with the day of order announcement. Orders that were placed by the same company within a period of seven consecutive days are excluded from the list of incidents, because the effects of the announcements on abnormal returns would overlap, i.e. no isolated impact of the single announcement could be measured.

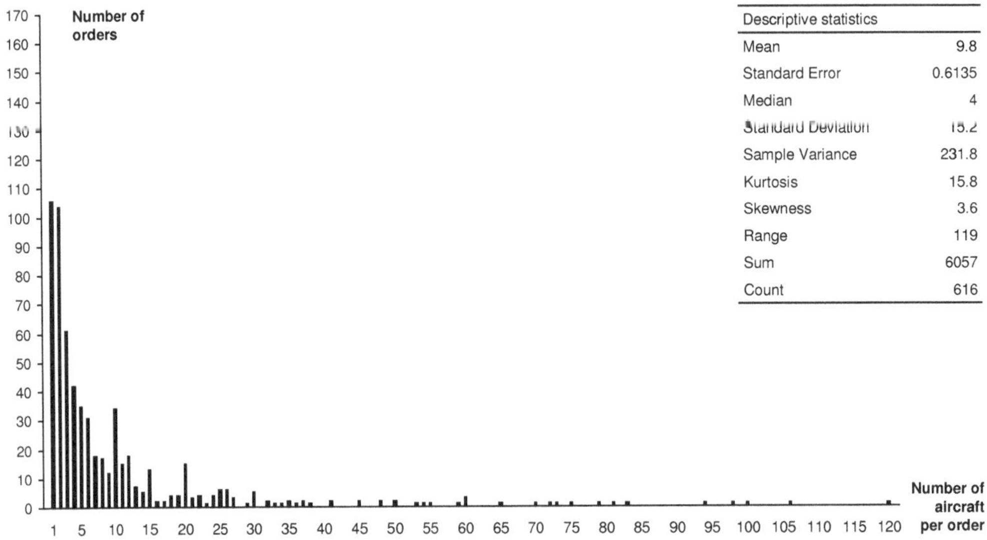

Descriptive statistics	
Mean	9.8
Standard Error	0.6135
Median	4
Standard Deviation	15.2
Sample Variance	231.8
Kurtosis	15.8
Skewness	3.6
Range	119
Sum	6057
Count	616

Figure 31: *Distribution of aircraft numbers per order placed 1994-2009 – Selected orders*

This figure presents the distribution of aircraft numbers per firm order placed at aircraft manufacturers between January 1, 1994 and December 31, 2009 by the aircraft operating and holding companies in scope of the analysis. One order is equal to a signal day at which purchase agreements are placed at one or several manufacturers. An order (announcement) can include one or more aircraft of the same or different types/manufacturers. Aircraft refers to commercial jets, excluding turbo props and small business jets. All sample firms acted as the direct order customer for the manufacturer and were stock listed when the order was announced, with at least six months of stock return data before and after the announcement as well as the full set of data for the explanatory and control variables used in the multivariate regressions. Order-to-order time was restricted to a minimum of eight consecutive days, i.e. the orders do not overlap with other order of the same company within a period of 7 days. Data was retrieved from Ascend Worldwide Ltd. (2010).

To create a manageable size for the regression analyses, the sample had to be further adjusted while paying attention to statistical significance and avoiding biases. Firstly, the sample was separated in orders placed within a 2σ (two times standard deviation) probability distribution of the mean and orders placed outside of this range. In other words, one sample was created containing aircraft numbers per order within the confidence level of the majority of firms (1-40 aircraft per order) and another sample includes the extreme outsiders (41-120 aircraft per order). Secondly, the number of orders within the 2σ range was reduced by the factor 10 (rounded to the next integer) in each aircraft per order category, thus keeping the original distribution of aircraft numbers per order. Further, it was ensured that the list contains all sample companies. This results in a final sample of 58 incidents within the 2σ probability of the mean. The orders outside the 2σ range, i.e. all orders of more than 40 aircraft per order, were taken as a stand-alone sample including 28 events.

Figure 32 illustrates the two separate samples for the analysis of stock market's reaction on aircraft orders. Tables 20 and Tables 21 list the respective incidents in scope.

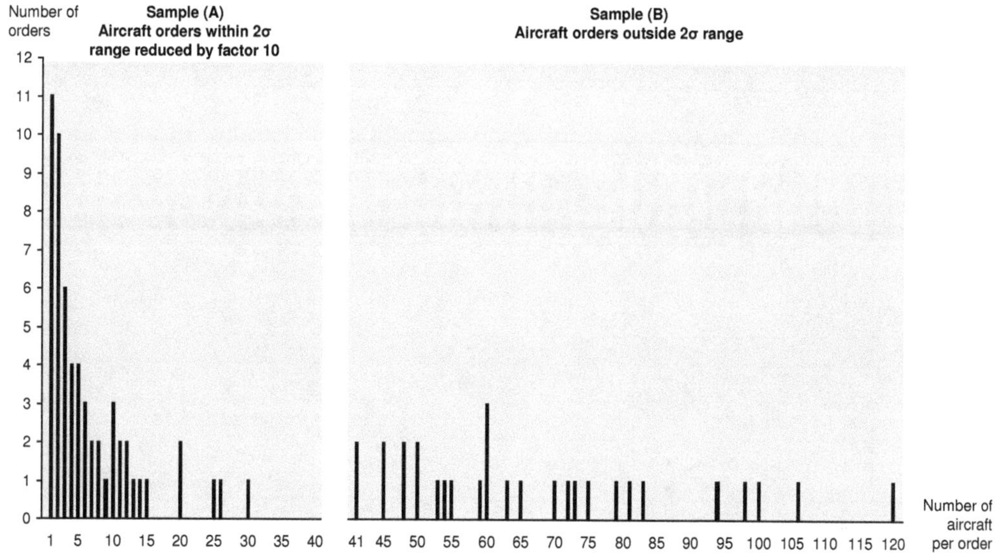

Figure 32: *Samples for multivariate regression analysis of stock market's reaction to aircraft firm orders*

This figure presents two samples of aircraft firm orders based on the overall distribution of aircraft numbers per firm order placed at aircraft manufacturers between January 1, 1994 and December 31, 2009. Sample (A) includes orders placed within a 2σ probability range (with σ equal to 15.2) of the mean (9.8). The number of orders in this sample was reduced by the factor 10 (rounded to the next integer) in each aircraft per order category to create a manageable size of 58 incidents for subsequent analysis while keeping the original distribution of aircraft numbers per order. Sample (B) contains all 28 orders placed outside the 2σ confidence level, i.e. orders with 41-120 aircraft per order. One order is equal to a signal day at which purchase agreements are placed at one or several manufacturers. An order (announcement) can include one or more aircraft of the same or different types/manufacturers. Aircraft refers to commercial jets, excluding turbo props and small business jets. All sample firms acted as the direct order customer for the manufacturer and were stock listed when the order was announced, with at least six months of stock return data before and after the announcement as well as the full set of data for the explanatory and control variables used in the multivariate regressions. Order-to-order time was restricted to a minimum of eight consecutive days, i.e. the orders do not overlap with other orders of the same company within a period of 7 days. Data was retrieved from Ascend Worldwide Ltd. (2010).

Count	Order Date	Company (Customer)	Company Cluster	Region	Operator	Aicraft types (number)	Aircraft usage	Total number of aircraft
1	June 16, 1994	Deutsche Lufthansa AG	MFSC	EMEA	Lufthansa City Line	BAE SYSTEMS RJ Avroliner	Passenger	3
2	October 13, 1994	Southwest Airlines Company	LCC	NORAM	Southwest Airlines	Boeing B737	Passenger	5
3	December 22, 1994	Federal Express/FedEx Corp	FREIGTHER	NORAM	Fedex	Boeing (McDonnell-Douglas) MD-11	Freight	2
4	June 12, 1995	Deutsche Lufthansa AG	MFSC	EMEA	Lufthansa	Airbus A319	Passenger	20
5	August 30, 1996	Federal Express/FedEx Corp	FREIGTHER	NORAM	Fedex	Airbus A300	Freight	11
6	September 2, 1996	British Airways PLC	MFSC	EMEA	British Airways	Boeing B747 (7), B757 (3), B777 (3)	Passenger	13
7	December 20, 1996	Singapore Airlines Limited	MFSC	APAC	Singapore Airlines	Boeing B777	Passenger	2
8	June 9, 1997	Atlas Air/Atlas Air Worldwide Holdings Inc	FREIGTHER	NORAM	Atlas Air	Boeing B747	Freight	10
9	June 9, 1997	Malaysian Airline System Berhad	MFSC	APAC	Malaysian Airline	Boeing B737	Passenger	1
10	July 1, 1997	Air France	MFSC	EMEA	Air France	Airbus A319	Passenger	1
11	October 20, 1997	Air Canada Inc	MFSC	NORAM	Air Canada	Airbus A330 (6), A340 (2)	Passenger	8
12	May 19, 1998	Delta Air Lines Inc	MFSC	NORAM	Delta Air Lines	Boeing B737 (1), B757 (4), B767 (1)	Passenger	6
13	November 23, 1998	Continental Airlines Inc	MFSC	NORAM	Continental Airlines	Boeing B767	Passenger	10
14	December 31, 1998	ATA Holdings	LCC	NORAM	ATA Airlines	Boeing B757	Passenger	1
15	June 1, 1999	Delta Air Lines Inc	MFSC	NORAM	Delta Air Lines	Boeing B767	Passenger	4
16	August 31, 1999	US Airways Group Inc	MFSC	NORAM	US Airways	Airbus A320	Passenger	2
17	October 20, 1999	FLYi, Inc.	NFSC	NORAM	Atlantic Cost Airlines	Bombardier CRJ Regional Jet	Passenger	3
18	November 30, 1999	AMR Corp.	MFSC	NORAM	American Airlines	Boeing B777	Passenger	3
19	June 27, 2000	EVA Airways Corp.	MFSC	APAC	Eva Air	Boeing B777	Passenger	7
20	August 1, 2000	UAL Corp.	MFSC	NORAM	United Airlines	Airbus A319 (6), A320 (6)	Passenger	12
21	November 30, 2000	America West Holdings	LCC	NORAM	America West	Airbus A319	Passenger	4
22	November 30, 2000	United Parcel Service, Inc	FREIGTHER	NORAM	UPS Airlines	Airbus A300	Freight	2
23	January 16, 2001	Northwest Airlines Corporation	MFSC	NORAM	Northwest Airlines	Boeing B747 (2), B757 (18)	Passenger	20
24	April 18, 2001	SAS AB	MFSC	EMEA	SAS	Airbus A330	Passenger	1
25	August 21, 2001	Airtran Holdings Inc	LCC	NORAM	Airtran Airways	Boeing B717	Passenger	1
26	September 25, 2001	Hawaiian Holdings Inc	NFSC	NORAM	Hawaiian Airlines	Boeing B767	Passenger	3
27	October 8, 2001	TAM SA	MFSC	LATAM	TAM Linhas Aereas	Airbus A320	Passenger	1
28	April 15, 2002	Midwest Express Holdings/Midwest Air Group,	NFSC	NORAM	Midwest Airlines	Boeing B717	Passenger	25
29	October 1, 2002	Iberia SA	MFSC	EMEA	Iberia	Airbus A320	Passenger	1
30	October 7, 2002	Japan Airlines Corp.	MFSC	APAC	Japan Airlines	Boeing B747	Passenger	2
31	November 25, 2002	Thai Airways International Public Compan	MFSC	APAC	Thai Airways	Boeing B747	Passenger	2
32	October 9, 2003	Westjet Airlines Limited	NFSC	NORAM	Westjet	Boeing B737	Passenger	2
33	December 17, 2003	Korean Air Lines Company Limited	MFSC	APAC	Korean Air Lines	Boeing B777	Passenger	9
34	August 25, 2004	Air New Zealand Limited	MFSC	APAC	Air New Zealand	Boeing B777 (4), B787 (2)	Passenger	6
35	November 23, 2004	EVA Airways Corp.	MFSC	APAC	Eva Air	Airbus A330	Passenger	1
36	June 13, 2005	Ryanair Holdings PLC	LCC	EMEA	Ryanair	Boeing B737	Passenger	5
37	July 13, 2005	China Eastern Airlines Corp. Limited	MFSC	APAC	China Cargo Airlines	Boeing B747	Freight	2
38	August 16, 2005	United Parcel Service, Inc	FREIGTHER	NORAM	UPS Airlines	Boeing B747	Freight	8
39	November 30, 2005	El Al Israel Airlines Limited	MFSC	EMEA	El Al	Boeing B777	Passenger	2
40	December 14, 2005	Cathay Pacific Airways Limited	MFSC	APAC	Cathay Pacific Airways	Boeing B777	Passenger	12
41	December 16, 2005	China Southern Airlines Company Limited	MFSC	APAC	China Southern Airlines	Boeing B787	Passenger	10
42	December 21, 2005	Easyjet PLC	LCC	EMEA	EasyJet	Airbus A319	Passenger	11
43	February 2, 2006	Alaska Air Group Inc	MFSC	NORAM	Alaska Airlines	Boeing B737	Passenger	3
44	March 30, 2006	Qantas Airways Limited	MFSC	APAC	Qantas Airways	Boeing B787	Passenger	30
45	April 1, 2006	Frontier Airlines, Inc.	LCC	NORAM	Frontier Airlines	Airbus A320	Passenger	6
46	December 14, 2006	All Nippon Airways Company Limited	MFSC	APAC	ANA - All Nippon Airways	Boeing B767	Passenger	1
47	February 21, 2007	British Airways PLC	MFSC	EMEA	British Airways	Airbus A320	Passenger	4
48	October 31, 2007	Lan Airlines SA	MFSC	LATAM	LAN	Boeing B787	Passenger	26
49	November 14, 2007	Air China Limited	MFSC	APAC	Air China	Boeing B777	Passenger	15
50	November 21, 2007	US Airways Group Inc	MFSC	NORAM	US Airways	Airbus A330	Passenger	5

Table 20: *Overview on aircraft firm orders of selected companies with 1-40 aircraft per order*

Count	Order Date	Company (Customer)	Company Cluster	Region	Operator	Aicraft types (number)	Aircraft usage	Total number of aircraft
51	December 3, 2007	Iberia SA	MFSC	EMEA	Iberia	Airbus A320	Passenger	7
52	December 12, 2007	Finnair OYJ	MFSC	EMEA	Finnair	Airbus A330	Passenger	1
53	January 15, 2008	Jetblue Airways Corp.	LCC	NORAM	Jetblue	Embraer 190	Passenger	3
54	January 22, 2008	China Airlines Limited	MFSC	APAC	China Airlines	Airbus A350	Passenger	14
55	March 31, 2008	AER Lingus Group PLC	LCC	EMEA	AER Lingus	Airbus A320	Passenger	4
56	June 13, 2008	Korean Air Lines Company Limited	MFSC	APAC	Korean Air Lines	Boeing B777	Passenger	1
57	March 26, 2009	Virgin Blue Holdings Limited	LCC	APAC	Virgin Blue Airlines	Boeing B737	Passenger	5
58	November 25, 2009	Air Berlin PLC	LCC	EMEA	Air Berlin	Embraer 190	Passenger	2

Table 20 (continued): *Overview on aircraft firm orders of selected companies with more than 40 aircraft per order*

This table presents selected aircraft firm orders placed at aircraft manufacturers between January 1, 1994 and December 31, 2009 by the aircraft operating and holding companies in scope of the analysis. All orders are within a 2σ probability distribution of the mean. The number of orders within the 2σ range was reduced by the factor 10 (rounded to the next integer) in each aircraft per order category, thus keeping the original distribution of aircraft numbers per order. The list contains all companies that ordered aircraft and incidents in all years 1994 to 2009. One order is equal to a signal day at which purchase agreements are placed at one or several manufacturers. An order can include one or more aircraft of the same or different types/manufacturers. Aircraft refers to commercial jets, excluding turbo props and small business jets. All sample firms acted as the direct order customer for the manufacturer and were stock listed when the order was announced, with at least six months of stock return data before and after the announcement as well as the full set of data for the explanatory and control variables used in the multivariate regressions. The operator can refer to the mother company or any subsidiary the company has a majority share in and that is consolidated in the stock listed company. Order-to-order time is restricted to a minimum of eight consecutive days, i.e. the orders do not overlap with other orders of the same company within a period of 7 days. Data was retrieved from Ascend Worldwide Ltd. (2010).

Count	Order Date	Company (Customer)	Company Cluster	Region	Operator	Aicraft types (number)	Aircraft usage	Total number of aircraft
1	July 25, 1996	Continental Airlines Inc	MFSC	NORAM	Continental Airlines	Boeing B737	Passenger	48
2	August 22, 1996	UAL Corp.	MFSC	NORAM	United Airlines	Boeing B747 (13), B757 (6), B777 (2), Airbus A319 (24)	Passenger	45
3	October 10, 1996	Continental Airlines Inc	MFSC	NORAM	Continental Airlines	Boeing B737	Passenger	60
4	November 21, 1996	AMR Corporation	MFSC	NORAM	American Airlines	Boeing B737 (75), B757 (12), B767 (4), B777 (7)	Passenger	98
5	June 10, 1997	Delta Air Lines Inc	MFSC	NORAM	Delta Air Lines	Boeing B737 (70), B757 (5), B767 (31)	Passenger	106
6	September 19, 1997	Northwest Airlines Corporation	MFSC	NORAM	Northwest Airlines	Airbus A319	Passenger	50
7	October 31, 1997	US Airways Group Inc	MFSC	NORAM	US Airways	Airbus A319 (66), A320 15)	Passenger	81
8	January 22, 1998	Southwest Airlines Company	LCC	NORAM	Southwest Airlines	Boeing B737	Passenger	59
9	October 26, 1998	British Airways PLC	MFSC	EMEA	British Airways	Airbus A319 (33), A320 (20)	Passenger	53
10	December 22, 1998	Delta Air Lines Inc	MFSC	NORAM	Delta Air Lines	Boeing B737 (30), B757 (14), B767 (3), B777 (1)	Passenger	48
11	February 18, 1999	Northwest Airlines Corporation	MFSC	NORAM	Northwest Airlines	Airbus A350	Passenger	54
12	June 29, 2000	Southwest Airlines Company	LCC	NORAM	Southwest Airlines	Boeing B737	Passenger	94
13	July 9, 2001	Northwest Airlines Corporation	MFSC	NORAM	Northwest Airlines	Airbus A350	Passenger	75
14	January 24, 2002	Ryanair Holdings PLC	LCC	EMEA	Ryanair	Boeing B737	Passenger	100
15	December 31, 2002	Easyjet PLC	LCC	EMEA	Easyjet	Airbus A319	Passenger	120
16	April 24, 2003	Jetblue Airways Corp.	LCC	NORAM	Jetblue	Airbus A320	Passenger	65
17	June 10, 2003	Jetblue Airways Corp.	LCC	NORAM	Jetblue	Embraer 190	Passenger	83
18	June 27, 2003	All Nippon Airways Company Limited	MFSC	APAC	All Nippon Airways	Boeing B737	Passenger	45
19	July 26, 2004	All Nippon Airways Company Limited	MFSC	APAC	All Nippon Airways	Boeing B787	Passenger	50
20	May 10, 2005	Japan Airlines Corp.	MFSC	APAC	Japan Airlines	Boeing B737 (30), B787 (30)	Passenger	60
21	May 12, 2005	Ryanair Holdings PLC	LCC	EMEA	Ryanair	Boeing B737	Passenger	70
22	April 20, 2006	Southwest Airlines Company	LCC	NORAM	Southwest Airlines	Boeing B737	Passenger	79
23	October 5, 2006	Northwest Airlines Corporation	MFSC	NORAM	Northwest Airlines	Embraer 170 (36), Bombardier CRJ 900 (36)	Passenger	72
24	December 22, 2006	Air Berlin PLC	LCC	EMEA	Air Berlin	Boeing B737	Passenger	60
25	September 5, 2007	China Southern Airlines Company Limited	MFSC	APAC	China Southern Airlines	Boeing B737	Passenger	55
26	September 20, 2007	Deutsche Lufthansa AG	MFSC	EMEA	Lufthansa	Airbus A319 (6), A320 (6), A321 (20), A330 (9)	Passenger	41
27	October 2, 2007	US Airways Group Inc	MFSC	NORAM	US Airways	Airbus A320 (31), A321 (10), A330 (10), A350 (22)	Passenger	73
28	February 14, 2008	TAM SA	MFSC	LATAM	TAM	Airbus A319 (3), A320 (9), A321 (3), A330 (4), A350 (20)	Passenger	41

Table 21: *Overview on aircraft firm orders of selected companies with more than 40 aircraft per order*

This table presents aircraft firm orders placed at aircraft manufacturers between January 1, 1994 and December 31, 2009 by the aircraft operating and holding companies in scope of the analysis. All orders are outside the 2σ confidence level with regard to the number of aircraft per order, i.e. these orders contain more than 40 aircraft per order. One order is equal to a signal day at which purchase agreements are placed at one or several manufacturers. An order can include one or more aircraft of the same or different types/manufacturers. Aircraft refers to commercial jets, excluding turbo props and small business jets. All sample firms acted as the direct order customer for the manufacturer and were stock listed when the order was announced, with at least six months of stock return data before and after the announcement as well as the full set of data for the explanatory and control variables used in the multivariate regressions. The operator can refer to the mother company or any subsidiary the company has a majority share in and that is consolidated in the stock listed company. Order-to-order time is restricted to a minimum of eight consecutive days, i.e. the orders do not overlap with other orders of the same company within a period of 7 days. Data was retrieved from Ascend Worldwide Ltd. (2010).

The samples of accidents and aircraft orders are used to test market' reaction on company specific, isolated events. More concretely the firms' stock performances on these days in terms of abnormal returns are analyzed with multivariate regression methodology. For that purpose the next sections focus on the shift in alpha and beta risk and the significance of abnormal returns caused by the events.

7.3.2 Special events – Alpha, beta, and the shift in risk

Alpha and beta are integral components of the calculation of abnormal returns in stocks (cf. Chapter 7.1.1.1). Also for the estimation of abnormal returns caused by accidents or aircraft orders, alpha and beta coefficients are computed for the time prior and after the incidents.

Calculation of α and β risk components for company specific isolated events[64]:

α_i = least square model parameter reflecting the risk prior to an aircraft accident or order; calculated over a period of 130 trading days ending on the day before the incident

$\alpha_i^{'}$ = least square model parameter reflecting a risk shift resulting from an aircraft accident or order; calculated as the difference between α_i and the alpha for the same i determined over a period of 131 trading days starting with the day of incident

β_i = least square model parameter reflecting the risk prior to an aircraft accident or order; calculated over a period of 130 trading days ending on the day before the incident

$\beta_i^{'}$ = least square model parameter reflecting a risk shift resulting from an aircraft accident or order; calculated as the difference between β_i and the beta for the same i determined over a period of 131 trading days starting with the day of incident.

The shift in risk is equal to the difference between the alpha and beta before and after the event, both estimated over a period of six months.

Alphas and betas ex-ante and ex-post aircraft accidents

Table 22 illustrates alpha and beta coefficients preceding aircraft accidents with hull loss between 1994 and 2009 of firms in scope of this analysis and shifts in risk after the incident, respectively. Coefficients are calculated using the least square market model. The market was adjusted for each event according to the event day and required data set prior and after the event. The table shows insignificant alphas and shift in alphas for almost all carriers and accidents. It reveals that most firms had significant betas at the 1% level prior to the

[64] The number of trading days mentioned is exemplary and refers to the trading days of the New York Stock Exchange (NYSE). Saturdays and Sundays are excluded as well as NYSE trading holidays, i.e. days with full closure of the exchange. For companies listed at other stock exchanges the actual number of trading days might vary.

accident, both above and below the market's beta of "1.0". With the accident, the majority of the firms experienced a significant change in the systematic risk, 2/3 of which with a positive and 1/3 with a negative sign. The adjustments range between -0.9499*** (FedEx) and 1.1796*** (Singapore Airlines).

At first view, alphas, betas, and the shift in risk caused by hull loss accidents show that the market does not react identically to an accident. After accidents, most companies experience a significant increase but others a decrease in betas. Even with the shift in risk some companies' systematic risk coefficients stay under the benchmark while others lie above. Further, the beta adjustment is not always constant for one company, e.g. though FedEx had to cope with several hull losses between 1994 and 2009, its beta sometimes increased and at other times decreased within the six months after the accident.

At a closer look, major full service carriers had the most extreme positive and negative betas before the incidents and also the most extreme positive and negative adjustments. Investing in North American based companies was on average more risky than investing in Asia Pacific firms. Generally betas seem to adjust towards the market after the accidents, i.e. on average betas higher than 1.0 experience a downward adjustment while betas below 1.0 experience upward adjustments. Yet, the overall distribution does not change significantly.

Additionally, Table 23 shows the correlation of beta, change in beta, percentage of fatalities or injuries, accident date, as well as carrier or region cluster a company belongs to. Table 23 generally supports the interpretation of Table 22, though the correlation coefficients are generally low.

Count	Accident Date	Company	Company Cluster	Region	α_i		α'_i		β_i		β'_i	
1	July 2, 1994	US Airways Group Inc	MFSC	NORAM	-0.0053 *	(0.0030)	0.0016	(0.0035)	0.7940	(0.5380)	-1.3375	(0.8791)
2	August 10, 1994	Korean Air Lines Company Limited	MFSC	APAC	0.0001	(0.0016)	0.0007	(0.0020)	0.2091	(0.3610)	0.0967	(0.4527)
3	September 8, 1994	US Airways Group Inc	MFSC	NORAM	-0.0028	(0.0028)	0.0018	(0.0038)	0.8169	(0.6715)	-0.8450	(0.8160)
4	December 20, 1995	AMR Corp.	MFSC	NORAM	-0.0008	(0.0013)	0.0035	(0.0014)	1.4842 ***	(0.3174)	-1.3706	(0.2542)
5	September 5, 1996	Federal Express/FedEx Corp	FREIGHTER	NORAM	0.0000	(0.0011)	0.0021	(0.0013)	1.4111 ***	(0.2407)	0.0915 ***	(0.2774)
6	July 6, 1997	Delta Air Lines Inc	MFSC	NORAM	0.0005	(0.0015)	0.0020 *	(0.0015)	0.9894 ***	(0.2576)	0.0995 ***	(0.1605)
7	July 31, 1997	Federal Express/FedEx Corp	FREIGHTER	NORAM	0.0004	(0.0016)	0.0001	(0.0018)	1.0691 ***	(0.2607)	0.3880 ***	(0.1870)
8	August 6, 1997	Korean Air Lines Company Limited	MFSC	APAC	0.0002	(0.0022)	-0.0083	(0.0065)	-0.1113	(0.3535)	1.0178	(0.6830)
9	December 16, 1997	Air Canada Inc	MFSC	NORAM	0.0031 *	(0.0016)	-0.0057	(0.0018)	1.1067 ***	(0.1770)	0.2597 ***	(0.2376)
10	December 19, 1997	Singapore Airlines Limited	MFSC	APAC	-0.0004	(0.0016)	-0.0013	(0.0027)	0.1617	(0.1820)	1.1796 ***	(0.3444)
11	February 9, 1998	AMR Corp.	MFSC	NORAM	0.0011	(0.0014)	-0.0012	(0.0018)	1.0597 ***	(0.1476)	-0.3223 ***	(0.2280)
12	February 16, 1998	China Airlines Limited	MFSC	APAC	-0.0029	(0.0025)	0.0013	(0.0020)	0.6004 **	(0.2583)	-0.0467 **	(0.2511)
13	August 5, 1998	Korean Air Lines Company Limited	MFSC	APAC	-0.0029	(0.0052)	0.0073	(0.0046)	1.7088 **	(0.6777)	-0.1231 ***	(0.3715)
14	December 11, 1998	Thai Airways International Public Company	MFSC	APAC	0.0041	(0.0050)	-0.0019	(0.0034)	0.2129	(0.4048)	0.5889 *	(0.4174)
15	March 4, 1999	Air France	MFSC	EMEA	-0.0003	(0.0027)	-0.0003	(0.0014)	0.1467	(0.2371)	-0.1264	(0.1923)
16	March 5, 1999	Air France	MFSC	EMEA	-0.0002	(0.0026)	-0.0003	(0.0014)	0.1204	(0.2358)	-0.0868	(0.1875)
17	March 15, 1999	Korean Air Lines Company Limited	MFSC	APAC	0.0067	(0.0045)	-0.0010	(0.0043)	1.6834 ***	(0.4143)	-0.7496	(0.6048)
18	April 15, 1999	Korean Air Lines Company Limited	MFSC	APAC	0.0069	(0.0045)	-0.0056	(0.0047)	2.0480 ***	(0.4856)	-1.1022	(0.6579)
19	June 1, 1999	AMR Corporation	MFSC	NORAM	-0.0009	(0.0024)	-0.0007	(0.0019)	1.4652 ***	(0.2898)	-0.0344 ***	(0.2603)
20	August 22, 1999	China Airlines Limited	MFSC	APAC	0.0002	(0.0020)	0.0003	(0.0015)	0.0394	(0.2788)	-0.3734 *	(0.1770)
21	October 17, 1999	Federal Express/FedEx Corp	FREIGHTER	NORAM	-0.0018	(0.0023)	0.0003	(0.0026)	1.8853 ***	(0.3096)	-0.9400 ***	(0.2673)
22	December 22, 1999	Korean Air Lines Company Limited	MFSC	APAC	-0.0035	(0.0044)	-0.0015	(0.0050)	0.1708	(0.5949)	0.6838 *	(0.4788)
23	January 31, 2000	Alaska Air Group Inc	MFSC	NORAM	-0.0029	(0.0018)	0.0016	(0.0027)	0.9059 ***	(0.2141)	-0.0404 ***	(0.2721)
24	March 5, 2000	Southwest Airlines Company	LCC	NORAM	-0.0003	(0.0020)	0.0017	(0.0022)	0.9738 ***	(0.2455)	-0.4636 **	(0.2375)
25	July 25, 2000	Air France	MFSC	EMEA	0.0001	(0.0021)	0.0017	(0.0021)	0.2557	(0.2177)	0.1730 *	(0.2309)
26	October 31, 2000	Singapore Airlines Limited	MFSC	APAC	-0.0002	(0.0021)	-0.0011	(0.0018)	0.3561	(0.2409)	0.0148 **	(0.1535)
27	October 8, 2001	SAS AB	MFSC	EMEA	-0.0039	(0.0027)	0.0063	(0.0021)	0.6085 **	(0.2620)	0.2875 ***	(0.2428)
28	November 12, 2001	AMR Corp.	MFSC	NORAM	-0.0031	(0.0041)	0.0041	(0.0023)	2.1669 ***	(0.4108)	-0.4923 ***	(0.2621)
29	May 25, 2002	China Airlines Limited	MFSC	APAC	0.0018	(0.0025)	-0.0018	(0.0025)	-0.0232	(0.2865)	0.3240 *	(0.1597)
30	July 26, 2002	Federal Express/FedEx Corp	FREIGHTER	NORAM	0.0006	(0.0018)	0.0001	(0.0016)	0.8343 ***	(0.1611)	0.1532 ***	(0.1085)

***Table 22:** Alpha, beta and the shift in risk with aircraft accidents (hull losses)*

(Table continued on next page)

31 August 30, 2002	TAM SA	MFSC	LATAM	-0.0023	(0.0018)	0.0015	(0.0014)	-0.0540	(0.1351)	0.3665 ***	(0.1032)
32 December 18, 2003	Federal Express/FedEx Corp	FREIGHTER	NORAM	0.0000	(0.0011)	0.0004	(0.0010)	1.0230 ***	(0.1677)	-0.1802 ***	(0.1392)
33 November 7, 2004	Deutsche Lufthansa AG	MFSC	EMEA	0.0004	(0.0005)	-0.0006	(0.0004)	0.2728 ***	(0.0823)	0.1237 ***	(0.0894)
34 August 2, 2005	Air France-KLM	MFSC	EMEA	-0.0010	(0.0010)	0.0027	(0.0012)	0.9403 ***	(0.2006)	0.2361 ***	(0.2226)
35 February 7, 2006	United Parcel Service, Inc	FREIGHTER	NORAM	-0.0004	(0.0009)	-0.0005	(0.0012)	0.7362 ***	(0.1602)	-0.2721 ***	(0.1573)
36 July 28, 2006	Federal Express/FedEx Corp	FREIGHTER	NORAM	-0.0001	(0.0012)	-0.0005	(0.0010)	0.9762 ***	(0.1589)	0.2675 ***	(0.2223)
37 July 17, 2007	TAM SA	MFSC	LATAM	0.0000	(0.0018)	-0.0023	(0.0025)	1.6721 ***	(0.2869)	0.3919 ***	(0.2466)
38 November 9, 2007	Iberia SA	MFSC	EMEA	-0.0001	(0.0017)	-0.0017	(0.0021)	1.5320 ***	(0.1972)	-0.4992 ***	(0.1843)
39 January 17, 2008	British Airways PLC	MFSC	EMEA	-0.0019	(0.0021)	0.0016	(0.0028)	1.6641 ***	(0.2115)	0.3876 ***	(0.2719)
40 February 2, 2008	Atlas Air/Atlas Air Worldwide Holdings Inc	FREIGHTER	NORAM	-0.0005	(0.0012)	0.0007	(0.0016)	0.7702 ***	(0.1148)	0.1623 ***	(0.1636)
41 December 20, 2008	Continental Airlines Inc	MFSC	NORAM	0.0039	(0.0079)	-0.0090	(0.0060)	0.2744	(0.2894)	-0.3301	(0.3372)
42 January 15, 2009	US Airways Group Inc	MFSC	NORAM	0.0150 *	(0.0088)	-0.0271 **	(0.0057)	1.7071 ***	(0.3180)	0.7066 ***	(0.3252)
43 March 23, 2009	Federal Express/FedEx Corp	FREIGHTER	NORAM	-0.0020	(0.0028)	0.0024	(0.0018)	1.0347 ***	(0.0965)	0.4735 ***	(0.1296)
44 June 1, 2009	Air France-KLM	MFSC	EMEA	0.0007	(0.0027)	-0.0030	(0.0019)	1.4241 ***	(0.1403)	0.3156 ***	(0.1741)
45 December 22, 2009	AMR Corp.	MFSC	NORAM	0.0024	(0.0036)	-0.0008	(0.0027)	1.5222 ***	(0.3432)	0.0040 ***	(0.2397)

** Statistically significant at the 10% level*

*** Statistically significant at the 5% level*

**** Statistically significant at the 1% level*

Table 22 (continued): *Alpha, beta and the shift in risk with aircraft accidents (hull losses)*

Table 22 presents the standard market model parameters α and β and standard errors (in parentheses) for each firm, estimated over a period of 130 trading days ending on the day before the incident. It also presents the market model parameters α′ and β′ which reflect a risk shift after the incident. α′ [β′] is calculated as the difference between the firm's α [β] before the incident and the firm's α [β] after the incident, estimated over a period of 131 trading days starting with the day of incident. Underlying daily stock data were retrieved from Thomson Financial Datastream (2009). Benchmark is the MSCI World Index. The number of trading days refers to the trading days of the New York Stock Exchange (NYSE). Statistical significance is based on t-statistics.

	β_i	β'_i	*Fatalities*	*Injuries*	*Date*	*MFSC*	*NFSC*	*LCC*	*FREIGHT*	*APAC*	*EMEA*	*LATAM*	*NORAM*
β_i	1												
β'_i	-0.3630	1											
Fatalities	-0.0742	0.0280	1										
Injuries	-0.0287	-0.0237	-0.1481	1									
Accident Date	0.2983	0.2341	-0.1250	-0.0787	1								
MFSC	-0.1743	0.0172	0.3000	-0.1538	-0.2113	1							
NFSC							1						
LCC	0.0275	-0.1224	-0.1168	-0.0374	-0.0297	-0.2843		1					
FREIGHTER	0.1713	0.0269	-0.2693	0.1737	0.2307	-0.9364		-0.0701	1				
APAC	-0.3746	0.1305	0.2838	-0.0711	-0.3949	0.3292		-0.0936	-0.3083	1			
EMEA	-0.0714	0.1343	-0.0749	-0.1217	0.2046	0.2632		-0.0748	-0.2464	-0.3292	1		
LATAM	-0.0139	0.1531	0.0585	-0.0721	0.1756	0.1070		-0.0304	-0.1002	-0.1338	-0.1070	1	
NORAM	0.4055	-0.2899	-0.2213	0.1929	0.1230	-0.5577		0.1586	0.5222	-0.5903	-0.4719	-0.1918	1

Table 23: *Correlation of beta and shift in beta with incident specific factors in aircraft accidents*

This table presents standard correlation coefficients between company stocks' betas preceding an aircraft accident, the shift in risk after the accident and selected descriptive factors such as the percentage of passenger or crew fatalities and injuries, the date of accident, and the carrier and region cluster the companies belong to.

Alphas and betas ex-ante and ex-post aircraft firm orders

Alphas and betas before and the shift in risk caused by aircraft firm orders are illustrated in Table 24 and Table 25 for orders including 1-40 aircraft and orders including 41-120 aircraft, respectively. Table 26 presents the standard correlations for a sample of all aircraft orders independent from the number of aircraft per order.

Before the order events, alphas and changes in alphas are usually not significant. Betas and their changes, on the other hand, show high significance again mostly at the 1% level. Similar to betas before and after aircraft accidents, and independent from the number of aircraft per order, NORAM based companies carry higher betas (on average >1) and APAC based companies lower betas (on average <1.0). Major full service carriers on average show the most intense positive and negative systematic risk and the most distinct change after an aircraft order. The conclusion that betas overall seem to adjust towards market's beta of 1.0 can be confirmed. Comparing Table 24 and Table 25, one could assume that companies ordering extreme numbers of aircraft per order have higher betas before the orders, because in the sample of aircraft orders with 41-120 aircraft 67% of the significant betas are >1.0, whereas in the sample of aircraft orders with 1-40 aircraft 76% of the significant betas are <1.0. However, the number of aircraft per order is neither correlated to the beta of a company's stock preceding the order nor to the algebraic sign or magnitude of the shift in risk afterwards (cf. Table 26).

Count	Order Date	Company (Customer)	Company Cluster	Region	α_i		α'_i		β_i		β'_i	
1	June 16, 1994	Deutsche Lufthansa AG	MFSC	EMEA	0.0009	(0.0017)	0.0001	(0.0013)	1.0743 ***	(0.3092)	0.1576 ***	(0.2986)
2	October 13, 1994	Southwest Airlines Company	LCC	NORAM	-0.0035 *	(0.0019)	0.0019	(0.0022)	1.5883 ***	(0.5034)	-0.4563 ***	(0.4260)
3	December 22, 1994	Federal Express/FedEx Corp	FREIGTHER	NORAM	-0.0019	(0.0015)	0.0020	(0.0011)	0.9852 ***	(0.3497)	-0.7799	(0.2118)
4	June 12, 1995	Deutsche Lufthansa AG	MFSC	EMEA	0.0008	(0.0013)	-0.0019	(0.0010)	1.0602 ***	(0.2410)	-0.3810 ***	(0.2295)
5	August 30, 1996	Federal Express/FedEx Corp	FREIGTHER	NORAM	0.0000	(0.0011)	0.0014	(0.0013)	1.4543 ***	(0.2403)	0.0306 ***	(0.2716)
6	September 2, 1996	British Airways PLC	MFSC	EMEA	0.0005	(0.0010)	0.0007	(0.0011)	0.5798 ***	(0.2169)	0.2937 ***	(0.2299)
7	December 20, 1996	Singapore Airlines Limited	MFSC	APAC	-0.0006	(0.0006)	-0.0002	(0.0007)	0.1346	(0.1201)	0.1918 **	(0.1298)
8	June 9, 1997	Atlas Air/Atlas Air Worldwide Holdings Inc	FREIGTHER	NORAM	-0.0044	(0.0038)	0.0039	(0.0029)	1.0699	(0.6456)	0.3646 ***	(0.3269)
9	June 9, 1997	Malaysian Airline System Berhad	MFSC	APAC	-0.0006	(0.0019)	-0.0066 *	(0.0041)	0.1190	(0.3295)	0.4579	(0.4688)
10	July 1, 1997	Air France	MFSC	EMEA	0.0045	(0.0072)	-0.0072	(0.0037)	0.8240	(1.2175)	-0.9710	(0.4001)
11	October 20, 1997	Air Canada Inc	MFSC	NORAM	0.0037 **	(0.0016)	-0.0059	(0.0018)	1.1738 ***	(0.2527)	-0.0129 ***	(0.1911)
12	May 19, 1998	Delta Air Lines Inc	MFSC	NORAM	-0.0002	(0.0016)	-0.0002	(0.0019)	0.7183 ***	(0.2111)	0.5774 ***	(0.1542)
13	November 23, 1998	Continental Airlines Inc	MFSC	NORAM	-0.0034	(0.0027)	0.0035	(0.0027)	0.2740	(0.2171)	-0.2526	(0.3270)
14	December 31, 1998	ATA Holdings	LCC	NORAM	0.0000	(0.0034)	-0.0012	(0.0028)	1.3727 ***	(0.2779)	-0.5686 **	(0.3510)
15	June 1, 1999	Delta Air Lines Inc	MFSC	NORAM	-0.0001	(0.0026)	-0.0021	(0.0020)	1.0529 ***	(0.3121)	0.4109 ***	(0.2774)
16	August 31, 1999	US Airways Group Inc	MFSC	NORAM	-0.0045 *	(0.0025)	-0.0001 *	(0.0026)	1.8235 ***	(0.3420)	-0.5199 ***	(0.3152)
17	October 20, 1999	FLYi, Inc.	NFSC	NORAM	-0.0028	(0.0038)	0.0040	(0.0035)	0.8940 *	(0.5188)	-0.1844 *	(0.3623)
18	November 30, 1999	AMR Corp.	MFSC	NORAM	-0.0019	(0.0019)	0.0029	(0.0030)	1.5167 ***	(0.2633)	-0.1249 ***	(0.2911)
19	June 27, 2000	EVA Airways Corp.	MFSC	APAC	0.0005	(0.0023)	-0.0012	(0.0027)	0.4472 **	(0.2232)	-0.2025	(0.2952)
20	August 1, 2000	UAL Corp.	MFSC	NORAM	-0.0004	(0.0025)	-0.0016	(0.0021)	0.8106 ***	(0.2537)	0.0640 ***	(0.2279)
21	November 30, 2000	America West Holdings	LCC	NORAM	-0.0041 *	(0.0023)	0.0051	(0.0025)	0.8897 ***	(0.2722)	0.0522 ***	(0.2180)
22	November 30, 2000	United Parcel Service, Inc	FREIGTHER	NORAM	0.0005	(0.0017)	-0.0002	(0.0013)	0.7059 ***	(0.1998)	0.0461 ***	(0.1148)
23	January 16, 2001	Northwest Airlines Corporation	MFSC	NORAM	0.0005	(0.0030)	-0.0001	(0.0020)	2.0616 ***	(0.3203)	-0.9168 ***	(0.1860)
24	April 18, 2001	SAS AB	MFSC	EMEA	0.0024	(0.0015)	-0.0056	(0.0027)	0.5387 ***	(0.1280)	0.0955 **	(0.2634)
25	August 21, 2001	Airtran Holdings Inc	LCC	NORAM	-0.0007	(0.0030)	0.0017	(0.0050)	0.9995 ***	(0.2807)	1.7711 ***	(0.4775)
26	September 25, 2001	Hawaiian Holdings Inc	NFSC	NORAM	0.0004	(0.0036)	0.0024	(0.0044)	1.0060 ***	(0.3317)	-1.1912	(0.4925)
27	October 8, 2001	TAM SA	MFSC	LATAM	-0.0017	(0.0011)	0.0030 *	(0.0007)	0.2550 **	(0.1045)	-0.0897 **	(0.0808)
28	April 15, 2002	Midwest Express Holdings/Midwest Air Group, Inc.	NFSC	NORAM	0.0033	(0.0024)	-0.0107 **	(0.0035)	1.0705 ***	(0.2731)	0.3627 ***	(0.2334)
29	October 1, 2002	Iberia SA	MFSC	EMEA	0.0008	(0.0024)	0.0000	(0.0024)	0.9251 ***	(0.1704)	0.0000 ***	(0.1704)
30	October 7, 2002	Japan Airlines Corp.	MFSC	APAC	-0.0010	(0.0016)	-0.0011	(0.0021)	0.1844	(0.1138)	0.0614	(0.1655)
31	November 25, 2002	Thai Airways International Public Compan	MFSC	APAC	-0.0003	(0.0028)	0.0000	(0.0021)	0.0760	(0.1772)	0.0721	(0.1952)
32	October 9, 2003	Westjet Airlines Limited	NFSC	NORAM	0.0028	(0.0018)	-0.0037	(0.0020)	0.5530 **	(0.2366)	0.5708 ***	(0.3341)
33	December 17, 2003	Korean Air Lines Company Limited	MFSC	APAC	0.0014	(0.0024)	-0.0044	(0.0027)	1.2760 ***	(0.3808)	0.4350 ***	(0.3895)
34	August 25, 2004	Air New Zealand Limited	MFSC	APAC	-0.0006	(0.0020)	-0.0001	(0.0013)	0.8104 ***	(0.2896)	-0.3636 *	(0.2617)
35	November 23, 2004	EVA Airways Corp.	MFSC	APAC	-0.0006	(0.0022)	0.0016	(0.0016)	0.5457	(0.3721)	0.3893 ***	(0.3024)
36	June 13, 2005	Ryanair Holdings PLC	LCC	EMEA	0.0008	(0.0014)	-0.0008	(0.0012)	0.9447 ***	(0.2735)	0.1224 ***	(0.2436)
37	July 13, 2005	China Eastern Airlines Corp. Limited	MFSC	APAC	-0.0050 **	(0.0025)	0.0057	(0.0019)	0.4341	(0.5007)	-0.1174	(0.3648)
38	August 16, 2005	United Parcel Service, Inc	FREIGTHER	NORAM	-0.0004	(0.0009)	0.0004	(0.0009)	1.1759 ***	(0.1871)	-0.4329 ***	(0.1630)
39	November 30, 2005	El Al Israel Airlines Limited	MFSC	EMEA	-0.0001	(0.0019)	-0.0009	(0.0014)	0.4980	(0.3877)	-0.0346 *	(0.2421)
40	December 14, 2005	Cathay Pacific Airways Limited	MFSC	APAC	-0.0007	(0.0009)	0.0011	(0.0009)	0.5816 ***	(0.1798)	-0.0437 ***	(0.1366)
41	December 16, 2005	China Southern Airlines Company Limited	MFSC	APAC	-0.0015	(0.0020)	0.0016	(0.0020)	0.2927	(0.4058)	-0.0465	(0.2923)
42	December 21, 2005	Easyjet PLC	LCC	EMEA	0.0020	(0.0019)	-0.0014	(0.0017)	1.3402 ***	(0.3726)	-0.0930 ***	(0.2492)
43	February 2, 2006	Alaska Air Group Inc	MFSC	NORAM	-0.0016	(0.0018)	0.0031	(0.0018)	0.9819 ***	(0.3236)	0.5571 ***	(0.2479)
44	March 30, 2006	Qantas Airways Limited	MFSC	APAC	-0.0003	(0.0013)	0.0012	(0.0013)	0.6656 ***	(0.2397)	0.0969 ***	(0.1801)
45	April 1, 2006	Frontier Airlines, Inc.	LCC	NORAM	-0.0028	(0.0037)	0.0030	(0.0023)	1.5775 **	(0.7029)	-0.3435 ***	(0.3105)
46	December 14, 2006	All Nippon Airways Company Limited	MFSC	APAC	-0.0006	(0.0012)	0.0004	(0.0009)	0.8218 ***	(0.1994)	-0.2803 ***	(0.1581)
47	February 21, 2007	British Airways PLC	MFSC	EMEA	0.0016	(0.0012)	-0.0037	(0.0015)	1.5206 ***	(0.2691)	0.2510 ***	(0.1941)
48	October 31, 2007	Lan Airlines SA	MFSC	LATAM	0.0009	(0.0011)	-0.0012	(0.0020)	0.9793 ***	(0.1342)	0.3223 ***	(0.1737)
49	November 14, 2007	Air China Limited	MFSC	APAC	0.0055	(0.0037)	-0.0066	(0.0039)	0.0310	(0.4467)	-0.0844	(0.3501)
50	November 21, 2007	US Airways Group Inc	MFSC	NORAM	-0.0042	(0.0031)	-0.0053 *	(0.0049)	1.4460 ***	(0.3446)	-0.2644 **	(0.4538)

***Table 24:** Alpha, beta and the shift in risk with aircraft orders (1-40 aircraft per order)*

(Table continued on next page)

Count	Order Date	Company (Customer)	Company Cluster	Region	αi		α'i		βi		β'i	
51	December 3, 2007	Iberia SA	MFSC	EMEA	-0.0007	(0.0018)	-0.0020	(0.0020)	1.3708 ***	(0.1959)	-0.2943 ***	(0.1904)
52	December 12, 2007	Finnair OYJ	MFSC	EMEA	-0.0008	(0.0018)	-0.0027 *	(0.0019)	1.0777 ***	(0.1937)	-0.2595 ***	(0.1795)
53	January 15, 2008	Jetblue Airways Corp.	LCC	NORAM	-0.0061 **	(0.0023)	0.0045	(0.0036)	1.1509 ***	(0.2405)	0.0479 ***	(0.3417)
54	January 22, 2008	China Airlines Limited	MFSC	APAC	0.0018	(0.0018)	-0.0058	(0.0028)	0.1947	(0.1737)	0.3851 **	(0.2829)
55	March 31, 2008	AER Lingus Group PLC	LCC	EMEA	0.0002	(0.0017)	-0.0017	(0.0028)	0.6135 ***	(0.1537)	0.4468 ***	(0.2214)
56	June 13, 2008	Korean Air Lines Company Limited	MFSC	APAC	-0.0028	(0.0026)	0.0024	(0.0054)	0.9701 ***	(0.2402)	-0.0219 ***	(0.1998)
57	March 26, 2009	Virgin Blue Holdings Limited	LCC	APAC	-0.0021	(0.0058)	0.0048	(0.0041)	0.7393 ***	(0.2009)	0.6502 ***	(0.3133)
58	November 25, 2009	Air Berlin PLC	LCC	EMEA	-0.0013	(0.0022)	0.0001	(0.0018)	0.8959 ***	(0.1987)	0.7296 ***	(0.1684)

** Statistically significant at the 10% level*

*** Statistically significant at the 5% level*

**** Statistically significant at the 1% level*

Table 24 (continued): *Alpha, beta and the shift in risk with aircraft orders (1-40 aircraft per order)*

This table presents the standard market model parameters α and β and standard errors (in parentheses) for each firm, estimated over a period of 130 trading days ending on the day before the incident. It also presents the market model parameters α′ and β′ which reflect a shift in risk after the incident. α′ [β′] is calculated as the difference between the firm's α [β] before the incident and the firm's α [β] after the incident, estimated over a period of 131 trading days starting with the day of incident, Underlying daily stock data were retrieved from Thomson Financial Datastream (2009). Benchmark is the MSCI World Index. The number of trading days refers to the trading days of the New York Stock Exchange (NYSE). Statistical significance is based on t-statistics.

Count	Order Date	Company (Customer)	Company Cluster	Region	αi		α'i		βi		β'i	
1	July 25, 1996	Continental Airlines Inc	MFSC	NORAM	0.0011	(0.0018)	-0.0006	(0.0022)	0.6480	(0.4022)	-0.0547	(0.4925)
2	August 22, 1996	UAL Corp.	MFSC	NORAM	0.0005	(0.0017)	-0.0001	(0.0019)	1.9042 ***	(0.3709)	-0.6134 ***	(0.4089)
3	October 10, 1996	Continental Airlines Inc	MFSC	NORAM	-0.0018	(0.0020)	0.0034	(0.0020)	0.9146 *	(0.4653)	-0.6778	(0.4060)
4	November 21, 1996	AMR Corporation	MFSC	NORAM	-0.0011	(0.0015)	0.0008	(0.0013)	1.3911 ***	(0.3335)	-0.1172 ***	(0.2254)
5	June 10, 1997	Delta Air Lines Inc	MFSC	NORAM	0.0007	(0.0015)	0.0012	(0.0015)	1.0735 ***	(0.2489)	0.0170 ***	(0.1684)
6	September 19, 1997	Northwest Airlines Corporation	MFSC	NORAM	-0.0008	(0.0021)	0.0023	(0.0021)	0.9416 ***	(0.3079)	0.8400 ***	(0.2296)
7	October 31, 1997	US Airways Group Inc	MFSC	NORAM	0.0022	(0.0026)	-0.0004	(0.0020)	1.6988 ***	(0.3169)	-0.7668 ***	(0.2370)
8	January 22, 1998	Southwest Airlines Company	LCC	NORAM	0.0037 *	(0.0021)	-0.0039	(0.0019)	1.2465 ***	(0.2231)	-0.3906 ***	(0.2622)
9	October 26, 1998	British Airways PLC	MFSC	EMEA	-0.0025	(0.0019)	0.0032	(0.0024)	1.2868 ***	(0.1574)	-0.7182 **	(0.2730)
10	December 22, 1998	Delta Air Lines Inc	MFSC	NORAM	-0.0023	(0.0021)	0.0025	(0.0025)	1.4189 ***	(0.1710)	-0.4085 ***	(0.3052)
11	February 18, 1999	Northwest Airlines Corporation	MFSC	NORAM	-0.0025	(0.0035)	0.0041	(0.0026)	1.8532 ***	(0.2863)	-0.9766 **	(0.3560)
12	June 29, 2000	Southwest Airlines Company	LCC	NORAM	0.0014	(0.0022)	0.0033 **	(0.0021)	0.6910 ***	(0.2068)	0.0896 ***	(0.2270)
13	July 9, 2001	Northwest Airlines Corporation	MFSC	NORAM	-0.0010	(0.0021)	-0.0005	(0.0040)	1.1554 ***	(0.1932)	1.4665 ***	(0.3925)
14	January 24, 2002	Ryanair Holdings PLC	LCC	EMEA	0.0009	(0.0027)	0.0001	(0.0023)	1.1625 ***	(0.2629)	-0.4102 ***	(0.2058)
15	December 31, 2002	Easyjet PLC	LCC	EMEA	-0.0002	(0.0035)	-0.0019	(0.0036)	0.9553 ***	(0.2220)	-0.2309 **	(0.3432)
16	April 24, 2003	Jetblue Airways Corp.	LCC	NORAM	0.0014	(0.0023)	0.0025 **	(0.0018)	1.0776 ***	(0.2049)	0.2045 ***	(0.2463)
17	June 10, 2003	Jetblue Airways Corp.	LCC	NORAM	0.0015	(0.0019)	-0.0016	(0.0026)	1.2510 ***	(0.1814)	0.3222 ***	(0.3939)
18	June 27, 2003	All Nippon Airways Company Limited	MFSC	APAC	0.0007	(0.0019)	-0.0005	(0.0020)	-0.2170	(0.1753)	1.7027 ***	(0.3239)
19	July 26, 2004	All Nippon Airways Company Limited	MFSC	APAC	0.0012	(0.0014)	-0.0003	(0.0010)	0.9384 ***	(0.2109)	-0.4859 **	(0.1936)
20	May 10, 2005	Japan Airlines Corp.	MFSC	APAC	0.0000	(0.0009)	-0.0010	(0.0010)	0.7699 ***	(0.1802)	-0.5511	(0.1996)
21	May 12, 2005	Ryanair Holdings PLC	LCC	EMEA	0.0007	(0.0014)	-0.0003	(0.0012)	1.2590 ***	(0.2727)	-0.4023 ***	(0.2504)
22	April 20, 2006	Southwest Airlines Company	LCC	NORAM	0.0002	(0.0013)	-0.0010	(0.0014)	0.5005 **	(0.2449)	0.6062 ***	(0.1867)
23	October 5, 2006	Northwest Airlines Corporation	MFSC	NORAM	0.0032	(0.0037)	-0.0054	(0.0101)	0.5618	(0.5076)	2.5597 *	(1.8064)
24	December 22, 2006	Air Berlin PLC	LCC	EMEA	0.0034	(0.0022)	-0.0048	(0.0017)	1.3238 ***	(0.3932)	0.7175 ***	(0.2838)
25	September 5, 2007	China Southern Airlines Company Limited	MFSC	APAC	0.0107 ***	(0.0031)	-0.0107	(0.0039)	-0.2582	(0.4110)	0.5680	(0.3794)
26	September 20, 2007	Deutsche Lufthansa AG	MFSC	EMEA	0.0001	(0.0003)	0.0007 *	(0.0004)	0.1416 ***	(0.0345)	0.0041 ***	(0.0394)
27	October 2, 2007	US Airways Group Inc	MFSC	NORAM	-0.0047 *	(0.0028)	-0.0024 *	(0.0041)	1.6422 ***	(0.3518)	-0.6707 ***	(0.3613)
28	February 14, 2008	TAM SA	MFSC	LATAM	0.0003	(0.0024)	-0.0002	(0.0026)	2.0911 ***	(0.2314)	-0.3689 ***	(0.2796)

** Statistically significant at the 10% level*

*** Statistically significant at the 5% level*

**** Statistically significant at the 1% level*

Table 25: *Alpha, beta and the shift in risk with aircraft orders (41-120 aircraft per order)*

This table presents the standard market model parameters α and β and standard errors (in parentheses) for each firm, estimated over a period of 130 trading days ending on the day before the incident. It also presents the market model parameters α′ and β′ which reflect a shift in risk after the incident. α′ [β′] is calculated as the difference between the firm's α [β] before the incident and the firm's α [β] after the incident, estimated over a period of 131 trading days starting with the day of incident, Underlying daily stock data were retrieved from Thomson Financial Datastream (2009). Benchmark is the MSCI World Index. The number of trading days refers to the trading days of the New York Stock Exchange (NYSE). Statistical significance is based on t-statistics.

	β_i	β'_i	Aircraft	Date	MFSC	NFSC	LCC	FREIGHT	APAC	EMEA	LATAM	NORAM
β_i	1											
β'_i	-0.4071	1										
Aircraft per order	0.1633	0.0148	1									
Order Date	-0.1178	0.2087	-0.0778	1								
MFSC	-0.1226	-0.0634	-0.0572	0.0245	1							
NFSC	-0.0736	0.0302	-0.1620	-0.1331	-0.3588	1						
LCC	0.1409	0.0952	0.2439	0.1475	-0.7417	-0.1494	1					
FREIGHTER	0.0758	-0.0762	-0.1540	-0.1781	-0.3256	-0.0656	-0.1356	1				
APAC	-0.5272	0.0928	-0.1886	0.3127	0.3612	-0.1494	-0.2465	-0.1356	1			
EMEA	0.0492	-0.0738	-0.0061	0.1533	-0.0454	-0.1448	0.2080	-0.1314	-0.2992	1		
LATAM	0.0695	-0.0245	-0.0218	0.1556	0.1399	-0.0502	-0.1038	-0.0456	-0.1038	-0.1006	1	
NORAM	0.3816	-0.0083	0.1731	-0.4497	-0.3194	0.2659	0.0731	0.2412	-0.5620	-0.5445	-0.1889	1

Table 26: *Correlation of beta and shift in beta with incident specific factors in aircraft orders*

This table presents standard correlation coefficients between company stocks' betas preceding an aircraft order, the shift in risk after the order and selected descriptive factors such as the number of aircraft per order the date of order, and the carrier and region cluster the ordering companies belong to.

Overall, it can be concluded that

- Betas and shifts in betas are highly significant; alphas and shifts in alphas are not
- NORAM companies on average carry higher and APAC firms lower betas
- Betas shift after aircraft accidents and after aircraft orders, and adjust towards market's beta of 1.0
- How severe the accident is in terms of fatalities and injuries or how many aircraft are ordered does not play a role in the change of risk

The company specific alphas and betas before and after accidents and firm orders are used to calculate the abnormal returns on the first trading day following the incident as well as for the five consecutive trading days. The abnormal returns are subsequently used as dependent variables in multivariate regressions to evaluate short term distinguishing factors between the individual companies in scope.

7.3.3 Special events – Analysis results: Stock market's reaction

Abnormal return as a reaction to aircraft accidents and firm orders

Abnormal returns were calculated for each firm and event – aircraft accident or firm order – using equation 2 in Chapter 7.1.1.1 and applying alphas and betas estimated in the previous section. The analysis focuses on the short term, i.e. the first trading day (y_1) after the incident and the five consecutive trading days following this day ($y_{2\text{-}6}$).

For aircraft accidents, y_1 is defined as the first day on which the stock market could react to the accident. Depending on the time of accident in relation to the opening hours of the home stock exchange market of the affected company, y_1 can be equal to the day of accident or

the day after the accident. For example, when a Europe based aircraft crashes on a Friday morning central European time, news will spread immediately in the media and the European stock market has the possibility to react on the same day. Does the aircraft crash on a Friday evening, the home stock exchange is already closed and the market participants will have to wait for its opening on Monday morning to respond to the incident.
Aircraft firm orders in the sample were all announced by the ordering company or the manufacturer on the day of order, i.e. during business hours, giving the home stock market enough time to react. Here, y_1 is equal to the day of announcement, which was obtained from Ascend Worldwide Ltd. (2010) and cross-checked with media reports and the companies' and manufacturers' homepages to make sure it is the first announcement day and no information was injected into the market prior to the day published by Ascend Worldwide Ltd.

All events were treated as isolated events, i.e. no carrier or region portfolio was created due to the fact that some airlines are represented with more than one accident or order in the sample which might lead to company-biased portfolios. Whether the market differentiated between the different company types is evaluated in subsequent regressions.

Table 27, Table 28, and Table 29 illustrate the abnormal returns y_1-y_6 and cumulated abnormal returns $y_{2\text{-}6}$ in the market's reaction on aircraft accidents, firm orders with 1-40 aircraft per order, and firm orders with 41-120 aircraft per order, respectively. The significance of the abnormal returns is based on t-statistics. Adjusted R^2 and F-statistics present the explanatory power of the regressions.

Not all accidents cause abnormal returns on the first trading day, but if so, the abnormal return is mainly negative ranging between -0.1639*** (Korean Air Lines, December 22, 1999) and -0.0267** (FedEx, December 18, 2003). On trading days y_2-y_6, the same stocks that reacted on the first trading day, show again abnormal returns though with both positive and negative sign. Abnormal returns seem to occur mainly for companies that had experienced more than one hull loss in the past, i.e. are top ranked in the list numbers of total loss accidents, namely American Airlines, China Airlines, Korean Air Lines, and FedEx (cf. Chapter 7.3.1, Table 19*Table*). Perhaps, the market becomes sensitized when a company repeatedly loses aircraft. This is then reflected in abnormal returns.

Table 28 and Table 29 show that neither aircraft orders with numbers of aircraft per order within a 2σ range (1-40 aircraft per order) nor extreme orders outside this range (41-120 aircraft per order) generally cause significant abnormal returns. In both samples only 35-40% of the incidents lead to significant abnormal returns on at least one of the days y_1-y_6 and the reaction can have both a positive or negative sign. Further, no clear reaction day can be identified. In the sample of orders with 1-40 aircraft per order, the significant abnormal returns are almost evenly distributed over the six trading days. In the sample of orders with

41-120 aircraft per order, most significant abnormal returns occur on the first trading days, though also some on the other days. Between the carrier types or regions no clear difference can be observed.

In a next step, the estimated abnormal returns are used as dependent variable in regression analysis to test against a series of independent explanatory and control variables to see how the stock market differentiated between the individual firms with regard to both aircraft accidents and firm orders. Based on the overall low significance of abnormal returns caused by aircraft accidents or orders, the explanatory power of the regression models is expected to be of less significance, too. It is questionable if conclusions can be drawn from the regressions at all.

Count	Accident Date	Company	Company Cluster	Region	y1	y2	y3	y4	y5	y6	R² adj.	F-stat.	∑y2-6
1	July 2, 1994	US Airways Group Inc	MFSC	NORAM	-0.0333	0.0224	-0.0168	0.0037	0.0079	0.0430	-0.01	0.46	0.0603
2	August 10, 1994	Korean Air Lines Company Limited	MFSC	APAC	0.0378 *	-0.0022	-0.0005	0.0124	-0.0168	-0.0167	0.00	0.84	-0.0238
3	September 8, 1994	US Airways Group Inc	MFSC	NORAM	-0.0777 **	-0.0200	-0.0200	0.0217	-0.0200	-0.0209	0.00	0.94	-0.0592
4	December 20, 1995	AMR Corp.	MFSC	NORAM	-0.0157	0.0091	0.0354 **	-0.0031	-0.0054	-0.0074	0.00	1.20	0.0287
5	September 5, 1996	Federal Express/FedEx Corp	FREIGHTER	NORAM	-0.0116	0.0198	-0.0043	0.0009	-0.0049	-0.0144	-0.01	0.70	-0.0028
6	July 6, 1997	Delta Air Lines Inc	MFSC	NORAM	-0.0172	-0.0081	-0.0152	-0.0113	-0.0241	0.0152	0.00	0.90	-0.0435
7	July 31, 1997	Federal Express/FedEx Corp	FREIGHTER	NORAM	-0.0120	0.0186	0.0220	-0.0007	-0.0214	-0.0126	-0.01	0.73	0.0059
8	August 6, 1997	Korean Air Lines Company Limited	MFSC	APAC	-0.0550	0.0212	0.0257	0.0133	0.0229	0.0223	-0.02	0.29	0.1054
9	December 16, 1997	Air Canada Inc	MFSC	NORAM	-0.0145	-0.0019	0.0231	-0.0201	0.0078	0.0075	-0.01	0.56	0.0165
10	December 19, 1997	Singapore Airlines Limited	MFSC	APAC	-0.0501 **	0.0229	0.0792 ***	0.0018	-0.0102	-0.0421 *	0.04	3.02 ***	0.0517
11	February 9, 1998	AMR Corp.	MFSC	NORAM	0.0100	-0.0103	0.0285	-0.0229	-0.0007	0.0245	0.00	1.10	0.0191
12	February 16, 1998	China Airlines Limited	MFSC	APAC	-0.0733 ***	-0.0723 ***	-0.0393 *	0.0077	0.1041 ***	-0.0530 **	0.13	7.65 ***	-0.0528
13	August 5, 1998	Korean Air Lines Company Limited	MFSC	APAC	-0.1289 **	0.0349	-0.0299	-0.0175	-0.0266	0.0107	0.00	1.08	-0.0284
14	December 11, 1998	Thai Airways International Public Company	MFSC	APAC	-0.0396	0.0252	0.0078	-0.0248	0.0065	-0.0253	-0.02	0.25	-0.0107
15	March 4, 1999	Air France	MFSC	EMEA	-0.0222	0.0043	0.0002	-0.0174	0.0187	-0.0345	-0.01	0.66	-0.0287
16	March 5, 1999	Air France	MFSC	EMEA	0.0000	-0.0175	0.0184	-0.0347	0.0099	-0.0005	-0.01	0.56	-0.0245
17	March 15, 1999	Korean Air Lines Company Limited	MFSC	APAC	-0.0773	0.0418	-0.0365	-0.0601	0.0460	-0.0360	0.00	1.08	-0.0448
18	April 15, 1999	Korean Air Lines Company Limited	MFSC	APAC	0.0888 *	-0.0115	-0.0154	-0.0122	-0.0984 *	0.0258	0.00	1.19	-0.1117
19	June 1, 1999	AMR Corporation	MFSC	NORAM	-0.0157	0.0208	-0.0070	0.0094	-0.0255	-0.0138	-0.01	0.45	-0.0162
20	August 22, 1999	China Airlines Limited	MFSC	APAC	-0.0535 ***	-0.0180	-0.0244	0.0221	-0.0284	-0.0077	0.03	2.18 **	-0.0565
21	October 17, 1999	Federal Express/FedEx Corp	FREIGHTER	NORAM	-0.0213	-0.0171	-0.0029	0.0165	-0.0085	-0.0108	-0.02	0.27	-0.0227
22	December 22, 1999	Korean Air Lines Company Limited	MFSC	APAC	-0.1635 ***	-0.1071 **	-0.0377	0.1300 **	0.0014	0.0010	0.06	3.54 ***	-0.0123
23	January 31, 2000	Alaska Air Group Inc	MFSC	NORAM	-0.0244	-0.0094	-0.0015	-0.0347	-0.0142	-0.0052	-0.01	0.54	-0.0649
24	March 5, 2000	Southwest Airlines Company	LCC	NORAM	-0.0566 **	0.0652 ***	0.0219	0.0263	0.0192	0.0027	0.04	2.70 **	0.1353
25	July 25, 2000	Air France	MFSC	EMEA	-0.0301	0.0126	-0.0024	-0.0069	-0.0082	0.0266	-0.01	0.54	0.0217
26	October 31, 2000	Singapore Airlines Limited	MFSC	APAC	-0.0113	0.0113	-0.0526 **	-0.0293	0.0291	0.0051	0.02	1.68	-0.0364
27	October 8, 2001	SAS AB	MFSC	EMEA	-0.0284	0.0209	-0.0042	0.0348	0.0118	0.0069	-0.01	0.60	0.0701
28	November 12, 2001	AMR Corp.	MFSC	NORAM	-0.0813 **	0.0070	0.0480	0.0380	0.0633 *	0.0187	0.02	1.78	0.1750
29	May 25, 2002	China Airlines Limited	MFSC	APAC	-0.0714 ***	-0.0646 **	-0.0632 **	-0.0112	-0.0570 **	-0.0087	0.06	3.72 ***	-0.2047
30	July 26, 2002	Federal Express/FedEx Corp	FREIGHTER	NORAM	0.0095	-0.0186	0.0324 *	-0.0165	-0.0294	-0.0117	0.01	1.25	-0.0438
31	August 30, 2002	TAM SA	MFSC	LATAM	0.0022	-0.0081	-0.0172	0.0028	-0.0135	0.0124	-0.01	0.37	-0.0236
32	December 18, 2003	Federal Express/FedEx Corp	FREIGHTER	NORAM	-0.0267 **	-0.0054	-0.0055	-0.0077	-0.0035	-0.0004	0.00	1.09	-0.0226
33	November 7, 2004	Deutsche Lufthansa AG	MFSC	EMEA	-0.0019	0.0006	-0.0042	-0.0008	0.0002	0.0048	-0.02	0.27	0.0008
34	August 2, 2005	Air France-KLM	MFSC	EMEA	-0.0110	0.0001	-0.0098	0.0343 ***	0.0000	0.0086	0.01	1.62	0.0334
35	February 7, 2006	United Parcel Service, Inc	FREIGHTER	NORAM	-0.0059	0.0160	-0.0026	0.0154	0.0060	0.0098	0.00	0.83	0.0446
36	July 28, 2006	Federal Express/FedEx Corp	FREIGHTER	NORAM	-0.0041	-0.0058	-0.0096	0.0234 *	-0.0155	-0.0019	0.00	1.04	-0.0093
37	July 17, 2007	TAM SA	MFSC	LATAM	-0.0789 ***	-0.0744 ***	-0.0130	-0.0049	0.0077	-0.0225	0.06	3.86 ***	-0.1071
38	November 9, 2007	Iberia SA	MFSC	EMEA	-0.0135	0.0093	0.0219	0.0068	0.0571 ***	0.0103	0.01	1.56	0.1054
39	January 17, 2008	British Airways PLC	MFSC	EMEA	0.0010	0.0108	0.0722 **	0.0277	0.0063	-0.0211	0.01	1.40	0.0960
40	February 2, 2008	Atlas Air/Atlas Air Worldwide Holdings Inc	FREIGHTER	NORAM	0.0010	0.0229	0.0064	0.0005	0.0000	0.0049	-0.01	0.38	0.0348
41	December 20, 2008	Continental Airlines Inc	MFSC	NORAM	-0.0061	0.0137	0.0132	0.0317	0.0056	0.0641	-0.02	0.15	0.1282
42	January 15, 2009	US Airways Group Inc	MFSC	NORAM	0.0586	0.0992	0.0295	0.0067	-0.0455	0.0498	-0.01	0.44	0.1396
43	March 23, 2009	Federal Express/FedEx Corp	FREIGHTER	NORAM	-0.0148	-0.0137	0.0600 **	0.0020	0.0237	-0.0149	0.00	1.18	0.0573
44	June 1, 2009	Air France-KLM	MFSC	EMEA	-0.0378	0.0305	-0.0191	-0.0203	-0.0090	-0.0305	0.00	0.98	-0.0484
45	December 22, 2009	AMR Corp.	MFSC	NORAM	-0.0107	-0.0091	-0.0007	-0.0568	-0.0010	0.0072	-0.01	0.47	-0.0605

** Statistically significant at the 10% level*

*** Statistically significant at the 5% level*

**** Statistically significant at the 1% level*

Table 27: *Abnormal returns y_1 - y_6 and cumulated abnormal returns $y_{2\text{-}6}$ after aircraft hull losses*

This table presents the abnormal returns of all firms with standard errors (in parentheses) estimated using equation 2 (cf. section 7.1.1) for the trading days y_1 - y_6. Standard market model parameters α, α', β, and β' used for the MVRM were estimated as presented in Table 22. This table also presents adjusted R^2 and F-statistics illustrating the explanatory power of the regression model as well as cumulative abnormal returns for the period $y_{2\text{-}6}$. Estimates of significance are based on t-statistics.

Count	Order Date	Company (Customer)	Company Cluster	Region	y1	y2	y3	y4	y5	y6	R² adj.	F-stat.	∑y2-6
1	June 16, 1994	Deutsche Lufthansa AG	MFSC	EMEA	-0.0333 **	-0.0022	-0.0521 ***	0.0579 ***	-0.0017	0.0244	0.08	4.87 ***	0.0264
2	October 13, 1994	Southwest Airlines Company	LCC	NORAM	-0.0219	-0.0032	-0.0312	0.0336	0.0350	-0.0201	0.01	1.32	0.0141
3	December 22, 1994	Federal Express/FedEx Corp	FREIGTHER	NORAM	-0.0093	0.0143	-0.0006	0.0058	0.0002	0.0031	-0.02	0.25	0.0228
4	June 12, 1995	Deutsche Lufthansa AG	MFSC	EMEA	0.0014	-0.0084	0.0142	-0.0091	0.0038	0.0114	-0.01	0.49	0.0119
5	August 30, 1996	Federal Express/FedEx Corp	FREIGTHER	NORAM	0.0021	0.0031	-0.0117	-0.0141	-0.0110	0.0204	0.00	0.82	-0.0132
6	September 2, 1996	British Airways PLC	MFSC	EMEA	-0.0027	-0.0211 *	0.0122	0.0018	-0.0121	-0.0037	0.00	0.95	-0.0230
7	December 20, 1996	Singapore Airlines Limited	MFSC	APAC	-0.0157 **	0.0136 *	-0.0037	0.0007	-0.0015	-0.0012	0.01	1.32	0.0079
8	June 9, 1997	Atlas Air/Atlas Air Worldwide Holdings Inc	FREIGTHER	NORAM	0.1105 ***	0.0500	0.0335	-0.0274	-0.0085	-0.0094	0.02	1.98 **	0.0383
9	June 9, 1997	Malaysian Airline System Berhad	MFSC	APAC	0.0338	0.0212	0.0047	0.0047	-0.0217	0.0033	-0.02	0.26	0.0122
10	July 1, 1997	Air France	MFSC	EMEA	0.0044	-0.0026	0.0050	-0.0008	0.0076	-0.0049	-0.02	0.01	0.0043
11	October 20, 1997	Air Canada Inc	MFSC	NORAM	-0.0017	-0.0061	0.0003	0.0181	-0.0033	-0.0110	-0.02	0.22	-0.0020
12	May 19, 1998	Delta Air Lines Inc	MFSC	NORAM	-0.0334 *	0.0011	-0.0031	0.0151	0.0004	0.0245	0.00	0.81	0.0381
13	November 23, 1998	Continental Airlines Inc	MFSC	NORAM	-0.0006	0.0099	-0.0469	0.0119	0.0341	-0.0554 *	0.00	1.18	-0.0465
14	December 31, 1998	ATA Holdings	LCC	NORAM	0.0045	0.0011	-0.0302	0.0209	-0.0002	0.0172	-0.02	0.22	0.0088
15	June 1, 1999	Delta Air Lines Inc	MFSC	NORAM	0.0293	-0.0086	-0.0062	0.0002	0.0228	-0.0133	-0.01	0.39	-0.0052
16	August 31, 1999	US Airways Group Inc	MFSC	NORAM	-0.0071	-0.0175	-0.0206	0.0063	-0.0005	-0.0260	-0.02	0.29	-0.0583
17	October 20, 1999	FLYi, Inc.	NFSC	NORAM	0.0390	-0.0197	-0.0264	0.0799 *	-0.0017	-0.0195	0.00	0.91	0.0125
18	November 30, 1999	AMR Corp.	MFSC	NORAM	0.0328	-0.0308	-0.0008	0.0034	-0.0157	0.0190	-0.01	0.54	-0.0248
19	June 27, 2000	EVA Airways Corp.	MFSC	APAC	-0.0151	0.0148	-0.0169	0.0063	-0.0052	-0.0189	-0.02	0.24	-0.0199
20	August 1, 2000	UAL Corp.	MFSC	NORAM	-0.0228	-0.0084	0.0145	-0.0063	0.0086	-0.0247	-0.01	0.37	-0.0163
21	November 30, 2000	America West Holdings	LCC	NORAM	-0.0284	0.0196	-0.0185	0.0324	0.0016	0.0097	-0.01	0.60	0.0448
22	November 30, 2000	United Parcel Service, Inc	FREIGTHER	NORAM	0.0145	-0.0020	-0.0132	-0.0087	0.0281	-0.0070	-0.01	0.74	-0.0029
23	January 16, 2001	Northwest Airlines Corporation	MFSC	NORAM	0.0091	0.0148	-0.0670 **	-0.0717 **	0.0012	0.0064	0.02	2.09 *	-0.1162
24	April 18, 2001	SAS AB	MFSC	EMEA	-0.0221	0.0199	0.0718 ***	0.0152	0.0121	0.0018	0.02	1.81 *	0.1208
25	August 21, 2001	Airtran Holdings Inc	LCC	NORAM	0.0065	-0.0885 *	-0.1733 ***	-0.0378	0.0095	0.0660	0.06	3.54 ***	-0.2242
26	September 25, 2001	Hawaiian Holdings Inc	NFSC	NORAM	-0.0242	-0.0273	0.0229	0.0476	-0.0503	-0.0153	-0.01	0.55	-0.0224
27	October 8, 2001	TAM SA	MFSC	LATAM	-0.0129	0.0030	-0.0024	-0.0053	-0.0019	0.0019	-0.02	0.34	-0.0047
28	April 15, 2002	Midwest Express Hlg./Midwest Air Group Inc	NFSC	NORAM	-0.0252	0.0072	0.0027	0.1271 ***	-0.0029	0.0245	0.04	2.72 **	0.1586
29	October 1, 2002	Iberia SA	MFSC	EMEA	-0.0263	0.0609 **	0.0198	0.0272	-0.0129	0.0148	0.01	1.47	0.1098
30	October 7, 2002	Japan Airlines Corp.	MFSC	APAC	-0.0278	0.0011	-0.0079	-0.0185	0.0213	0.0015	-0.01	0.59	-0.0025
31	November 25, 2002	Thai Airways International Public Compan	MFSC	APAC	0.0211	-0.0247	-0.0029	0.0542 *	0.0205	0.0136	0.00	0.98	0.0606
32	October 9, 2003	Westjet Airlines Limited	NFSC	NORAM	-0.0156	0.0044	-0.0040	-0.0026	0.0037	0.0591 ***	0.01	1.43	0.0607
33	December 17, 2003	Korean Air Lines Company Limited	MFSC	APAC	-0.0478 *	-0.0212	-0.0078	-0.0209	0.0314	0.0016	0.00	0.84	-0.0170
34	August 25, 2004	Air New Zealand Limited	MFSC	APAC	-0.0385 **	-0.0021	0.0211	-0.0047	0.0206	0.0062	0.00	1.13	0.0412
35	November 23, 2004	EVA Airways Corp.	MFSC	APAC	0.0221	-0.0182	0.0257	0.0172	0.0077	-0.0038	-0.01	0.64	0.0285
36	June 13, 2005	Ryanair Holdings PLC	LCC	EMEA	-0.0048	-0.0096	0.0023	-0.0158	0.0110	-0.0215	-0.01	0.75	-0.0336
37	July 13, 2005	China Eastern Airlines Corp. Limited	MFSC	APAC	-0.0262	0.0034	-0.0627 **	0.0358	-0.0069	0.0226	0.02	1.78	-0.0076
38	August 16, 2005	United Parcel Service, Inc	FREIGTHER	NORAM	-0.0063	0.0039	0.0022	-0.0060	0.0073	0.0000	-0.02	0.24	0.0074
39	November 30, 2005	El Al Israel Airlines Limited	MFSC	EMEA	-0.0179	-0.0035	-0.0055	0.0032	-0.0113	0.0229	-0.01	0.48	0.0059
40	December 14, 2005	Cathay Pacific Airways Limited	MFSC	APAC	-0.0066	0.0097	-0.0018	0.0164	0.0038	0.0056	-0.01	0.74	0.0338
41	December 16, 2005	China Southern Airlines Company Limited	MFSC	APAC	-0.0009	0.0384 *	0.0070	-0.0159	0.0023	-0.0039	-0.01	0.58	0.0279
42	December 21, 2005	Easyjet PLC	LCC	EMEA	0.0064	-0.0036	-0.0019	-0.0014	0.0068	-0.0093	-0.02	0.08	-0.0095
43	February 2, 2006	Alaska Air Group Inc	MFSC	NORAM	0.0281	-0.0022	-0.0259	-0.0033	0.0160	0.0093	-0.01	0.73	-0.0061
44	March 30, 2006	Qantas Airways Limited	MFSC	APAC	-0.0061	-0.0140	0.0097	0.0045	0.0052	-0.0070	-0.02	0.32	-0.0016
45	April 1, 2006	Frontier Airlines, Inc.	LCC	NORAM	-0.0449	0.0380	-0.0105	-0.0379	0.0530	-0.0431	0.01	1.34	-0.0006
46	December 14, 2006	All Nippon Airways Company Limited	MFSC	APAC	-0.0032	-0.0110	-0.0097	-0.0135	0.0032	-0.0051	-0.01	0.51	-0.0360
47	February 21, 2007	British Airways PLC	MFSC	EMEA	-0.0039	0.0059	-0.0071	-0.0115	0.0110	0.0123	-0.02	0.36	0.0106
48	October 31, 2007	Lan Airlines SA	MFSC	LATAM	-0.0027	0.0185	-0.0186	-0.0131	-0.0191	-0.0252	0.00	0.95	-0.0575
49	November 14, 2007	Air China Limited	MFSC	APAC	0.0222	0.0111	0.0012	-0.0759 *	-0.0277	-0.0184	-0.01	0.65	-0.1097
50	November 21, 2007	US Airways Group Inc	MFSC	NORAM	0.0677	0.0060	0.0149	-0.0204	0.0011	0.0590	-0.01	0.66	0.0606

Table 28: *Abnormal returns y_1 - y_6 and cumulated abnormal returns $y_{2\text{-}6}$ after aircraft orders (1-40 aircraft per order)*

(Table continued on next page)

Count	Order Date	Company (Customer)	Company Cluster	Region	y1	y2	y3	y4	y5	y6	R² adj.	F-stat.	∑y2-6
51	December 3, 2007	Iberia SA	MFSC	EMEA	0.0028	0.0103	-0.0058	-0.0061	0.0100	-0.0067	-0.02	0.11	0.0016
52	December 12, 2007	Finnair OYJ	MFSC	EMEA	-0.0278	-0.0158	-0.0261	-0.0257	-0.0040	-0.0452 **	0.02	1.71	-0.1168
53	January 15, 2008	Jetblue Airways Corp.	LCC	NORAM	0.0086	0.0666 *	0.0312	-0.0338	0.0376	0.0200	0.00	1.21	0.1216
54	January 22, 2008	China Airlines Limited	MFSC	APAC	-0.0718 ***	-0.0410	0.0230	-0.0077	-0.0701 ***	-0.0085	0.05	3.05 ***	-0.1043
55	March 31, 2008	AER Lingus Group PLC	LCC	EMEA	-0.0043	-0.0061	0.0205	-0.0459 *	0.0156	-0.0194	-0.01	0.75	-0.0351
56	June 13, 2008	Korean Air Lines Company Limited	MFSC	APAC	-0.0179	0.0402	0.0046	0.0344	-0.0094	0.0370	-0.02	0.34	0.1068
57	March 26, 2009	Virgin Blue Holdings Limited	LCC	APAC	-0.0761	0.0143	-0.0057	-0.0037	0.0133	0.1276 **	0.00	1.17	0.1459
58	November 25, 2009	Air Berlin PLC	LCC	EMEA	0.0095	-0.0214	0.0233	-0.0110	-0.0175	0.0082	-0.01	0.52	-0.0184

** Statistically significant at the 10% level*

*** Statistically significant at the 5% level*

**** Statistically significant at the 1% level*

Table 28 (continued): *Abnormal returns y_1-y_6 and cumulated abnormal returns $y_{2\text{-}6}$ after aircraft orders (1-40 aircraft per order)*

This table presents the abnormal returns of all firms with standard errors (in parentheses) estimated using equation 2 (cf. section 7.1.1) for the trading days y_1 - y_6. after an aircraft firm order including 1-40 aircraft Standard market model parameters α, α′, β, and β′ used for the MVRM were estimated as presented in Table 22. This table also presents adjusted R^2 and F-statistics illustrating the explanatory power of the regression model as well as cumulative abnormal returns for the period $y_{2\text{-}6}$. Estimates of significance are based on t-statistics.

Count	Order Date	Company (Customer)	Company Cluster	Region	y1	y2	y3	y4	y5	y6	R² adj.	F-stat.	∑y2-6
1	July 25, 1996	Continental Airlines Inc	MFSC	NORAM	-0.0001	0.0218	0.0112	0.0223	0.0037	-0.0354	-0.01	0.74	0.0236
2	August 22, 1996	UAL Corp.	MFSC	NORAM	-0.0192	-0.0354 *	0.0111	0.0057	0.0034	0.0112	-0.01	0.78	-0.0039
3	October 10, 1996	Continental Airlines Inc	MFSC	NORAM	-0.0013	0.0120	-0.0028	0.0073	0.0081	-0.0170	-0.02	0.17	0.0075
4	November 21, 1996	AMR Corporation	MFSC	NORAM	-0.0045	-0.0017	0.0131	-0.0195	-0.0081	0.0023	-0.01	0.42	-0.0139
5	June 10, 1997	Delta Air Lines Inc	MFSC	NORAM	-0.0459 ***	-0.0025	-0.0181	0.0125	-0.0250	0.0134	0.02	2.10 *	-0.0197
6	September 19, 1997	Northwest Airlines Corporation	MFSC	NORAM	0.0101	-0.0071	-0.0085	0.0193	-0.0009	-0.0365	-0.01	0.57	-0.0337
7	October 31, 1997	US Airways Group Inc	MFSC	NORAM	0.0110	0.0125	-0.0084	0.0035	0.0048	-0.0063	-0.02	0.10	0.0061
8	January 22, 1998	Southwest Airlines Company	LCC	NORAM	-0.0334	-0.0361	0.0033	-0.0322	0.0695 ***	-0.0278	0.04	3.02 ***	-0.0233
9	October 26, 1998	British Airways PLC	MFSC	EMEA	-0.0284	0.0607 **	0.0510 **	-0.0534 **	0.0309	0.0247	0.05	3.35 ***	0.1139
10	December 22, 1998	Delta Air Lines Inc	MFSC	NORAM	0.0017	-0.0250	0.0069	-0.0010	0.0032	-0.0186	-0.02	0.25	-0.0345
11	February 18, 1999	Northwest Airlines Corporation	MFSC	NORAM	0.0021	0.0175	-0.0062	-0.0173	0.0460	-0.0205	-0.01	0.43	0.0196
12	June 29, 2000	Southwest Airlines Company	LCC	NORAM	-0.0121	-0.0277	0.0150	-0.0045	0.0368	-0.0094	-0.01	0.76	0.0101
13	July 9, 2001	Northwest Airlines Corporation	MFSC	NORAM	-0.0086	0.0080	0.0230	0.0055	-0.0134	0.0523	-0.01	0.46	0.0755
14	January 24, 2002	Ryanair Holdings PLC	LCC	EMEA	-0.0177	0.0161	0.0310	0.0221	-0.0373	0.0474 *	0.00	1.20	0.0792
15	December 31, 2002	Easyjet PLC	LCC	EMEA	-0.0239	0.0021	0.0340	0.0301	-0.0354	-0.0097	-0.01	0.40	0.0210
16	April 24, 2003	Jetblue Airways Corp.	LCC	NORAM	0.0460 *	-0.0038	0.0092	-0.0119	-0.0219	-0.0190	0.00	0.96	-0.0475
17	June 10, 2003	Jetblue Airways Corp.	LCC	NORAM	-0.0553 **	0.0269	0.0181	0.0189	-0.0053	0.0239	0.01	1.25	0.0826
18	June 27, 2003	All Nippon Airways Company Limited	MFSC	APAC	0.0017	-0.0079	0.0369 *	0.0126	0.0208	-0.0247	0.00	0.93	0.0378
19	July 26, 2004	All Nippon Airways Company Limited	MFSC	APAC	-0.0209	-0.0081	-0.0099	-0.0206	0.0366 ***	0.0060	0.02	2.11 ***	0.0040
20	May 10, 2005	Japan Airlines Corp.	MFSC	APAC	0.0138	0.0124	-0.0145	0.0078	-0.0167	0.0059	0.01	1.35	-0.0051
21	May 12, 2005	Ryanair Holdings PLC	LCC	EMEA	0.0204	0.0211	-0.0090	0.0091	0.0037	0.0031	0.00	0.80	0.0279
22	April 20, 2006	Southwest Airlines Company	LCC	NORAM	-0.0515 ***	-0.0337 **	0.0402 ***	-0.0190	-0.0051	0.0097	0.08	4.86 ***	-0.0080
23	October 5, 2006	Northwest Airlines Corporation	MFSC	NORAM	-0.0241	0.0234	-0.0013	0.0124	0.0083	-0.0267	-0.02	0.04	0.0161
24	December 22, 2006	Air Berlin PLC	LCC	EMEA	-0.0170	0.0024	-0.0033	0.0207	-0.0040	0.0000	-0.02	0.25	0.0157
25	September 5, 2007	China Southern Airlines Company Limited	MFSC	APAC	0.0033	-0.0087	0.0075	0.0237	0.0379	0.0306	-0.02	0.31	0.0910
26	September 20, 2007	Deutsche Lufthansa AG	MFSC	EMEA	0.0082 **	-0.0008	-0.0008	0.0014	-0.0016	-0.0001	-0.01	0.72	-0.0020
27	October 2, 2007	US Airways Group Inc	MFSC	NORAM	0.0489	0.0221	0.0227	0.0151	0.0306	0.0310	-0.01	0.60	0.1215
28	February 14, 2008	TAM SA	MFSC	LATAM	-0.0346	-0.0329	0.0024	-0.0824 ***	0.0173	-0.0099	0.02	1.96 *	-0.1055

** Statistically significant at the 10% level*

*** Statistically significant at the 5% level*

**** Statistically significant at the 1% level*

Table 29: *Abnormal returns y_1 - y_6 and cumulated abnormal returns $y_{2\text{-}6}$ after aircraft orders (41-120 aircraft per order)*

This table presents the abnormal returns of all firms with standard errors (in parentheses) estimated using equation 2 (cf. section 7.1.1) for the trading days y_1 - y_6 after an aircraft firm order including 41-120 aircraft. Standard market model parameters α, α', β, and β' used for the MVRM were estimated as presented in Table 23. This table also presents adjusted R^2 and F-statistics illustrating the explanatory power of the regression model as well as cumulative abnormal returns for the period $y_{2\text{-}6}$. Estimates of significance are based on t-statistics.

Market's reaction on aircraft accidents and aircraft firm orders

Compared to the analysis of stock market's reaction to shock events the list of explanatory and control variables is adjusted. The variables covering the market and business shares of the individual companies (RPKMKTSHR, FTKMKTSHR, PINT, PFREIGHT) are excluded from the list as no significant correlation is expected. In return, three new variables are added to the regressions of aircraft accidents: FATALITY and INJURY refer to the percentage of passengers and crew killed or injured in the incident, and LOSTVALUE reflects the generic book value of the lost aircraft. One new factor was added to the explanatory variables in regressions of abnormal returns caused by aircraft firm orders: ACPORDER which refers to the number of aircraft per order.

Table 30 illustrates the explanatory power of all variables in the analysis of abnormal returns on trading day one (y_1) and cumulated abnormal returns on trading days two to six ($y_{2\text{-}6}$) caused by aircraft accidents (Model U), aircraft firm orders with 1-40 aircraft per order (Models V1 and V2), and aircraft firm orders with 41-120 aircraft per order (Models W1 and W2).

Given the low significance of the abnormal returns caused by the incidents in scope of the analysis, the findings of the regressions are of equally low descriptive strength. This is shown by adjusted R^2 of maximum 0.29 and F-statistics limited between 2.0 and 6.0 mostly with a statistical significance at the 10% and 5% level. For a review of the test statistics cf. Chapter 7.1.1.

In aircraft accidents, stock market's reaction on the first trading day can be interpreted with good will as linked to the percentage of passengers and crew killed by the incident. The higher the FATALITY rate, the more negatively affected are abnormal returns. Further, regional stock markets seem to make a difference. The regression results give the impression that the Asia Pacific stock market (APAC) penalizes their carriers more for an aircraft hull loss than the European and North American market.

		Model U1	Model U2	Model V1	Model V2	Model W1	Model W2
Observation period		Post a/c accident	Post a/c accident	Post a/c firm order	Post a/c firm order	Post a/c firm order	Post a/c firm order
Sample		All hull losses 1994-2009	All hull losses 1994-2009	1-40 a/c p. order 1994-20(	1-40 a/c p. order 1994-2009	41-120 a/c p. order 94-09	41-120 a/c p. order 94-09
Sample size		45	45	58	58	28	28
Dependent variable		Abnormal returns (AR) y1	Cumulated ARs y2-6	Abnormal returns (AR) y1	Cumulated ARs y2-6	Abnormal returns (AR) y1	Cumulated ARs y2-6
Cluster	Variable						
Financial	SIZE		+	+	+		
	LIQUIDITY			+			+
	NDTEBITDA			+	-		-
	EBITDAMAR			++			--
	EQITYRAT			-		+	++
	INTRSTCOVRG					-	+
Aircraft fleet	TOTALAC		+				
	OPSLEASE					+	
	STORAC		-				
	nYRORDER			+	-		
	nYROPTION		+			+	
	AVGAGE					-	
Carrier	MFSC		--	-	-		
	NFSC	n/a	n/a	-	+	n/a	n/a
	LCC	n/a	n/a	-	-		
	FREIGHT		--	n/a	n/a	n/a	n/a
Region	APAC	-	-	-			
	EMEA	+					+
	LATAM		--			n/a	n/a
	NORAM	+	+	+			
Event	FATALITY	-		n/a	n/a	n/a	n/a
	INJURY			n/a	n/a	n/a	n/a
	LOSTVALUE			n/a	n/a	n/a	n/a
	ACPORDER						-
	R^2 (adjusted)	≤ 0.13	≤ 0.19	≤ 0.29	≤ 0.12	≤ 0.18	≤ 0.21
	F-statistic	2.07* - 5.25**	1.90* - 3.39**	2.87** - 6.01***	2.14* - 4.23**	2.48* - 4.63**	2.22* - 2.92*

+/- Positive/negative impact on abnormal returns < 0.1/>-0.1
++/-- Positive/negative impact on abnormal returns ≥ 0.1/≤ -0.1
+++/--- Positive/negative impact on abnormal returns ≥ 1.0/≤ -1.0

xxx Statistically significant at the 10% level
xxx Statistically significant at the 5% level
xxx Statistically significant at the 1% level

Table 30: *Overview on regression results for stock market's reaction on aircraft accidents and firm orders*

This table presents a consolidated overview of cross-sectional regression results for the stock market's reaction on aircraft accidents (U), aircraft firm orders with 1-40 aircraft per order (V), and aircraft firm orders with 41-120 aircraft per order (W). Two time windows are observed: the abnormal returns on the first trading day after the incident (y_1) and the cumulated abnormal returns of the five following trading days ($y_{2\text{-}6}$). Accidents refer to all aircraft hull losses of stock traded aircraft operating and holding companies between January 1, 1994 and December 31, 2009. Aircraft firm orders refer to all orders placed by the same company sample in the same time horizon. Orders were split in orders inside and orders outside the 2σ confidence level with regard to the number of aircraft per order. Companies in the sample are selected based on the full availability of data throughout all years in scope. SIZE is the natural logarithm of total assets, LIQUIDITY is cash & equivalents over current liabilities, NDTEBITDA is net debt over EBITDA, EBITDAMAR is EBITDA over total operating revenue, EQITYRAT is owners equity over total assets, INTRSTCOVRG is interest expenses for debt over EBIT, TOTALAC is the total number of jet aircraft, OPSLEASE is the ratio of operating leased aircraft over total aircraft count, STORAC is the ratio of stored aircraft to total aircraft count, nYRORDER and nYROPTION are the number of aircraft orders and purchase options to existing fleet in the next years, and AVGAGE is the average age of existing aircraft. Also, eight dummy variables are included which are equal to one if the firm meets the requirements and equal to zero otherwise: MFSC if the firm is a major full service carrier, NFSC if the firm is a non-major full service carrier, LCC if the firm is a low cost carrier, FREIGHT if the firm is a freight only carrier, APAC, if the firm is Asia Pacific based, EMEA if the firm is based in Europe Middle East or Africa, LATAM if the firm is Latin America based, and NORAM if the firm is North American based. FATALITY and INJURY refer to the percentage of passengers and crew killed and injured in the incident, and LOSTVALUE reflects the generic book value of the lost aircraft. ACPORDER is the number of aircraft per order. The magnitude of the positive and negative influence of the variables on abnormal returns refers to the regression coefficient. Statistical significance is based on t-statistics.

On the five trading days following the incident, the market participants appear to consider accidents as less severe for a company that holds a larger asset base (SIZE), a higher number of aircraft in its fleet (TOTALAC), or a company that holds options for new aircraft purchases. The regional differences remain. The source for differences between the carrier clusters can most likely be found in the correlation between the variables.

In aircraft firm orders, the interpretation of stock market's reaction is equally difficult. SIZE and LIQUIDITY seem to play a positive role, but generally all carrier types' abnormal returns were equally negatively affected. The findings for the remaining variables are not consistent; therefore no further assumptions are made concerning factors that differentiate between companies' abnormal returns in market's reaction on aircraft firm orders.

Looking at the analysis of abnormal returns caused by aircraft accidents and aircraft firm orders of stock traded aircraft operating and holding companies in the years 1994-2009, merely few statements can be made to avoid deceptive conclusions:

(1) Aircraft accidents and aircraft firm orders cause abnormal returns for some but definitively not all companies in scope of the analysis
(2) No clear reaction day can be made out, i.e. not all stocks show abnormal returns on the first trading day but rather spread over the period of six trading days
(3) If abnormal returns occur, they are mostly negative in aircraft accidents but with no clear sign in aircraft firm orders
(4) The low statistical significance of the abnormal returns leads to equally low significance of the regression results
(5) Concluding statements on differencing factors between the companies are not possible because of the low explanatory power of the findings

Overall the analysis of company specific isolated positive and negative events shows that stock markets occasionally respond to aircraft accidents and firm orders but the reaction is mostly of no or low statistical significance. Hence, in strategic capacity planning companies do not have to fear a strong ad hoc market reaction to aircraft firm orders, independent from the order size.

7.4 Business cycle – Analysis of long term financial performance

The evaluation of companies' performance and market's reaction over a long term business cycle bears two challenges: Choosing the right performance tracker and choosing the right observation period. On one hand the results of the analyses should be comparable to the outcome of the evaluation of stock market's reaction in shock events and to company specific isolated events, on the other hand to sufficiently evaluate a part of a normal business cycle, a wider time window has to be chosen which immediately raises the risk that the individual companies and respectively their stock values in scope can be exposed to different influencing factors that do not simultaneously affect all firms in the industry. Especially long term share price development is a very weak financial performance tracker as it is subject to speculative market behavior. Also, share price development does not describe how successful a business runs in terms of stability in growth and profitability.

Therefore, the evaluation of companies' financial performance in the long term business cycle is not based on abnormal returns. Instead, three dependent variables were chosen for the regression analyses of a company's long term success, which are mainly considered by analysts and investors when evaluating a company's sustainability and enterprise value (cf. Chapter 7.1.1.2):

(1) Average annual revenue growth – a company's business growth tracker
(2) Average EBITDA margin – a company's asset-neutral profitability tracker
(3) Average EBIT margin – a company's bottom line profitability tracker

In contrast to external shocks, no specific time window was pre-defined when observing the long term. Nevertheless, concrete time scopes are needed to analyze companies' long term performance including economic shocks and excluding economic shocks. These two observation windows were defined: the 15-years period 1995 to 2009 and the 6-years sub-period 2002 to 2007.

All necessary data to define the three dependent variables are frequently published by all stock listed companies in annual profit and loss statements. Because the companies in scope do not have the same financial reporting cycle, data were annualized to the year ending December 31.

7.4.1 Business cycle – Observation period and company sample

The time window defined as the long term business cycle represents the 15-years period 1995 to 2009. As described in Chapter 3.1, Figure 13, during this period the aviation industry went through several full cycles of recession, depression, recovery, prosperity and boom. However, two of these cycles were heavily influenced by the shocks of 9/11 and the Financial Crisis 2008. A subsection of this 15-year period, the years 2002 to 2007 represents a time of "business as usual" between the two world economic shocks 2001 and 2008. Between these shocks no significant other external event influenced the aviation industry other than the "normal" dependency on the world economic growth and the oil price development.

One restriction of a long term observation period is the sample size, i.e. the number of companies that operated and reported their financial results consistently over all years. From the initial sample of 56 companies (cf. Chapter 6.4, Table 2) only 13 firms remain that were already active 1995, did not file for bankruptcy after 9/11, and did not change their accounting or reporting policies in a way that makes it impossible to retrieve reliable data for dependent and independent variables. During the period 2002 to 2007 a bigger sample of 41 companies can be analyzed in comparison.

Figure 33 illustrates the observation periods and samples evaluated in subsequent regression analysis of long term business growth and profitability.

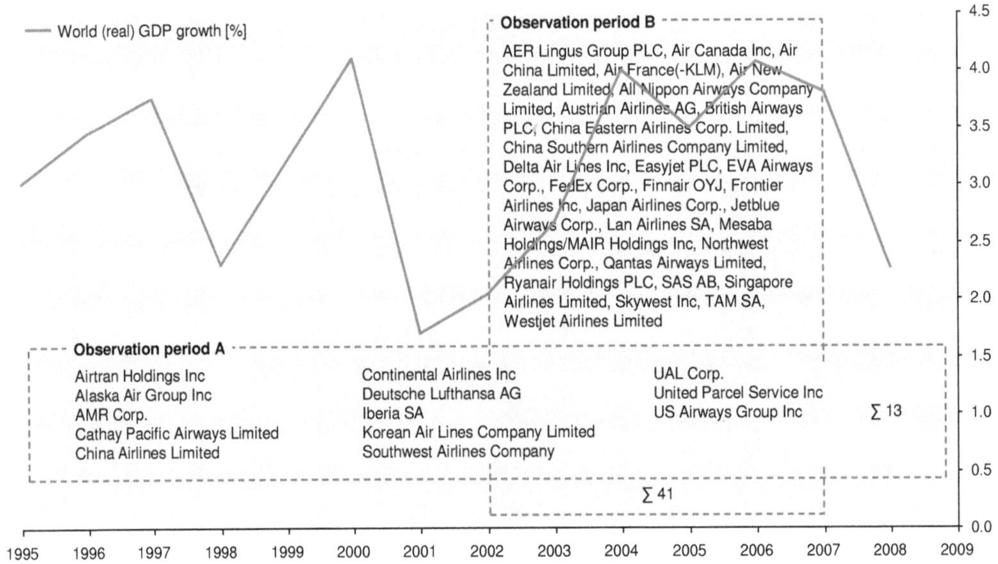

Figure 33: *Overview on observation periods and company samples for analysis of long term business cycles*

This figure presents two long term observation periods (A) 1995 to 2009 and (B) sub-period 2002 to 2007 in comparison to the world (real) GDP growth rate as well as the sample companies matching the two observation periods. Observation period (A) includes several economic cycles and the two economic shocks (terrorist attacks on September 11, 2001 and Financial Crisis 2008). The analysis of this full 15-years period includes a total of 13 companies that consistently operated and reported their financial results. Observation period (B) is analyzed with a sample of 41 companies that all fulfill the data requirements for the planned regression analyses during this 6-year time horizon.

7.4.2 Business cycle – Analysis results: companies' long term performance

Average annual revenue growth, EBITDA margin, and EBIT margin – all measures of companies' financial long term success – are tested in regressions against a variety of explanatory and control variables. Aim of the analysis is to identify whether basic aircraft fleet and fleet planning factors have significant impact on the financial success of a company. Control variables include financial ratios and carrier as well as regional dummy variables. Inter-variable correlation can be found in Appendix 37 and Appendix 38.

Each dependent variable was tested in two different observation periods and company samples as described in the last section. Table 31 summarizes the results of the analysis of companies' financial success factors over the long term business cycle. For detailed findings of the regression models please refer to Appendix 39 to Appendix 44.

		Model X1	Model X2	Model Y1	Model Y2	Model Z1	Model Z2
Observation period		2002-2007	1995-2009	2002-2007	1995-2009	2002-2007	1995-2009
Sample		Selected companies	Selected companies	Selected companies	Selected companies	Selected companies	Selected companies
Sample size		41	13	41	13	41	13
Dependent variable		Avg. p.a revenue growth	Avg. p.a. revenue growth	Avg. p.a. EBITDA margin	Avg. p.a. EBITDA margin	Avg. p.a. EBIT margin	Avg. p.a. EBIT margin
Cluster	Variable						
Financial	SIZE	-	-	+	+	+	+
	LIQUIDITY		++	+		+	++
	NDTEBITDA	+	-			-	
	EBITDAMAR	++	--	n/a	n/a	n/a	n/a
	EBITMAR		--	n/a	n/a	n/a	n/a
	EQITYRAT		++	++	++	++	++
	INTRSTCOVRG		+				
Aircraft fleet	TOTALAC	-	-				
	OPSLEASE	++	++	--	--	-	--
	STORAC		+	-		-	
	nYRORDER	++	++	+		+	++
	nYROPTION	++		+		+	
	AVGAGE	-	+		-		+
Carrier	MFSC		--	--		-	
	NFSC	++	n/a		n/a	+	n/a
	LCC		++	-	+	-	--
	FREIGHT	++	--	+	++	++	++
Region	APAC		+	+		+	-
	EMEA				-		--
	LATAM		n/a		n/a		n/a
	NORAM			-			+
	R^2 (adjusted)	≤ 0.53	≤ 0.96	≤ 0.54	≤ 0.79	≤ 0.61	≤ 0.81
	F-statistic	2.57* - 12.21***	5.15** - 36.11***	2.45** - 18.82***	2.94* - 12.22***	3.15** - 13.52***	3.38* - 11.34***

+/- Positive/negative impact on abnormal returns < 0.1/>-0.1
++/-- Positive/negative impact on abnormal returns ≥ 0.1/≤ -0.1
+++/--- Positive/negative impact on abnormal returns ≥ 1.0/≤ -1.0

xxx Statistically significant at the 10% level
xxx Statistically significant at the 5% level
xxx Statistically significant at the 1% level

Table 31: *Overview on regression results for financial performance in the long term business cycle*

This table presents a consolidated overview of cross-sectional regression results for the long term financial success indicators: (X) Average annual revenue growth, (Y) Average annual EBITDA margin, and (Z) Average annual EBIT margin of aircraft operating and holding companies. Two time windows are observed: the 6-years period 2002-2007 which does not include industry-external economic shocks and the 15-years period 1995-2009 including the economic shocks of the terrorist attacks on September 11, 2001 and the Financial Crisis 2008. The sample size is adjusted according to the observation period. Companies in the sample are selected based on the full availability of data throughout all years in scope. SIZE is the natural logarithm of total assets, LIQUIDITY is cash & equivalents over current liabilities, NDTEBITDA is net debt over EBITDA, EBITDAMAR is EBITDA over total operating revenue, EQITYRAT is owners equity over total assets, INTRSTCOVRG is interest expenses for debt over EBIT, TOTALAC is the total number of jet aircraft, OPSLEASE is the ratio of operating leased aircraft over total aircraft count, STORAC is the ratio of stored aircraft to total aircraft count, nYRORDER and nYROPTION are the number of aircraft orders and purchase options to existing fleet in the next years, and AVGAGE is the average age of existing aircraft. Also, eight dummy variables are included which are equal to one if the firm meets the requirements and equal to zero otherwise: MFSC if the firm is a major full service carrier, NFSC if the firm is a non-major full service carrier, LCC if the firm is a low cost carrier, FREIGHT if the firm is a freight only carrier, APAC, if the firm is Asia Pacific based, EMEA if the firm is based in Europe Middle East or Africa, LATAM if the firm is Latin America based, and NORAM if the firm is North American based. The magnitude of the positive and negative influence of the variables on abnormal returns refers to the regression coefficient. Statistical significance is based on t-statistics.

Models X1 and X2 show mostly the expected patterns. Align with the hypotheses, the variables SIZE, TOTALAC, and MFSC are all negatively correlated to average annual revenue growth, i.e. companies with a high asset base, many aircraft, and those classified as major full service carriers grew on average less than other companies. Naturally, the bigger a company the lower is the remaining growth potential given a saturated market with relatively constant market shares of the big players. For smaller companies and new business models growth is the key to success, reflected in higher growth rates for NFSC and LCC. Among the regions, APAC and its aircraft operating and holding companies experienced an economic boom in the past 15 years. EMEA and NORAM grew relatively less and LATAM's economic upswing has only just begun.

The financial variables LIQUITITY, EQUITRAT, and INTRSTCOVRG are positively linked to revenue growth when looking at the full 15-years horizon 1995-2009. Although also EBITDA margin seems to have a significant correlation to revenue growth, in the financial world no direct link between these measures is known. More easily can be assumed that the profit margins highly correlate with the underlying business models of the companies which then are reflected in the findings (cf. correlation table in Appendix 38). NDTEBITDA shows a positive sign in Model X1, i.e. long term debt was used to finance the growth (capital expenditures). The negative sign in Model X2 is caused by the strongly U.S. (NORAM) biased company sample for the years 1995-2009 and by the negative correlation of -0.42 between NDTEBITDA and NORAM. Further, the U.S. carriers were founded well before 1995 and might have experienced their high-growth years before the years analyzed.

All aircraft fleet and fleet planning variables show significant correlation with average annual revenue growth. As hypothesized, OPSLEASE, nYRORDER, and nYROPTIONS show a positive relationship with revenue increase. Companies that focus on growth rely on aircraft orders and purchase options to secure future capacity and if necessary quickly gain capacity by entering aircraft operating leases.

The aircraft fleet age (AVGAGE) is negatively linked to revenue growth when looking at the years 2002-2007 while it shows a positive relationship over the full 15-years horizon 1995-2009. Reason for this is most likely the correlation of young aircraft fleets with young companies. Especially the low cost carriers – of which more companies have been operating in the 21st century than in the late 1990's (cf. Figure 33) – base their business model on new, efficient, and low-maintenance aircraft. Hence, the businesses with the highest growth rate operate the youngest fleets.

A significant and positive connection of revenue growth with number of aircraft stored (STORAC) is found in the regression analysis for the full period 1995-2009, indicating that stored aircraft might be a lever to ensure capacity. Intuitively a negative correlation was anticipated as one would expect strong growing companies to generally face capacity shortage.

The models Y and Z illustrate the correlation of the explanatory and control variables with average annual EBITDA margin and EBIT margin, respectively. Again, for each dependent variable one model summarizes the findings from the regressions based on a sample of 41 companies in the time period 2002-2007 (Y1 and Z1) and a second model gives an overview on the results from the regressions including 13 companies over the years 1995-2009 (Y2 and Z2).

Independent of profit measure and time horizon, the regressions result in a very consistent picture. In all models the financial variables LIQUIDITY and EQUITYRAT show positive correlation with the two profit measures EBITDA margin and EBIT margin.

Also, SIZE is positively related to a higher EBITDA margin and EBIT margin. As SIZE is the natural logarithm of a company's assets book value, it seems like assets not only increase the EBITDA margin (which is expected because less operating expenses occur and depreciation and amortization are not yet deducted from the earnings), but also allow a markup in EBIT margin. This conclusion is underlined by the negative correlation found for OPSLEASE to both EBITDA margin and EBIT margin. Those companies in the sample with highest profit margins run their operations with the lowest portion of operating leased aircraft in their fleet. Further, they make use of aircraft orders (nYRORDER) and purchase options (nYROPTION), both positively connected with profit margins, to secure future capacity need by increasing the number of owned aircraft in their fleet. As described in Chapter 2.2.2 and Chapter 3 some companies even show opportunistic buying behavior in placing orders and options, i.e. act ahead of the market when aircraft prices are low and capacity demand is yet to come.

STORAGE does not confirm the hypothesized positive correlation to profit, most likely because stored aircraft do not generate revenue but fix costs and the benefits of flexible grounding and re-activating aircraft when demand requires do not outweigh the lost revenue. AVGAGE shows the expected trend, i.e. the higher the average age the higher the EBIT margin. Further, a correlation with EBITDA margin is found. The lower the average age of aircraft the higher is the EBITDA margin. Reason for this could be that new aircraft usually run on lower operating costs which positively affect EBITDA and old aircraft have low depreciation or even have been taken off the books which both positively affect EBIT.

Among the carrier and region variables, the major full service carriers (MFSC) in the sample seem to have lower average profit margins compared to non-major full service carriers (NFSC) and freight carriers (FREIGHT). Low cost carriers do not necessarily generate high profit margins. Here, small variations in the business model appear to make a difference when it comes to EBITDA margin and EBIT margin. Further, APAC based companies were able to generate higher profit margins compared to other regions. Conclusions drawn from carrier and fleet variables generally have to be judged with caution, because they might be biased by the correlations between the individual explanatory and control variables tested.

Overall, the regression analysis of the three long term financial success measures (X) average annual revenue growth, (Y) average annual EBITDA margin, and (Z) average annual EBIT margin, can be summarized in the following statements:

(1) All explanatory and control variables correlate significantly with revenue growth, EBITDA margin, and EBIT margin, and mostly show the hypothesized trends with varying explanatory power
(2) Companies with high liquidity and a high equity ratio grew more and had higher profit margins and vice versa
(3) Assets of aircraft operating and holding companies are positively connected to profit margins
(4) The bigger a company the lower the annual growth
(5) Aircraft operating leases are used by those sample companies that grew faster, but have a negative relationship with both EBITDA margin and EBIT margin
(6) Aircraft orders and purchase options show a positive relationship to all three measures revenue growth, EBITDA, and EBIT margin

The analysis of company's financial performance over the long term business cycle reveals that basic aircraft fleet and fleet planning parameters play a significant role in a company's success. Those companies which generated the highest EBITDA margin and EBIT margin secured aircraft capacity in form of own assets and planned future capacity strategically with aircraft orders and purchase options. Operating leases were used by companies to enhance revenue growth, but are negatively correlated to profit margins.

7.5 Summary of success factors for aircraft operating and holding companies

Three different observation periods were chosen to test the influence of basic aircraft fleet and fleet planning variables on a company's financial success represented by stock development and long term growth and profitability: (1) shocks and crises such as the terrorist attacks on September 11, 2001 and the Financial Crisis 2008, (2) company specific isolated negative and positive events such as aircraft accidents and aircraft firm orders, and (3) the long term business cycles including and excluding shocks & crisis.

The aircraft fleet and fleet planning variables in focus of the analyses were the two basic sourcing and financing alternatives of "on-demand capacity acquisition versus future-oriented aircraft orders and purchase options" and "own versus operating lease of aircraft". Beside these key variables the influence of the fleet size, the portion of active versus stored aircraft, the age of the fleet, and a variety of financial, market, carrier, and region variables (cf. Table 3) were tested to increase the statistical significance of the regressions and identify those variables that had the power to explain the differences between the 56 companies in scope.

Figure 34 summarizes the results of all analyses conducted and illustrates the factors having a statistically significant positive or negative impact on aircraft operating and holding companies' financial success in shocks & crises, company specific isolated events and over long term business cycles.

The illustration focuses on financial, fleet, and selected market variables from which a general conclusion can be drawn and that are not influenced by event specifics. Based on the findings of the analyses, the variables can be re-clustered into six success categories that have influence on a company's stock development in crises and on its long term financial success in terms of revenue growth and profitability (EBITDA margin, EBIT margin): (1) investment in property, (2) financial risk minimization, (3) future oriented fleet strategy, (4) profitability[65], (5) liquidity, and (6) operational flexibility and diversity. Each success factor may include one or several levers (variables).

[65] The correlation of profitability was tested against abnormal returns in stocks and against long term revenue growth, but not against long term EBITDA and EBIT margins

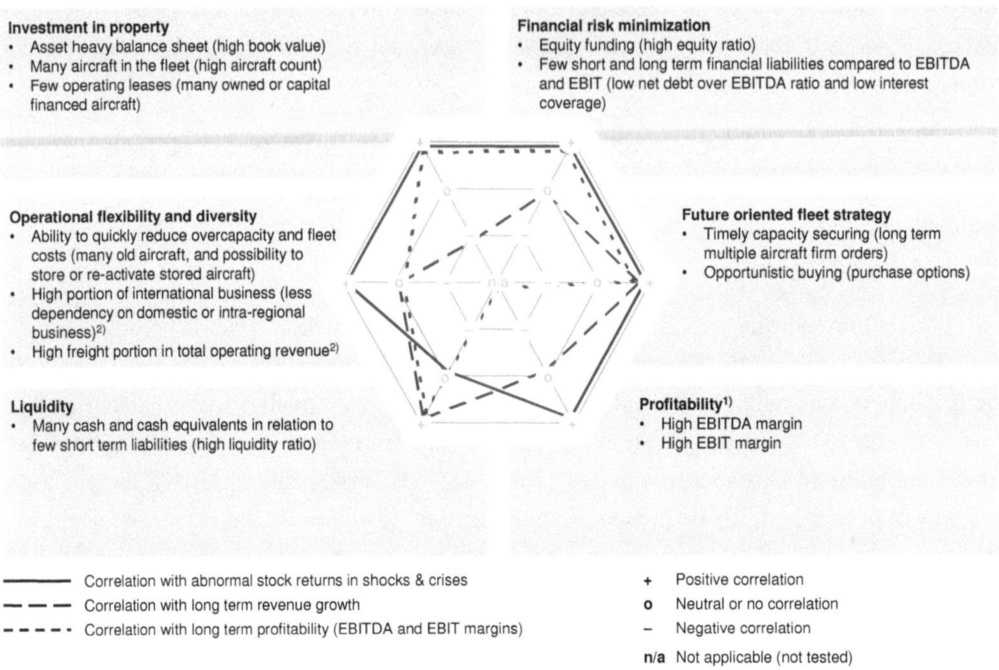

[1] *Only tested for abnormal returns caused by shocks & crises 2001 and 2008, and for the analysis of long term revenue growth*

[2] *Only tested for abnormal returns caused by shocks & crises 2001 and 2008; for the analysis of long term revenue growth and profitability, no reliable PINT and PFREIGHT data for all years in scope was available.*

Figure 34: *Summary of results – Correlation of key financial and aircraft fleet factors with abnormal returns in stocks, revenue growth and profitability*

This figure presents the correlation of key financials and aircraft fleet factors with abnormal returns in stock during shocks & crises, with long term revenue growth, and with long term profitability. All factors listed showed statistical significance in multivariate and cross-sectional regressions and allow for a general statement for all observation periods in scope (exceptions not included in the figure). Abnormal returns were evaluated for the initial, short-, and mid term reaction of the stock market to two external shocks: the terrorist attacks on September 11, 2001 and the Financial Crisis 2008. The performances of long term revenue growth, EBITDA margin, and EBIT margin, were tested over a period of 15 years 1995-2009 (including the two shocks) and a period of 6 years 2002-2007 (excluding the two shocks). The illustration summarizes the regression results in positive (+), neutral or no (o), or negative (–) correlation of the six dependent variable clusters with stock performance, revenue growth and profitability. The six categories include: (1) Investment in property, (2) Financial risk minimization, (3) Future oriented fleet strategy, (4) Profitability (not tested in regressions on EBITDA margin and EBIT margin), (5) Liquidity, and (6) Operational flexibility and diversity (market variables including portion of international and freight business in total revenue only tested in regressions on abnormal stock returns). For more details on the variables cf. Table 3.

Which factors had a positive correlation with company's stock price development in shocks & crises? Both shocks, 9/11 and the Financial Crisis 2008, caused abnormal returns in company's stocks compared to the MSCI World Index. The abnormal returns were combined non-zero and were non-equal for the company's in scope. The findings show that investment in property, financial risk minimization, future-oriented fleet strategy, high profitability, operational flexibility and diversity had a positive impact on abnormal returns in stock market's reaction. More concretely, a company's stock experienced less negative or even positive abnormal returns as a result of the shock when the company held a high asset book value, operated many aircraft, and preferred ownership over operating lease. Further, a low financial risk, i.e. high equity ratio and low short and long term liability to 3rd party, a future oriented fleet strategy in terms of many aircraft orders and purchase options, and high EBITDA and EBIT margins were rewarded by investors. With respect to operational flexibility and diversity, a mix of international and domestic business as well as passenger and freight business was of advantage. Old aircraft and the ability to quickly ground aircraft, thus reducing operating costs, were beneficial.

Which factors had a positive correlation with a company's long term revenue growth rates? Not all companies grew with the same rate as the general air transport market over the last decades. Some grew more, some less. A company that already ranks among the top players cannot achieve the same growth rates as e.g. a new business model. This is also reflected in the findings of the cross sectional regressions with focus on companies' average annual revenue growth rate. Companies with high growth rates had fewer assets (lower book values), a smaller aircraft fleet and made use of operating leases to quickly access capacity as well as of aircraft orders and purchase options to secure future capacity. The same companies took more risk with short and long term financial liabilities to finance the growth, generated high profit margins, and were highly solvent.

Which factors had a positive correlation with a company's long term profitability? Companies that generated the highest average EBITDA and EBIT margins had the highest investment in property (asset book value) and the smallest portion of operating leased aircraft in their fleet. These companies' fleet strategies all included long term strategic capacity securing and opportunistic buying with aircraft firm orders and purchase options up to 20 years into the future. Further these companies ran their businesses with a high degree of liquidity and avoided financial risk in liabilities to 3rd parties both short and long term. The portion of inactive aircraft was low and the age of aircraft generally high. Especially the freight carriers UPS, FedEx, and Atlas Air meet all criteria above, consequently rank high among the financially most successful air transport operating and holding companies.

Which factors have a positive correlation with stock market's reaction to company specific isolated events? The results of this analysis are not displayed in Figure 34. The estimation of abnormal returns as a result of aircraft accidents or aircraft firm orders reveals no or only weak abnormal returns, i.e. the stock market did not react significantly to these events, independent of how severe the accident was or how many aircraft were ordered in one order placement. Consequently, one cannot conclude on any significant differences between the individual companies in stock's reaction to aircraft accidents and firm orders.

8. Discussion of results against hypotheses and literature

This chapter builds on the hypotheses and the literature consulted to support the rationales as described in Chapter 6.3. It summarizes and substantiates the first discussion of the analysis results already included in the description of the findings within the last sections (cf. Chapter 7) by focusing on the impact and correlation of aircraft fleet and fleet variables on stock prices, revenue growth, and profit margins. It may be important at this point to mention again that the impact of basic aircraft fleet and fleet planning variables on financial performance from an investors or top management point of view had not yet or only insufficiently been investigated and hence only few supporting literature could be consulted. Further it needs to be recapitulated that the findings in regression models of 9/11, the Financial Crisis 2008 as well as the normal business cycle show high statistical significance while the abnormal returns in times of aircraft acquisitions and losses are less significant resulting in a weaker explanatory power of these regressions. The discussion of the influence of the financial, market, carrier type, region variables, and special event day variables on companies' financial performance is not summarized in this chapter (for details on these variables please refer to the description of results in Chapter 7).

Recap of the research hypotheses and scope

Key hypothesis was that basic aircraft financing and sourcing options have a statistically significant positive or negative impact on the financial performance of airlines. The five null and alternative testable hypotheses included the anticipated impact of the two major fleet variables [1] ratio of leased to total aircraft and [2] ratio of planned to total aircraft, as well as of the three minor fleet variables [3] total number of aircraft, [4] ratio of stored to total aircraft, and [5] average age of aircraft.

Companies' financial performance was defined as the performance from an investor and top management point of view, i.e. measured by short to mid term abnormal stock returns in times of crisis and company specific events such as aircraft hull losses and aircraft acquisitions, as well as long term revenue growth, EBITDA, and EBIT margins. The sample included 56 major full service carriers, non-major full service carriers, low cost carriers, and freight carriers from all regions. The observation periods contained the terrorist attacks on September 11, 2001, the Financial Crisis 2008, aircraft losses and aircraft acquisitions 1994-2009, as well as the normal business cycles between 1995-2009 and the sub-period 2002-2007.

R. Günther, *Impact of Aircraft Sourcing & Financing on Financial Success*,
Edition KWV, https://doi.org/10.1007/978-3-658-24094-3_8

All null hypotheses were expected to be rejected. All alternative hypotheses were expected not to be rejected. For review of the individual hypotheses please refer back to Chapter 6.3.

Discussion of hypothesis [1] – Ratio of leased to total aircraft

The findings reject the null hypothesis [$H_0$1] and validate the alternative hypotheses [H_A1]-[H_C1] as expected, i.e. the ratio of operating leased aircraft is not independent of financial performance. The analyses provide evidence that a higher ratio of operating leased aircraft (lower ratio of owned aircraft) in the fleet has an impact on abnormal stock returns in times of crisis that is negative and significant up to the 1% level. This pattern only changed when market's behavior was influenced by governmental actions, e.g. bailout packages. Further the results show a positive correlation of operating lease to revenue growth statistically significant at the 1% level and a positive correlation to EBITDA margin and EBIT margin at the 1-10%, depending on the sample and observation period. Also as expected, the ratio of operating leased to total aircraft does not have a (or only a very weak) significant influence on abnormal stock returns caused by aircraft losses or acquisitions.

Oum et al. (2000) examined the optimal use of operating lease from an airlines' perspective considering both the premium on lease and the flexibility in capacity management. Their "model suggested that the optimal demand [for operating lease] by [their sample of] 23 major airlines in the world would range between 40%-60% of their total fleet, for the reasonable range of premiums of operating leases [between 5% and 30%]" (Oum et al., 2000, p. 17). This would mean that the flexibility needed in capacity management would be extremely high as the result of this thesis suggests that – ignoring flexibility in capacity management – the share of own aircraft should be as high as possible, ideally 100%. Eventually, the tradeoff has still to be made to account for unexpected or seasonal demand fluctuations, but any airline should strive to minimize the use of operating lease by more carefully forecasting capacity peaks and find more cost sensitive alternatives to manage capacity changes, e.g. through storage of old and owned aircraft.

Discussion of hypothesis [2] – Ratio of planned to total aircraft

Also the null hypothesis [$H_0$2], formulating that the ratio of planned to total aircraft is independent from financial performance, is rejected. The findings are mostly but not fully in line with the alternative hypotheses [H_A2]-[H_C2] that future-oriented fleet planning has a positive impact. Both, a high number of aircraft order and a higher number of purchase options have a positive impact at the 1-5% level on stock market's reaction on 9/11 and the Financial Crisis 2008, especially in the short- and mid term (less in the initial reaction on the shock). Aircraft options further have a positive impact on stock market's short term reaction on aircraft losses, but only at a 10% level. With revenue growth the correlation is highly positive and significant at the 1% level. Unexpectedly, there is also a correlation observed between ordered or optioned aircraft and market's reaction to aircraft acquisitions. However, this reaction is indifferent in direction (positive or negative) and statistically significant (at the 5-10% level). Further, a positive correlation at the 1% level with EBITDA margin (at least in a recent normal business cycle 2002-2007) and EBIT margin can be observed, both not anticipated.

The results provide strong evidence to the conclusion of Liehr et al.'s research conducted at Lufhansa and German Wings that "aircraft orders are a key element in the cycle-generating structure of the airline market. Growing slower in the capacity than your competitor means losing market share [...]." "In this situation counter-cyclical orderings yield several advantages for a single carrier, most of all lower prices and shorter lead times for aircraft, which result in quicker reaction times". (Liehr et al., 2001, p. 321) This thesis provides the evidence, that not only investors are in favor of future-oriented (not necessarily only counter-cyclical) fleet planning with options and orders, but also that future-oriented fleet planning seems to be positively correlated with company's long term growth and profitability.

Discussion of hypothesis [3] – Total number of aircraft

The total number of aircraft shows a dependency on financial performance, as already indicated by the literature, rejecting the null hypothesis [$H_0$3]. The analysis results fully support the alternative hypotheses [H_A3]-[H_C3].
The number of aircraft positively influenced abnormal stock returns in the short term reaction on 9/11 at the 1-5% level, depending on the different sample scopes tested. The results for the first trading day after 9/11 and the mid term are indifferent and not significant enough for a conclusion. In contrast, in reaction on the Financial Crisis, the regressions reveal a strong positive impact of the number of aircraft on stock market's initial reaction, but less in the short- and mid term. Overall, it is valid to conclude that this fleet variable has a significant positive effect in times of crisis. The findings in the stock prices are in line with the conclusions of Chalk (1987), Carter & Simkins (2004), Walker (2005), and Merkert & Hensher (2011) that the probability of survival in crisis is linked to the company's size, not only represented by assets or market capitalization, but in case of airlines also strongly correlated with fleet size.
With regard to abnormal returns as a result of aircraft hull loss, fleet size has a positive impact at the 5% level, validating the hypothesis that the stock market judges the loss and the airline's possibility to compensate it in relation to the overall number of aircraft in the fleet.

Also, at the 5% level, revenue growth and fleet size have the predicted negative relationship reflecting the maturity of the business, i.e. small business is equal to small fleet size is equal to high growth and vice versa a mature business is equal to a big fleet is equal to a high market share and a stable business with less growth (potential).

As expected, there is no statistical proof for a correlation of fleet size with stock price changes when a new aircraft is acquired or with a company's profit margin (EBITDA and EBIT).

Discussion of hypothesis [4] – Ratio of stored to total aircraft

The null hypothesis [$H_0$4] is equally rejected, as also the ratio of stored to total number of aircraft in the fleet is not independent of a company's financial performance. The alternative hypotheses [H_A4]-[H_C4] are partially validated and partially rejected, still providing some evidence for Liehr et al.'s (2001, p. 322) argument that maintaining old aircraft in the fleet "opens margins and flexibility for fleet planning", because when stored they can be quickly and cost-sensitively activated in times of capacity shortage and vice versa retired in times of capacity surplus. In the majority of the models tested, a ratio of stored to total aircraft of up to 20% (maximum portion of stored aircraft observed in the observation periods and sample) was positively considered by the stock market in its reaction to 9/11, with high coefficients, but not always the highest statistical significance. The positive influence is displayed in the abnormal returns on the first trading days and in the short term (both at the 5%-10% level) in which stored aircraft can be considered as beneficial as they are grounded at fix costs and do not fly empty. The flexibility to store aircraft is acknowledged by the stockholders. However, the ratio negatively influenced the market in the mid term of 9/11 (at the 5% level), when general demand seemed to increase again but aircraft remained stored. With this an airline provided a clear signal to the market: despite market growth, the airline did not have sufficient own business demand (volumes) to re-activate the stored fleet. Although the negative impact in the mid term is only visible in few regression models on 9/11, the findings of the Financial Crisis 2008 analysis show the same pattern. In the Financial Crisis 2008, the ratio of stored to total aircraft negatively impacted abnormal returns from the market's initial reaction to the mid term (up to the 1% level), penalizing the missing revenue of the companies.

No strong statistical evidence is found that the stock market considers the amount of remaining stored aircraft in case of an aircraft hull loss (only in few models a very low significance is observed).

Initially not expected is the positive correlation of stored aircraft to revenue growth, which is even highly significant at the 1% level over the time horizon 1993-2009 (the long term business cycle including the crises). A negative correlation was expected as a fast and strong growing company is believed to rather operate a capacity shortage than to store aircraft; the ex-ante counterintuitive finding could nevertheless – in light of the other results – be considered logically because, similar to the positive correlation of firm orders and options with revenue growth, stored aircraft is another mean for airlines to manage a capacity surplus for future demand.

Further not expected was the negative relation in the regression against EBIT margin (though with low explanatory power at the 10% level) and against EBITDA margin (at the 5% level over the years 2002-2007). Predicted were a positive EBITDA margin and EBIT margin correlation with stored aircraft, mainly because of the lower cost of storing, activating and grounding of old, owned aircraft compared to costs associated with balancing changes in capacity by leasing. Despite this cost argument, a too high percentage of stored aircraft seem to diminish profit more than they benefit a flexible capacity management.

Overall, the stock market appears to observe the ratio of stored to total aircraft and to rationally consider whether it ascribes it as a benefit or disadvantage to the airline, depending on the time during the crisis as well as growth times. This means that a certain percentage of stored aircraft is indeed suggested to be kept by airlines at certain times. However this percentage has to be chosen in tradeoff to the sustention of non-revenue-making capacity and consequently lower profit margins. With the results of this thesis, the overall discussion of Liehr et al. can be supported. The optimal percentage of stored aircraft in a fleet cannot be concluded. The maximum of 20% in the sample data is too high; the average of 2-3% could be too low. With Liehr et al.'s suggestion to keep a defined percentage (10-15%) of old aircraft in the fleet, more flexibility is provided to capacity management by adding the possibility to store and re-activate old aircraft at relatively lower cost. The tradeoff between young and old aircraft is discussed in more detail in hypothesis [5].

Discussion of hypothesis [5] – Average age of aircraft

As indicated in the discussion of hypothesis [4], the age of aircraft can be used as a strategic lever for flexible fleet management. To further test the argumentation of Liehr et al. (2001) described above, the average age of aircraft in the fleet was chosen as a separate independent variable. The null hypothesis [$H_0$5] is rejected. The average age of aircraft in a fleet is not independent of a company's financial performance. The alternative hypotheses [H_A5]-[H_C5] are generally validated.

High average fleet age is clearly positively perceived by the stock market in the initial reaction to and in the short term after both crises, 9/11 and Financial Crisis 2008, strongly significant in the majority of the regression models up to the 1% level. This finding clearly supports the hypothesis [H_A5] that the stock market sees old aircraft as being of benefit in times of dramatic capacity drops, most likely because of the opportunity to quickly and efficiently retire capacity. However, it needs to be mentioned that in the mid term either no

or, in a few models, a negative influence on abnormal returns is observed at the 5-10% level.
The positive effect of an old fleet on EBIT margin in [H_B5] is validated. So, the logical argument that old, fully or almost fully depreciated aircraft operate at a relatively higher EBIT margin than younger aircraft with high depreciation, is statistically proven right.

As expected, no correlation of average aircraft fleet age with stock market's reaction on aircraft losses is observed. The test against stock market's reaction on aircraft acquisition indicates some (negative) relation, but does not provide enough explanatory power to conclude on significant correlation.
Yet, against revenue growth and EBITDA margin, average fleet age shows a dependency that was not predicted to be significant. With regards to revenue growth a negative correlation (at the 5% level) is identified in the regression over the years 2002-2007 contrary to a positive correlation (equally at the 5% level) in the regression over the full business cycle, including the crises, from 1995-2009. Rationale for the result could be that the sample of firms 2002-2007 simply includes younger companies with consequently younger fleet (if new aircraft were acquired). When looking at the full observation period, including times of strong demand disruptions (1995-2009), it seems like the positive effect of flexibility in capacity management already mentioned in hypotheses [H4] becomes also visible in this variable. The possibility to re-activate old aircraft that were stored when demand declined could have provided a mean to accelerate capacity and realize growth faster and with potentially higher growth rates compared to companies that had to newly acquire capacity.
An unexpected negative correlation (at the 5% level) of old aircraft to EBITDA margin is observed in the regression of the full business cycle 1995-2009. Compared to the positive correlation with EBIT margin this gives room for speculation that old aircraft might – despite the lower depreciation – require higher costs in terms of maintenance and other operating costs. With this finding, the analysis does not support Merkert & Hensher's (2011) outcome that fleet age has a small but very significant positively correlation with cost efficiency; the initial suspicion concerning this statement proves to be right.
Discussing the results of [H4] and [H5] tests, it can be concluded that maintaining a certain number of old aircraft in the fleet is definitively advisable, but only a limited number should be stored as long as demand allows.

With the rejection of the null hypotheses and the validation of most alternative hypotheses, this thesis has provided evidence that basic aircraft fleet and fleet planning characteristics have statistically significant impact on and correlation with stock market's reaction in times of crisis as well as with average revenue growth, EBITDA margin, and EBIT margin over the long term business cycle. The findings in the analysis of stock market's reaction on aircraft acquisition and aircraft losses are of less explanatory power.

After the analysis and the discussion of the results against hypotheses and consulted literature, interesting questions remain. New research could build on the findings that owned or capital leased aircraft and future-oriented fleet planning with firm orders and purchase of options ahead of demand are of benefit to companies. It would be exiting to know whether ideal ratios can be found for these major fleet characteristics and perhaps also for the minor fleet variables storage and age. Apart from testing the results in business life, which always bears the risk of wrong decisions, it might be worth trying whether mathematical optimization models could help to determine the ideal ratios of own versus lease, existing versus planned, active versus stored, and old versus young aircraft in a fleet.

Further, in this thesis the special case of aircraft as key asset in capacity management for air passenger and cargo transport companies was chosen. However, it would be interesting to see whether the findings can also be applied to other transport capacity assets, e.g. ocean freight containers.

9. Conclusion and recommendation

The aim of this thesis was to analyze whether basic aircraft fleet and fleet planning decisions have an influence on or show correlation to stock development and financial performance of aircraft operating and holding companies.

Nowadays, air transport companies follow different strategies to source and finance their air capacity. Some of these strategies include a focus on aircraft ownership and long term aircraft fleet planning, the latter with aircraft firm orders and use of purchase options for opportunistic buying way ahead of the market. But, are these strategies better than those concentrating more on operating lease aircraft and on ad hoc, on-demand capacity procurement?

To answer this question it is important to take the right perspective. In this thesis the perspective of the investor and shareholder is chosen who is interested in a sustainable long term financial success of a company that is neither jeopardized by external shocks and crises nor by company specific events. Key financial success parameters investors consider are typically revenue growth and profitability in terms of EBITDA and EBIT margins. Further, the stock market might react with abnormal returns depending on how it sees a company's individual readiness to face unexpected situations. Consequently, a company's top management will and should consider all factors positively influencing long term financial success as well as increasing the chance of survival in unexpected crises in its overall strategy and decision making process to maximize investors' and shareholders' value.

The analysis results show that basic aircraft sourcing and financing decisions indeed coincide with a company's financial success and prove those companies right that invest in aircraft ownership and run a long term aircraft fleet strategy. Owned (or capital financed) aircraft, long term aircraft orders, and purchase options for opportunistic buying not only correlate highly positive with a company's long term profitability, but also positively influence the stock market in times of shocks and crises. Operating lease and ad hoc capacity supply are verified as levers of fast growth and may sometimes be beneficial when governmental financial aid actions influence stock market's behavior, but generally correlate negatively with the company's financial success.

The risks taken by investing in assets and long term aircraft acquisitions are clearly awarded. Considering non-aircraft fleet success factors such as financial risk minimization and liquidity, the ideal capacity seems to be an aircraft that is cash funded and purchased opportunistically ahead of the market, i.e. avoiding external liabilities and high prices.

R. Günther, *Impact of Aircraft Sourcing & Financing on Financial Success*,
Edition KWV, https://doi.org/10.1007/978-3-658-24094-3_9

What does that mean for air transport and holding companies, assuming that air transport demand will continue to grow and air capacity supply will decrease as expected by industry experts? It means that some companies did and are still doing very well when it comes to the sourcing and acquisition of aircraft and others seem to do exactly the opposite of what the findings of this thesis suggest. Looking into the future, the latter will probably face a supplier market with rising prices for short term available capacity which will further decrease their already today lower profit margins in comparison to their competitors. Additionally, these companies will suffer more from shocks and crises.

Thus, this thesis recommends to air transport companies which historically relied on a high portion of operating leased aircraft and on-demand capacity acquisition to critically review their basic aircraft sourcing and financing strategy towards more asset ownership and long term aircraft fleet planning in order to secure future capacity and stay competitive throughout the business cycles and economic crises.

"An airline [and any air transport company] is often bound by decisions made by earlier management teams that are difficult to unravel. […] Will o' the wisp decisions can be costly in the long term. So, once a choice is made, there is often no economic prospect of changing [for] some time."

(Clark, 2007, p 230)

Literature references

List of references not exhaustive: When available, annual reports of all companies in scope and the years 1993-2009 were retrieved from the respective companies' webpages or were available in hardcopy and are not listed individually. The Annual reports were used to selectively validate data retrieved from Ascend Worldwide Ltd. and Thomson Reuters Datastream.

Aberle, G. (2003). *Transportwirtschaft – Einzelwirtschaftliche und gesamtwirtschaftliche Grundlagen* (4th ed.). München: Oldenbourg Wissenschaftsverlag

Abeyratne, R.I.R (2001). *Aviation Trends in the New Millennium*. Hants, United Kingdom: Ashgate

Airbus (2008a). *Aircraft Families – Product Viewer*. Retrieved January 21, 2010, from the World Wide Web: http://www.airbus.com/en/aircraftfamilies/productcompare

Airbus (2008b). *Airbus Aircraft Range of 2008 List Prices (mio USD).* Blagnac Cedex, France: Airbus S.A.S.

Airbus (2009). *Global Market Forecast 2009-2028.* Blagnac Cedex, France: Airbus S.A.S.

Airbus (2011). *Delivering the Future – Global Market Forecast 2011-2030.* Blagnac Cedex, France, September 2011: Airbus S.A.S.

Aircraft Value Analysis Company (2008). Historic r*aw data on aircraft sales and lease price specifically requested from and provided by the Aircraft Value Analysis Company for the purpose of this thesis.*

Air Transport Association (2008). *U.S. Airline Bankruptcies & Service Cessations.* Washington, DC, United States: Airlines for America (A4A), formerly known as Air Transport Association

Andrade, G. Mitchell, M. & Stafford, E. (2001). *New evidence and perspectives of mergers.* Journal of Economic Perspectives, Vol. 15, pp.103-120

Ascend Worldwide Ltd. (2008), (2009), (2010). Accessed via DHL Express Global Aviation (business sponsor of the doctoral thesis project).

Assaf, A. (2009). *Are U.S. Airlines really in Crisis?*. Tourism Management, Vol. 30, pp. 916-921

Assaf, A.G. & Josiassen, A. (2011). *The Operational Performance of UK Airlines: 2002-2007.* Journal of Economic Studies, Vol. 38, Issue 1, pp. 5-16

R. Günther, *Impact of Aircraft Sourcing & Financing on Financial Success*, Edition KWV, https://doi.org/10.1007/978-3-658-24094-3

Aviation Week Business Intelligence Service (2002). *The Aviation & Aerospace Almanac 2002*. New York: Aviation Week, McGraw-Hill

Aviation Week Business Intelligence Service (2003). *The Aviation & Aerospace Almanac 2003*. New York: Aviation Week, McGraw-Hill

Barber, B.M. & Lyon, J.D. (1997). *Detecting long-run abnormal stock returns: The empirical power and specification of test statistics.* Journal of Financial Economics, Vol. 43, pp. 341-372

Barbot, C., Costa, Á. & Sochirca, E. (2008). *Airlines Performance in the New Market Context: A Comparative Productivity and Efficiency Analysis.* Journal of Air Transport Management, Vol. 14, pp. 270-274

Bard, J.F., Yu, G. & Argüello, M.F. (2001). *Optimizing aircraft routings in response to groundings and delays.* IIE Transactions, Vol. 33, Issue 10, October 2011, pp. 931-947

Barnhart, C., Belobaba, P. & Odoni, A.R. (2009). *Applications of Operations Research in the Air Transport Industry.* Transportation Science, Vol. 37, No. 4, November 2003, pp. 368-391

Bartlik, M. (2007). *The Impact of EU Law on the Regulation of International Air Transportation.* Hampshire, United Kingdom: Ashgate

Becher, D.A., Jensen, G.R. & Mercer, J.M. (2008). *Monetary Policy Indicators as Predictors of Stock Returns.* Journal of Financial Research, Vol. 31, Issue 4, pp. 357-379

Belsley, D.A., Kuh, E. & Welsch, R.E. (2004). *Regression Diagnostics – Identifying Influential Data and Sources of Collinearity.* Hoboken, NJ, United States: John Wiley & Sons

Binder, J.J. (1985). *On the Use of Multivariate Regression Model in Event Studies.* Journal of Accounting Research, Vol. 23, Spring 1985, pp. 370-383

Binder, J.J. (1998). *The Event Study Methodology Since 1969.* Review of Quantitative Finance and Accounting, Vol. 11, pp. 111-137

Bloomberg (2011). *Index Profiles.* Retrieved December 15, 2011 from the World Wide Web: http://www.bloomberg.com

Blume, M.E. & Stambaugh, R.F. (1983). *Biases in Computed Returns – An Application to the Size Effect.* Journal of Financial Economics, Vol. 12, pp. 387-404

Boeing (2008). *Commercial Airplanes – Products [and] Jet Prices*. Retrieved January 21, 2010, from the World Wide Web: http://www.boeing.com/commercial/products.html; http://www.boeing.com/commercial/prices/

Boeing (2009). *Current Market Outlook 2009-2028.* Seattle, WA, United States: Boeing Commercial Airplanes.

Boeing (2011). *Current Market Outlook 2011-2030.* Seattle, WA, United States: Boeing Commercial Airplanes.

Bowen, J.T. and Slack, B. (2007). *Shifting modes and spatial flows in North American freight transporation.* In: Leinbach, T.R. & Capineri, C. (2007)

Bowerman, B.L. & O'Connell, R.T. (2003). *Business Statistics in Practice (3rd ed.).* New York, NY, United States: McGraw-Hill

Brealey, R.A., Myers, S.C. & Marcus, A.J. (2007). *Fundamentals of Corporate Finance (5th ed.).* New York, NY, United States: McGraw-Hill Irwin

Butler, G.F. & Keller, M.R. (2000). *Handbook of Airline Operations*. Washington, D.C, United States: Aviation Week

Button, K. & Kilpi, J. (2007). *Fleet composition of commercial jet aircraft 1952-2005: Developments in uniformity and scale.* Journal of Air Transport Management, Vol. 13, pp. 81-89

Canina, L., Michaely, R. Thaler, R. & Womack, K (1998). *Caveat Compounder: A Warning about Using the Daily CRSP Equally-Weighted Index to Compute Long-Run Excess Returns.* Journal of Finance, Vol. 53, Issue 1, February 1998, pp. 409-416

Carhart, M.M. (1997). *On Persistence in Mutual Fund Performance*. Journal of Finance, Vol. 52, Issue 1, March 1997, pp. 57-82

Carhart, M.M., Carpenter, J.N., Lynch, A.W. & Musto, D.K. (2002). *Mutual Fund Survivorship.* Review of Financial Studies, Vol. 15, No. 5, Winter 2002, pp. 1439-1463

Carter, D.A. & Simkins, B.J. (2004). *The market's reaction to unexpected, catastrophic events: the case of airline stock returns and the September 11th attacks.* Quarterly Review of Economics and Finance, Vol. 44, July 2004, pp. 539-558.

Caves, R.E. (1989). *Mergers, takeovers, and economic efficiency: Foresight vs. hindsight.* International Journal of Industrial Organization, Vol. 7, pp. 151-174

Chalk, A.J. (1987). *Market Forces and Commercial Aircraft Safety.* Journal of Industrial Economics, Vol. 36, No. 1, September 1987, pp. 61-81

Chan, L.K.C., Jegadeesh, N. & Lakonishok, J. (1996). *Momentum Strategies.* Journal of Finance, Vol. 51, Issue 5, December 1996, pp. 1681-1713

Chen, Z. & Knez, P.J. (1996). *Portfolio Performance Measurement: Theory and Applications.* Review of Financial Studies, Vol. 9, Issue 2, Sommer 1996, pp. 511-555

Chiavi, R. (2005). *Airfreight Development Supporting the Strategy of Global Logistics Companies.* In: Delfmann, W., Baum, H., Auerbach, S. & Albers, S. (2005)

Christopherson, J.A., Ferson, W.E. & Glassmann, D.A (1998). *Conditioning Manager Alphas on Economic Information: Another Look at the Persistence of Performance.* Review of Financial Studies, Vol. 11, Issue 1, Spring 1998, pp. 111-142

Clark, P. (2007). *Buying the Big Jets – Fleet Planning for Airlines (2nd ed.).* Hampshire, United Kingdom: Ashgate

COMAC (2010). Company Webpage. Retrieved October 22, 2010 from the World Wide Web: http://english.comac.cc/

COMAC (2012). Company Webpage. Retrieved April 23, 2012 from the World Wide Web: http://english.comac.cc/

Conrad, J. & Kaul, G. (1993). *Long-Term Market Overreaction or Biases in Computed Returns?.* Journal of Finance, Vol. 48, Issue 1, March 1993, pp. 39-63

Cowan, A.R. & Sergeant, A.M.A (2001). *Interacting Biases, Non-normal Return Distributions and the Performance Tests for Long-Horizon Event Studies.* Journal of Banking and Finance, Vol. 25, Issue 4, April 2001, pp. 741-765

Crans, B. (2004). *How to Make Sure your Aircraft Lease Agreement Covers (Almost) Everything.* Air & Space Law, Vol. 29, Issue 1, February 2004

Dellavigna, S. & Pollet, J.M. (2009). *Investor Inattention and Friday Earnings Announcements.* Journal of Finance, Vol. 64, Issue 2, April 2009, pp. 709-749

Delfmann, W., Baum, H., Auerbach, S. & Albers, S. (2005). *Strategic Management in the Aviation Industry.* Hampshire, United Kingdom: Ashgate, co-published by Kölner Wissenschaftsverlag

DHL Express Global Aviation (2007). *Strategic Plan Aviation.* Bonn, Germany: DHL Express, unpublished

Doganis, R. (2006). *The Airline Business (2nd ed.).* New York, United States: Routledge.

Duso, T., Gugler, K. & Yurtoglu, B. (2010). *Is the event study methodology useful for merger analysis? A comparison of stock market and accounting data.* International Review of Law and Economics, Vol. 30, Issue 2, June 2010, pp. 186-192

Fama, E.F., Fisher, L., Jensen, M. & Roll, R. (1969). *The Adjustment of Stock Prices to New Information.* International Economic Review, Vol. 10, February 1969, pp. 1-21

Fama, E.F. & French, K.R. (1993). *Common Risk Factors in the Returns on Stocks and Bonds.* Journal of Financial Economics, Vol. 33, pp. 3-56

Fama, E.F. & French, K.R. (1996). *Multifactor Explanations of Asset Pricing Anomalies.* Journal of Finance, Vol. 51, Issue 1, March 1996, pp. 55-84

Federal Aviation Administration (2001a). *FAA advises air travellers on airport, airline security measures.* Press release APA 65-01, October 8, 2001. Washington, D.C., United States: Federal Aviation Administration, U.S. Department of Transportation

Federal Aviation Administration (2001b). *FAA to boost security staff.* Press release APA 65-01, October 8, 2001. Washington, D.C., United States: Federal Aviation Administration, U.S. Department of Transportation

Federal Aviation Administration (2008). *FAA Aerospace Forecast Fiscal Years 2008-2025.* Washington, D.C., United States: Federal Aviation Administration, U.S. Department of Transportation

Federal Aviation Administration (2009). *FAA Aerospace Forecast – Fiscal Years 2009-2025.* Washington, D.C., United States: Federal Aviation Administration, U.S. Department of Transportation

Federal Aviation Administration (2011). *FAA Aerospace Forecast – Fiscal Years 2011-2031.* Washington, D.C., United States: Federal Aviation Administration, U.S. Department of Transportation

Fisher, F.M. & McGowan, J.J. (1983). *On the misuse of accounting rate of return to inter monopoly profits.* American Economic Review, Vol. 73, pp. 82-97

Fisher, L., Weaver, D.G. & Webb, G. (2010). *Removing biases in computed returns.* Review of Quantitative Finance and Accounting, Vol. 35, January 2010, pp. 137-161

Flouris, T. & Walker, T.J. (2005). *The financial performance of low-cost and full-service airlines in times of crisis.* Canadian Journal of Administrative Sciences, Vol. 22, Issue 1, pp. 3-20. Montreal: ASAC

Frost & Sullivan (2005). *Aircraft World Leasing Industry – Investment Analysis and Growth Opportunities, A873-F1.* Palo Alto, CA, United States

Gavazza, A. (2010). *Asset liquidity and financial contracts: Evidence from aircraft leases.* Journal of Financial Economics, Vol. 95, Issue 1, January 2010, pp. 62-84

Gavazza, A. (2011). *Leasing and Secondary Markets: Theory and Evidence from Commercial Aircraft.* Journal of Political Economy, Vo. 119, Issue 2, April 2011, pp. 325-377

Gibson, W. & Morrell, P.S. (2004). *Theory and practice in aircraft financial evaluation.* Journal of Air Transport Management, Vol. 10, pp. 427-433

Good, W.A. (2000). *Flight Crew Scheduling Update: The Strategic Management of Airline Intellectual Capital and Core Competencies.* In: Butler, G.F. & Keller, M.R. (2000).

Gorjidooz, J. & Vasigh, B. (2010). *Aircraft Valuation in Dynamic Air Transport Industry.* Journal of Business & Economics Research, Vol. 8, Issue 7, July 2010, pp. 1-16

Government Accounting Office (2001a). *Airline Industry Emergency Assistance, Report GAO-02-133R, October 5.* Washington, D.C., United States: United States General Accounting Office

Government Accounting Office (2001b). *Testimony before the committee on commerce, science, and transportation, U.S. Senate, September 20, 2001, Commercial aviation: A framework for considering federal financial assistance.* Washington, D.C., United States: United States General Accounting Office

Grinhold, R.C. & Kahn, R.N. (2000). *Active portfolio management – A quantitative approach for providing superior returns and controlling risk (2nd ed.).* New York, United States: McGraw-Hill

Guenther, R. (2005). *Airline Stock's reaction to 9/11: Full Service versus Low Cost Carriers.* Maastricht, Netherlands: University of Maastricht, Master Thesis

Gugler, K., Mueller, D.C., Yurtoglu, B.B. & Zulehner, C. (2003). *The effects of mergers: An international comparison.* International Journal of Industrial Organization, Vol. 21, pp. 625-653

Henstra, D., Ruijgrok, C. & Tavasszy, L. (2007). *Globalized trade, logistics and intermodality: European perspectives.* In: Leinbach, T.R. & Capineri, C. (2007)

Hirshleifer, D., Myers, J.N., Myers, L.A. & Siew, H.T. (2008). *Do Individual Investors Cause Post-Earnings Announcement Drift? Direct Evidence from Personal Trades.* Accounting Review, Vol. 83, Issue 6, November 2008, pp. 1521-1550

Hoberg, G. & Phillips, G. (2010). *Real and Financial Industry Booms and Busts.* Journal of Finance, Vol. 65, Issue 1, February 2010, pp. 45-86

Holloway, S. (1998). *Changing Planes: A Strategic Management Perspective on an Industry in Transition*. Ashgate Publishing Ltd.

Hu, Q. (2010). *Network Game and Capacity Investment Under Market Uncertainty*. Production and Operations Management, Vol. 19, No. 1, January-February 2010, pp. 98-110

ICAO (2001). *Aircraft Accident and Incident Investigation*. International Standards and Recommended Practices. Annex 13 to the Convention on International Civil Aviation (9th ed.). Montréal, Quebec, Canada: International Civil Aviation Organization

ICAO (2010). *Annual Report of the Council 2010*. Documentation for the session of the Assembly in 2013, Doc 9952: Montréal, Quebec, Canada: International Civil Aviation Organization

International Monetary Fund (2009). *World Economic Outlook – Crisis and Recovery (Apr 09)*. Washington, D.C., United States: IMF Multimedia Services Division

Jarrah, A.I. (2000). *An Efficient Airline Re-Fleeting Model for the Incremental Modification of Planned Fleet Assignments*. Transportation Science, Vol. 34, No. 4, November 2000, pp. 349-363

Jegadeesh, N. & Titman, S. (1993). *Returns to Buying Winners and Selling Losers: Implications for Stock Market Efficiency*. Journal of Finance, Vol. 48, Issue 1, March 1993, pp. 65-91

Jensen, M.C. (1968). *Problems in Selection of Security Portfolios – The Performance of Mutual Funds in the Period 1945-1964*. Journal of Finance, Vol. 23, May 1968, pp. 389-416

Jensen, G.R. & Johnson, R.R. (1995). *Discount Rate Changes and Security Returns in the U.S. 1962-1991*. Journal of Banking & Finance, Vol. 19, pp. 79-95

Jensen, G.R., Mercer, J.M. & Johnson, R.R. (1996). *Business Conditions, Monetary Policy, and Expected Security Returns*. Journal of Financial Economics, Vol. 40, pp. 213-237

Jensen, G.R. & Mercer, J.M. (2002). *Monetary Policy and the Cross-Section of Expected Stock Returns*. Journal of Financial Research. Vo. 25, Issue 1, Spring 2002, pp. 125-139

Joint Aviation Authority (2007). *JAR-OPS 1: Commercial Air Transportation (Aeroplanes)*. Hoofddorp, Netherlands: Joint Aviation Authority, Amendment 13, May 1, 2007

Kaps, R. W. (2000). *Fiscal Aspects of Aviation Management*. Carbondale and Edwardsville, United States: Southern Illinois University Press

Kedem, B. & Fokianos, K. (2002). *Regression Models for Time Series Analysis*. Hoboken, NJ, United States: John Wiley & Sons

Koch, B. & Kraus, A. (2005). *Integrator Network Strategies And Parameters Of Airport Choice In The European Air Cargo Market*. In: Delfmann, W., Baum, H., Auerbach, S. & Albers, S. (2005)

Leinbach, T.R. & Capineri, C. (2007). *Globalized Freight Transport – Intermodality, E-Commerce, Logistics and Sustainability*. Cheltenham, United Kingdom.: Edward Elgar

Lie, E. & Lie, H.J. (2002). *Multiples Used to Estimate Corporate Value*. Financial Analysts Journal, Vol. 58, Issue 2, March/April 2002, pp. 44-54

Liehr, M., Größler, A., Klein, M. & Milling, P.M. (2001). *Cycles in the sky: understanding and managing business cycles in the airline market*. System Dynamics Review, Vol. 17, No. 4, Winter 2001, pp. 311-322

Littlejohns, A. & McGairl, S. (2003). *Aircraft Financing (3rd ed.)*. London, United Kingdom: Euromoney Books

Listes, O. & Dekker, R. (2005). *A Scenario Aggregation-Based Approach for Determining a Robus Airline Fleet Composition for Dynamic Capacity Allocation*. Transportation Science, Vol. 39, No. 3, August 2005, pp. 367-382

Livnat, J. & Mendenhall, R.R. (2006). *Comparing the Post-Earnings Announcement Drift for Surprises Calculated from Analyst and Time Series Forecasts*. Journal of Accounting Review, Vol. 44, Issue 1, March 2006, pp. 177-205

Liu, Y., Szewczyk, S.H. & Zantout, Z. (2008). *Underreaction to Dividend Reductions and Omissions*. Journal of Finance, Vol. 63, Issue 2, April 2008, pp. 987-1020

Mazouz, K., Nathan, L.J. & Joulmer, J. (2009). *Stock Price Reaction Following Large One-Day Price Changes*. Journal of Banking & Finance, Vol 33, pp. 1481-1493

Merkert, R. & Hensher, D. (2011). *The impact of strategic management and fleet planning on airline efficiency – A random effects Tobit model based on DEA efficiency scores*. Transporation Research Part A: Policy and Practice, Vol. 45, Issue 7, August 2011, pp. 686-695

Morrell, P.S. (2007). *Airline Finance (3rd ed.)*. Hampshire, United Kingdom: Ashgate

MSCI (2010). MSCI World Index – Index Fact Sheet. MSCI Inc.

Neidl, R.E. (2000). *A New Idea Is Born and Developed by a Visionary: Atlas Air, Inc*. In: Butler, G.F. & Keller, M.R. (2000)

Netessine, S., Dobson, G. & Shumsky, R.A. (2002). *Flexible Service Capacity. Optimal Investment and the Impact of Demand Correlation.* Operations Research, Vol. 50, No. 2, March-April 2002, pp. 375-388

OECD (2009). *OECD Economic Outlook, Volume 2009/1, No. 85.* Organization for Economic Co-operation and Development (OECD)

Otten, R. & Bams, D. (2004). *How to Measure Mutual Fund Performance: Economic versus Statistical Relevance.* Accounting and Finance, Vol. 44, Issue 2, July 2004, pp. 203-222

Oum, T.H., Zhang, A. & Zhang, Y. (2000). *Optimal demand for operating lease of aircraft.* Transportation Research Part B: Methodological, Vol. 24, Issue 1, January 2000, pp. 17-29

Pan, A.G. de Borges & Santo, A. Espirito (2004). *Developing a Fleet Standardization Index For Airline Pricing.* Journal of Air Transportation, Vol. 9, Issue 2, 2004

Pulvino, T.C. (1998). *Do Asset Fire Sales Exist? An Empirical Investigation of Commercial Aircraft Transactions.* Journal of Finance, Vol. 53, Issue 3, June 1998, pp. 939-978

Reinhart, C.M. & Rogoff, K.S. (2008). *The Aftermath of Financial Crisis.* Draft paper as of December 19, 2008; presented at the American Economic Association meetings in SanFrancisco, January 3, 2009

Reuters (2009). *Three Top Economists Agree 2009 Worst Financial Crisis Since Great Depression; Risks Increase if Right Steps are Not Taken.* Article as of February 27, 2009. Business Wire 2009. Retrieved December 15, 2009 from the World Wide Web: http://www.reuters.com/article/idUS193520+27-Feb-2009+BW20090227

Rexing, B., Barnhart, C. & Kniker, T. (2000). *Airline Fleet Assignment with Time Window.* Transportation Science, Vol. 34, No. 1, February 2000

Rhoades, D.L. (2003). *Phoenix rising.* Aldershot, Hants, United Kingdom: Ashgate.

Ross, S.A., Westerfield, R.W. & Jaffe, J. (2005). *Corporate Finance (7th ed.).* New York, NY, United States: McGraw-Hill

Schwenk, W. & Giemulla, E. (2005). *Handbuch des Luftverkehrsrechts (3rd ed.).* (Manual of Aeronautic Laws). Cologne, Germany: Carl Heymanns Verlag

Shleifer, A. (2000). *Inefficient Markets: An Introduction to Behavioral Finance.* Oxford, United Kingdom: Oxford University Press

Shleifer, A. & Vishny, R.W. (1992). *Liquidation Values and Debt Capacity: A Market Equilibrium Approach*. Journal of Finance, Vol. 47, Issue 4, September 1992, pp. 1343-1366

Sterzenbach, R., Conrady, R. & Fichert, F (2009). *Luftverkehr (4th ed.)*. Muenchen, Germany: Oldenbourg Wissenschaftsverlag GmbH

Smith, B.C. & Johnson, E.L. (2006). *Robust Airline Fleet Assignment: Imposing Station Purity Using Station Decomposition.* Transportation Science, Vol. 40, No. 4, November 2006, pp. 407-516

Sunshine, R.A. & Woodward, G.T. (2001). *H.R. 2926, Air Transportation Safety and system Stabilization Act. U.S. Congressional Budget Office Pay-as-you-go estimate, November 30, 2001*. Washington, D.C., United States: U.S. Congress

Thomson Reuters Datastream (2009), (2010), (2011).

TNT (2009). *TNT Annual Report 2009 – Weathering the Storm.* Amsterdam, The Netherlands: TNT N.V.

U.S. Congress (2001). *Public Law 107-42. Air Transportation Safety and System Stabilization Act.* Congressional Record, Vol. 147 (2001): Sept. 21, considered and passed House and Senate. Weekly Compilation of Presidential Documents, Vol. 37 (2001): Sept. 22, Presidential statement

U.S. Courts (2009). *Bankruptcy Basics – Applicable to Cases Filed on or After October 17, 2005 (Revised 3rd ed.).* Bankruptcy Judges Division, Administrative Office of the United States Courts, December 2009

Walker, T.J., Thiengtham, D.J. & Lin, M.Y. (2005). *On the Performance of Airlines and Airplane Manufacturers Following Aviation Disasters.* Canadian Journal of Administrative Sciences, Vol. 22, Issue 1, March 2005, pp. 21-34

World Economic Forum (2008). *The Financial Development Report 2008*. World Economic Forum USA Inc.

Wensveen, J.G. (2007). *Air Transportation – A Management Perspective. (6th ed.).* Hampshire, United Kingdom: Ashgate

Interview references

Atlas Air (2009). *Interviews with William Flynn, CEO Atlas Air Worldwide Holdings, USA, and Jason Grant, SVP and CFO Atlas Air Worldwide Holdings, USA.* Telephone interviews: February 10, 2009 and February 16, 2009.

AWAS (2009). *Interview with Carter White, SVP Aircraft Trading AWAS, Ireland.* Telephone interview: February 4, 2009.

DVB Bank (2009). *Interview with Stephan Sayre, Investment Adviser to Deucalion Aviation Funds, DVB Bank SE, UK.* Telephone interview: February 9, 2009.

LCI Aviation (2009). *Interviews with Crispin Maunder, CEO Lease Corporation International, UK, and Jaspal Jandu, CFO Lease Corporation International, UK.* Telephone interview: February 2, 2009.

Macquarie AirFinance (2009). *Interview with Harry Forsythe, SVP Sales and Marketing Macquarie AirFinance, Australia.* Telephone interview: February 19, 2009.

Titan Aviation Leasing (2009). *Interview with Ray Sisson, CEO Titan Aviation Leasing Ltd., Ireland.* In same telephone interview as Atlas Air (2009): February 10, 2009

R. Günther, *Impact of Aircraft Sourcing & Financing on Financial Success*, Edition KWV, https://doi.org/10.1007/978-3-658-24094-3

Appendices

R. Günther, *Impact of Aircraft Sourcing & Financing on Financial Success*,
Edition KWV, https://doi.org/10.1007/978-3-658-24094-3

Date	**Carrier**	**Chapter**
2/29/2000	Tower Air	11
5/1/2000	Kitty Hawk	11
9/19/2000	Pro Air	11
9/27/2000	Fine Air Services	11
12/3/2000	Legend Airlines	11
12/6/2000	National Airlines	11
12/13/2000	Allegiant Air	11
1/10/2001	Trans World Airlines	11
8/13/2001	Midway Airlines	11
1/2/2002	Sun Country Airlines	7
7/30/2002	Vanguard Airlines	11
8/11/2002	US Airways	11
12/9/2002	United Airlines	11
3/21/2003	Hawaiian Airlines	11
10/30/2003	Midway Airlines	7
1/23/2004	Great Plains Airlines	11
1/30/2004	Atlas Air/Polar Air Cargo	11
09/12/2004	US Airways	11
10/26/2004	ATA Airlines	11
12/1/2004	Southeast Airlines	7
12/30/2004	Aloha Airlines	11
9/14/2005	Delta Air Lines	11
9/14/2005	Comair	11
9/14/2005	Northwest Airlines	11
9/29/2005	TransMeridian Airlines	7
10/13/2005	Mesaba Airlines	11
11/07/2005	Independence Air (originally Atlantic Coast Airlines)	11
12/28/2005	Era Aviation	11
1/6/2006*	Independence Air	7
2/21/2006	Florida Coastal Airlines	11
10/15/2007	Kitty Hawk Aircargo	11
12/24/2007	MAXjet Airways	11
1/7/2008	Big Sky	7
3/31/2008	Champion Air (orig. MGM Grand Air)	11
3/31/2008	Aloha Airlines	7
4/2/2008	ATA Airlines	11
4/7/2008	Skybus Airlines	11
4/11/2008	Frontier Airlines	11

4/26/2008	Eos Airlines	11
5/14/2008	Air Midwest	7
6/18/2008	Gemini Air Cargo	11
7/18/2008	Vintage Props & Jets	11
8/12/2008	Gemini Air Cargo	7
10/06/2008	Sun Country	11
10/15/2008	Primaris Airlines	11

Appendix 1: *U.S. airline bankruptcies & service cessations 2000-2008*

This table presents U.S. airlines that filed for liquidation (chapter 7) or reorganization (chapter 11) under the U.S. Bankruptcy Code between 2000 and 2008. Source of the information is Air Transport Association (2008) based on an unofficial compilation of research. The information is not used as an authoritative source.

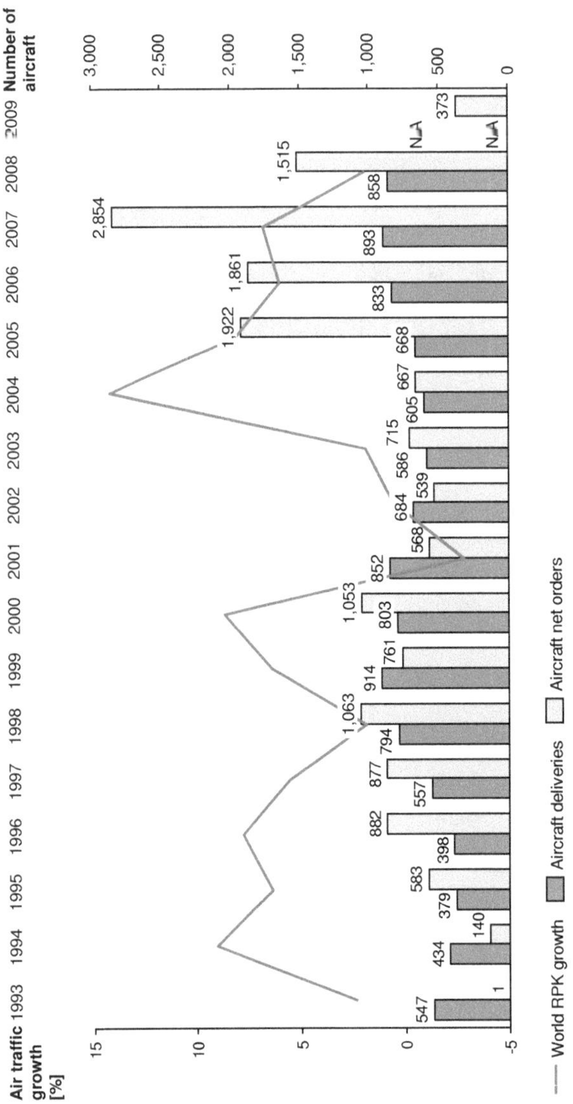

Appendix 2: *Deliveries and net orders of Airbus and Boeing aircraft versus air traffic growth 1993-2009*

This figure presents deliveries and net orders (total gross orders minus total cancellations) of Airbus and Boeing aircraft in the years 1993 to 2009 in comparison to the percentage growth of air traffic (year on year) based on world revenue passenger kilometers (RPKs). Boeing includes McDonnell-Douglas. Source of aircraft data is Ascend Worldwide Ltd. (2009). Information on RPK growth rates is retrieved from Airbus (2009), based on Global Insight and ICAO. RPK figures post 2000 are validated with information from the Federal Aviation Administration (2008 and 2009), based on ICAO. Information pre 2000 could not be validated with other sources.

	SIZE	LIQUIDITY	NDTEBITDA	EBITDAMAR	EQITYRAT	INTRSTCOV.	RPKMKTSHR	FTKMKTSHR	PINT
SIZE	1								
LIQUIDITY	-0.38	1							
NDTEBITDA	0.24	-0.28	1						
EBITDAMAR	-0.10	0.57	-0.29	1					
EQITYRAT	-0.33	0.49	-0.41	0.38	1				
INTRSTCOVRG	-0.09	-0.08	-0.08	-0.11	-0.06	1			
RPKMKTSHR	0.70	-0.25	0.03	-0.15	-0.29	-0.11	1		
FTKMKTSHR	0.54	-0.20	-0.09	0.08	0.06	-0.09	0.28	1	
PINT	0.52	-0.39	0.42	-0.23	-0.36	-0.19	0.33	0.28	1
PINT1	0.44	-0.27	0.49	-0.10	-0.25	-0.19	0.20	0.19	0.91
PFREIGHT	0.11	0.03	0.01	0.26	0.10	-0.09	-0.21	0.38	0.18
TOTALAC	0.67	-0.26	-0.08	-0.16	-0.23	-0.15	0.87	0.41	0.17
OPSLEASE	-0.35	-0.18	-0.02	-0.13	-0.03	0.09	-0.26	-0.26	-0.07
STORAC	0.17	-0.15	-0.13	-0.14	-0.13	-0.19	0.06	0.21	0.25
nYRORDER	-0.51	0.35	-0.21	0.24	0.31	0.03	-0.27	-0.26	-0.34
nYROPTION	-0.40	0.20	-0.18	0.28	0.25	-0.03	-0.09	-0.27	-0.34
1YROPTION	0.16	-0.02	-0.05	-0.07	-0.10	-0.03	0.23	0.10	0.10
AVGAGE	-0.11	-0.15	-0.23	-0.10	-0.10	0.05	-0.09	0.08	-0.17
AMR/UAL	0.22	-0.05	0.03	-0.19	-0.24	-0.21	0.40	0.07	0.01
MFSC	0.68	-0.41	0.39	-0.27	-0.46	-0.12	0.53	0.17	0.70
NFSC	-0.66	0.34	-0.26	-0.06	0.38	-0.12	-0.33	-0.27	-0.43
LCC	-0.37	0.13	-0.17	0.22	0.10	0.35	-0.20	-0.27	-0.43
FREIGHT	0.12	0.12	-0.13	0.26	0.18	-0.07	-0.26	0.37	-0.13
APAC	0.29	-0.22	0.38	0.10	-0.12	-0.05	0.00	0.06	0.41
EMEA	0.08	0.07	0.02	-0.09	0.05	-0.11	0.02	0.08	0.08
LATAM	-0.13	-0.14	0.01	0.02	-0.09	-0.04	-0.15	-0.11	0.27
NORAM	-0.27	0.19	-0.35	-0.02	0.10	0.15	0.04	-0.07	-0.53

	PINT1	PFREIGHT	TOTALAC	OPSLEASE	STORAC	nYRORDER	nYROPTION	1YROPTION	AVGAGE
SIZE									
LIQUIDITY									
NDTEBITDA									
EBITDAMAR									
EQITYRAT									
INTRSTCOVRG									
RPKMKTSHR									
FTKMKTSHR									
PINT									
PINT1	1								
PFREIGHT	0.16	1							
TOTALAC	0.00	-0.08	1						
OPSLEASE	-0.10	-0.12	-0.24	1					
STORAC	0.16	0.32	0.21	-0.11	1				
nYRORDER	-0.33	-0.24	-0.29	0.12	-0.16	1			
nYROPTION	-0.34	-0.24	-0.07	0.21	-0.07	0.74	1		
1YROPTION	0.02	-0.07	0.19	0.13	0.05	-0.06	-0.09	1	
AVGAGE	-0.25	0.28	0.11	-0.22	0.34	-0.14	0.05	-0.07	1
AMR/UAL	-0.06	-0.10	0.44	-0.08	0.03	-0.09	-0.05	-0.04	0.01
MFSC	0.66	-0.07	0.31	-0.03	0.11	-0.42	-0.36	0.16	-0.37
NFSC	-0.42	-0.23	-0.31	-0.02	-0.12	0.43	0.35	-0.09	0.06
LCC	-0.35	-0.25	-0.15	0.22	-0.21	0.30	0.26	-0.09	0.08
FREIGHT	-0.18	0.73	0.05	-0.20	0.24	-0.18	-0.15	-0.06	0.47
APAC	0.56	0.13	-0.25	-0.16	-0.12	-0.22	-0.30	-0.12	-0.33
EMEA	0.14	-0.14	-0.05	0.00	0.13	-0.01	-0.02	0.12	-0.15
LATAM	0.18	0.09	-0.12	0.46	-0.03	0.05	0.11	-0.04	-0.04
NORAM	-0.66	-0.03	0.30	-0.05	0.00	0.17	0.23	0.02	0.42

	AMR/UAL	MFSC	NFSC	LCC	FREIGHT	APAC	EMEA	LATAM	NORAM
SIZE									
LIQUIDITY									
NDTEBITDA									
EBITDAMAR									
EQITYRAT									
INTRSTCOVRG									
RPKMKTSHR									
FTKMKTSHR									
PINT									
PINT1									
PFREIGHT									
TOTALAC									
OPSLEASE									
STORAC									
nYRORDER									
nYROPTION									
1YROPTION									
AVGAGE									
AMR/UAL	1								
MFSC	0.16	1							
NFSC	-0.09	-0.53	1						
LCC	-0.09	-0.53	-0.17	1					
FREIGHT	-0.06	-0.39	-0.12	-0.12	1				
APAC	-0.12	0.45	-0.24	-0.24	-0.17	1			
EMEA	-0.11	0.19	-0.21	0.08	-0.15	-0.30	1		
LATAM	-0.04	0.16	-0.09	-0.09	-0.06	-0.12	-0.11	1	
NORAM	0.21	-0.60	0.41	0.18	0.30	-0.58	-0.51	-0.21	1

Appendix 3: *Correlation of explanatory and control variables for analysis of stock market's reaction on 9/11 (as of Ye 2000)*

Observation period: y1 (RoW) September 11, 2001
Sample: Non-U.S.
Sample size: 25 (incl. Air Canada as only NORAM company)

Cluster	Variable	Model 1	Model 2	Model 3	Model 4	Model 5	Model 6	Model 7
	Constant	0.0420 (0.0540)	0.1122 *** (0.0326)	0.1741 (0.2862)	-0.0747 *** (0.0180)	0.0749 ** (0.0326)	-0.0674 (0.0452)	-0.0275 (0.0553)
Financial	SIZE			-0.0172 (0.0180)				
	LIQUIDITY	-0.0789 * (0.0382)		-0.0372 (0.0353)				
	NDTEBITDA						[illegible]	
	EBITDAMAR						0.2826 (0.2776)	
	EQITYRAT	0.1889 * (0.1035)						
	INTRSTCOVRG			-0.0237 (0.0177)		-0.0246 (0.0163)		
Market	RPKMKTSHR	-7.1559 ** (2.8667)	-6.1524 ** (2.7703)					-4.4847 ** (2.1452)
	FTKMKTSHR	-1.4259 ** (0.5697)	-1.0182 * (0.4872)					
	PINT			-0.0917 (0.0959)				
	PINT1							
	PFREIGHT			-0.1291 (0.1412)		-0.1512 (0.1182)		
Aircraft fleet	TOTALAC	0.0008 ** (0.0003)	0.0007 ** (0.0003)					
	OPSLEASE	-0.2538 ** (0.0869)	-0.2018 *** (0.0687)					-0.1932 ** (0.0890)
	STORAC	-0.9921 *** (0.3103)	-0.6269 * (0.2982)					-0.7280 * (0.3680)
	nYRORDER	0.0999 (0.0850)						
	nYROPTION	-0.0966 (0.0752)		-0.0407 (0.0456)		-0.0301 (0.0332)		
	1YROPTION							
	AVGAGE	0.0103 * (0.0055)		0.0096 (0.0066)				
Carrier	AMR/UAL							
	MFSC							0.1306 ** (0.0604)
	NFSC							
	LCC						-0.0815 (0.0722)	
	FREIGHT							
Region	APAC			0.1517 *** (0.0346)	0.1038 *** (0.0260)			
	EMEA	-0.1219 *** (0.0288)	-0.1307 *** (0.0261)			-0.1290 *** (0.0300)		
	LATAM			0.0775 (0.0615)				
	NORAM	-0.1382 ** (0.0626)	-0.1273 * (0.0628)					
	R^2 (adjusted)	0.63	0.58	0.40	0.38	0.44	-0.04	0.23
	F-statistic	4.46 ***	5.72 ***	2.80 **	15.88 ***	5.62 ***	0.67	2.77 *

Appendix 4: *Regression models for stock market's initial reaction after 9/11 – Sep 11, non-U.S. sample*

Observation period: y1 (U.S.) September 17, 2001
Sample: U.S.
Sample size: 23

Cluster	Variable	Model 1	Model 2	Model 3	Model 4	Model 5	Model 6	Model 7
	Constant	-0.4514 *** (0.1156)	-0.5671 *** (0.0852)	-0.6194 *** (0.1050)	-0.4163 *** (0.0469)	-0.2658 *** (0.0530)	-0.9930 (0.8819)	-0.4728 *** (0.0829)
Financial	SIZE						0.0461 (0.0662)	
	LIQUIDITY			0.1369 * (0.0725)				0.1499 * (0.0748)
	NDTEBITDA	-0.0811 *** (0.0169)	-0.0749 *** (0.0166)			-0.0612 *** (0.0197)		
	EBITDAMAR	1.3156 *** (0.3333)	1.3772 *** (0.2957)					
	EQITYRAT			0.2828 (0.2469)			0.2260 (0.2667)	
	INTRSTCOVRG	-0.0057 (0.0056)						
Market	RPKMKTSHR	-10.3539 *** (2.2795)	-10.2534 *** (2.4023)					
	FTKMKTSHR							4.2558 ** (1.8847)
	PINT	0.7990 ** (0.3122)	0.9679 *** (0.3077)					
	PINT1							
	PFREIGHT			-0.3901 (0.2826)			0.2370 (0.1818)	
Aircraft fleet	TOTALAC						-0.0004 (0.0005)	
	OPSLEASE	-0.2743 ** (0.0993)	-0.2524 ** (0.1012)			-0.3374 ** (0.1360)		
	STORAC			4.4931 ** (1.9659)				
	nYRORDER	-0.0606 (0.0385)						-0.0529 (0.0763)
	nYROPTION			-0.0704 (0.0632)			-0.0242 (0.0714)	
	1YROPTION							
	AVGAGE	0.0075 ** (0.0034)	0.0093 ** (0.0034)					
Carrier	AMR/UAL							-0.2401 (0.1627)
	MFSC	0.2908 *** (0.0948)	0.3028 *** (0.0992)					
	NFSC	-0.0428 (0.0742)						
	LCC						-0.1502 (0.1250)	
	FREIGHT			0.3816 * (0.1990)	0.3630 *** (0.1124)	0.2924 *** (0.0897)		
Region	APAC							
	EMEA							
	LATAM							
	NORAM							
	R^2 (adjusted)	0.83	0.81	0.37	0.30	0.58	0.10	0.21
	F-statistic	11.43 ***	14.09 ***	3.13 **	10.44 ***	11.33 ***	1.40	2.50 *

Appendix 5: *Regression models for stock market's initial reaction after 9/11 – Sep 17, U.S. sample*

Observation period: y5 (RoW) September 17, 2001
Sample: Non-U.S.
Sample size: 25 (incl. Air Canada as only NORAM company)

Cluster	Variable	Model 1	Model 2	Model 3	Model 4	Model 5	Model 6	Model 7
	Constant	-0.8662 *** (0.2778)	-0.3414 ** (0.1255)	-0.4592 (0.8389)	0.1131 ** (0.0452)	0.0442 (0.0293)	-0.1227 * (0.0603)	-0.6033 (0.3646)
Financial	SIZE			0.0409 (0.0555)				0.0366 (0.0231)
	LIQUIDITY			-0.0213 (0.0591)				
	NDTEBITDA	0.0070 (0.0042)		0.0030 (0.0032)				
	EBITDAMAR	1.7142 ** (0.5556)	0.8165 ** (0.3120)					0.5968 * (0.2933)
	EQITYRAT	-0.3561 (0.2047)						
	INTRSTCOVRG	-0.0675 ** (0.0268)	-0.0719 *** (0.0235)			-0.0549 ** (0.0251)		
Market	RPKMKTSHR						-3.6052 (5.0569)	
	FTKMKTSHR	1.9106 * (0.8856)		-0.8744 (1.2962)				
	PINT	-0.1450 (0.1269)		-0.3386 ** (0.1433)	-0.2500 ** (0.1107)			
	PINT1							
	PFREIGHT			0.6260 * (0.3194)	0.4218 ** (0.1713)			
Aircraft fleet	TOTALAC			-0.0003 (0.0005)			0.0008 (0.0005)	
	OPSLEASE			-0.4800 ** (0.1964)	-0.4600 *** (0.1241)			
	STORAC	0.7637 (0.5103)		1.0886 * (0.5684)	0.8560 * (0.4252)			
	nYRORDER						-0.0819 (0.1944)	
	nYROPTION	0.1962 * (0.0925)					0.1284 (0.1499)	
	1YROPTION							
	AVGAGE	0.0260 * (0.0119)						
Carrier	AMR/UAL							
	MFSC	0.3682 ** (0.1504)	0.1648 * (0.0904)					
	NFSC							
	LCC			0.0727 (0.1439)			0.0580 (0.1399)	
	FREIGHT							
Region	APAC			-0.2397 *** (0.0624)	-0.1888 *** (0.0394)	-0.1279 *** (0.0402)		-0.1899 *** (0.0444)
	EMEA	0.1497 ** (0.0527)	0.1587 *** (0.0447)					
	LATAM	-0.0327 (0.0960)		0.1965 (0.1243)	0.1889 * (0.0969)			
	NORAM	0.2061 * (0.1009)	0.2938 *** (0.0962)					
	R^2 (adjusted)	0.59	0.51	0.53	0.62	0.42	-0.01	0.40
	F-statistic	3.65 **	6.01 ***	3.24 **	7.48 ***	9.71 ***	0.94	6.32 ***

Appendix 6: *Regression models for stock market's initial reaction after 9/11 – Sep 17, non-U.S. sample*

Observation period: y1 (U.S.) = y5 (RoW) September 17, 2001
Sample: All companies
Sample size: 48

Cluster	Variable	Model 1	Model 2	Model 3	Model 4	Model 5	Model 6	Model 7
	Constant	-0.0928 (0.2160)	-0.1099 (0.0879)	-0.7315 (0.8361)	-0.0863 * (0.0485)	-0.7507 (0.6025)	0.0410 (0.0570)	-0.2681 *** (0.0919)
Financial	SIZE			0.0258 (0.0546)		0.0184 (0.0379)		
	LIQUIDITY			0.0708 (0.0579)		0.0842 (0.0747)		
	NDTEBITDA					0.0044 (0.0081)		
	EBITDAMAR	0.6572 * (0.3285)	0.6507 ** (0.2798)					0.7905 ** (0.3222)
	EQITYRAT	0.0794 (0.1457)		0.1978 (0.1996)		0.2481 (0.2583)		
	INTRSTCOVRG	-0.0132 * (0.0071)	-0.0138 ** (0.0066)					-0.0158 ** (0.0076)
Market	RPKMKTSHR			-6.1239 * (3.0827)	-6.2780 *** (1.9763)			-8.7861 *** (1.9063)
	FTKMKTSHR			0.1227 (1.4200)		0.4901 (1.9022)		
	PINT	0.0221 (0.1843)		0.2797 (0.2166)		0.4064 (0.2661)		
	PINT1							
	PFREIGHT	-0.0778 (0.1584)				0.1306 (0.1873)		
Aircraft fleet	TOTALAC	-0.0005 *** (0.0002)	-0.0005 *** (0.0002)				-0.0001 (0.0002)	
	OPSLEASE	-0.3882 *** (0.1174)	-0.3779 *** (0.0944)					-0.3776 *** (0.1069)
	STORAC	1.0356 (0.6865)	1.0161 * (0.5885)					
	nYRORDER			0.0592 (0.0891)		0.0472 (0.1107)		
	nYROPTION			-0.0368 (0.0742)		-0.0719 (0.0912)		
	1YROPTION							
	AVGAGE	0.0024 (0.0046)		0.0070 (0.0049)		0.0045 (0.0069)		
Carrier	AMR/UAL	-0.2216 * (0.1219)	-0.2350 ** (0.1123)				-0.2007 (0.1409)	
	MFSC	0.2463 ** (0.0945)	0.2339 *** (0.0761)					0.2339 *** (0.0668)
	NFSC			-0.2061 (0.1748)	-0.2614 *** (0.0840)			-0.0941 (0.0834)
	LCC			-0.2257 (0.1351)	-0.3037 *** (0.0793)		-0.1272 (0.0770)	
	FREIGHT	0.2462 * (0.1370)	0.2196 ** (0.0834)				0.2843 *** (0.0979)	
Region	APAC	-0.3132 ** (0.1300)	-0.2545 *** (0.0608)				-0.1666 ** (0.0724)	
	EMEA			0.2473 *** (0.0718)	0.2496 *** (0.0670)			0.2109 *** (0.0583)
	LATAM	-0.0807 (0.1370)		0.1249 (0.1640)		0.1767 (0.2004)		
	NORAM	-0.2969 * (0.1506)	-0.2230 *** (0.0678)				-0.3690 *** (0.0659)	
	R^2 (adjusted)	0.67	0.70	0.40	0.43	0.04	0.50	0.59
	F-statistic	7.32 ***	12.16 ***	3.44 ***	9.86 ***	1.16	8.70 ***	10.59 ***

Appendix 7: *Regression models for stock market's initial reaction after 9/11 – Sep 11, all companies*

Observation period y1 (U.S.) = y1 (RoW) September 17 = September 11, 2001
Sample All companies
Sample size 48

Cluster	Variable	Model 1	Model 2	Model 3	Model 4	Model 5	Model 6	Model 7
	Constant	0.5181 (0.6400)	-0.0915 (0.0698)	-0.7418 (0.5062)	-0.2196 *** (0.0638)	-0.3158 *** (0.0477)	0.3600 *** (0.0807)	0.2400 ** (0.1000)
Financial	SIZE	-0.0391 (0.0444)		0.0339 (0.0348)				
	LIQUIDITY	-0.0224 (0.0550)		-0.0274 (0.0676)				
	NDTEBITDA	-0.0031 (0.0047)		0.0017 (0.0057)				
	EBITDAMAR	0.2323 (0.4337)		1.3270 ** (0.5448)	0.9403 *** (0.3067)		0.1566 (0.1849)	0.7582 ** (0.3267)
	EQITYRAT							
	INTRSTCOVRG	-0.0176 ** (0.0083)	-0.0246 *** (0.0069)					
Market	RPKMKTSHR	-2.5805 (4.4341)		-5.2638 * (2.9204)			0.3732 (1.2982)	
	FTKMKTSHR			-1.0414 (1.3190)				
	PINT2			0.2104 (0.2117)		0.5022 *** (0.1711)		
	PINT1						0.4713 *** (0.1254)	
	PFREIGHT			-0.0695 (0.1456)		0.2560 * (0.1392)		
Aircraft fleet	TOTALAC	-0.0002 (0.0004)	-0.0008 *** (0.0001)					-0.0005 ** (0.0002)
	OPSLEASE	-0.4465 *** (0.1216)	-0.3687 *** (0.0955)					-0.3056 *** (0.1113)
	STORAC						0.3305 (0.9025)	
	nYRORDER			0.0910 (0.0780)				
	nYROPTION			-0.1178 (0.0707)				
	1YROPTION							
	AVGAGE			0.0116 ** (0.0050)	0.0108 ** (0.0041)			0.0095 ** (0.0043)
Carrier	AMR/UAL	-0.2659 ** (0.1233)	-0.3244 *** (0.1133)					
	MFSC	0.2532 ** (0.1036)	0.2541 *** (0.0631)					0.1807 ** (0.0848)
	NFSC	-0.1104 (0.1054)	-0.1588 * (0.0802)					
	LCC			-0.2109 ** (0.0863)	-0.2121 *** (0.0691)			
	FREIGHT	0.2547 * (0.1369)	0.2133 ** (0.0936)					
Region	APAC			-0.0076 (0.0880)				
	EMEA	-0.0520 (0.0791)						
	LATAM	0.0816 (0.1366)		-0.0727 (0.1544)				
	NORAM	-0.1703 (0.1130)		-0.2533 *** (0.0724)	-0.3386 *** (0.0522)			-0.2123 *** (0.0783)
	R^2 (adjusted)	0.67	0.68	0.56	0.56	0.21	0.20	0.57
	F-statistic	7.35 ***	15.24 ***	4.94 ***	16.19 ***	7.24 ***	4.01 ***	11.54 ***

Appendix 8: *Regression models for stock market's initial reaction after 9/11 – Sep 11 = Sept 17, all companies*

Observation period y2-6 (RoW) September 12-18, 2001
Sample Non-U.S.
Sample size 25 (incl. Air Canada as only NORAM company)

Cluster	Variable	Model 1	Model 2	Model 3	Model 4	Model 5	Model 6	Model 7
	Constant	-0.2443 (0.2250)	-0.3251 *** (0.0765)	0.3933 (0.2266)	0.2156 (0.1689)	1.0288 (0.8495)	-0.2980 (0.2097)	-0.3251 *** (0.0765)
Financial	SIZE					-0.0874 (0.0605)		
	LIQUIDITY	-0.3165 ** (0.1403)		-0.0714 (0.0681)				
	NDTEBITDA					-0.0031 (0.0049)		
	EBITDAMAR	1.4950 * (0.7250)	0.6815 * (0.3637)					0.6815 * (0.3637)
	EQITYRAT						0.2025 (0.2371)	
	INTRSTCOVRG	-0.1061 ** (0.0449)	-0.0953 *** (0.0320)					-0.0953 *** (0.0320)
Market	RPKMKTSHR					9.5975 (6.8220)		
	FTKMKTSHR						0.6160 (1.3969)	
	PINT	-0.2377 (0.1960)		-0.3242 * (0.1740)				
	PINT1							
	PFREIGHT	0.3590 (0.3277)		0.3702 (0.2729)				
Aircraft fleet	TOTALAC	0.0004 (0.0005)	0.0008 ** (0.0003)					0.0008 ** (0.0003)
	OPSLEASE	-0.1585 (0.3040)		-0.5837 ** (0.2263)	-0.4188 ** (0.1989)			
	STORAC					0.3153 (0.7777)		
	nYRORDER	-0.2504 (0.1821)						
	nYROPTION						0.0426 (0.1301)	
	1YROPTION							
	AVGAGE	0.0243 (0.0156)						
Carrier	AMR/UAL							
	MFSC						0.0054 (0.1799)	
	NFSC							
	LCC	0.2310 (0.2687)						
	FREIGHT							
Region	APAC	-0.1854 * (0.0903)		-0.5169 *** (0.1597)	-0.4217 ** (0.1488)			
	EMEA			-0.3165 * (0.1538)	-0.2616 * (0.1408)			
	LATAM	0.0449 (0.1803)					0.1305 (0.1405)	
	NORAM	-0.2040 (0.1513)		-0.5486 ** (0.2166)	-0.4867 ** (0.1992)			
	R^2 (adjusted)	0.42	0.30	0.32	0.27	0.00	-0.09	0.30
	F-statistic	2.31 *	4.48 **	2.64 **	3.21 **	0.97	0.59	4.48 **

Appendix 9: *Regression models for stock market's short term reaction after 9/11 – Sep 12-18, non-U.S. sample*

Observation period y2-6 (U.S.) September 18-24, 2001
Sample U.S.
Sample size 23

Cluster	Variable	Model 1	Model 2	Model 3	Model 4	Model 5	Model 6	Model 7
	Constant	-1.0636 *** (0.2864)	-1.1618 *** (0.2445)	-0.7559 *** (0.1127)	0.0140 (0.0876)	-0.0742 *** (0.0229)	-0.1207 (0.0752)	-0.0297 (0.0414)
Financial	SIZE	0.0564 ** (0.0216)	0.0667 *** (0.0177)	0.0374 *** (0.0076)				
	LIQUIDITY	0.0210 (0.0347)			-0.0316 (0.0442)			-0.0695 ** (0.0316)
	NDTEBITDA	0.0068 (0.0158)			-0.0158 (0.0137)			-0.0225 (0.0161)
	EBITDAMAR	-0.0880 (0.2404)			0.0370 (0.3657)		0.1882 (0.2606)	
	EQITYRAT	0.2923 * (0.1458)	0.2444 *** (0.0547)	0.1867 *** (0.0477)				
	INTRSTCOVRG	-0.0059 (0.0031)	-0.0064 ** (0.0021)	-0.0057 *** (0.0019)				
Market	RPKMKTSHR	7.5640 ** (2.8300)	6.8699 *** (1.5360)	6.7817 *** (0.7599)				
	FTKMKTSHR	-0.2955 (0.9905)			-1.8752 (1.1775)			
	PINT	-0.8635 *** (0.2233)	-0.8910 *** (0.1288)	-0.8852 *** (0.1260)				
	PINT1							
	PFREIGHT	-0.0915 (0.0897)					-0.0029 (0.0833)	
Aircraft fleet	TOTALAC	-0.0002 (0.0003)	-0.0002 (0.0002)		0.0004 ** (0.0002)	0.0003 *** (0.0001)	0.0004 ** (0.0001)	
	OPSLEASE	0.1373 * (0.0623)	0.1367 *** (0.0358)	0.1203 *** (0.0348)				
	STORAC	1.4758 (0.8169)	1.0399 ** (0.3871)	0.7015 * (0.3461)				
	nYRORDER	-0.0050 (0.0376)			0.0721 * (0.0370)		-0.0229 (0.0349)	
	nYROPTION	-0.0053 (0.0287)			-0.0586 (0.0408)			0.0575 * (0.0282)
	1YROPTION							
	AVGAGE	0.0087 ** (0.0030)	0.0087 *** (0.0013)	0.0076 *** (0.0013)				
Carrier	AMR/UAL							0.1420 (0.0844)
	MFSC				-0.0826 (0.0951)			0.1183 ** (0.0532)
	NFSC				-0.0824 (0.0869)		0.0427 (0.0752)	
	LCC		-0.0208 (0.0234)		-0.0679 (0.0816)		0.0459 (0.0679)	
	FREIGHT		-0.0860 * (0.0439)					0.0771 (0.0564)
Region	APAC							
	EMEA							
	LATAM							
	NORAM							
	R^2 (adjusted)	0.82	0.90	0.89	0.49	0.46	0.34	0.32
	F-statistic	7.30 **	18.75 ***	22.63 ***	3.15 **	19.89 ***	2.88 **	2.72 *

Appendix 10: *Regression models for stock market's short term reaction after 9/11 – Sep 18-24, U.S. sample*

Observation period y6-10 (RoW) September 18-24, 2001
Sample Non-U.S.
Sample size 25 (incl. Air Canada as only NORAM company)

Cluster	Variable	Model 1	Model 2	Model 3	Model 4	Model 5	Model 6	Model 7
	Constant	-1.2107 *** (0.3930)	-1.3303 *** (0.3760)	-0.8840 *** (0.2251)	-0.7944 *** (0.2208)	-0.0795 (0.1539)	0.0372 (0.0418)	-0.0982 (0.0688)
Financial	SIZE	0.0907 *** (0.0247)	0.0935 *** (0.0244)					
	LIQUIDITY			0.1694 (0.1173)				
	NDTEBITDA	-0.0108 *** (0.0032)	-0.0093 *** (0.0029)				-0.0087 ** (0.0036)	
	EBITDAMAR			1.8250 ** (0.7008)	2.1197 *** (0.6563)			
	EQITYRAT	-0.2025 (0.1579)		-0.6461 ** (0.2666)	-0.6186 ** (0.2661)			
	INTRSTCOVRG	-0.1328 *** (0.0278)	-0.1216 *** (0.0265)				-0.0928 *** (0.0312)	
Market	RPKMKTSHR			-4.2653 (5.0966)				-2.1630 (5.6887)
	FTKMKTSHR						1.3509 (1.0034)	
	PINT	-0.3521 ** (0.1382)	-0.2504 ** (0.1090)					
	PINT1							
	PFREIGHT	0.1925 (0.1967)		-0.2885 (0.2551)				
Aircraft fleet	TOTALAC			0.0011 (0.0006)				0.0010 (0.0006)
	OPSLEASE	0.1980 (0.1187)						-0.0655 (0.1545)
	STORAC					0.7771 (0.7117)		
	nYRORDER			0.6094 *** (0.1816)	0.4248 *** (0.1436)			
	nYROPTION					0.0298 (0.0967)		
	1YROPTION							
	AVGAGE			0.0245 (0.0150)	0.0349 ** (0.0138)			
Carrier	AMR/UAL							
	MFSC					0.0038 (0.1420)		
	NFSC							
	LCC			-0.9009 *** (0.2762)	-0.7003 *** (0.2040)			
	FREIGHT							
Region	APAC			0.3876 ** (0.1389)	0.2427 ** (0.1026)			
	EMEA			0.4349 *** (0.1396)	0.4166 *** (0.1152)			
	LATAM			0.1577 (0.1442)			-0.0228 (0.0869)	
	NORAM							-0.2635 * (0.1322)
	R^2 (adjusted)	0.55	0.56	0.40	0.30	-0.07	0.28	0.17
	F-statistic	5.26 ***	7.02 ***	2.34 *	2.47 *	0.44	3.31 **	2.26 *

Appendix 11: *Regression models for stock market's short term reaction after 9/11 – Sep 18-24, non-U.S. sample*

Observation period	y2-6 (U.S.) = y6-10 (RoW)	September 18-24, 2001
Sample	All companies	
Sample size	48	

Cluster	Variable	Model 1	Model 2	Model 3	Model 4	Model 5	Model 6	Model 7
	Constant	-0.4116 (0.2604)	-0.2562 (0.2104)	-0.0611 ** (0.0239)	0.0639 (0.0593)	0.0663 *** (0.0206)	0.0472 (0.0400)	-0.0005 (0.0373)
Financial	SIZE	0.0231 (0.0172)	0.0152 (0.0149)					
	LIQUIDITY						-0.0622 (0.0430)	
	NDTEBITDA	-0.0018 (0.0033)			-0.0056 * (0.0030)	-0.0053 * (0.0028)		
	EBITDAMAR						0.6034 * (0.3227)	
	EQITYRAT	0.0588 (0.0982)						
	INTRSTCOVRG	-0.0068 (0.0048)	-0.0065 (0.0043)					
Market	RPKMKTSHR	4.7748 *** (1.5823)	5.1529 *** (1.3682)	5.0484 *** (1.0070)				
	FTKMKTSHR				-0.6490 (0.6850)			
	PINT	-0.3923 *** (0.1215)	-0.4601 *** (0.1035)	-0.2743 *** (0.0820)				-0.3444 *** (0.0981)
	PINT1							
	PFREIGHT						-0.0604 (0.0842)	
Aircraft fleet	TOTALAC				0.0005 *** (0.0001)	0.0004 *** (0.0001)		0.0005 *** (0.0001)
	OPSLEASE	0.0271 (0.0793)						
	STORAC	0.6763 (0.4579)	0.7659 * (0.4164)	0.9623 ** (0.3996)				0.6993 * (0.4001)
	nYRORDER						-0.0359 (0.0392)	
	nYROPTION	0.0148 (0.0273)			0.0281 (0.0269)			
	1YROPTION							
	AVGAGE	0.0045 (0.0028)	0.0040 (0.0025)		0.0038 (0.0026)			
Carrier	AMR/UAL						0.1719 * (0.0936)	
	MFSC				-0.0428 (0.0544)			
	NFSC						0.0079 (0.0668)	
	LCC	0.0192 (0.0479)						
	FREIGHT							
Region	APAC						-0.0775 (0.0462)	
	EMEA						0.0425 (0.0506)	
	LATAM	0.1076 (0.0884)	0.1317 * (0.0725)					
	NORAM	-0.0654 (0.0390)	-0.0665 * (0.0368)		-0.1073 ** (0.0504)			-0.0965 ** (0.0371)
	R^2 (adjusted)	0.42	0.47	0.38	0.34	0.31	0.06	0.40
	F-statistic	3.61 ***	6.14 ***	10.71 ***	4.47 ***	11.42 ***	1.39	9.00 ***

Appendix 12: *Regression models for stock market's short term reaction after 9/11 – Sep 18-24, all companies*

Observation period	y2-6 (U.S.) = y2-6 (RoW)	September 18-24 = September 12-18, 2001
Sample	All companies	
Sample size	48	

Cluster	Variable	Model 1	Model 2	Model 3	Model 4	Model 5	Model 6	Model 7
	Constant	-0.1512 (0.4321)	-0.1926 *** (0.0393)	-0.1159 ** (0.0532)	-0.0642 ** (0.0266)	-0.1179 *** (0.0303)	-0.0368 (0.0696)	-0.0501 * (0.0252)
Financial	SIZE	-0.0122 (0.0275)						
	LIQUIDITY			-0.0176 (0.0336)				
	NDTEBITDA			-0.0027 (0.0037)		-0.0110 *** (0.0039)		
	EBITDAMAR	0.2050 (0.2806)						
	EQITYRAT	0.1196 (0.1193)		0.1531 (0.1197)				
	INTRSTCOVRG						-0.0063 (0.0080)	
Market	RPKMKTSHR			3.1832 ** (1.3562)	3.6647 *** (1.1281)	3.6981 ** (1.4268)		
	FTKMKTSHR	-0.3583 (0.9143)						
	PINT	-0.1499 (0.1440)						
	PINT1							
	PFREIGHT	0.0136 (0.0983)	-0.4013 *** (0.0936)	0.0558 (0.0792)				
Aircraft fleet	TOTALAC	0.0005 ** (0.0002)						
	OPSLEASE	-0.0306 (0.1031)	0.0006 *** (0.0001)					
	STORAC						0.5080 (0.6981)	
	nYRORDER	-0.0507 (0.0562)		-0.0778 (0.0507)				
	nYROPTION	0.0443 (0.0494)		0.0759 * (0.0428)				
	1YROPTION							
	AVGAGE	0.0043 (0.0038)						
Carrier	AMR/UAL	0.0874 (0.0971)	0.0063 ** (0.0026)	0.1043 (0.0944)				
	MFSC						-0.1125 (0.0738)	
	NFSC						-0.0349 (0.0923)	
	LCC							-0.0067 (0.0571)
	FREIGHT						-0.0067 (0.1104)	
Region	APAC			-0.2192 *** (0.0472)	-0.2534 *** (0.0403)			-0.2205 *** (0.0465)
	EMEA	0.0767 (0.0578)		-0.0998 ** (0.0448)	-0.1215 *** (0.0430)			
	LATAM	0.1946 * (0.1116)						
	NORAM	0.1044 (0.0759)	0.1949 ** (0.0854)					
	R^2 (adjusted)	0.50	0.53	0.51	0.50	0.20	0.00	0.31
	F-statistic	4.19 ***	14.42 ***	5.95 ***	16.84 ***	7.06 ***	0.96	11.78 ***

Appendix 13: *Regression models for stock market's short term reaction after 9/11 – Sep 18-24 = Sep 12-18, all companies*

Observation period y7-36 (RoW) September 19 - October 30, 2001
Sample Non-U.S.
Sample size 25 (incl. Air Canada as only NORAM company)

Cluster	Variable	Model 1			Model 2			Model 3			Model 4			Model 5			Model 6			Model 7		
	Constant	-0.3139		(0.2427)	0.1258	**	(0.0500)	-3.1291	***	(0.9737)	-0.1393		(0.0993)	-0.7142		(0.9375)	0.1052	*	(0.0597)	0.0597		(0.0515)
Financial	SIZE							0.1562	**	(0.0604)				0.0607		(0.0609)						
	LIQUIDITY										0.0103		(0.1703)									
	NDTEBITDA	-0.0126	*	(0.0057)	-0.0119	***	(0.0041)										-0.0118	**	(0.0042)			
	EBITDAMAR													0.1110		(0.6957)						
	EQITYRAT										0.2323		(0.3860)									
	INTRSTCOVRG	-0.0804		(0.0660)																		
Market	RPKMKTSHR	6.8862		(8.4942)																		
	FTKMKTSHR	4.8903	*	(2.2237)																2.1603		(1.4378)
	PINT	0.3438		(0.2379)																		
	PINT1																					
	PFREIGHT	-1.4812	**	(0.5363)	-0.6954	***	(0.2349)										-0.7050	***	(0.2387)	-0.9210	***	(0.3016)
Aircraft fleet	TOTALAC	-0.0004		(0.0009)																		
	OPSLEASE	0.7318		(0.4405)				0.5413	*	(0.2812)							0.0935		(0.1430)			
	STORAC													-0.1934		(1.1301)						
	nYRORDER	-0.0093		(0.2071)										0.0362		(0.2063)						
	nYROPTION										-0.0251		(0.1961)									
	1YROPTION																					
	AVGAGE	0.0124		(0.0172)																		
Carrier	AMR/UAL																					
	MFSC													-0.3291		(0.2829)						
	NFSC																					
	LCC	0.2435		(0.2849)				0.5804	***	(0.1995)	0.2072		(0.3314)									
	FREIGHT																					
Region	APAC	0.2153	*	(0.1141)				0.5101	***	(0.1651)												
	EMEA							0.5360	***	(0.1708)												
	LATAM	-0.0817		(0.1983)				0.4931	*	(0.2439)												
	NORAM	-0.3968	*	(0.2050)	-0.6411	***	(0.1424)										-0.6308	***	(0.1452)	-0.6324	***	(0.1607)
	R^2 (adjusted)	0.54			0.57			0.43			-0.05			-0.08			0.56			0.45		
	F-statistic	3.00	**		11.57	***		4.06	***		0.73			0.65			8.55	***		7.67	***	

Appendix 14: *Regression models for stock market's mid term reaction after 9/11 – Sep 19 to Oct 30, non-U.S. sample*

Observation period y7-36 (U.S.) September 25 - November 5, 2001
Sample U.S.
Sample size 23

Cluster	Variable	Model 1			Model 2			Model 3			Model 4			Model 5			Model 6			Model 7		
	Constant	0.3297	*	(0.1669)	0.0330		(0.0834)	0.1160		(0.1096)	0.3600		(0.8086)	-0.0795		(0.1049)	0.0425		(0.0765)	-0.0143		(0.0564)
Financial	SIZE										-0.0318		(0.0539)									
	LIQUIDITY	-0.3185	***	(0.0946)	-0.1950	**	(0.0761)							0.0556		(0.0831)	-0.0821		(0.0665)			
	NDTEBITDA	-0.0721	***	(0.0231)	-0.0685	**	(0.0245)															
	EBITDAMAR	1.9977	***	(0.5555)	1.7748	***	(0.5524)										1.1417	*	(0.5418)			
	EQITYRAT										0.0515		(0.2986)									
	INTRSTCOVRG	-0.0259	***	(0.0075)	-0.0259	***	(0.0077)										-0.0339	***	(0.0072)			
Market	RPKMKTSHR							-10.3847	**	(4.8268)				-2.4615		(2.9712)				-3.4578		(2.4099)
	FTKMKTSHR							-3.8280		(2.9797)	1.2512		(2.8155)									
	PINT							1.3882		(0.9487)												
	PINT1																					
	PFREIGHT							-0.0943		(0.2037)												
Aircraft fleet	TOTALAC	-0.0014	***	(0.0003)	-0.0011	***	(0.0003)										-0.0009	***	(0.0003)			
	OPSLEASE	-0.1533		(0.1511)																		
	STORAC	1.8338		(1.2957)				2.4752		(2.3090)												
	nYRORDER													0.0177		(0.0902)						
	nYROPTION										-0.0151		(0.0759)				-0.0637		(0.0419)			
	1YROPTION																					
	AVGAGE	-0.0156	**	(0.0065)				-0.0094		(0.0074)												
Carrier	AMR/UAL																-0.4260	***	(0.1265)			
	MFSC	0.5384	***	(0.1320)	0.4705	***	(0.1329)										0.3927	***	(0.1127)			
	NFSC										0.0452		(0.1724)									
	LCC							-0.1036		(0.1266)												
	FREIGHT	0.0848		(0.1061)										0.0323		(0.1516)						
Region	APAC																					
	EMEA																					
	LATAM																					
	NORAM																					
	R^2 (adjusted)	0.61			0.56			0.04			-0.20			-0.07			0.63			0.05		
	F-statistic	4.51	***		5.58	***		1.13			0.28			0.64			6.36	***		2.06		

Appendix 15: *Regression models for stock market's mid term reaction after 9/11 – Sep 25 to Nov 5, U.S. sample*

Observation period y11-40 (RoW) September 25-November 5, 2001
Sample Non-U.S.
Sample size 25 (incl. Air Canada as only NORAM company)

Cluster	Variable	Model 1	Model 2	Model 3	Model 4	Model 5	Model 6	Model 7
	Constant	-0.2263 (0.9020)	-0.4679 *** (0.1095)	0.5449 ** (0.2357)	0.2705 ** (0.1028)	0.7807 (1.2344)	-0.1266 ** (0.0452)	0.3378 ** (0.1428)
Financial	SIZE	-0.0270 (0.0007)				-0.0602 (0.0823)		
	LIQUIDITY					0.1687 (0.1157)		
	NDTEBITDA	-0.0109 * (0.0037)	-0.0142 *** (0.0035)					
	EBITDAMAR			-0.6770 (0.5818)				
	EQITYRAT	0.3546 (0.1996)		0.3023 (0.2781)				
	INTRSTCOVRG			0.1506 *** (0.0403)	0.1178 *** (0.0372)		0.1038 ** (0.0423)	
Market	RPKMKTSHR					5.5928 (8.8289)		
	FTKMKTSHR			-2.0675 (1.3497)				
	PINT	0.7806 *** (0.1701)	0.6689 *** (0.1618)					
	PINT1							
	PFREIGHT	-0.9707 *** (0.2796)	-0.8775 *** (0.2280)					
Aircraft fleet	TOTALAC	0.0008 (0.0006)						0.0006 (0.0006)
	OPSLEASE	0.8309 *** (0.1715)	0.6865 *** (0.1291)			0.3785 (0.2919)		0.6021 ** (0.2638)
	STORAC	-1.9602 ** (0.6335)	-1.6536 ** (0.5820)					-0.7597 (0.8652)
	nYRORDER	0.0460 (0.1746)						
	nYROPTION	-0.1785 (0.1372)		-0.1937 (0.1257)				
	1YROPTION							
	AVGAGE					-0.0131 (0.0180)		
Carrier	AMR/UAL							
	MFSC			-0.6082 *** (0.1937)	-0.3881 *** (0.1086)			-0.4672 *** (0.1542)
	NFSC							
	LCC	0.5375 ** (0.2049)	0.3859 *** (0.0931)				0.3997 *** (0.1246)	
	FREIGHT							
Region	APAC	0.4209 *** (0.0963)	0.4406 *** (0.0845)					
	EMEA	0.1604 * (0.0872)	0.2384 ** (0.0827)					
	LATAM			0.2064 (0.1369)				-0.2987 (0.1880)
	NORAM			-0.4324 ** (0.1576)	-0.4244 *** (0.1497)			-0.3960 ** (0.1745)
	R^2 (adjusted)	0.77	0.75	0.52	0.50	0.05	0.33	0.38
	F-statistic	7.10 ***	9.82 ***	4.20 ***	8.87 ***	1.25	7.04 ***	3.12 **

Appendix 16: *Regression models for stock market's mid term reaction after 9/11 – Sep 25 to Nov 5, non-U.S. sample*

Observation period y7-36 (U.S.) = y11-40 (RoW) September 25 - November 5, 2001
Sample All companies
Sample size 48

Cluster	Variable	Model 1	Model 2	Model 3	Model 4	Model 5	Model 6	Model 7
	Constant	0.0219 (0.1280)	-0.0004 (0.0306)	1.4203 ** (0.6947)	-0.1771 *** (0.0578)	0.0569 (0.2155)	0.2993 (0.2937)	0.0287 (0.0369)
Financial	SIZE			-0.1052 ** (0.0490)			-0.0255 (0.0191)	
	LIQUIDITY					0.0556 (0.0675)		
	NDTEBITDA	-0.0124 * (0.0068)		-0.0080 (0.0065)				-0.0083 (0.0052)
	EBITDAMAR	0.5675 (0.4209)		0.6214 (0.4299)	0.9201 ** (0.3685)		0.5700 (0.3567)	
	EQITYRAT	-0.2108 (0.1967)						
	INTRSTCOVRG	-0.0267 *** (0.0096)	-0.0234 ** (0.0089)				-0.0218 ** (0.0088)	-0.0246 *** (0.0089)
Market	RPKMKTSHR	-2.9652 (2.5780)						
	FTKMKTSHR					-0.4374 (1.5201)		
	PINT	0.2135 (0.2232)		0.2684 (0.2341)				
	PINT1							
	PFREIGHT			-0.3638 (0.2204)				
Aircraft fleet	TOTALAC			0.0004 (0.0004)				
	OPSLEASE	0.1681 (0.1534)						
	STORAC	-1.2258 (0.8890)						
	nYRORDER	0.0668 (0.0839)						
	nYROPTION	-0.0522 (0.0767)						
	1YROPTION				53.9449 * (30.2337)			
	AVGAGE					-0.0040 (0.0065)		
Carrier	AMR/UAL	-0.3068 * (0.1636)	-0.4152 *** (0.1428)				-0.3251 ** (0.1449)	-0.4125 *** (0.1423)
	MFSC					-0.1018 (0.1623)		
	NFSC					-0.0551 (0.1684)		
	LCC					-0.0890 (0.1743)		
	FREIGHT			0.4037 * (0.2076)				-0.0147 (0.1018)
Region	APAC			0.1399 (0.1010)				
	EMEA					0.0197 (0.0855)		
	LATAM	-0.1611 (0.1776)						
	NORAM			-0.1661 (0.1035)				
	R^2 (adjusted)	0.20	0.19	0.13	0.13	-0.10	0.23	0.20
	F-statistic	2.00 *	6.36 ***	1.81 *	4.42 **	0.41	4.53 ***	3.86 ***

Appendix 17: *Regression models for stock market's mid term reaction after 9/11 – Sep 25 to Nov 5, all companies*

Observation period y7-36 (U.S.) = y7-36 (RoW) September 25 - November 5 = September 19 - October 30, 2001
Sample All companies
Sample size 48

Cluster	Variable	Model 1	Model 2	Model 3	Model 4	Model 5	Model 6	Model 7
	Constant	-0.0679 (0.0853)	0.0139 (0.0299)	-0.0106 (0.1648)	-0.1543 *** (0.0570)	0.0131 (0.9645)	-0.0719 ** (0.0290)	-0.0248 (0.0332)
Financial	SIZE					-0.0027 (0.0655)		
	LIQUIDITY	0.0502 (0.0484)						
	NDTEBITDA	-0.0108 ** (0.0050)	-0.0124 *** (0.0044)					
	EBITDAMAR			1.1137 ** (0.5051)	0.7206 * (0.3674)			
	EQITYRAT					0.1175 (0.2140)		
	INTRSTCOVRG	-0.0245 *** (0.0080)	-0.0256 *** (0.0075)					-0.0240 *** (0.0086)
Market	RPKMKTSHR					0.9856 (5.8688)		
	FTKMKTSHR					0.6630 (1.7223)		
	PINT					-0.1209 (0.2652)		
	PINT1							
	PFREIGHT	-0.1459 (0.1673)						
Aircraft fleet	TOTALAC					-0.0003 (0.0006)		
	OPSLEASE	0.0655 (0.1169)		0.2247 (0.1741)				
	STORAC					0.2405 (1.0198)		
	nYRORDER	0.0352 (0.0566)						
	nYROPTION			-0.0507 (0.0631)				
	1YROPTION	57.2674 ** (26.3992)	60.8190 ** (24.3232)				70.1115 ** (29.6276)	
	AVGAGE			0.0038 (0.0064)				
Carrier	AMR/UAL	-0.3839 *** (0.1274)	-0.3831 *** (0.1190)					-0.3919 *** (0.1372)
	MFSC	0.0493 (0.0770)		-0.1546 (0.1092)				
	NFSC					-0.0155 (0.1909)		
	LCC			-0.2262 * (0.1215)		-0.0700 (0.1523)		
	FREIGHT	0.1408 (0.1602)		-0.1466 (0.1637)				
Region	APAC			-0.1353 (0.0942)		-0.0496 (0.1079)		
	EMEA							0.0457 (0.0665)
	LATAM			-0.2034 (0.1885)				
	NORAM			-0.1528 * (0.0902)				
	R^2 (adjusted)	0.34	0.39	0.01	0.06	-0.18	0.09	0.20
	F-statistic	3.39 ***	8.50 ***	1.03	3.85 *	0.27	5.60 **	4.95 ***

Appendix 18: *Regression models for stock market's mid term reaction after 9/11 – Sep 25 to Nov 5 = Sept 19 to Oct 30, all companies*

	SIZE	LIQUIDITY	NDTEBITDA	EBITDAMAR	EQITYRAT	NTRSTCOVRC	RPKMKTSHR	FTKMKTSHR	PINT
SIZE	1								
LIQUIDITY	-0.31	1							
NDTEBITDA	0.18	-0.28	1						
EBITDAMAR	0.26	0.22	0.33	1					
EQITYRAT	0.08	0.51	-0.27	0.31	1				
INTRSTCOVRG	-0.03	-0.01	0.06	-0.05	0.04	1			
RPKMKTSHR	0.71	-0.16	0.07	0.10	-0.23	0.05	1		
FTKMKTSHR	0.50	-0.27	0.00	0.18	0.38	-0.04	0.11	1	
PINT	0.37	-0.34	-0.19	0.01	-0.02	-0.11	0.26	0.38	1
PINT1	0.29	-0.24	-0.21	0.16	0.10	-0.14	0.14	0.31	0.84
PFREIGHT	-0.13	-0.04	0.08	0.08	0.17	-0.09	-0.30	0.51	0.11
TOTALAC	0.71	-0.20	0.11	-0.05	-0.19	0.05	0.80	0.24	0.09
OPSLEASE	-0.52	0.12	-0.18	-0.41	-0.09	0.13	-0.26	-0.50	-0.27
STORAC	0.06	-0.18	0.12	-0.14	-0.14	-0.05	-0.06	0.16	0.09
nYRORDER	-0.03	0.23	0.13	0.33	0.16	0.11	-0.03	-0.16	-0.34
nYROPTION	-0.24	0.39	0.08	0.15	0.06	0.17	-0.05	-0.34	-0.32
1YROPTION	-0.18	0.09	0.00	-0.05	0.05	0.03	-0.11	-0.11	-0.16
AVGAGE	0.17	-0.13	-0.02	-0.14	-0.05	-0.01	0.09	0.40	0.14
AMR/UAL									
MFSC	0.47	-0.44	-0.01	0.05	-0.19	-0.12	0.48	0.16	0.71
NFSC	-0.38	0.18	0.06	0.12	-0.14	0.18	-0.26	-0.23	-0.38
LCC	-0.29	0.37	-0.07	-0.09	0.20	0.05	-0.16	-0.37	-0.48
FREIGHT	-0.03	0.07	0.05	-0.07	0.19	-0.04	-0.35	0.47	-0.17
APAC	0.15	-0.31	-0.05	0.20	0.04	-0.06	0.00	0.23	0.33
EMEA	0.00	0.24	-0.04	0.00	0.28	-0.06	-0.04	-0.12	0.05
LATAM	-0.13	-0.01	0.00	-0.03	-0.07	0.02	-0.12	-0.08	0.16
NORAM	-0.08	0.09	0.08	-0.18	-0.26	0.11	0.09	-0.08	-0.42

	PINT1	PFREIGHT	TOTALAC	OPSLEASE	STORAC	nYRORDER	nYROPTION	1YROPTION	AVGAGE
SIZE									
LIQUIDITY									
NDTEBITDA									
EBITDAMAR									
EQITYRAT									
INTRSTCOVRG									
RPKMKTSHR									
FTKMKTSHR									
PINT									
PINT1	1								
PFREIGHT	0.13	1							
TOTALAC	-0.08	-0.14	1						
OPSLEASE	-0.24	-0.37	-0.36	1					
STORAC	0.01	0.50	0.20	-0.33	1				
nYRORDER	-0.18	-0.14	-0.19	0.22	-0.26	1			
nYROPTION	-0.28	-0.19	-0.14	0.31	-0.20	0.41	1		
1YROPTION	-0.16	-0.09	-0.13	0.21	-0.09	0.15	0.01	1	
AVGAGE	0.00	0.66	0.32	-0.50	0.71	-0.38	-0.23	-0.15	1
AMR/UAL									
MFSC	0.64	-0.08	0.17	-0.17	-0.02	-0.17	-0.21	-0.20	0.04
NFSC	-0.37	-0.18	-0.17	0.12	-0.18	-0.14	0.29	-0.04	-0.21
LCC	-0.37	-0.27	-0.12	0.40	-0.25	0.41	0.17	0.30	-0.43
FREIGHT	-0.22	0.71	0.03	-0.38	0.55	-0.15	-0.16	-0.04	0.74
APAC	0.43	0.09	-0.23	-0.12	-0.25	0.15	-0.14	0.22	-0.15
EMEA	0.10	-0.18	-0.16	0.13	-0.09	0.03	-0.13	-0.08	-0.18
LATAM	0.21	0.08	-0.13	0.16	0.21	0.24	0.20	-0.03	-0.09
NORAM	-0.57	0.03	0.40	-0.06	0.23	-0.26	0.16	-0.12	0.33

	AMR/UAL	MFSC	NFSC	LCC	FREIGHT	APAC	EMEA	LATAM	NORAM
SIZE									
LIQUIDITY									
NDTEBITDA									
EBITDAMAR									
EQITYRAT									
INTRSTCOVRG									
RPKMKTSHR									
FTKMKTSHR									
PINT									
PINT1									
PFREIGHT									
TOTALAC									
OPSLEASE									
STORAC									
nYRORDER									
nYROPTION									
1YROPTION									
AVGAGE									
AMR/UAL	1								
MFSC		1							
NFSC		-0.41	1						
LCC		-0.65	-0.14	1					
FREIGHT		-0.41	-0.09	-0.14	1				
APAC		0.39	-0.20	-0.20	-0.20	1			
EMEA		0.02	-0.17	0.22	-0.17	-0.38	1		
LATAM		0.15	-0.06	-0.10	-0.06	-0.14	-0.12	1	
NORAM		-0.44	0.36	0.04	0.36	-0.55	-0.47	-0.17	1

Appendix 19: *Correlation of explanatory and control variables for analysis of stock market's reaction on the Financial Crisis 2008 (as of Ye 2007)*

Observation period y1 September 15, 2008
Sample All companies
Sample size 49

		Model 1			Model 2			Model 3			Model 4			Model 5			Model 6			Model 7		
Cluster	Variable	Coefficient	P-v	Standard en	Coefficient	P-v	Standard en	Coefficient	P-v	Standard en	Coefficient	P-v	Standard en	Coefficient	P-v	Standard en	Coefficient	P-v	Standard en	Coefficient	P-v	Standard en
	Constant	-0.0142		(0.0192)	0.0036		(0.0093)	-0.0567	*	(0.0320)	-0.0239		(0.0201)	-0.3122	***	(0.1024)	0.0170		(0.0211)	-0.0712		(0.1304)
Financial	SIZE													0.0221	***	(0.0067)				0.0057		(0.0089)
	LIQUIDITY	0.0063		(0.0140)				0.0128		(0.0145)												
	NDTEBITDA							0.0007		(0.0006)												
	EBITDAMAR																0.0276		(0.1289)			
	EQITYRAT																-0.0334		(0.0582)			
	INTRSTCOVRG													-0.0022		(0.0039)						
Market	RPKMKTSHR							1.0469	**	(0.4822)	1.4459	***	(0.4408)							0.7677		(0.6496)
	FTKMKTSHR													-0.2145		(0.2163)						
	PINT																0.0242		(0.0362)			
	PFREIGHT										0.0280		(0.0346)									
Aircraft	TOTALAC	0.0001	**	(0.0000)	0.0001	***	(0.0000)													0.0000		(0.0001)
	OPSLEASE	0.0229		(0.0346)				0.0334		(0.0350)	0.0236		(0.0328)									
	STORAC	-0.2466		(0.2277)																		
	nYRORDER													-0.0061		(0.0182)						
	nYROPTION																0.0180		(0.0184)			
	AVGAGE							0.0021		(0.0014)												
Carrier	AMR/UAL																					
	MFSC							0.0255		(0.0218)												
	NFSC	-0.0608	**	(0.0259)	-0.0411	**	(0.0203)													-0.0408	*	(0.0217)
	LCC	-0.0236		(0.0183)				0.0233		(0.0252)												
	FREIGHT																0.0026		(0.0245)			
Region	APAC													-0.0224	*	(0.0131)				-0.0271	*	(0.0136)
	EMEA	0.0247		(0.0169)							0.0199		(0.0154)									
	LATAM	0.0412		(0.0325)										0.0277		(0.0302)						
	NORAM	0.0224		(0.0187)							0.0110		(0.0132)									
	R^2 (adjusted)	0.20			0.22			0.13			0.15			0.16			-0.08			0.25		
	F-statistic	2.34	**		7.71	***		2.06	*		2.66	**		2.57	**		0.33			4.14	***	

Appendix 20: *Regression results of stock market's initial reaction on the Financial Crisis 2008 – Sep 15 (y_1)*

Observation period y2 September 16, 2008
Sample All companies
Sample size 49

		Model 1			Model 2			Model 3			Model 4			Model 5			Model 6			Model 7		
Cluster	Variable	Coefficient	P-v	Standard en	Coefficient	P-v	Standard en	Coefficient	P-v	Standard en	Coefficient	P-v	Standard en	Coefficient	P-v	Standard en	Coefficient	P-v	Standard en	Coefficient	P-v	Standard en
	Constant	-0.0613	***	(0.0179)	-0.0253		(0.0280)	-0.0342	***	(0.0116)	0.0618	***	(0.0110)	-0.0707	**	(0.0307)	0.0467		(0.0300)	-0.0225		(0.0231)
Financial	SIZE																					
	LIQUIDITY	0.0255	*	(0.0139)																		
	NDTEBITDA													0.0005		(0.0007)	-0.0001		(0.0008)			
	EBITDAMAR													-0.1772		(0.1575)				0.0363		(0.1414)
	EQITYRAT													0.1658	**	(0.0734)	0.0087		(0.0725)			
	INTRSTCOVRG													0.0019		(0.0044)				0.0056		(0.0049)
Market	RPKMKTSHR													1.8170	***	(0.5209)	2.7409	***	(0.6389)			
	FTKMKTSHR													-0.4645	*	(0.2726)				-0.1144		(0.3098)
	PINT													0.0380		(0.0565)				0.0195		(0.0532)
	PFREIGHT	-0.1456	***	(0.0487)	-0.1217	**	(0.0459)							-0.0634		(0.0465)	-0.0786	*	(0.0449)			
Aircraft	TOTALAC	0.0002	***	(0.0001)	0.0001	**	(0.0001)	0.0002	***	(0.0001)												
	OPSLEASE				0.0534		(0.0356)															
	STORAC													0.2681		(0.2626)				0.2973		(0.2965)
	nYRORDER													0.0139		(0.0277)	-0.0324		(0.0273)			
	nYROPTION	0.0492	**	(0.0191)	0.0357	*	(0.0182)	0.0613	***	(0.0203)												
	AVGAGE	0.0044	**	(0.0018)	0.0037	**	(0.0017)															
Carrier	AMR/UAL																					
	MFSC																-0.0764	***	(0.0260)			
	NFSC																			-0.0504		(0.0305)
	LCC													-0.0129		(0.0218)	-0.0369		(0.0320)			
	FREIGHT																			-0.0910	**	(0.0425)
Region	APAC				-0.0458	***	(0.0162)				-0.0867	***	(0.0172)									
	EMEA				-0.0363	**	(0.0160)				-0.0585	***	(0.0185)									
	LATAM													0.0377		(0.0371)	0.0701		(0.0427)			
	NORAM													0.0817	***	(0.0177)				0.1007	***	(0.0181)
	R^2 (adjusted)	0.52			0.60			0.42			0.34			0.54			0.29			0.41		
	F-statistic	11.21	***		11.27	***		18.17	***		13.58	***		5.28	***		3.44	***		5.16	***	

Appendix 21: *Regression results of stock market's initial reaction on the Financial Crisis 2008 – Sep 16 (y_2)*

Observation period y3 September 17, 2008
Sample All companies
Sample size 49

		Model 1			Model 2			Model 3			Model 4			Model 5			Model 6			Model 7		
Cluster	Variable	Coefficient	P-v	Standard error	Coefficient	P-v	Standard error	Coefficient	P-v	Standard error	Coefficient	P-v	Standard error	Coefficient	P-v	Standard error	Coefficient	P-v	Standard error	Coefficient	P-v	Standard error
	Constant	-0.2627		(0.2105)	0.0636	***	(0.0149)	-0.0550	**	(0.0215)	-0.0177		(0.0137)	0.0146		(0.0179)	-0.7033	***	(0.1892)	-0.5114	***	(0.1368)
Financial	SIZE	0.0205		(0.0137)													0.0438	***	(0.0129)	0.0309	***	(0.0095)
	LIQUIDITY																					
	NDTEBITDA							0.0005		(0.0006)												
	EBITDAMAR							0.1278		(0.1241)												
	EQITYRAT							0.0739		(0.0578)												
	INTRSTCOVRG																					
Market	RPKMKTSHR	-1.6253	**	(0.6129)	-1.1325	***	(0.3734)							-0.8564	*	(0.4950)						
	FTKMKTSHR	-0.3478		(0.3305)													-0.4580		(0.3179)			
	PINT																0.0890	**	(0.0435)	0.0860	*	(0.0439)
	PFREIGHT	0.0849		(0.0505)													0.1222	***	(0.0429)	0.0784	**	(0.0295)
Aircraft	TOTALAC																-0.0003	***	(0.0001)	-0.0002	***	(0.0001)
	OPSLEASE	-0.0891	**	(0.0358)	-0.1267	***	(0.0286)							-0.0869	**	(0.0326)						
	STORAC	-0.6277	***	(0.2242)	-0.4200	**	(0.1900)							-0.3236		(0.2015)						
	nYRORDER																-0.0205		(0.0169)	0.0427	*	(0.0217)
	nYROPTION																0.0415	*	(0.0215)			
	AVGAGE																					
Carrier	AMR/UAL																					
	MFSC							-0.0428	**	(0.0180)	-0.0534	***	(0.0178)	-0.0237		(0.0227)						
	NFSC																0.0769	***	(0.0260)	0.0610	**	(0.0247)
	LCC							-0.0601	***	(0.0200)	-0.0671	***	(0.0204)	-0.0387		(0.0236)						
	FREIGHT																					
Region	APAC							0.0757	***	(0.0152)	0.0859	***	(0.0148)	0.0637	***	(0.0168)						
	EMEA							0.0573	***	(0.0160)	0.0683	***	(0.0153)	0.0551	***	(0.0157)						
	LATAM																-0.0593	*	(0.0314)	-0.0626	*	(0.0314)
	NORAM	-0.0436	***	(0.0117)	-0.0494	***	(0.0112)															
	R^2 (adjusted)	0.49			0.49			0.47			0.44			0.50			0.46			0.44		
	F-statistic	7.65	***		12.31	***		7.13	***		10.37	***		7.74	***		5.47	***		6.39	***	

***Appendix 22:** Regression results of stock market's initial reaction on the Financial Crisis 2008 – Sep 17 (y_3)*

Observation period y4 September 18, 2008
Sample All companies
Sample size 49

		Model 1			Model 2			Model 3			Model 4			Model 5			Model 6			Model 7		
Cluster	Variable	Coefficient	P-v	Standard err	Coefficient	P-v	Standard err	Coefficient	P-v	Standard err	Coefficient	P-v	Standard err	Coefficient	P-v	Standard err	Coefficient	P-v	Standard err	Coefficient	P-v	Standard err
	Constant	-0.1304	***	(0.0322)	-0.0863	***	(0.0246)	-0.3683	**	(0.1512)	-0.3803	***	(0.1135)	-0.0923	***	(0.0205)	-0.1219	***	(0.0231)	-0.3550	**	(0.1557)
Financial	SIZE							0.0185	**	(0.0089)	0.0183	**	(0.0070)							0.0188	**	(0.0092)
	LIQUIDITY	0.0318		(0.0192)				0.0371	**	(0.0175)	0.0361	**	(0.0151)							0.0339	**	(0.0167)
	NDTEBITDA	0.0018	**	(0.0007)	0.0013	**	(0.0006)										0.0011	*	(0.0006)			
	EBITDAMAR													0.2065		(0.1403)						
	EQITYRAT	0.1591	**	(0.0768)	0.2086	***	(0.0628)										0.2017	***	(0.0638)			
	INTRSTCOVRG													0.0023		(0.0050)						
Market	RPKMKTSHR													0.9937	**	(0.4904)						
	FTKMKTSHR	-0.5767	*	(0.3145)	-0.8023	***	(0.2604)										-0.6408	**	(0.2448)			
	PINT	0.1124	*	(0.0562)	0.1122	*	(0.0564)													0.0336		(0.0471)
	PFREIGHT	-0.0537		(0.0578)																		
Aircraft	TOTALAC	0.0002	**	(0.0001)	0.0002	***	(0.0000)										0.0002	***	(0.0000)			
	OPSLEASE							-0.0143		(0.0480)										-0.0366		(0.0420)
	STORAC													0.3727		(0.2441)						
	nYRORDER							0.0115		(0.0241)												
	nYROPTION							-0.0175		(0.0229)												
	AVGAGE	0.0032		(0.0021)				0.0045	**	(0.0022)	0.0033	**	(0.0012)				0.0025	*	(0.0014)			
Carrier	AMR/UAL																					
	MFSC	-0.0328		(0.0262)	-0.0579	**	(0.0235)															
	NFSC																			0.0372		(0.0302)
	LCC	-0.0543	*	(0.0280)	-0.0837	***	(0.0236)										-0.0443	**	(0.0196)			
	FREIGHT							-0.0556		(0.0427)												
Region	APAC							-0.0346	*	(0.0204)												
	EMEA	-0.0140		(0.0165)				-0.0299		(0.0197)												
	LATAM																					
	NORAM													0.0246		(0.0155)						
	R^2 (adjusted)	0.38			0.37			0.21			0.24			0.14			0.34			0.13		
	F-statistic	3.72	***		5.02	***		2.40	**		5.96	***		2.54	**		5.16	***		2.46	**	

***Appendix 23:** Regression results of stock market's initial reaction on the Financial Crisis 2008 – Sep 18 (y_4)*

Observation period y2-12 September 16-30, 2008
Sample All companies
Sample size 49

		Model 1			Model 2			Model 3			Model 4			Model 5			Model 6			Model 7		
Cluster	Variable	Coefficient	P-v	Standard err	Coefficient	P-v	Standard err	Coefficient	P-v	Standard err	Coefficient	P-v	Standard err	Coefficient	P-v	Standard err	Coefficient	P-v	Standard err	Coefficient	P-v	Standard err
	Constant	-0.1426		(0.1011)	-0.1048	*	(0.0542)	-0.1368	**	(0.0393)	-0.5335		(0.3732)	-0.0833		(0.0786)	-0.4492		(0.4188)	-0.1454	**	(0.0618)
Financial	SIZE										0.0248		(0.0223)				0.0216		(0.0247)			
	LIQUIDITY	-0.0189		(0.0510)													-0.0154		(0.0434)			
	NDTEBITDA	-0.0018		(0.0022)	-0.0016		(0.0020)	-0.0020		(0.0018)												
	EBITDAMAR													-0.3411		(0.4353)						
	EQITYRAT													0.0825		(0.1882)				0.1275		(0.1715)
	INTRSTCOVRG	0.0108		(0.0142)	0.0120		(0.0140)	0.0124		(0.0133)										0.0113		(0.0133)
Market	RPKMKTSHR	-2.4679		(2.7686)	-2.2056		(3.2195)															
	FTKMKTSHR													0.1151		(0.7490)						
	PINT	0.1214		(0.1518)	0.0724		(0.1708)															
	PFREIGHT	-0.0735		(0.1224)	-0.1459		(0.1622)															
Aircraft	TOTALAC	0.0003		(0.0003)	0.0002		(0.0003)	0.0001		(0.0001)												
	OPSLEASE	0.0326		(0.1253)							0.1122		(0.1177)				0.0836		(0.1118)			
	STORAC													-0.0522		(0.9731)						
	nYRORDER	0.0363		(0.0703)										0.0058		(0.0691)						
	nYROPTION	-0.0131		(0.0621)										-0.0052		(0.0593)						
	AVGAGE													0.0002		(0.0060)						
Carrier	AMR/UAL																					
	MFSC				0.0575		(0.0757)	0.0247		(0.0413)										0.0377		(0.0415)
	NFSC																0.0185		(0.0779)			
	LCC										-0.0356		(0.0558)									
	FREIGHT				0.0486		(0.1368)															
Region	APAC				-0.0402		(0.0590)															
	EMEA				-0.0665		(0.0566)													-0.0562		(0.0467)
	LATAM										0.0773		(0.1024)									
	NORAM										0.0479		(0.0404)									
	R^2 (adjusted)	-0.13			-0.09			-0.02			-0.04			-0.15			-0.06			-0.02		
	F-statistic	0.44			0.60			0.78			0.67			0.11			0.31			0.73		

Appendix 24: *Regression results of stock market's short term reaction on the Financial Crisis 2008 – Sep 16-30 (y_{2-12})*

Observation period y13-18 October 1-8, 2008
Sample All companies
Sample size 49

		Model 1			Model 2			Model 3			Model 4			Model 5			Model 6			Model 7		
Cluster	Variable	Coefficient	P-v	Standard err	Coefficient	P-v	Standard err	Coefficient	P-v	Standard err	Coefficient	P-v	Standard err	Coefficient	P-v	Standard err	Coefficient	P-v	Standard err	Coefficient	P-v	Standard err
	Constant	-0.1938		(0.4838)	-0.0261		(0.0384)	-0.0312		(0.0345)	0.0103		(0.0401)	-0.6093	*	(0.3034)	-0.0982	**	(0.0460)	-0.0141		(0.0303)
Financial	SIZE	0.0141		(0.0329)										0.0386	**	(0.0184)						
	LIQUIDITY	-0.0439		(0.0349)	-0.0562	*	(0.0302)	-0.0961	***	(0.0266)	-0.0794	***	(0.0272)							-0.0502	*	(0.0295)
	NDTEBITDA													-0.0022		(0.0014)						
	EBITDAMAR	-0.7291	**	(0.2819)	-0.5526	**	(0.2293)	-0.5403	**	(0.2227)	-0.5104	**	(0.2166)									
	EQITYRAT	0.2677	*	(0.1436)	0.3033	**	(0.1250)	0.4291	***	(0.1104)	0.3284	***	(0.1198)									
	INTRSTCOVRG	-0.0184	**	(0.0076)	-0.0202	***	(0.0073)	-0.0219	***	(0.0073)	-0.0193	**	(0.0072)							-0.0169	*	(0.0092)
Market	RPKMKTSHR	-4.7969	**	(1.7807)	-3.9383	***	(1.3332)															
	FTKMKTSHR	0.5360		(0.6970)	0.9502	*	(0.4981)															
	PINT	0.0470		(0.0821)													0.0643		(0.1257)			
	PFREIGHT	-0.2150	*	(0.1062)	-0.2343	***	(0.0801)	-0.2620	***	(0.0785)	-0.3084	***	(0.0800)									
Aircraft	TOTALAC	0.0003		(0.0002)	0.0003	*	(0.0001)															
	OPSLEASE	-0.0782		(0.0831)										0.0510		(0.0962)						
	STORAC	-1.9073	***	(0.5003)	-1.6858	***	(0.4540)	-2.0778	***	(0.4444)	-2.0963	***	(0.4311)							-2.6244	***	(0.5419)
	nYRORDER	0.1144	***	(0.0415)	0.0990	***	(0.0348)	0.0866	**	(0.0344)	0.0674	*	(0.0349)							0.0645		(0.0417)
	nYROPTION	-0.0066		(0.0332)													-0.0147		(0.0491)			
	AVGAGE													-0.0079	**	(0.0032)						
Carrier	AMR/UAL																					
	MFSC													-0.0734	*	(0.0377)						
	NFSC																-0.0041		(0.0731)			
	LCC																0.0836		(0.0547)			
	FREIGHT							0.1865	***	(0.0602)	0.2488	***	(0.0671)							0.1188	*	(0.0594)
Region	APAC													0.0654		(0.0397)						
	EMEA													0.0624		(0.0381)						
	LATAM																-0.0387		(0.0870)			
	NORAM																					
	R^2 (adjusted)	0.59			0.61			0.60			0.63			0.27			-0.03			0.37		
	F-statistic	5.95	***		8.53	***		10.15	***		9.98	***		3.51	***		0.71			6.55	***	

Appendix 25: *Regression results of stock market's mid term reaction on the Financial Crisis 2008 – Oct 1-8 (y_{13-18})*

Observation period y19-24 October 9-16, 2008
Sample All companies
Sample size 49

		Model 1			Model 2			Model 3			Model 4			Model 5			Model 6			Model 7		
Cluster	Variable	Coefficient	P-v	Standard er	Coefficient	P-v	Standard er	Coefficient	P-v	Standard er	Coefficient	P-v	Standard er	Coefficient	P-v	Standard er	Coefficient	P-v	Standard er	Coefficient	P-v	Standard er
	Constant	-0.0159		(0.1456)	-0.3748	***	(0.1055)	0.8139		(0.9324)	0.0017		(0.0372)	0.1430		(0.1058)	-0.2877		(0.5404)	-0.0848		(0.1245)
Financial	SIZE							-0.0416		(0.0632)							0.0299		(0.0353)			
	LIQUIDITY	0.1211	*	(0.0698)	0.0958	*	(0.0504)															
	NDTEBITDA	0.0028		(0.0024)				0.0025		(0.0030)												
	EBITDAMAR																-0.4173		(0.6889)			
	EQITYRAT	-0.1804		(0.2764)										-0.3106		(0.2304)						
	INTRSTCOVRG	0.0074		(0.0167)																		
Market	RPKMKTSHR							12.1425	***	(3.3993)	7.1061	***	(3.5260)							4.9275	**	(1.8770)
	FTKMKTSHR							-0.9338		(1.5801)												
	PINT							-0.1302		(0.2944)												
	PFREIGHT																-0.2443		(0.2047)			
Aircraft	TOTALAC	0.0001		(0.0002)																		
	OPSLEASE	0.0209		(0.1519)				0.1622		(0.2040)				0.0055		(0.1305)						
	STORAC																1.0441		(1.3286)			
	nYRORDER	0.0059		(0.0906)				-0.1461		(0.1057)												
	nYROPTION	0.0587		(0.0766)																		
	AVGAGE	0.0089		(0.0088)																		
Carrier	AMR/UAL																					
	MFSC	0.2863	**	(0.1186)	0.3344	***	(0.0912)	-0.2201		(0.1903)										0.0914		(0.0673)
	NFSC							-0.1330		(0.1808)												
	LCC	0.2057	*	(0.1153)	0.2050	**	(0.0935)	-0.1682		(0.1921)												
	FREIGHT	-0.2050		(0.2083)	-0.1013		(0.1050)															
Region	APAC	-0.4031	***	(0.0966)										-0.0914		(0.0698)				-0.1233		(0.1183)
	EMEA	-0.3478	***	(0.0832)																-0.0135		(0.1230)
	LATAM	-0.3758	**	(0.1425)																		
	NORAM				0.4522	***	(0.0518)							0.2367	***	(0.0675)				0.2593	**	(0.1273)
	R^2 (adjusted)	0.57			0.61			0.23			0.19			0.40			-0.01			0.57		
	F-statistic	5.19	***		15.72	***		2.47	**		12.43	***		8.97	***		0.83			13.60	***	

Appendix 26: *Regression results of stock market's mid term reaction on the Financial Crisis 2008 – Oct 9-16 (y_{19-24})*

Observation period y13-35 October 1-31, 2008
Sample All companies
Sample size 49

		Model 1			Model 2			Model 3			Model 4			Model 5			Model 6			Model 7		
Cluster	Variable	Coefficient	P-v	Standard er	Coefficient	P-v	Standard er	Coefficient	P-v	Standard er	Coefficient	P-v	Standard er	Coefficient	P-v	Standard er	Coefficient	P-v	Standard er	Coefficient	P-v	Standard er
	Constant	-2.6860	**	(1.0647)	-2.2814	***	(0.6423)	0.3964	***	(0.0874)	0.4109	***	(6.0010)	0.0588		(0.1189)	0.1463		(0.1046)	-0.0791		(0.0953)
Financial	SIZE	0.1606	**	(0.0717)	0.1300	***	(0.0381)															
	LIQUIDITY	0.1649		(0.1035)																		
	NDTEBITDA	0.0036		(0.0040)																		
	EBITDAMAR	-0.8311		(0.9076)				-0.9574		(0.7091)												
	EQITYRAT	-0.6477		(0.3948)																		
	INTRSTCOVRG																			-0.0010		(0.0247)
Market	RPKMKTSHR													5.1365		(3.1937)						
	FTKMKTSHR							2.8824	**	(1.3133)							1.9955		(1.6592)			
	PINT	0.4480	*	(0.2629)																		
	PFREIGHT													-0.5337	**	(0.2406)						
Aircraft	TOTALAC	-0.0003		(0.0005)																		
	OPSLEASE	0.4878	**	(0.2324)	0.6201	***	(0.2010)													0.1335		(0.1922)
	STORAC	-2.7096	**	(1.2617)	-2.8425	**	(1.1722)															
	nYRORDER							0.2166	*	(0.1138)				0.0101		(0.1314)						
	nYROPTION	0.1446		(0.1068)																		
	AVGAGE																0.0080		(0.0138)			
Carrier	AMR/UAL																					
	MFSC																-0.1183		(0.1360)			
	NFSC							-0.1898		(0.1382)	-0.2820	**	-(2.0590)	0.0502		(0.1739)						
	LCC	0.1679		(0.1121)																		
	FREIGHT							-0.8092	***	(0.1556)	-0.6486	***	-(4.7358)				-0.7257	**	(0.3464)	-0.5368	***	(0.1508)
Region	APAC							-0.5841	***	(0.0967)	-0.5143	***	-(5.5978)				-0.2781	**	(0.1031)	-0.0584		(0.0940)
	EMEA							-0.4537	***	(0.0945)	-0.4341	***	-(4.4821)	-0.1330		(0.1035)						
	LATAM							-0.5856	***	(0.1809)	-0.4928	***	-(2.7201)	-0.0799		(0.2213)						
	NORAM	0.3580	***	(0.1017)	0.3721	***	(0.0695)													0.3743	***	(0.0912)
	R^2 (adjusted)	0.48			0.46			0.48			0.44			0.15			0.17			0.39		
	F-statistic	4.64	***		11.31	***		6.56	***		8.43	***		2.40	**		2.98	**		7.04	***	

Appendix 27: *Regression results of stock market's mid term reaction on the Financial Crisis 2008 – Oct 1-31 (y_{13-35})*

	SIZE	*LIQUIDITY*	*NDTEBITDA*	*EBITDAMAR*	*EQITYRAT*	*NTRSTCOVAG*	*TOTALAC*	*OPSLEASE*
SIZE	1							
LIQUIDITY	-0.19	1						
NDTEBITDA	-0.20	-0.15	1					
EBITDAMAR	0.03	-0.14	-0.28	1				
EQITYRAT	0.10	0.25	-0.01	0.23	1			
INTRSTCOVAG	0.36	0.12	-0.10	0.34	0.11	1		
TOTALAC	0.68	-0.19	-0.15	-0.24	-0.16	0.02	1	
OPSLEASE	-0.35	0.17	-0.07	-0.45	-0.21	-0.49	-0.15	1
STORAC	0.41	-0.25	-0.04	-0.34	-0.07	-0.11	0.53	-0.23
nYRORDER	-0.46	0.43	-0.10	0.34	-0.05	-0.01	-0.53	0.35
nYROPTION	-0.30	0.23	-0.01	-0.23	-0.05	-0.71	0.05	0.56
AVGAGE	0.27	0.06	-0.11	-0.21	0.27	0.06	0.28	-0.31
MFSC	-0.10	0.00	0.11	-0.06	-0.49	-0.05	-0.05	0.35
NFSC								
LCC	-0.08	0.01	-0.03	0.18	0.18	0.01	0.03	-0.08
FREIGHTER	0.13	0.00	-0.11	0.00	0.45	0.04	0.04	-0.33
APAC	-0.30	-0.26	0.26	0.54	-0.07	0.21	-0.57	-0.23
EMEA	0.29	0.29	-0.11	-0.29	0.01	0.12	-0.05	0.21
LATAM	-0.44	0.12	0.00	-0.14	-0.04	-0.65	-0.21	0.70
NORAM	0.22	-0.05	-0.14	-0.19	0.07	-0.01	0.63	-0.25
FATALITY	-0.07	-0.07	-0.09	0.15	0.07	0.17	-0.10	0.12
INJURY	0.07	-0.15	0.10	-0.04	0.10	0.01	0.13	-0.15
LOSTVALUE	0.01	0.03	0.09	0.14	-0.01	0.16	-0.28	-0.08

	STORAC	*nYRORDER*	*nYROPTION*	*AVGAGE*	*MFSC*	*NFSC*	*LCC*	*FREIGHTER*
SIZE								
LIQUIDITY								
NDTEBITDA								
EBITDAMAR								
EQITYRAT								
INTRSTCOVAG								
TOTALAC								
OPSLEASE								
STORAC	1							
nYRORDER	-0.55	1						
nYROPTION	-0.20	0.40	1					
AVGAGE	0.55	-0.42	-0.22	1				
MFSC	-0.36	0.33	0.28	-0.85	1			
NFSC						1		
LCC	-0.10	0.03	-0.09	-0.09	-0.28		1	
FREIGHTER	0.41	-0.35	-0.26	0.91	-0.94		-0.08	1
APAC	-0.37	0.38	-0.09	-0.49	0.32		-0.09	-0.30
EMEA	-0.15	-0.11	-0.17	-0.19	0.27		-0.08	-0.25
LATAM	-0.15	0.40	0.62	-0.18	0.12		-0.03	-0.11
NORAM	0.51	-0.42	-0.04	0.66	-0.55		0.15	0.51
FATALITY	-0.04	0.18	-0.03	-0.34	0.31		-0.12	-0.28
INJURY	0.40	-0.19	-0.07	0.21	-0.16		-0.04	0.18
LOSTVALUE	-0.24	0.05	-0.16	-0.22	0.15		-0.10	-0.12

	APAC	*EMEA*	*LATAM*	*NORAM*	*FATALITY*	*INJURY*	*LOSTVALUE*
SIZE							
LIQUIDITY							
NDTEBITDA							
EBITDAMAR							
EQITYRAT							
INTRSTCOVAG							
TOTALAC							
OPSLEASE							
STORAC							
nYRORDER							
nYROPTION							
AVGAGE							
MFSC							
NFSC							
LCC							
FREIGHTER							
APAC	1						
EMEA	-0.30	1					
LATAM	-0.13	-0.11	1				
NORAM	-0.59	-0.49	-0.21	1			
FATALITY	0.28	-0.04	0.06	-0.24	1		
INJURY	-0.05	-0.15	-0.07	0.20	-0.15	1	
LOSTVALUE	0.35	0.21	-0.12	-0.43	-0.01	-0.13	1

Appendix 28: *Correlation of explanatory and control variables for analysis of stock market's reaction on the aircraft accidents (data as of Ye of the respective year of accident)*

Observation period: Trading day y1 after aircraft accidents 1994-2009
Sample: All companies with hull losses
Sample size: 45
Dependent variable: Abnormal returns y1

Cluster	Variable	Model 1		Model 2		Model 3		Model 4		Model 5		Model 6		Model 7	
	Constant	-0.0532 **	(0.0229)	-0.0317 *	(0.0177)	-0.0682	(0.0605)	-0.0179 **	(0.0072)	-0.1592	(0.1330)	-0.1284	(0.1190)	-0.0481 **	(0.0111)
Financial	SIZE									0.0084	(0.0082)	0.0071	(0.0074)		
	LIQUIDITY					[illegible]	[illegible]								
	NDTEBITDA	-0.0002	(0.0003)												
	EBITDAMAR					-0.0506	(0.1476)								
	EQITYRAT					0.0025	(0.0456)								
	INTRSTCOVRG					-0.0003	(0.0027)								
Aircraft fleet	TOTALAC					0.0000	(0.0001)								
	OPSLEASE	0.0697	(0.0495)							0.0695	(0.0472)				
	STORAC					-0.0005	(0.0008)								
	nYRORDER					0.0673	(0.0692)								
	nYROPTION	0.0237	(0.0238)												
	AVGAGE	0.0020	(0.0014)	0.0014	(0.0013)										
Carrier	MFSC					0.0434	(0.0516)								
	NFSC														
	LCC														
	FREIGHT					0.0793	(0.0585)								
Region	APAC					-0.0327	(0.0305)	-0.0319 **	(0.0139)						
	EMEA													0.0321 *	(0.0177)
	LATAM	-0.0667	(0.0446)							-0.0356	(0.0429)				
	NORAM													0.0313 **	(0.0142)
Event specific	FATALITY	-0.0278 *	(0.0141)	-0.0280 *	(0.0139)					-0.0345 **	(0.0132)	-0.0323 **	(0.0132)		
	INJURY					0.0421	(0.0480)								
	LOSTVALUE					0.0002	(0.0003)								
	R^2 (adjusted)	0.13		0.12		-0.13		0.09		0.11		0.11		0.07	
	F-statistic	2.07 *		3.86 **		0.61		5.25 **		2.40 *		3.68 **		2.78 *	

Appendix 29: *Regression models for stock market's initial reaction on aircraft hull losses – Trading day* y_1

Observation period: Trading days y2-7 after aircraft accidents 1994-2009
Sample: All companies with hull losses
Sample size: 45
Dependent variable: Cumulated abnormal returns y2-6

Cluster	Variable	Model 1		Model 2		Model 3		Model 4		Model 5		Model 6		Model 7	
	Constant	-0.5168 **	(0.2444)	-0.4152 *	(0.2158)	-0.0262	(0.0328)	0.0026	(0.0232)	0.1142	(0.0736)	-0.4401 **	(0.2079)	0.0180	(0.0278)
Financial	SIZE	0.0312 **	(0.0154)	0.0256 *	(0.0137)	0.0001 **	(0.0001)					0.0301 **	(0.0133)		
	LIQUIDITY	0.0423	(0.0289)												
	NDTEBITDA					-0.0005	(0.0005)								
	EBITDAMAR													-0.0633	(0.1600)
	EQITYRAT									-0.0217	(0.0579)				
	INTRSTCOVRG	-0.0076	(0.0047)												
Aircraft fleet	TOTALAC							0.0001 **	(0.0001)						
	OPSLEASE	0.1121	(0.0856)							0.0379	(0.0899)				
	STORAC	-0.0016 *	(0.0009)	-0.0015 *	(0.0009)										
	nYRORDER									0.0586	(0.0712)				
	nYROPTION									0.0774 *	(0.0406)				
	AVGAGE					0.0025	(0.0023)								
Carrier	MFSC	-0.0158	(0.0313)							-0.1407 *	(0.0717)				
	NFSC														
	LCC														
	FREIGHT									-0.1294 *	(0.0702)				
Region	APAC									-0.0700 **	(0.0303)				
	EMEA													0.0202	(0.0295)
	LATAM	-0.1648 *	(0.0837)							-0.2023 **	(0.0764)				
	NORAM	0.0394	(0.0270)	0.0513 **	(0.0240)										
Event specific	FATALITY													-0.0215	(0.0246)
	INJURY													-0.0325	(0.0707)
	LOSTVALUE					0.0005	(0.0004)			0.0004	(0.0003)				
	R^2 (adjusted)	0.14		0.11		0.11		0.10		0.19		0.10		-0.05	
	F-statistic	1.90 *		2.74 *		2.09 *		3.35 **		2.17 **		3.39 **		0.51	

Appendix 30: *Regression models for stock market's short term reaction on aircraft hull losses – Trading days* $y_{2\text{-}6}$

	SIZE	LIQUIDITY	NDTEBITDA	EBITDAMAR	EQITYRAT	NTRSTCOVAC	TOTALAC
SIZE	1						
LIQUIDITY	-0.20	1					
NDTEBITDA	0.05	-0.08	1				
EBITDAMAR	0.09	0.25	0.22	1			
EQITYRAT	0.00	0.47	-0.04	0.31	1		
INTRSTCOVAG	0.10	-0.08	0.12	0.12	-0.21	1	
TOTALAC	0.53	-0.20	-0.17	0.00	-0.09	-0.12	1
OPSLEASE	-0.39	0.22	-0.29	-0.25	0.15	-0.21	-0.23
STORAC	-0.04	-0.03	0.00	-0.02	0.13	-0.11	0.34
nYRORDER	-0.27	0.36	-0.03	0.10	0.22	-0.16	-0.20
nYROPTION	-0.13	0.39	-0.15	0.09	0.30	-0.11	0.05
AVGAGE	-0.14	-0.13	-0.05	-0.10	-0.26	0.07	0.18
MFSC	0.54	-0.47	0.20	-0.03	-0.34	0.23	0.20
NFSC	-0.61	0.10	0.02	-0.08	0.12	-0.06	-0.13
LCC	-0.35	0.38	-0.28	-0.10	0.16	-0.22	-0.19
FREIGHTER							
APAC	0.24	-0.33	-0.18	0.16	0.03	0.17	-0.25
EMEA	0.08	0.33	0.07	-0.29	0.05	-0.25	-0.12
LATAM	-0.13	-0.15	0.03	0.09	-0.09	0.00	-0.13
NORAM	-0.24	0.07	0.09	0.07	-0.04	0.06	0.38
AC per order	0.11	-0.08	0.03	-0.09	0.04	-0.09	0.07

	OPSLEASE	STORAC	nYRORDER	nYROPTION	AVGAGE	MFSC	NFSC
SIZE							
LIQUIDITY							
NDTEBITDA							
EBITDAMAR							
EQITYRAT							
INTRSTCOVAG							
TOTALAC							
OPSLEASE	1						
STORAC	-0.09	1					
nYRORDER	0.29	-0.18	1				
nYROPTION	0.27	-0.14	0.39	1			
AVGAGE	-0.30	0.12	-0.40	-0.06	1		
MFSC	-0.26	-0.10	-0.29	-0.33	-0.27	1	
NFSC	-0.03	0.34	0.22	0.06	0.25	-0.38	1
LCC	0.50	-0.15	0.37	0.47	-0.16	-0.67	-0.13
FREIGHTER							
APAC	-0.13	-0.22	-0.05	-0.19	-0.33	0.39	-0.18
EMEA	0.11	0.07	-0.01	0.05	-0.25	0.07	-0.15
LATAM	0.29	-0.04	0.04	0.10	-0.06	0.14	-0.05
NORAM	-0.08	0.16	0.04	0.09	0.54	-0.47	0.31
AC per order	-0.05	-0.03	-0.18	0.22	0.17	0.10	0.07

	LCC	FREIGHTER	APAC	EMEA	LATAM	NORAM	AC per order
SIZE							
LIQUIDITY							
NDTEBITDA							
EBITDAMAR							
EQITYRAT							
INTRSTCOVAG							
TOTALAC							
OPSLEASE							
STORAC							
nYRORDER							
nYROPTION							
AVGAGE							
MFSC							
NFSC							
LCC	1						
FREIGHTER		1					
APAC	-0.21		1				
EMEA	0.14		-0.36	1			
LATAM	-0.09		-0.12	-0.11	1		
NORAM	0.11		-0.56	-0.49	-0.16	1	
AC per order	-0.17		0.05	-0.10	0.20	-0.03	1

Appendix 31: *Correlation of explanatory and control variables for analysis of stock market's reaction on the aircraft firm orders with 1-40 aircraft per order (data as of Ye preceding the year of order)*

Observation period	Trading day y1 after aircraft orders 1994-2009
Sample	All companies 1-40 aircraft per order
Sample size	58
Dependent variable	Abnormal returns y1

		Model 1		Model 2		Model 3		Model 4		Model 5		Model 6		Model 7	
Cluster	Variable														
	Constant	-0.0211	(0.0455)	-0.0362	(0.0621)	-0.0006	(0.0046)	-0.0322 ***	(0.0091)	-0.0311 ***	(0.0076)	0.0202	(0.0125)	-0.0038	(0.0136)
Financial	SIZE	0.0002	(0.0029)	0.0010	(0.0041)			0.0217 ***	(0.0079)						
	LIQUIDITY	[illegible]	[illegible]							[illegible]	[illegible]				
	NDTEBITDA	0.0001 **	(0.0001)					0.0001 *	(0.0001)	0.0001 **	(0.0001)				
	EBITDAMAR	0.1333 ***	(0.0494)					0.0931 *	(0.0488)	0.1024 **	(0.0467)				
	EQITYRAT	-0.0594 **	(0.0274)	0.0154	(0.0328)										
	INTRSTCOVRG	-0.0016	(0.0032)	0.0015	(0.0039)										
Aircraft fleet	TOTALAC													0.0000	(0.0000)
	OPSLEASE							0.0165	(0.0188)					-0.0092	(0.0223)
	STORAC			-0.0003	(0.0004)									-0.0003	(0.0004)
	nYRORDER			0.0191	(0.0139)							0.0273 **	(0.0114)		
	nYROPTION							-0.0090	(0.0088)					-0.0031	(0.0102)
	AVGAGE			0.0008	(0.0011)									0.0006	(0.0008)
Carrier	MFSC			0.0116	(0.0128)							-0.0334 **	(0.0135)		
	NFSC							-0.0176	(0.0145)			-0.0445 **	(0.0198)		
	LCC							-0.0183	(0.0116)			-0.0507 ***	(0.0163)		
	FREIGHT														
Region	APAC			-0.0217 *	(0.0118)	-0.0144 *	(0.0084)								
	EMEA			-0.0106	(0.0116)									-0.0022	(0.0102)
	LATAM													0.0017	(0.0246)
	NORAM							0.0182 **	(0.0073)	0.0127 *	(0.0068)				
Event specific	ACPORDER													-0.0002	(0.0007)
	R² (adjusted)	0.25		-0.02		0.03		0.29		0.26		0.12		-0.13	
	F-statistic	4.17 ***		0.87		2.93 *		3.86 ***		6.01 ***		2.87 **		0.21	

Appendix 32: *Regression models for stock market's initial reaction on aircraft orders (1-40 aircraft per order) – Trading* day y_1

Observation period	Trading days y2-6 after aircraft orders 1994-2009
Sample	All companies 41-120 aircraft per order
Sample size	58
Dependent variable	Cumulated abnormal returns y2-6

		Model 1		Model 2		Model 3		Model 4		Model 5		Model 6		Model 7	
Cluster	Variable														
	Constant	-0.3526 *	(0.1801)	-0.0017	(0.0084)	0.0730	(0.0912)	-0.0334	(0.0254)	-0.1297	(0.1625)	-0.0095	(0.0162)	0.0170	(0.0182)
Financial	SIZE	0.0225 *	(0.0117)							0.0087	(0.0103)				
	LIQUIDITY													0.0082	(0.0180)
	NDTEBITDA	-0.0003 **	(0.0002)	-0.0004 **	(0.0001)					-0.0004 **	(0.0002)				
	EBITDAMAR					-0.1866	(0.1307)							-0.1305	(0.1166)
	EQITYRAT							0.0583	(0.0599)						
	INTRSTCOVRG					0.0040	(0.0083)	0.0068	(0.0081)						
Aircraft fleet	TOTALAC	-0.0001	(0.0001)					0.0000	(0.0001)						
	OPSLEASE	0.0753	(0.0465)			0.0781	(0.0541)	0.0569	(0.0422)			0.0544	(0.0394)		
	STORAC	0.0009	(0.0008)			0.0006	(0.0008)	0.0010	(0.0008)			0.0010	(0.0007)		
	nYRORDER					-0.0528 *	(0.0310)			-0.0295	(0.0250)				
	nYROPTION					0.0415	(0.0249)								
	AVGAGE					-0.0031	(0.0025)								
Carrier	MFSC					-0.0716 **	(0.0323)								
	NFSC	0.0957 **	(0.0464)	0.0538 *	(0.0317)					0.0903 *	(0.0471)				
	LCC					-0.0916 **	(0.0392)			0.0108	(0.0283)				
	FREIGHT														
Region	APAC					0.0608	(0.0535)								
	EMEA					0.0331	(0.0562)								
	LATAM	-0.0423	(0.0459)											-0.0275	(0.0479)
	NORAM					0.0355	(0.0544)								
Event specific	ACPORDER					-0.0020	(0.0015)					-0.0008	(0.0013)		
	R² (adjusted)	0.12		0.10		0.05		0.00		0.09		0.02		-0.02	
	F-statistic	2.15 *		4.23 **		1.21		1.04		2.14 *		1.42		0.62	

Appendix 33: *Regression models for stock market's short term reaction on aircraft orders (1-40 aircraft per order) – Trading days* $y_{2\text{-}6}$

	SIZE	LIQUIDITY	NDTEBITDA	EBITDAMAR	EQITYRAT	NTRSTCOVAC	TOTALAC
SIZE	1						
LIQUIDITY	-0.69	1					
NDTEBITDA	0.32	-0.45	1				
EBITDAMAR	-0.54	0.66	-0.39	1			
EQITYRAT	-0.51	0.56	-0.43	0.68	1		
INTRSTCOVAG	0.12	-0.17	0.40	-0.08	-0.07	1	
TOTALAC	0.69	-0.57	-0.07	-0.28	-0.45	-0.20	1
OPSLEASE	-0.58	0.15	-0.23	-0.07	0.16	0.07	-0.48
STORAC	0.27	-0.19	-0.01	-0.40	-0.67	-0.08	0.45
nYRORDER	-0.72	0.46	-0.08	0.34	0.43	-0.01	-0.72
nYROPTION	-0.56	0.58	-0.36	0.44	0.38	-0.24	-0.37
AVGAGE	0.53	-0.35	0.19	-0.41	-0.66	-0.24	0.57
MFSC	0.15	0.03	-0.13	0.15	0.02	-0.28	0.18
NFSC							
LCC	-0.15	-0.03	0.13	-0.15	-0.02	0.28	-0.18
FREIGHTER							
APAC	0.27	0.13	0.15	0.02	0.06	0.03	-0.24
EMEA	-0.17	0.10	-0.14	0.03	0.28	0.13	-0.07
LATAM							
NORAM	-0.05	-0.18	0.01	-0.04	-0.29	-0.13	0.24
AC per order	-0.38	0.47	-0.40	0.45	0.40	-0.27	-0.02

	OPSLEASE	STORAC	nYRORDER	nYROPTION	AVGAGE	MFSC	NFSC
SIZE							
LIQUIDITY							
NDTEBITDA							
EBITDAMAR							
EQITYRAT							
INTRSTCOVAG							
TOTALAC							
OPSLEASE	1						
STORAC	-0.15	1					
nYRORDER	0.57	-0.34	1				
nYROPTION	0.32	-0.22	0.72	1			
AVGAGE	-0.47	0.44	-0.69	-0.52	1		
MFSC	-0.11	-0.19	-0.21	-0.03	0.14	1	
NFSC							1
LCC	0.11	0.19	0.21	0.03	-0.14	-1.00	
FREIGHTER							
APAC	-0.26	-0.16	0.11	0.13	-0.07	0.30	
EMEA	0.33	-0.19	0.27	0.26	-0.31	-0.34	
LATAM							
NORAM	-0.09	0.28	-0.31	-0.32	0.32	0.07	
AC per order	0.00	0.00	0.13	0.24	-0.19	-0.08	

	LCC	FREIGHTER	APAC	EMEA	LATAM	NORAM	AC per order
SIZE							
LIQUIDITY							
NDTEBITDA							
EBITDAMAR							
EQITYRAT							
INTRSTCOVAG							
TOTALAC							
OPSLEASE							
STORAC							
nYRORDER							
nYROPTION							
AVGAGE							
MFSC							
NFSC							
LCC	1						
FREIGHTER		1					
APAC	-0.30		1				
EMEA	0.34		-0.21	1			
LATAM					1		
NORAM	-0.07		-0.55	-0.70		1	
AC per order	0.08		-0.24	0.15		0.04	1

Appendix 34: *Correlation of explanatory and control variables for analysis of stock market's reaction on the aircraft firm orders with 41-120 aircraft per order (data as of Ye preceding the year of order)*

Observation period	Trading day y1 after aircraft orders 1994-2009
Sample	Orders of 41-120 aircraft per order
Sample size	28
Dependent variable	Abnormal returns y1

Cluster	Variable	Model 1		Model 2		Model 3		Model 4		Model 5		Model 6		Model 7	
	Constant	0.0184	(0.0113)	0.0121	(0.0100)	-0.0152	(0.0324)	-0.0236 **	(0.0086)	-0.1432	(0.1115)	-0.0152 **	(0.0062)	-0.0110	(0.0130)
Financial	SIZE									0.0076	(0.0067)				
	LIQUIDITY					-0.0073	(0.0155)							0.0025	(0.0078)
	NDTEBITDA					-0.0016	(0.0017)							-0.0015	(0.0014)
	EBITDAMAR					-0.0263	(0.0874)								
	EQITYRAT									0.0424 *	(0.0223)				
	INTRSTCOVRG									-0.0038 *	(0.0021)				
Aircraft fleet	TOTALAC					0.0000	(0.0001)								
	OPSLEASE									0.0553 *	(0.0279)				
	STORAC	-0.0001	(0.0003)												
	nYRORDER					0.0064	(0.0314)								
	nYROPTION					0.0138	(0.0199)	0.0166 *	(0.0086)			0.0162 *	(0.0087)		
	AVGAGE	-0.0019 *	(0.0010)	-0.0019 **	(0.0009)										
Carrier	MFSC					0.0126	(0.0128)	0.0127	(0.0092)					0.0088	(0.0114)
	NFSC														
	LCC	-0.0142	(0.0095)												
	FREIGHT														
Region	APAC					0.0020	(0.0173)							0.0058	(0.0152)
	EMEA					-0.0065	(0.0142)							-0.0011	(0.0128)
	LATAM														
	NORAM														
Event specific	ACPORDER					0.0001	(0.0003)								
	R^2 (adjusted)	0.15		0.12		-0.20		0.11		0.18		0.08		-0.06	
	F-statistic	2.58 *		4.63 **		0.55		2.75 *		2.48 *		3.45 *		0.71	

Appendix 35: *Regression models for stock market's initial reaction on aircraft orders (41-120 aircraft per order) – Trading days* y_1

Observation period	Trading days y2-6 after aircraft orders 1994-2009
Sample	All orders with 41-120 aircraft per order
Sample size	28
Dependent variable	Cumulated abnormal returns y2-6

Cluster	Variable	Model 1		Model 2		Model 3		Model 4		Model 5		Model 6		Model 7	
	Constant	-0.1101	(0.1901)	0.0245	(0.0147)	0.0626 *	(0.0320)	0.0613 **	(0.0276)	0.0737 **	(0.0350)	0.0286	(0.0371)	0.0161 *	(0.0088)
Financial	SIZE	0.0085	(0.0115)												
	LIQUIDITY	0.0255	(0.0169)					0.0322 **	(0.0138)						
	NDTEBITDA	-0.0027	(0.0024)			-0.0050 **	(0.0023)								
	EBITDAMAR	-0.2979 **	(0.1385)	-0.2074	(0.1298)										
	EQITYRAT	0.0960 *	(0.0481)	0.1160 **	(0.0480)										
	INTRSTCOVRG	0.0084 *	(0.0040)			0.0079 *	(0.0042)							0.0055	(0.0041)
Aircraft fleet	TOTALAC									-0.0001	(0.0001)				
	OPSLEASE											-0.0129	(0.0558)		
	STORAC									-0.0001	(0.0006)				
	nYRORDER							-0.0288	(0.0233)	-0.0312	(0.0327)				
	nYROPTION											-0.0104	(0.0206)		
	AVGAGE											-0.0020	(0.0023)		
Carrier	MFSC											0.0156	(0.0203)		
	NFSC														
	LCC									-0.0068	(0.0194)				
	FREIGHT														
Region	APAC											0.0142	(0.0287)		
	EMEA							0.0377 *	(0.0198)			0.0352	(0.0247)		
	LATAM														
	NORAM									-0.0293	(0.0193)				
Event specific	ACPORDER					-0.0005	(0.0004)	-0.0009 **	(0.0004)						
	R^2 (adjusted)	0.21		0.12		0.13		0.16		-0.04		-0.09		0.03	
	F-statistic	2.22 *		2.92 *		2.35 *		2.29 *		0.80		0.63		1.83	

Appendix 36: *Regression models for stock market's short term reaction on aircraft orders (41-120 aircraft per order) – Trading days* $y_{2\text{-}6}$

	SIZE	LIQUIDITY	NDTEBITDA	EQUITYRAT	INTRSTCOVRG	TOTALAC	OPSLEASE
SIZE	1						
LIQUIDITY	-0.43	1					
NDTEBITDA	0.17	-0.40	1				
EQUITYRAT	-0.27	0.36	-0.45	1			
INTRSTCOVRG	0.24	-0.12	-0.02	0.01	1		
TOTALAC	0.70	-0.20	0.12	-0.51	0.11	1	
OPSLEASE	-0.59	0.20	-0.17	0.11	-0.10	-0.34	1
STORAC	0.50	-0.20	0.32	-0.64	-0.12	0.81	-0.24
nYRORDER	-0.32	0.42	-0.09	0.28	-0.01	-0.33	0.24
nYROPTION	-0.26	0.55	-0.12	0.14	-0.13	-0.09	0.30
AVGAGE	0.64	-0.41	0.23	-0.32	-0.03	0.60	-0.39
MFSC	0.44	-0.63	0.29	-0.47	0.14	0.18	-0.10
NFSC	-0.41	0.35	-0.05	0.12	-0.03	-0.20	-0.17
LCC	-0.41	0.60	-0.25	0.34	-0.10	-0.17	0.39
FREIGHT	0.30	-0.14	-0.12	0.27	-0.08	0.17	-0.26
APAC	0.18	-0.39	0.21	0.13	0.07	-0.29	-0.25
EMEA	-0.01	0.30	-0.30	0.27	0.17	-0.14	0.16
LATAM	-0.28	-0.10	-0.11	-0.05	-0.10	-0.17	0.33
NORAM	0.04	0.09	0.12	-0.33	-0.14	0.43	-0.11

	STORAC	nYRORDER	nYROPTION	AVGAGE	MFSC	NFSC
SIZE						
LIQUIDITY						
NDTEBITDA						
EQUITYRAT						
INTRSTCOVRG						
TOTALAC						
OPSLEASE						
STORAC	1					
nYRORDER	-0.33	1				
nYROPTION	-0.08	0.68	1			
AVGAGE	0.71	-0.48	-0.28	1		
MFSC	0.17	-0.40	-0.35	0.17	1	
NFSC	-0.13	-0.04	0.11	-0.24	-0.44	1
LCC	-0.27	0.61	0.45	-0.41	-0.71	-0.13
FREIGHT	0.27	-0.15	-0.18	0.65	-0.35	-0.06
APAC	-0.32	-0.01	-0.21	-0.14	0.41	-0.18
EMEA	-0.23	0.06	0.02	-0.19	-0.01	-0.16
LATAM	-0.08	0.06	0.08	-0.03	0.15	-0.06
NORAM	0.48	-0.03	0.15	0.31	-0.37	0.30

	LCC	FREIGHT	APAC	EMEA	LATAM	NORAM
SIZE						
LIQUIDITY						
NDTEBITDA						
EQUITYRAT						
INTRSTCOVRG						
TOTALAC						
OPSLEASE						
STORAC						
nYRORDER						
nYROPTION						
AVGAGE						
MFSC						
NFSC						
LCC	1					
FREIGHT	-0.10	1				
APAC	-0.29	-0.15	1			
EMEA	0.20	-0.13	-0.37	1		
LATAM	-0.10	-0.05	-0.15	-0.13	1	
NORAM	0.10	0.24	-0.38	-0.53	-0.21	1

Appendix 37: *Correlation of explanatory and control variables for analysis of companies' performance over the business cycle 2002-2007*

	SIZE	LIQUIDITY	NDTEBITDA	EQUITYRAT	INTRSTCOVRG	TOTALAC	OPSLEASE
SIZE	1						
LIQUIDITY	-0.60	1					
NDTEBITDA	-0.13	-0.35	1				
EQUITYRAT	-0.08	0.37	0.12	1			
INTRSTCOVRG	0.15	-0.22	0.18	0.04	1		
TOTALAC	0.64	-0.36	-0.33	-0.48	-0.03	1	
OPSLEASE	-0.78	0.49	-0.03	-0.33	-0.14	-0.30	1
STORAC	0.60	0.43	0.00	0.06	0.20	0.05	-0.21
nYRORDER	-0.70	0.30	0.11	0.14	0.08	-0.54	0.62
nYROPTION	-0.04	0.13	-0.11	-0.25	-0.22	0.40	0.24
AVGAGE	0.22	-0.03	-0.39	-0.07	-0.23	0.29	-0.04
MFSC	0.25	-0.34	0.26	-0.50	0.02	0.11	-0.06
NFSC							
LCC	-0.54	0.53	-0.23	0.32	0.01	-0.10	0.34
FREIGHT	0.34	-0.18	-0.10	0.36	-0.04	-0.05	-0.37
APAC	0.00	-0.18	0.62	0.27	0.30	-0.51	-0.19
EMEA	0.08	0.15	-0.16	0.12	-0.25	-0.07	-0.15
LATAM							
NORAM	-0.06	0.05	-0.42	-0.32	-0.07	0.49	0.28

	STORAC	nYRORDER	nYROPTION	AVGAGE	MFSC	NFSC
SIZE						
LIQUIDITY						
NDTEBITDA						
EQUITYRAT						
INTRSTCOVRG						
TOTALAC						
OPSLEASE						
STORAC	1					
nYRORDER	-0.66	1				
nYROPTION	0.28	0.12	1			
AVGAGE	0.54	-0.22	0.15	1		
MFSC	0.20	-0.39	-0.06	-0.55	1	
NFSC						1
LCC	-0.37	0.64	0.19	0.06	-0.78	
FREIGHT	0.18	-0.25	-0.16	0.80	-0.53	
APAC	-0.47	0.17	-0.29	-0.54	0.30	
EMEA	-0.10	-0.11	-0.21	-0.13	0.23	
LATAM						
NORAM	0.48	-0.07	0.41	0.56	-0.43	

	LCC	FREIGHT	APAC	EMEA	LATAM	NORAM
SIZE						
LIQUIDITY						
NDTEBITDA						
EQUITYRAT						
INTRSTCOVRG						
TOTALAC						
OPSLEASE						
STORAC						
nYRORDER						
nYROPTION						
AVGAGE						
MFSC						
NFSC						
LCC	1					
FREIGHT	-0.12	1				
APAC	-0.23	-0.16	1			
EMEA	-0.18	-0.12	-0.23	1		
LATAM					1	
NORAM	0.34	0.23	-0.69	-0.54		1

Appendix 38: *Correlation of explanatory and control variables for analysis of companies' performance over the business cycle 1995-2009*

Observation period	2002-2007
Sample	All companies
Sample size	41
Dependent variable	Average annual revenue growth

Cluster	Variable	Model 1	Model 2	Model 3	Model 4	Model 5	Model 6	Model 7
	Constant	0.2333 *** (0.0743)	-0.6909 (0.7484)	-0.0038 (0.0449)	0.2428 *** (0.0725)	0.1574 *** (0.0319)	0.7077 ** (0.3314)	0.0180 (0.0279)
Financial	SIZE		0.0452 (0.0490)				-0.0368 * (0.0205)	
	LIQUIDITY	0.0298 (0.0393)					0.0641 (0.0454)	
	NDTEBITDA	0.0099 *** (0.0032)						0.0061 ** (0.0025)
	EBITDAMAR		0.5475 (0.3914)	0.7459 ** (0.2844)				
	EBITMAR							
	EQITYRAT				-0.0875 (0.1293)			
	INTRSTCOVRG				0.0073 (0.0134)			
Aircraft fleet	TOTALAC		-0.0003 (0.0003)		-0.0003 (0.0002)	-0.0002 ** (0.0001)		
	OPSLEASE		0.3065 ** (0.1248)	0.2971 *** (0.0803)				0.2015 *** (0.0680)
	STORAC		0.0025 (0.0024)		0.0009 (0.0027)			
	nYRORDER	0.1095 ** (0.0467)						0.1708 *** (0.0360)
	nYROPTION				0.1033 ** (0.0396)	0.1214 *** (0.0366)		
	AVGAGE	-0.0176 *** (0.0064)						
Carrier	MFSC				-0.0752 (0.0466)			
	NFSC		0.2289 ** (0.1107)	0.1393 ** (0.0651)				0.1842 *** (0.0533)
	LCC		0.1099 (0.0730)					
	FREIGHT	0.1856 * (0.1001)						
Region	APAC	-0.0616 (0.0379)						
	EMEA						-0.0288 (0.0572)	
	LATAM		0.0337					
	NORAM						0.0002 (0.0469)	
	R^2 (adjusted)	0.45	0.28	0.32	0.25	0.27	0.14	0.53
	F-statistic	6.50 ***	2.92 **	7.29 ***	3.21 **	8.31 ***	2.57 *	12.21 ***

Appendix 39: *Regression models for companies' long term revenue growth 2002-2007*

Observation period	1995-2009
Sample	All companies
Sample size	13
Dependent variable	Average annual revenue growth

Cluster	Variable	Model 1	Model 2	Model 3	Model 4	Model 5	Model 6	Model 7
	Constant	1.0104 *** (0.1226)	-0.0146 (0.0382)	0.0659 (0.0631)	0.9290 *** (0.2244)	0.1582 * (0.0710)	0.0194 (0.0647)	0.5194 * (0.1709)
Financial	SIZE	-0.0770 *** (0.0080)			-0.0696 *** (0.0140)			-0.0497 ** (0.0096)
	LIQUIDITY						0.1590 * (0.0762)	0.0595 (0.0294)
	NDTEBITDA	-0.0034 *** (0.0007)						-0.0013 (0.0006)
	EBITDAMAR	-0.6882 ** (0.1924)						
	EBITMAR						-0.1750 (0.5820)	-0.5608 ** (0.1745)
	EQITYRAT	0.4515 *** (0.0630)			0.2839 ** (0.0825)			0.3848 *** (0.0628)
	INTRSTCOVRG	0.0245 *** (0.0031)			0.0177 ** (0.0052)			0.0241 *** (0.0030)
Aircraft fleet	TOTALAC			-0.0002 *** (0.0001)			-0.0001 (0.0001)	-0.0002 ** (0.0000)
	OPSLEASE		0.2169 *** (0.0614)			0.2271 ** (0.0841)		
	STORAC	0.0076 *** (0.0010)			0.0054 *** (0.0015)			0.0085 *** (0.0012)
	nYRORDER	0.6846 *** (0.1028)			0.5316 ** (0.1766)			0.8150 *** (0.1166)
	nYROPTION		-0.0579 (0.0574)			-0.0639 (0.0734)		
	AVGAGE		0.0065 (0.0038)	0.0165 ** (0.0063)		-0.0019 (0.0075)		
Carrier	MFSC			-0.1078 *** (0.0262)		-0.1199 *** (0.0321)		
	NFSC							
	LCC		0.1283 *** (0.0271)					
	FREIGHT			-0.2564 *** (0.0609)		-0.0547 (0.0913)		
Region	APAC	0.0804 ** (0.0218)						
	EMEA					0.0106 (0.0317)	-0.0521 (0.0572)	
	LATAM							
	NORAM		-0.0421 (0.0258)					
	R^2 (adjusted)	0.96	0.78	0.79	0.84	0.67	0.23	0.96
	F-statistic	36.11 ***	9.45 ***	11.96 ***	13.21 ***	5.15 **	1.92	34.32 ***

Appendix 40: *Regression models for companies' long term revenue growth 1995-2009*

Observation period 2002-2007
Sample All companies
Sample size 41
Dependent variable Average annual EBITDA margin

Cluster	Variable	Model 1	Model 2	Model 3	Model 4	Model 5	Model 6	Model 7
	Constant	-0.0279 (0.1124)	0.1173 *** (0.0176)	0.0735 ** (0.0323)	0.0693 *** (0.0123)	0.1470 *** (0.0325)	0.0518 *** (0.0128)	0.1354 *** (0.0155)
Financial	SIZE	0.0139 * (0.0074)						
	[illegible]		[illegible] ** [illegible]					
	NDTEBITDA			0.0011 (0.0019)				
	EBITDAMAR							
	EBITMAR							
	EQITYRAT			0.1808 *** (0.0578)	0.1751 *** (0.0404)		0.1415 *** (0.0392)	
	INTRSTCOVRG			0.0005 (0.0062)				
Aircraft fleet	TOTALAC			0.0000 (0.0001)		-0.0001 (0.0001)		
	OPSLEASE		-0.1201 *** (0.0365)			-0.1564 *** (0.0399)		-0.1314 *** (0.0391)
	STORAC		-0.0018 *** (0.0006)			-0.0010 (0.0011)		
	nYRORDER		0.0444 ** (0.0214)			0.0159 (0.0285)	0.0425 ** (0.0197)	
	nYROPTION	0.0575 *** (0.0159)				0.0540 ** (0.0227)		0.0698 *** (0.0179)
	AVGAGE			-0.0003 (0.0028)		0.0013 (0.0029)		
Carrier	MFSC	-0.1215 *** (0.0237)						
	NFSC			0.0293 (0.0348)				
	LCC	-0.0701 ** (0.0268)						
	FREIGHT		0.0617 * (0.0358)					
Region	APAC	0.0599 *** (0.0165)					0.0347 ** (0.0164)	
	EMEA			-0.0160 (0.0223)				
	LATAM			-0.0177 (0.0423)				
	NORAM	-0.0525 *** (0.0156)						-0.0442 *** (0.0161)
	R^2 (adjusted)	0.54	0.43	0.23	0.31	0.43	0.41	0.34
	F-statistic	8.77 ***	7.13 ***	2.45 **	18.82 ***	5.93 ***	10.24 ***	7.82 ***

***Appendix 41:** Regression models for companies' long term EBITDA margin 2002-2007*

Observation period 1995-2009
Sample All companies
Sample size 13
Dependent variable Average annual EBITDA margin

Cluster	Variable	Model 1	Model 2	Model 3	Model 4	Model 5	Model 6	Model 7
	Constant	-0.6821 *** (0.1595)	0.2238 *** (0.0572)	0.0986 *** (0.0198)	-0.1049 (0.4462)	0.0846 ** (0.0282)	0.0660 *** (0.0180)	0.1110 *** (0.0280)
Financial	SIZE	0.0532 *** (0.0104)						
	LIQUIDITY				-0.0638 (0.1028)	-0.0441 (0.0476)		0.0579 (0.0528)
	NDTEBITDA				-0.0008 (0.0025)			
	EBITDAMAR							
	EBITMAR							
	EQITYRAT				0.3591 (0.3968)	0.1822 ** (0.0684)	0.1618 ** (0.0675)	
	INTRSTCOVRG				0.0094 (0.0106)	0.0083 (0.0060)		
Aircraft fleet	TOTALAC	-0.0002 (0.0000)						
	OPSLEASE			-0.0560 (0.0692)				-0.1544 * (0.0779)
	STORAC				0.0017 (0.0058)			
	nYRORDER				0.3878 (0.8338)			
	nYROPTION				0.0074 (0.1401)			
	AVGAGE		-0.0136 ** (0.0060)					
Carrier	MFSC				0.0547 (0.1274)			
	NFSC							
	LCC	0.0621 ** (0.0210)						
	FREIGHT		0.1789 ** (0.0653)					
Region	APAC			0.0588 ** (0.0262)				
	EMEA	-0.0730 *** (0.0166)						-0.0799 ** (0.0303)
	LATAM							
	NORAM				0.0264 (0.0660)			
	R^2 (adjusted)	0.79	0.32	0.28	-0.53	0.37	0.28	0.33
	F-statistic	12.22 ***	3.77 *	3.31 *	0.54	3.40 *	5.75 **	2.94 *

***Appendix 42:** Regression models for companies' long term EBITDA margin 1995-2009*

Observation period	2002-2007
Sample	All companies
Sample size	41
Dependent variable	Average annual EBIT margin

Cluster	Variable	Model 1	Model 2	Model 3	Model 4	Model 5	Model 6	Model 7
	Constant	0.0341 (0.0298)	-0.0216 (0.0147)	0.0146 (0.0132)	0.0055 (0.0103)	-0.2298 (0.1368)	0.0134 (0.0101)	0.0389 ** (0.0172)
Financial	SIZE					0.0226 ** (0.0093)		
	LIQUIDITY		0.0593 *** (0.0139)					
	NDTEBITDA							-0.0026 * (0.0014)
	EBITDAMAR							
	EBITMAR							
	EQITYRAT			0.1363 *** (0.0360)	0.1509 *** (0.0340)			
	INTRSTCOVRG							-0.0014 (0.0054)
Aircraft fleet	TOTALAC	-0.0001 (0.0001)				-0.0002 (0.0001)		
	OPSLEASE	-0.0743 * (0.0366)		-0.0519 (0.0371)				
	STORAC	-0.0005 (0.0010)	-0.0008 * (0.0005)					
	nYRORDER	0.0262 (0.0262)				0.0537 ** (0.0203)		0.0638 *** (0.0192)
	nYROPTION	0.0518 * (0.0208)	0.0340 ** (0.0137)				0.0608 *** (0.0154)	
	AVGAGE	0.0034 (0.0027)						
Carrier	MFSC					-0.0852 *** (0.0191)		
	NFSC			0.0510 * (0.0262)	0.0481 * (0.0258)			
	LCC			0.0349 (0.0210)		-0.0520 * (0.0265)		
	FREIGHT		0.1180 *** (0.0259)				0.0827 ** (0.0334)	
Region	APAC		0.0400 *** (0.0141)					
	EMEA							-0.0153 (0.0215)
	LATAM			0.0432 (0.0337)				
	NORAM							-0.0085 (0.0177)
	R^2 (adjusted)	0.37	0.61	0.38	0.37	0.50	0.30	0.21
	F-statistic	4.90 ***	13.52 ***	5.98 ***	12.77 ***	8.94 ***	9.39 ***	3.15 **

Appendix 43: *Regression models for companies' long term EBIT margin 2002-2007*

Observation period	1995-2009
Sample	All companies
Sample size	13
Dependent variable	Average annual EBIT margin

Cluster	Variable	Model 1	Model 2	Model 3	Model 4	Model 5	Model 6	Model 7
	Constant	-0.1004 * (0.0461)	0.0802 (0.0443)	-0.1396 (0.1432)	0.0344 (0.0445)	-0.5460 ** (0.1963)	0.0314 *** (0.0087)	-0.3174 ** (0.1210)
Financial	SIZE			0.0076 (0.0088)		0.0393 ** (0.0123)		0.0157 * (0.0067)
	LIQUIDITY	0.1553 ** (0.0482)						
	NDTEBITDA				-0.0001 (0.0013)	0.0004 (0.0010)		
	EBITDAMAR							
	EBITMAR							
	EQITYRAT			0.1586 ** (0.0542)	0.1010 (0.0918)			0.1347 *** (0.0285)
	INTRSTCOVRG				0.0050 (0.0057)			
Aircraft fleet	TOTALAC					-0.0001 (0.0001)		
	OPSLEASE	-0.3335 *** (0.0889)						
	STORAC				0.0006 (0.0011)	-0.0014 (0.0012)		
	nYRORDER	0.7729 ** (0.2447)						0.2018 * (0.0910)
	nYROPTION		0.0782 (0.0540)					
	AVGAGE		-0.0075 (0.0051)					0.0041 ** (0.0016)
Carrier	MFSC				-0.0352 (0.0283)	-0.0298 (0.0223)		
	NFSC							
	LCC	-0.1125 ** (0.0441)						
	FREIGHT		0.1571 ** (0.0561)				0.0838 ** (0.0315)	
Region	APAC	-0.0601 * (0.0258)						
	EMEA	-0.1128 *** (0.0252)						-0.0573 *** (0.0127)
	LATAM							
	NORAM			0.0366 * (0.0178)		0.0591 * (0.0262)		
	R^2 (adjusted)	0.62	0.39	0.37	0.14	0.55	0.34	0.81
	F-statistic	4.26 *	3.53 *	3.38 *	1.41	3.40 *	7.08 **	11.34 ***

Appendix 44: *Regression models for companies' long term EBIT margin 1995-2009*

FSC
www.fsc.org
MIX
Papier | Fördert gute Waldnutzung
FSC® C083411

Kolibri 360 GmbH
Ferdinand-Jühlke-Straße 7
99095 Erfurt, Deutschland
produktsicherheit@kolibri360.de